BRITISH
WRITERS
Classics

VOLUME II

ISSN 1541-8995

BRITISH WRITERS
Classics

VOLUME II

EDITED BY JAY PARINI

CHARLES SCRIBNER'S SONS®

New York • Detroit • San Diego • San Francisco • Cleveland • New Haven, Conn. • Waterville, Maine • London • Munich

THOMSON

GALE

British Writers Classics, Volume II
Jay Parini, Editor in Chief

Permissions Department
The Gale Group, Inc.
27500 Drake Rd.
Farmington Hills, MI 48331-3535
Permissions Hotline:
248 699-8006 or 800 877-4253, ext. 8006
Fax: 248 699-8074 or 800 762-4058

ISBN 0-684-31269-7 (volume 2)
ISSN 1541-8995

Printed in the United States of America
10 9 8 7 6 5 4 3 2 1

Editorial and Production Staff

Project Editor
PAMELA PARKINSON

Copyeditors
SHANE DAVIS
MELISSA DOBSON
LINDA SANDERS

Proofreader
CAROL HOLMES

Indexer
CYNTHIA CRIPPEN

Composition Specialist
GARY LEACH

Buyer
STACY MELSON

Publisher
FRANK MENCHACA

v

Acknowledgments

Acknowledgment is gratefully made to those publishers and individuals who have permitted the use of the following material in copyright. Every effort has been made to secure permission to reprint copyrighted material.

Crow
Excerpts from "Ted Hughes and *Crow*" by Ekbert Faas. *The London Magazine,* v. 10, January 1971. © London Magazine, 1971. Reproduced by permission. Hughes, Ted. From *Crow: From the Life and Songs of the Crow.* Faber and Faber, 1970. Copyright © 1970 by Ted Hughes. All rights reserved. Reproduced by permission. Hughes, Ted. From *Three Contemporary Poets: Thom Gunn, Ted Hughes and R.S. Thomas: A Casebook.* Macmillan, 1990. Selection and editorial matter copyright © 1990 by A.E. Dyson. All rights reserved. Reproduced by permission of Palgrave Macmillan. Hughes, Ted. From *Winter Pollen: Occasional Prose.* Edited by William Scammell. Picador USA, 1995. Copyright © 1994, 1995 by Ted Hughes. Introduction copyright © 1994 by William Scammell. All rights reserved. Reproduced by permission.

Jane Eyre
Shuttleworth, Sally. From *Jane Eyre.* Edited by Margaret Smith. Oxford World's Classics, 1969, revised edition 2000.

Text copyright © 1969, 1975 by Oxford University Press. Introduction, chronology, bibliography, and notes copyright © 2000 by Sally Shuttleworth. All rights reserved. Reproduced by permission.

Mrs. Dalloway
Woolf, Virginia. From *The Captain's Death Bed and Other Essays.* Edited by Leonard Woolf. Harcourt, Brace and Company, 1950. Copyright © 1950, 1978 by Harcourt, Brace and Company, Inc. All rights reserved. Reproduced by permission.

Possession
Byatt, A.S. From *In Possession: A Romance.* Chatto and Windus, 1990. Copyright © 1990 by A.S. Byatt. All rights reserved. Reproduced in the U.K. by permission of Random House UK Limited, in the rest of the world by permission of Random House, Inc.

Waterland
Rosenberg, Scott, "GLOWing in the Ashes," <www.salon.com>. Reproduced by permission of Salon, http://www.salonmagazine.com.

List of Subjects

Introduction

This is the second volume in a series that we hope will continue for a long time. It represents a further development of *British Writers*, which had its origin in a sequence of monographs called *The Minnesota Pamphlets on American Writers*. These biographical and critical monographs were incisively written and informative, treating ninety-seven American writers in a format and style that attracted a devoted following. It proved invaluable to a generation of students and teachers, who could depend on the reliable and interesting critiques of major figures that were offered in those pages.

The idea of reprinting the Minnesota pamphlets occurred to Charles Scribner, Jr. Soon four volumes entitled *American Writers: A Collection of Literary Biographies* (1974) appeared, and it was widely acclaimed by students, teachers, and librarians. To this was added *British Writers*, a parallel series that deals with major writers from the United Kingdom and Anglophone countries, such as Ireland, South Africa, India, Australia, Canada, and New Zealand. The series continues, with volumes added yearly as supplements and retrospectives. The articles in these collections all consider the whole career of an important writer, supplying biographical and cultural context as well as taking careful look at the shape of the individual achievement.

This new series provides substantial articles that focus on a single masterwork of British or Anglophone literature, whether it be a novel, a volume of stories, a play, a long poem or sequence of poems, or a major work of autobiography or nonfiction. The idea behind the series is simple: to provide close readings of landmark works. These readings, written by well-known authors and professors of literature, will in each case examine the text itself, explaining its internal dynamics, and consider the cultural, biographical, and historical dimensions of the work. Some effort will be made to place the work within the author's overall career, though the main focus in each essay will be on the chosen text.

In the past twenty-five years or so, since the advent of post-structuralism, the emphasis in most critical writing has been largely theoretical. What was called "close reading" during the days of the so-called New Criticism—a movement that had its origins in formalist criticism of the twenties and thirties, and which reigned supreme in university English departments for several decades—was often immensely useful to students and teachers, who wanted careful and detailed analyses of individual texts. Every effort has been made in these articles to provide useful and patient readings of important works without sacrificing theoretical sophistication.

Our hope is that students and teachers, as well as the general reader, will find these articles both informative and stimulating. Each essay will introduce a reader to a major text and offer a subtle analysis of its formal properties without ignoring the historical and cultural dimensions of the work. The bibliographies attached to the end of each article offer a guide to further reading on each work.

This second volume of *British Writers Classics* is largely concerned with novels. We take up a fair number of novels that must be considered central to the British tradition of literary fiction, and a fair number of these were written during the nineteenth century, when the novel as a genre came into its own, and when novelists were just discovering the range and power of fiction. (It was also a time, of course, when the audience for fiction expanded dramatically with the increase in literacy that ushered in the modern era.) The novels discussed from this era are *Frankenstein, Jane Eyre, Bleak House, Vanity Fair, Daniel Deronda,* and *The Mayor of Casterbridge.* We also look at Kipling's first collection of Anglo-Indian stories, *Plain Tales from the Hills.* Each of these must be considered a touchstone of English fiction.

We also explore several key novels from the twentieth century, including *Mrs. Dalloway, The Picture of Dorian Grey, Lord of the Ring, Things Fall Apart, Possession,* and *Waterland.* As anyone can see, the range of works discussed is broad, though each text can lay claim to cultural significance. Each of these texts has also managed to attract a wide audience—another factor in their inclusion here.

Three poets are included here, represented by studies of their major long poems or poem-sequences. Robert Herrick's *Hesperides* was an important contribution to seventeenth century poetry. The same could be said for Byron's *Don Juan,* a major Romantic poem, and *Crow* by Ted Hughes, one of the most savagely powerful sequences of the postwar era. In each case, a good deal of background material is provided to make these complex works accessible.

Two plays are discussed: *Waiting for Godot* and *Copenhagen.* Beckett's play remains a seminal work of modern drama, one of the most widely performed and widely imitated theatrical texts of all time. Michael Frayn's recent play about the reunion in Copehagen during World War Two of physicists Niels Bohr and Werner Heisenberg has been a huge hit and has quickly established itself as a contemporary classic.

Our hope is that these articles will encourage readers to return to the texts, thoughtfully, and better informed than they were before. That is, after all, one of the traditional functions of criticism. My own sense is that we have achieved a good deal in this first volume, and that readers will go away pleased and edified.

—JAY PARINI

Contributors

Paul Bibire. Writer and lecturer. Formerly a lecturer in the School of English, University of St. Andrews in Scotland, and of the Department of Anglo-Saxon, Norse, and Celtic, University of Cambridge, England. Since retirement he has been an honorary lecturer in Mediaeval History at the University of St. Andrews. Research includes Old English and Old Norse language and literature; Germanic philology; the development of Germanic legend and its representation in early English and Scandinavian poetry; Norse paganism and pagan mythology; Icelandic sagas and other prose; Norse court poetry. THE LORD OF THE RINGS

Fred Bilson. Lecturer. Studied moral sciences at Cambridge University, England, and has since lectured in English, linguistics and computer studies. He freelances as a support worker for dyslexic students at the university. COPENHAGEN

Sandie Byrne. Fellow in English at Balliol College, Oxford. Her publications include works on eighteenth and nineteenth-century fiction and twentieth-century poetry. JANE EYRE and VANITY FAIR

Clare Connors. Lecturer in English language and literature at the Queen's College and Merton College, Oxford, where she teaches literature from 1740 to the present day. She has published widely on various aspects of literary theory and criticism, including an essay on the early Freud in Whitehead and Rossington, eds., *Between the Psyche and the Polis: Refiguring History* (2000). She has lectured on Victorian literature in both the United States and Japan. DANIEL DERONDA

Gareth Cornwell. Senior Lecturer in the Department of English at Rhodes University in South Africa, Dr. Cornwell has published many essays and reviews, mainly in the field of South African literature and culture. He was for some years editor of the journals *New Coin Poetry* and *English in Africa*. He is currently working on a *Guide to South African Literature in English Since 1945* for Columbia University Press. THINGS FALL APART

Thomas D'Evelyn. Independent scholar and editorial consultant. His publications include *Called to Mind: Some Odes of Horace* (2001). HESPERIDES

Joseph Dewey. Associate professor of American literature for the University of Pittsburgh, Dewey is the author of *In a Dark Time: The Apocalyptic Temper in the American Novel of the Nuclear Age; Novels from Reagan's America: A New Realism;* and *Understanding Richard Powers,* as well as numerous articles and critical reviews on post-World War II literature and culture. He has also coedited casebooks on Henry James's short fiction and Don DeLillo's *Underworld*. He is completing a study on DeLillo. WATERLAND

Amy Edwards. Instructor. Educated at University College London and Worcester College, Oxford. In 2003 she completed a doctorate thesis on recent developments in contemporary British fiction. She teaches at Oxford University and is writing a monograph on the work of A.S. Byatt. POSSESSION

Peter Filkins. Associate Professor of English at Simon's Rock College of Bard. He is the author of numerous reviews and essays, as well as two volumes of poetry, *What She Knew* (1998) and *After Homer* (2002). His translation of the collected poems of Ingeborg Bachmann, *Songs in Flight* (1994), received an Outstanding Translation Award from the American Literary Translators Association. He is the recipient of grants and fellowships from the Fulbright Commission, Massachusetts Cultural Council, Yaddo, MacDowell, and the Millay Colony for the Arts. DON JUAN and MRS. DALLOWAY

James A. Knapton. Writer. Educated at the Universities of Durham and Oxford. In 2003 he was completing his doctoral thesis on politics and national identity in English poetry since the Second World War. He helped to research the Faber edition of Ted Hughes's *Collected Poems* (forthcoming, 2003). CROW

Phillip Mallett. Senior Lecturer in English at the University of St Andrews in Scotland. His main interests are in the field of Victorian studies. He has edited three collections of essays on Thomas Hardy, as well as editions of three of Hardy's novels, and a collection of essays on Kipling, *Kipling Considered*, as well as a critical biography, *Rudyard Kipling: a Literary Life*. PLAIN TALES FROM THE HILLS

Neil Powell. Poet, biographer, and editor. His books include five collections of poetry—*At the Edge* (1977), *A Season of Calm Weather* (1982), *True Colours* (1991), *The Stones on Thorpeness Beach* (1994) and *Selected Poems* (1998)—as well as *Carpenters of Light* (1979), *Roy Fuller: Writer and Society* (1995) and *The Language of Jazz* (1997). His critical biography of Crabbe, *George Crabbe: An English Life*, will be published in March 2004. He lives in Suffolk, England. BLEAK HOUSE and THE MAYOR OF CASTERBRIDGE

Sophie Ratcliffe. Lecturer. After studying at Oxford and Cambridge, Sophie Ratcliffe gained the post of Lecturer in English at Jesus College, Oxford University, where she teaches undergraduates and researches twentieth century literature. She has a particular interest in Joyce, Beckett, T.S. Eliot, and W.H. Auden. Her most recent article on Beckett is published in the 2003 volume of the journal *Samuel Beckett Today/Aujourd'hui* and she is currently working on the develpment of the dramatic monologue form. She also reviews contemporary fiction for the National Press in the United Kingdom. WAITING FOR GODOT

Lewis Robinson. Writer. Author of *Officer Friendly and Other Stories* (HarperCollins, 2003), he has published short stories in *Tin House, The Missouri Review, Open City,* and other periodicals. He is a graduate of Middlebury College and the Iowa Writers' Workshop, where he was a Teaching/Writing Fellow and winner of the Glenn Schaeffer Award. FRANKENSTEIN

N. S. Thompson. Lecturer in English at Christ Church, Oxford. He is the author of *Chaucer, Boccaccio and the Debate of Love* (1997) and articles on medieval and modern literature for a variety of journals, as well as many reviews for the *Times Literary Supplement*. He has translated several works from the Italian and a selection of his poetry was included in *Oxford Poets 2001: An Anthology.* THE RING AND THE BOOK

Thomas Wright. Freelance writer and editor. Editor of *Table Talk: Oscar Wilde*, the first anthology of Wilde's spoken stories. As a freelance writer, he has published numerous articles in the *Times Literary Supplement, The Independent,* and *The Daily Telegraph.* He has contributed to the *British Writers* series the entries on Oscar Wilde and Peter Ackroyd, whose journalism and miscellaneous pieces he has also edited and introduced in the anthology *The Collection.* THE PICTURE OF DORIAN GREY

Charles Dickens's
Bleak House

∾

NEIL POWELL

CHARLES DICKENS PLANNED his most ambitious novel, *Bleak House,* in 1851, during the renovation of his recently acquired London home, Tavistock House; but he was unable to start writing until the building work was finished and he could move in. The delays drove him frantic; the chaos was unbearable. Having fled to Broadstairs, on the Kentish coast, Dickens told his old friend Henry Austin: "I am perpetually wandering (in fancy) up and down the house and tumbling over the workmen . . . I smell paint in the sea. Phantom lime attends me all day long" (p. 388). The door between his study and the drawing-room was to be painted with dummy books, to create an illusion of continuous shelves, and Dickens amused himself by inventing titles for them: for instance, *The Gunpowder Magazine, Noah's Arkitecture, Cat's Lives* (in nine volumes), and *History of a Short Chancery Suit* (in twenty-one volumes). Houses, ghostly presences, strange meetings on staircases, and the law's delays in the Court of Chancery were all to find their way into his new book.

In other respects, however, *Bleak House* would be a novel notably purged of autobiographical themes. Charles Dickens, the second of eight children, was born in Portsmouth in 1812; his father was a clerk in the Navy Office and his childhood years in Chatham, Kent, were both peaceful and promising, thanks to the encouragement of his teacher, William Giles. But in 1822 John Dickens was transferred to London and the family's fortunes swiftly declined: he ended up in the debtors' prison, the Marshalsea, while Charles was sent to earn his living at Warren's blacking factory. He subsequently resumed his education and in 1827 became a solicitor's clerk; by 1833, he was parliamentary correspondent for *The Morning Chronicle.* A hopeless four-year courtship of Maria Beadnell was succeeded by his marriage to Catherine Hogarth in April 1836, the month in which the first installment of *The Pickwick Papers* appeared; this was followed by a succession of novels, including *Oliver Twist* (1838), *Nicholas Nickleby* (1839), *Barnaby Rudge* (1841) and *Dombey and Son* (1848). *David Copperfield* (1850) essentially tells the story of its author's own early life; when he turned to his next novel, *Bleak House* (1853), he could draw on altogether different resources.

He thoroughly researched and made extensive use of two particular kinds of source material (much of it helpfully assembled in A. E. Dyson's "Casebook" critical anthology on *Bleak House*). On the one hand were accounts of London poverty, such as those in Friederich Engels's *The Working Class in England in 1844*, Henry Mayhew's *London Labour and the London Poor*, and the Simon Report into the "Sanitary Condition of the City" of 1850. In Engels he found the description of St Giles—"Scarcely a whole window-pane can be found, the walls are crumbling, doorposts and window-frames loose and broken, door of old boards nailed together, or altogether wanting in this thieves' quarter, where no doors are needed, there being nothing to steal"—on which he based Tom-all- Alone's. From Simon he drew background information on fatal diseases (including smallpox) among the urban poor, as well the "putrefactive process" in the "saturated soils" of old city burial-grounds. Dickens's other source—to which his own experience in law and journalism drew him— was the continuing debate on the Court of Chancery in *The Times* during 1850 and 1851, which has been discussed by John Butt and Kathleen Tillotson in "The Topicality of *Bleak House*" (reprinted in Dyson, pp. 105–131). An article of 24 December 1850 is much to the point: "If a house be seen in a peculiarly dilapidated condition, the beholder at once exclaims, 'Surely that property must be in Chancery'," the writer reported; "the lingering and expectant suitors waste their lives as well as their substance in vain hopes, and death robs them of their wished-for triumph, if ruin have not already rendered it impossible." And, on 28 March 1851: ". . . the Court of Chancery is a name of terror, a devouring gulf, a den whence no footsteps return. . . A suit in that court is endless, bottomless, and insatiable." In addition, *The Times* supplied Dickens with further material about the living conditions of the poor: its leading article of 4 September 1851 argued that "In English towns generally half the attainable period of life is lost to all who are born. . . The destroying agent is typhus fever, generated by localised filth and excessive moisture. . . ."

CHRONOLOGY

1812	Charles Dickens born at Portsmouth, 7 February, second child of John Dickens, a naval clerk, and his wife Elizabeth (neé Barrow).
1817	Family moves to Chatham, where John Dickens works at the Royal Dockyards.
1822	Family moves to London.
1824	John Dickens in Marshalsea Prison; Charles sent to work at Warren's blacking factory; then attends Wellington House Academy.
1827	Clerk to Ellis and Blackmore, solicitors, Gray's Inn.
1832	Parliamentary reporter, *The Mirror of Parliament.*
1833	Parliamentary reporter, *The Morning Chronicle.*
1836	Publishes *Sketches by Boz*; marries Catherine Hogarth.
1837	*The Pickwick Papers* published.
1838	*Oliver Twist* published.
1838	*Nicholas Nickleby* published.
1841	*The Old Curiosity Shop* and *Barnaby Rudge* published.
1842	Visits North America and publishes *American Notes.*
1844	*Martin Chuzzlewit* published.
1848	*Dombey and Son* published.
1850	Founds *Household Words*, which he continues until 1859, and publishes *David Copperfield.*
1853	*Bleak House* published.
1854	*Hard Times* published.
1856	Buys Gad's Hill Place.
1857	*Little Dorrit* published.
1859	*A Tale of Two Cities* published.
1861	*Great Expectations* published.
1865	*Our Mutual Friend* published.
1867	Second American reading tour.
1870	*The Mystery of Edwin Drood* published in monthly installments but remains incomplete when Dickens dies on 9 June.

In these and several other ways, *Bleak House* is an intensely topical novel. Its continuing vein of parliamentary satire can be tracked to historical events: the hiatus at the start of chapter 40, for instance, in which "Lord Coodle would go out, Sir Thomas Doodle wouldn't come in, and there being nobody in Great Britain (to speak of) except Coodle and Doodle, there has been no Government" (p. 638), took place after the fall of Russell's administration in February 1851. The appearance of Dickens's literary acquaintances—Leigh Hunt as Skimpole, Walter Savage Landor as Boythorn—and of various thinly disguised charitable persons (such as Mrs Caroline Chisholm, of the Family Colonization Loan Society) further anchors the novel in its time and place. So too does the triumphant conversion of Dickens's friend Inspector Field, the subject of several essays in *Household Words*, into Inspector Bucket, who is probably the first detective in English fiction—a distinction often wrongly assigned to Sergeant Cuff in Wilkie Collins's *The Moonstone* (1868). Such correlations between the novel and its origins will help to account for the immense energy and urgency of this huge book, but they should not obscure the fact that *Bleak House* is much greater than its topicality and enjoyable without reference to it.

Dickens struggled to choose a title for so wide-ranging a novel. Most of his candidates were variations on "Tom-all-Alone's," the name of a derelict house near Chatham, remembered from his Kentish childhood, which he now transferred to the London slums. Interestingly, he supplemented many of these with over-restrictive subtitles: "The Solitary House where the Grass Grew," "The Solitary House where the Wind Howled," or "The Ruined House that Got into Chancery and Never Got Out." Penultimately, he abandoned Tom-all-Alone's and came up with the impossibly cumbersome "Bleak House and the East Wind: How They Both Got into Chancery and Never Got Out." At this point, he must have realized that wind was exactly the opposite of the novel's dominant image, fog, and settled simply for "Bleak House."

After finishing *Bleak House*, Dickens turned his attention from London poverty and the interminable processes of the law to the state of industrial England in *Hard Times* (1854). Other major novels—including *Little Dorrit* (1857), *Great Expectations* (1861) and the book which most obviously rivals *Bleak House* in scope and scale, *Our Mutual Friend* (1865)—followed. Exhausted both by writing and by his extensive international reading tours, Dickens died at Gad's Hill, the house near Rochester he had bought in 1856, in June 1870 at age 58.

BLEAK HOUSE

MAKING CONNECTIONS

Bleak House is a novel about nothing less than the entire fabric of mid-nineteenth-century England, its connections and its disconnections.

> What connexion can there be, between the place in Lincolnshire, the house in town, the Mercury in powder, and the whereabout of Jo the outlaw with the broom, who had that distant ray of light upon him when he swept the churchyard-step? What connexion can there have been between many people in the innumerable histories of this world, who, from opposite sides of great gulfs, have, nevertheless, been very curiously brought together?
>
> (p. 256)

Connections are what the fortunate possess—we speak of people as being "well-connected" or "connected by marriage"—and the unfortunate, the disenfranchised, lack; at another level, they are what the novelist must invent or discover to hold his novel together. Dickens is as ruthless as Grandfather Smallweed, whom he describes as "a horny-skinned, two-legged, money-getting species of spider" (p. 332), and as prodigious as Sir Leicester Dedlock, who "like a glorious spider, stretches his threads of relationship" (p. 446), in spinning his own web of connections: there are moments in *Bleak*

House when even the most admiring reader will greet with weary dismay the revelation that one more character is another's long lost relative. Sometimes this interconnectedness is a source of astonishment to individuals at the very heart of it: "Why, Esther!" says John Jarndyce smilingly, after a visit from Sir Leicester Dedlock, "our visitor and you are the two last persons on earth I should have thought of connecting together!" (p. 685). Meanwhile, beyond the connections of kinship and coincidence, there is at the core of the book a further tangle: the hopeless and (for at least nine hundred pages or so) seemingly interminable Chancery case of Jarndyce and Jarndyce. Dickens was attempting, as Edgar Johnson puts it, "an anatomy of modern society. *Bleak House* articulates its institutions, from government and law to philanthropy and religion—on every level, from Sir Leicester Dedlock's Lincolnshire estates to the rotting tenements of Tom-all-Alone's—as a corrupt and entangled web of vested interests and power" (*Charles Dickens: His Tragedy and Triumph*, p. 385).

But *Bleak House* is also a novel of disconnections, of curious and sinister ends, as Jo the crossing-sweeper knows all too well: "'They dies everywheres,'" said the boy. "'They dies in their lodgings—she knows where; I showed her—and they dies down in Tom-all-Alone's in heaps. They dies more than they lives, according to what *I* see'" (p. 492). Those whose final disconnections shape the novel's course include not only impoverished victims such as Jo and Gridley, the "man from Shropshire," but Krook (who in this connective world turns out to have been Mrs Smallweed's brother), Lady Dedlock (who dies precisely because she is discovered to be Esther's mother), the enigmatic lawyer Tulkinghorn, and the ward-in-Jarndyce Richard Carstone; Esther and her maid Charley both narrowly escape dying of smallpox. Krook's death by spontaneous combustion—as bizarre an end as any in English fiction—is mirrored by the eventual conclusion of Jarndyce and Jarndyce, when it is found that the entire estate has been absorbed by legal costs. In each case, there is literally nothing left: the disconnections are total.

The web like construction of *Bleak House*—and the tangled, shadowy use Dickens makes of it—ought to warn us against expecting too much in the way of a conventional linear plot. In fact, the novel has two main strands of plot, both of which are notably arbitrary in nature. One is the mystery of Esther Summerson and her parentage: it is essentially a fairy story, in which a pauper is discovered to have been a princess all along, except that its conclusion is bleakly ironic. The fact that Esther is found to be Lady Dedlock's daughter is irrelevant to her own happiness (neither John Jarndyce's nor Allan Woodcourt's love for her depends on it) and ruinous to her mother's. Moreover, as a source of suspense for the reader, it lasts for little more than half the novel: Lady Dedlock's disclosure in the woods at Chesney Wold—"O my child, my child, I am your wicked and unhappy mother!"—occurs in chapter 36 (p. 579), and the remainder of this plot consists of her doomed attempts to keep the secret from her husband and the fashionable world. The other main plot strand is feebler still, for although the case of Jarndyce and Jarndyce manages to touch almost everyone in the book, its whole point is that no one knows what on earth it is about: "it was about a Will when it was about anything," John Jarndyce explains to Esther, but "[i]t's about nothing but Costs, now" (p. 118). It is simply there, an inscrutable time-wasting cause, eating up money and lives. Krook recalls Tom Jarndyce's "restless habit of strolling about," talking about Chancery to anyone who would listen: "'For,' says he, 'it's being ground to bits in a slow mill; it's being roasted at a slow fire; it's being stung to death by single bees . . . it's going mad by grains'" (p. 71). And yet it is the backbone of the book, and so when "the suit lapses and melts away" (p. 975) the novel must end too.

To understand the greatness of this huge and ambitious novel, we shall need to concentrate less on its linear progress than on the significance Dickens attaches to his carefully chosen locations and, above all, his extraordinary cast of characters.

BLEAK HOUSES

The book begins in fog and ends in sunlight: it opens in London, in Lincoln's Inn Hall, and it ends in Yorkshire, in the second of two places called Bleak House. And the first thing to say about the places in this novel is that almost all of them are bleak, apart from the two houses which bear that ominous name: they, on the contrary, are scenes of the most radiant happiness. Dickens's symbolism of place, therefore, is not straightforward nor without irony.

The opening chapter is justly famous and has been much analyzed. It is an achievement in advance of its time: the density is reminiscent of Henry James, the spectral city, of James Joyce. Dickens's paradoxical achievement is to describe in immense detail a world where detail is foggily invisible; and this fog, which seems to be centered on Temple Bar ("that leaden-headed old obstruction, appropriate ornament for the threshold of a leaden-headed old corporation") and the Lord Chancellor himself (he is "at the very heart" of it), reaches out to embrace the whole of London, as well as "the Essex Marshes" and "the Kentish heights." It is—like poverty, disease, and the fog-bound case of Jarndyce and Jarndyce—a spreading contagion. Moreover, it is a state which the Londoner-lawyers we meet readily accept as their natural, habitual environment. When Esther arrives in the capital, in chapter 3, she is greeted by Mr. Guppy, a "young gentleman who had inked himself by accident," corresponding to the blurry and murky weather, and who cheerfully assures her: "This is a London particular." A little later, when Mr. Guppy gives Esther, Ada, and Richard directions to Mrs Jellyby's, he is magnificently oblivious to the fact that the places he names cannot actually be seen:

"Only round the corner," said Mr Guppy. "We just twist up Chancery Lane, and cut along Holborn, and there we are in four minutes time, as near as a toucher. This is about a London particular now, ain't it, miss?" He seemed quite delighted with it on my account.

(p. 51)

With this we are swiftly conveyed to the dirty, disorganized home of Mrs Jellyby, the "telescopic philanthropist," who lives with her ragged family and her distant benevolence in "a narrow street of tall houses, like an oblong cistern to hold the fog."

Hers is the first, and in some ways the mildest, of Dickens's grotesque London locations. Of a very different order is Krook's "Rag and Bottle Warehouse," at which, as Esther comments, "Everything seemed to be bought, and nothing to be sold" (p. 67); it has "the air of being in a legal neighbourhood, and of being, as it were, a dirty hanger-on and disowned relation of the law" (p. 68). Krook himself has a more elevated view of the matter: "they call me the Lord Chancellor, and call my shop Chancery," he explains, because "I have so many old parchmentses and papers in my stock. And I have a liking for rust and must and cobwebs. And all's fish that comes to my net. And I can't bear to part with anything I once lay hold of. . . ." (p. 70). His shop's correlation to the actual Court of Chancery even extends to his lodgers: one, Miss Flite, is a hopelessly impoverished suitor in the court; the other, known only as Nemo (we subsequently discover him to be Captain Hawdon), a transcriber of legal documents. It is characteristic of Dickens to be fascinated as well as appalled by this scene of cobwebbed stagnation: readers of *Great Expectations* will recall a similar ambivalence in his approach to Satis House.

Krook's premises establish the dominant motifs for a cluster of other London locations: poverty, dereliction, gloom, and confusion. Nearby, in Cook's Court, Cursitor Street, is Snagsby's, the law stationer's, once Peffer and

Snagsby's; but Peffer "has been recumbent this quarter of a century in the churchyard of St Andrews, Holborn" and "smoke, which is the London ivy, had so wreathed itself round Peffer's name, and clung to his dwelling-place, that the affectionate parasite quite overpowered the parent tree" (p. 155). In Bell Yard, "a narrow alley" towards the Strand, above a chandler's shop, are Gridley, "the man from Shropshire" and, above him, the fatherless children of Harold Skimpole's debt-enforcing pursuer Neckett. A further short distance away is Tom-all-Alone's, "a black, dilapidated street, avoided by all decent people. . . . these tumbling tenements contain, by night, a swarm of misery" (p. 256). All these places are close to the law courts, as are the far more respectable but no less sinister chambers of Mr. Tulkinghorn (Dickens stresses the proximity, as the crow flies, by having an actual crow "skim westward over the leaden slice of sky belonging to Cook's Court" (p. 158) across Chancery Lane to Lincoln's Inn Fields). Meanwhile, Tulkinghorn's rather less successful legal colleague, Mr. Vholes, occupies an office in Symond's Inn, which is "squeezed up in a corner, and blinks at a dead wall"; there, "[a] smell as of unwholesome sheep, blending with the smell of must and dust, is referable to the nightly (and often daily) consumption of mutton fat in candles, and to the fretting of parchment forms in greasy drawers" (p. 621). The taint of Krook's rag-and-bottle shop, which is also the taint of Chancery, infects each of these closely linked locations.

The geographical compactness of his London scenes, almost all of which can be identified in the *A–Z* street atlas, is important for Dickens's plotting in the later stages of the novel; five more locations are within a few minutes' walk of the Inns of Court. Mr. Turveydrop's Academy is in Newman Street, a decent enough address, but it occupies part of "a sufficiently dingy house" shared with "a drawing-master, a coal-merchant (there was, certainly, no room for his coals), and a lithographic artist" (p. 222). George's Shooting Gallery is in "the curious region lying about the Haymarket and Leicester Square, which is a centre of attraction to indifferent foreign hotels and indifferent foreigners, racket-courts, fighting-men, swordsmen, footguards, old china, gaming-houses, exhibitions, and a large medley of shabbiness and shrinking out of sight" (pp. 349–50); Dickens's affection for the random oddities of the Victorian city is once again self-evident. Further away, but no distance at all for a fit man like Trooper George, is the musical instrument shop of his friend and former army colleague, Matthew Bagnet: it is across the river, near the Elephant and Castle, which even a non-Londoner will immediately recognize as an unpromising place to sell musical instruments. To the north of the Inns of Court lies "a rather ill-favoured and ill-savoured neighbourhood, though one of its rising grounds bears the name of Mount Pleasant;" and there, "in a little narrow street, always solitary, shady, and sad, closely bricked in on all sides like a tomb" (p. 332), live the Smallweed family. Lastly, a little to the west is Somers Town, where Harold Skimpole—who is as innocent of money as Grandfather Smallweed is obsessed by it—lives in a house whose condition comes as no surprise to Esther, or to the reader:

> It was in a state of dilapidation quite equal to our expectation. Two or three of the area railings were gone; the water-butt was broken; the knocker was loose; the bell handle had been pulled off a long time, to judge from the rusty state of the wire; and dirty footprints on the steps were the only signs of its being inhabited.
>
> (p. 672)

This remarkable catalogue of decaying and derelict places—to which may be added, as a symbolic extension of London, the brickmaker's cottage near St Albans—forms the novel's solid foundation, its recurring ground bass.

But there is another world in the novel, infinitely more grand though every bit as gloomy:

While Esther sleeps, and while Esther wakes, it is still wet weather down at the place in Lincolnshire. The rain is ever falling, drip, drip, drip, by day and night, upon the broad flagged terrace-pavement, The Ghost's Walk. The weather is so very bad, down in Lincolnshire, that the liveliest imagination can scarcely apprehend its ever being fine again. Not that there is any superabundant life of imagination on the spot, for Sir Leicester is not here (and, truly, even if he were, would not do much for it in that particular), but is in Paris, with my Lady; and solitude, with dusky wings, sits brooding upon Chesney Wold.

(p. 103)

This little paragraph—the opening one of chapter 7—is a fine example of Dickens's technique at its most subtly suggestive. It is all about absence. It begins with Esther, who has never been to Chesney Wold and has, as far as we are aware at this point in the novel, no connection with it; it ends with the Dedlocks, who are not there either. In between, we have the weather (the London fog has organized itself into rain) and the unforgettable image of The Ghost's Walk, with which Dickens introduces an entirely new dimension to *Bleak House*: the idea of the past coming back to haunt the present. We are told almost nothing, and yet we sense almost everything, about Chesney Wold: its name, its weather and its ghosts are more than enough.

Finally, there are three more houses which need to be mentioned in this tour of the novel's geography. Two of them bear the book's title. John Jarndyce's Bleak House, which had been called The Peaks when it originally belonged to his great uncle, the suicidal Tom Jarndyce, is near St Albans. It is, from the moment we (and Esther) first see it, an image of easy, unconstrained domesticity, "one of those delightfully irregular houses where you go up and down steps out of one room into another, and where you come upon more rooms when you think you have seen all there are, and where there is a bountiful provision of little halls and passages, and where you find still older cottage-rooms in unexpected places, with lattice windows and green growth pressing through them" (p. 85). This description continues for two pages, so there is no mistaking Dickens's determination to create a scene of natural happiness which is in every respect the opposite of fog-bound London. The other Bleak House, at the very end of the book, is in effect John Jarndyce's wedding-present to Esther and Allan Woodcourt: approached via "a pretty little orchard, where the cherries were nestling among the green leaves, and the shadows of the apple-trees were sporting on the grass" (p. 962), it is almost impossibly edenic in its idealized goodness. Between these two comes Lawrence Boythorn's house which, in direct contrast to the neighboring Chesney Wold, is also a place of tranquility and plenty: "everything about the place wore an aspect of maturity and abundance. . . Such stillness and composure reigned within the orderly precincts of the old red wall, that even the feathers hung in garlands to scare the birds hardly stirred. . . ." (p. 288). It is a commonplace to remark that these somewhat over-sugared pastoral retreats in Dickens are a response to his own ruined childhood; but Boythorn's home, which is emblematic of his goodness (and which he lends to Esther for her convalescence), ought to remind us of a literary antecedent, the strikingly similar house and garden of the admirable Mr. Wilson, who turns out to be the hero's father, in Henry Fielding's *Joseph Andrews*. The sources of *Bleak House* are both various and surprising.

To focus on some of the major characters in *Bleak House*, I shall now need to make a few rough-and-ready distinctions. There are the "Emblems and Hypocrites," who represent clear if often indefensible values and interests; the "Pursuers and Victims," who drive forward the book's narrative movement; and a somewhat problematic group, including Esther herself, who embody Dickens's own moral perspectives. In such an immense and fluid novel as this, some will necessarily belong in more than one of these arbitrary divisions, which should nevertheless serve as helpful starting- points.

EMBLEMS AND HYPOCRITES

Krook is the clearest instance in *Bleak House* of a purely emblematic figure: he is so much an emblem that, as we have seen, he is indistinguishable from the place he inhabits. He possesses few human attributes beyond generalized malice: he is defined by the objects he has collected around him, by his unfortunate lodgers, and by his malevolent cat. Viewed in this light, his grotesque death seems altogether apt, for he is less a person than part of the atmosphere into which, as Dickens gleefully demonstrates, he is assimilated. Mr. Snagsby thinks the greasy air comes from tainted chops grilling at the Sol's Arms, while Mr. Guppy at first surmises that a chimney is on fire and then discovers a "thick, yellow liquor . . . a stagnant, sickening oil" (p. 516) dripping from the window-sill; and thus Krook melts away, exactly like a Chancery case, in "Spontaneous Combustion, and none other of all the deaths that can be died" (p. 519). After his death, when the Smallweeds arrive with "[a]n air of haste and excitement," Grandfather Smallweed thanks Mr. Guppy "for discharging the melancholy office of discovering the ashes of Mrs Smallweed's brother": the word "ashes" has a special resonance in this context, and the revelation that Krook could have been related to anyone at all is astonishing. "We were not on terms," Grandfather Smallweed explains, and adds, exactly echoing Miss Flite's original description of her landlord, "He was eccentric—he was very eccentric" (p. 529).

An inquest is promptly held and Krook's remains are absurdly despatched in a "much admired" six-foot coffin; Jo, though absent and already ill on this occasion, had been present at the inquest (or, as he has it, "Inkwhich") which followed the law-writer's death in the same house:

Name, Jo. Nothing else that he knows on. Don't know that everybody has two names. Never heerd of sich a think. Don't know that Jo is short for a longer name. Thinks it long enough for him.—He don't find no fault with it. Spell it? No. He can't spell it. No father, no mother, no friends. Never been to school. What's home? Knows a broom's a broom, and knows it's wicked to tell a lie. Don't recollect who told him about the broom, or about the lie, but knows both. Can't exactly say what'll be done to him arter he's dead if he tells a lie to the gentlemen here, but believes it'll be something wery bad to punish him, and serve him right—and so he'll tell the truth.

(p. 177)

Like Krook, Jo is an emblem; and, like him, he is an image of contagion. In Jo's case, however, since he is forever being "moved on," the contagion moves on with him. As his self-description before the coroner suggests, he is more cause than character: others' kindnesses—Esther's, George Rouncewell's—will be measured against his misfortunes. He remains destitute and uncomprehending—"*We* never know nothink. *I* never knowd what it wos all about" (p. 733)— and his death provokes Dickens to the most passionate anger he displays in the entire book: "Dead, your Majesty. Dead, my lords and gentlemen. Dead, Right Reverends and Wrong Reverends of every order. Dead, men and women, born with Heavenly compassion in your hearts. And dying thus around us, every day" (p. 734). The point is wholly justified, but the tone suffers as the polemicist momentarily elbows the novelist out of the way.

It is Jo's bad luck, and the subject of Dickens's most sardonic humor, that he was born in London instead of in some remote country where he might have been the grateful recipient of telescopic philanthropy:

He is not one of Mrs Pardiggle's Tockahoopo Indians; he is not one of Mrs Jellyby's lambs, being wholly unconnected with Borrioboola-Gha; he is not softened by distance and unfamiliarity; he is not a genuine foreign-grown savage; he is the ordinary home-made article. Dirty, ugly, disagreeable to all the senses, in body a common creature of the common streets, only in soul a heathen. Homely filth begrimes him, homely parasites devour him, homely sores are in him, homely rags are on him; native ignorance, the growth of English soil and climate, sinks his immortal nature lower than the beasts that perish. Stand forth, Jo, in uncompromising colours! From the sole of thy foot to the crown of thy head, there is nothing interesting about thee.

(p. 724)

In one sense this is scathingly ironic for, quite apart from Esther and George, who attempt to help him, a surprising number of people are interested in Jo: to Bucket, Snagsby, and Tulkinghorn, he is the vital witness who (to his bewilderment, though not the reader's) will eventually have seen three separate incarnations of Lady Dedlock, while to the evangelical Mr. Chadband he is a fit subject for conversion. But in another sense, there is indeed nothing interesting about him: he is simply an emblem of the London poor, equally invisible to the wealthy Dedlocks and to the telescopically charitable Mrs Jellyby.

The connection—or, more usually, the failure of connection—between urban poverty and those who might alleviate it is the great subterranean theme of *Bleak House*: Dickens's most consistent satire is directed towards the hypocrites who, while they appear to make life better, actually do exactly the opposite—Mrs. Jellyby and Mrs. Pardiggle, Chadband, Turveydrop, and Skimpole. The two charitable ladies have much in common: both fix their attention on distant good deeds at the expense of their own families. But Mrs. Jellyby, altogether the more subtly drawn character, is in her combination of obsession and absent-mindedness one of Dickens's finest comic creations:

"You find me, my dears," said Mrs Jellyby, snuffing the two great office candles in tin candlesticks which made the room taste strongly of hot tallow (the fire had gone out, and there was nothing in the grate but ashes, a bundle of wood, and a poker), "you find me, my dears, as usual, very busy; but that you will excuse. The African project

at present employs my whole time. It involves me in correspondence with public bodies, and with private individuals anxious for the welfare of their species all over the country. I am happy to say it is advancing. We hope by this time next year to have from a hundred and fifty to two hundred healthy families cultivating coffee and educating the natives of Borrioboola-Gha, on the left bank of the Niger."

(p. 53)

As her long-suffering daughter Caddy remarks, on the eve of her own marriage to Prince Turveydrop (an occasion noticed by her mother merely as an inconvenience, since she will now have to employ a boy to help her): "Ma and Africa, together, upset the whole house. . . . Ma's ruinous to everything." Meanwhile Mr. Jellyby, who has acquired the habit of opening his mouth without saying anything, manages to utter a momentous piece of advice to his daughter: "Never have a Mission, my dear child" (p. 481).

Mrs. Jellyby is monstrously wrong-headed, and John Jarndyce finds her a great provoker of the east wind ("I am much obliged to Mrs Jellyby. O dear me! This is a very trying wind!" [p. 217]), but Mrs. Pardiggle is a hectoring bully, as Esther observes: "She was a formidable style of lady, with spectacles, a prominent nose, and a loud voice, who had the effect of wanting a great deal of room. And she really did, for she knocked down little chairs with her skirts that were quite a great way off" (p. 124). Her five disgruntled and mutinous sons, by whom she is invariably accompanied, have been coerced into donating their pocket-money to causes ranging from the Tockahoopo Indians to the Great National Smithers Testimonial, while the youngest ("who was stolidly and evenly miserable") has enrolled in the Infant Bonds of Joy: "It was not merely that they were weazen and shrivelled—though they were certainly that too—but they looked absolutely ferocious with discontent" (p. 125). Whereas Mrs. Jellyby confines her charitable attentions to distant subjects, Mrs. Pardiggle has "a mechanical way of taking possession of people" (p. 133) such as the brickmaker and his family. She is not only moralizing but invasive, as is the appalling Mr. Chadband, "a large yellow man, with a fat smile, and a general appearance of having a good deal of train oil in his system" (pp. 304–305), whose "stern, severe-looking, silent" wife turns out to be the former Mrs. Rachael who, packing the young Esther off for London, had been "too good to feel any emotion at parting" (p. 35). That is perhaps too glib a coincidence even for Dickens to carry off, but the scene in which Chadband expounds on the "the light of Terewth" before an audience which includes Jo (baffled and wholly unenlightened) and Mrs. Snagsby (who "sees it all" and misunderstands everything) is a triumph of merciless parody:

> "Of Terewth," says Mr. Chadband . . . "Say not to me that is *not* the lamp of lamps. I say to you, it is. I say to you, a million of times over, it is. It is! I say to you that I will proclaim it to you, whether you like it or not; nay, that the less you like it, the more I will proclaim it to you. With a speaking-trumpet! I say to you that if you rear yourself against it, you shall fall, you shall be bruised, you shall be battered, you shall be flawed, you shall be smashed."
>
> (p. 412)

He matches Mrs. Pardiggle in his ability to disguise hectoring as self-sacrifice—"You can't tire me, good people," she tells the brickmaker and his family, "I enjoy hard work; and the harder you make mine, the better I like it" (p. 132)—but in each case their ministrations prefigure death. Jenny's child dies after Mrs. Pardiggle's visit; Jo's fatal illness begins after Mr. Chadband's.

In this company, Mr. Turveydrop must count as a lesser evil, though he is no less a hypocrite. There is, indeed, nothing at all genuine about him:

> He was a fat old gentleman with a false complexion, false teeth, false whiskers, and a wig. He had a fur collar, and he had a padded breast to his coat, which only wanted a star or a broad blue ribbon to be complete. He was pinched in, and swelled out, and got up, and strapped down, as much as he could possibly bear. He had such a neck-cloth on (puffing his very eyes out of their natural shape), and his chin and even his ears were so sunk into it, that it seemed as though he must inevitably double up, if it were cast loose. He had, under his arm, a hat of great size and weight, shelving downward from the crown to the brim; and in his hand a pair of white gloves, with which he flapped it, as he stood poised on one leg, in a high-shouldered round-elbowed state of elegance not to be surpassed. He had a cane, he had an eye-glass, he had a snuff-box, he had rings, he had wristbands, he had everything but any touch of nature; he was not like youth, he was not like age, he was like nothing in the world but a model of Deportment.
>
> (p. 225)

As is often the case with Dickens's comic characters, the ludicrous exterior masks a more serious problem: Mr. Turveydrop, who leaves his overworked son to manage the dancing-school while he promenades around town and takes his meals in hotels, is as selfish and as self-deluding as Mrs. Jellyby. Yet he is unexpectedly redeemed: after his son's marriage to Caddy Jellyby, he finds in the unhappy Mr. Jellyby a grateful audience for his endless tales about the Prince Regent. Esther wryly reflects: "That old Mr Turveydrop should ever, in the chances and changes of life, have come to the rescue of Mr Jellyby from Borrioboola-Gha, appeared to me to be one of the pleasantest of oddities" (p. 613).

Harold Skimpole's is the opposite trajectory. When he is first introduced to Esther, Ada, and Richard, he explains his philosophy in terms which are, ironically, very close to Mrs. Pardiggle's or Mr. Chadband's: "I don't feel any vulgar gratitude to you. I almost feel as if *you* should be grateful to *me*, for giving you the opportunity of enjoying the luxury of generosity" (p. 91). But Skimpole is his own charitable cause, and the reader quickly perceives his childlike innocence to be self-serving indolence: his befriending of Richard, who is already well on the way to sharing Skimpole's less desirable qualities, is—as Esther at least recognizes—likely to prove disastrous. The sagacious Inspector Bucket has his measure too: "'No idea of money,' observed Mr. Bucket.—'He takes it though!'" (p. 874). He has indeed taken it, from Bucket himself, with consequences for Jo, Esther, and Skimpole that reverberate through the rest of the book. We may find it hard to forgive John Jarndyce for his misplaced patience in putting up with Skimpole's tomfoolery for so long and for his tardiness in severing the connection: when that comes, it is the necessary rejection by the hero of the buffoon, like Prince Hal's of Falstaff.

PURSUERS AND VICTIMS

Bleak House begins as a notably static book, in fog-bound London and rain-soaked Lincolnshire, but it modulates into something very different: a novel of pursuit. And crucial to this modulation is Dickens's invention of Detective Inspector Bucket: "Time and place cannot bind Mr Bucket. Like man in the abstract, he is here today and gone tomorrow—but, very unlike man indeed, he is here again the next day" (p. 803). Seemingly ubiquitous, he is in fact merely cunning, resourceful, and speedy—as his nocturnal pursuit of Lady Dedlock makes abundantly clear. He can also seem omniscient, whereas on closer inspection his intelligence turns out to be limited but highly focused, reinforced by a variety of tactical strategies. With Mr. Snagsby, for instance, his ruse is a confiding flattery which the reader (unlike poor Snagsby) at once recognizes as outrageous:

"Yes! and lookee here, Mr Snagsby," resumes Bucket, taking him aside by the arm, tapping him familiarly on the breast, and speaking in a confidential tone. "You're a man of the world, you know, and a man of business, and a man of sense. That's what *you* are."

"I am sure I am much obliged to you for your good opinion," returns the stationer, with his cough of modesty, "but—"

"That's what you *are*, you know," says Bucket. "Now, it an't necessary to say to a man like you,

engaged in your business, which is a business of trust and requires a person to be wide awake and have his senses about him, and his head screwed on tight (I had an uncle in your business once)—it ain't necessary to say to a man like you, that it's the best and wisest way to keep little matters like this quiet. Don't you see? Quiet!"

(p. 356)

Bucket's manner and speech-rhythms provide the template for numerous literary (and screen) detectives who have followed him. His imaginary stationer-uncle is a recurrent trick: needing information from Sir Leicester's footman, he creates a friend who is a Royal Academy sculptor, for whom the footman should model; about to arrest George Rouncewell at Matthew Bagnet's musical instrument shop, he suddenly remembers another friend "in want of a second-hand wiolinceller, of a good tone" (p. 759). Yet—and this is a redeeming feature in a character who is otherwise at best morally neutral and at worst devious—when Bucket is confronted with a true villain, such as the murderous Mademoiselle Hortense or the money-grubbing Grandfather Smallweed, he becomes mercilessly direct. He is the only person in the novel to intimidate Smallweed, in the splendid chapter ("Springing a Mine") that culminates in Hortense's arrest: "'I am Inspector Bucket of the Detective, I am; and this,' producing the top of his convenient little staff from his breast-pocket, 'is my authority. . . Your name, old gentleman, is Smallweed; that's what your name is; I know it well'" (pp. 822–823). Dickens's characters are usually more joked about than joking, but Bucket goes on to compare Smallweed to a pig ("You don't happen to know why they killed the pig, do you? . . . on account of his having so much cheek. Don't *you* get into the same position. . . .") and even succeeds in preventing the old man from shouting at everyone as if they were his deaf wife.

Smallweed, despite his grotesquely comical immobility, is a pursuer too, hounding his debtors (among them the admirable George Rouncewell) and at last, while going through his late brother-in-law's effects, accidentally unlocking the Jarndyce case by discovering a missing will. The Smallweeds illustrate one of Dickens's most ambiguous strengths: they are despicable and repulsive, yet they provide such irresistible slapstick comedy (and such vigorous writing) that the reader will delightedly welcome their reappearances. Bart Smallweed's tall hat, which invariably presents itself to our view before he does, or Grandfather Smallweed's extravagantly resourceful verbal abuse of his wife, accompanied by his hurling of increasingly dangerous missiles, are the stuff of farce. By the time we reach Krook's inquest the inoffensive cushion seems likely to be replaced by a quart pot:

> ". . . I am speaking of your brother, you brimstone black-beetle, that was seventy-six years of age."
>
> Mrs Smallweed instantly begins to shake her head, and pipe up, "Seventy-six pound seven and sevenpence! Seventy-six thousand bags of money! Seventy-six hundred thousand million of parcels of bank notes!"
>
> "Will somebody give me a quart pot?" exclaims her exasperated husband, looking helplessly about him, and finding no missile within his reach. "Will somebody obleege me with a spittoon? Will somebody hand me anything hard and bruising to pelt at her? You hag, you cat, you dog, you brimstone barker!"
>
> (p. 530)

In the absence of a suitable object, Grandfather Smallweed throws his granddaughter Judy at her grandmother, which is both less damaging and much funnier.

Krook is not Smallweed's only connection with the law. Precisely because he is so single-minded in his pursuit of money, he needs a ruthless lawyer; and, in one of the novel's most bizarre and sinister connections, Tulkinghorn acts both for Lord Dedlock and for Smallweed. (This is, of course, also a convenience of plot, enabling Tulkinghorn to trade off George's debt for the document that confirms the law-writer's

identity as Captain Hawdon.) And Smallweed and the whole legal hierarchy have something else in common: "The one great principle of the English law is, to make business for itself. There is no other principle distinctly, certainly, and consistently maintained through all its narrow turnings. Viewed by this light it becomes a coherent scheme, and not the monstrous maze the laity are apt to think it" (p. 621). Whether its avenues are "narrow turnings" or a "monstrous maze," they are conduits of pursuit: the image is so entrenched in actual law that "to pursue" is a proper synonym for "to prosecute." Dickens explicitly compares the black-suited Tulkinghorn to a bird of prey: he is "like a larger species of rook" (p. 191), while his vampirish legal inferior, Mr. Vholes, is also "a bird of ill omen" (p. 696). Birdlike, too, Tulkinghorn has a room in a turret at Chesney Wold and chambers at the top of a staircase in London; he belongs everywhere and nowhere. He is omniscient in a manner far more disturbingly enigmatic than that of the apparently straightforward Inspector Bucket. Even the book's authorial present-tense narrator purports to find him unfathomable: "Therefore, while Mr Tulkinghorn may not know what is passing in the Dedlock mind at present, it is very possible that he may" (p.25).

There is indeed a sense in which Tulkinghorn is, or at least seeks to be, the author of the novel's main events. He is the common thread in all the strands of plot, most of which he attempts to manipulate; he is killed not by any of the persons who might predictably and reasonably wish him dead but by a crazed and aggrieved servant whose actions he has failed to predict. When Allan Woodcourt asks George Rouncewell, whose judgments of his fellow-men are usually generous, to describe Tulkinghorn, he is understandably astonished by the reply he receives:

> "Why, then I'll tell you, sir," returns the trooper, stopping short, and folding his arms on his square chest, so angrily that his face fires and flushes all over; "he is a confoundedly bad kind of man. He is a slow-torturing kind of man. He is no more

like flesh and blood, than a rusty old carbine is. He is a kind of man—by George!—that has caused me more restlessness, and more uneasiness, and more dissatisfaction with myself, than all other men put together. That's the kind of man Mr Tulkinghorn is!"

(p. 727)

It is an answer in all respects but one: *why* Tulkinghorn is as he is, what drives him in his lonely and ultimately self-destructive quest, remains a mystery. Both inscrutable and purposeless, he is the perfect symbol for the legal system he represents.

The other legal figures in the novel all have one touch of Tulkinghorn or another. There is the oily, verbose Conversation Kenge, who cannot believe that there is anyone who has "never heard of Jarndyce and Jarndyce" (p. 33); the pathetic Mr. Guppy, whose hopeless pursuit of Esther ironically mirrors Tulkinghorn's of her mother, Lady Dedlock; the bloodsucking Mr. Vholes, with "his dead glove" and "his long thin shadow" (p. 698); and lesser hangers-on to the legal profession, such as Jopling (or Weevle) and Bart Smallweed. All of them are parasitic, in the exact sense that their existence within the world of *Bleak House* depends on their clinging to the misfortunes of other and more admirable characters. When they fail, they crumple and disappear, like Mr. Guppy after Esther's rejection, or come to sudden and grotesque ends, like Tulkinghorn—and, of course, like the figure who stands as emblem for Chancery, Krook.

Their most obvious victims include the various casualties of Chancery: Gridley, the man from Shropshire; Miss Flite and her caged birds; and, above all, Richard Carstone, who is drawn inexorably into Miss Flite's desolate orbit:

He had even begun to haunt the Court. He told us how he saw Miss Flite there daily; how they talked together, and he did her little kindnesses; and how, while he laughed at her, he pitied her from his heart. But he never thought—never, my poor, dear, sanguine Richard, capable of so much happiness then, and with such better things before him!—

what a fatal link was riveting between his fresh youth and her faded age; between his free hopes and her caged birds, and her hungry garret, and her wandering mind.

(p. 369)

This short passage illustrates one difficulty with Richard and another with Esther's narrative. We are required to accept that all Richard's troubles stem from Chancery, whereas the sceptical reader may simply see an amiably feckless young man who is indulged in his half-hearted attempts at a series of careers; meanwhile, Esther's view of him here raises the question of her suppressed hindsight (as she is telling her story in the past tense, she knows perfectly well that Richard does not have "such better things before him"). Apart from his own folly, Richard is also morally culpable in his disregard for John Jarndyce's impassioned advice: "'Rick, Rick!' cried my guardian, with a sudden terror in his manner, and in an altered voice, and putting up his hands as if he would have stopped his ears, 'for the love of God, don't found a hope or expectation on the family curse'" (p. 389). His subsequent, Chancery-induced antagonism towards John Jarndyce is recognized by the latter, in a metaphor which connects with another of the book's major themes, as a form of contagious disease: "[I]t is in the subtle poison of such abuses to breed such diseases. His blood is infected, and objects lose their natural aspects in his sight" (p. 560). Once again, the law is seen as not merely a corrupting but a denaturing force; and by turning first to Skimpole—"Richard could scarcely have found a worse friend than this" (p. 594)—and then to Vholes, Richard compounds his illness. Appropriately, it is his physician, Allan Woodcourt, who provides the most perceptive diagnosis:

"It is not," said Mr Woodcourt, "his being so much younger or older, or thinner or fatter, or paler or ruddier, as there being upon his face such a singular expression. I never saw so remarkable a look in a

13

young person. One cannot say that it is all anxiety, or all weariness; yet it is both, and like ungrown despair."

(p. 707)

That subtle analysis is a finer note on which to leave Richard than the perilously sententious one, the idea of "beginning the world," on which Dickens actually ends.

There remains the victim of the parallel pursuit, Lady Dedlock. Some readers find it a fault that her downfall is not bound in with the Chancery plot, as it might conceivably have been; but the apartness of her death satisfactorily reflects the apartness of her life, and for once a failure to tie up loose ends neatly works to the book's advantage. Her transition is from ennui to panic: her destruction seems likely from the moment she discovers that her daughter is still alive; and, once her secret has been fathomed by both Tulkinghorn and Guppy, it is certain. True to the book's symbolic structure, she must both don a pauper's costume—disguising herself in Jenny's clothes during her flight to St. Albans—and die a pauper's death: that even her daughter Esther should not at first recognize her in death ("I saw, with a cry of pity and horror, a woman lying—Jenny, the mother of the dead child" [p. 913]) precisely counterbalances Lady Dedlock's failure to recognize her daughter in life.

GOODNESS

Goodness causes problems for Dickens: his virtuous characters are often too sweet for modern taste, and it is perhaps not until *Great Expectations* that he creates, in Pip, a hero whom readers invariably find both good and likeable. Esther labors under two special disadvantages. She carries substantial portions of the narrative herself, in the past tense, continually qualifying her own faultless conduct with self-deprecation; and she is burdened by a series of nicknames which sound diminishing to modern ears: "This was the beginning of my being called Old Woman, and Little Old Woman, and Cobweb,

and Mrs Shipton, and Mother Hubbard, and Dame Durden, and so many names of that sort, that my own name soon became quite lost among them" (p. 121). But both the self-deprecation and the nicknames are so characteristic of their time that Dickens's readers must learn to put up with them. More local difficulties, perhaps less easily excused, occur when John Jarndyce gives Charley Neckett to Esther as a "present"—"If you please, miss, I'm a present to you, with Mr Jarndyce's love" (p. 385)—and when, having proposed to Esther and been accepted, he steps aside for Allan Woodcourt (and a different Bleak House) in a scene of Pandarus-like manipulation.

Those are the blemishes; apart from them, Esther is a far more complicated and convincing portrait of goodness than is generally conceded. The key to her remarkable personality is, as Inspector Bucket observes, not saintliness but balance:

> "You're a pattern, you know, that's what you are," said Mr Bucket, warmly; "you're a pattern."
>
> I told him I was very glad, as indeed I was, to have been no hindrance to him; and that I hoped I should be none now.
>
> "My dear," he returned, "when a young lady is as mild as she's game, and as game as she's mild, that's all I ask, and more than I expect. She then becomes a Queen, and that's about what you are yourself."

(p. 902)

Esther is incontestably "mild," but "game"? That may come as a surprise, until we reflect on how precisely right it is: she has been game since the day Mrs. Rachel sent her off like a parcel on the coach to London (on which journey she bravely outfaced a strange fellow-passenger). She is game enough to visit the poor and to care for the sick, at terrible cost to her own health; she continually undertakes expeditions which are risky (to the brickmakers' cottages or to Bell Yard) or which require unusual tact (informing Mrs. Jellyby and Mr. Turveydrop of their children's impending marriage, intervening on

Richard's behalf with Skimpole); and of course she accompanies Bucket on the gruelling night journey in search of her mother. When in her epilogue she expresses modest surprise that she is so well-liked "as the doctor's wife" (p. 988), it is clear to the reader that her entire career in the novel has been a preparation for just this role.

Esther is calm and plucky; but she is also intelligent. Her judgments of other characters strike us as trustworthy, not simply because she is an authorial mouthpiece but because they are grounded in careful observation and good sense. There are, indeed, occasions on which she is simply too well-informed, when Dickens not only stretches but entirely neglects the restricted point of view of a first-person narrator (for instance, in the opening pages of chapter 51, where she gives a long verbatim account of a meeting between Vholes and Woodcourt at which she was not present). Finally, there is her remarkable discretion: while those whose professional business it is to keep secrets continually divulge them, Esther discloses her two momentous burdens—the discovery of her parentage and John Jarndyce's proposal—only to the proper confidants, Jarndyce and Ada respectively.

Elsewhere in *Bleak House,* as elsewhere in Dickens, goodness tends to shade into weakness and simplicity. Ada, though her gentleness fully deserves Esther's devotion, is nevertheless foolish to marry Richard and, having married him, to exert so little influence on him. The Rouncewell family are triumphantly reunited towards the end of the book, yet George Rouncewell's admirable qualities are compromised by his inability to organize his business life; his friend Matthew Bagnet, who has continually to defer to his wife to speak for him, is equally hopeless in his business affairs. When these two innocents visit Grandfather Smallweed, Dickens very justly comments: "Whether there are two people in England less likely to come satisfactorily out of any negotiation with Mr Smallweed than Mr George and Mr Matthew Bagnet, may be very reasonably

questioned" (p. 544). Their eventual survival is wholly dependent on luck, not on judgment.

There is, however, one more good character in *Bleak House* who needs to be mentioned, and that is Sir Leicester Dedlock. At the beginning of the book, he is an emblem, though a complex one, of the decaying aristocracy: "He is an honourable, obstinate, truthful, high-spirited, intensely prejudiced, perfectly unreasonable man" (p. 22). His appearances invariably exemplify his intransigence (in his dealings with Boythorn) and his snobbery (with Rouncewell, the "Ironmaster"). We know, however, that he married for love, and his forgiveness—while recovering from the stroke which almost kills him—of his missing wife is one of the most moving passages in the entire novel:

> Therefore I desire to say, and to call you all to witness . . . that I am on unaltered terms with Lady Dedlock. That I assert no cause whatever of complaint against her. That I have ever had the strongest affection for her, and that I retain it undiminished. Say this to herself, and to every one. If you ever say less than this, you will be guilty of deliberate falsehood to me.
>
> (p. 895)

The legal phraseology is, of course, appropriate to the texture of *Bleak House*; but the vital point is that Dickens has allowed Sir Leicester to learn through suffering and to grow into goodness.

CONCLUSION

To write about *Bleak House,* at almost any length, is to be conscious of how much one has left out. It is so various and prolific a novel that any one approach to it immediately suggests others. Q. D. Leavis, understandably struggling to compress the diversity of the novel into a single sentence, wrote of it: "There is this extraordinary combination of the painfully serious that tends towards the macabre even, which yet consorts with a high-spirited, witty and sometimes humorous apprehension of life without discordance, and runs to a finer awareness of the quality of personality and human relations. . . ." (*Dickens the Novelist,* p. 227) That struggle is instructive. The all-embracing scope and the dazzling interconnections of *Bleak House* mean that any summarizing sentence is likely, like Mrs. Leavis's, to start spinning its own web.

Perhaps the case could be put more simply. On British radio, there is a long-running program called "Desert Island Discs," in which a "castaway" is invited to choose eight records to take to a desert island. The imaginary island is also provided with copies of the Bible and the works of Shakespeare, and the castaway is allowed one further book. Clearly, this would have to be endlessly rereadable, continually surprising, enormously wide-ranging, profoundly moving, and hilariously funny. I would nominate *Bleak House.*

Selected Bibliography

EDITIONS

Bleak House was first published between March 1852 and September 1853 in nineteen monthly installments; the first edition in book form appeared in 1853.

Bleak House, edited by Norman Page, with an introduction by J. Hillis Miller. Harmondsworth: Penguin English Library, 1971.

Bleak House, edited by George Ford and Sylvère Monod. New York: Norton Critical Edition, 1977.

Bleak House, edited by Nicola Bradbury. London: Penguin Classics, 1996. Page references are to this edition.

SECONDARY WORKS

Ackroyd, Peter. *Dickens.* London: Sinclair- Stevenson, 1991.

Bloom, Harold (editor), *Charles Dickens's Bleak House.* New York: Chelsea, 1987.

Butt, John, and Kathleen Tillotson, *Dickens at Work.* London: Methuen, 1957.

Dyson, A. E. (editor), *Bleak House: A Casebook.* London: Macmillan, 1969.

Engel, Monroe, *The Maturity of Dickens.* London: Oxford University Press, 1959.

Garis, Robert, *The Dickens Theatre: A Reassessment of the Novels.* Oxford: Clarendon Press, 1965.

Gilbert, Eliot L. (editor), *Critical Essays on Charles Dickens's Bleak House.* Boston: Prentice Hall, 1989.

Harvey, W. J., *Character and the Novel.* London: Chatto and Windus, 1965.

Hawthorn, Jeremy, *Bleak House: The Critics Debate.* London: Macmillan, 1987.

House, Humphrey, *The Dickens World.* Oxford: Clarendon Press, 1941.

Johnson, Edgar, *Charles Dickens: His Tragedy and Triumph.* Revised edition. London: Allen Lane, 1977.

Leavis, F. R., and Q. D., *Dickens the Novelist.* London: Chatto and Windus, 1970; Harmondsworth: Pelican, 1972.

McMaster, Juliet, *Dickens the Designer.* London: Macmillan, 1987.

Miller, J. Hillis, *Charles Dickens: The World of His Novels.* Cambridge, Mass.: Harvard University Press, 1959.

Page, Norman, *Bleak House: A Novel of Connections.* Boston: Twayne, 1990.

Schlicke, Paul, *Dickens and Popular Entertainment.* London: Allen and Unwin, 1985.

Stone, Harry, *Dickens and the Invisible World.* London: Macmillan, 1980.

Welsh, Alexander. *The City of Dickens.* Cambridge, Mass.: Harvard University Press, 1986.

Michael Frayn's
Copenhagen

FRED BILSON

MICHAEL FRAYN'S *COPEN-HAGEN*, first produced in London in 1998 and in New York in 2000, is a brilliantly imagined account of a real meeting that took place in September 1941 between Werner Heisenberg, Germany's most distinguished nuclear physicist, and his old friend and mentor, the Danish physicist Niels Bohr. In the 1920s the two men had worked together developing a view of nuclear physics that remains the orthodox theory. Called the Copenhagen interpretation, it was based on two principles: Heisenberg's uncertainty principle and Bohr's complementarity principle. Heisenberg's uncertainty principle held that since the act of observation in itself interfered with the phenomenon being observed, accuracy in establishing the position of an electron leads to loss of accuracy in establishing its velocity, and vice versa. Bohr's complementarity principle held that any account of electron behavior must take into consideration both the model that saw it as a particle and the model that saw it as a wave. Uncertainty is extended metaphorically in the play—the more certain we are of one thing in the past, the less certain we become of others, and Heisenberg's behavior is an example of his own principle. Complementarity too is a feature of relationships between opposites, especially the stolid Bohr and the mercurial Heisenberg. Heisenberg, a professor at Leipzig, was leading a team working on a nuclear reactor. A reactor is not an atomic weapon, but the technology of one can contribute to the other, and there were rumors of work to develop a bomb in both Britain and the United States (at the time still neutral in World War II). At this critical juncture, Heisenberg went to Copenhagen to visit Bohr. But, as the play relates, in later life, the two men could not agree on what took place at the meeting they had, and Heisenberg's motives in making the trip remain unclear.

Copenhagen has only three characters: Heisenberg, Bohr, and Bohr's wife, secretary, and confidante Margrethe. Through these characters, and through dialogue that combines highly serious subject matter with an often comic tone, the play deals first with the difficulty of memory and the difficulty of establishing what took place in the past. It has been likened by some critics to a detective story: the fact of the meeting is known, but the motivation for it is yet to be established. Above the encounter hangs the question of whether an atomic bomb can be created. In 1939 Bohr had shown that only the Uranium isotope U-235 could create a chain reaction—in ordinary uranium, there is a second isotope U-238 that inhibits any reaction. The major question is the size of the critical mass—the amount of U-235 necessary to create a bomb. Frayn holds to the view that, throughout the war, Heisenberg thought the answer was about a ton—a thousand pounds, which would take about 200,000 years to separate out. For Heisenberg, then, there can be no atomic weapon, but he is desperate to check if Bohr has picked up any rumors about developments in Britain or the United States.

In 1958 Robert Jungk published *Brighter than a Thousand Suns,* on the theme of the creation of the bomb, and this book was known to Frayn at the time of writing. In it Jungk quotes Heisenberg as saying that he went to see Bohr to persuade him to join in a general refusal by all scientists to work on projects designed to use atomic power for military purposes. This is clearly nonsensical. Bohr had no access to the German government, and the Danes were not in a position to engage in such work. Most alarmingly, to suggest to a government that you don't want to use atomic power for military purposes implies that such use is possible. If Heisenberg really had this conversation, was he probing Bohr on the question of the size of the critical mass? No wonder he reports Bohr as being cold and unresponsive.

Heisenberg is clearly not planning a social visit; Germany is at this stage doing well in the war, and he expects ultimate victory. Any information he receives from Bohr must help Germany's war effort—either in enabling Heisenberg to make the German reactor more efficient, or in increasing German access to the resources of the Danish Institute for Theoretical Physics. The question for the Bohrs is what agenda Heisenberg will set, and what pressures he will bring to bear to get what he wants given the status of Bohr as a citizen of a conquered state, and a Jew.

What Frayn did not know at the time of writing was Bohr's response to the Jungk book.

CHRONOLOGY

1933	Michael Frayn born in Mill Hill, London on 8 September. His father, Thomas Allen Frayn, is an asbestos salesman: Frayn has commented on the contrast between the mildness of his father's temper and the lethalness of the work he did. Frayn's mother, Violet Alice Frayn, had given up a career as a concert violinist to work as a shop assistant to help support the family. Later they move to Ewell, a more prosperous suburb, and Frayn is sent to private schools.
1945	Frayn's mother dies and his father is compelled to employ a housekeeper so cannot afford school fees. Frayn transfers to a state school, Kingston Grammar. He is much happier here, and qualifies to go to Cambridge University.
1952–1954	Frayn does two years military service where he learns Russian.
1954–1957	Frayn is a student at Emmanuel College, Cambridge, where he studies Moral Sciences (Philosophy) and starts his career as a writer.
1957	On graduating, Frayn becomes a journalist on the *Manchester Guardian,* writing humorous columns.
1965	Frayn's first novel *The Tin Men,* which wins the Somerset Maugham prize, includes a discussion of the nature of machine intelligence. He continues to write novels including fantasy, satire, and social reportage.
1968–1969	BBC Television broadcasts two plays by Frayn, *Jamie on a Flying Visit* and *Birthday,* which are successful, but rejects two further scripts as unproduceable. Unlike most of his generation of writers, Frayn does not have a substantial body of TV work.
1970	Frayn's first stage play, *The Two of Us,* is a disaster.
1974	Frayn publishes *Reflections,* a collection of thoughts on writing and philosophy, where he reflects on Heisenberg's Uncertainty Principle.

1975	Successful opening in London of *Clouds, Alphabetical Order* (each based on one of the rejected TV scripts), and of *Donkey's Years*.
1980	Frayn meets Claire Tomalin, widow of a contemporary of his at Cambridge. Subsequently, he divorces his wife and marries her.
1982	Frayn's most commercially successful play *Noises Off* opens in London.
1998	*Copenhagen* opens in London on 28 May, and subsequently in New York on 11 April 2000.
January 2003	Frayn and Tomalin are both winners of the Whitbread prize: he for his novel *Spies,* she for her biography of Samuel Pepys.

Deeply distressed, Bohr composed a memorandum to Heisenberg saying that his recollection of the meeting (which was in his office, not at his home) was characterized by Heisenberg's aggressive attitude and triumphalism, which included the suggestion that Heisenberg was prepared to work on military applications, and this explained Bohr's reserve. Bohr preserved this memorandum, but did not send it.

There is no reason to doubt Bohr's account, but in a sense it only increases the confusion, for Heisenberg did nothing during the war to create a German bomb; in fact, he regarded himself as having sabotaged it. Possibly the whole encounter was a charade managed by Heisenberg in case they were either overheard or subsequently interrogated by the gestapo.

Subsequently Bohr composed several letters to Heisenberg urging him to meet and agree on an account of their encounter in 1941. These letters are warm in their personal regard for Heisenberg and his family, but none were ever sent. In direct response to Frayn's play, Bohr's family published all these documents, which are available on the Internet at www.nbi.dk

The play ends with an uncomfortable discussion of who is guilty and who is innocent. For,

as it turned out, while Heisenberg had done nothing to help develop an atomic bomb, Bohr had worked on the Manhattan Project, responsible for the Hiroshima and Nagasaki bombs. It is an uncomfortable inversion.

> HEISENBERG: You were a good man from first to last . . . Whereas I—
> BOHR: Whereas you, my dear Heisenberg never managed to contribute to the death of one single solitary person in all your life.
>
> (*Copenhagen*, page 91)

It is also a play about friendship, especially the friendship of two people who work closely together: it deals with how such a friendship is built up, about the strains that are put on it, and how it may eventually collapse, as well as how a close marriage adapts to accommodate such a friendship. Finally, it looks at the existential state in which we live. Bohr, a child of the nineteenth century, had hoped that his work would put man back at the center of the universe. Bohr proclaims that the new physics (relativistic in the Einsteinian sense) puts our power to observe at the center of science and marks the end of the systems of classic Newtonian science that have dwarfed man; ". . . we're suddenly forced to rise from our knees again . . . the universe exists only. . . . through the understanding lodged inside the human head" (*Copenhagen,* pp. 71-72). Heisenberg, a streetfighter from the twentieth century, has less exalted views: to him what we do is survive, live day by day. Frayn was eleven years old when Hiroshima was bombed in 1945: the day before it had seemed that, no matter how bad World War II was, something must survive. That day we learned that perhaps nothing would. Yet even with the burden of this knowledge, we have somehow managed—so far—to keep living. The play ends on this note.

FRAYN'S BACKGROUND

Michael Frayn has had a long and productive career as journalist, playwright, and novelist.

The combination of serious purpose and comic tone in *Copenhagen* is less paradoxical than it may seem, for he has always been a deeply serious philosopher from his time at Cambridge University.

At Cambridge, Frayn initially studied French and Russian, but he soon switched to Moral Sciences, a broad-based philosophy course that he found congenial. Moral Sciences covers ethics and problems in philosophy, the history of philosophy, and formal logic, concentrating particularly on the problem of knowledge. How can we be sure of what we know? How far is language misleading in its description of the world? The presiding geniuses at this time included A. J. Ayer, whose book *Language, Truth and Logic* was seminal to the course, and Ludwig Wittgenstein. A central tenet of the course was that all we could know was the data our senses presented to us, and there was a distrust of all formalized systems: Marxism, Freudianism, even the American systems of Charles Sanders Peirce and William James were not considered to be much more than metaphysical and were therefore not fit objects for discussion. The function of philosophy was to specify how language came to have meaning.

Wittgenstein had taught at Cambridge until his death in 1951, and his influence on the philosophy of language continued to be a dominant force during Frayn's years there. His work *Philosophical Investigations* was published posthumously in 1956 and was a major revision of his earlier thinking. Here he proposed the notion of the language game. We don't have to play some particular game at all, but if we do play chess, for example, we must play by the rules of chess, even though they are arbitrary: otherwise we aren't truly playing chess. So if we use language, we must abide by the rules of language use even though they are arbitrary. Furthermore, language games cover a variety of functions, and relate in some way to an external world; they are purposeful. Frayn is fascinated by this "epistemology of intention" as he calls it (in "*Copenhagen* Revisited"), and his work is full of language games.

At Cambridge, many people found the view of philosophy studied in Moral Sciences abstract and arid. Those like Frayn who took to it ended up as convinced pragmatists, very much in tune with the political thinking of the 1960s, for example, which saw politics as presenting a series of problems to be solved empirically, and out of tune with the conviction politics of the 1980s, which believed in programs designed to remold society. Politically Frayn has always been a leftist, liberal supporter of the Labour Party.

Frayn's plays before *Copenhagen* were commercially successful and vastly entertaining in a comic sense. He is both a shrewd commentator on English middle class manners (*Alphabetical Order, Donkey's Years*) and a master of stagecraft: he is, rarely, an achieved writer of farce (*Donkey's Years, Noises Off*). At the same time, his plays are deeper because they are concerned with a philosophical problem—the problem of epistemology, that is, our knowledge of the world and how we construct it. He says of his earlier plays that they are about the way in which we impose our ideas on the world around us (*Plays One*, p. xiii). This might include the way in which we construct a personality for ourselves, the way we balance the contrasting urges to Order and Disorder in our behavior or the way in which we represent what we perceive in the language we use.

Copenhagen is both continuous with the earlier work and a departure from it. The comic element is now subordinate to a more serious overall preoccupation. Frayn abandons comedy for something closer to a Shakespearean chronicle play. Margrethe, Bohr, and Heisenberg were real people. Their representations in the play are bound by historical fact, and so are less free to engage in that semi-autonomous dialog with the author that marks the drama or the novel at its best. But the central preoccupation of the play remains epistemological. We cannot have a sense of our present without a sense of our past; what does it mean if we cannot agree with others who were there on what the past was like? And how is the re-creating of the past influenced by the creative tension that exists between those of us who represent Order (the Bohrs) and those of use who represent Disorder (Heisenberg)?

HISTORICAL BACKGROUND TO THE PLAY

When Frayn chose to write about a historical incident involving people whom many in the audience would have known, he knew that judgments of the play would partly depend on that fact. He describes, for example, an encounter with Heisenberg's son, Jochen. Frayn writes, "'Of course, your Heisenberg is nothing like my father,' he told me. 'I never saw my father express emotion about anything except music. But I understand that the characters in a play have to be rather more forthcoming than that'" ("*Copenhagen* Revisited").

First let us consider the elder of the two scientists, Niels Bohr, born in 1885. His father was an academic at Copenhagen University and his mother a member of a prominent Jewish banking family. Bohr had renounced religion at the age of eighteen. But in Nazi terms he remained a Jew. Bohr's work in atomic physics earned him the Nobel Prize in 1922; he gave the gold medal to charity. He later tried to persuade Roosevelt and Churchill to renounce the use of atomic weapons and after the war was awarded the Atoms for Peace prize in 1956 by the Ford Foundation. He died in 1962, venerated both as a scientist and as a man.

Central to Bohr's life and career was his wife, Margrethe, the second character of *Copenhagen*. Born in 1890, she married Bohr in 1910; they were totally devoted to each other, had six sons together (two of whom died young, one from illness, one from a boating accident), and their marriage lasted until Niels's death in 1962.

Margrethe had initially been engaged by Niels as a typist, and all through his life she would type his manuscripts. Clearly she had an understanding of his work and acted as a sounding board for his ideas. More, it is obvious that, despite the clarity of his thinking, Niels was often almost incoherent in expression, and she was important in helping him express himself. Friends stressed that the importance of Margrethe as an enabler cannot be overexaggerated.

In 1941 the Bohrs were living in a villa in the grounds of the Carlsberg brewery, granted them in 1931 by the king on the grounds that Bohr was Denmark's most distinguished scientist. Clearly, both the Germans and the Danes would be aware of Heisenberg's visit, and the Bohrs would be at risk from both sides as a result.

In 1943 the family was smuggled out of Denmark along with other Danes at risk under the German racial laws. Niels and their son Aage went first to Sweden (where he met up with Margrethe), then to England, then to the United States. Traveling separately, Margrethe and the other sons (who were of course themselves marked down for extermination) remained in Sweden.

Back in 1924, when their son Ernest was a week old, Bohr had gone off on a walking tour with Heisenberg. Frayn renders their reminiscence of it this way:

BOHR: . . .One week, yes. And you really didn't mind?

MARGRETHE: Not at all. I was pleased you had an excuse to get away. And you always went off hiking with your new assistants. You went off with Kramers when he arrived in 1916.

BOHR: Yes, when I suppose Christian was still only . . .

MARGRETHE: One week.

(p. 57)

This is an important exchange, of the sort Frayn has written many times. How ironic is-

Margrethe, and how far is she genuinely putting Bohr first, enabling his work and thinking? The play suggests the remark is non-ironic, for Margrethe is totally devoted to Bohr's interests and needs.

Describing the escape to Sweden in 1943 she tells Heisenberg, "It's my dear, good, kind husband who's on his hands and knees! Literally. Crawling down to the beach in the darkness in 1943, fleeing like a thief in the night from his own homeland to escape being murdered" (p. 78). So much is she centered on Bohr that she does not even mention she and the children had to do the same.

Margrethe died in 1984, an eminence in Danish life. She remained implacable in her contempt for Heisenberg.

The third character, Werner Heisenberg, was born in 1901, the son of an academic family and a brilliant student who became a right-winger in his attitudes, dividing his time between youth politics and study. In 1924 he came to Copenhagen to work with Bohr. He won the Nobel Prize for physics in 1933.

Under the Third Reich, he remained in Germany, despite invitations to work abroad, but he was discriminated against and attacked in the press as an exponent of "Jewish Science" (Einstein's theory of relativity). He conscientiously continued to teach relativity as professor at Leipzig. After the war and his detention at Farm Hall in England, he continued to work in academic life, heading the Max Planck Institute, Germany's leading center for the study of science.

In the historical circumstances of the Third Reich, Heisenberg found himself a clever man compelled to outwit the Nazis, who as well as being inhumanely cruel were often among the stupidest members of society. He comes across, in the play as in his memoirs, as a Till Eulenspiegel figure. Till is the central figure of a set of German stories—half history, half folk-myth—about how an ingenuous peasant posing as a

simpleton outwits the authorities of his day. In Nazi Germany he was an exemplar of how to survive, and Heisenberg played the role to the hilt—outwitting Albert Speer, persuading the Nazis to let him visit Copenhagen, continuing his work under their very noses.

To dispose of an old cliché of literary interpretation, it is not that the complex and slightly corrupt Heisenberg is a more interesting person than the worthy Bohrs: he isn't. They have their own complexities and subtleties, and they have a deep, dark interior place where they mourn their two dead sons—their "Elsinore" (*Copenhagen*, p. 76). But one of the moral points Frayn insists on is that it is a duty to survive, and Heisenberg enshrines this. Still, ultimately Heisenberg's anecdotal approach trivializes human endeavor. Bohr had led and inspired the work that extended Einstein's original conceptualization into the picture of physics that became known as the Copenhagen Interpretation. He believed that it placed man back at the center of the universe and gave him a new dignity.

Beyond the real-life background of *Copenhagen*'s characters, two other historical issues are central to an understanding of the play: the persecution of the Jews throughout the Nazi regime of 1933 to 1945 that culminated in the Holocaust; and the developing science of atomic physics itself, which brought Bohr and Heisenberg together.

First, it is impossible to judge Bohr or Heisenberg without taking account of the pressures each was under in the wake of the Nazi racial laws of 1936. These laws categorized as a Jew anyone who had a single grandparent of Jewish descent: in practice this included many people who were denounced by neighbors on the basis of old gossip. Bohr, then, despite the fact that he was not a practicing Jew in the religious sense, was a target. Heisenberg, for his part, while not a Jew in the "racial" sense, was still subject to the pressures that applied to everyone in the Reich: he underwent gestapo interrogation because he was teaching a "Jewish" science and was called a "White Jew." Had he left Germany, his family would have been held hostage.

The racial laws were applied in the occupied territories, often with the support of local people. Denmark is a shining exception. Only seventy-seven Danish Jews died in the Holocaust, and the evacuation of the rest is a part of the story of *Copenhagen*. The success of the evacuation was due in large part to Georg Duckwitz. Duckwitz had been a Nazi even before 1933. He was an official in the Foreign Ministry and part of the Nazi administration of Denmark. In 1943 he picked up a rumor that two freighters were due to arrive to take off Denmark's 5,500 Jews for deportation and extermination. Travelling to Stockholm, he persuaded the Swedes to accept any Jews that could be got across to Sweden. He then tipped off the Danish resistance, who organized a fleet to evacuate the Jews to Sweden. Finally, he used his influence with friends in the German Navy to ensure that all the U-boats that might have interrupted the evacuation were kept in harbor on the excuse that they were in need of repair.

Only 500 Jews remained to be rounded up. They were sent to Theresienstadt, and the Danes kept up the pressure to ensure their safety. As a result, fewer than fifty were killed. Heisenberg's part in all this is problematical, but it seems clear that Bohr and his sons owe their lives to the Nazi Duckwitz and to some degree to Heisenberg.

After the war, Duckwitz was German ambassador to Denmark, and Bohr mentions in the unsent memorandum to Heisenberg that he plans to take Duckwitz into his confidence, possibly in the hope of enlisting his mediation.

Frayn is acutely aware of the arbitrariness of the Nazi definition of Jewishness (it is one of the themes of his novel *Spies*) as someone who is in part Jewish.

At certain expansive moments, having about a third of a pint of Jewish blood in my veins, I like to claim to be a Jew. But only to Gentiles. I haven't yet met a Jew I thought would believe me.

(*Constructions* no. 101)

The arbitrariness of the Nazis' definition of who is and who is not a Jew, illustrated by Hermann Göring's remark "Wer ein Jude ist, dass sage ich" ("I say who's Jewish"), is a central issue in the Bohr-Heisenberg relationship in *Copenhagen*. Heisenberg, not Jewish by birth, is discriminated against as a friend of Jewish science. Bohr, not Jewish in sentiment or practice, is in danger of his life.

Finally, although a thorough knowledge of nuclear physics is not necessary for an appreciation of the play, it is important enough that, in the published version of *Copenhagen*, Frayn provides a chart detailing its development from Sir Joseph Thomson's discovery of the electron in 1895 to Hiroshima in 1945 (pp. 133–134). The play takes up two particular threads from this, summarized below: the way in which Bohr's work and Heisenberg's influenced each other, and the notions of uncertainty and complementarity.

Frayn defines Max Planck's 1900 quantum theory thus: "Heat energy is not continuously variable. . . . There is a smallest common coin in the currency, the quantum, and all transactions are in multiples of it" (p. 134). In 1915 Bohr applied this theory to matter itself, showing that the orbits of electrons around the nucleus of the atom have a limited number of possibilities.

In 1925, Heisenberg characterized electron orbits as unobservable, leading Max Born to substitute a matrix model based on the effects of orbits on the absorption and emission of light. In 1927, Heisenberg formulated the uncertainty principle—better, suggests Frayn, the "indeterminability" principle (p. 100). This states that the more certainly the position of a particle is known, the less certainly its velocity is known, and vice versa.

In 1928, Bohr defined complementarity, building on the Heisenberg-Born formulation of the particle and the de Broglie-Schrödinger formulation of the wave, to posit the need to define electrons in terms of both particle and wave. Complementarity is the principle that both models (the electron seen as particle and the electron seen as wave) are needed for a complete explanation, and neither is privileged over the other. Uncertainty and complementarity define the Copenhagen interpretation.

As early as 1974 Frayn had been interested in the philosophical implications of the uncertainty principle:

> The . . . question "What is the case?" to which it was once thought that sense-data statements might provide plausible answers, has an artificial air when we make its application universal. This conception of things was destroyed by Heisenberg for a start . . .
>
> (*Constructions* no. 283)

In *Copenhagen* Frayn found a dramatic potentiality; he points out that Heisenberg's life is in itself an illustration of the uncertainty principle, which is also reflected in the structure of the play. The more clear the Bohrs' story seems to be, the less clear Heisenberg's is, and vice versa, and often it is Margrethe who provides the opposite pole to Heisenberg, rather than Bohr. It is interesting to read Frayn's description of the items he felt obliged to leave out of the play "for fear of making [it] even more tangled than it is." He sees this as part of the "indeterminacy of human memory, or at any rate the indeterminability of the historical record" (*Copenhagen*, p. 124). As for complementarity, the older Bohr and the younger Heisenberg are of course complementary in the intellectual sense; their friendship is of a very intense sort as a result. There is another complementarity too: the complementarity of Germany and the rest of the world of science as it had been in the 1920s. In the play, Heisenberg never

quite realizes how far the Third Reich has destroyed both of these complementarities.

HEISENBERG'S VISIT TO COPENHAGEN

Frayn had originally intended to write a more naturalistic play based on the debriefing of Heisenberg and other German nuclear scientists by British Intelligence at Farm Hall in 1945–1946; in effect, they were kidnapped and brought to England, leaving their families behind. However, his interest moved to the 1941 visit.

Thus the immediate background of the play is as follows: At this time, 1941, Heisenberg's chief rival is Kurt Diebner, the head of Germany's second nuclear research team run by the army; Diebner is a convinced Nazi, who wishes to take over Heisenberg's work. Reports have appeared in the Swedish press that teams in Britain and the still-neutral United States are attempting to build a nuclear weapon. The Nazis are suspicious of theoretical physics as a "Jewish science"; this both enables Heisenberg to minimize its potential to Hitler and Albert Speer and attracts the suspicion of the gestapo. Clearly, whatever else Heisenberg is, he cannot survive in this world if he is naïve.

That September he and his assistant, Carl von Weiszäcker, arrive in Copenhagen, capital of Nazi-occupied Denmark. Denmark has a special status among occupied countries; the king is still in the country and there is a vestige of civilian administration. The occasion for the visit is a lecture Heisenberg is to give at the German Cultural Institute, but he has also been scheduled to visit the (Danish) Institute for Theoretical Physics where he had worked in the 1920s with Bohr, the doyen of nuclear physics. Heisenberg intends to make a call on Bohr at his home.

STAGING

The set is minimalist, and the cast of three are onstage throughout. In the first London production, the back of the stage was occupied by a high-walled area with seating for part of the audience, who thus suggested a tribunal in some afterlife where the dead may be finally judged.

This minimalist staging avoids the need to provide a set to locate the action more firmly in the Bohrs' home, which would privilege their account and their memories, particularly of the 1941 visit. However, this is not simply a radio play for voices—all three actors have by physical set, gesture, and voice to convey a complex relationship that is as close as parents and child at one point, as distant as enemies at war at another point. Technically it is essential for them to make clear at each point whether they are addressing one or both of the other actors onstage or whether the line represents an internal monologue.

The cost of the minimalist staging, however, is to make the play very static, reminding some of Beckett's *Waiting for Godot*, emphasizing the lack of any resolution to the central question of the play: Why did Heisenberg come to Copenhagen? In fact, the play does reach a resolution. Uncertainty means we must take all accounts into consideration, and if our survival is only conditional, it is no less real for all that. It is not a nihilistic work. As a result, there have also been productions which have taken a more representational approach.

SYNOPSIS

Unusually, there is no developmental narrative line in the play: the circumstances are known in advance and no single solution to the question of why Heisenberg visited Copenhagen is proposed—we are left with a variety of different readings of the incident. The play is in two acts. Though they regularly revisit incidents, the two acts are distinguished: act 1 establishes the historical context of the 1941 visit; act 2 considers how the friendship of Bohr and Heisenberg was built up as they worked on the Copenhagen interpretation and the strains placed on this friendship by the events of World War II—especially the development of the atom bomb and the defeat of Germany.

Act 1 opens with a short scene in which Margrethe, Bohr, and Heisenberg are visualized after death. Margrethe and Bohr do not at first relate onstage to Heisenberg, but their speeches interconnect and relate, partly because Heisenberg appears able to overhear and comment on what Margrethe and Bohr are saying. Margrethe is still perplexed by the problem of why Heisenberg came to Copenhagen in 1941.

> BOHR: Does it matter, my love, now we're all three of us dead and gone?
> MARGRETHE: Some questions remain long after their owners have died. Lingering like ghosts.

She is unforgiving of Heisenberg: he was a German and an enemy. To Bohr he was still one of their oldest friends (p. 3).

Heisenberg is happy to make one more attempt to explain his actions back in 1941, for "Now no one can be hurt, now no one can be betrayed." Ironically one of the lessons the play will make clear is that some hurts and betrayals are so deep they last forever (p. 4).

There follows a scene that recalls the joy of the early 1924 relationship, when Heisenberg first came to Copenhagen. Margrethe claims that "I never entirely liked him, you know," but for Bohr it was complementarity that marked that first encounter (pp. 4–6). Heisenberg remembers arriving on the night train to Copenhagen in 1941, with all the personnel in uniform—a stark reminder of the facts of the occupation. He attends a lunch at the Institute for Theoretical Physics and claims that the occupation of Poland is justified. Germany will win the war. Bohr recounts the story of the lunch, though whether he was actually there himself is never made clear (pp. 7–8). But Heisenberg is invited to visit the Bohrs at the villa. His arrival marks the end of the first part of act 1, with the first appearance of what will become a refrain:

BOHR: My dear Heisenberg!
HEISENBERG: My dear Bohr!

(p. 13)

The warmth of the greeting turns quickly, in Margrethe's phrase, to "cold ashes." Heisenberg's attempts at friendly conversation strike raw nerves with the Bohrs, because he has not allowed for the facts of the occupation. He suggests to Bohr that they go out for a walk, on which they might talk freely. At first reluctant, Bohr eventually agrees, but they are back from the walk within minutes. Heisenberg excuses himself and leaves, and it is the question of what happened on that walk that is the mystery of the play. What did Heisenberg say? The play is silent on this point.

In a postlude set after the war, the question of how feasible it was in 1941 that an atomic weapon should be made leads Heisenberg to claim innocence: he had had no interest in the atomic bomb; his reactor was principally a source of power.

The first part of act 2 deals with the interconnection of the development of the Copenhagen interpretation and the professional friendship of Bohr and Heisenberg. When Heisenberg first arrived in 1924 he was almost a son to the Bohrs, but he matures into a Nobel Prize winner and a professor submissive to, but not wholly trusted by, the Nazi regime. Margrethe points out to the men that they had in fact both worked alone; though they cooperated in sharing ideas, each of them had written their major papers in isolation (pp. 61–64) and the nature of the work meant there had often been bitter quarrels between them (pp. 64–67). It is now that Margrethe's resentment of Heisenberg is seen most clearly as she recounts Bohr's escape in 1943. Along with the discussion is the question of whether Heisenberg had been capable of calculating the critical mass, that is, the exact weight of material that would create a chain reaction. If he could not have done this—and in fact in 1945 he was still mistaken on the point and thus could claim no credit for refusing to make a bomb—then he did not realize one could be made (pp. 80–82).

The play closes by centering on Heisenberg, whose life remains a classic of uncertainty. His part in saving the Danish Jews and in preserving the independence of the Danish Institute for Theoretical Physics is established. But above all, in a magnificent solo, which Frayn based on Heisenberg's reminiscences, he describes his journey across the ruined Germany of 1945, culminating in an encounter with an SS man who was about to shoot him but settled for a pack of cigarettes—Lucky Strike, Heisenberg points out. I loved my country, he says: How much would I have been justified in doing to save her from this? As you would have been prepared to destroy German cities to bring victory, I might have done the same to some other city on your side. Perhaps even Copenhagen. But so far, we have been spared this.

COPENHAGEN WITHIN THE FRAMEWORK OF FRAYN'S DRAMATIC TECHNIQUE

By the time he came to write *Copenhagen*, Frayn had developed a number of techniques, three of which are considered here.

In *Copenhagen*, Heisenberg at one point refers to "their importunate guest, stumbling from one crass and unwelcome thoughtfulness to the next" (p. 87), and indeed the disruptive visitor has been a frequent component in Frayn's drama: initially welcome, he often brings problems with him. For Frayn, the visitor from the past who rekindles old joy is almost archetypal: in such company we become again the happier, more carefree people that our memories present to us as our past condition. This is a delusion, of course: as the playwright makes clear, the past had its own grief and troubles.

Heisenberg's arrival (especially in his own eyes) is potentially such a joyous irruption, bringing with it memories of the days when he was almost a son to the Bohrs and shared holidays skiing, sailing, or walking. But they are bitter memories to his hosts, who are now barred from enjoying such sports and are living under the occupation. It is a massive misjudgment on his part: we have to ask, can Heisenberg really be this naive? Or has a genuine affection overcome his better judgment?

Another theme in Frayn's work is the contrast between order and disorder, a polarity often associated with the importunate visitor. In *Alphabetical Order* (1975) Leslie arrives to work in the clippings room of a provincial newspaper. Finding chaos and disorganization, she imposes a ruthless order, first on the library, then on the personal lives of the staff. When the announcement comes that the paper is going to close, the rest of the staff trashes the clippings room and slips back into the pattern of pre-Leslie relationships. But Leslie returns to shame them into joining a plan to take over the newspaper as a cooperative. For Frayn the moral is not just that order and disorder contrast, but that they need each other.

In *Copenhagen* the first need the Bohrs feel as they look back to that 1941 meeting is to establish order by establishing the facts that lay behind Heisenberg's visit. But this is never achieved because of the disorder created by the impossibility of accurate recall. Further, Frayn suggests, scientific progress itself comes from a mix of order and disorder. Heisenberg surrounds himself with disorder—his recall of Germany disintegrating in 1945 is but a macrocosm of the disorder that surrounded the research program he ran at Haigerloch. If it had gone critical, says Bohr, you'd have vanished into the center of the earth.

> HEISENBERG: Not at all. We had a lump of cadmium to hand.
> BOHR: A *lump* of cadmium? What were you proposing to do with a *lump* of cadmium?
> HEISENBERG: Throw it into the water.

> BOHR: What water?
> HEISENBERG: The heavy water.

> (p. 50)

Bohr, the man of order, is appalled at the sloppiness. The description of the cadmium as a "lump" is terribly unscientific, as is the lack of proper care and attention to detail. But Heisenberg is unrepentant; he had come so close: "Two more weeks, two more blocks of uranium" (p. 51).

Another technique in Frayn's plays (one that is found in John Osborne's *Look Back in Anger*) is that of the "revisited scene." This is a technique where some representation on stage strongly suggests an earlier scene to the audience. It can be done by mise-en-scène or by dialog. Frayn pays his tribute to the revisited scene in *Alphabetical Order,* for example, where act 1 opens in the clippings room as Leslie arrives, and act 2 opens in the transformed office on which she has imposed order.

Frayn later developed the technique of revisiting a scene a number of times within the same play. He reports that a member of his audience once pointed out to him that the structure of *Copenhagen* mirrored the structure of *Noises Off,* Frayn's most commercially successful play. In that piece, a stock theater company is depicted as either rehearsing or performing a bedroom farce called *Nothing On.* In each of three acts an identical portion of the play is seen: in acts 1 and 3 from in front of the stage, in act 2 from backstage. The dramatic interest of the play *Noises Off* lies in the personal relationships within the company. Their conversations offstage are the "noises off" of the play's title, and they come to be more important than the farce *Nothing On* that they are performing. Thus the effect created in *Noises Off* is one of cycling through time. At each of the three cycles, the kaleidoscope of relationships has shifted, but each of the three patterns is present in the other two.

Memory operates in a similar way in that it embeds later memories, and it is memory that is foregrounded in *Copenhagen*. It is almost impossible to recapture a single given experience. Those of us who remember 22 November 1963 can hardly strip away from our memories of it all our subsequent memories of the Kennedy family, or what we have learned since of John F. Kennedy himself. Consequently we often find we remember the assassination slightly differently from others who were also conscious of it at the time. And revisiting it, watching that few seconds of video, does not help to revive the original memory. We are left with two problems. What did we really feel then? Would we have felt the same way then if we had known what we know now?

In *Copenhagen,* the characters similarly try to re- create the events of September 1941 across the subsequent memory of Hiroshima and Nagasaki, as they cycle through the events of the evening of Heisenberg's visit. This cycling is marked by the appearance of that short refrain mentioned earlier—the dramatic equivalent of *Nothing On*—when Heisenberg first knocks on the front door and for a minute or two everything is as it had been before the war:

> BOHR: My dear Heisenberg!
> HEISENBERG: My dear Bohr!
> BOHR: Come in, come in. . .

After this first meeting, this dialogue occurs two more times: at the close of act 1, suggesting that act 2 will take up the theme of the meeting again; and once more during act 2. But where act 2 had opened with a warm recall of the building up of a friendship, we now have the tale of how it was lost because of the war. Tellingly, Bohr's line after Heisenberg's account of the end of the war is the opening of the exchange "My dear Heisenberg!" But this time Heisenberg does not respond (p. 93). For Bohr, Heisenberg's account revives the old feelings of warmth towards Heisenberg, but Heisenberg cannot respond. Instead there is, as Margrethe says, the silence "we always in the end return to"; the silence in which they contemplate the lost children—the

German children on the road; Heisenberg himself "wandering the world like a lost child himself," as Bohr says; the drowned son, Christian Bohr.

FRAYN AND CHEKHOV

Chekhov has been central to Frayn's development as a dramatist. Frayn's fluency in Russian has led him to translate a number of Chekhov's plays, including the four major plays (*The Seagull, Uncle Vanya, Three Sisters, The Cherry Orchard*), and they are published in a collected edition with a perceptive introduction by the translator.

The problems that Frayn set himself in *Copenhagen* are illuminated by his reading of Chekhov's success in handling similar problems. First, Frayn points out in his introduction to the collected *Chekhov* that a major problem for a writer of prose attempting drama is "the loss of authorial voice" (*Chekhov*, p. xiii): characters must speak for themselves and there can be no editorializing. Chekhov is distinguished by the "detachment" he achieves (p. xiv), and the detachment of the author complements the passion of the characters (p. xiv). It is one of the strengths of *Copenhagen* that Margrethe, Bohr, and Heisenberg speak for themselves. Their words are not editorialized or framed ironically; the horror of the Holocaust or Hiroshima is not editorially underlined.

Chekhov's dramas are located, rather contrary to the general view, in a world where people must support themselves by hard work (p. xiv); often his plays are located in rare moments of leisure for the characters. Frayn creates in *Copenhagen* (especially in act 2) an outstanding picture of a friendship based on solid, hard, difficult work.

Many, possibly most, readers of Chekhov see his plays as comedies. For Frayn this view is mistaken: for example, he is particularly savage with those who see the abandonment and probable death of Firs at the end of *The Cherry Orchard* as a comic touch because they delude themselves that he will be saved by some miraculous intervention (p. xxii). Comedies are comedies, in everyday terms, either because they are comic in tone or because they end optimistically. For Frayn, the optimistic ending is just not there in Chekhov, and this raises the question of the ending of *Copenhagen*. Does the play end happily? Both Bohr and Heisenberg, against high odds, survive the war. No European city is atom bombed. Is this not an optimistic ending? Margrethe mourns for "our ruined and dishonoured and beloved world" which will one day be lost and forgotten, and Heisenberg replies that we must be content that it has been preserved so far:

> But in the meanwhile . . . there it is. . . . Preserved, just possibly, by that one short moment in Copenhagen. . . . By that final core uncertainty at the heart of things.
>
> (p. 94)

This is the fact with which we have lived since Hiroshima. But there is loss, and Frayn characterizes Chekhov's four great plays in terms that might apply to his own:

> In all the plays, too, something is being lost. All attempts at forward motion—all the brave forays into the world of work and endeavour—are counterbalanced by the undertow of regret; there is some loss that will never be made good.
>
> (*Chekhov*, p. xxv)

COMIC TONE

Of course, there are moments in Chekhov's plays when the tone is comic, but for Frayn the purpose of such scenes is part of the plays' dramatic structure, giving change of pace and suggesting the futility of human endeavor:

> Part of what Chekhov wanted when he insisted on the comedy in his plays was surely a different style of acting; he was looking for lightness, speed,

indifference, and irony; something that suggested not the inexorable tolling of fate but the absurdity of human intentions and the meaningless of events.
>
> (p. xxiv)

In particular, there are passages in which the dialogue in Chekhov is happy and rapid, and passages where a slower pace with longer speeches introduces a somber note. Often characters are given speeches that other characters onstage appear to ignore.

It is not hard to trace this influence of Chekhov in *Copenhagen*. First, we note the control of pace and mood through the rhythms of language. Consider the early scene of the play that opens with Bohr and Margrethe remembering the old days with Heisenberg, then moves on to Heisenberg's first account of his 1941 visit. The language at first is fast paced, excited, and happy, though even here Margrethe is cautious: "I never entirely liked him."

> BOHR: Yes, you did. . . . On the beach at Tisvilde with us and the boys? He was one of the family.

Her qualms are almost lost in the flood of Bohr's happy reminiscences. She adopts his speech cadences, but her reservations are clear. Lines consist of short phrases of four of five words each:

> BOHR: So quick and eager.
> MARGRETHE: Too quick. Too eager.
>
> (p. 4)

They all remember the closeness:

> BOHR: Heisenberg usually led the way.
> HEISENBERG: Bohr made sense of it all. . . . Chairman and managing director.
> MARGRETHE: Father and son.
>
> (p. 5)

Then this pace is lost as we approach the uncertainty of 1941. It is introduced by a failure of memory on Heisenberg's part: "September, 1941. For years I had it down in my memory as

October." This is followed by a passage that might have come from *Three Sisters*. Each character now has a longer line for each speech, full sentences with a complexity of imagery and structure:

> BOHR: A curious sort of diary memory is.
> HEISENBERG: You open the pages, and all the neat headings and tidy jottings dissolve around you.
> BOHR: You step through the pages into the months and days themselves.
> MARGRETHE: The past becomes the present inside your head.
>
> (p. 6)

This is followed by Heisenberg's Chekhovian reminscence of his arrival at Copenhagen station on the night train, among Wehrmacht and SS men, with a lecture in his bag and a message in his head. As if they had not heard this, Bohr and Margrethe resume their dialogue considering whether they should respond to an invitation to Heisenberg's lecture. Finally Frayn puts together two reminiscences, one by Heisenberg, one by Bohr, describing the same lunch at the institute; the speeches do not connect with each other and thus emphasize the distance between the two men. Bohr's description does not even clear up the uncertainty Heisenberg experiences about whether Bohr was actually present or whether Bohr is recounting what he had been told about the occasion.

Comic structure, then, but too dark for comic tone in the circumstances of this encounter in 1941. There is even at one point a classic Jewish joke by Bohr, at which no one will ever laugh:

> HEISENBERG: I still have my old ski-hut. . . . So if by any chance . . . at any time . . . for any reason . . .
> BOHR: Perhaps Margrethe will be kind enough to sew a yellow star on my ski-jacket.
> HEISENBERG: Yes. Yes. Stupid of me.
>
> (p. 16)

But *Copenhagen* does not lack comic tone and even comic scenes. In act 1, they are particularly

associated with the recollections of the 1920s, when Heisenberg arrived as a bright young man in the Bohrs' middle-aged household, with its sorrow and its Elsinore at the center. At one point Heisenberg reminds Bohr that he shot one of his assistants (pp. 26–28), and there follows a cross-talk act in which Bohr insists it was Gamow and Heisenberg insists it was Casimir:

> BOHR: Before his gun is even out of his pocket, mine is in my hand.
> HEISENBERG: And poor Casimir has been blasted out of existence.

It's a compact piece of writing. Heisenberg doesn't realize till the middle of the conversation that they're talking cap pistols, and the scene ends with Bohr complacently giving the picture of himself as a western gun-slinger. The confusion as to whether it was Gamow or Casimir mirrors other confusions in the play and leads to a masterly one-liner:

> HEISENBERG: Both of them simultaneously alive and dead in our memories.
> BOHR: Like a pair of Schrödinger cats. . . .

In act 2 there is a Chaplinesque routine where Bohr is on a train to Leiden and a question of particle behavior has been raised in a paper. At Hamburg, Pauli and Stern meet Bohr's train to canvass his opinion. At Leiden, Einstein meets Bohr, and persuades him to change his mind on the paper. The progress continues on the home journey, where Bohr detours to meet Heisenberg and then Pauli catches up with him again at Berlin (pp. 59–60).

Both these routines catch the rapidity and the excitement of the making of the Copenhagen interpretation, and contrast with the elegiac tone of such passages as Heisenberg's trip across Germany in 1945.

CRITICAL REACTION AND WIDER RESPONSE

The initial critical reaction to *Copenhagen* was almost universally positive. The London press was lavish in its praise, seeing this as an important play of ideas, and it won both the *Evening Standard* and the Critics' Circle awards for best play of the year.

One of the features of a play of ideas is that the ideas may be discussed as widely as the play. Even Frayn was surprised at the reception awarded to *Copenhagen*. Both its commercial success and the reaction to it in the United States astonished him, as he described in his article "*Copenhagen* Revisited":

> The reaction in New York, both positive and negative, took me by surprise. When I wrote the play I thought it unlikely that anyone would want to produce it. Even if I sometimes hoped I might find some small theater somewhere that would take it on, I can't remember ever thinking that anyone would come to see it, much less have strong views about it.

Two of the responses to the play have come to affect our reading of it. The first is the decision of the Bohr family to publish the drafts of Bohr's memorandum and subsequent letters already detailed above. Frayn concedes that he had not allowed for the extent of Bohr's continuing anger against Heisenberg, for all the personal affection he continued to feel.

The second response is the condemnation voiced by some Holocaust scholars. To attempt to contextualize this, Frayn is of his generation in that he did not come to see the Nazis as evil because he learned about the Holocaust. His early years were spent in the shadows of this evil regime; for example, he lived in a London that was regularly bombed by the Luftwaffe. For him, this evil is taken for granted; the extermination policy when it became known in spring 1945 confirmed the reading; it did not create it. So he does not foreground the extermination program in the play. In human terms, the Holocaust was experienced as a series of individual encounters—one Danish scientist and his family escape, another scientist's family left behind in the Reich perishes. No one can claim

that *Copenhagen* ignores this basic fact of the Bohrs' existence in 1941.

The substantive charges made against the play are first that it whitewashes Heisenberg. Claims are made that he had in fact calculated the critical mass needed to produce a bomb during the war. Frayn's response is a careful consideration of the Farm Hall transcripts (of recordings of the talk of the interned German scientists taken unawares) and the fact that Heisenberg did no work toward a bomb. Second, Heisenberg knew the circumstances in which the uranium was mined by slave labor in Czechoslovakia. On this, there is no evidence that Heisenberg bears any individual responsibility, over and above a share in the general responsibility of the German war effort.

The other substantive charge concerns the way the play foregrounds the fact that so many who contributed to the Manhattan Project (Einstein, Bohr, Peierls for example) were Jews in the extended Nazi sense, and that Frayn is contributing to an anti- Jewish revisionism by foregrounding this, especially by having Margrethe voice the fact. Frayn dismisses this claim (by Professor Rose of Pennsylvania State University) as fantastic.

Even if Frayn were in fact completely mistaken about the historical Heisenberg, the play would still stand up for its consideration of what he has called the epistemology of intention (the understanding of how we can know what people intend by their actions). He puts the matter like this:

> Let me make it absolutely unambiguous: my Heisenberg is saying that we do have to make assessments of intention in judging people's actions. (The epistemology of intention is what the play is about!) He is saying that Bohr will continue to inspire respect and love, in spite of his involvement in the building of the Hiroshima and Nagasaki bombs; and he himself will continue to be regarded with distrust in spite of his failure to kill anyone.

Finally, in "*Copenhagen* Revisited," Frayn bids his characters adieu in these terms:

Whatever was said at the meeting, and whatever Heisenberg's intentions were, there is something profoundly characteristic of the difficulties in human relationships, and profoundly painful, in that picture of the two aging men, one in Copenhagen and one in Göttingen, puzzling for all those long years over the few brief moments that had clouded if not ended their friendship. It's what their shades do in my play, of course. At least in the play they get together to work it out.

Selected Bibliography

EDITIONS

Copenhagen. London: Methuen Drama, 1998.

OTHER WORKS BY FRAYN

Constructions. (Philosophical essays.) London: Wildwood House, 1974.

Plays One. London: Methuen, 1986. Contains *Alphabetical Order, Donkey's Years, Clouds, Make and Break, Noises Off.*

Chekhov: Plays. (Translated and introduced by Frayn.) London: Methuen, 1988.

"Copenhagen Revisited." *New York Review of Books* (28 March 2002).

SECONDARY WORKS

Staub, August. "The Scientist as Byronic Hero: Michael Frayn's Copenhagen." *Journal of Dramatic Theory and Criticism* 16, no. 2 (spring 2002): 133–141.

Stewart, Victoria. "A Theatre of Uncertainties: Science and History in Michael Frayn's Copenhagen." *New Theatre Quarterly* 15, no. 4 (November 1999): 301–307.

Ted Hughes's
Crow

JAMES A. KNAPTON

CROW: FROM THE Life and Songs of the Crow is a book-length poem. First published in 1970, it is rated by many critics as Hughes's most important work, and indeed as one of the central Anglophone texts to be written since World War II. Prompted in part by the suicide of the author's first wife, the American poet Sylvia Plath (1932–1963), *Crow* attempts to salvage something from Hughes's private ruins. The poem's hybrid mythic universe—loaded with violence, desecration and sexuality—is the locus for an idiosyncratic quest narrative that aims to repair man's relations with women, with the spiritual realm, and with history. Originating in Hughes's psychic crucible of suffering and grief, *Crow* also is a text of its times, weighted with the global and civic anxieties of the 1960s. The book's primitivist stylistic experimentation, its range of demotic and authoritative voices, and its black humor—coupled with Hughes's skilful layering of the universal, the political, and the personal–together have contributed to its uninterrupted popularity among readers of all ages and nationalities.

TED HUGHES: LIFE AND WORKS

Edward (Ted) James Hughes was born in the village of Mytholmroyd in the Yorkshire Pennines, England, in 1930. His father, a carpenter by trade, fought in the Gallipoli campaign during World War I; his mother was a dedicated wife and homemaker. He was the youngest of three children: his brother Gerald emigrated to Australia, while his sister Olwyn pursued various careers before becoming a literary agent. When Ted was seven the family moved to Mexborough, a mining town in South Yorkshire, where his parents opened a newsdealer's shop. As a child, Hughes was fascinated by the natural world, and he enjoyed shooting and fishing expeditions with his brother. In 1948 he won a scholarship to read English at Pembroke College, Cambridge, although later he changed his course of studies to archaeology and anthropology. Before taking up his university place he completed two years' national service in the Royal Air Force, during which he read and reread the complete works of William Shakespeare. After graduating from Cambridge in 1954, he performed various jobs—gardener, night watchman, zoo attendant, movie script-reader, and schoolteacher—designed to support his writing life.

In 1956 he met the American poet Sylvia Plath, who was studying at Cambridge on a Fulbright scholarship. The couple was married later that year. They moved to the United States in 1957, where Plath worked at her alma mater, Smith College, while Hughes taught in the creative writing program at the University of Massachusetts at Amherst. They traveled across the United States in summer 1959, spent the fall at the writers' colony of Yaddo in Saratoga Springs, New York, and returned to settle in London, England, in December of that year.

Hughes's first book, *The Hawk in the Rain*, appeared in September 1957. Publication by Harper and Brothers was Hughes's prize for receiving an award from the Poetry Center of the Young Men's and Young Women's Hebrew Association of New York for the best first collection of poems—a competition judged by W. H. Auden, Marianne Moore, and Stephen Spender. The poems, many of which highlight Hughes's preoccupations with the natural world and with English history, sometimes bear the influence of his formative literary passions: Shakespeare, W. B. Yeats, Gerard Manley Hopkins, and John Crowe Ransom. Meanwhile, he and Plath became interested in experiments with Ouija boards, horoscopes, and hypnosis. Hughes further explored the hybrid traditions of cabalistic and folkloric wisdom, especially those detailed in Robert Graves's idiosyncratic book *The White Goddess* (1948).

In 1960 Hughes's second volume, *Lupercal*, was published. The verses again predominantly focus on natural phenomena, but the Roman festival alluded to in the title poem, "Lupercalia," hints at Hughes's growing fascination with ancient myth and the supernatural realm. Like *The Hawk in the Rain*, the lyrics of *Lupercal* use strong, muscular, and alliterative rhythms, and often they highlight the discrepancies between the cerebral world of humanity and the instinctual workings of the animal kingdom.

CHRONOLOGY

1930	17 August: Born in Mytholmroyd, a village in the Yorkshire Pennines, England, to William Henry and Edith Hughes (nee Farrar). Siblings: brother Gerald, ten years older; sister Olwyn, two years older.
1937	Family moves to Mexborough, South Yorkshire.
1948	Wins scholarship to read English at Cambridge University.
1949–1951	National service in the RAF.
1951–1954	At Pembroke College, Cambridge. Two years into his studies he changes his major to archaeology and anthropology.
1955	Lives in London. Starts to publish poems in little magazines.
1956	February: Meets Sylvia Plath at the *St Botolph's Review* launch party in Cambridge. June: Marries Sylvia Plath.
1957	February: The manuscript of *The Hawk in the Rain* wins the award for the best first collection of poems from the Poetry Center of the Young Men's and Young Women's Hebrew Association of New York. (June) Moves with Plath to the United States. (September) *The Hawk in the Rain* published.
1959	Summer–Fall: Travels across the United States and spends time at the writers' colony of Yaddo in Saratoga Springs, NY. (December) Returns to England and settles in London.
1960	March: *Lupercal* published. (April) Frieda Rebecca Hughes born.
1961	April: *Meet My Folks!*, the first of Hughes's many volumes of poetry and prose for children, published. Starts regular book reviewing for the British press. (August) Moves with Plath to North Tawton, Devon.
1962	January: Nicholas Farrar Hughes born. (June) Began affair with Assia Wevill (nee Gutman).
1963	February: Suicide of Plath in London.
1967	January: Alexandra Tatiana Eloise Wevill—known as Shura—born. (May) *Wodwo* published.

1968	Becomes involved with the creative writing workshops run by the Arvon Foundation.
1969	March: Suicide of Assia Wevill and death of Shura. May: Death of Hughes's mother.
1970	August: Marries Carol Orchard. Settles in North Tawton. October: First edition of *Crow: From the Life and Songs of the Crow* published.
1971	May–September: Accompanies the theatre director Peter Brook to the Shiraz Festival in Iran, where they produce the epic play *Orghast*. (November) Edited and introduced *With Fairest Flowers While Summer Lasts: Poems from Shakespeare*.
1972	Buys Moortown Farm, Devon, and runs it in partnership with his father-in-law Jack Orchard. December: Second edition of *Crow: From the Life and Songs of the Crow* published.
1977	May: *Gaudete* published.
1978	September *Cave Birds: An Alchemical Cave Drama* published. (October) *Moortown Elegies* published.
1979	May: *Remains of Elmet: A Pennine Sequence* published.
1981	February: Death of Hughes's father.
1983	September: *River* published.
1984	December: Appointed Poet Laureate of the United Kingdom.
1986	October: *Flowers and Insects: Some Birds and a Pair of Spiders* published.
1987	Epistolary disputes with feminists about Sylvia Plath's estate and grave conducted in the British press.
1989	September: *Wolfwatching* published.
1992	April: *Shakespeare and the Goddess of Complete Being* published. June: *Rain-Charm for the Duchy and Other Laureate Poems* published. September: *A Dancer to God: Tributes to T. S. Eliot* published.
1994	March: *Winter Pollen: Occasional Prose*, ed. William Scammell published.
1995	March: *New Selected Poems, 1957–1994* published. October: *Difficulties of a*
	Bridegroom: Collected Short Stories published.
1996	September: Translation of Lorca's *Blood Wedding* published.
1997	May: *Tales from Ovid* published. Diagnosed with cancer of the colon.
1998	January: *Birthday Letters* published. September: Translation of Racine's *Phèdre* published. October: Appointed a member of the Order of Merit by Queen Elizabeth II. 28 October: Dies, at London Bridge Hospital, of a heart attack.
1999	13 May: Memorial service in Westminster Abbey, London. September: Translation of Aeschylus's *Oresteia* published. November: Translation of Euripides's *Alcestis* published.

Frieda Rebecca, the first child of Hughes and Plath, was born later in 1960, and the Hugheses were absorbed into metropolitan literary life, befriending many other young writers and meeting established figures including T. S. Eliot. Hughes also wrote lively book reviews for newspapers and magazines, he broadcast many of his poems on the radio, and he gave frequent public readings of his work—all practices that he continued throughout his life.

In August 1961 Hughes and Plath moved to North Tawton, a small village in Devon. Hughes worked on film scripts, opera librettos, and translations, and published the first of numerous volumes for children, *Meet My Folks!* In January 1962 Plath gave birth to a son, Nicholas Farrar Hughes. The couple's relationship, however, was strained, partly due to Hughes's affair with a thrice-married German-Jewish émigré, Assia Wevill. Later that year, Plath left her husband and relocated to London, determined to seek a divorce. In February 1963 she committed suicide.

Hughes took over the guardianship of Frieda and Nicholas as well as Plath's literary estate. He continued to complete radio scripts, literary-critical articles, and short plays, but the trauma of his wife's death caused a form of writer's block. Hughes's next major volume for adults, *Wodwo* (1967), principally contains verse composed between 1960 and 1963. Although the formal structures of these poems are freer and more associative than those employed in Hughes's first two books, *Wodwo's* concentration on the interactions between humans, animals, and landscapes places the text firmly within the writer's "early" period. When Hughes started to compose poetry again, in 1967, his imagination descended into a wretched mythic universe of bodily desecration and absurd destruction—the universe of *Crow.*

In 1969 Assia Wevill, with whom Hughes had been living since Plath's death, killed herself along with Shura, their two- year-old daughter. Principally as a result of this upheaval, Hughes stopped writing the *Crow* poems, although a selection appeared in 1970 as *Crow: From the Life and Songs of the Crow.* In the same year, Hughes married Carol Orchard, the daughter of a Devon farmer. They settled in Hughes's North Tawton house, and Carol provided a stable environment that allowed the poet's hitherto turbulent emotional and literary life to progress in relative peace.

In 1971 Hughes wrote the script for a stage work titled *Orghast,* produced that year in Iran under the direction of Peter Brook. The epic production used an imaginary primitive language created by Hughes. In the same year, Hughes wrote an introduction to a selection of Shakespearean verse in which he formulated his distinctive view of the playwright's psychological, political, and legendary evolution. Twenty years later, he expanded this text into the huge critical study *Shakespeare and the Goddess of Complete Being* (1992).

Hughes's lyric verse of the mid-1970s predominantly is housed, like *Crow,* within elaborate, mythical poetic sequences. *Gaudete* (1977) and *Cave Birds: An Alchemical Cave Drama* (1978) are central examples. Toward the end of the decade, though, Hughes returned to the poetry of natural phenomena and regional territory with which he had launched his career. *Moortown Elegies* (1978) is a journal-like sequence recording his time working on a livestock farm with Carol Orchard's father; *Remains of Elmet* (1979) commemorates the Yorkshire region in which he spent his childhood; *River* (1983) contains exhilarated lyrics about fishing and the flora and fauna of waterways.

In 1984 Hughes became the Poet Laureate of the United Kingdom. The appointment commemorated not only his verse, but also his long-standing commitment to numerous literary and social causes: his preparation of poetry editions (including those of Plath's work) and anthologies; his efforts to promote foreign verse in Britain, both through his own translations and through his administrative and editorial support for the work of others; his gifts of time and money to the creative writing workshops run by the Arvon Foundation; his involvement with numerous environmental projects; and his attempts to encourage poetic composition in schools. The pressures of the laureateship—responding to mail, attending poetry festivals, writing prefaces and contributions for various books, patronizing charities and initiatives—might have caused Hughes's creative output to diminish. In fact, the reverse was true. In the late 1980s he produced two new volumes of verse for adults, *Flowers and Insects: Some Birds and a Pair of Spiders* (1986) and *Wolfwatching* (1989), and in 1992 he gathered together his laureate poems as *Rain-Charm for the Duchy.* Additionally, he collected many of his miscellaneous prose writings in *A Dancer to God: Tributes to T. S. Eliot* (1992), *Winter Pollen: Occasional Prose* (1994), and *Difficulties of a Bridegroom: Collected Short Stories* (1995).

Following the publication of his *New Selected Poems, 1957–1994* in 1995, Hughes's energies were directed along two main routes. The first was translation, and he produced versions of many canonical plays—Lorca's *Blood Wedding* (1996), Racine's *Phèdre* (1999), Aeschylus's *Oresteia* (1999), and Euripides's *Alcestis* (1999)—as well as the nondramatic *Tales from Ovid* (1997), his rendition of twenty-four stories from the *Metamorphoses*. The second major creative enterprise of Hughes's last years was the completion of his verse memoirs about Plath, *Birthday Letters,* which appeared in 1998 to huge publicity, acclaim, and sales. By the time the book was published, Hughes knew that he was losing his battle with cancer. He died on 28 October 1998, shortly after receiving the prestigious honor of the Order of Merit from Queen Elizabeth II.

CROW: TEXT, NARRATIVE, AND RECEPTION

The above summary of Hughes's life and works, abbreviated from Elaine Feinstein's *Ted Hughes: The Life of a Poet* (2001), suggests the centrality of *Crow* to the writer's oeuvre. Its openly mythical superstructure recurs in *Cave Birds,* in *Gaudete,* and years later in *Tales from Ovid*; its oblique response to Sylvia Plath's life, death, and legacy complements the more direct treatment of these events in *Birthday Letters*; and its title and much of its imagery highlight the natural energies probed in Hughes's first three collections and in his work from the 1980s. At the same time, it is a pivotal text, marking Hughes's firm eschewal of his tightly focused early lyrics, and his embarkation upon the ambitious mythic journeys of the 1970s.

Given its important position in Hughes's corpus, it is surprising that the idea for *Crow* came not from the poet but from his friend, the artist Leonard Baskin. In 1967 Baskin asked Hughes to contribute some poems to accompany Baskin's engravings of crows. Hughes saw this invitation as a vehicle by which he could resume writing adult verse after the upheaval of Plath's suicide, and gradually he realized that the symbolic and totemic properties of the crow could be used to mobilize his most urgent psychological, religious, and political concerns. As a result, Hughes developed an extensive mythical narrative in which to frame the poems.

The *Crow* project gripped Hughes's imagination for at least three years, and he produced hundreds of verse and prose manuscript drafts, most of which are now held in the Ted Hughes archive at Emory University in Atlanta, Georgia. Before the appearance of the volume *Crow* in 1970, Hughes published many of these poems in private-press pamphlets, journals, and newspapers. He continued to release further *Crow* poems after 1970, and a small number of these were included in the 1971 American edition of the book and in the augmented British version published in 1972. Others, though, appeared in later Hughes volumes, or remained (and remain) uncollected. It is important to recognize, then, that *Crow* is an unstable and provisional text, and that many more poems exist—in both published and unpublished states—besides those that appear in the American or British book-length editions. This fact is highlighted by the volume's subtitle (*From the Life and Songs of the Crow*), which suggests that the work is culled from a vast cache of material.

Hughes never gave a definitive version of the mythic tale that lies behind the *Crow* poems, although he outlined sections of it at readings, in letters, and to interviewers. Nonetheless, it remains salient to an understanding of the text, and merits a brief recapitulation. The following summary draws upon Keith Sagar's description in *The Laughter of Foxes: A Study of Ted Hughes* (2000), and intersperses some comments from Hughes's retrospective prose writings about *Crow*.

The narrative starts in heaven, with God exhausted from the labors of creation. As he dozes, he has a recurrent Nightmare, which mocks his inventions, especially mankind. God and the Nightmare argue about man's worth, but during their dispute a male ambassador arrives in heaven asking God to take life away from humanity. Furious at these events, God challenges the Nightmare to improve upon his handiwork. The result is the half-man, half-bird called Crow, who is sent to earth and put through various adventures and tribulations. (It is at this point in the story that the volume *Crow* opens.) God initially befriends Crow, but soon he sees that the creature repeatedly meddles in his work, and so he tries to thwart Crow's reckless activities. Crow wanders the earth, causing both creative and destructive mayhem and frequently annihilating himself—yet surviving—in the process. He soon becomes more intelligent, testing things out, and learning the entire history of humanity, its cultures, religions, and stories. Gradually, though, his thoughts center on one main theme: the origins of his existence.

As Hughes explained in 1979 in "A Reply to Critics" (collected in A. E. Dyson, ed., *Three Contemporary Poets: Thom Gunn, Ted Hughes and R. S. Thomas,* 1990), Crow's journeying ultimately becomes a quest "for marriage with [his] creator, a marriage that will be a self-immolation in new, greater and other life" (p. 111). Repeatedly he encounters horrific female beings, but he cannot accept that a woman might have engendered him. He then meets the ghost of an Eskimo Hunter, who becomes Crow's guide and teacher, leading the protagonist to a river. Sitting on the bank is a hideous Ogress who demands that Crow carry her across the river on his back. As he does so, she asks him a series of cryptic riddles about the relations between men and women, and about love. Crow's answers at first are very flawed and he sinks under the Ogress's weight. As he starts to answer more positively, however, her load lightens, and they reach the far riverbank. As Hughes told Ekbert Faas in a 1977 interview ("Ted Hughes and *Gaudete,*" collected in Faas's *Ted Hughes: The Unaccommodated Universe,* 1980), "[Crow's] answers move from one pole of total disaster in the relationship between him and the female to the opposite pole of totally successful, blissful union" (p. 213). The Ogress then transforms herself into a beautiful young woman and Crow joyfully chases her into a wood where she consents to become his wife. In the 1980 essay "On Images in *Crow*" (collected in A. E. Dyson, ed., *Three Contemporary Poets*),

Hughes affirms that "What Crow is grappling with is not 'something dangerous,' but what becomes—at the end of his mistakes and errantry—his bride and his almost-humanity" (p. 114).

The background story behind the *Crow* poems, then, is one of creation, disintegration, and reconstruction. In a radio broadcast dating from July 1970, which was published partially in *The Listener* later that month ("Ted Hughes's *Crow*"), Hughes summarized the progress of his protagonist in such terms: "he's put through various adventures and disasters and trials and ordeals, and the effect of these is to alter him not at all, then alter him a great deal, completely transform him, tear him to bits, put him together again, and produce him a little bit changed" (p. 149). Crow's adventures chart his attempts to dilute his powerful ego and to become a more complete, rounded member of the human species. Primarily, he must learn that women are beings to be regarded not with fear and loathing but with acceptance and love. Of course, the published volume does not complete this narrative, since it closes around the time when Crow meets the ghost of the Eskimo Hunter. For this reason, *Crow* can appear to be a life-denying, pessimistic book, since the hero's emotional reformation and rehabilitation barely begins. Hughes, in fact, found that he could not write the restorative and affirmative ending following the suicide of Assia Wevill in 1969. The tragic events of his own life made it impossible for him to sanction his fictional creature's rebirth into a raw, healed wisdom.

The implications of this detailed framework are vital for the reader's experience of *Crow*. For instance, the poems as they are published constitute an open-ended and cyclical series—reflecting the ceaseless exploits of the indestructible protagonist—but the presence of the quest-narrative turns them into successive fragments of a closed, teleological sequence. Some critics have insisted upon the separation of the poems and the myth; others have argued that the two cannot be divorced. The debates over this issue cannot be resolved by reference to the author's own opinions. In his ephemeral glosses to the text, Hughes's attitudes to *Crow*'s underlying fable are equivocal. To Ekbert Faas in 1971 (in the interview "Ted Hughes and *Crow*," collected in Faas's *The Unaccommodated Universe*), he stated: "The story is not really relevant to the poems as they stand. . . . I think the poems have a life a little aside from it" (p. 206). Eight years later, in his essay "A Reply to Critics," Hughes's stance was quite different: "a more graphic idea of the context—of the traditional convention I set out to exploit, as far as I could, and of the essential line and level of the narrative, which might make some misreadings less likely—ought to have been part of those published fragments" (p.113). Significantly, Hughes here states that his volume has been the subject of "misreadings." It is likely that he was thinking, at least in part, of the book's early reviews, which cleared the ground for many years of contentious critical discussion.

Crow was reviewed widely in the British and American press. Many critics greeted the book as Hughes's major work to date, its poems distilling his distinctive postwar and post-Holocaust vision. A. Alvarez, writing in the London *Observer* in 1970, offered a typically enthusiastic response: "With *Crow*, Hughes himself now joins the select band of survivor-poets whose work is adequate to the destructive reality we inhabit" (p. 33). Other commentators, though, recoiled from the book's howls of anguished laughter and apocalyptic despair. In a 1971 *Times Literary Supplement* review titled "A Mouthful of Blood," Ian Hamilton referred to *Crow*'s "wholly artificial" atmosphere, and stated: "there can be no disguising the fact that the central energies of this book are, in their eager pursuit of blood and thunder, only minimally tempered by poetic caution" (p. 30).

Such polarized reactions have determined *Crow*'s subsequent reception history. David Holbrook, in his book *Lost Bearings in English Poetry* (1977), interprets *Crow* as a facile, paranoid, and "schizoid" text, characterized by a nihilistic destructiveness that constitutes an assault on creativity. Other readers have been more tempered in their hostility: A. K. Weatherhead and Anthony Thwaite both criticize the volume on formal grounds, complaining of its monotonous and flat language. Despite such negative reactions, many academic commentators have followed Alvarez in praising the book's technical and thematic experimentation. P. R. King, in his study *Nine Contemporary Poets: A Critical Introduction* (1979), argues that the verse's vitality and vigor itself counteracts the story's destructive and pessimistic impulses, while Neil Corcoran, in *English Poetry Since 1940* (1993), applauds the volume's transgressive questioning of traditional religious and sexual boundaries.

The interpretive mayhem surrounding *Crow* is more understandable when one remembers the subversive originality of the book, in terms both of its overarching concerns and its energetic aesthetic procedures. Hughes himself accepted the difficulties and challenges offered by his creation. In a short essay dating from 1980, "On Images in *Crow*" (collected in *Three Contemporary Poets*), he stated: "Parables of this sort, I know, are bald fantasies without a certain sort of subjective experience in the reader. And I know, too, that in all writings of this sort it is very difficult to tell what is authentic and what is only imagined" (p. 115). In an unpublished letter to his brother Gerald, dated 27 October 1969, Hughes was more forthright about the obstacles situated between his text and its reader:

But since my tradition—what I set my writing against—is the primitive literatures, the absolute bedrock productions of nature, which I find most congenial anyway, and which seem to me the vital and unchangeable tradition, then I think what I'm doing will always be there. It will be invisible to all those who hardly know that tradition exists (almost all litterateurs) and whose brains have been constructed by the aberrations of recent civilisation. But since I've seen my other books gradually create an audience out of people who to begin with were full of superior opinions I guess this will do the same though it might take longer.

This passage shows that Hughes was prepared for the negative responses and "misreadings" that his book might receive. In discussing the "tradition" of primitive literatures in which he felt himself to be writing, the letter also highlights those specific techniques of style and language that are so central to the creative boldness of *Crow,* and which have caused such a wide spectrum of critical assessments.

STYLE, TEXTURE, AND LANGUAGE

In 1971 Hughes remarked in the interview with Faas: "The first idea of *Crow* was really an idea of style. . . . The idea was originally just to write his songs, the songs that a Crow would sing. In other words, songs with no music whatsoever, in a super-simple and a super-ugly language which would in a way shed everything except just what he wanted to say without any other consideration" (p. 208). This comment seems concisely to gloss many sections of the book, such as the opening of "A Kill":

> Flogged lame with legs
> Shot through the head with balled brains
> Shot blind with eyes
> Nailed down by his own ribs
> Strangled just short of his last gasp
> By his own windpipe
> Clubbed unconscious by his own heart
>
> (p. 16)

This poem is one of the apocryphal versions of Crow's mythical creation that feature at the beginning of the volume. The language of these lines appears to be "super-simple" and "super-ugly," as Hughes described it during his 1971 interview. There are no compound words or dialect terms, both features that Hughes favors elsewhere in his verse. There is no metrical scheme, and the plain discourse is devoid of simile, metaphor, and punctuation—stylistic and organizational devices that appear rarely throughout the text.

However, it is important to notice that Hughes's comments to the interviewer, however true as a description of the poems' inspirational genesis, downplay his artistry in the book. This is true even of lines, like those quoted from "A Kill," that appear to be somewhat flavorless and superficial. When read slowly, or aloud, the passage has a pulsating, incantatory intensity that recalls the rhythms of the King James Bible. The verbs that open all of the lines excepting the penultimate one give the passage an internal, cyclical coherence that, in some ways, is stronger than the external constraints of metrical form. There is a pervasive alliterative pulse, as the labial *l* sounds of the first line—"Flogged," "lame," and "legs"—resonate later in the passage through the words "balled," "blind," "Nailed," "last," and "Clubbed." (There are, too, resonant patterns of sibilants and plosives.) It is quite false, then, to argue that the start of "A Kill" has "no music whatsoever," as Hughes stated in the interview, and as many antipathetic critics also have concluded. It is also wrong to suggest that the apparently simplistic passage holds no intertextual resonance. The reference in the fourth line to Crow being "Nailed down by his own ribs," for instance, clearly recalls Christ's Crucifixion—an appropriate allusion in a poem whose cadences are so indebted to the litanies and chants of the Christian Church and its holy texts.

Many of Hughes's comments about *Crow* echo the casual, self-deprecatory tone of the statement cited from the 1971 interview. In the same interview he claimed that the poems "wrote themselves quite rapidly" (p. 207), for instance, and in his 1977 interview with Faas he argued that he was returning in *Crow* to a style that he had used "for a while when I was about nineteen" (p. 212). Such assertions should be treated with caution. A much more incisive commentary by Hughes on the mechanics of his *Crow* poems may be found in his contemporaneous essay, first published in 1969, on the Yugoslav poet Vasko Popa (collected in Hughes's *Winter Pollen: Occasional Prose*, 1994). This piece merits lengthy quotation:

> There is a primitive pre-creation atmosphere about his work, as if he were present where all the dynamisms and formulae were ready and charged, but nothing created—or only a few fragments. . . . His poetry is near the world of music, where a repository of selected signs and forms, admitted from the outer world, act out fundamental combinations that often have something eerily mathematical about their progressions and symmetries, but which seem to belong deeply to the world of spirit or of the heart. Again like music, his poems turn the most grisly confrontations into something deadpan playful: a spell, a riddle, a game, a story. It is the Universal Language behind language, and when the poetic texture of the verbal code has been cancelled . . . we are left with solid hieroglyphic objects and events, meaningful in a direct way, simultaneously earthen and spiritual, plain-statement and visionary.
>
> (pp. 223–224)

These sentences, which incidentally illustrate the driven and cumulative power of Hughes's critical prose, could be describing the poetics and symbolism of *Crow* rather than those of Popa's verse. The "primitive pre- creation atmosphere" of the volume is foregrounded in the passage from "A Kill" discussed earlier—a passage that operates formally not through metrical stanzas but through musical and "mathematical . . . progressions and symmetries." More generally, the book again and again tells "a spell, a riddle, a game, a story" in rhetoric which is both "plain-statement and visionary."

However illuminating these phrases from the Popa essay may be, it would be wrong to suggest that *Crow* has a single, monolithic style or cadence that is repeated in every poem. While certain image clusters—blackness, nothingness, laughter—remain constant, there is considerable variation between the stylistic imperatives driving the different lyrics. "Lineage," for example,

draws on the archaic language used in the Bible's ancestral catalogues:

> In the beginning was Scream
> Who begat Blood
> Who begat Eye
> Who begat Fear
> Who begat Wing
>
> (p. 14)

The poem following "Lineage" in the volume, "Examination at the Womb-door," employs the discourse of catechismal interrogation:

> Who owns these scrawny little feet? *Death.*
> Who owns this bristly scorched-looking face? *Death.*
> Who owns these still-working lungs? *Death.*
>
> (p. 15)

Later in the book, "Crow and the Birds" gestures toward a neo-Romantic register:

> When the eagle soared clear through a dawn
> distilling of emerald
> When the curlew trawled in seadusk through a
> chime of wineglasses
> When the swallow swooped through a woman's
> song in a cavern
> And the swift flicked through the breath of a
> violet
>
> (p. 37)

The Hopkins-like cadences of these lines recall the aesthetic strategies employed in Hughes's early verse. Significantly, the end of the poem undercuts and ironizes the unabashed beauty of these descriptions, as the reader confronts "Crow spraddled head-down in the beach-garbage, guzzling a dropped ice-cream" (p. 37). The poem focuses on the contrast between the protagonist and the other birds, but its finale should not detract from Hughes's mobilization of a rhetoric that is quite different from the "super-simple" and "super-ugly" squawk of the Crow.

In other poems, Hughes draws upon a quite different discursive tradition—that of comic strips and cartoons. "The Battle of Osfrontalis" alludes, for example, to a Walt Disney character: "Words came with blank cheques— / He drew Minnie Mice on them" (p. 34). Elsewhere, in the poem "In Laughter," Hughes engages more fundamentally with the performative strategies of the popular visual arts. As David Lodge first noted in his influential 1971 article "*Crow* and the Cartoons," this lyric sets highly staged images of violence and pain against a refrain-like soundtrack of canned laughter:

> Cars collide and erupt luggage and babies
> In laughter
> The steamer upends and goes under saluting like a
>   stuntman
> In laughter
> The nosediving aircraft concludes with a boom
> In laughter

> (p. 48)

The reference to "a stuntman" highlights the text's indebtedness to the realms of televisual and movie culture. The poem deliberately aims to shock and unsettle the reader with its robust, surreal humor. But such strategies are not employed throughout the volume. Parts of "Crow and the Birds," as illustrated above, employ rhetorical procedures that establish an atmosphere of natural grace and harmony rather than farcical destruction. *Crow,* then, employs a multitude of discourses and registers—from cartoon violence to mythic genesis, from self-conscious extravagance to simple clarity—and this has led some critics, such as Paul Bentley in his *The Poetry of Ted Hughes: Language, Illusion and Beyond* (1998), to employ the theories of the Russian critic Mikhail Bakhtin (1895–1975) in their readings of Hughes's text. Bakhtin's writings focus on the "Carnivalesque" blending of "high" and "low" cultural forms, and they highlight patterns of discourse that suggest a plurality of speakers and linguistic registers. Such Bakhtinian interpretations of *Crow* seem especially prescient when set against

Hughes's own critical essays, which frequently praise writers for their impulsive, extempore linguistic adaptability. In 1971 for example, in his introduction to *With Fairest Flowers While Summer Lasts: Poems from Shakespeare* (collected in *Winter Pollen* as "The Great Theme: Notes on Shakespeare"), Hughes discussed Shakespeare's verse texture, anatomizing its "air of being invented in a state of crisis, for a terribly urgent job, a homely spur-of-the-moment improvisation out of whatever verbal scrap happens to be lying around" (*Winter Pollen,* p. 105).

Bakhtin's theoretical model—highlighting vocal plurality, rhetorical excess, and verbal play—both shadows Hughes's criticism and helps to illuminate his poems. Crow's mobilization of a wide range of discourses and styles is offset, however, by Hughes's awareness of linguistic poverty and the limitations of representation. The comfortless and negative character of language is emphasized in "Crow Goes Hunting":

> Crow
> Decided to try words.
> . . .
> He pointed out the hare and away went the
>   words
> Resounding.
> Crow was Crow without fail, but what is a hare?
>
> It converted itself to a concrete bunker.
> The words circled protesting, resounding.
>
> Crow turned the words into bombs—they blasted
>   the bunker.
> The bits of bunker flew up—a flock of starlings.

> (p. 54)

These lines highlight the absence of authoritative signifying procedures in *Crow*'s absurd universe. Far from providing a link between one's consciousness and the world, the words destabilize the things that they attempt to name and delimit. In his 1967 prose book for children,

Poetry in the Making: An Anthology of Poems and Programmes from "Listening and Writing," Hughes likened the process of imaginative composition to the intense effort required when hunting animals:

The special kind of excitement, the slightly mesmerized and quite involuntary concentration with which you make out the stirrings of a new poem in your mind, then the outline, the mass and colour and clean final form of it, the unique living reality of it in the midst of the general lifelessness, all is too familiar to mistake. This is hunting and the poem is a new species of creature, a new specimen of the life outside your own.

(p. 17)

Crow's own hunt, though, goes awry because he is ignorant of the conventions of meaning and understanding that allow human beings to communicate with one another. The poem's events leave Crow "Speechless with admiration" (p. 54), and elsewhere in the book he strains to utter meaningful language. "Crow's First Lesson" opens:

God tried to teach Crow how to talk.
'Love,' said God. 'Say, Love.'
Crow gaped, and the white shark crashed into the
     sea
And went rolling downwards, discovering its own
     depth.

(p. 20)

The poem continues in this vein, with Crow trying to utter the word "love" but only causing the inception of predatory, disease-ridden, or violent aspects of creation. Crow's recurrent struggles with God's alien tongue parallel the hermeneutic difficulties facing the volume's reader. One hindrance is that *Crow* frequently frustrates and reverses the reader's assumptions of meaning and understanding. Love is described in the idiom of hate, as in the lines from "Crow's First Lesson" quoted above, or creation is figured through the rhetoric of apocalypse, beauty in the style of ugliness, laughter using the

vocabulary of pain, and so on. Language in *Crow*, then, is severed from its established contracts of representation. This does not appear especially anomalous or strange because the book's episodes occur not in any recognizable modern or historical landscape but instead in an indeterminate realm that Hughes creates from various mythical traditions and beliefs.

MYTH: RESOURCES AND RELIGIONS

Hughes was interested in mythic stories, primitive cultures, and aboriginal beliefs throughout his life, and he reviewed numerous books of folklore, anthropology, and oral literature. In "Tricksters and Tar Babies," an article written for the *New York Review of Books* in 1965 (collected in *Winter Pollen*), Hughes observed that the explorers and missionaries who recorded the tales and poems of oral societies were the very people whose colonial presence destroyed such untouched tribal cultures. He ended the piece, though, by praising the "seminal," "inspired and astonishing" nature and the "elemental autonomy" of the North American Winnebago "Trickster Cycle" collected by Paul Radin (pp. 77–78). Critical essays by Graham Bradshaw and Jarold Ramsey explore how these primitive Native American legends in large part inspired the mythic universe of *Crow*.

Trickster folklore tells of wild escapades, violent confrontations, incessant transformations, and repeated deaths and rebirths. The (anti-)hero of these narratives, the trickster himself, is both creative and destructive, both victim and perpetrator. He is not immoral, but rather amoral: he exists before the categories of good and evil have been formulated by the conscious mind. He has a liminal, self-contradictory, metamorphic identity and he is transgressive, defying sexual taboos and socioreligious authorities. His sole genius is his will to live and his ability to survive whatever his opponents contrive for him. In his 1985 essay

"Crow on the Beach" (collected in *Winter Pollen*), Hughes emphasized his understanding of this: "Trickster, demon of phallic energy, bearing the spirit of the sperm, is repetitive and indestructible" (p. 241). In the Winnebago cycle of narratives, the trickster often is figured as a raven, and hence *Crow*'s protagonist fits effortlessly into this mythological tradition. In a radio program broadcast in 1970, "Ted Hughes's *Crow*," Hughes drew on trickster motifs to describe his character: "The crow is the most intelligent of the birds. He lives in just about every piece of land on earth, and there's a great body of folklore about crows, of course. . . . The crow is the indestructible bird who suffers everything, suffers nothing" (p. 149).

The poem "A Childish Prank" clearly illustrates Crow's trickster credentials. The lyric opens with the soulless bodies of man and woman lying down in Eden. While God ponders what to do, Crow operates instinctively:

Crow laughed.
He bit the Worm, God's only son,
Into two writhing halves.

He stuffed into man the tail half
With the wounded end hanging out.

He stuffed the head half headfirst into woman
And it crept in deeper and up
To peer out through her eyes
Calling its tail-half to join up quickly, quickly
Because O it was painful.

(p. 19)

By his unthinking, irresponsible actions, Crow initiates the trials of sexuality and destroys the nascent hope that human beings might possess souls. Typically, he leaves the world transformed, for better or for worse. Dissolving the boundary between eros and agape, Crow's activities also include an explicit scatological element.

Elsewhere in the text, Crow is the casualty rather than the perpetrator of such cosmic crimes. "Truth Kills Everybody," a poem from the end of the volume, describes Crow's battle with the shape-shifting character Proteus. Crow clings on to Proteus through his hybrid metamorphoses, and the poem ends in disaster:

The ankle of a rising, fiery angel—he held it

Christ's hot pounding heart—he held it

The earth, shrunk to the size of a hand grenade

And he held it he held it and held it and

BANG!

He was blasted to nothing.

(p. 83)

Despite his total erasure in these lines, Crow reappears at the beginning of the next poem in the book, "Crow and Stone." Astonishingly, given his experience of being "blasted to nothing," this subsequent poem describes Crow as "nimble," and as "*he who never has been killed / . . . / And is only just born*" (p. 84). In his 1979 essay "A Reply to Critics," Hughes described his hero as "destruction prone but indestructible, and more than happy, . . . blundering through every possible mistake and every possible sticky end, experimenting with every impulse, like a gambling machine of mutations, but inaccessible to despair" (p. 111).

These retrospective comments succinctly gloss the action of "A Childish Prank" and "Truth Kills Everybody," and they help to link both lyrics to the trickster tradition. But it is important to recognize that throughout the volume, and indeed in the passages quoted from these two poems, Hughes looks beyond the Winnebago legends in order to activate a heterogeneous spectrum of mythological and folkloric material. In "A Childish Prank," for instance, Hughes revisits the biblical narrative of Adam and Eve in the Garden of Eden, and he turns the serpent of temptation into an aggressively eroticized "Worm" who also symbolizes Christ, "God's only son." Again and again in *Crow*, Hughes rewrites and deconstructs the totemic stories of the Christian religion—the

Creation, the Fall, the Nativity, and the Passion. Such irreverent poems elucidate his observation to Ekbert Faas in the 1971 interview that "Christianity is just another provisional myth of man's relationship with the creator and the world of spirit" (p. 205).

In "Truth Kills Everybody," Hughes again alludes to the explicitly Christian symbols of "a rising, fiery angel" and "Christ's hot pounding heart," but this poem's central mythical scenario derives from ancient Greek legend. The text narrates a version of the Homeric fable about the all-knowing, form-changing sea-god Proteus, who will provide answers to riddles and queries only if the questioner holds him while he adopts several terrifying disguises. The echoes of Christian and classical culture in "A Childish Prank" and "Truth Kills Everybody" are conspicuous, and they should be relatively familiar to most informed readers. Elsewhere, though, Hughes utilizes more arcane mythical and religious sources, such as Tibetan Buddhist beliefs, Celtic legends, and Inuit fables. Hughes's myriad debts to such materials are explored fully in the relevant chapters of several book-length studies of his oeuvre, such as Keith Sagar's *The Art of Ted Hughes* (1975) and Leonard Scigaj's *Ted Hughes* (1991).

THEORIES OF THE GODDESS

Just as *Crow* employs multiple stylistic discourses, then, Hughes's imagination ranges geographically and chronologically over numerous myths and stories. This leaves the book fissured by a central paradox: the poems' apparently crude, uncivilized, and archaic texture is achieved only through the activation of Hughes's hugely learned creative psyche. Partly as a result of this incongruity, many critics have debated the fundamental authority and status of *Crow*. Some, like Rand Brandes in his 2001 essay "Ted Hughes: *Crow*," have argued that the book itself constitutes a "modern myth," continuing the tradition of Mary Shelley's

Frankenstein, Joseph Conrad's *Heart of Darkness,* and T. S. Eliot's *The Waste Land.* Others, following the seminal work of Terry Gifford and Neil Roberts in *Ted Hughes: A Critical Study* (1981), have insisted that Hughes's text, although engaging with a myriad hoard of anthropological resources and devices, does little or nothing to synthesize these fragmentary materials into an original vision of its own.

Whether or not one labels them a "myth," it is important for the reader of *Crow* to recognize that these poems are rooted within a core set of convictions and preoccupations that resonate throughout Hughes's oeuvre. When he published his critical magnum opus, *Shakespeare and the Goddess of Complete Being,* Hughes took his leading epigraph from Yeats's *Ideas of Good and Evil* (1903): "The Greeks, a certain scholar has told me, considered that myths are the activities of the Daimons, and that the Daimons shape our characters and our lives. I have often had the fancy that there is some one myth for every man, which, if we but knew it, would make us understand all he did and thought" (p. xv). The fact that Yeats's words introduce Hughes's monumental Shakespeare study is significant, because this book— whatever its merits or limitations as an interpretation of the playwright—openly demonstrates Hughes's intrinsic beliefs about the world and the functions of the poetic imagination. In short, it embodies Hughes's own "some one myth."

The texture of *Shakespeare and the Goddess of Complete Being* is complex, multilayered, and saturated with esoteric knowledge about classical mythology, English religious history, and the traditions of Elizabethan occult wisdom. At the same time, though, its principal argument is quite simple to follow. Hughes suggests that Shakespeare's two long narrative poems, *Venus and Adonis* and *The Rape of Lucrece,* together constitute a concise mythic narrative that may be traced, with some variants, throughout his mature plays. In Hughes's reading, Shakespeare's works return incessantly to "the image of the beautiful youth Adonis, rejecting the voluptuous, besotted Goddess, then being bloodily, sumptuously slain by the Boar, before being restored as a flower between the breasts of the Goddess as she flies to heaven" (p. 40). Alongside this private narrative, Hughes suggests that Shakespeare's myth symbolizes the energies both of recusant Elizabethan Catholicism (the rejection of Venus parallels the Reformation's destruction of the ancient, sacred figure of the Great Goddess), and of Puritanism's ascendant tyranny (the puritanical Adonis's sexual repression later explodes as Tarquin's execution of rape). As such, Shakespeare's texts mirror and embody the religious crises of their time, and the playwright emerges from Hughes's account as a prophetic visionary akin to the seers of classical culture:

> In both the Greek world and Shakespeare's the archaic reign of the Great Goddess was being put down, finally and decisively, by a pragmatic, sceptical, moralizing, desacralizing spirit: in Greece by the spirit of Socrates, and in England by the spirit of the ascendant, Puritan God of the individual conscience, the Age of Reason cloaked in the Reformation. For England, as for Greece, it was a supernova moment, which, it seems, can happen only once in a nation, as in a star. . . . Maybe this is how the *Complete Works* come to be (with whatever else they may be) modern England's creation story, our sacred book, closer to us than the Bible.

(p. 85.)

This idiosyncratic literary and historical analysis may seem a long way from the universe of *Crow*. It is significant, though, that Hughes's reading of Shakespeare's mythic superstructure was advanced first in 1971, in the introduction to his anthology *With Fairest Flowers While Summer Lasts* (collected in *Winter Pollen* as "The Great Theme"). This anthology, of course, is contemporaneous with the initial appearance of *Crow* in 1970, and the two texts share the same underlying obsessions and convictions. In the *With Fairest Flowers* introduction, for instance, Hughes refers to "the agonies of an

ancient Dionysus in a world of suddenly hardening sceptical intellect and morality"—and this is the basic mythical DNA that determines the plot of *Crow* (*Winter Pollen*, p. 111).

Central to Hughes's poetic vocation, as suggested by the summary of *Shakespeare and the Goddess of Complete Being* given above, is a desire to dismantle Western man's adherence to codes of behavior and understanding grounded in dogmatic Judeo-Christian morality, Platonic rationalism, and objective, scientific materialism. These psychological and cultural conditions, Hughes thinks, have created a chronically sick society that has devalued the primitive, the pagan, the natural (encompassing the physical body as well as the organic environment), the instinctual, and the feminine. Like Shakespeare as he understands him, Hughes aims to unite the two sides of humanity's split psyche, and thus to heal the divisions—between male and female, Puritan and Catholic, rational and emotional—that afflict the modern self.

An early *Crow* poem, "The Door," sets up a palpable opposition between "a body" that "is growth of the solid world" and "The eye's pupil" which stands as a doorway out of that body (p. 18). The "eye" here sonically elides into the "I" of consciousness, and the poem therefore stages the comprehensive detachment of the self's mental operations from its corporeal existence—a detachment that the rest of the volume aims to mend. This medicinal narrative is not fully successful, as a poem from the end of the volume, "Crow's Last Stand," makes clear. This lyric again employs the "eye-pupil" image: "Limpid and black— / Crow's eye-pupil, in the tower of its scorched fort" (p. 81). These lines figure Crow's body as a burnt-out "fort," with only the "tower" of the conscious "eye" / "I" avoiding the flames by retaining some moisture (the word "limpid" often is used to describe clear or transparent water). Hughes draws here on the extensive Platonic-Protestant tradition in Anglophone literature that portrays the sovereign, solipsistic self as a "tower"—from Milton's "high lonely tower" through Shelley's "starlit tower" to Yeats's book- length collection *The Tower.* Hughes's coded allusion to the ontology of solitude and isolation promoted by these poets compactly details Crow's failure to abnegate the absolute power of his own ego. If, then, the underlying story of *Crow* delineates the self's search for its own restorative synthesis, it is important to notice that the volume's "premature" ending leaves many of the wounds still rupturing and barely healed.

Crow personifies many of the things that Hughes's God has tried to eliminate from his universe—spontaneous actions, bodily felicities, and absurd responses. Typically, Crow exaggerates all of these qualities, so that his noteworthy efforts to balance and correct some of God's sterile laws merely seem to be acts of empty, childish rebellion. "Crow Blacker than ever," for instance, opens:

> When God, disgusted with man,
> Turned towards heaven.
> And man, disgusted with God,
> Turned towards Eve,
> Things looked like falling apart.
>
> But Crow   Crow
> Crow nailed them together,
> Nailing Heaven and earth together—
>
> (p. 69)

Crow in these lines becomes a sort of godhead himself, since the triple repetition of his name openly echoes the Christian Trinity of Father, Son, and Holy Spirit, and the verb "nailed" obliquely recalls Christ's Crucifixion. Crow's efforts, well-meaning though they may be, predictably end in catastrophe:

> The agony
> Grew.
> Crow
> Grinned Crying: 'This is my Creation,'
> Flying the black flag of himself.
>
> (p. 69)

While God wishes to distance himself from the universe, Crow laudably aims to unite the two.

However, his instinctive attempt to weld humanity to its spiritual roots causes pain for all parties involved, meaning that his actions appear not as commendable, selfless attempts to neutralize God's aloof reserve, but rather as irresponsible eruptions of adolescent defiance.

Furthermore, it would be wrong to suggest that Crow embodies only "positive" qualities to set against God's "negative" ones. An important structuring device of the book's quest myth concerns the protagonist's developing attitudes toward the female figures that he meets—all of whom emblematize the mythic Great Goddess. In *Shakespeare and the Goddess of Complete Being,* Hughes marshals a prodigious quantity of anthropological data to conclude that the primitive goddess has "three aspects: the Mother, the Sacred Bride, and the Queen of the Underworld" (p. 7). It is a cornerstone of Hughes's mythic understanding that the female simultaneously embodies all three of these identities; the dominant personality at any one moment depends upon the perceptive and hermeneutic powers of the interacting male. In *Crow,* the protagonist figures the first female bodies that he encounters as hellish Mothers, before imaging them as Queens of the Underworld, and then—finally—as Sacred Brides.

The poem "Crow and Mama" appears early in the volume:

> When Crow cried his mother's ear
> Scorched to a stump.
>
> When he laughed she wept
> Blood her breasts her palms her brow all wept
>   blood.
>
> (p. 17)

Crow and his "Mama," then, exist not in harmonic union but in a dialectic relationship of mutual torment. Later in the volume, Crow's disposition toward the female has become even more hostile and sardonic. "Revenge Fable" tells of a man's desire to "get rid of his mother":

So he pounded and hacked at her
With numbers and equations and laws
Which he invented and called truth.
He investigated, incriminated
And penalized her, like Tolstoy,
Forbidding, screaming and condemning,
Going for her with a knife

(p. 70)

Significantly, the unnamed man tries to kill the goddess- figure with the instruments of rational, scientific understanding—"numbers and equations and laws"—which for Hughes exemplify Western man's divorce from his unadulterated spiritual self. In "Revenge Fable," then, the goddess materializes as a dangerously sexual and illogical Queen of the Underworld who must be destroyed so that man can continue his illusory progress toward greater detachments and more discriminating abstractions. However, there are a small number of *Crow* poems in which the protagonist apparently looks forward to the final, reconstructive phase of his mythic journey, when his outlook toward the female has matured into something more positive and reciprocative. In "Fragment of an Ancient Tablet," the speaker recognizes that the goddess is a complex entity to be loved as well as feared: "Above—the well-known lips, delicately downed. / Below—beard between thighs" (p. 85). The book's closing poem, "Littleblood," ends with a request to "Sit on my finger, sing in my ear, O littleblood" (p. 94). This poised line may be interpreted as Crow's invocation to the female muse who will become (in the narrative that continues beyond the bounds of the volume) his Sacred Bride.

The regenerative arc of Crow's opinions about the goddess—which complements his own faltering endeavors to become a "complete being"—has not prevented some critics from attacking Hughes for apparently luxuriating in his sadistic, virile portrayals of violence against women. The end of "Song for a Phallus" provides one example:

He split his Mammy like a melon
    He was drenched with gore

He found himself curled up inside
    As if he had never been bore
                Mamma   Mamma
                    (p. 77)

At first, there seems to be some merit in the thoughtful censures contained in a book like Calvin Bedient's *Eight Contemporary Poets* (1974). Even the vitriolic denunciations of David Holbrook, in his *Lost Bearings in English Poetry* (1977), seem partially understandable. Other objections to Hughes's brutal, murderous imagery have been rooted in personal hostility toward the poet, who for a small number of feminist writers and academics always will remain the man who precipitated Sylvia Plath's suicide. Setting aside such biographical considerations, it is clear that all of these critics have made two errors of appreciation in assessing Hughes's work. The first is that they have mistaken Crow's unreconstructed masculine voice for the voice of Hughes himself—despite the fact that the book mobilizes an extensive spectrum of linguistic registers and speakers. More significantly, they have ignored Hughes's own understanding of the "violence" in his poetry. In his 1971 interview with Ekbert Faas he stated: "Any form of violence—any form of vehement activity—invokes the bigger energy, the elemental power circuit of the Universe" (p. 200). This "power circuit," in Hughes's imagination, is energized not by a male God but by the female Goddess of Complete Being—variously manifested in his writings as Mother Earth, Gaia, the Great Goddess, the Virgin Mary, and so on. The worst acts of brutal criminality in *Crow* may be executed by the pseudo-male protagonist, but primarily he is following the rhythms of the Great Goddess in her infernal aspect. Furthermore, this Queen of the Underworld identity is a visage of the goddess that becomes less pronounced as the volume progresses, since Crow gradually ameliorates his understanding of the female. One cannot write a shamanistic narrative of creation, dissolution, and rebirth without incorporating some cathartic conflict, yet certain readers of

Crow have failed to probe beyond the text's superficial portrayals of violence into that savagery's mythic origins, its feminine loyalties, and its progressive effects.

HISTORY, NATION, AND TRAUMA

Much of the foregoing discussion of *Crow* has focused on the book's status as a universal narrative designed to encode a spiritual corrective for the human psyche. It can, however, be read through some more specific interpretive lenses: as a text engaging with the global political culture of the mid-to-late 1960s; as a book continuing its author's complex dialogue with England and Englishness; and as an interior narrative that obliquely rehearses Hughes's mourning for his first wife, Sylvia Plath.

The violence of *Crow* may be justified, as above, by recourse to Hughes's central mythical beliefs and models. Additionally, however, it may be related to the text's particular historical moment. The *Crow* universe exists as a sort of postmodern bricolage, in which the entire history of the gods and of mankind takes place within the present instant. Alongside the "sophisticated" anthropological materials quarried from ancient civilizations, for example, Hughes utilizes the "lowbrow" language and imagery of contemporary popular culture. Some lines from "Crow Tries the Media" concisely illustrate this technique:

> He wanted to sing very clear
>
> But this tank had been parked on his voice
> And his throat was nipped between the Roman
>   Emperor's finger and
> thumb
> Like the neck of a linnet
> While King Kong in person
> Held the loop of his blood like a garotte
> And tycoons gambled his glands away in a fog of
>   cigar smoke

> (p. 46)

Ranging allusively from a "Roman Emperor" to the movie character "King Kong," this passage demonstrates *Crow*'s illusion of temporal synchrony. However, it contains two references that work to situate the poem within its own historical time—the "tank" of the second line, and the tycoons' "cigar smoke" at the end of the quotation. Both of these images give "Crow Tries the Media" a distinctive twentieth-century atmosphere. The "tank" in particular is significant, since its presence effaces the fantasy of ahistorical timelessness and sites the text within the agitated and anxious global mood of the 1960s—the decade of the cold war and the Cuban missile crisis, the Vietnam War, the outbreak of the Troubles in Northern Ireland, and numerous conflicts in postcolonial Africa.

The atomic threats of the cold war are confronted in Hughes's *Crow* poem "A Disaster," which narrates the destructive exploits of a voracious "word" which tries to consume the entire earth:

> But its effort weakened.
> It could digest nothing but people.
> So there it shrank, wrinkling weaker,
> Puddling
> Like a collapsing mushroom.
> Finally, a drying salty lake.

> (p. 33)

The simile of the "collapsing mushroom" recalls the mushroom cloud caused by an atomic bomb, and the "drying salty lake" concisely illustrates the ecological effects of total war. Critics such as Neil Roberts, in his book *Narrative and Voice in Postwar Poetry* (1999), have focused their attentions on *Crow*'s complex, ambivalent relations to its era. They suggest that images like the "pistol muzzle oozing blue vapour," which opens "That Moment," or the "nuclear glare" of the post-holocaust landscape sketched in "Notes for a Little Play," cannot be understood without reference to the worldwide social contexts in which Hughes composed his verse (pp. 22, 86). In the 1976 essay "Myth and Education" (collected in *Winter Pollen*), Hughes praised Shakespeare's *King Lear* as a text that "has somehow focused all the pressures of an age—

collisions of spirit and nature and good and evil" (p. 153). Many writers on Hughes's work similarly have explored the ways in which his verbal cadences and image clusters work not only to signify the poet's universal mythic preoccupations, but also to emblematize "all the pressures of an age."

Another growing branch of political criticism concentrates more narrowly on Hughes's engagement with his native land. In his prose writings, Hughes returns obsessively to three seminal events of English history: the Reformation, the Industrial Revolution, and World War I. All three, for Hughes, were occasions when man's rational, mechanical nature overtook, with disastrous effects, his instinctive awareness of spiritual and natural life. The causes and consequences of these historical pressures erupt in many of the *Crow* poems. In "Crow's Account of St George," for instance, Hughes represents England's patron saint as a soulless, cerebral technocrat for whom "everything in the Universe / Is a track of numbers racing towards an answer." George's mathematical, intellectual outlook leads him to murder a female creature who, to him, represents a Queen of the Underworld: "A belly-ball of hair, with crab-legs, eyeless." Only at the end of the poem, when the saint's murderous frenzy has passed, does the "eyeless"—or "I"-less—goddess reveal herself to be "his wife" and Sacred Bride (pp. 31–32). Saint George, in Hughes's idiosyncratic retelling of the legend, incarnates the energies both of the Puritan Reformation and of the scientific Enlightenment that precipitated the Industrial Revolution in eighteenth-century England.

The most recent of Hughes's three formative events in English history held personal associations for the poet, who grew up in a household headed by his withdrawn, war veteran father. Hughes began his 1965 review of Great War verse, entitled "National Ghost" (collected in *Winter Pollen*), with the words: "The First World War goes on getting stronger—our number one national ghost. It's still everywhere, molesting everybody. It's still politically alive,

too, in an underground way" (p. 70). Nearly thirty years later, when writing the notes to accompany *Rain-Charm for the Duchy and Other Laureate Poems*, Hughes returned to this theme. He described himself as "the son of an infantryman of the First World War," and figured the conflict as "virtually the Creation Story, and such a shattering, all-inclusive, grievous catastrophe that it was felt as a national *defeat,* though victory had somehow been pinned on to it as a consolation medal" (p. 58). The trope of the "Creation Story" employed in this note directly echoes Hughes's analysis, in *Shakespeare and the Goddess of Complete Being,* of Shakespeare's plays as "modern England's creation story" (p. 85). Hughes's seismic understanding of World War I recurs in the lyrics of *Crow,* where the various battles and conflicts act as ciphers that allow him to write a latter-day, displaced war poetry.

Numerous *Crow* poems allude directly to the global, and especially European, hostilities of 1914 to 1918. "Dawn's Rose" describes "the dull gunshot and its after-râle / Among conifers, in rainy twilight"—an image that might have been composed by one of the soldier-poets who experienced trench warfare in northern France (p. 59). In "Crow's Account of the Battle," the presence of "cartridges" and "pocket-books" helps to situate the cosmic conflict simultaneously within the period of World War I. The battle, caused by a "mishmash of scripture and physics," seems to be the logical outcome of Western man's adherence to codes of behavior initiated by Reformation "scripture" and confirmed by the revolutions of eighteenth-century "physics" that enabled the development of mechanized, industrial weaponry (p. 26).

Crow, then, amasses its prodigious range of mythic materials not only to tell a universal story of mankind's spiritual suffering and redemption, but also to probe the dynamics of English history and contemporary global politics. The text also operates, though, on a more intimate level—as a trauma narrative designed to help its author overcome the death of his first wife. Although the composition of the text's regenerative myth was suspended after the copycat suicide of Assia Wevill in 1969, there is some evidence that *Crow* helped Hughes to exorcize a number of his private demons. In 1979, in "A Reply to Critics," he described the book as "a means of domesticating many things that interested me, and that I could find no other way of coming to terms with at the time. And I was conscious, too, that the overall theme offered a good outcome for me personally" (p. 112). Throughout his retrospective prose defenses of *Crow,* as in the 1985 essay "Crow on the Beach" (collected in *Winter Pollen*), Hughes dismisses those readers who bemoan the text's "animal despair and suicidal nihilism," arguing that its energies instead are driven by an "unkillable, biological optimism" (p. 239) that constitutes "an all-out commitment to salvaging life against the odds" (p. 240). He states that his hero "works to redeem us, to heal us, and even, in a sense, to resurrect us, in our bad times" (p. 241). This final quotation echoes Hughes's frequent remarks about the purposes of art dating from the last decade of his life, many of which seem colored by the events of his marriage to Plath. In a 1996 interview with Eliat Negev, for instance, he observed: "Every work of art stems from a wound in the soul of the artist. . . . When a person is hurt, his immune system comes into operation, and the self- healing process takes place, mental and physical. Art is a psychological component of the auto-immune system that gives expression to the healing process. That is why great works of art make us feel good" (p. 4).

Crow is one such "great work of art." The fixed, rictus smile that it wears while destruction and apocalypse threaten should not blind the reader to the fact that, at times, it helps to "make us feel good." One must approach Hughes's own statements about his work with caution, but he seems correct to highlight the book's curative, redemptive subtexts. Even if one sets aside the unwritten regenerative finale that crowns the book's underlying myth, there are moments in the published volume when Crow unreservedly embarks on his transformative journey. The end of "Crow's Undersong" is the foremost instance of this:

> She has come amorous it is all she has come for
>
> If there had been no hope she would not have
>   come
>
> And there would have been no crying in the city
>
> (There would have been no city)
>
> (p. 56)

In these lines, Crow initially views the goddess solely as a sexual being, who has "come amorous"—a phrase containing a clear pun on the orgasmic meaning of "come." His concluding parenthetical statement, though, accepts her role as partial creator of the universe, and as a female principle to balance the male godhead. *Crow*'s world, then, is not simply one of anarchy, negation, and despair. The final line of Hughes's last work, his posthumously released translation of Euripides's *Alcestis,* reads: "Let this give man hope" (p. 83). The positive, procreative energies of Hughes's poetic imagination continued to flow until his death, and they swirl too—powerfully, majestically, expectantly—in *Crow*: "If there had been no hope she would not have come."

Selected Bibliography

EDITIONS

Crow: From the Life and Songs of the Crow. London: Faber, 1970; New York: Harper and Row, 1971; 2d ed. London: Faber, 1972. The second British edition is generally regarded as the canonical version to date. Page references to *Crow* given herein are to this edition of the text.

OTHER WORKS BY HUGHES

The Hawk in the Rain. London: Faber; New York: Harper, 1957.

Lupercal. London: Faber; New York: Harper, 1960.

Meet My Folks! London: Faber, 1961.

Wodwo. London: Faber, 1967.

Poetry in the Making: An Anthology of Poems and Programmes from "Listening and Writing." London: Faber, 1967.

Autograph letter to Gerald and Joan Hughes, 27 October 1969. Ted Hughes: Letters to Gerald Hughes 1952–1991 (MSS 854). Ted Hughes Collection. Robert W. Woodruff Library, Emory University. Box 1, folder 18.

With Fairest Flowers While Summer Lasts: Poems from Shakespeare. Edited and introduced by Hughes. Garden City, N.Y.: Doubleday, 1971.

Gaudete. London: Faber, 1977.

Cave Birds: An Alchemical Cave Drama. London and Boston: Faber, 1978. Includes drawings by Leonard Baskin.

"Ted Hughes's *Crow.*" *Listener* 84, no. 2157 (30 July 1970): 149. Extract from *Poetry Now,* a radio program broadcast on 6 July 1970 by BBC Radio 3.

Moortown Elegies. London: Rainbow Press, 1978.

"A Reply to Critics." 1979. Collected in A. E. Dyson, ed., *Three Contemporary Poets: Thom Gunn, Ted Hughes and R. S. Thomas: A Casebook.* Basingstoke and London: Macmillan, 1990, pp. 108–114.

Remains of Elmet: A Pennine Sequence. London: Faber, 1979. Includes photographs by Fay Godwin.

"On Images in *Crow.*" 1980. Collected in A. E. Dyson, ed., *Three Contemporary Poets: Thom Gunn, Ted Hughes and R. S. Thomas: A Casebook.* Basingstoke and London: Macmillan, 1990, pp. 114–115.

River. London and Boston: Faber in association with James and James, 1983. Includes photographs by Peter Keen.

Flowers and Insects: Some Birds and a Pair of Spiders. New York: Knopf, 1986. Includes drawings by Leonard Baskin.

Wolfwatching. London and Boston: Faber, 1989.

Shakespeare and the Goddess of Complete Being. New York: Farrar, Straus and Giroux, 1992.

Rain-Charm for the Duchy and Other Laureate Poems. London: Faber, 1992.

A Dancer to God: Tributes to T. S. Eliot. London: Faber, 1992. New York: Farrar, Straus and Giroux, 1993.

Winter Pollen: Occasional Prose. Edited by William Scammell. London: Faber, 1994.

Difficulties of a Bridegroom: Collected Short Stories. London: Faber, 1995.

New Selected Poems, 1957–1994. London: Faber, 1995.

Blood Wedding. Lorca. Translation. London: Faber, 1996.

Tales from Ovid. London: Faber; New York: Farrar, Straus and Giroux, 1997.

Birthday Letters. London: Faber; New York: Farrar, Straus and Giroux, 1998.

Phèdre. Racine. Translation. New York: Farrar, Straus and Giroux, 1999.

The Oresteia. Aeschylus. Translation. New York: Farrar, Straus and Giroux, 1999.

Alcestis. Euripides. Translation. New York: Farrar, Straus and Giroux, 1999.

INTERVIEWS WITH HUGHES

Faas, Ekbert. "Ted Hughes and *Crow.*" In Appendix 2 of Faas, *Ted Hughes: The Unaccommodated Universe.* Santa Barbara, Black Sparrow Press, 1980, pp. 197–208. Conducted in 1970.

———. "Ted Hughes and *Gaudete.*" In Appendix 2 of Faas, *Ted Hughes: The Unaccommodated Universe.* Santa Barbara: Black Sparrow Press, 1980, pp. 208–215. Conducted in 1977.

Negev, Eilat. "My Life with Sylvia Plath, by Ted Hughes." *Daily Telegraph* (31 October 1998): 4. Conducted in 1996.

SECONDARY WORKS

Alvarez, A. "Black Bird." *Observer* (11 October 1970): 33.

Bedient, Calvin. *Eight Contemporary Poets.* London: Oxford University Press, 1974.

Bentley, Paul. *The Poetry of Ted Hughes: Language, Illusion and Beyond.* London and New York: Longman, 1998.

Bradshaw, Graham. "Ted Hughes' 'Crow' as Trickster-Hero." In Paul V. A. Williams, ed., *The Fool and the Trickster: Studies in Honour of Enid Welsford.* Cambridge: D. S. Brewer, 1979, pp. 83–108.

Brandes, Rand. "Ted Hughes: *Crow.*" In Neil Roberts, ed., *A Companion to Twentieth-Century Poetry.* Oxford: Blackwell, 2001, pp. 513–523.

Corcoran, Neil. *English Poetry Since 1940.* London and New York: Longman, 1993.

Feinstein, Elaine. *Ted Hughes: The Life of a Poet.* London: Weidenfeld and Nicolson, 2001.

Gifford, Terry, and Neil Roberts. *Ted Hughes: A Critical Study.* London: Faber, 1981.

Hamilton, Ian. "A Mouthful of Blood." *Times Literary Supplement* 3593 (8 January 1971): 30.

Holbrook, David. *Lost Bearings in English Poetry.* London: Vision Press, 1977.

King, P. R. *Nine Contemporary Poets: A Critical Introduction.* London and New York: Methuen, 1979.

Lodge, David. "*Crow* and the Cartoons." *Critical Quarterly* 13, no. 1 (spring 1971): 37–42.

Ramsey, Jarold. "*Crow,* or the Trickster Transformed." In Keith Sagar, ed., *The Achievement of Ted Hughes.* Manchester, U.K.: Manchester University Press, 1983, pp. 171–185.

Roberts, Neil. *Narrative and Voice in Postwar Poetry.* London and New York: Longman, 1999.

Sagar, Keith. *The Art of Ted Hughes.* Cambridge, U.K.: Cambridge University Press, 1975.

———. *The Laughter of Foxes: A Study of Ted Hughes.* Liverpool, U.K.: Liverpool University Press, 2000.

Sagar, Keith, and Stephen Tabor. *Ted Hughes: A Bibliography, 1946–1995.* 2d ed. London and New York: Mansell, 1998.

Scigaj, Leonard M. *Ted Hughes.* Boston: Twayne Publishers, 1991.

Smith, A. C. H. *Orghast at Persepolis, an Account of the Experiment in Theatre Directed by Peter Brook and Written by Ted Hughes.* London: Eyre Methuen, 1972.

Thwaite, Anthony. *Poetry Today: A Critical Guide to British Poetry, 1960–1984.* London and New York: Longman, 1985.

Weatherhead, A. K. "Ted Hughes, *Crow,* and Pain." *Texas Quarterly* 19, no. 3 (autumn 1976): 95–108.

George Eliot's
Daniel Deronda

CLARE CONNORS

Was she beautiful or not beautiful? And what was the secret of form or expression which gave the dynamic quality to her glance? Was the good or the evil genius dominant in those beams?

(Daniel Deronda, p. 7)

THE NOTE OF fascinated ambivalence struck in the opening sentences of George Eliot's last novel, *Daniel Deronda,* was echoed by the book's first readers. Following the fortunes of both the enigmatic Gwendolen Harleth and the eponymous hero Deronda as they were revealed volume by volume in 1876, the public pondered the book's merits as engrossedly as Daniel mused over Gwendolen's beauty and virtue. The author of *Adam Bede* and *Middlemarch* already had an enthusiastic readership eagerly awaiting her next novel and anticipating the blend of wit, wisdom, psychologically insightful characterization, and compelling plotting that she had made her own. However, as *Daniel Deronda's* intricate double plot unwound, its critics displayed increasingly divided feelings. Although the story of the bewitching Gwendolen met with almost universal approval, its "Jewish plot" proved controversial. This is not to say that the book was condemned out of hand. Indeed, far from causing the novel to sink into oblivion, the

impassioned critical discussion over its merits made it the hot topic of literary London. As Eliot's publisher John Blackwood wrote to her: "People keep discussing the book like a great historical event about which there is a difference of opinion" (Haight, *Letters,* vol. 6, 5 November 1876).

It was not the first time that this celebrated author had prompted discussion and controversy. Indeed, while she never courted scandal, Eliot's personal history had contained several events that caused severe differences of opinion both among those close to her and in Victorian society at large.

Mary Anne Evans, as "George Eliot" was christened, had shocked her father in 1842 by voicing doubts about the historical veracity of Christianity and refusing to go to church. Upon her father's death Evans moved from her native Warwickshire to London, where she began to write reviews and articles for the *Westminster Review.* Here she flouted convention again by "eloping" to Germany with the married man George Lewes: respectable London society was shocked. It was perhaps in part because of the unacceptable connotations attaching to her own name that Evans adopted the pseudonym

57

George Eliot when, encouraged by Lewes, she published her first story, "The Sad Fortunes of Amos Barton," in 1857. The name was certainly to serve her well. While the true authorship of her work quickly became known after her first full-length novel, *Adam Bede,* appeared in 1859 to warm critical acclaim, it was as George Eliot that she continued, for the rest of her life, to produce both her novels and poetry. Despite the fact that "Mrs. Lewes" remained a figure of dubious morality to whom many men refused to introduce their wives (Tennyson obliterated from his memoirs references to his wife's visits to the Lewes house), her literary fame gave her increasing public acceptance. Queen Victoria and her daughters were admirers, and many among the reading public regarded the author as a sage. From financially straitened beginnings, Eliot made her fortune by her pen. By 1879 *Middlemarch* alone, generally acclaimed a masterpiece, had netted the author £9000—riches if we consider that the character Deronda views himself as wealthy on £700 a year. *Daniel Deronda* was to be Eliot's last novel, although she subsequently published a collection of essays written while her beloved Lewes was dying in 1878. One further surprise was in store for those who followed the author's life, however. In 1880 she married John Cross, a man twenty years her junior. The marriage was only to last for a few months. In December of the same year, Eliot died.

Despite the impressive list of publications Eliot amassed in her lifetime, writing did not come easily to her. This was as true of her last novel, *Daniel Deronda,* as of any of the others. She habitually lacked faith in her work and had to be encouraged, cosseted, and praised both by George Lewes and by her faithful publisher John Blackwood. The novel had a long gestation: the inspiration for its brilliant opening scene is often linked to an event that took place in 1872, when Eliot narrates in a letter how she watched Byron's grandniece gambling in a casino. "It made me cry," she writes, "to see her young fresh face among the hags and brutally stupid

CHRONOLOGY

1819	Mary Ann Evans born on 22 November at South Farm, Arbury, Warwickshire, third child of Robert and Christiana Evans.
1824–1832	Attends school.
1836	Mother dies. Leaves school to help her father.
1842	The "holy wars"—Mary Ann refuses to go to church.
1844	Begins to translate D. F. Strauss's *Das Leben Jesu* (The Life of Jesus Critically Examined).
1849	Father dies. Travels in Switzerland with her friends the Brays.
1850	Returns to England.
1851	Moves to London. Lodges with the publisher John Chapman. Has an affair with Chapman and in March is thrown out of the house by his wife. Moves back in September and becomes assistant editor of Chapman's journal the *Westminster Review.* Meets George Henry Lewes for the first time.
1843	Leaves Chapman's house to take up independent lodgings.
1854	Translation of Feuerbach's *Das Wesen des Christentums.* On 20 July "elopes" to Germany with Lewes.
1855	Returns to London and moves into a house in Richmond with Lewes.
1856	Publishes articles in the *Westminster Review* including "Silly Novels by Lady Novelists." Begins writing fiction. "Amos Barton," the first of *The Scenes of Clerical Life,* is accepted for publication in *Blackwood's Edinburgh Magazine* under the pseudonym George Eliot.
1857	"Mr. Glifil's Love Story" and "Janet's Repentance" published in *Blackwood's Edinburgh Magazine.* Breaks with brother Isaac over news of her relationship with Lewes.
1858	The three *Scenes of Clerical Life* are published together in a two-volume edition.

1859	*Adam Bede* is published in three volumes and sells well, receiving excellent reviews. "The Lifted Veil" is published in *Blackwood's Edinburgh Magazine.*
1860	*The Mill on the Floss* published. Between March and June travels in Europe. Writes "Brother Jacob."
1861	*Silas Marner* published.
1862	*Romola* serialized in *Cornhill* (Eliot's only novel not to be published by John Blackwood).
1863	With Lewes buys a house in Regent's Park called The Priory. Begins to hold "Sunday afternoons" to which distinguished writers and thinkers are invited.
1866	*Felix Holt: The Radical* published.
1868	*The Spanish Gypsy* published.
1871	Meets the Tennysons. The poem "Armgart" and the first book of *Middlemarch* published.
1872	Books 2 through 8 of *Middlemarch* published; her reputation grows. Travels to Germany.
1873	Returns to Germany to visit the synagogues.
1874	*The Legend of Jubal and Other Poems* published. Becomes ill with kidney trouble, from which she will suffer until her death.
1876	*Daniel Deronda* published. She and Lewes buy a country home in Surrey.
1878	Lewes dies of cancer on 30 November.
1879	*The Impressions of Theophrastus Such* published. Prepares Lewes's *Problems of Life and Mind* for publication.
1880	Marries John Cross on 6 May; dies on 22 December.

men around her" (*Letters,* vol. 5, 4 October 1872). If this image provided a serendipitous model for the tragic Gwendolen Harleth, whose whole life becomes a terrible gamble, other material for the novel was acquired through scholarly slog rather than inspired chance. Eliot's notebooks for 1872–1875 show an extraordinary breadth of reading not only in

legal questions of inheritance and articles on gambling and the calculation of probabilities but also in the Cabala, Jewish history and culture, and Hebrew poetry. As Lewes wrote proudly in a letter to Blackwood, "only learned Rabbis are so profoundly versed in Jewish history and literature as she is" (*Letters,* vol. 6, 1 December 1875).

Her hesitations and self-doubt notwithstanding, Eliot was able to record in the Christmas entry of her diary in 1875 that the first book of *Daniel Deronda* was "to be published on February 1" (*Letters,* vol. 6, p. 200). She finished writing it the next June. The novel was initially published in eight monthly parts, its final volume appearing in September 1876, before being gathered together in four-volume book form. This serial publication allowed for public opinion and debate on the novel to grow gradually, changing as new elements in the novel emerged. Thus Henry James, for example, reviewed the first installments enthusiastically in an unsigned review in the *Nation* as early as February 1876, likening the "threads of the narrative" to "long electric wires capable of transmitting messages from mysterious regions" (in Carroll, ed., *George Eliot: The Critical Heritage,* p. 363). His later responses, once the full text had appeared, were to be more equivocal. Eliot's diary entry in December 1876 captures well the conflicting feelings the book aroused.

> 1 December 1876. Since we came home at the beginning of September I have been made aware of much repugnance or else indifference towards the Jewish part of Deronda, and of some hostile as well as adverse reviewing. On the other hand there have been the strongest expressions of interest—some persons adhering to the opinion, started during the early numbers, that the book is my best—delighted letters have here and there been sent to me, and the sale both in America and in England has been an unmistakeable guarantee that the public has been touched.
>
> (*Letters,* vol. 6, p. 314)

The story of Gwendolen Harleth was certainly almost unanimously well received.

Eliot's account of the "splendid girl" (p. 325), whose initial narcissism undergoes a series of blows through her marriage to the reptilian and sadistic Grandcourt, was both recognizable and captivating to readers who had followed the similar education and eventual happy ending of Dorothea Brooke in *Middlemarch*. The rapturous response of Eliot's publisher Blackwood is typical. "I did not know what a hold the mermaid witch had got of me until I felt inclined to kick Herr Klesmer for his criticism on her singing" he writes (*Letters*, 25 May 1875). But what were readers to make of the book's "Jewish plot," which contains not only the English gentleman Deronda but the visionary and consumptive Mordecai with his dream of a Jewish homeland? Many critics (among the book's Christian readership at least) found it oppressive and preachy and were disinclined to participate in what appeared to be its idealization of Judaism. What, asked an anonymous reviewer in the *Saturday Review* in September 1876, could "be the design of this ostentatious separation from the universal instinct of Christendom, this subsidence into Jewish hopes and aims?" (Carroll, ed., *The Critical Heritage*, p. 377). Moreover, the story of Daniel's espousal of the cause of Jewish nationalism seemed (as indeed it did to the self-obsessed character herself) bafflingly unrelated to the Gwendolen plot—especially when, as the novel reached its close, it became clear that there was to be no happy ending for Gwendolen but instead a marriage "according to the Jewish rite" (p. 809) between Daniel and the young Jewish singer Mirah.

Not all its readers disliked *Daniel Deronda*'s "Jewish plot," however. George Eliot reported delightedly to Blackwood that she had received a letter from the chief rabbi expressing his "warmest appreciation of the fidelity with which some of the best traits of the Jewish character have been depicted" (*Letters*, vol. 6, 2 September 1876). A portion of the book was translated into Hebrew and published in a German-Jewish newspaper. And despite the equivocation of some critics, *Daniel Deronda* continued to sell.

Eliot reported in her diary at the start of December 1876 that the four-volume form of the book had already outperformed the sales of the same format of the acknowledged masterpiece *Middlemarch*.

Clearly then, Eliot's last novel was as perplexing and bewitching as its troubled heroine Gwendolen Harleth. While most critics today rate it as one of the novelist's finest achievements, vexed discussion about its two plots and how they are to be related continues. Is the book an aesthetically and thematically convincing whole? Or should we excise the romantic, messianic Deronda story and focus our attention solely on the sharply observed novel about the education of a middle-class Englishwoman? A close reading of *Daniel Deronda*'s political, ethical, and symbolic meanings might help us decide.

GWENDOLEN AND DANIEL

"I meant everything in the book to be related to everything else" protested George Eliot, railing against those critics "who cut the book into scraps and talk of nothing in it but Gwendolen" (*Letters*, vol. 6, 2 October 1876). The book, after all, does not bear her name. What then is the relationship of Gwendolen to the eponymous hero of *Daniel Deronda*? Their "plots" are very different. The beautiful and accomplished Gwendolen, facing impecunity when her mother's investments fail, contracts an unhappy marriage and ends the novel a widow. The handsome and charismatic Deronda, on the other hand, having been brought up by the benign Sir Hugo Mallinger and possessing a private income, discovers his true Jewish parentage—and along with it a vocation—and ends the novel marrying his adored Mirah.

In terms of their character traits the two are deliberately contrasted on a number of points. Gwendolen, while beautiful and captivating, is self-obsessed and shallow. She is driven by an "inborn energy of egoistic desire" (p. 41) and a deluded sense of the extent of her own power. Eliot describes at the start of the novel how, when she hears of her family's bankruptcy,

Gwendolen makes immediate plans to return to them and then sits gazing at herself in the mirror.

> Her beautiful lips curled into a more and more decided smile, till at last she took off her hat, leaned forward and kissed the cold glass which had looked so warm. How could she believe in sorrow? If it attacked her, she felt the force to crush it, to defy it, or run away from it, as she had done already.
>
> (p. 18)

An all-sufficient self-love is seen here to go hand in hand with a belief in the limitless extent of one's own powers. Gwendolen's gradual education into an understanding of viewpoints and claims other than her own will happen alongside a decrease in her sense of absolute mastery. While later readers might see a prescient foreshadowing of Freud's "his Majesty the ego" in the description of this self-described "princess in exile" (p. 41), Eliot's deliberate invocation is of the Narcissus myth. Like the beautiful youth of Greek legend, Gwendolen is in love with her own image. Although she, unlike Narcissus, does not literally drown, drowning is a key motif in the book. Mirah is prevented from trying to end her life in the Thames, and the odious Grandcourt meets his death while out yachting. Metaphorically, however, Gwendolen too risks submersion in her sorrows. The only moments of fear she knows in her early life are feelings of engulfment and panic at the "immeasurable existence aloof from her, in the midst of which she was helplessly incapable of asserting herself" (p. 64). This dread is actualized when, having ignored the claims of another, Grandcourt's mistress Lydia Glasher, she marries Grandcourt only to find all her own desires and her very will obliterated. When Daniel visits Gwendolen to attempt to counsel her in her distress he perceives her as "a vessel in peril of wreck—the poor ship with its many-lived anguish beaten by the inescapable storm" (p. 610).

If Gwendolen's narcissism results in her coming adrift in the storms of life, Deronda, then, is defined by an altruism that saves others from foundering. He pulls Mirah from the brink literally and Gwendolen metaphorically. His acts of charity begin indeed in his youth. While at Cambridge he helps his friend Hans Meyrick win a scholarship that will support his family, ruining his own chances of academic success as a consequence. Meyrick tells him that he has helped "save an ugly mongrel from drowning" (p. 183). Whereas Gwendolen fears the vastness and indifference of the world as a force that will overthrow her own desires and submerge her ego, Deronda positively craves immersion in the wider world. His favorite pastime is rowing (suggesting a more intuitive relationship to the waves than Gwendolen's or Grandcourt's), and Eliot describes a particular moment of mystical communion as Daniel watches the sunset from his boat.

> He was forgetting everything else in a half-speculative, half-involuntary identification of himself with the objects he was looking at, thinking how far it might be possible habitually to shift his centre till his own personality would be no less outside him than the landscape.
>
> (p. 189)

While Gwendolen fears "otherness," wanting only to conquer it, Daniel desires to encounter it, to displace himself into the landscape. Significantly too it is while he is out rowing that he meets Mirah and, later on, is recognized by Mordecai as the "new self" (p. 494) the latter has been awaiting. Deronda's symbolic desire to identify himself with objects in the landscape leads to enriching encounters with other people, whereas Gwendolen's narcissism can only produce a sterile and lonely solipsism.

It seems then that the predominant mode in which Gwendolen and Deronda are related is through thematic and symbolic oppositions. A further list of opposed terms might be drawn up. Gwendolen is a Gentile, Deronda turns out to be Jewish. Gwendolen takes pleasure in being a spectacle, having all eyes on her, while Deronda is a silent observer of scenes. In-marrying Grandcourt, Gwendolen links her fortunes to an exhausted and etiolated aristocracy, whereas Deronda's marriage to Mirah is the prelude to the founding of a new Jewish nation. Gwendolen's parental and marital inheritance is financial, whereas the chest Deronda is bequeathed by his grandfather is a rich repository of cultural and religious documents.

These oppositions participate in a more general difference between the materialistic, superficial world of high society, emblematized by the figures at the gaming table in Leubronn who looked "as if they had all eaten of some root that for the time compelled the brains of each to the same narrow monotony of action" (p. 9) and the spiritually nourishing and meaningful environments to which Deronda is drawn. Deronda's world comprises both the fervid idealism of the consumptive Mordecai and the gentle domesticity of the self- sufficient Meyricks, who combine quiet industry with culture, imagination, and sympathy for others. Ironically it is from just the sort of humble and straitened circumstances in which the contented Meyricks live that Gwendolen imagines she is saving her family when she contracts her misguided but socially elevating marriage.

It is not Gwendolen, however, who epitomizes the worst tendencies of the selfish and materialistic world opposed to Deronda's ideals but rather her husband, Henleigh Grandcourt. With his lizardlike features, his sybaritic sidekick Lush, and his perpetual ennui, he is so different from the warm- blooded and often impassioned Deronda, who possesses "a calm intensity of life," that Eliot suggests the two "might have been a subject for those old painters who liked contrasts of temperament" (p. 162). Like the protagonist of a morality play, Gwendolen is poised between two possibilities: death or life, entrapment in the self or enlargement through others. In an image the novel employs several times, "the scale could dip on the wrong side" (p. 253). Everything is in the balance for Gwendolen. We first encounter her through Deronda's

eyes, as he watches her at the gambling table debating whether or not it is evil or good that predominates in her character. It is the answer to this question that the book will unfold, charting slowly the progress of the beautiful young woman through a series of trials and temptations to her final melancholy promise: "I shall live. I shall be better" (p. 807). The reader is invited to watch over Gwendolen as Deronda does, monitoring her progress and willing her toward goodness. Daniel's role is therefore not simply to be a foil to Gwendolen at the level of narrative structure but to intervene in the life of this "ill-educated, worldly girl" (p. 413) as her monitor, guide, and "outer conscience" (p. 763).

ETHICAL RELATIONS

The relatedness of everything to everything else in *Daniel Deronda* could in fact be understood to happen in three ways. At the most literal level, in terms of plot, Daniel is an agent in both "worlds." While he might turn out to be most at home in the company of Mirah, Mordecai, and the Meyricks, he is also a part of genteel society. Thus his becoming a moral counselor to Gwendolen and helping her find the resources to transcend the stultifying confines of her world is at its most banal a plot device that links their two otherwise divergent fates. Other characters too cross from one of the book's plots to the other. Mirah, for example, sings in the salons of grand ladies, Gwendolen's included. Conversely Anna Gascoigne, Gwendolen's shy country cousin, coincidentally makes the acquaintance of the Meyrick family. The brilliant composer and pianist Klesmer, who describes himself ironically as "the Wandering Jew" (p. 242), is at home in both worlds. Indeed his marriage to the heiress Caroline Arrowpoint, based upon a mutual passion for music, is a rare instance of material success supplementing rather than supplanting spiritual striving.

More frequently, materialism and spiritualism are opposed in this novel. Secondly, then, the relatedness between the two plots Eliot sought to effect happens at a symbolic or structural level, the contrast between Daniel's and Gwendolen's worlds functioning to encapsulate the series of oppositional values upon which the book's moral system is based. Matter and spirit, ennui and enthusiasm, the past and the future are thematically ranged against one another in a densely woven mesh of imagery and incident.

Thirdly and most significantly, the book's ethos itself is precisely one of relatedness. The interimplication of different stories in *Daniel Deronda* is in the last analysis neither simply a technical matter nor merely an aesthetic or moral system of comparisons and contrasts. More fundamentally than either of these considerations, the book's "relatedness" embodies the very humanist philosophy its author espoused. Gwendolen's suffering in her marriage to Grandcourt arises not primarily because her husband turns out to be a cruel and brutish tyrant but because she has stood in another's way to gain him and the life of financial ease he provides. Lydia Glasher's terrifying letter, sent with the diamonds that should have been her own wedding gift, concludes with the words "the willing wrong you have done me will be your own curse" (p. 359), and this proves to be true. *Daniel Deronda,* with its worldview stretching from West to East and its characters spanning all classes from the wealthy aristocrat Sir Hugo Mallinger to Joel Dagge the blacksmith's son, suggests that our fates and destinies cannot be separated as easily as the arbitrary divisions of geography and rank would have us believe. The wrong we do to others can therefore easily come back to haunt us. This being the case, the challenge for individuals is to learn both to acknowledge and moderate the impact of their actions upon those of others. One must respect the difference of other people rather than simply assimilate them to one's own schemes and desires.

The motif of gambling with which the novel opens encapsulates the interrelatedness of society and the mutual dependence of people's happiness within it. Daniel tells Gwendolen that he dislikes gambling precisely because it dramatizes so acutely the way in which happiness can come at the expense of others' suffering.

> There are enough inevitable turns of fortune which force us to see that our gain is another's loss:—that is one of the ugly aspects of life. One would like to reduce it as much as one could, not get amusement out of exaggerating it.
>
> (p. 337)

Indirectly it is through her gambling that Gwendolen is driven to marry Grandcourt. As she tells her mother, had she known of the family's financial losses sooner she would have brought home the "nearly two hundred pounds" (p. 232) she had won instead of staying to lose them again. The family's penury itself arises from a sort of gambling. As Mrs. Davilow explains to her daughter of their stockbroker, "there were great speculations: he meant to gain" (p. 233). With Gwendolen's own initial "gain" of two hundred pounds she could have provided a degree of comfort for her family and staved off the immediate choice between marriage or becoming a governess. In a telling dramatic irony, we learn that the indifferent Grandcourt "brought away about two hundred" (p. 161) from the gaming table. The point is not labored but the symmetry is clear. Gwendolen's loss is Grandcourt's gain in all senses. Her marriage itself comes to seem a colossal speculation: it is a "hard, unfair exclusion of others" (p. 335).

As Gwendolen's conscience develops and she becomes more ethically mature, the very values of losing and winning are inverted. Waiting to learn the details of Grandcourt's will and fearing that her position will harm the fortunes of Mrs. Glasher's son, whose image haunts her, she reflects upon this "new gambling in which the losing was not simply a *minus,* but a terrible *plus*" (p. 598). Daniel, conversely, reaps the rewards for submission and self-sacrifice. The early sacrifices he makes to Hans pay dividends late in the novel when Hans, himself in love with Mirah, generously tells Deronda of her love for him, thus smoothing the obstacles in the path of true love. Daniel's disinterested rescue of Mirah brings him a wife. His respectful submission to Mordecai's views brings him a vocation.

The novel as a whole, then, maps out a general economy in which the merciless pursuit of profit is punished and disinterested sacrifice is rewarded. Those who lose win and vice versa. Given this systematic interrelation of the novel's diverse parts and characters it is difficult to see how it is possible to "cut the book into scraps and talk of nothing in it but Gwendolen."

GENERIC DOUBLENESS: ROMANCE AND REALISM

Two objections present themselves, however, to this neatly organic reading of *Daniel Deronda*. The first derives from its very neatness. The providential economy of gains and losses we have charted might be all very well in a fairy story. It surely sits ill, though, in the work of a novelist who in *Adam Bede* likened her literary method to the minutely lifelike paintings of the Dutch realists and who in this novel is careful to embed her characters in the sociohistorical context of the mid-1860s, complete with outbreaks of rinderpest among cattle and of rebellion in Jamaica (p. 331). The suspiciously neat patterning of the text seems to tug against its aspirations to verisimilitude, giving us a generic rather than a character-based version of the "two novels" argument. Instead of *Daniel Deronda* versus *Gwendolen Harleth*, we have a chasm between the novel as romance and the novel as realist narrative.

The second objection we might raise to the "organic" reading of *Daniel Deronda* is that there is an imbalance not in terms of the attention given by the author to Gwendolen and Daniel but in the interest these two characters arouse in the reader. While the situation of general interpersonal involvement the novel describes is as true for the Deronda plot as for

Gwendolen's story, it is only Gwendolen who has to learn from this a moral lesson. As is evident from Deronda's very first action in the novel, his restitution to Gwendolen of her pawned necklace, he has a highly developed moral sense. Indeed he says to his mother that what he has most been "trying to do for fifteen years is to have some understanding of those who differ" from himself (p. 630). Daniel, then, has no need of the harsh schooling Gwendolen receives in the claims others may make upon oneself. An apt scholar, he has learned these lessons before our story begins. If we want to view this book as being truly interrelated in all its parts in an aesthetically and ethically satisfying way, it is surely not enough, however, for Daniel's participation in the novel to be confined to the role of a slightly pious spiritual adviser to Gwendolen. That would indeed be to unbalance the book's internal dynamic and fuel claims that its center of interest lies solely in its flawed heroine. Once again we seem in danger of cutting the book into scraps and talking only of Gwendolen.

In what, then, lies the interest of Deronda's story? Whereas with Gwendolen the appeal for the reader is in the minute shades of her emotional and psychological maturation, Deronda's story seems to appeal to more atavistic readerly desires for adventure, revelation, serendipity, and happy endings. His is not so much a bildungsroman, charting the process of a character's education and development, as a romance plot in which the hero discovers the secret of his birth, rescues a damsel in distress, reunites her with her long-lost sibling, and embarks on a perilous but glorious mission. Here our first objection to the "organic" reading of *Daniel Deronda*—that it undermines its own claims to versimilitude—joins up with our second objection. Through trying to right the imbalance between Gwendolen's story and Daniel's by exploring the specificity of the latter, we end up positing another dichotomy, which again takes the form of a distinction between realism and romance.

The novel's apparent separation into romantic and realistic elements, moreover, seems to perpetuate terrible unfairness toward its characters. Indeed it might be said to connive in a punitive and repressive sexual politics at odds both with what one might expect from the unconventional and freethinking George Eliot and, more tellingly, with the book's overt ethical position. "Realism" in Gwendolen's case seems to entail not simply the achievement of a more equitable view of her own relations to others but a series of violent chastisements by fate (or the novel's author) in which not only are all her selfish desires and hopes thwarted but she is left distraught and "forsaken" by her spiritual guide Deronda. Gwendolen seems to be punished at every turn. She is humiliated by Deronda's return of her necklace. Her family's bankruptcy means she has to come back from Europe alone. Herr Klesmer publicly criticizes her singing and later administers a stern dose of "realism" to her desire to make her living on the stage. And then, not relishing the prospect of becoming a governess but, quite laudably one would suppose, wanting to support her mother in comfort, she makes a marriage in which she is tyrannized over by a cold-blooded and quietly sadistic man, witnesses his drowning, and is humiliatingly treated in her husband's will, which leaves most of his wealth to his mistress. Other people in the "Gwendolen" plot are similarly thwarted. Her mother is described as habitually looking sorrowful, Gwendolen's family becomes impoverished, Rex Gascoigne is not only turned down by Gwendolen but has his shoulder painfully dislocated.

Daniel Deronda, on the other hand, seems to live not in the harsh world of realist fiction but in a magical, romance-filled environment in which all needs are met and every wish fulfilled. He is brought up in an atmosphere of both material comfort and affection, educated at Cambridge and given an inherited income of £700 a year. He craves a friend, and Mordecai appears. He falls in love with a Jewish woman who will only marry a fellow Jew, and his ancestry magically turns out to be Jewish. Similarly Mab is just "wishing something wonderful would happen" (p. 199) when there is a knock at the door bringing the waif Mirah, a damsel in distress to be cared for as in the best fairy tales. Of this last coincidence Eliot writes: "Mab looked rather awe-stricken, as if this answer to her wish were something preternatural" (p. 200). These happy coincidences do indeed seem to belong to a world that does not obey the "natural" laws of realism but the "preternatural" imperatives of romance.

READING ROMANCE AND REALISM

A variety of readings of the novel's generic duplicity are open to a twenty-first-century reader. From a post-Freudian point of view Gwendolen seems to have to negotiate the Oedipus complex or, in another model that describes a similar transition, to regulate the conflicting demands of the pleasure principle and the reality principle. Having had an exclusive relationship with her adored mother and been accorded "assiduous apologetic attention" from all the minions in her "domestic empire" (p. 41), Gwendolen must encounter "that unmanageable world which was independent of her wishes" (p. 251). Immediate gratifications must be postponed, sacrificed to the imperious demands of the world, represented in Freud's Oedipal narrative by the father and in *Deronda* by Grandcourt.

In Deronda's case, on the other hand, there seems to be a fantastical return to a pre-Oedipal state in which all one's needs are met by the nurturing mother. Literally, of course, this is far from the case. Indeed his earliest memory could be read as a textbook case of the transition from pleasure to reality and of the harsh fracturing of the child's initial sense of oneness with the mother. "Daniel . . . had a dim sense of having been kissed very much, and surrounded by thin, cloudy scented drapery, till his fingers caught in something hard, which hurt him, and he began to cry" (p. 165). Moreover, when he does once again find his lost mother, she does not fulfill his yearnings and rejects his affectionate overtures, saying "I am not a loving woman. That is the truth. It is a talent to love—I lacked it" (p. 666). However, there may be said to be a symbolic return to the mother in the form of Mordecai and Judaism. Metaphorically speaking Daniel is restored in several ways to a pre-Oedipal state in which every wish produces immediate gratification. When he announces his Jewish birth to Mordecai and Mirah, Eliot writes that he is "enjoying one of those rare moments when our yearnings and our acts can be completely one, and the real we behold is our ideal good" (p. 748). Eliot describes Mordecai's "consumptive glance" at Deronda as having "something of the slowly dying mother's look when her one loved son visits her bedside" and suggests that his desire for "spiritual perpetuation" in Daniel resembles the "maternal transference of self" (p. 495). And when Mordecai anticipates the news of Deronda's Jewishness, he exclaims "You are even as my brother that sucked the breasts of my mother" (p. 570). Thus while Daniel's literal return to his mother is as thwarting as any Oedipal wounding would be, at the level of symbol Eliot seems to be implying that he has achieved a state of perfect coincidence between need and satisfaction via a blissful restitution of lost mother figures. It is almost as though the novel's two genres play out two different modes of psychic life. The romance plot recalls the infantile state we yearningly recall while the realist plot shows the world as we must accept it if, like Gwendolen, we are to say "I shall live."

The distinction between a "real" cruel mother and an imaginary beneficent one might also be interestingly related to another twentieth-century account of the divide between romance and realism in the novel: this time a feminist reading. The separating out of an idealized, incorporeal "romantic" figure of the mother from a flawed, fleshly "real" mother participates in the good woman/bad double dichotomies

famously identified by the critics Sandra Gilbert and Susan Gubar in their work of criticism *The Madwoman in the Attic* (1979). Similarly the "realist" requirement that Gwendolen be chastened in her desires and aspirations could be said to be complicit with the patriarchal suppression of women.

Conversely Deronda's own triumphs, on the one hand figured as a return to an idealized mother, also entail taking on his paternal inheritance. His romantic quest does lead, like many fairy stories and Gothic tales, to finding a lost mother. But it also puts him in touch with the wishes of his dead grandfather, so powerful that they haunt his dying mother's conscience, obliging her against her will to inform Daniel of his parentage and ethnic origins. To that extent the romance plot installs Deronda resolutely in a tradition of patriarchs. Even the sounds of the novel endorse this gendered reading. Deronda is ensconced in a world of alliterative M's—the Mallingers, Mirah, Mordecai, and the Meyricks, including the "little mother" Mrs. Meyrick. His own strikingly alliterative name seems to mark itself out as overtly masculine in contrast with these maternal ménages.

The presentation of meek Mirah makes it hard not to view the book as endorsing and even idealizing female submission. "It is not her nature to run into planning and devising: only to submit" (p. 224) reports Mrs. Meyrick approvingly of Mirah, only a few pages before the narrator says of the troubled Gwendolen, "she did not mean to submit" (p. 229). Deronda's mother, Princess Leonora Halm-Eberstein, protests against the idea that "a woman's heart must be of such a size and no larger, else it must be pressed small, like Chinese feet" (p. 631) and seeks artistic success on her own terms as a world-famous musician. Mirah, on the other hand, though musical, has no ambition to go on the stage. Appropriately her voice is only strong enough for small rooms. Nor do her feet need to be bound: these extremities are fetishized by the narrative, or least by Mab, for their petiteness. The latter has "some pride in the effect produced by a pair of tiny felt slippers which she had rushed out to buy because there were no shoes in the house small enough for Mirah" (p. 209). Mirah's littleness stands in contrast also to Gwendolen's more statuesque fleshliness.

We might be tempted to assert, then, that the less space women take up in this novel the better. On the other hand it would be wrong to suggest that Eliot is simply endorsing the constraints contemporary society placed upon women. The book is too fascinated by its less submissive female characters for that to be the case: from the "witch" Gwendolen Harleth to young Adelaide Rebekah in her Sabbath frocks, we are captivated by more obtrusive, less quiescent instances of femininity. The Princess Halm-Eberstein, in her final parting from her son, asks, "Had I not a rightful claim to be something more than a mere daughter and mother? . . . Whatever else was wrong, acknowledge that I had a right to be an artist, though my father's will was against it." To this Deronda answers, "I do acknowledge that" (p. 664–665). Another way to think about *Daniel Deronda*'s generic bifurcation, then, would be to link it to its conflicting "acknowledgements" about gender. On the one hand women should submit to duty and tradition; on the other hand the constraints tradition and socially determined notions of duty place upon women are unjust. We might attribute this ambivalence to Eliot herself. As an unconventional and successful professional writer, she seemed to resist the traditional constraints of Victorian society. As an ethical thinker, however, she argued that tradition and a sense of duty were necessary. Women in *Daniel Deronda* are not allowed the consolations of romance, but by employing romantic elements the book itself betrays a strong desire for the unconstrained happiness of romantic fulfillment.

While both the psychoanalytic and the feminist readings we have outlined are important and illuminate the novel in different ways, both do tend to see the novel's generic doubleness as a problem to be resolved or accounted for. To view the realism/romance divide as one that simply befalls the narrative of *Daniel Deronda* or arises purely out of the symptoms and circumstances of the author's life would be naive, however. Frequently the text contains overt allusions to both the realistic and the romantic that suggest that these genres are being thematized and reflected upon rather than simply unwittingly deployed. It therefore cannot simply be a case of "reading" romantic and realistic elements within the text. Rather *Daniel Deronda* itself supplies clues for the proper reading of romance and realism.

Gwendolen, for example, is defined as having an inauthentic relationship to romance. Eliot writes of her that "Her horizon was that of the genteel romance where the heroine's soul poured out in her journal is full of vague power, originality and general rebellion, while her life moves strictly in the sphere of fashion" (p. 53). The "genteel romance" here connotes a debased version of the romance tradition, one that plays at moving beyond the quotidian but is unable to imagine any mode of existence not materially determined and socially acceptable. Gwendolen does not, Eliot suggests, have the resources or disposition to transcend her circumstances. Indeed, in imagining her future relationship to Grandcourt she represents it as a parody of the romance tradition: "I shall send him round the world to bring me back the wedding-ring of a happy woman. . . . he will come back Lord Grandcourt—but without the ring—and fall at my feet. I shall laugh at him" (p. 95). The romantic here is nothing but a pretext for fantasies of her own omnipotence. There is, of course, an occasion when Gwendolen's wishes do come true. Of the moment when Grandcourt drowns she tells Deronda, "I saw my wish outside me" (p. 696). Her terrible education is to learn that wishes can have an effect upon other people in the world. Romance is not to do simply with the self, and neither is it risible.

Her own reading, interestingly, is not so much of romances as of novels that purport to be realistic. Writing of her first shocking encounter with Mrs. Glasher, Eliot says that "Gwendolen's uncontrolled reading, though consisting chiefly in what are called pictures of life, had somehow not prepared her for this encounter with reality" (p. 155). Realism, then, can be as debased a form as romance, sensationalizing gritty reality in a way that provides its reader with a frisson of illicit excitement without promoting sympathy or enlarging the understanding. "What horrors of damp huts, where human beings languish, may not become picturesque through aerial distance!" (p. 155) the narrator exclaims with heavy irony. Bad realist novels, just like bad romances, simply reinforce solipsism rather than allowing for encounters with the world.

Daniel's relationship to the romantic and realistic is harder initially to gauge. The narrator seems on the one hand to criticize the idea that he is romantic ("To say that Deronda was romantic would be to misrepresent him," p. 205) and yet on the other hand to endorse the very same idea ("if you like, he was romantic," p. 515). This apparent ambivalence in fact comes about because the novel itself is in the process of redefining what romance is. Gwendolen is "romantic" in a negative sense. Her "romances" tend to self-glorification and do not extend her relationship to the world. Daniel's romanticism, on the other hand, lies in his spiritually enlarging openness to other people and his environment, not in dreams of personal heroism or success.

> under his calm and somewhat self-repressed exterior there was a fervour which made him easily find poetry and romance among the events of everyday life. And perhaps poetry and romance are as plentiful as ever in the world except for those phlegmatic natures who I suspect would in any age have regarded them as a dull form of erroneous thinking.
>
> (p. 205)

Again we abut upon a question of relationship—here the relationship between realism and romance. This is not presented simply as a happy synthesis. Eliot does not seem to be saying that we should take our reality with a judicious admixture of romance. That is the sort of stance taken by Lady Pentreath, "an easy, deep-voiced old lady" who says of the marriage between Klesmer and Caroline Arrowpoint: "I'm glad to find a little romance left among us. I think our young people now are getting too worldly wise" (p. 407). While this benign, liberal tolerance is, it is suggested, better than narrow-minded condemnation, it does not in itself manifest the capacity for imaginative transformation of self and world that a truly and "really" romantic stance would have. It is Daniel's relationship to the real events of everyday life that allows them to be romantic.

REALIZING ROMANCE: JUDAISM AND THE FUTURE

What does this mean in practice? How does the novel suggest that one finds the "poetry and romance among the events of everyday life" and what are the implications of doing so? An almost incidental moment, which occurs as Daniel Deronda is helping Sir Hugo show a party of visitors around the abbey, captures some of what this utopian aspiration might mean in all its strangeness. Daniel points out the arches of the former chapel, carved with leaves, and wonders aloud "whether one oftener learns to love real objects through their representations, or the representations through the real objects." He continues: "When I was a little fellow these capitals taught me to observe, and delight in, the structure of leaves" (p. 422). Ordinarily we might imagine that we appreciate realistic representations because we recognize real life in them. In the case of literature, realist fiction would thus confirm what we already know; it would be "what oft was thought but ne'er so well expressed," to quote Pope. Such a view of reading and writing would, however, in the terms of the ethical schema Eliot outlines in *Daniel Deronda*, amount to little more than solipsism. In confirming the already known, such ostensible realism would simply enforce the status quo in all its indolent banality. Deronda suggests, on the other hand, a model of representation in which we move from an image outward to an object in the world, appreciating it in its uniqueness and beauty for the first time. Realism thus points out the romance in the real.

If here we might assume that the sculptor at least had to see the "real" leaves before he replicated them in stone, the strangest interlinkings of realism, romance, and representation in *Daniel Deronda* come when representations seem absolutely to precede what they ought logically only to come after. This is what happens in the part of the story dealing with Mordecai and more generally in the recurrent motif of "second sight." These uncanny or occult themes are initially introduced relatively prosaically. Anna Gascoigne's fears about her brother Rex's involvement with Gwendolen are said to have "gifted her with second sight." Her distressed whisper "she will not care for you one bit" has, the narrator remarks, "the unwelcomeness which all unfavourable fortune-telling has" (p. 67). Gwendolen habitually lacks such prescience. Moving off after her first condescending encounter with Mirah, she is "entirely without presentiment that this Jewish protégée would ever make a more important difference in her life than the possible improvement of her singing" (p. 561). The ostensibly magical phenomenon of second sight or fortune-telling, far from being an embarrassing "romantic" excrescence in the story, is seen to be precisely what is missing in the too materialistic "real" world Gwendolen inhabits.

Eliot's longest excursus on second sight comes, however, when she is first explaining to the reader Mordecai's convictions about the arrival of someone who will bear his ideas about Judaism into the future.

> "Second-sight" is a flag over disputed ground. But it is matter of knowledge that there are persons whose yearnings, conceptions—nay, travelled conclusions—continually take the form of images which have a foreshadowing power; . . . the event they hunger for or dread rises into vision with a seed-like growth feeding itself fast on unnumbered impressions.

(p. 471)

This might be read, banally, as an embarrassed apology for the introduction of an unrealistic character into a realistic narrative, if it weren't for the fact that we have already seen a fully "realistic" representation of "second sight" in Anna's care for Rex. That must prepare us to take Mordecai's visions more seriously. Eliot is saying that "second sight" is real—or rather, that it is what makes way for or creates the real. It is Mordecai's conjuring of a "friend to come" (p. 475) that brings about Daniel's arrival. We need not understand this absolutely literally. What Eliot implies, however, is that it is Mordecai's sensitive, imaginative projections that enable him to recognize in Daniel the potential he is seeking and act as midwife to it.

The actualization of something not hitherto recognized as "real" is also seen when Daniel meets his grandfather's friend Joseph Kalonymos, who asks him whether he will call himself a Jew and profess the faith of his fathers. Eliot writes that Deronda's "respect for the questioner would not let him decline to answer, and by the necessity to answer he found out the truth for himself" (p. 725). The truth comes into being as it is solicited, in what philosophers of language call a "performative utterance." Performatives are phrases like "I promise," which enact a reality as they are uttered rather than describing it after the fact. As in the case of the "sincere acting" of Deronda's mother, in whom "experience immediately passed into drama, and she acted her own emotions" (p. 629), so here Daniel enacts the truth as he utters it. The novel's fascination with a variety of performances (Gwendolen's acting of Hermione, Mirah's and the princess's singing, Klesmer's playing) culminates in this moment in the idea of an authentic and original acting that brings into the world what it asserts.

It is vital to insist that this acting is an action of Daniel's own free will. He does not experience Kalonymos's question or Mordecai's vision as violently coercive, for two reasons. First, because of his desire to avoid the "moral stupidity" that can only conceive of these things as happening in a long distant past, he is open to the "momentous and sacred" in the present (p. 509). This stance, like Mordecai's, is one of remaining hospitable to what is "to come" rather than seeing it as something threatening to the self. Second, however, Daniel does not necessarily take Mordecai's visions for their future as absolutely determining. This is not evasive slyness on Deronda's part. It arises rather because a part of the duty to the future is not to close down its possibilities. This is the stance he makes explicit in his response to Kalonymos: "I shall call myself a Jew. . . . But I will not say that I shall profess to believe exactly as my fathers have believed. Our fathers themselves changed the horizon of their belief and learned of other races" (p. 725). Cultural and racial inheritance here is not imagined as an exhausted and impotent repetition (as it is with the British aristocracy represented by Sir Hugo, who resembles his ancestors in all but his disappointingly short nose) but as a fidelity precisely to a capacity for change.

Judaism itself is figured as a religion with an open relationship to the future, in ironic counterpoint to the prejudiced Gentile image of it "as a sort of eccentric fossilised form" (p. 363). Its futurity indeed is interwoven with its relationship to tradition. In an impassioned urging of the importance of a Jewish state, Mordecai asserts: "The divine principle of our race is action, choice, resolved memory. Let us . . . help to will our own better future and the better future of the world" (p. 538). On the one hand, Mordecai seems here to suggest that Jews possess certain determining characteristics. On the other hand, these characteristics are those that will allow for change, development, and the arrival of the new and the unexpected. The past as a transformative possibility thus allows a passage to the future.

The founding of a state of Israel, to which the novel looks forward at its end, is the political embodiment of the relationship Eliot seems to be proposing between the romantic and the real, the future and the past. Daniel and Mirah head for the East, charged with a vision they will seek to realize. At the historical moment at which Eliot was writing, a Jewish nation was, of course, only a possibility; indeed it was not to be actualized for more than another half century. *Daniel Deronda* is thus both politically and artistically avant-garde. Politically its sympathies were far in advance of many among Eliot's contemporary Christian readership. Artistically her conclusion, by pointing toward an uncertain and unknowable future, avoids the easy gratifications of the "happily ever after" endings that undermine the claims to authenticity of many realist novels. Just as Judaism is presented in *Daniel Deronda* as both retaining its identity and having the capacity to transform itself, so the novel itself both retains many of the conventions of realism and simultaneously puts them to work in new ways. Ironically Eliot's gesturing toward what is not yet "real" in the form of what is "to come" seems more realist than the artificial closures of traditionally realist works.

Here then we have a further, and stranger, answer to the abiding question of the relatedness of the generic elements of this novel. The uncanny, romantic elements of *Daniel Deronda*, which insist on an imaginative relationship to the future that is not simply an extrapolation from the present, seem both antirealist and suprarealist. In this case the "romantic" and "realist" elements of the novel are neither bound in an organic unity nor simply antagonistic to one another. Rather, each part of the novel both displaces and encapsulates the other. There is no true realism without romantic second sight and a pointing toward the future beyond realism's own grasp. At the same time, as Gwendolen's failed romances testify, there is no authentic romance without a realistic relationship to the world and its claims. This is a model of relatedness rather different from the liberal ideal of "separateness and communication" (p. 724) that Deronda himself overtly endorses. Appropriately, perhaps, it finds its expression in Mordecai's philosophizing. In expounding to Mirah the Shemah, the Hebrew devotional exercise of the divine unity, he argues that "in complete unity a part possesses the whole as the whole possesses every part" (p. 734). This idea of a mutual possession between part and whole is, "realistically" speaking, impossible: a part cannot literally possess the whole of which it is a part. As a figure, however, Mordecai's image captures the mutually deferring relationship between the realistic and the romantic the novel itself seems to enact.

It is no wonder, then, that *Daniel Deronda*'s first readers "kept discussing the book like a great historical event about which there [was] a difference of opinion." No ultimate decision about it seems possible, yet rather than frustrating reading or discussion, this recalcitrance to a definitive solution seems to prompt such engagement. Indeed re-reading is demanded: this is a novel whose secrets are revealed gradually. A first reading gives the simple pleasures of suspense. We turn the pages to discover the outcome of Deronda's relationship with Gwendolen and Mirah, to find out about his ancestry, and to see whether Gwendolen will find a way out of her entrapping marriage. Subsequent readings provide other pleasures, as the novel's ironies and symbolic patternings emerge. The novel also discusses re-reading. Mordecai argues that while Gentiles undersand Judaic law as something dark, unbending, and unchanging, in fact the true tradition of Judaism is "to use records as a seed . . . enlarging and illuminating with fresh-fed interpretation" (p. 532). Thus *Daniel Deronda* itself, in being hospitable to the possibilities of new readings, seems to look forward to its own afterlife and the readings it will continue to engender across the centuries.

IMPORTANCE AND INFLUENCE

Appropriately enough, given the lively discussion *Daniel Deronda* engendered among its readers, one of the most important early responses to the whole novel, by Henry James, took the form not of a mono-vocal review but of a dramatic conversation. Published in *Atlantic Monthly,* the young writer's "Daniel Deronda: A Conversation" stages a debate between Pulcheria, who finds the novel "protracted, pretentious, pedantic"; Theodora, who has "enjoyed the novel deeply, from beginning to end"; and Constantius, a reviewer and novelist who takes the middle ground (in Carroll, ed., *The Critical Heritage,* p. 419, 421). James is thus able to satirize some of the extreme reactions the book received. He gives Pulcheria, for example, an anti-Semitic obsession with the idea that Deronda might have a "horrid big Jewish nose" (p. 417) but similarly suggests that Theodora, who is "consumed with a hopeless passion" (p. 420) for Deronda, is naively romantic. At the same time, Constantius's ostensible syntheses seem implausible. As Pulcheria points out, his response "I understand that" to both positive and negative criticisms of the novel becomes irritating (p. 419). It seems that James employed the conversational format as much to give expression to his own ambivalence about *Daniel Deronda* as to find a singular response to the novel's dualisms.

If his critical reactions were divided, it is nevertheless clear that Eliot's final novel had a profound effect on James's own writing. His depiction in *The Portrait of a Lady* of Isabel Archer, who rejects a variety of suitors before contracting an oppressive marriage to the cruel Gilbert Osmond, owes much to Eliot's story of Gwendolen Harleth's unhappy marital career. Stylistically *Daniel Deronda* was an inspiration rather than a direct influence. Its testings of realism pointed the way to new possibilities in the novel form, which James was to be the first to exploit. In this way *Daniel Deronda* can be situated on the cusp between realism and modernism, testing the limits of the former in ways that led to the emergence of the latter. At a longer distance, the strange blend of realism and romance—the way in which visions and second sight coexist with the world of drawing rooms and musical parties—anticipates the later twentieth-century genre of magic realism.

After her death, Eliot's star waned. In the heyday of modernism she represented for many the epitome of stuffy Victorianism and, despite *Daniel Deronda*'s critical distance from the tradition of novelistic realism, it was lumped in with her other more conventionally realistic masterpieces and went unread. When the Cambridge critic F. R. Leavis revived her fortunes in his monumental *The Great Tradition* in 1948, *Daniel Deronda* was discussed in remarkably similar terms to those used by its Gentile critics upon its reception. Situating Eliot in relation to her literary successors, Leavis writes:

> Henry James wouldn't have written *The Portrait of a Lady* if he hadn't read *Gwendolen Harleth* (as I shall call the good part of *Daniel Deronda*), and, of the pair of closely comparable works, George Eliot's has not only the distinction of having come first, it is decidedly the greater. . . . As for the bad part, there *is* nothing to do but cut it away.
>
> (pp. 85, 122)

One might well disagree with almost everything Leavis says, but he did at least bring Eliot's last novel back to the attention of literary critics. In 1959 Barbara Hardy's influential *The Novels of George Eliot: A Study of Form* shifted the focus away from the Leavisite emphasis upon a text's moral qualities toward an analysis of the formal properties of Eliot's work. Over the following decades understanding of the book was enriched with (in Mordecai's words) "fresh-fed interpretation" from a variety of other critical perspectives. Feminism, emerging in Eliot's day as an important political movement, began in the twentieth century to inform literary criticism. Writers as diverse as Gillian Beer, Catherine Gallagher, and Sandra Gilbert and Susan Gubar considered the novel's treatment of gender and femininity, differing in their views on Eliot's stance and the "feminism" or otherwise of the book but united in a sense of its

literary as well as political importance. The work of Freud, who began publishing (albeit pre-psychoanalytic work) only a year after *Daniel Deronda* arrived in the world, provided in the later twentieth century an important resource for critics of Eliot's novel, including Jacqueline Rose and Dianne Sadoff. For its treatment of Gwendolen's hysteria, its repetitions of the Oedipus complex, and its presentation in Deronda of a "proto-psychoanalyst," psychoanalytic critics continue to be fascinated by *Daniel Deronda*. The novel's inversion of causality, where truth is effected by utterance and performance has an originating function, resonates also with deconstructive critics. Deronda meets Derrida and de Man in the work of Cynthia Chase and telepathically communicates with Nicholas Royle, sharing his critical fascination with occult phenomena, second sight, and visions.

More recently *Daniel Deronda* has proven to be a televisual as well as a telepathic novel. In 2003 a two-part television adaptation of the book was aired. The tension in the text between realism and romance was well suited to the medium. Mirah's suicide attempt was eerily lit, giving it a Gothic quality, and through variations of pace and idiosyncratic cutting Lydia Glasher's appearance to Gwendolen conveyed some of the sickening shock we sense in the novel. What generations of critics have perceived as the book's flaws were also remarked in the adaptation: Mark Lawson pointed out in a review in the *Guardian*, for example, that "Hugh Dancy as Daniel has little to do except project integrity and handsomeness." Nevertheless, the presentation of the book to a new audience at the start of the twenty-first century shows that, just as it promotes openness to the future, so it remains open to future readings.

One of the risks of celebrating or leaving open the future is that that future might turn out to be less benign that one would hope. The events of the last decades of the twentieth century and the first years of the twenty-first have shown that nationalism can often become-violent separatism. Certainly the founding of a state of Israel has not been the irenic event the seer Mordecai dreamed of. If we are to take Eliot seriously on the subject of second sight, then we must hold her to account for a lack of clairvoyance here. Indeed, one of the notable omissions of the novel seems to be in its imagination of "the East," which is treated almost as empty terrain, simply a tabula rasa on which a new Jewish nation can be inscribed. If Eliot could not completely predict the future, however, her last novel remains remarkable as a statement of the need to approach the future thoughtfully, imaginatively, and nonviolently. *Daniel Deronda*'s own future, both as literary masterpiece and ethico-political reflection, seems assured.

Selected Bibliography

EDITIONS

Daniel Deronda. London and Edinburgh: William Blackwood and Sons, 1876.

Daniel Deronda. Edited and introduced by Terence Cave. London: Penguin, 1995. The Penguin edition, to which this essay refers throughout, is based on the corrected and slightly amended three-volume Cabinet edition, which appeared in 1878.

OTHER WORKS BY ELIOT

Adam Bede. Edinburgh and London: William Blackwood and Sons, 1858.

Middlemarch: A Study of Provincial Life. Edinburgh and London: William Blackwood and Sons, 1871.

The George Eliot Letters. 9 vols. Edited by Gordon S. Haight. New Haven, Conn.: Yale University Press, 1954–1978. Volumes 5–7 contain material relevant to *Daniel Deronda.*

George Eliot's Daniel Deronda *Notebooks.* Edited by Jane Irwin. Cambridge: Cambridge University Press, 1996.

The Journals of George Eliot. Edited by Margaret Harris and Judith Johnston. Cambridge: Cambridge University Press, 1998.

SECONDARY WORKS

Ashton, Rosemary. *George Eliot: A Life.* London: Hamish Hamilton, 1996. Ashton's biography is perfectly respectable but adds little to Haight's.

Beer, Gillian. *George Eliot.* Bloomington: Indiana University Press, 1986; Brighton, U.K.: Harvester Press, 1986. Part of the Key Women Writers series.

Carroll, David. "The Unity of *Daniel Deronda.*" *Essays in Criticism* 9 (1959): 369–380.

———. *George Eliot and the Conflict of Interpretations: A Reading of the Novels.* Cambridge and New York: Cambridge University Press, 1992.

Carroll, David, ed. *George Eliot: The Critical Heritage.* London: Routledge and Kegan Paul, 1971. Contains a selection of contemporary reviews of *Daniel Deronda.*

Chase, Cynthia. "The Decomposition of the Elephants: Double-Reading *Daniel Deronda.*" *PMLA* 93 (1978): 215–227.

Gallagher, Catherine. "George Eliot and *Daniel Deronda*: The Prostitute and the Jewish Question." In *Sex, Politics, and Science in the Nineteenth-Century Novel.* Edited by Ruth Bernard Yeazell. Baltimore and London: Johns Hopkins University Press, 1986.

Gilbert, Sandra, and Susan Gubar. *The Madwoman in the Attic: The Woman Writer and the Nineteenth-Century Literary Imagination.* New Haven, Conn.: Yale University Press, 1979.

Haight, Gordon S. *George Eliot: A Biography.* Oxford: Clarendon Press, 1968. This is the standard biography.

Hardy, Barbara. *The Novels of George Eliot: A Study in Form.* London: Athlone Press, 1959.

Lawson, Mark. "Rethinking the Classics." *Guardian* (18 November 2002). A review of Andrew Davies's television adaptation of the novel.

Leavis, F. R. *The Great Tradition.* London: Chatto and Windus, 1947.

Royle, Nicholas. *Telepathy and Literature.* Oxford and Cambridge, Mass.: Blackwell, 1991.

Newton, K. M., ed. *George Eliot.* London: Longman, 1991. This work, in the Longman Critical Readers series, reprints a selection of critical material on Eliot.

Rose, Jacqueline. "George Eliot and the Spectacle of the Woman." In her *Sexuality in the Field of Vision.* London: Verso, 1986.

Sadoff, Dianne F. *Monsters of Affection: Dickens, Eliot & Brontë on Fatherhood.* Baltimore and London: Johns Hopkins University Press, 1982.

Semmel, Bernard. *George Eliot and the Politics of National Inheritance.* Oxford and New York: Oxford University Press, 1994.

Shalvi, Alice, ed. *Daniel Deronda: A Centenary Symposium.* Jerusalem: Jerusalem Academic Press, 1976. A selection of essays including Shmuel Werses's "The Jewish Reception of *Daniel Deronda.*"

Stone, Wilfred. "The Play of Chance and Ego in *Daniel Deronda.*" *Nineteenth Century Literature* 53 (June 1998): 25–55.

Lord Byron's
Don Juan

PETER FILIKINS

NO LITERARY MASTERPIECE seems more fittingly "unfinished" than Lord Byron's *Don Juan.* Written between 1816 and 1823 in several different cities, published by two different publishers, abandoned entirely after its first five cantos only to be taken up again in secret several months later, and containing as many "digressions" and "speculations" as its author could muster, *Don Juan* remains a brilliant work despite its checkered incubation. Though it will never be known just how long Byron's "epic" would have run had he not died of a fever at age thirty-seven in 1824, we are told early on that it "is meant to be / Divided in twelve books" (I. 200). Yet when we actually get to the twelfth canto the narrator admits that "If my Pegasus should not be foundered / I think to canter gently through a hundred" (XII. 55). Whether twelve, one hundred, or the sixteen and one half cantos that have come down to us, it is no matter. *Don Juan*'s true end, as many critics have pointed out, could only occur with the death of its author, for it is not so much a poem about its hero as it is a manifestation of the remarkable consciousness that first set it in motion.

In some ways this could be said to be true of all poems, if not any work of art. But in reading *Don Juan*, we quickly discover the subject to be Byron himself. The nature of this self, however, is not simply autobiographical. Rather, the complexity and uniqueness of *Don Juan* rest in the poem's ability to consume a seemingly infinite array of ideas and subjects, but in a manner consistent with the idea of a single consciousness behind it. Though Byron told Thomas Medwin that his "spirits, both good and bad, must serve for the machinery" (*Conversations of Lord Byron*, p. 165), and though the author draws heavily upon his personal experience, the poem is not merely a record of that experience. Instead, it is the arrangement of those events and the narrator's commentary about them, and how the conflation of the two engages, entertains, and surprises us with the richness found in good conversation, which creates the uncanny sense of a mind caught in the formless yet rhythmic activity of thought itself.

Byron's purpose in forwarding such a "nondescript and ever varying rhyme" (VII. 2) involves a different conception of poetry than the self-containment of the traditional lyric poem. At times it seems that the poet asks that we create the poem he is writing along with him, claiming that "I rattle on exactly as I talk / With any body in a ride or walk" (XV. 19), and that

> I never decide what I shall say, and this I call
>   Much too poetical. Men should know why
> They write, and for what end; but, note or text,
> I never know the word which will come next.
>
> (IX. 41)

Because we do not know what "will come next," Byron demands from us an engagement that supersedes the usual passive appreciation of linear meaning. Instead, our reading becomes a kind of action in and of itself, one that is required if any meaning is to emerge from the poem, for Byron makes clear his reluctance to serve it up for us:

> I won't describe—that is, if I can help
>   Description; and I won't reflect—that is,
> If I can stave off thought, which, as a whelp
>   Clings to its teat, sticks to me through the abyss
> Of this odd labyrinth; or as the kelp
>   Holds by the rock; or as a lover's kiss
> Drains its first draught of lips:—but, as I said,
> I *won't* philosophize, and *will* be read.
>
> (X. 28)

The result is a high wire act in which both the reader and poet balance on the thread of a story in order to perform shared acrobatic leaps of consciousness before landing again on solid ground, renewed and invigorated, if only because "'Tis better on the whole to have felt and seen / That which humanity may bear, or bear not" (XIV. 49).

Though Byron told his publisher that the purpose of his poem was "to be a little quietly facetious upon every thing" (*Byron's Letters and Journals* VI. 67), his underlying project also involves a serious commentary on the foibles and failures of his time. Emphasizing that his "Muse . . . mostly sings of human things and acts" (XIV. 13), much of *Don Juan* consists of Byron's disgust with the hypocrisy and corruption of his native England, as well as the

CHRONOLOGY

1788	George Gordon Byron is born on 22 January in London.
1789	Catherine Gordon Byron and her son move to Aberdeen, Scotland.
1791	His father, Captain John Byron, dies.
1794	Upon the death of a cousin, George becomes heir to the title of Lord Byron.
1801	Enters Harrow School.
1805	Enters Trinity College, Cambridge.
1806	*Fugitive Pieces,* his first book of poems, is privately printed.
1807	*Poems on Various Occasions,* privately printed. *Hours of Idleness* is published. Leaves Cambridge for London.
1808	*Hours of Idleness* is ridiculed by Henry Brougham in *The Edinburgh Review.*
1809	Joins the Whig Party and takes his seat in the House of Lords. *English Bards and Scotch Reviewers* published. Travels with John Cam Hobhouse through Portugal, Spain, Malta, Greece, Albania, and Turkey. Begins work on *Childe Harold's Pilgrimage.*
1810	Visits Troy and swims the Hellespont. Hobhouse returns to England and Byron stays in Greece. Begins *Hints from Horace* and writes *The Curse of Minerva,* protesting the removal of the Elgin Marbles from the Acropolis to London.
1811	Returns to England. Death of his mother. Death of two friends from Trinity, C. S. Matthews and the choirboy John Edleston.
1812	Delivers his first speech in the House of Lords, attacking the Frame Bill, and a second speech supporting Catholic emancipation. John Murray publishes the first two cantos of *Childe Harold's Pilgrimage,* which is an instant success. Has affairs with Lady Caroline Lamb and Lady Oxford. Proposes to Annabella Milbanke, but is rejected. Tries to sell Newstead Abbey, the family seat.
1813	Publishes *The Giaour.* Delivers third and last speech to House of Lords in support of parliamentary reform. Begins affair

with his half-sister, Augusta Leigh. Publishes *The Bride of Abydos.* Begins a journal.

1814   *The Corsair* sells 10,000 copies on the first day of publication. Proposes again to Annabella Milbanke, and she accepts. Publishes *Lara.*

1815   Marries Annabella in January. Joins subcommittee of management of Drury Lane Theater. A daughter, Augusta Ada, is born in December.

1816   Annabella and Ada leave London. Annabella asks for a legal separation. Publication of *The Siege of Corinth* and *Parisina.* Leaves England in April. Travels through Belgium to Switzerland, where he spends the summer at Villa Diodati on Lake Geneva. Befriends Percy Bysshe Shelley, his wife, Mary, and Claire Clairmont, who live nearby. Writes *Childe Harold III* and *The Prisoner of Chillon.* Tours the Alps and Italy with Hobhouse and settles in Venice. Begins affair with Marianna Segati.

1817   Allegra, his daughter by Claire Clairmont, is born in England. Finishes *Manfred.* Tours Rome and returns to Venice. Begins *Childe Harold IV.* Finishes *Beppo.* Affair with Margarita Cogni.

1818   Publishes *Childe Harold IV* and *Beppo.* Begins *Don Juan.* Shelley and Claire Clairmont visit him in Venice. Writes his "Memoirs."

1819   Sells Newstead Abbey. Falls in love with Teresa Guiccioli, who remains his principle lover until his death, despite her being married. Cantos I and II of *Don Juan* are published anonymously. Follows the Guicciolis to Ravenna and Bologna. Begins Cantos III and IV of *Don Juan.* Gives his "Memoirs" to Thomas Moore, who returns with them to England.

1820   Translates first canto of Pulci's *Morgante Maggiore.* Writes *Prophecy of Dante* and *Marino Faliero.* Completes Canto V of *Don Juan.* The Pope grants Countess

Guiccioli a separation. Becomes involved with the Carbonari.

1821   Writes *Sardanapalus, The Two Foscari, Cain, Heaven and Earth,* and *The Vision of Judgement.* Tells Murray that he has decided to abandon *Don Juan* because of Teresa's objections. Leaves Ravenna for political reasons. Spends time with Shelley at Pisa. Cantos III–V of *Don Juan* are published.

1822   Finishes *Werner,* begins *The Deformed Transformed,* secretly starts work on *Don Juan* again. His daughter Allegra dies of a fever. Shelley drowns. Completes six new cantos of *Don Juan.* Moves to Genoa. John Hunt becomes his new publisher.

1823   Writes *The Island.* Completes Cantos XIII–XVI, and begins Canto XVII, of *Don Juan.* Serves as representative of the London Greek Committee and goes to Greece to fight for Greek independence. Cantos VI–VIII, IX–XI, and XII–XIV of *Don Juan* are published.

1824   Travels to Missolonghi. Cantos XV–XVI of *Don Juan* are published. On 9 April Byron is caught in a heavy rain while out riding and becomes feverish. He dies on 19 April, and his body is transported to England for burial at Hucknall church near Newstead. Moore burns his "Memoirs." The fragment of Canto XVII found in his papers is later published in 1907.

repressive climate that accompanied the Restoration of the Bourbons in France. Over the poem's long meandering course the poet deflates the seemingly untouchable Admiral Wellington, who defeated Napolean at Waterloo, and pokes fun at mad King George III, the obesity of George IV, and one "whom glory still adores / As greatest of all sovereigns and w———s" (VI. 92), the licentious tyrant, Catherine of Russia. Byron's most blistering attack, however, is reserved for Castlereagh, Foreign Secretary of England, and in the poet's view the "Cold-blooded, smooth-faced, placid miscreant"

(Dedication. 12) responsible for England's repressive rule of Ireland in his pursuit of "States to be curbed, and thoughts to be confined / . . . Cobbling at manacles for all mankind" (Dedication. 14).

Yet if the politics of his day were the only target of Byron's razor sharp wit, *Don Juan* would remain a poem of little more than historical interest. Byron's political aims, however, are deeply interlaced with a revolutionary aesthetic bent on attacking the foundations of the Romantic movement that the poet himself helped to forge. In fact, the two are linked from the very start, for before Byron goes on to vilify Castlereagh in the Dedication, it is "the Lakers" such as William Wordsworth, Samuel Coleridge, and Robert Southey who fall victim to his mocking address:

> You, Gentlemen! By dint of long seclusion
> From better company have kept your own
> At Keswick, and through still continued fusion
> Of one another's minds at last have grown
> To deem as a most logical conclusion
> That Poesy has wreaths for you alone;
> There is a narrowness in such a notion
> Which makes me wish you'd change your lakes
> for ocean.
>
> (Dedication. 5)

Byron had many problems with the Romantics, the first being what he perceived as their unwillingness to write of the everyday world about them, choosing instead to invoke a spiritual, dreamy world based upon a solitary and meditative appreciation of Nature. Their disdain of the wit and engagement of poets like Alexander Pope and John Milton also irked Byron, as well as the tendency of the Romantics to turn toward conservative Tory politics later in life. Finally, Byron's jest that the Romantics "change your lakes for ocean" relates to his dictum that "Experience is the chief philosopher" (XV. 17). His own life of travel, debauchery, physical courage, political engagement, and general restlessness had long

convinced him that the flux and chaos of life's "ocean" was a more valid subject for poetry than the studied placidity and potentially narcissistic "lake" inhabited by the Romantic's more somber Muse.

Be it Byron's playful urge for "mere speculation" (XIV. 7) in the range of subjects he touches upon, or his drive to "show things really as they are" (XII. 40), and thus ridicule his native "low, newspaper, humdrum, law-suit / Country" (XII. 65), or his wish to wander "with pedestrian Muses" (Dedication. 8) rather than in the ethereal realms of the Romantics—all of this contributes to the fabric of the poem. *Don Juan*, however, is a poem whose pattern and shape remains continually elusive and ungraspable. Many a critic has laid this to the extraordinary nature of Byron's own personality, but other scholars notice more method to Byron's madness. In *"Don Juan" in Context*, Jerome McGann was one of the first to argue that the violation of the aesthetic synthesis we expect from the poem as an "epic" is not something merely idiosyncratic to the poet's personality. According to McGann, Byron "opposes a discourse ruled by symbols, which drive into silence and ecstatic revelation, with a discourse of 'conversational facility' (XV. 20)" (p. 111). Hence, as Byron states,

> This narrative is not meant for narration,
> But a mere airy and fantastic basis,
> To build up common things with common places
>
> (XIV. 7)

through the symbiotic relationship of language, thought, and experience that is both the poem's complexity and its charm.

THE REAL VS. THE IDEAL

Byron's irrepressible urge for invention also applies to the hero of his epic, for we are given a very different Don Juan than the original created by Tirso da Molina in 1630 and later made famous by Molière and Mozart. Even the pronunciation of his name is different, as Byron makes sure to rhyme "true one" and "new one" with "Juan" in the poem's first stanza, thus forcing an anglicized pronunciation, throughout. Though Byron announces that "I want a hero" in the very first line, the effect of taking "our ancient friend Don Juan" and turning him into a kind of caricature announces that the poet is the one in control of his legend and myth, rather than the poem being in service to either.

Byron toys with the relationship he has to his material as early as the seventh stanza of Canto I, as he disingenuously informs us:

> My way is to begin with the beginning;
> The regularity of my design
>   Forbids all wandering as the worst of sinning,
> And therefore I shall open with a line
>   (Although it cost me half an hour of
> spinning)
> Narrating somewhat of Don Juan's father,
> And also of his mother, if you'd rather.
>
> (I. 7)

There is much slyness at work here, for Byron well knows that a great deal of "wandering" will take place in his poem. Though he claims to be writing an "epic," his commitment to "begin with the beginning" also cuts against the epic tradition to begin in medias res, thus making the "regularity" of his "design" suspect. Add to this the odd feel of the poet announcing "I shall open with a line . . ." as if the opening of the poem had not already occurred, or that we are not already reading the very poem that he says he is about to begin, and a strange kind of mirroring sets in between the poem as an object we read and ourselves as present subjects reading it. This is further underscored when Byron implies that he can begin "Narrating somewhat of Don Juan's father, / And also of his mother, if you'd rather," as if the reader really did have any choice in the matter. Of course we do not, for the poem has already been written by the time we read it, a fact acknowledged by Byron's disingenuous admission that even a single line has "cost me

half an hour of spinning." What did or did not actually happen in the composition of the poem, however, is of little consequence. Byron seeks to compose a different kind of event, one that happens right here on the page as we find ourselves reading about the make up of the character Don Juan only to discover that the real subject of the stanza is ourselves reading about how Byron controls our reading.

Whether or not it is Byron who is narrating the poem is initially confusing. In a prose preface that the poet later abandoned, Byron planned for the narrator to be a Spanish gentleman who would retell the poem's adventure while drinking wine in a village between Monasterio and Seville. Even without the preface, the narrator claims to have known Juan and his parents personally, to have had "a pail of housemaid's water" (I. 24) dumped on him by Juan as a boy, and to have seen him carried off by the devil as the legend goes. But a third of the way into Canto I, the Spanish gentleman disappears entirely and is replaced by Byron himself. Unlike a lyric poem in which the poet is merely the "voice" that speaks the poem, Byron's presence is an active one as he comments on the writing of the poem or inevitably drifts into his countless asides. As Anne Barton points out, he is in many ways the replacement for the sidekick traditionally given to Don Juan, such as Sganarelle in Molière or Leporello in Mozart, though clearly his is a more mercurial and controlling presence.

Such changing of tack midstream lends a haphazard feel to *Don Juan,* and a sense of the poem being composed on the fly with barely any revision. Yet T. G. Steffan's analysis of the poem's manuscript has revealed that Byron revised extensively, and that such discrepancies are meant to stand by themselves. The poem's purpose, then, is not to provide us with a fully fleshed-out narrative of the life of Don Juan, but rather to make use of Don Juan as a character in order to fully flesh out the erratic genius of life. "[I]t may be profligate," Byron wrote to his first publisher, John Murray, "but is it not *life,* is it not *the thing*?—Could any man have written it—who has not lived in the world?" (*Byron's Letters and Journals*, VI. 232). The answer of course would seem to be no, for there is a great deal of "living" within it, indeed.

Nonetheless, Byron does have a story to tell, no matter how wildly discursive it may be. Unlike his predecessors, Byron's Don Juan is not a sinister womanizer, but rather is himself seduced by only five women over the course of the poem. This alone turns the legend on its head, but Byron goes further by mocking both traditional notions of romance and modes of depicting it. Like the poet's questioning of the Romantic ethos, this poses a struggle between the ideal and the real. His mother, Donna Inez, raises Juan such that "his breeding be strictly moral," but the hypocrisy of her ideal for him is revealed when she sets him up with Donna Julia, the wife of one of her own former lovers. The comic seduction of Juan turns on Julia's own self-delusion as Byron delights in skewering the subtle shift in her allegiance from her husband to Juan:

> Julia had honor, virtue, truth, and love,
>   For Don Alfonso; and she inly swore,
> By all the vows below to powers above,
>   She never would disgrace the ring she
>   wore,
> Nor leave a wish which wisdom might reprove;
>   And while she pondered this, besides
>   much more,
> One hand on Juan's carelessly was thrown,
> Quite by mistake—she thought it was her own;
>
> Unconsciously she lean'd upon the other,
>   Which play'd within the tangles of her
>   hair;
> And to contend with thoughts she could not
>   smother,
>   She seem'd by the distraction of her air.
>   (I. 109–110)

Byron's ability here to stretch the sentence over two stanzas and thus place more emphasis on

"Unconsciously" and its corresponding irony is a microcosm of how the poet manipulates Don Juan's tale to suit his own needs. The ottava rima form that Byron imitated after reading John Hookham Frere's *Whistlecraft*, which itself came from Luigi Pulci's *Morgante Maggiore*, written in 1485, may at first seem a limited mechanism, given its use of only three rhymes in an eight-line stanza. Yet in Byron's hands it seems to spur him on to outlandish rhymes such as "Homer" and "misnomer," or "Bottle" and "Aristotle," which then engage us with the poem's self-mockery, while also allowing to spill over from one stanza into another. This invites the narrator's own wry commentary on the preceding action, such as here when the next lines to follow tell us with a knowing smile,

> 'Twas surely very wrong in Juan's mother
>   To leave together this imprudent pair,
> She who for many years had watched her son
>   so—
> I'm very certain *mine* would not have done so.

Such comic undermining also occurs in the poem's macrocosm as Juan moves from one hapless adventure in love to the next. When his affair with Julia is revealed, Juan is sent on a voyage to Cadiz by his mother in order to escape the scandal and become a man of the world. But once again such ideal intentions are thrown asunder, literally, when Juan's vessel encounters the very real experience of a storm that shipwrecks him. In describing the event, Byron mixes the language of high tragedy with low comedy, the most famous, or infamous passage occurring in stanza 61 of Canto II as the poet describes the occupants of Juan's lifeboat as they watch their ship go down: "They grieved for those who perish'd with the cutter, / And also for the biscuit casks and butter" (II. 61). The sacrilege of this last line caused contemporary critics to nearly burst at the seams with anger and spurred John Keats to throw the poem aside in disgust. But such antics remain at the heart of Byron's open rebellion against "cant" announced in the poem's first stanza. Similarly, just as we find Don Juan mooning over his lost Julia, only to succumb to seasickness at the same time, or when the men in the long boat take "by force from Juan Julia's letter" (II. 79) in order to rip it up and draw lots for who will be eaten first, Byron sticks a pin in each airy balloon of sentimentality. Instead, the poet opposes the necessity of the real against the delusion of an ideal that is casually or automatically assumed to be valid and true, but in reality is easy prey to hypocrisy. As the ship goes down, Byron's sardonic wit turns suddenly serious as he tells us "a wreck she roll'd, / At mercy of the waves, whose mercies are / Like human beings during civil war" (II. 42). Civil wars, after all, are often fought over entrenched ideals, and no doubt England and Europe had seen plenty of both before and during Byron's time. The poet's shipwreck of Juan's woozy notions of romantic love also implies the disastrous results fostered by the blind obedience to ideals.

"FIERCE LOVES AND FAITHLESS WARS"

Distorting a line from book 1 of Spenser's *The Faerie Queene,* Byron proclaims his true subject to be "'Fierce loves and faithless wars'" (VII. 8) in this his "versified Aurora Borealis / which flashes o'er a waste and icy clime" (VII. 2). Indeed, the twin subject to love and its failings throughout *Don Juan* is the misery and destruction of war. Though Juan is granted brief respite when he washes up on the Cyclades and falls in love with the beautiful Haidée, it is a relationship almost doomed by Time itself. To them there seems "no life beneath the sky/ Save theirs, and that their life could never die" (II. 188), but we are not at all surprised when Haidée's pirate father shows up and sells Juan into slavery, only to have his own daughter die in sorrow. In addition, Juan's adventure in the Turkish court amid Princess Gulbeyaz's cold-hearted attempt to turn him into her sexual slave also further undermines any notion of love as an ideal realm of nourishment and trust. Whatever respite is gained with Haidée is only the result of the

violence of the shipwreck that lands Juan on her shores, just as the sweetness of his night with the odalisque Dudù is only a prelude to Gulbeyaz's ire and his expulsion to the siege of Ismail.

Some critics have read into such scenes a distrust of women and relationships on Byron's part, citing the poet's legendary debauchery and numerous affairs as further support for his inherent misogyny. Clearly *Don Juan* is directed at a male audience, nor is it a surprise that the women of the time almost universally condemned its licentious escapades. To write off the poem as the flawed product of a misogynist, however, risks an oversimplification and a misreading of the poem's characters as deep psychological portraits rather than the caricatures that they are. The narrator in fact expresses his sympathy for the plight of women when he notes:

Poor Thing of Usages! Coerc'd, compell'd,
    Victim when wrong, and martyr oft when
  right,
Condemned to child-bed, as men for their sins
Have shaving too entailed upon their chins,—

A daily plague which in the aggregate
    May average on the whole with
  parturition.
But as to women, who can penetrate
    The real sufferings of their she condition?
Man's very sympathy with their estate
    Has much of selfishness and more
  suspicion.
Their love, their virtue, beauty, education,
But form good housekeepers to breed a nation.
                                    (XIV. 23–24)

Granted, the comparison of "shaving" to "parturition" makes the narrator's sympathies highly suspect, but he himself acknowledges the same in attesting to his own "selfishness" and "suspicion." Nor is Byron's Don Juan the scandalous rake of legend out to manipulate and dominate women. As Anne Barton argues, the poem values the importance and validity of pleasure for both men and women, as seen in the open passion between Haidée and Juan, as well as offering the portrait of a woman able to inspire and renew "The love of higher things and better days" (XVI. 108), as does Aurora Raby at the poem's end.

At the heart of Byron's attack on romantic love is an awareness that man's best intentions often end up turning into his worst nightmares. "Man's a strange animal," Byron tells us,

> . . . and makes strange use
> > Of his own nature, and the various arts,
> And likes particularly to produce
> > Some new experiment to show his parts.
>
> > > > (I. 128)

The lewd pun at the end here should be enough to question the "strange use" made of our "various arts," but if there is any doubt about it, Byron makes clear his skepticism when a few stanzas later he reminds his reader that

> This is the patent-age of new inventions
> > For killing bodies, and for saving souls,
> All propagated with the best intentions,

only to become "ways to benefit mankind, as true, / Perhaps, as shooting them at Waterloo" (I. 132). Against such unnatural "invention," Byron seeks to return both men and women to their own "nature," though he concedes "Few mortals know what end they would be at, / But whether glory, power, or love, or treasure, / The path is through perplexing ways . . ." (I. 133).

The pursuit of "Glory," however, often disguises the violence of war as an end in itself controlled by those who use it to maintain their own power. Such corruption was not inherent to Byron's age alone, and he knew it, admitting that in

> > > . . . every age and every year,
> And almost every day, in sad reality,
> > > Some sucking hero is compelled to rear,
> Who, when come to sum up the totality

> Of deeds to human happiness most dear,
> Turns out to be a butcher in great business,
> Afflicting young folks with a sort of dizziness.
>
> > > > (VII. 83)

Noting that "An uniform to boys, is like a fan / To women" (VII. 84), Byron continues to connect the hollowness of "Glory" with the vanity and disillusionment attached to romantic "Love," though it is for the leaders of war that Byron saves his greatest disdain. At Ismail, the Russian general Suwarrow is depicted as both a "Harlequin in uniform" (VII. 55) and "the greatest Chief / That ever peopled hell with heroes slain, / Or plunged a province or a realm in grief" (VII. 68). Elsewhere Byron condemns "Buonaparte's cancer" that could "dash on / Through fifty victories to shame or fame, / Without a stomach . . ." (IX. 14). Not even Napoleon's nemesis is spared Byron's acid, for in his all-out effort to see "Glory's dream / Unriddled" (VIII. 1), the poet fearlessly lays out Admiral Wellington, England's greatest hero:

> You are "the best of cut- throats:"—do not start;
> > The phrase is Shakespeare's, and not
> misapplied:—
> War's a brain-spattering, windpipe- slitting art,
> > Unless her cause by Right be sanctified.
> If you have acted *once* a generous part,
> > The World, not the World's masters, will
> decide,
> And I shall be delighted to learn who,
> Save you and yours, have gained by Waterloo?
>
> > > > (IX. 4)

Originally written to appear as an introduction to Cantos VI–VIII, the attack was so ferocious that John Murray not only refused to publish it, but also informed Byron that he could not go on with the poem as a whole. Choosing the more radical John Hunt as publisher, Byron still found a way to weave the stanzas on Wellington into the beginning of Canto IX after abandoning them initially. They in fact serve as a fine coda to the massacre at Ismail, as well as Byron's own vehement protest against the times. As he explained to his friend Thomas Moore, he felt it "necessary, in the present clash of philosophy and tyranny, to throw away the scabbard," (*Byron's Letters and Journals,* IX:191), and there is little doubt that he does so in these middle cantos.

Byron, however, was not simply a pacifist. He himself sought a soldier's death in going to Greece to help in the fight for Greek independence. On the one hand, this illustrates Byron's own quicksilver, paradoxical nature, whose spirit informs the many conflicting views expressed in *Don Juan.* On the other hand there is his deep sympathy with any struggle for liberty and independence, thus accounting for his admiration of "Leonidas and Washington, / Whose every battle- field is holy ground, / Which breathes of nations saved, not undone" (VIII. 5). For though "War's a brain- spattering, windpipe-slitting art," all bets are off if "her cause by Right be sanctified." Byron's principle motivation is that "I wish men to be free / As much from mobs and kings—from you as me" (IX. 25), and the reference to the threat of tyranny between individuals makes his cause as philosophical as it is concrete. For Byron's real enemy is not Wellington or Castlereagh, but rather the narrow- mindedness and repression that gives rise to either, as he states:

> And I will war, at least in words (and—should
>   My chance so happen—deeds) with all
>   who war
> With Thought;—and of Thought's foes by far
>   most rude,
>   Tyrants and Sycophants have been and are.
> I know not who may conquer: if I could
>   Have such a presence, it should be no bar
> To this my plain, sworn, downright detestation
> Of every despotism in every nation.
>
>   (IX. 24)

Byron's is not only a war of words, but one also fought within the action of words on the page. In the end, war—like Love, like Don Juan or Haidée or Wellington—becomes the material of Byron's real battle, namely against those who oppose the free-flowing, paradoxical nature of thought. Only by forwarding the rigor and integrity of genuine thought against the laziness of "cant" is he able to succeed in his mission to "teach, if possible, the stones / To rise against the Earth's tyrants" (VIII. 135).

TIME AND MOBILITY

As the cantos concerned with war attest, Byron's satire is more serious than he lets on. Yet many a critic has pointed out that *Don Juan* is a poem entirely without pattern, its progress and scope seeming to remain at the whim of its creator. Writing to his publisher in 1819, Byron chided John Murray for being "too earnest and eager about a work never intended to be serious." Having pointed out that "the Soul of such writing is its licence—at least the *liberty* of that *licence* if one likes," the poet concludes, "[D]o you suppose that I could have any intention but to giggle and make giggle?—a playful satire with as little poetry as could be helped—was what I meant" (*Byron's Letters and Journals,* VI. 208). Nowhere is Byron's playfulness more evident than in his many digressions, the number of which increase in frequency and length as the poem continues. "For me, I know nought; nothing I deny, / Admit, reject, contemn" (XIV. 3), maintains the poet, and more importantly the same can be said for his poem and its ability to absorb a wide array of ideas and subjects, as well as contradictions in the narrator's own thinking. His penchant for "mere speculation" (XIV. 7), is in itself a philosophical stance, as he explains:

> You know or don't know, that great Bacon saith,
>   'Fling up a straw, 'twill show the way the
>   wind blows;'
> And such a straw, borne on by human breath,
>   Is Poesy, according as the mind glows;
> A paper kite, which flies 'twixt life and death,
>   A shadow which the onward Soul behind
>   throws:

And mine's a bubble not blown up for praise,
But just to play with, as an infant plays.

(XIV. 8)

"One system eats another up" (XIV. 1), and if nothing else, it is the hegemonic regularity of any system that Byron seeks to deride. This includes his own poem, for the free play of the thinking behind it is much more vital to him than any structure employed to prop it up. The fact that *Don Juan* was written over five years and published in six installments also serves the same cause. Byron never attempted to square its many plot discrepancies, to account for the disappearance of the Spanish narrator or several characters within it, or even to fully account for how Juan gets from one place to the next. These are matters for a narrative epic to worry about, not the episodic mélange of philosophical "speculation" that is *Don Juan.*

Byron also extends such free play to the poem's narrative time. As Jerome McGann has illustrated in "The Book of Byron and the Book of a World," three different time periods overlap each other in the poem. The first is the era of the French Revolution running from roughly 1787 to 1793, which is when Juan's adventures take place. Byron, in fact, told Thomas Medwin that his plan was for Juan to meet his death at the guillotine in France, an irony in itself, given that the French Revolution had promised liberty for all. Meanwhile, the second time period runs from 1808 to 1816 and corresponds to Byron's years of fame in the English court, as well as the rise and fall of Napoleon. Finally, 1816 to 1823 are the years of the poem's composition which are also directly referenced by the narrator, particularly when he refers to Byron's own immediate experience and the repression that accompanied the Restoration. Throughout, the poet makes no effort to distinguish between any of these times, but rather moves from one event to another as if all were happening simultaneously in the poem's present. Even Juan, who begins the poem as a sixteen-year-old and should be no more than seventeen when he gets

to England, ends up being the "junior by six weeks" (XIV. 51) to Lady Adeline Amundeville, who is twenty-one.

The compulsion to confound time's linear "system" is more serious than wanton lapses in Byron's control of the poem's narrative. What is created after all is a new time, one that is controlled entirely by Byron in writing the poem. As Bernard Beatty notes in *Byron's "Don Juan,"* "It is in the gaps and jumps of the narrator's artfully mirrored consciousness that we come into closest contact with Lord George Gordon Byron himself" (p. 122). It is Byron's own experience of time through memory and present awareness that we experience while reading the poem. Thus, according to Beatty, "the poem is not simply a mimesis of life but is, so to say, as directly impelled by it as it is possible for a work of art, remaining a work of art, to be" (p. 121).

The famed *ubi sunt* passage of Canto XI that mourns the passage of time illustrates Byron's deep awareness of mortality, which in many ways provides the motivation for the poet to manipulate time throughout *Don Juan.* With Juan having moved on from the sexual slavery imposed on him by Catherine of Russia after he escapes the siege of Ismail, he arrives in England on a diplomatic mission, but also as a courier to and from Byron's past. The "English" cantos that account for over a third of the poem's length draw directly from Byron's years at court. Throughout them there is a mix of both nostalgia and disdain for "This Paradise of Pleasure and *Ennui*" (XIV. 17), as he recounts the beauty of London and Newstead Abbey, as well as warning, "Ill / Can tender souls relate the rise and fall / Of hopes and fears which shake a single ball" (XI. 72). Then quite suddenly, at the end of Canto XI, the tone turns deeply melancholic:

"Where is the world," cries Young, "at *eighty*?
    Where
        The world in which a man was born?"
    Alas!

Where is the world of *eight* years past? *'Twas
    there*—
I look for it—'tis gone, a Globe of Glass!
Cracked, shivered, vanished, scarcely gazed on,
    ere
        A silent change dissolves the glittering
mass.
Statesmen, chiefs, orators, queens, patriots, kings,
And dandies, all are gone on the wind's wings.

                          (XI. 76)

What would seem at first to be one of Byron's sardonic attacks on "that glittering sea / Of gems and plumes, and pearls and silks" (XI. 70) suddenly explodes into anguish over the "silent change" that "dissolves the glittering mass." Byron, in fact, continues on for fourteen more stanzas, listing all of the political and historical change that has occurred in the last seven years, until even he who "knew that nought was lasting" finds that "Change grows too changeable, without being new" (XI. 82). Predictably, the narrator's only advice for Juan is "'Carpe diem,' Juan, 'Carpe, carpe!'" before concluding with the dictum, "Be hypocritical, be cautious, be / Not what you *seem,* but always what you *see*" (XI. 86).

Juan, however, is a character in a tale and therefore does not actually suffer the mutability and passing of time. Instead, Byron does, and so too the reader. What both the poet and the reader *see* are the words before them, and it will be those words that will seize hold of and shape Juan's life as well. Byron speaks to this by wondering aloud how he "shall . . . relate in other Cantos / Of what befell our hero in the land" (XI. 87), only to concede that Juan's fate "Is yet within the unread events of time" (XI. 90). What the poet is adamant about, however, is that whatever happens will be what *he* intends, even "Though every scribe, in some slight turn of diction, / Will hint allusions never *meant,*" adding that, "Ne'er doubt / *This*—when I speak, I *don't hint,* but *speak out*" (XI. 88). Complaining that his poem is "the subject of attack / As ever yet was any work sublime," Byron

concludes with a defiant gesture in support of his right to maintain control of Juan's story, as he states, "So much the better!—I may stand alone, / And would not change my free thoughts for a throne" (XI. 90).

But even Byron knows that he will not be around forever to further the adventures of his hero, nor can he control entirely how his poem is read. Furthermore, the comic rhymes and sexual innuendo with which the poem is riddled not only invite the reader to participate in their meaning, they often inspire the search for those very "allusions never *meant*" which the poet protests against. Instead, it will be his reader who through "some slight turn of diction" will uncover meaning within the poem, and thus bring both the poem and poet alive in our consciousness once again. Indeed, it would seem as if Byron means here to encourage our own "free thought" as much as he wishes to avow the sanctity of his own. For if the reader's "free thought" is really engaged throughout this passage, we see that he cannot possibly mean it at all. This does not make the passage untrue or a deception. Rather, as Byron points out earlier in the same canto, ". . . after all, what is a lie? 'Tis but / The truth in masquerade" (XI. 37). Ironically, and quite magically, the "truth" uncovered in this passage is our very own the moment we realize Byron's insistence on control is unfeasible. The narrator may feel that "I will fall at least as fell my hero," Juan having become "my Moscow" (XI. 56), as he compares the disparaging of his poem to Napoleon's defeat, but so long as we remain vigilant and responsive to the action and ironies of the poem, we are freed by the direct experience of "Poesy, according as the mind glows" (XIV. 8) through the act of interpretation that liberates the "truth" Byron has prepared for us.

Thus, in the operation of the poem's "action" the reader's role is paramount, nor has there ever been a poem that more directly speaks to and involves its reader than *Don Juan.* Throughout we are not only told the motivations of the poet in his approach and handling of the poem; we are also required to question those motivations in order to arrive at true meaning. "I am but a mere spectator, / And gaze where'er the palace or the hovel is, / Much in the mode of Goethe's Mephistopheles" (XIII. 7), claims the narrator rather modestly, if not mischievously. We as readers, however, cannot afford to gape on as mere "spectators," for we are in the arch hands of a Mephistopheles who reminds us:

Oh, reader! If that thou canst read,—and know,
    'Tis not enough to spell, or even to read,
To constitute a reader; there must go
    Virtues of which both you and I have
    need.
Firstly, begin with the beginning—(though
    That clause is hard); and secondly,
    proceed;
Thirdly, commence not with the end—or, sinning
In this sort, end at least with the beginning.

                    (XIII. 73)

Though the "Virtues" listed here would at first seem a lot of playful nonsense, they underscore the fact that Byron's poem is constantly beginning and ending, only to begin over again. Because any notion of "the end" is here equated with "sinning," the narrator requests that we "end at least with the beginning," and thus commence the poem's action all over again through our reading. To this "end," we are the poet's lifeboat keeping his poem (and thus the poet as well) afloat by our engagement with it. Nor does it seem any accident that the above request comes at the end of seventeen stanzas enumerating the riches and beauty of "Norman Abbey," Byron's fictional stand-in for Newstead Abbey, his family's former seat. In attempting to capture "The mansion's self" (XIII. 66), Byron also seeks to set down his own. But even that "self" must come to an end with the completion of the poem. That is, unless the reader is there to return to it over time and once more "end at least with the beginning."

The need for the reader to help both poet and poem travel across time, as well as to accept the narrative's conflation of different times, is what makes "mobility" the poem's central cause and effect. As a negative trait, it is the source of Adeline's ability to pay lip service to her husband while becoming increasingly interested in Juan. This allows her to maintain "vivacious versatility / Which many people take for want of heart," as Byron remarks that "mobility" is "A thing of temperament and not of art, / Though seeming so, from its supposed facility" (XVI. 97). In a note to the passage, Byron goes further and says, "It may be defined as an excessive susceptibility of immediate impressions—at the same time without *losing* the past; and is, though sometimes apparently useful to the possessor, a most painful and unhappy attribute." Hence, because it helps keep up appearances and thus conceals those "Icebergs in the hearts of mighty men, / With Self-love in the centre as their Pole" (XIV. 102), mobility can be seen as the source of the hypocrisy and decadence inherent to Adeline and her class, and which Byron's entire poem remains bent on criticizing.

The poet, however, protests too much. Though "mobility" may seem more a sinister "temperament" than a redeeming "art," he also adds in the same stanza that it is "false—though true; for surely they're sincerest, / Who are strongly acted on by what is nearest" (XVI. 97). Similarly, Byron continually makes his reader susceptible to "immediate impressions," be they comic innuendoes or the immediacy of the poet's digressions and addresses to the reader. What's more, his effort to stop "*losing* the past" is, as we have seen, at the heart of his battle against "the weight of human hours" (IV. 15), this being a poet who reminds us that "if I laugh at any mortal thing, / 'Tis that I may not weep" (IV. 4). Though Juan may be freed to bound through time and space undeterred, the poet knows that he possesses no such liberty, but like the rest of us must suffer "The death of friends, and that which slays even more— / The death of friendship, love, youth, all that is" (IV. 12). Against time's force, the poet's best weapon is his art, for only that has the requisite mobility to sustain character and voice beyond the fixed parameters of life. Such mobility is not employed for deceit and duplicity, but rather to remain "false—though true" in the way that art partakes of each. When this happens the reader is "strongly acted on by what is nearest," namely the immediacy of Byron's extraordinary personality as evoked by the poem's words. The result is that, indeed, "the end of fame . . . 'tis but to fill / A certain portion of uncertain paper" (I. 218), for only there are poet and reader alike granted the possibility of outrunning time when

> . . . words are things, and a small drop of ink,
>   Falling like dew, upon a thought, produces
> That which makes thousands, perhaps millions,
>   think;
>   'Tis strange, the shortest letter which man
>   uses
> Instead of speech, may form a lasting link
>   Of ages; to what straits old Time reduces
> Frail man, when paper—even a rag like this,
> Survives himself, his tomb, and all that's his.
>
>   (III. 88)

IMPORTANCE AND INFLUENCE

Don Juan was the most popular poem of its time. It sold in the thousands when published, as did numerous pirate editions and imitations which unscrupulous publishers claimed were written by Byron. More importantly, *Don Juan* struck a chord with both the upper class that its author so brilliantly satirized and the general reading public. William St. Clair has demonstrated that, based on copies published and sold, it remained Byron's best selling work throughout the nineteenth century and was probably read by thousands who read none of Byron's other books.

By the twentieth century, however, both Byron and *Don Juan* fell out of favor. Ironically enough, Wordsworth's *The Prelude* has come to seem the more central work of the time, the

Romantics having survived Byron's attack on their work as "dropsies, taken for divinities" (III. 95). Instead, the charge that within their work were "things which in this century don't strike / The public mind" (III. 95) has come to seem more generally true of Byron's own. Few students of writing or poetry know *Don Juan*, and it enjoys neither the regard among contemporary writers shown to poems by Wordsworth and Keats, nor the enduring influence of Coleridge's criticism. After the arrival of modernism and the "difficulty" advocated by T. S. Eliot as necessary for capturing the complexity of modern life, Byron's jocularity and wit seemed less trenchant, less inventive, and less true to experience in a world sunk in the cataclysms of two world wars and the Holocaust. Add to this the poem's "unfinished" state and our propensity to value only the completed art work, whole and ready to dispense its meaning like gum from a machine, and it is easy to see why *Don Juan*'s fame has waned.

Oddly enough, the same cannot be said of Byron, for, of all of the figures of the Romantic movement, his life and death remain the epitome of the popular conception of the classic Romantic hero. "Byronic" has even entered the dictionary and come to stand for a person or work characterized by melancholy, passion, cynicism, and the libertine spirit made famous by the poet himself. Even his good looks, seen in portraits where he is in eastern costume or courtly dress, are more readily recognized by the general reader than the face of Wordsworth or Keats. One cannot help but wonder how Byron would respond to being turned into a caricature of himself. "If I sneer sometimes, / It is because I cannot well do less" (XIII. 8), he admits, nor would we expect him to do less than sneer if he were here.

Though his poems have lost the vast readership they once enjoyed, and though his life has too often been reduced to a cliché, in other ways Byron's poetic spirit remains very much alive.

Both the whimsy and the complexity of *Don Juan* stand at the heart of the work of postmodern writers such as John Ashbery or Paul Muldoon, who themselves are descended from the sophistication and verbal range of Wallace Stevens and Hart Crane. Byron's worldliness and melancholy are also evident in the work of Joseph Brodsky and Derek Walcott, and they would trace their lineage back to Horace and Catullus much as Byron did. John Berryman's jarring and mercurial epic *The Dream Songs,* Robert Lowell's sprawling sequence of loose sonnets, *History,* and even James Merrill's *The Changing Light at Sandover* share with Byron the effort to create a poem of epic reach out of the flux of the quotidian. One would doubt that any of these poets would put Byron at the top of their list of recommended reading, but their work owes much to *Don Juan* as the first modern epic.

Where both Byron and *Don Juan* have been well served is by criticism. Breakthrough work by scholars such as Jerome McGann, T. G. Steffan, W. W. Pratt, Ernest J. Lovell, and Michael Cooke helped to reinvigorate Byron studies in the 1960s following the publication of Leslie Marchand's seminal biography in 1957. This led to closer critical scrutiny of the poem, as well as more scholarly editions of the work accompanied by useful notes and appendices. Female critics such as Anne Barton, Caroline Franklin, and Susan J. Wolfson also provided astute readings that increased *Don Juan*'s interest to women. Given the increased appreciation for the poem's complex demands upon the reader, as well the tantalizing way in which its "unfinished" state has come to seem an integral part of its poetic strategy, one hopes that it will soon enjoy a revival among both writers and critics.

What will remain true is the way in which, as Jerome McGann says, "*Don Juan* encourages almost endless commentary but frustrates almost every sort of formal analysis" ("*Don Juan*" *in Context,* p. 107). "I was born for op-position" (XV. 22), Byron tells us, and the same is true of *Don Juan* the moment one tries to wrestle it into any particular critical cage. Though the narrator informs us early on that "I hate inconstancy—I loathe, detest, / Abhor, condemn, abjure the mortal made / Of such quicksilver clay that in his breast / No permanent foundation can be laid" (II. 209), nothing would seem further from the truth when it comes to the nature of both the poet and his poem. Indeed, the quixotic nature of *Don Juan*'s ever-unfolding mix of narrative, thought, and comic digression is its very lifeblood. "*Difficile est proprie communia dicere*" ("'Tis no slight task to write on common things") is the epigraph from Horace which Byron chose for *Don Juan,* and the source of its genius lies in its ability to show us that common things also contain great complexity in their very nature. Not to know this is to lay oneself open to the reductive nature of "cant," whether it be found in politics, philosophy, the media, or the hallowed halls of academia. "There's no such thing as certainty, that's plain / As any of Mortality's Conditions" (IX. 17), Byron reminds us, and his is an effort to counter our well-worn tendency to "speculate both far and wide, / And deem, because we *see,* we are *all-seeing*" (IX. 16). To this end *Don Juan*'s unfinished state serves well its purpose, for when Byron says that "I leave the thing a problem, like all things" (XVII. 13) it is an open invitation to "solve" it for ourselves. Only then can we discover and tap into the poem's own remarkable life force so that we, like Byron, and in some odd way with him, can say,

And wherefore this exordium?—Why, just now,
    In taking up this paltry sheet of paper,
My bosom underwent a glorious glow,
    And my internal Spirit cut a caper:
And though so much inferior, as I know,
    To those who, by the dint of glass and va-
  pour,
Discover stars, and sail in the wind's eye,
I wish to do as much by Poesy.

                                (X. 3)

Selected Bibliography

EDITION

The Complete Poetical Works. 7 vols. Ed. Jerome J. McGann. Oxford: Clarendon, 1980–1993. (*Lord Byron: The Major Works.* Jerome J. McGann, ed. Oxford and New York: Oxford University Press, 2000, is cited in this essay.)

OTHER WORKS

Byron's "Don Juan": A Variorum Edition. Ed. T. G. Steffan and W. W. Pratt. Austin: University of Texas Press, 1957. (Contains extensive information about the writing, revision, and sources of the poem.)

Byron's Letters and Journals. 12 vols. Ed. Leslie A. Marchand. London: John Murray, 1973–1982.

Medwin, Thomas. *Conversations of Lord Byron.* Ed. Ernest J. Lovell. Princeton, N.J.: Princeton University Press, 1966.

SECONDARY WORKS

Barton, Anne. *Byron. Don Juan.* Cambridge: Cambridge University Press, 1992. (An excellent introduction and concise discussion of the poem's themes and formal strategies.)

Beatty, Bernard. *Byron's "Don Juan."* Totowa, N.J.: Barnes and Noble, 1985. (An insightful account of the demands the poem makes on the reader in its unfolding.)

Beaty, Frederick L. *Byron the Satirist.* DeKalb: Northern Illinois University Press, 1985. (Includes several chapters on the satiric style and content of the poem.)

Blessington, Marguerite. *Lady Blessington's Conversations of Lord Byron.* Ed. Ernest J. Lovell. Princeton, N.J.: Princeton University Press, 1969. (A record of conversations with Byron by one of his contemporaries, though somewhat suspect in its accuracy.)

Bloom, Harold, ed. *Lord Byron's "Don Juan."* New York: Chelsea House, 1987. (A concise critical collection that reprints key work by George M. Ridenour, McGann, Cooke, and Peter J. Manning.)

Bold, Alan, ed. *Byron: Wrath and Rhyme.* London and Tottowa, N.J.: Vision Press and Barnes and Noble, 1983. (Contains Jenni Calder's article, "The Hero as Lover: Byron and Women" that explores Byron's double standard in his treatment of women, as well as Walter Perrie's "The Byronic Philosophy," a useful overview of the Byronic hero.)

Bostetter, Edward E., ed. *Twentieth Century Interpretations of "Don Juan."* Englewood Cliffs, N.J.: Prentice-Hall, 1969. (Collects important essays by Lovell, Ridenour, Steffan, and Andrew Rutherford, as well as critical observations by Virgina Woolf, T. S. Eliot, W. B. Yeats, and W. H. Auden on Byron's place and significance as a poet.)

Boyd, Elizabeth F. *Byron's "Don Juan": A Critical Study.* New York: The Humanities Press, 1958. (Discusses the sources Byron used for his poem.)

Cooke, Michael. *The Blind Man Traces the Circle.* Princeton, N.J.: Princeton University Press, 1969. (An important discussion of the ideas and themes running throughout all of Byron's work.)

Franklin, Caroline. *Byron's Heroines.* Oxford: Clarendon Press, 1992. (An insightful and thorough feminist study.)

Gleckner, Robert F. *Critical Essays on Lord Byron.* New York: G.K. Hall, 1991. (Contains key essays by McGann, Cooke, Ridenour, and Beatty, as well as Susan J. Wolfson's "'Their She Condition': Cross- Dressing and the Politics of Gender in Don Juan.")

Grosskurth, Phyllis. *Byron: The Flawed Angel.* Boston: Houghton Mifflin, 1997. (Psychoanalytic biography.)

Joseph, M. K. *Byron the Poet.* London: Gollancz, 1964. (Thorough and well-rounded introduction.)

Jump, John D. *Byron.* London and Boston: Routledge and Kegan Paul, 1972. (Contains useful chapter on the history the poem draws on.)

Graham, Peter W. *Lord Byron.* New York, Twayne, 1998. (Concise overview of Byron's life and major works.)

Levine, Alice, and Robert N. Keane, eds. *Rereading Byron.* New York: Garland, 1993. (Reprints essays from Hofstra University's Byron Bicentennial Conference, including works by McGann, Graham, and Alan Richardson.)

Longford, Alice. *The Life of Byron.* Boston: Little, Brown, 1976. (One-volume biography).

MacCarthy, Fiona. *Byron: Life and Legend.* New York: Farrar, Straus and Giroux, 2002.

Manning, Peter J. *Byron and His Fictions.* Detroit: Wayne State University Press, 1978. (A well respected psychoanalytic approach.)

Marchand, Leslie A. *Byron: A Biography.* 3 vols. New York: Knopf, 1957. (The definitive biography.)

———. *Byron: A Portrait.* New York: Knopf, 1970. (One-volume abridgement of the biography.)

McGann, Jerome J. *"Don Juan" in Context.* Chicago: University of Chicago Press, 1976. (A superb study that traces Byron's thought and approach.)

———. *Fiery Dust: Byron's Poetical Development.* Chicago: University of Chicago Press, 1968. (One of the breakthrough works in Byron studies.)

Ridenour, George M. *The Style of "Don Juan."* New Haven, Conn.: Yale University Press, 1960. (Reads the poem as a search for redemption after The Fall.)

Rutherford, Andrew. *Byron: A Critical Study.* Stanford, Calif.: Stanford University Press, 1961. (Well-rounded study that considers Byron's response to the history and politics of his time.)

———. *Byron: The Critical Heritage.* New York: Barnes and Noble, 1970. (Collects reviews of Byron's work from his time and the late nineteenth century.)

Rutherford, Andrew, ed. *Byron: Augustan and Romantic.* London: MacMillan,1990. (Contains William St. Clair's "The Impact of Byron's Writing" that details how widely Byron's works were read in the nineteenth century.)

West, Paul. *Byron and the Spoiler's Art.* New York: St. Martin's, 1960. (Lively, well-written discussion of Byron's urge to violate decorum and disrupt normative meaning.)

West, Paul, ed. *Byron: A Collection of Critical Essays.* Englewood Cliffs, N.J.: Prentice-Hall, 1963. (Reprints important essays from 1930 to 1960.)

Mary Shelley's
Frankenstein

LEWIS ROBINSON

WHEN MARY WOLLSTONE-CRAFT Godwin began writing the novel *Frankenstein* in 1816, she was an eighteen-year-old existing very much in the shadow of her lover, the Romantic poet Percy Bysshe Shelley, and of her parents, the writers and social reformers Mary Wollstonecraft and William Godwin. In the years following its publication, however, *Frankenstein* emerged as an important Romantic text and as indispensable commentary on Milton's *Paradise Lost,* on creation and motherhood, and on the act of writing. The story of the writing of *Frankenstein* is nearly as well known as the novel's plot. As the daughter of two literary celebrities—her mother was the renowned author of *A Vindication of the Rights of Woman* (1792), and her father was a radical philosopher (author of *Enquiry Concerning Political Justice,* 1793)—Mary Godwin was exposed to England's literary hierarchy early in her life. She was only fifteen when she first met Percy Shelley, and just two years later, she traveled with him to France and Switzerland, where they fell in love. In her introduction to *Frankenstein* (first published in 1831, in the third edition of the text), Mary Shelley recognizes how her relationship with Percy Shelley added greatly to the pressures she inevitably endured as a literary heiress:

> [He was] from the first very anxious that I should prove myself worthy of my parentage and enrol myself on the page of fame. He was forever inciting me to obtain literary reputation, which even on my own part I cared for then. . . . At this time he desired that I should write, not so much with the idea that I could produce anything worthy of notice but that he might himself judge how far I possessed the promise of better things hereafter.
>
> (p. xxv)

In addition to bearing Percy Shelley's expectations, the young Mary Wollstonecraft Godwin was also preoccupied with other literary constellations. She was fascinated by Milton and Blake and Coleridge, and she was a tireless reader of her parents' work—in fact, she and Shelley spent a good deal of time together studying their books. Her mother had died during childbirth, and as soon as Mary took up with Shelley, her father played a significantly less important role in her life. So it was through reading—assembling the literary evidence, as it were—that she found a way to explore her origins and forge an identity. As the critics

Sandra Gilbert and Susan Gubar suggest (in the 1979 text *The Madwoman in the Attic: The Woman Writer and the Nineteenth-Century Literary Imagination*), "books appear to have functioned as [Mary Shelley's] surrogate parents, pages and words standing in for flesh and blood" (p. 223).

The late eighteenth and early nineteenth centuries were a time of great political, social, scientific, and economic upheaval; the era's revolutions (Industrial, American, and French) availed new beginnings, with lingering instability. These were Mary Shelley's formative years, and while she was studying her parents' books and familiarizing herself with her other literary forebears, she was also continuously pregnant or nursing. In this time of curiosity and becoming, when her sexuality and literariness represented new and uncharted terrain, she embarked on her first novel, which would be her only enduring work.

During the summer of 1816, young Mary and Percy Shelley—with their illegitimate baby William—visited Lord Byron and his doctor, Polidori, in Switzerland. Here, she was given an opportunity to prove her talents. As she explains in *Frankenstein*'s introduction, in the midst of a "wet, ungenial summer, [when] incessant rain often confined [them] for days to the house" (p. xxv), Lord Byron suggested that each vacationer in the house compose a ghost story. Thereafter, Mary "busied [herself] to think of a story," but she "felt that blank incapability of invention which is the greatest misery of authorship, when dull Nothing replies to our anxious invocations" (p. xxvii).

While Mary Godwin endured this case of writer's block—born undoubtedly of the expectations with which she unwittingly tortured herself—the literary landscape was shifting throughout Europe. While Milton was still in the forefront of many writers' minds, the Romantic poets were in vogue. Prompted by political revolution and social upheaval, the form and order of neoclassic writers such as Alexander Pope had yielded to poets such as William

CHRONOLOGY

1797	30 August: Mary Godwin born in London, England, to William Godwin and Mary Wollstonecraft Godwin.
	10 September: Mary Wollstonecraft Godwin dies from postpartum hemorrhage.
1789	14 July: storming of the Bastille.
1801	21 December: William Godwin remarries (Mary Jane Clairmont).
1812	11 November: Mary meets Percy Bysshe Shelley. Mary resides with Baxter family in Dundee, 1812–1814.
1814	5 May: Mary's second contact with Percy Shelley, in London. 28 July, Mary and Percy Shelley travel to France and Switzerland.
1815	22 February: Mary gives birth to premature female child, who dies 6 March. 19 March: Mary writes in her journal: "Dream that my little baby came to life again; that it had only been cold, and that we rubbed it before the fire, and it lived."
	August: Mary and Percy settle at Bishopsgate, Windsor.
1816	24 January: Mary gives birth to William Shelley. 3 May, Percy and Mary leave for Switzerland, arriving ten days later at Geneva, where they stay with Lord Byron and his doctor, Polidori. 15–16 June, probable dates for Byron's proposed "story-telling" competition, after which Mary, in a waking dream, claims to see "the pale student of unhallowed arts."
	9 October: Fanny Imlay, Mary's half sister, kills herself.
	10 December, Harriet Shelley (Percy's wife) discovered drowned in the Serpentine, Hyde Park.
	30 December: Percy and Mary married, London.
1817	22 August: Percy Shelley contracts for publication of *Frankenstein* with Lackington, Allen and Company.
	2 September: Mary gives birth to Clara Shelley.

1818	January: *Frankenstein* published anonymously. Percy forwards presentation volumes to Sir Walter Scott.
	24 September: Clara Shelley dies in Venice.
1819	7 June: William Shelley dies in Rome.
	12 November: Percy Florence, Mary's only child to survive, is born.
1822	16 June: Mary miscarries and nearly dies.
	8 July: Percy Bysshe Shelley drowned in Gulf of Spezia.
1823	Mary publishes autobiographical novel *Valperga*.
1826	Mary publishes *The Last Man*.
1830	Mary publishes *Perkin Warbeck*.
1835	Mary publishes *Lodore*.
1836	7 April: William Godwin dies.
1837	Mary publishes *Falkner*.
1838	28 June: coronation of Queen Victoria.
1851	1 February: Mary Shelley dies.

Wordsworth, who put greater emphasis on feeling, individuality, and passion. "Imagination," the individual's mental reservoir, was proving itself a strong force in the wake of the expansive rationalism and structured forms of the Enlightenment.

In her 1831 introduction, Mary asserts that "Invention, it must be humbly admitted, does not consist in creating out of void, but out of chaos. . . . Invention consists in the capacity of seizing on the capabilities of a subject and in the power of moulding and fashioning ideas suggested by it" (p. xxviii). After listening to a discussion between Lord Byron and Percy Shelley about science and the supernatural—specifically, about the ways in which a corpse might be reanimated—Mary Wollstonecraft Godwin retired to bed, where she was unable to sleep:

My imagination, unbidden, possessed and guided me, gifting the successive images that arose in my mind with a vividness far beyond the usual bounds of reverie. I saw—with shut eyes, but acute mental vision—I saw the pale student of unhallowed arts kneeling beside the thing he had put together. I

saw the hideous phantasm of a man stretched out, and then, on the working of some powerful engine, show signs of life and stir with an uneasy, half-vital motion.

(p. xxix)

It was then, in essence, that the monster who wreaks havoc in *Frankenstein* was born. The dream had terrified Mary, but she claimed to be still unable to conceive of a worthy ghost story—until, of course, she realized that the dream she had endured *was* her story. "What terrified me will terrify others!" she presumed (p. xxx). Accordingly, she embarked on her literary career, commingling her own becoming with the act of creation, writing a story that has at its heart the problems of becoming and creating. She spent the next few months writing the novel and caring for her child. In December of that same year, less than three weeks after his wife drowned in Hyde Park, Percy Shelley and Mary Godwin were married. *Frankenstein* was the only ghost story resulting from Lord Byron's contest.

THE ROMANTIC AND GOTHIC IN *FRANKENSTEIN*

The novel *Frankenstein* is not easily categorized. Many critics have been quick to place it in the company of other gothic novels, which is to suggest that the novel's chief concern is its element of fear, its gloomy setting, and its dealings with the supernatural. After all, Mary Shelley admits in her introduction that she hoped to create a tale that would "awaken thrilling horror—one to make the reader dread to look round, to curdle the blood, and quicken the beatings of the heart" (p. xxvii). Later in her introduction, though, she touches upon this fear's deeper source, when describing a vision of her protagonist, Victor Frankenstein, the creator of a monster: "Frightful must it be, for supremely frightful would be the effect of any human endeavour to mock the stupendous mechanism of the Creator of the world" (p. xxix). This casts Mary Shelley's endeavor in an entirely human, moral context—which suggests that *Frankenstein* has more significant Romantic, not simply gothic, underpinnings. The narrators in *Frankenstein*—Robert Walton, Victor Frankenstein, and the monster himself—share an ambition that is characteristically Romantic. All of them, including the monster, have an appetite for intense feeling and human perfectibility—they are all striving for the sublime, and they are doing so within the confines of human (or near human) imagination, human (or near human) emotion. This is not the Christian ideal; the narrators of *Frankenstein* are not striving to be bound to God (and unbound by flesh). Unlike protagonists of the previous literary era, *Frankenstein*'s characters do not look to God for strength, they look within themselves. They are unable to control their ambition, and their human passions—which, more than anything else, defines them as Romantic protagonists.

If we understand William Wordsworth's long poem *The Prelude* (completed in 1805) to be emblematic of the Romantic period, it may be helpful to compare the sensibility presented in *Frankenstein* to Wordsworth's view of poetry. Both Victor Frankenstein and the voice of the poet in *The Prelude* are seeking transcendence; they both aspire to be unbound by the specifics of time and space. This is not the paradigm of classical poetry, in which the Divine is the source of such transcendence; rather, the protagonists of *Frankentstein* and the speaker in *The Prelude* rely on their own ambitious imaginations. Both Victor Frankenstein and Wordsworth are passionate, striving individuals, and they both depend on the potentialities of the human will.

Where they diverge is in the practice of such passion. Wordsworth relies on the spontaneous overflow of powerful emotion recollected in tranquility. Victor Frankenstein, though, does not approach any of his endeavors tranquilly. Throughout the novel, he subjects himself to a barrage of trauma and torment. Mary Shelley's novel critiques the idealized Romantic sensibility by suggesting that imagination—art and creation—should be kept as a personal, human pleasure. When such bounds are overstepped, by intertwining the aesthetic with the moral (as Victor Frankenstein does by creating his near-human monster) the consequences are disastrous.

MONSTROUS AUTHORSHIP IN *FRANKENSTEIN*

Mary Shelley had high expectations for herself as an intellectual heiress, as the soon-to-be-bride of a famous Romantic poet, and as a young writer with dreams of literary anointment. These expectations may have come to bear on the structure of *Frankenstein* and the novel's preoccupation with writing and reading. Among its other shades of meaning, *Frankenstein* is a story about the desire to create (to write) and the role of reading and writing, as ways to fend off isolation and to inspire sympathetic connection.

Robert Walton's voice is the first of *Frankenstein*'s three narratives, and his voice serves as the novel's frame. Walton's letters to his sister Margaret introduce Victor Frankenstein's story and provide its afterword. This structure self-consciously asserts that the entire tale—from Walton's setting of scene, to Victor Frankenstein's telling of his story, to the monster's self-explanation to his creator—is contained within Walton's missives to his sister. All of the visceral aspects of the story—from the cold upon Walton's cheeks, to Victor Frankenstein's sweaty toils of "filthy creation," to the monster's fiendish murders—come to the reader by way of Walton's written document. Here, Mary Shelley reveals human imagination's potential: her own imagination's potential, as the writer of *Frankenstein,* and Walton's, as an isolated ship captain penning letters to his sister. It is interesting to note, though, that the premise of Walton's narrative is not that he is inventing the story, but that he is *retelling* it, that he is documenting the stories of others. This premise, of a story within a story, is situated within the Romantic sensibility, which understands imagination to well up from introspective Wordsworthian moments of contemplation. Walton observes in Letter 1 that "the phenomena of the heavenly bodies undoubtedly are in those undiscovered solitudes" (p. 6). After resolving to seek the North Pole, Walton endures six years of preparation, which puts great strains on his body and his mind. He is isolated in his pursuit, both before and after he sets sail. He is surrounded by a desolate frozen landscape when he is visited by Victor Frankenstein and the story he tells (and, in turn, the monster and the story the monster tells). Just as Walton foresees his destination to be a place where "the sun is for ever visible; its broad disk just skirting the horizon, and diffusing a perpetual splendour" (p. 7), so too do Victor Frankenstein's and the monster's vivid stories come to him virtually out of nowhere, from an unforeseen spot on the horizon.

Walton, like all writers, is an isolated entity; he uses his imagination to take him to more visual, sensual places, and his imagination fuels his ambition. His own story concerns a man seeking unforeseen truth and beauty in a desolate, frozen wasteland.

"I try in vain to be persuaded that the pole is the seat of frost and desolation; it ever presents itself to my imagination as the region of beauty and delight" (p. 6).

Walton's exploration, in the face of great adversity, coupled with his reliance on imagination, provides a premise for the entire novel. "This expedition has been the favourite dream of my early years" (p. 7), he says—and he is only the first of three dreaming narrators in the novel. Victor Frankenstein is a magnified, more visceral version of Walton, and the monster is a magnified version of Victor Frankenstein. The three concentric circles of narration—Walton on the outside, Victor Frankenstein's narrative within Walton's, and the monster's narrative within Frankenstein's—provides a structure to express the ideas of artistic potential with which Mary Shelley was preoccupied during the writing of *Frankenstein.* Each narrator is fueled by

imagination and ambition. Walton, as a writer, is the outermost narrator, plumbing the depths of the human spirit, but only theoretically. Victor Frankenstein provides the next narrative layer: he acts out Walton's curiosity—not in Walton's contemplative, Wordsworthian manner, but in a chaotic, dangerous, overreaching way. Finally, at the center of the story, is the monster's narrative—the heart of the novel. The monster is the primordial writer, nameless and isolated, yearning for a mode of expression but languageless. The monster educates himself from scratch, by witnessing the lives of those more developed than he (the De Lacey family) and by reading *Paradise Lost* and other seminal texts. By structuring her novel in three layers, Mary Shelley presents a model of imagination and ambition and their affects on the human spirit.

Like Victor Frankenstein and the monster, Walton is a self-educated orphan.

"I perused . . . those poets whose effusions entranced my soul, and lifted it to heaven. I also became a poet, and for one year lived in a Paradise of my own creation; I imagined that I also might obtain a niche in the temple where the names of Homer and Shakespeare are consecrated" (p. 7).

Here, Walton describes a "Paradise" of introspection, a desire to imagine and create. This Paradise is an Eden of innocence; Walton hasn't yet experienced the isolation of his expedition, and he hasn't yet met Victor Frankenstein and the monster. There is, however, a hint of danger: Walton's hope to "obtain a niche in the temple" where the great poets are consecrated foreshadows his weakness, and his fall from innocence. Later, as he writes in Letter 2, when he is "encompassed . . . by frost and snow" (p. 10), he tells his sister of "a most severe evil. . . . I have no friend, Margaret: when I am glowing with the enthusiasm of success, there will be none to participate in my joy." At this point, Walton begins his departure from Eden; he is no longer sustained by his own imaginings. His ambition, and his desire to be recognized for his successes, is taking over. To stem his isolation, he seeks solace in writing: "I shall commit my thoughts to paper, it is true; but that is a poor medium for the communication of feeling" (p. 10). According to Walton, writing is an imperfect, incomplete mode of expression; what would be better, he knows, is being in the company of a friend "whose eyes would reply to mine." With no friend in sight, he returns again to poetry—to "the most imaginative of modern poets" (p. 14), Samuel Taylor Coleridge, and Coleridge's poem "The Rime of the Ancient Mariner."

He refers to the poem affectionately, and while he claims to know of the warnings presented in the poem—the "dangerous mysteries of the ocean" and the consequences of ambition—Robert Walton remains stubbornly attached to his "love for the marvellous, a belief in the marvelous . . . which hurries me out of the common pathways of men" (p. 14). He seems seduced by the emotion of "The Rime of the Ancient Mariner," but unable to heed its warnings. The Wedding Guest, witness to the story of ghastly death told in the poem, is changed by what the Ancient Mariner tells him; he turns from the bridegroom's door "a sadder and a wiser man." Robert Walton, though, is optimistic in the face of great adversity; he seems to take no cues from the death and despair in Coleridge's poem, despite his attachment to its emotion. In his last letter before meeting Victor Frankenstein (Letter 3), his ambition has reached a fever pitch:

> Success *shall* crown my endeavours. Wherefore not? Thus far I have gone, tracing a secure way over the pathless seas: the very stars themselves being witnesses and testimonies of my triumph. Why not still proceed over the untamed yet obedient element? What can stop the determined heart and resolved will of man?
>
> (p. 17)

As though in answer to his question, Walton's next letter (Letter 4) reports of his first sight of the monster—"a being which had the shape of a man, but apparently of gigantic stature" (p. 19). The monster, Mary Shelley will have her readers know, is that which "can stop the determined heart and resolved will of man." After Walton sees the monster in the distance, he meets the monster's creator, Victor Frankenstein.

Walton has already described his dissatisfaction with writing as a form of expression, while also showing his reverence for (and naive understanding of) poetry. Essentially, he uses writing as a "secure way over the pathless seas," though his perception of writing changes, as does his ambition, after meeting Victor Frankenstein and retelling his story. Once Walton has written down Frankenstein's account, Frankenstein edits the document to his liking. Similarly, Walton himself is changed: in the second-to-last missive he writes ("Walton, in Continuation"), he notes that, "the die is cast; I have consented to return if we are not destroyed. Thus are my hopes blasted by cowardice and indecision; I come back ignorant and disappointed. It requires more philosophy than I possess to bear this injustice with patience" (p. 293). Here Walton's entry is abrupt; his brevity reflects his exasperation. Writing and ambition are again portrayed as parallel pursuits.

When Walton asks for a friend, someone sympathetic to his ambitious quest ("whose eyes would reply to mine"), he receives Victor Frankenstein. As the outermost narrative, Walton's story is the least self-conscious, the most naive. As we move toward the heart of the novel, the narrators (Victor Frankenstein and the monster) become increasingly more forthcoming with their flaws, their fallen natures. Despite the guilt they feel, they are conscious of the choices they have made, and continue to make. As writer-creators, they have greater power—while also being more isolated and vulnerable. Frankenstein edits Walton's story as he sees fit; similarly, the monster edits Frankenstein's story, telling him the ways in which his assumptions have been incorrect, asking him to see the events of his story more honestly.

As *Frankenstein* progresses, its outer, obscuring narrative layer is peeled away. The ambition that Walton displays may at first appear admirable, but once Victor Frankenstein takes over as the "creator" of the story, we see that Frankenstein's version of ambition—his revision—is better informed, as Frankenstein has seen its damaging effects firsthand. Accordingly, Victor Frankenstein, as the new author of the text, steers the novel in a new direction. First, he explains how he, like Walton, was tempted by ambition, but later, his narrative leads us to the heart of the matter: the consequences of overreaching ambition.

In telling his story to Walton in chapter 2, Victor Frankenstein describes his relationship with Elizabeth Lavenza, the childhood friend to whom he becomes engaged, and we quickly notice that he describes her just as Walton has been described:

> Elizabeth was of a calmer and more concentrated disposition; but, with all my ardour, I was capable of a more intense application, and was more deeply smitten with the thirst for knowledge. She busied herself with following the aerial creations of the poets; and in the majestic and wondrous scenes which surrounded our Swiss home. . . . While my companion contemplated with a serious and satisfied spirit the magnificent appearances of things, I delighted in investigating their causes.
>
> (p. 36)

Victor Frankenstein's pursuit—educational at first, then creational—is unlike both Walton's and Elizabeth's: it is less tempered, more susceptible to wildness and chaos. In his studies, he turns first to the occult sciences, whose chimerical works ignite his ambition. Quickly, though (chapter 3), he becomes disillusioned: "[He] entertained the greatest disdain for a would-be science, which could never even step within the threshold of real knowledge" (p. 43). Furthermore, when Victor's professor of natural philosophy condemns Victor's early interest in alchemy, Victor seems fully resolved to put such studies behind him. However, when he turns to so-called real knowledge (chapter 4), he realizes that he "was required to exchange chimeras of boundless grandeur for realities of little worth" (p. 51). He is a young ambitious creator under various influences, and his activity is volatile. He reveals this instability by explaining his decision to follow "the steps already marked" while also declaring that he will "pioneer a new way, explore unknown powers, and unfold to the world the deepest mysteries of creation" (p. 53). The conflict revealed here foreshadows the trouble that plagues him throughout the course of the novel, as a man with creative ambitions. Ultimately, he ignores his forebears when choosing to break new ground as a scientist. The novel proves this type of self-isolation to be destructive.

Just prior to executing his plans to bestow "animation upon lifeless matter" (p. 59), Victor Frankenstein changes his narration. Instead of simply relating the events of his story, he reminds us that he is telling the story to Walton (who, in turn, is writing the story in a letter to his sister):

> I see by your eagerness, and the wonder and hope which your eyes express, my friend, that you expect to be informed of the secret with which I am acquainted; that cannot be: listen patiently until the end of my story, and you will easily perceive why I am reserved upon that subject. I will not lead you on, unguarded and ardent as I then was, to your destruction and infallible misery. Learn from me, if not by my precepts, at least by my example, how dangerous is the acquirement of knowledge.
>
> (p. 60)

This self-conscious allusion to the novel's narrative structure reminds us that writing—Victor Frankenstein telling his story, and Walton writing it down—is primarily an attempt to stave off the destructive consequences of isolation. At sea, Walton is without a sympathetic companion until he meets Victor Frankenstein, who has traveled to the pole in pursuit of the monster and is similarly isolated. The story of

Frankenstein is one of linked narration; each narrator, in telling his story, is attempting to save himself from dehumanizing detachment.

The act of telling his story provides Victor Frankenstein with new hope for life; his previous creative act—reconstructing dead body parts, then reanimating them—nearly kills him. "My cheek had grown pale with study, and my person had become emaciated with confinement" (p. 62), he says, describing his "secret toil" in "a solitary chamber, or rather cell, at the top of the house." Much of his work is conducted during the "beautiful . . . plentiful" summer months (which was also when Mary Shelley engaged in the story-writing competition), though his "eyes were insensible to the charms of nature." He ignores the affections of his family and friends while "the great object, which swallowed up every habit of [his] nature, should be completed" (p. 64). Life and death are not opposites; they are presented as two closely linked states of being.

Just as Victor Frankenstein is enumerating the ways in which isolation and hard-nosed ambition have destroyed cultures throughout history, he again shifts gears in his narration, addressing Walton directly: "I forget that I am moralizing in the most interesting part of my tale; and your looks remind me to proceed." Again, the story reveals a reverence for storytelling itself, which is portrayed as a more creative act than Victor Frankenstein's reanimation of decaying body parts. "I appeared rather like one doomed by slavery to toil in the mines . . . than an artist occupied by his favourite employment" (p. 65). Near the end of the novel, after completing his story of the monster, Victor Frankenstein enjoys only one comfort: imagining conversations with his friends, whom he considers to be "not the creations of his fancy, but the beings themselves who visit him from the regions of a remote world" ("Walton, in Continuation," p. 286). With both Clerval, his dearest friend, and Elizabeth, dead, his only solace is tranquil imagination, and relating these imaginings to Walton.

After Victor Frankenstein creates his monster, the monster escapes the "solitary chamber" where he was given life. When the two are reunited, Victor wants only to kill his creation, but the monster eludes him, and says (chapter 10), "Be calm! I entreat you to hear me" (p. 127). Victor, at first, rejects this request by saying, "There can be no community between you and me" (p. 128)—intending to deny the "community" of author and reader. The monster continues to plead his case: "But am I not alone, miserably alone? . . . Listen to my tale: when you have heard that, abandon or commiserate me, as you shall judge that I deserve. But hear me." Whereas the "community" formed by Victor Frankenstein and Walton (the novel's first author/reader "community") was an amicable arrangement, the union of monster and creator is contentious and painful. "Why do you call to my remembrance . . . circumstances, of which I shudder to reflect, that I have been the miserable origin and author?" asks Victor Frankenstein. The monster responds with a threat: "On you it rests whether I quit for ever the neighbourhood of man, and lead a harmless life, or become the scourge of your fellow-creatures, and the author of your own speedy ruin" (p. 130). Here, both Victor Frankenstein and his monster are authors, and it appears at first that Victor Frankenstein must make a choice, either to acknowledge his own authorship (by allowing his creation a voice) or to ignore the monster's voice—thus invigorating the monster's violent authorship.

Essentially, authorship for both is inevitable, and Mary Shelley reveals her two protagonists' interchangeability, the "community" between them. The monster is a primordial, inner version of his creator; Victor Frankenstein is a more deliberate, guilt-ridden version of the monster. They despise each other, and yet they are inextricably bound: the monster must tell his story to Victor Frankenstein—he is the only one who will hear it. This exchange becomes the innermost (and most important) of the novel's three concentric circles of narration, but the community between them provides no solace;

their dialogue resembles the isolated imaginings of *one* mind, not two.

The monster's actions—and his narration—are at the heart of *Frankenstein.* The monster's rendition of authorship, as the novel's innermost, internal story, is appropriately transparent, raw and visceral. Most of the novel's action springs from the monster's activity (and the affect these activities have on Victor Frankenstein). Mary Shelley charts the development of this "author," her monstrous, primordial creator, from his beginnings. At first, he is as innocent as any wide-eyed human child. When in chapter 11 he recalls the "original era of [his] being," he tells that "a strange multiplicity of sensations seized me, and I saw, felt, heard, and smelt, at the same time. . . . it was, indeed, a long time before I learned to distinguish between the operations of my various senses" (p. 131). As a product of Victor Frankenstein's laboratory, he is physically and intellectually capable of authorship, but he is new to the world—everything must be experienced and learned. "Sometimes I tried to imitate the pleasant songs of the birds, but was unable. Sometimes I wished to express my sensations in my own mode, but the uncouth and inarticulate sounds which broke from me frightened me into silence again" (p. 133). Living in isolation, he is unable to acquire language, but soon, he finds a way to spy on the De Lacey family, from whom he learns how to speak, and, concurrently, how to feel: "I felt sensations of a peculiar and overpowering nature: they were a mixture of pain and pleasure, such as I had never before experienced" (pp. 139–140). As he watches them in their cottage (from an adjoining level), the monster longs to join the family—young Agatha and Felix, brother and sister, and their blind father—but dares not to, because all who see him are horrified by his appearance.

From this safe distance, he continues to become emotionally attached to the De Lacey family. In chapter 12 he makes the following observation: "These people possessed a method of communicating their experience and feelings to one another by articulate sounds. I perceived that the words they spoke sometimes produced pleasure or pain, smiles or sadness, in the minds and countenances of the hearers. This was indeed a godlike science, and I ardently desired to become acquainted with it" (p. 144).

There is a conspicuous lack of references to God in *Frankenstein,* but here, even a new-to-the-world monster recognizes the sanctity of language. Soon, he sees Felix De Lacey reading to his father (chapter 12), and he discerns "that [Felix] found on the paper signs for speech which he understood, and I ardently longed to comprehend these also" (p. 147). By witnessing this act of reading—which he sees as an expression of love—the monster becomes all the more attached to the De Laceys, wanting "to discover the motives and feelings of these lovely creatures" (p. 149). He imagines presenting himself to them, and winning them over—despite his horrific appearance—with his "gentle demeanour and conciliating words." Fresh to the world, the monster has great faith in the power of language as a form of communication and reconciliation. He witnesses the education of a young Arabian woman (Safie, Felix's lover, who visits the De Laceys while the monster is spying on them) and diligently acquires enough fluency with language to mirror her studies of history, government, and religion. But what he realizes, then, is that by better understanding the world, he is better able to recognize his isolation. In chapter 13 he states, "When I looked around, I saw and heard of none like me. . . . I cannot describe to you the agony that these reflections inflicted upon me: I tried to dispel them, but sorrow only increased with knowledge" (p. 157). The more he knows, the less satisfied he is as a witness—the more he feels "shut out from intercourse with them." As a being denied any ability to communicate, his introspection becomes increasingly painful and desperate. "I had never yet seen a being resembling me, or who claimed any intercourse with me. What was I?" These thoughts are the seed for the monster's later transgressions.

In chapter 15, the monster's fall from innocence is further spurred when, while walking in the woods, he happens upon a leather trunk containing "*Paradise Lost*, a volume of *Plutarch's Lives*, and the *Sorrows of Werther*." (p. 167). Just as the monster grows attached to the De Laceys as he learns their language, so too does he assign great emotional significance to the reading of these texts.

> As I read . . . I applied much personally to my own feelings and condition. I found myself similar, yet at the same time strangely unlike to the beings concerning whom I read, and to whose conversation I was a listener. I sympathized with, and partly understood them, but I was unformed in mind; I was dependent on none and related to none. "The path of my departure was free;" and there was none to lament my annihilation. My person was hideous and my stature gigantic. What did this mean? Who was I? What was I? Whence did I come? What was my destination?
>
> (p. 169)

Here, the act of reading is seen as a communion of souls, a way to love and be loved. By reading these texts, he realizes exactly what he longs for: he wants his feelings of sympathy to be received by another, and for others to understand him. *Paradise Lost*, which he reads as "a true history," affects him profoundly; he interprets the text as a path to help him find his way in the world. The monster speaks of Milton's poem and Victor Frankenstein's journal (a text found by the monster which specifies the details of his origin) in a similar way; they are both essential texts to be studied, and they both elicit a passionate reaction. They create great introspection, and great longing. By knowing what he is (from the journal) and what his role might be (from *Paradise Lost*), his ambition is piqued. Like Walton and Victor Frankenstein, he desires to reach well beyond his limitations.

PARADISE LOST

The cautionary aspect of *Frankenstein*—in addition to the multiple references to *Paradise Lost* throughout the text (including the novel's epigraph)—reveals Mary Shelley's preoccupation with Milton's poetic tale of Promethean ambition. All three narrators in *Frankenstein* have a Miltonic inclination to question their existence, to solve the problem of their being. Just after the monster asks, "Who was I? What was I? Whence did I come? What was my destination?" he reads *Paradise Lost*—he stumbles upon it, and he receives it as an answer to his questions. It becomes the monster's most important instructional text (just as it was, perhaps, Mary Shelley's most important literary point of reference when writing *Frankenstein*; she read it with Percy Shelley, and she studied it on her own). The monster's longings ruin him; by the end of the novel, he and his creator remain horribly isolated, alone, and left to die. Just as Milton's Satan is punished for his desire, so too is the monster (as well as Frankenstein). By the end of *Paradise Lost*, Adam and Eve are fallen, isolated entities; so too are Victor Frankenstein and his monster.

After the monster reads Milton's poem, he begins to explore his relationship to the poem's characters:

> Like Adam, I was apparently united by no link to any other being in existence; but his state was far different from mine in every other respect. He had come forth from the hands of God a perfect creature, happy and prosperous, guarded by the especial care of his Creator; he was allowed to converse with, and acquire knowledge from, beings of a superior nature: but I was wretched, helpless, and alone. Many times I considered Satan as the fitter emblem of my condition; for often, like him, when I viewed the bliss of my protectors, the bitter gall of envy rose within me.
>
> (p. 170)

Hell is a parody of heaven, and hell's creations are deformed imitations of heaven's creations. The monster recognizes that his circumstance is similar to Adam's, but he also knows he has not "come forth from the hands of God a perfect creature"—he has no comforting ties to anyone.

His dissatisfaction, and envy, is similar to Satan's, though "Satan had his companions, fellow-devils, to admire and encourage him; but I am solitary and abhorred" (p. 171). As Gilbert and Gubar show in *The Madwoman in the Attic,* the monster's confusion is indicative of his changing nature—both he and Victor Frankenstein, at different stages in the novel, are similar to each one of the major characters in *Paradise Lost.* Early on in their respective stories, they are both characterized as Adam-like innocents: Victor Frankenstein appears guileless, and the monster is an unformed, primordial creature. When he creates the monster, Victor Frankenstein is doing work which is normally left to God—while the monster, once he begins to wield control as Victor Frankenstein's "master," also becomes God-like. Victor, too, is similar to Satan—both he and Satan are tormented overreachers, while the monster and Satan are both envious, vengeful demons. Perhaps the most telling likeness, though, is found between *Frankenstein*'s two protagonists and Eve, the fallen woman—the antihero of *Paradise Lost.* Eve was not formed in God's image, she was a distortion of Adam's form. She was not allowed Adam's connection to "beings of a superior nature"; she was alone. In addition, as Milton shows us, she further deforms herself—morally—by desiring knowledge. The monster reads *Paradise Lost* and wonders why he isn't allowed Adam's privilege; it seems Mary Shelley casts him as the unfortunate inheritor of Eve's sin.

After creating his monster, Victor Frankenstein is overwhelmed with feelings of guilt; every evil deed that is attributed to the monster, Victor attributes to himself. Like Victor, Eve is a reservoir for guilty feelings; she, too, suffers the consequences of being afflicted by a dangerous hunger for knowledge. In chapter 4 Victor asks himself, "Whence . . . did the principle of life proceed? It was a bold question, and one which has ever been considered as a mystery; yet with how many things are we upon the brink of becoming acquainted, if cowardice or carelessness did not restrain our inquiries" (p. 58). He challenges himself to act brazenly, just as the serpent challenges Eve. Because we are told the story in retrospect—it is a story Victor is telling Robert Walton—we learn of Victor's naïveté and his regret simultaneously. He says to Walton, "Listen patiently until the end of my story, and you will easily perceive why I am reserved upon that subject. Learn from me, if not by my precepts, at least by my example, how dangerous is the acquirement of knowledge" (p. 60). Like Victor, Eve unknowingly eats the fruit by which she has been tempted, availing death and despair and isolation. Perhaps the most defining shared characteristic of Eve and Victor's, though, is that they both have the ability to create—they are both mothers. (Most female writers of the time were *not* mothers. Given her pregnancies—those that miscarried and those that were brought to term—it is not surprising that Mary Shelley was preoccupied with procreation and its ramifications.) For both Eve and Victor, reproduction and death are inextricably bound, a bind rife throughout *Frankenstein.*

The language that Mary Shelley uses to describe Victor Frankenstein's creation is unmistakably similar to the language used to describe birth. Victor tells us of his "incredible labour and fatigue" (p. 59), explaining that "after so much time spent in painful labour, to arrive at once at the summit of my desires was the most gratifying consummation of my toils." Victor's creation, though, is an explicit perversion. Mary Shelley has rewritten Milton's Eve in an exaggerated, distorted form—a man who is at once obsessed and repulsed by his "filthy creation." The being Victor creates is not merely a fallen being but a murderous fiend. By accentuating Victor's fallen nature, while also casting him as an Eve-like character, Mary Shelley reminds us that in *Paradise Lost,* femaleness—the ability to give birth—is an imperfect state. With every birth, the necessity of isolation and death is born, too. The monster becomes an amplified version of Victor, and of Eve: at first innocent, then, after stumbling upon self- consciousness, an outcast.

Much of Eve's guilt stems from her creation—not as a perfect being in God's image, as Adam was created, but as a distortion, a less-than-pure birth. She is born of Adam's rib, just as the monster is assembled from various body parts of others. ("The dissecting room and the slaughterhouse furnished many of my materials" [p. 63], says Victor Frankenstein in chapter 4.) As an exaggeration of Eve's moral deformity, the monster is a grotesque construction, large and unwieldy: "As the minuteness of the parts formed a great hindrance to my speed, I resolved, contrary to my first intention, to make the being of gigantic stature; that is to say, about eight feet in height, and proportionally large" (p. 61). The physicality of the monster—its enormity, its horrific appearance, its superhuman strength—becomes an expression of Victor's sin, his ambition, and another representation of "filthy creation." The monster's grotesque appearance describes Mary Shelley's conflicting thoughts about the distention of pregnancy and the way in which birth and death are inextricably bound. While writing *Frankenstein,* Mary was pregnant out of wedlock, and had already been the mother of a premature illegitimate baby who died at two weeks, before being named. Her mother, whose name Mary shared, had died giving birth to Mary. For Mary Shelley, birth was associated with death—at its starkest, birth is simply a way to bring more death into the world.

The monster, as an Eve-like creation, bears the burden of Victor's sin, just as Eve is blamed for the human desire for knowledge. In both cases, blame and punishment is displaced. When the monster visits Victor Frankenstein and Elizabeth Lavenza on their wedding night, Mary Shelley provides another opportunity for displaced punishment. Throughout the novel, Elizabeth is presented as selfless and innocent, perfect in all ways. "Every one loved Elizabeth," says Victor in chapter 1. "The passionate and almost reverential attachment with which all regarded her became, while I shared it, my pride and delight." (p. 35). Later, he admits: "I would die to make her happy" (p. 255). The monster understands that to best punish Victor Frankenstein, he must kill Elizabeth rather than Victor himself, on the night of their wedding. The most explicitly feminine character in *Frankenstein*—like Eve—becomes the victim, while the crime makes Victor Frankenstein even more isolated.

"Filthy creation"—an aesthetic born of moral corruption—runs parallel to Victor Frankenstein's failed authorship. Despite Victor's efforts of creation, his stubborn desire to retreat from others leads only to destruction. Throughout the novel, isolation (most often expressed as an inability to communicate) is the unrelenting catalyst of death and despair.

THE BLASTED TREE

Elizabeth's murder becomes another example in the novel of the inextricable connection between birth and death. Victor Frankenstein's creation, the birth of a monster, leads to many deaths; by killing Elizabeth, the monster ensures the end of further procreation. Elizabeth's death becomes the necessary result of the monster's birth—it is the monster's crowning achievement, his most perfect revenge.

However, the monster's turn to violence is not immediate; at first, his intentions are innocent. Before he is discovered by the De Lacey family, the monster speaks repeatedly of his great affection for them: "I tenderly love these friends; I have, unknown to them, been for many months in the habits of daily kindness towards them" (p. 176). Just after he utters these words, though, Felix, Safie, and Agatha find him alone with the elder, blind Mr. De Lacey; Agatha faints, Safie flees, and Felix beats the monster with a stick. The monster can no longer maintain an imagined connection to the family, and he desires their destruction for the first time. "My feelings were those of rage and revenge. I could with pleasure have destroyed the cottage and its inhabitants, and have glutted myself with their shrieks and misery" (p. 179). Once the monster realizes that his love for the De Lacy family is not reciprocated, his imaginings become chaotic and violent: "I, like the arch- fiend, bore a hell within me; and finding myself unsympathised with, wished to tear up the trees, spread havoc and destruction around me, and then to have sat down and enjoyed the ruin. . . . There was none among the myriads of men that existed who would pity or assist me. . . . from that moment I declared everlasting war against the species" (pp. 179–180). Clearly, this is a drastic shift from his earlier sentiments, and his new feelings of abomination arise entirely from his inability to relate his existence with another. "Unfeeling, heartless creator!" he cries to Victor Frankenstein in chapter 16, "You had endowed me with perceptions and passions, and then cast me abroad an object for the scorn and horror of mankind" (p. 184).

While the Romantic sensibility celebrates the individual expression of perception and passion, the monster's existence—and his violence—is determined by his inability to express such things. In chapter 15, in pleading with Victor Frankenstein to create a female companion for him, the monster says, "If I cannot inspire love, I will cause fear" (p. 192). The monster suggests, though, that if Victor Frankenstein creates a female monster, there will be no cause for violence, and the pair will retreat to "the vast wilds of South America," in peace. "The love of another will destroy the cause of my crimes, and I shall become a thing of whose existence every one will be ignorant." Despite this promise, Victor Frankenstein, as a fallen being himself, is wary; he does not believe such retreat is possible. Having heard the monster's story, he admits in chapter 19, "I saw an insurmountable barrier placed between me and my fellow-men; this barrier was sealed with the blood of William and Justine" (pp. 211–212). (William is the boy

whom the monster accidentally kills; the boy's mother, Justine, is falsely accused of murder and is sentenced to death.) He knows that the isolation he witnesses in the monster is his own; they are similarly fallen, wrecked, beings—and Victor sees no possible reconciliation with the world. For a time after the monster's proposition, the hope of a happy marriage with Elizabeth flickers, but to recognize such happiness would necessitate ignoring his isolating work, his promise to the monster—to create a mate— which would ensure the destruction of his marriage and himself. Seeing no way out, Victor Frankenstein nevertheless returns to his studies—his isolation, his ambition—for comfort. "Company was irksome to me; when alone, I could fill my mind with the sights of heaven and earth. . . . I could thus cheat myself into a transitory peace" (p. 211). However, this "transitory peace" makes him all the more despairing because it reminds him of his childhood.

> I was formed for peaceful happiness. During my youthful days discontent never visited my mind; and if I was ever overcome by ennui, the sight of what is beautiful in nature, or the study of what is excellent and sublime in the productions of man could always interest my heart, and communicated elasticity to my spirits. But I am a blasted tree; the bolt has entered my soul; and I felt then that I should survive to exhibit, what I shall soon cease to be—a miserable spectacle of wrecked humanity, pitiable to others, and intolerable to myself.
>
> (p. 214)

Victor Frankenstein first mentions this "blasted tree" earlier in his narrative, describing in chapter 2 the onset of his interest in science, when he was fifteen. "We witnessed a most violent and terrible thunderstorm. . . . I beheld a stream of fire issue from an old and beautiful oak . . . and so soon as the dazzling light vanished the oak had disappeared, and nothing remained but a blasted stump. . . . I never beheld anything so utterly destroyed" (pp. 42–43). This occasion reveals to him the power of evidentiary science—and while it makes an impression on him, he chooses instead a more isolating, heretical path. He interprets his witnessing of the blasted tree as "the last effort made by the spirit of preservation to avert the storm that was even then hanging in the stars, and ready to envelop me." By not heeding the lesson of the blasted tree, he becomes a blasted tree himself—just as he becomes a monster (when he accepts blame for the murder of William, Justine, Clerval, and Elizabeth) by creating the monster and not heeding the monster's warnings.

"ATROCIOUS SELFISHNESS"

Repeatedly, Mary Shelley reminds her readers of Victor Frankenstein's stubborn isolation, which ultimately destroys him. Even after the monster murders Frankenstein's closest friend, Henry Clerval, Frankenstein refuses to share the details of his "filthy creation" with anyone, including his father and his soon-to-be wife. In chapter 22 he states, "I could not bring myself to disclose a secret which would fill my hearer with consternation, and make fear and unnatural horror the inmates of his breast" (p. 250). Accordingly, his fate and the monster's are the same: they are silenced, and their silence torments them. "I checked . . . my impatient thirst for sympathy, and was silent when I would have given the world to have confided the fatal secret. Yet still words like those I have recorded would burst uncontrollably from me. I could offer no explanation of them; but their truth in part relieved the burden of my mysterious woe" (p. 250). The human desire to express and be heard is subverted, and the result is uncontrolled, distorted, monstrous.

Tragically, though, the more Victor Frankenstein is in need of quenching his "thirst for sympathy," the more fearful he is to share anything. Imprisoned by this inability to be understood, Victor Frankenstein is the monster's "slave," while the truth of the monster's destructive capabilities is his "master." No one but

Robert Walton, alone on the desolate Arctic Ocean, is privy to Victor's story. "The sun and the heavens," says Victor Frankenstein, "who have viewed my operations, can bear witness of my truth" (p. 251). Resigned to such isolation—for which only the sky offers silent sympathy—Victor Frankenstein turns inward. "Sufficient for me was the consciousness of [my crimes]" (251), he says. Before her death Elizabeth gives Victor a final opportunity to be heard, a last chance to avoid isolation by sharing his secrets. Victor resists; again, he fears the consequences of expression. Throughout the novel, his torment becomes increasingly transparent. When Justine is wrongly sentenced to death for a murder the monster committed, Victor says (chapter 8), "A thousand times would rather I have confessed myself guilty of the crime" (p. 101), but he does not confess, and Justine is killed. When he finds that his dear friend Clerval has been killed by the monster (chapter 21), Victor asks himself, "Why did I not die?" (p. 237), and yet it was his own choice to remain isolated, as it was his choice to create the monster. At nearly every turn, Mary Shelley reveals an opportunity for Victor to save himself from destruction, but he is unable to do so. He repeatedly admits that he would rather die himself than be bound to the monster, though others die while he remains under the monster's rule. "The threat I had heard weighed on my thoughts, but I did not reflect that a voluntary act of mine could avert it" (p. 229). He decides his own fate by overstepping his bounds as a scientist-author, yet he claims to be a victim of fate, too. By keeping his secret from Elizabeth, he ensures her death; he refers to his enslavement to the monster as a "miserable marriage"—and yet he embraces the isolation resulting from the keeping of secrets, rather than seeking the refuge of communion (of an actual marriage) with Elizabeth. Victor Frankenstein never re-linquishes his role as an overreacher; to the end, he believes that he can will himself to be saved, while never recognizing the danger of such unrelenting will.

THE ENDURANCE OF *FRANKENSTEIN*

Mary Shelley wrote *Frankenstein* in the wake of the Industrial Revolution in Britain, a time of rapid development spurred by the introduction of machines. This was a chaotic time in the West: governments had been overthrown and remained unsettled, cities were growing, and productivity was accelerating. The will of the individual was becoming increasingly obscured by the machinations of industrial society. *Frankenstein* issued from this new environment; the novel expressed the vitality of the human will amid such industrial progress.

However, *Frankenstein* was embraced by only a few critics during the first hundred years it was printed, and most of these critics attacked the tale's debased morality and its visceral, graphic details. As Johanna Smith states in "A Critical History of *Frankenstein*" (in *Frankenstein: Complete, Authoritative Text with Biographical, Historical, and Cultural Contexts,* 2000), one early critic focused on the novel's "impiety" and was concerned that it would encourage those with a "desperately inflamed . . . appetite . . . for every sort of wonder" (p. 329). The concern was, it seems, that if a primordial creature, such as Victor Frankenstein's monster, is susceptible to the ill affects of an overindulgence of sensation, readers might be vulnerable to such moral deformity, too. While it was Mary Shelley's intention to look beyond the merely tranquil passions of conventional Romanticism, her audiences may not have been ready to admit their appetite for "impiety." Near the end of the nineteenth century, some critics were at least ready to acknowledge the ambiguity of *Frankenstein*'s moral message—in 1886 the Reverend Hugh Haweis wrote in his introduction to *Frankenstein* that his reservations concerned the fact that the novel's "moral thrust—if there is any—is vague and indeterminate." Modern readers, though, seem more comfortable with this indeterminacy; we can sympathize with Victor Frankenstein's passions while also judging him for the path he

chooses. His obsession with searching for an authentic self in a world of seductive technology is perhaps more resonant today than it was when *Frankenstein* was first published.

The novel's structure emphasizes the idea of the magnification of self; as the narration moves from Robert Walton to Victor Frankenstein to the monster, the reader is presented with three versions of a single identity, each new version a magnification of its predecessor. The technology of monster-making is presented as an expression of self—despite Mary Shelley's use of what was once deemed lurid, inhuman language to describe such technology. The destructive power of lightning, as an example of the effects of evidentiary science, is that which first seduces young Victor Frankenstein, and Mary Shelley uses similarly powerful, energetic language to describe his later acts of "filthy creation." The seduction of discovery—described first by Robert Walton in an early letter penned to his sister ("I feel my heart glow with an enthusiasm which elevates me to heaven")—is shared by all three narrators. While the alluring power of discovery may steer the narrators of *Frankenstein*, readers find that the only true "discoveries" to be made in the novel are Victor's humanity, his fallibility, his mortality. Technological achievement parallels the discovery of the authentic self. This concept remains relevant, and is in part responsible for the endurance of *Frankenstein*.

In the last chapter, Victor Frankenstein notes that his search for the monster in the Arctic expanse marked the point when his "wanderings began" (p. 273), though such wanderings—for human righteousness amid seductive technologies—occupy him throughout the novel. Even in the end, close to death, he continues to look back in wonder at his prior ambition: "I cannot recollect without passion my reveries while the work was incomplete. I trod heaven in my thoughts, now exulting in my powers, now burning with the idea of their effects" ("Walton, In Continuation," p. 285). While Victor fears he is defined by the monster's rule, the reader recognizes the monster as an expression of Victor himself—not a threatening "other" but a manifestation of his fallen self.

In the early part of the nineteenth century, Mary Shelley was attributing to earthbound matter what had previously only been attributed to "spirit"; she imbued man with the powers of God. It was a radical idea at the time, one that was met with a great deal of skepticism, but her idea—her dream vision—was prophetic. Essentially, Mary Shelley had written a new version of Milton's *Paradise Lost,* without devils or angels or God; these roles were played by humans, and the products of human imagination. She had also written a novel that can be received as a critique of Wordsworth's *Prelude* and other Romantic texts—a novel in which "Spots of Time" are not revealing, contemplative moments but rather repetitious, chaotic warnings that are never heeded.

Mary Shelley's story continues to live in the modern imagination. Numerous film adaptations (including 1931's *Frankenstein,* staring Boris Karloff, and 1994's *Mary Shelley's Frankenstein,* staring Robert DeNiro and Kenneth Branagh) exemplify the modern taste for a story in which a man suffers from the choices he makes. Today, a "Frankenstein" (a thing that becomes terrifying to its creator) holds a common place in our lexicon and in our culture.

In the modern world, while technological progress continues to accelerate, the ideas in *Frankenstein* remain relevant. The claim that man himself, not the technology he creates, is responsible for corruption in the world remains a reminder of the power of human will and the dangers of ignorance.

Selected Bibliography

EDITIONS

All citations are from the Modern Library edition.

Frankenstein, or, The Modern Prometheus. Edited by Wendy Steiner. New York: Modern Library, 1999.

Frankenstein: The 1818 Text, Contexts, Nineteenth-Century Responses, Modern Criticism. Edited by J. Paul Hunter. New York: Norton, 1996.

Frankenstein: Complete, Authoritative Text with Biographical, Historical, and Cultural Contexts, Critical History, and Essays from Contemporary Critical Perspectives. Edited by Johanna M. Smith. Boston: Bedford/ St. Martin's, 2000. Includes an introduction to psychoanalytic, feminist, gender, Marxist, and cultural criticism.

OTHER WORKS BY MARY SHELLEY

The Journals of Mary Shelley: 1814–1844. Edited by Paula R. Feldman and Diana Scott-Kilvert. New York: Oxford University Press, 1987.

The Letters of Mary Wollstonecraft Shelley. Edited by Betty T. Bennett. 3 vols. Baltimore: Johns Hopkins University Press, 1980–1988.

The Novels and Selected Works of Mary Shelley. Edited by Nora Crook, with Pamela Clemit. London and Brookfield, Vt.: W. Pickering, 1996.

RELATED PRIMARY WORKS

Coleridge, Samuel Taylor. *Poetical Works.* Edited by J. C. C. Mays. Princeton, N.J.: Princeton University Press, 2001.

Godwin, William. *Enquiry Concerning Political Justice, with Selections from Godwin's Other Writings.* Edited by K. Codell Carter. Oxford: Clarendon, 1971.

Milton, John. *Complete Poems and Major Prose.* Edited by Merritt Y. Hughes. New York: Odyssey Press, 1957.

Shelley, Percy Bysshe. *The Letters of Percy Bysshe Shelley.* Edited by Betty Bennett. 3 vols. Baltimore: Johns Hopkins University Press, 1980–1988.

———. *Shelley's Poetry and Prose: Authoritative Texts, Criticism.* Edited by Donald H. Reiman and Neil Fraistat. New York: Norton, 2002.

Wollstonecraft, Mary. *A Vindication of the Rights of Woman.* New York: Penguin, 1992.

Wordsworth, William. *The Prelude, 1799, 1805, 1850.* Edited by Jonathan Wordsworth, M. H. Abrams, and Stephen Gill. New York: Norton, 1979.

SECONDARY WORKS

Baldick, Chris. *In Frankenstein's Shadow: Myth, Monstrosity, and Nineteenth-Century Writing.* New York: Oxford University Press, 1987.

Bann, Stephen, ed. *Frankenstein, Creation, and Monstrosity.* London: Reaktion Books, 1994.

Behrendt, Stephen C., ed. *Approaches to Teaching Shelley's Frankenstein.* New York: Modern Language Association of America, 1990. A helpful, thorough guide for teachers.

Bennett, Betty T., and Stuart Curran, eds. *Mary Shelley in Her Times.* Baltimore: Johns Hopkins University Press, 2000.

Botting, Fred. *Making Monstrous: Frankenstein, Criticism, Theory.* New York: St. Martin's Press, 1991.

Bump, Jerome. "Mary Shelley's Subversion of Male Myths of Creativity in *Frankenstein.*" In *The Ethics of Popular Culture: From "Frankenstein" to Cyberculture.* Edited by Ingo R. Stoehr. Kilgore, Tex.: Second Dimension, 1995.

Cason, James B. "Bringing the Author Forward: *Frankenstein* through Mary Shelley's Letters." *Criticism* 30, no. 4 (fall 1988): 431–453.

Forry, Steven Earl. *Hideous Progenies: Dramatizations of Frankenstein from Mary Shelley to the Present.* Philadelphia: University of Pennsylvania Press, 1990.

Frantz, Andrea Breemer. *Redemption and Madness: Three Nineteenth-Century Feminist Views on Motherhood and Childbearing.* Las Colinas, Tex.: Ide House, 1993.

Gilbert, Sandra M., and Susan Gubar. *The Madwoman in the Attic: The Woman Writer and the Nineteenth-Century Literary Imagination.* London and New Haven: Yale University Press, 1979.

Haweis, Hugh Reginald. Introduction to *Frankenstein, or, The Modern Prometheus.* By Mary Shelley. London: George Routledge, 1886. Pp. 5–9.

Kaplan, Morton. "Fantasy of Paternity and the Doppleganger: Mary Shelley's *Frankenstein.*" In *The Unspoken Motive: A Guide to Psychoanalytic Literary Criticism.* Edited by Morton Kaplan and Robert Kloss. New York: Free Press, 1973. Pp. 119–145.

Ketterer, David. *Frankenstein's Creation: The Book, the Monster, and Human Reality.* Victoria, B.C.: University of Victoria Press, 1979.

Levine, George, and U. C. Knoepflmacher. *The Endurance of Frankenstein: Essays on Mary Shelley's Novel.* Berkeley: University of California Press, 1979. An important survey of *Frankenstein* criticism.

Lowe-Evans, Mary. *Critical Essays on Mary Wollstonecraft Shelley.* New York: G. K. Hall, 1998.

Marshall, David. *The Surprising Effects of Sympathy: Marivaux, Diderot, Rousseau, and Mary Shelley.* Chicago: University of Chicago Press, 1988.

McWhir, Anne. "Teaching the Monster to Read: Mary Shelley, Education and *Frankenstein.*" In *The Educational Legacy of Romanticism.* Edited by John Willinsky. Waterloo, Canada: Wilfrid Laurier University Press, 1990. Pp. 73–92.

Mellor, Anne K. *Mary Shelley: Her Life, Her Fiction, Her Monsters.* New York: Methuen, 1988.

Newman, Beth. "Narratives of Seduction and the Seductions of Narrative: The Frame Structure of *Frankenstein.*" *ELH* 53, no. 1 (spring 1986): 141–163.

Shaw, Debra Benita. *Women, Science, and Fiction: The Frankenstein Inheritance.* New York: Palgrave, 2000.

St. Clair, William. *The Godwins and the Shelleys: The Biography of a Family.* New York: Norton, 1989.

Thornburg, Mary K. Patterson. *The Monster in the Mirror: Gender and the Sentimental/ Gothic Myth in Frankenstein.* Ann Arbor: University of Michigan Research Press, 1987.

Veeder, William. *Mary Shelley and Frankenstein: The Fate of Androgyny.* Chicago: University of Chicago Press, 1986.

Robert Herrick's
Hesperides

TOM D'EVELYN

WHEN *HESPERIDES* WAS published in 1648, Robert Herrick may well have felt that his career was behind him. In 1647, after refusing to submit to ecclesiastical authority, he had been stripped of his post as vicar by the new Puritan government, and the Stuart monarch who had appointed him, Charles I, was in exile. Twenty years earlier, Charles had bestowed on Herrick the vicarage of Dean Prior, in rural Devonshire, after Herrick had served the king in the role of chaplain to the duke of Buckingham, during a 1627 military expedition to the Île de Ré. Herrick dedicated *Hesperides* to Prince Charles, the king's son, an act for which he was branded a royalist. In 1649, Charles I was beheaded.

As we shall see, Herrick's vision of order as embodied in *Hesperides* is deeply rooted in the past. But it is also a response to changes that make the seventeenth century a pivotal period in modern history. These changes may be discussed in terms of religion and politics, but they were broadly cultural. Above all they exhibit a new emphasis on certainty born of anxiety about self and society. As James Simpson says in *Reform and Cultural Revolution,* " 'Renaissance' poetry manifests these two defining features of

modernity: historical solitude and the consciousness of self as open to construction" (127). While this notion of "self" may say more about our postmodernism than about Renaissance selfhood, it does appear that when a poet creates a world like *Hesperides* out of pieces like epigrams, something like "construction" is going on. In any event, a brief review of what we now think of as the English Revolution provides essential background for a reading of Herrick's *Hesperides.* In order to appreciate the complexity of Herrick's response, it is important to see the broad outlines of the changes he witnessed.

The changes which would later break out in civil war are easily identifiable at least as early as the sixteenth century. As queen and supreme governor of the Church of England, Queen Elizabeth followed her father Henry VIII, who, after naming himself "Head" of the Church of England, redistributed monastic properties to his supporters. This involved wholesale dismembering of churches and monasteries. Elizabeth maintained a state-established church under the somewhat tolerant Act of Uniformity, while the pillaging and destruction of church property, including magnificent pieces of medieval art, continued. In foreign policy,

Elizabeth tried to avoid taking sides in continental disputes (yet she was excommunicated by Pius V in 1570) while encouraging colonialization. In short, under Henry and Elizabeth, England grew from a cultural province of France to a European power, with colonies and trade protected by a formidable navy; along with these, the Tudor heritage included a heavy national debt (caused in part by the dissolution of monastic estates, which had been a source of taxation), an increasing reliance on Parliament for revenues (it is said that Elizabeth refused to reform the fiscal system out of dislike for novelty), and religious divisions of enduring intrigue.

The changes that took hold during the Tudors would come to haunt the house of Stuart. In 1603, without incident, Elizabeth was succeeded by James VI of Scotland. As James I, he skirted Parliament in raising revenues and enhanced the Anglican episcopacy. Financial stringencies did not allow for a professional standing army or a trained bureaucracy. With much of the material culture of the old religion destroyed, Puritans wished to purge the Sabbath of traditional customs of holiday. But, in his *Book of Sports* (1618), James rather reasonably reasoned that traditional recreations made the Church of England more attractive to Roman Catholics and also played a crucial role in the political economy by restoring strength and zest for life to the working people. These "sports" included practices well known to readers of *Hesperides*: dancing, hay-games, Whitsun-ales, Morris-dances, and maypoles. As it was, the clergy resisted James's call for "lawful recreation" and he withdrew it. The *Book of Sports* would be revived by his son, Charles I.

During the reign of Charles I, finance and religion, the problems plaguing the reign of James I, continued to weaken the crown. Regarding religion, Charles would turn out to be less tolerant on the whole than his father, James, had been. When Charles sought funds to pursue a continental war with Spain (a war avoided by James and favored now by

CHRONOLOGY

1591	Robert Herrick is born in London and baptized on 24 August, the seventh child of Nicholas Herrick, a prosperous goldsmith, and Julian Stone Herrick. Family has connections to the crown and lives comfortably in London's "Goldsmith's Row."
1592	Death of Nicholas Herrick, possibly by suicide. The family moves to the country to avoid the plague.
1607	Herrick returns to London to learn goldsmith's trade, apprenticed to his uncle Sir William Herrick.
1613	Enters St. John's College, Cambridge University. Awarded bachelor of arts degree in 1617. Transfers to Trinity Hall at Cambridge to study law. Awarded master of arts in 1620.
1623	Ordained a deacon and priest of the Church of England. Moves to London, where he is one of the "sons of Ben," a literary circle surrounding Ben Jonson.
1627	Chaplain to the duke of Buckingham on military expedition to the French Île de Ré.
1628	Buckingham assassinated.
1630	Herrick becomes vicar of Dean Prior, a parish in rural Devonshire, where over the course of fourteen years he composes many of the poems collected in *Hesperides*.
1640	William Laud, archbishop of Canterbury, impeached.
1647	Herrick ousted from vicarage for royalist sympathies. Probably lives in London until 1660, supported by relatives.
1648	Publishes *Hesperides*, dedicated to Prince Charles, son of King Charles I.
1649	Charles I beheaded. Commonwealth of England declared.
1660	English monarchy restored. Prince Charles named King Charles II. Herrick reinstated as vicar of Dean Prior.
1674	Herrick dies, buried at Dean Prior 15 October.

Parliament), Parliament negotiated with him for the "Petition of Right." The petition was Parliament's reply to the King's arbitrary use of power—not only had he imposed unparliamentary taxes, he had coerced freedmen and quartered troops in private homes.

Charles had to agree to the petition. But the petition did not extend to Scotland, and while his father, James, had allowed a wide variety of religious observances in Scotland, Charles tried to impose the English Episcopal system and the prayer book there. The Presbyterian Scots invaded England and defeated an English army at the Battle of Newburn in 1640. In London, landowners and merchants as well as Puritans combined forces in opposition to Charles and his officers. In 1642, Charles invaded Parliament, hoping to arrest key opponents, but they escaped. Soon Parliament had its own army, eventually reorganized by Oliver Cromwell, a Huntingdonshire squire who would become a virtual king through military skill and passionate leadership. In 1649, Parliament executed Charles and abolished the monarchy, the House of Lords, and the Anglican Church. Between 1649 to 1660, England became a Puritan republic; for most of that time, this "republic" was a military dictatorship. During the seventeeth century, the misery of the majority of people in England was deepened by inflation and policies that sent them from the country into London where their plight worsened; even Cromwell, as gentry, had found it hard to maintain his heritage. When Cromwell died in 1658, England was ready to restore the monarchy. Charles II came to the throne in 1660.

Herrick's relationship to these changes was complex. *Hesperides* vividly portrays the misery of life in the country. The label "Royalist" suggests too uniform a commitment on his part to the king's party, policies, and opinions. While the "old religion" of *Hesperides* evokes cultural space occupied and indeed furnished by Roman Catholicism, Herrick was an Anglican, opposing Calvinist predestination, opposing indeed the general drift toward intolerance about

differences of opinion over troubled points of free will, free grace, and predestination, an intolerance that increasingly characterized his times. Yet, as we shall see, Herrick's recognition of "hierarchy" extended from the lowest to the highest creatures; the symbols that embodied the belief in the divine right of kings were, as symbols, part of his heritage as a poet, as was his dependency on those above him in the social order for his livelihood. This system was no ideology, however, and allowed him to criticize as well as praise the King.

As we shall see, Herrick made room in *Hesperides* for subtle analysis of the king's failings as a leader. While we explore his profound appreciation of traditions under seige, we acknowledge that Herrick was not a party man. He could be unruly. In her biography, Marchette Chute suggests that in 1640 Herrick fell foul of church authorities when he spent some time in London without permission. Chute suggests he went to London without dispensation from his bishop to see about publishing a book of poems (nothing came of it). Furthermore, in the report that cites him for nonresidence, it is implied that he was the father of an illegitimate child. The charge seems not to have been followed up by Herrick's local bishop in Exeter. It could well be, Chute adds, that in 1640, the Church of England was in such "serious trouble" that the authorities had no time to pursue the matter.

As for the cultural politics of *Hesperides,* in her chapter on Herrick in *The Politics of Mirth,* Leah Marcus notes that Herrick "sometimes contemplates traditional observances in melancholy retrospect, as though grieving for their passing; but more often, he proposes and 'stage-manages' them through authorial directives to an imagined audience" (p. 141). While contrasting complexity, nuance, and distance of Herrick's world to the irrepressible energies of Jonson's comedy, Marcus also notes that "*Hesperides* is remarkable for its accommodation of sexual energies" that were overlooked by the king and his ministers who pressed for the use of "sports." "A recurring idea in *Hesperides*," Marcus writes, "is 'cleanly-Wantonnesse,' a sexual liberty 'licensed' by its enclosure within a recurrent cycle of sacred events. . . ." (p. 142). In what follows, we shall integrate these observations into an interpretation of Hesperides as a fictive "world," an imaginary order rooted in resistance to change but also in recognition of enduring sources of order beyond change. No more than Plato or Thomas More was Herrick interested in providing a blueprint for action; like Plato and More, his "utopia" or imaginative world is meant as a mirror for the contemplation of the present in light of eternity.

Hesperides, long considered a work of divinity (though anyone who now dips into the text as such is in for a surprise), was, in its dedication, indeed prophetic. In 1660, the English monarchy was restored, Prince Charles became King Charles II, and Herrick's petition to return to his vicarage in Devonshire met with success. However, Herrick's personal restoration as a poet was longer in coming. *Hesperides* had sold moderately well, but the political and social climate of the period ensured that there would be no second edition for a hundred and seventy-five years. After living the last years of his life in virtual silence, Herrick died in 1674. *Hesperides* would wait two centuries for a critical revival.

Herrick has traditionally been praised primarily for his formal accomplishments. He is grouped with Ben Jonson, whom he associated with and was influenced by, and the Cavalier (also called royalist) poets, known for their resurrection of classical poetic forms. Herrick was a master of classical allusion, especially to the Roman poets Horace, Catullus, Martial, the Anacreontic poems, and the epigrams of the Greek Anthology. He is praised for the wide variety of genres he practiced: among the more than fourteen hundred poems making up *Hesperides* are elegies, epitaphs, epigrams, anacreontics, hymns, and songs. Also praised is Herrick's range of tone, from the vulgar to the lofty. Given his fixation on form and verbal craftsmanship, it is no surprise that critics have traditionally

considered him shallow. The English literary critic F. R. Leavis damned him with faint praise for his "charm"; T. S. Eliot failed to discover "unity" in his vast output of poems. He has suffered by contrast to the more "difficult" poets of the metaphysical school, the other dominant movement in seventeenth-century poetry, whose major practitioners were John Donne and George Herbert.

It was only in the late twentieth century that scholars began to explore the cultural contexts of Herrick's poems. Herrick's celebrations of festivity, far from being simple allusions to Horace and other "pagan" authors, directly engage the religious and political controversy of his time, including, as we have seen, King James's arguments in favor of traditional sabbath pastimes. Likewise, his allegiance to the Stuart cause is now seen to be compromised by an acute awareness of the king's limitations as a politician.

THE WORLD OF *HESPERIDES*

If Herrick's formal perfection looks forward to the neoclassicism of the eighteenth century, his imagination is profoundly traditional, with roots in both classical and biblical worlds. *Hesperides* requires us to imagine a community, a community that is profoundly rooted in traditions, classical, Christian, native. *Hesperides* is, in a word, a Christian humanist project. According to Deborah Kuller Shuger in *The Renaissance Bible: Scholarship, Sacrifice, and Subjectivity* (1994), such a project, in "giving aesthetic form to sacred objects, itself seems to efface the boundaries dividing culture from holiness" (p. 159).

Herrick often writes in *Hesperides* of his own death, yet throughout the book, there is a palpable sense not of gloom but of self-transcendence. Among the meanings of *Hesperides* is the western garden, the realm of the dead. In *A History of English Literature* (1987), Alastair Fowler writes: "Even [Herrick's] antiquarian classicism served an ideal of civility that he pursued in response to the challenge of his own time—the engulfing of traditions in disorder and change. The ancient world offered hope of an uncontroversial social model" (p. 105).

Herrick was far from offering "an uncontroversial social model," classical or otherwise. *Hesperides* offers a "world" not of oblivion but of resistance to disorder and the illumination of difference. There can be no doubt that *Hesperides* is the site of resistance to the strategy of Protestantism as described by Deborah Shuger in *Political Theologies in Shakespeare's England: The Sacred and the State in "Measure for Measure"* (2001):

> Protestantism rejected the papal church's claim to be the earthly kingdom of Christ, and abolished or demoted all the traditional loci where the sacred had penetrated the temporal order: anchorites, relics, shrines, images, holy water, consecrated Host. Protestant responses to this second withdrawal of the visible gods and holy shepherds diverged along multiple trajectories, but almost always in search of those loci where the sacred remained or might be reconstituted.
>
> (p. 43)

Shuger defines a Christian society not in terms of the state religion but in terms of the presence of "transcendent principles" ("grace and peace and eternal righteousness") "at work in its midst, taming the powers of evil" (p. 47). In Herrick's time, the "sacral loci" had been devastated by waves of iconoclasm. Eamon Duffy's *The Stripping of the Altars: Traditional Religion in England, c. 1400–c. 1580* (1992), leaves no doubt as to the thoroughness of the abolition and demotion of "all the traditional loci where the sacred had penetrated the temporal order." Since the 1530s, as targets of reform, the main features of popular religion—"the cult of the saints, images, lights, relics, holy days, pilgrimage, pardon, and Purgatory" (p. 370)—were categorized by the reformers with the holidays that deprived the working poor of hours of profitable labor

along with the various encouragements of drunkenness, dancing, and idleness. *Hesperides* gives free rein to such festivities. In *Hesperides,* secular and sacred are mixed together; we see this mix in what Duffy calls the "ritual calendar, in which secular and sacred themes, the polarities of fast and feast and downright misrule, were difficult to disentangle." The mix of "secular and sacred" defines the community of *Hesperides.*

As we shall see, in *Hesperides,* the poems themselves, secular and sacred, become sacral loci; at times it seems that the whole is a work of restoration and a living source of Christian community. Herrick framed his world not in terms of the modern distinction between secular and religious, but in terms of the *"saeculum"*: the time of the world before the end. John Milbank, in *Theology and Social Theory: Beyond Secular Reason* (1991) explains: "Once, there was no 'secular.' . . . The *saeculum,* in the medieval era, was not a space, a domain, but a time—the interval between fall and *eschaton*" (p. 1).

Briefly, then, *Hesperides* belongs to what Shuger, in an essay in *Religion and Culture in Renaissance England* (1997), called "the parochial landscape of early modern England," as one of the "imagined and improvised communities," the "local experiments in sacred community," typical of this period (p. 134). Against the oblivion to which the ways of the old religion had been consigned by Protestant iconoclasts, *Hesperides* is a book of memory.

But Herrick's "memory" is not to be confused with the modern conception of memory, as a power to recall "things." As the popular culture was suppressed, with immense loss of cultural memory, Herrick's literary memory, like that of generations of students, was shaped by curricular emphasis on memorization, by frequent rereading of a small canon of texts, by imitation of those texts in a way that interprets them in terms of some "present," by a method of interpreting texts that calls for the hermeneutic application of principles to new circumstances. His was a highly structured memory.

If *Hesperides* presents a world of sacral loci which taken together help us create an imaginary community, the sense of time in this world needs attention. In our reading of Herrick's book, we will see, in its dedication to Charles, how the world of *Hesperides* begins in the presence of the prince. Next we see, in our reading of Herrick's "Argument of His Book," the hierarchical structuring of this world. Time and space for Herrick are ordered according to revelation, not according to "science." In addition, Herrick exploited the fundamental fact of the text: it unfolds in linear time. The time of the text draws on other orders of time; a play, for example, may "allude" to diurnal time, and "take up" in its hours just that many hours in the time of its characters. In a work as long as *Hesperides*, it is easy to lose track of time. It was only in the late twentieth century that critics began to read *Hesperides* as a temporal whole: that is, with a view to the "flow" of poems and any shape or meaning that flow might have. By definition, "sacral loci" connect the flow of time to transcendence; the sacred and the secular are like the chaff and the wheat in the Gospel parable: hard to separate until the harvest. And this Christian humanist concept of time complicates and enriches our response to *Hesperides*.

PARTAKING IN THE SACRED

The full title of Herrick's book is *Hesperides: or, The Works Both Humane and Divine of Robert Herrick, Esq.* As the title suggests, the book has two parts. The second part has its own title page: *His Noble Numbers: or, His Pious Pieces, Wherein (amongst other things), he sings the Birth of his Christ: and sighes for his Saviours suffering on the Crosse.* This page gives a separate publication date of 1647, but "His Noble Numbers" appears last in the final text as published in 1648. The title *Hesperides* is usually taken to refer to classical mythology, to the garden of golden apples that Hercules gathered as one of his twelve labors; as mentioned, Hesperides is also another name for the Islands of the Blessed, the mythological islands at the western end of the world to which the souls of the worthy are transported after death.

The dedication of *Hesperides* "To the Most Illustrious and Most Hopefull Prince, Charles, Prince of Wales" was, as we have seen, both tactful and timely. Herrick did not dedicate his long-considered volume to the soon-to- be-executed king but to his son, the future King Charles II (although in 1648 he might have found it difficult to find others who thought the prince had much of a chance of succeeding his father). Here is the book's prefatory poem:

> WEll may my Book come forth like Publique
>   Day,
> When such a *Light* as *You* are leads the way:
> Who are my Works *Creator,* and alone
> The *Flame* of it, and the *Expansion.*
> And look how all those heavenly Lamps acquire
> Light from the Sun, that *inexhausted Fire:*
> So all my *Morne,* and *Evening Stars* from You
> Have their *Existence,* and their *Influence* too.
> Full is my Book of Glories; but all These
> By You become *Immmortall Substances.*

(p. 9)

The analogy of the prince and the sun was an analogy under suspicion from the opponents of the Stuart ideology of the divine right of kings, which would include the Puritans. The immortalizing influence of the prince flows from his position at the top of the hierarchy, under God. This transcendent light illuminates all lesser lights; by reflection (participation), even the poet's "glories" become "Immortal Substances." Under the pressure of popular interpretations of the new science of Francis Bacon and Sir Isaac Newton, the belief that all truths may be communicated with mathematical clarity, that analogy and that hierarchy, which, in several forms, were traditional, were about to disappear from public view, along with *Hesperides,* a book that they informed. But *Hesperides* persists as a work of literature, full of moments when mundane events, such as the publication of a book, open up views of the influence—the inflowing or overflowing—of the sacred onto the human scene.

Hesperides has often been discussed as a world unto itself. The title helps us grasp the nature of this world. Hesperus is the evening star. It appeared within an hour of the birth of Prince Charles on 29 May 1630. Since English Reformation political ideology identified royalty and the sacred, the appearance of Hesperus at this moment recalled the appearance of the Star of Bethlehem, heralding the birth of Christ. In addition, by adding a diminutive to the end of the word "Hesperus," Herrick suggests that his poems are "little" stars. "So all my *Morne*, and *Evening Stars* from You / Have their *Existence*." That is, *Hesperides* participates in the sacred event of the birth of the prince. The polysemous quality of the title captures many themes which will become relevant at different times during a reading of *Hesperides* and on different levels of interpretation of the whole.

The second poem in *Hesperides*, "The Argument of His Book," flows naturally from the dedication. Its scope includes everything under the sun.

> I Sing of *Brooks*, of *Blossomes*, *Birds*, and *Bowers*:
> Of *April*, *May*, of *June*, and *July*-Flowers.
> I sing of *May-poles*, *Hock-carts*, *Wassails*, *Wakes*,
> Of *Bride-grooms*, *Brides*, and of their *Bridall-*
>   *cakes*.
> I write of *Youth*, of *Love*, and have Accesse
> By these, to sing of cleanly-*Wantonnesse*.
> I sing of *Dewes*, of *Raines*, and piece by piece
> Of *Balme*, of *Oyle*, of *Spice*, and *Amber-Greece*.
> I sing of *Times trans-shifting*; and I write
> How *Roses* first came *Red*, and *Lillies White*.
> I write of *Groves*, of *Twilights*, and I sing
> The Court of *Mab*, and of the *Fairie- King*.
> I write of *Hell*; I sing (and ever shall)
> Of *Heaven*, and hope to have it after all.

(p. 11)

This poem continues the triumphalism of the dedication by asserting the poet's capacity to "sing" the whole universe. The poem reveals the hierarchical ordering of this universe. The first couplet establishes the realm of nature; the second of culture; the third of erotic energies; the fourth of blessings natural and refined; the fifth of the political realm; the sixth of the realm of fairy; and last, the realm of the *eschaton*, the last things. Even a cursory look at the more than fourteen hundred poems in *Hesperides* suggests the comprehensiveness of this catalog. The title, if we see it as referring to islands at the edge of the world, reaches beyond *Hesperides* into the second part of Herrick's book, "His Noble Numbers."

Finally, there is a note of defiance in the last verbs: "I sing (and ever shall) / Of *Heaven*, and hope to have it after all"—a defiance at once humble before God and proud before man. The astringent quality of Herrick's faith will be fully explored in "His Noble Numbers."

The mention of "*May-poles, Hock-carts, Wassails, Wakes*" reminds us of the emphasis placed on these things by the Stuart regime. In 1618, as mentioned earlier, King James had issued the *Book of Sports*. This volume was directed at the Puritan attitude toward holidays. It supported pastimes such as Herrick lists here, pastimes traditional and sanctified by the traditional church. The *Book of Sports* was reissued by Charles I in 1633. Herrick would live to see such "sports" violently suppressed and was no doubt criticized in 1648 for celebrating, or "singing," them by the very people who had just stripped him of his vicarage.

Under such circumstances, the complex tone of the final couplet suggests that *Hesperides* not only "sings" "*Times trans-shifting*" but defies them. The isolation that Herrick felt under Puritanism is vividly captured in the next poem, "To His Muse":

> WHither *Mad maiden* wilt thou roame?
> Farre safer 'twere to stay at home:
> Where thou mayst sit, and piping please
> The poore and private *Cottages*.

Since *Coats*, and *Hamlets*, best agree
With this thy meaner Minstralsie.
There with the Reed, thou mayst expresse
The Shepherds Fleecie happinesse:
And with thy *Eclogues* intermixe
Some smooth, and harmlesse *Beucolicks.*
There on a Hillock thou mayst sing
Unto a handsome Shephardling;
Or to a Girle (that keeps the Neat)
With breath more sweet then Violet.
There, there, (perhaps) such Lines as These
May take the simple *Villages.*
But for the Court, the Country wit
Is despicable unto it.
Stay then at home, and doe not goe
Or flie abroad to seeke for woe.
Contempts in Courts and Cities dwell;
No *Critick* haunts the Poore mans Cell:
Where thou mayst hear thine own Lines read
By no one tongue, there, censured.
That man's unwise will search for Ill,
And may prevent it, sitting still.

(p. 12)

This poem is based on a stock epigram situation, the author complaining of the delinquency of his muse. The poem serves to enlighten us with respect to Herrick's own political situation. For him, the countryside meant privacy and a freedom to live as he wished; in London, the conservative scowl of his superior, William Laud, archbishop of Canterbury, on the one hand, and the growing power of the Puritans on the other would have made life uneasy for him. Laud, though vehemently opposed to the Puritans, was determined to impose conformity on the Church of England. After the collapse of the regime of Charles I, Laud was impeached and executed. Herrick's conclusion? Given the tenor of the times, there was something to be said for "sitting still."

HESPERIDES AND THE LITERARY TRADITION

The tradition appealed to in "To His Muse" is the tradition of pastoral. As a genre, pastoral had been developed by Elizabethan poets such as Edmund Spenser and Sir Philip Sidney. It goes back to Hellenistic times, to the Greek poet Theocritus and the Roman poet Virgil. In classical pastoral, we see familiar shepherds singing of lost love and hear their complaints about the poverty and dislocation caused by war. Unhappy in love and confused as to purpose, the shepherds take consolation in song. In pastoral, resolutions are formal; a well-sung song prevails, for the moment, against the chaos of public and private disaster. The world of *Hesperides* is a pastoral world.

Throughout *Hesperides*, the interplay of country and city is subtle. In "To His Muse," Herrick chides his muse for wandering away from Dean Prior. His muse—strikingly modern in her stylish couplets—longs for the court. The poet reminds her of her pastoral duties: to sing "with the Reed" (or pipe) "The Shepherds Fleecie happinesse: / And with thy *Eclogues* intermixe / Some smooth, and harmlesse *Beucolicks.*" The phrasing suggests the tenderness of the reproof: "Fleecie happinesse" conveys the poet's awareness of the limitations as well as the seductiveness of the pleasures afforded by the country. If he urges his muse to mix "eclogues" and "beucolicks," the distinction is a learned one, but seems to reflect the idea that within pastoral eclogues, the bucolic is more base. As even a dip into *Hesperides* suggests, Herrick recognizes in base things something essential to his community.

While defining his muse in terms of the pastoral tradition, Herrick reflects the political decorum of the time. "Free speech" is out of the question. The court is a dangerous place. He serves at the mercy of the crown, and in matters religious, the crown means William Laud. Charles I depended on Laud to discipline the clergy, and Laud fought fire with fire, making a list dividing the English world between Puritans and Orthodox, or the Church of England. Laud could have little sympathy for Herrick's profound sense of play, and his poetry frequently violated Laud's emphasis on "decency." But Laud's toleration of "sport," condemned by the Puritans as "pagan," connected him with the popular culture and with the pastoral tradition that Herrick embraced.

In addition, "To His Muse" draws on the traditions of epigram, best illustrated in the work of the Roman poet Martial, whose satirical poems are marked by brevity and urbanity. It is a style that would grow in favor as the revolutions of the seventeenth century—the rage for "method" and the "language of mathematics" (Galileo)—shattered the old world of analogy and allegory. A second, nonsatirical, tradition of epigram, associated with the Greek Anthology and in particular Anacreon, is more subjective, erotic, elegiac. Herrick drew equally from both traditions. It should be noted that, according to Alastair Fowler, the influence of the epigram led to a "revolution in literature; for it achieved a new closeness of texture and economy of language, setting benchmarks for all subsequent literature. The new scale is one we take for granted" (p. 105). Naturalized by Surrey in the sixteenth century, the epigram is a "short, pointed, compressed form" (Fowler, p. 42) brought to perfection by Herrick.

"To His Muse" is followed by a set of epigrams, beginning with "To His Booke," which picks up where "To His Muse" left off:

> WHile thou didst keep thy *Candor* undefil'd,
> Deerely I lov'd thee; as my first-borne child:
> But when I saw thee wantonly to roame
> From house to house, and never stay at home;
> I brake my bonds of Love, and bad thee goe,
> Regardless whether well thou sped'st, or no.
> On with thy fortunes then, what e're they be;
> If good I'le smile, if bad I'le sigh for Thee.
>
> (pp. 12–13)

While such a speech to one's wayward muse is, again, a staple in the classical tradition, this particular poem echoes with the Bible. "Walking in the way of the Lord" is a central motif of biblical righteousness, and as a motif it would speak to Puritan and Orthodox alike. Herrick's playful mixing of the sacred Biblical tradition of "walking" and the "wandering" tradition of the classical epigram—the pose of the flaneur—illustrates the keen sense of fairness that prevails in *Hesperides.* The epigrammatic balance of smiles and sighs elegantly captures Herrick's bemusement.

Herrick's point becomes sharper in the next poem, which is a classic epigram of two rhyming couplets. Titled simply "Another," it illustrates the tendency in epigram to create a scene that dramatizes a witty distinction. It's as if the "Virgin shie" were reading the poem just read, about the "wanton" muse, and identifying with her:

> TO read my Booke the Virgin shie
> May blush, (while *Brutus* standeth by:)
> But when He's gone, read through what's writ,
> And never staine a cheeke for it.
>
> (p. 13)

The psychological assumption is that "the virgin shie" is a hypocrite (and we should note that for Herrick, the term "virgin," like "maid," had a looser relationship to gender than it does now); when in the presence of Virtue, the shy virgin acts one way; when Virtue has gone, she's not so shy. Note that the "blush" is under the virgin's conscious control.

This kind of epigram—short and directed at a "humour" or type—was practiced widely in Herrick's time and would be Alexander Pope's bread and butter. For Herrick this style of writing was seen at its best in the epigrams of Ben Jonson. Herrick, a self-described "son of Ben," acknowledged Jonson's rank among poets, admiring the great delicacy as well as brutal directness in Jonson's poems, such as "To My Muse":

> Away, and leave me, thou thing most abhorred,
> That has betrayed me to a worthless lord,

Made me commit most fierce idolatry
To a great image through thy luxury.

(p. 35)

The poem goes on to suggest that Jonson has paid dearly for his muse's idolatry: "With me thou leav'st a happier muse than thee, / And which thou brought'st me, welcome poverty." After a couplet on his newfound honesty, the poet pulls back: "But I repent me: stay. Whoe'er is raised / For worth he has not, he is taxed, not praised" (p. 35).

In Jonson's inner dialogue, the poet criticizes himself, then stops. Arguing that though he has praised his subjects beyond their deserts, the distance between the ideal and the application will be obvious. The claim of idolatry is irrelevant: Jonson's idealism would never be applied to a real person. He can't lose.

This self-defense of a most self-conscious poet was not unanimously persuasive. Shakespeare, for one, objected to it. Jonson's idealism and tendency to lash out at what threatens it became an issue on the London stage when Herrick was growing up. Between 1599 and 1601 Jonson and Shakespeare explored the issues of nature and art and the self in a series of plays that would eventually include some of Shakespeare's most famous, including *As You Like It, Twelfth Night, Hamlet,* and *Troilus and Cressida.* Jonson attacked what he considered Shakespeare's absurd plots, subversive couplings of high and low, and foolish fools. Jonson in turn was parodied for narcissism, even for his efforts to banish self-love. Shakespeare's use of chance and accidental events in his plots and his parti-colored celebration of sexual desire seem to have been aimed at Jonson's ideal of rational self-control. Shakespeare's use of the pastoral conventions in his festive comedies challenges Jonson's emphasis on rational art.

In Shakespeare, art and nature are not ultimately opposed but thrive on—and in—difference. As much as Herrick was indebted to Ben Jonson, he seems to be of Shakeseare's camp.

Herrick's own festive, ironic spirit concludes the opening sequence of poems in *Hesperides.* Here is "When He Would Have His Verses Read."

IN sober mornings, doe not thou reherse
The holy incantation of a verse;
But when that men have both well drunke, and
    fed,
Let my Enchantments then be sung, or read.
When Laurell spirts 'ith fire, and when the
    Hearth
Smiles to it selfe, and guilds the roof with mirth;
When up the *Thyrse* is rais'd, and when the sound
Of sacred *Orgies* flyes, A round, A round.
When the *Rose* raignes, and locks with ointments
    shine,
Let rigid *Cato* read these Lines of mine.

(p. 14)

The "Cato" of the last line, like the "critick" in "To His Muse," represents for Herrick reason inappropriately applied. Cato identifies with the "sober" morning. Cato, the Roman culture hero Jonson most identified with, becomes a creature of "mirth" only in the mirthful hour. We have seen how the pastimes of mirth—like maypoles and wassails—figure both in Herrick's "Argument" and in Stuart anti-Puritan policy. Here, with allusions to Horace's odes, Herrick portrays a moment of release from the day's cares, and provides the footnotes himself: *Thyrse,* he explains, is "A *Javelin* twind with Ivy"; and *Orgies* refers to "Songs to *Bacchus,*" the god of wine. Herrick's learning is essential to his vision of imagined community. The mood is so inclusive that even Cato would, in the right circumstances, provide a suitable reading of Herrick's mirthful verses.

Hesperides produced many anthology favorites: "Delight in Disorder," "Corinna's Going a Maying," "To the Virgins, To Make Much of Time," "His Prayer to Ben Jonson," "Upon Julia's Clothes," "A Thanksgiving to God, for His House," and so on. To literary historians, Herrick is known as a perfecter of the epigram and as a pastoral poet. But the relationship between his poems and his place in literary history is not always clear and not always addressed. There are good reasons for this. Many of his best poems are short; his art is, in a sense, an art of miniaturization; and his world is not ours. It is not obvious to us what unifies *Hesperides,* if anything. Is it, in our sense, a book?

We have noted in passing how his very short poems, his epigrams, reflect both his attention to classical tradition and his allegiance to Ben Jonson. Herrick inserted himself in the canon, as it were, by proclaiming his loyalty to Jonson, twice in a row. Here is the first poem:

> *Upon* Ben Jonson
> HEre lies *Johnson* with the rest
> Of the Poets; but the Best.
> Reader, wo'dst thou more have known?
> Aske his Story, not his Stone.
> That will speake what this can't tell
> Of his glory. *So farewell.*
>
> (p. 380)

Herrick combines several traditional themes in this laconic verse. Its very brevity is definitive: the ancient epigram, which it imitates, never quite loses its reference to originally being cut into stone, the marmoreal finality of it all. "Here lies" is the most common generic beginning in the epigram-as-epitaph tradition. Herrick playfully turns that into a compliment. Then he turns to the reader. Once again, he plays with the convention of the material of the text by using it as foil for the spirit of the letter, "the story." Finally, he exploits a rhyme and pushes off the sound of the word "story" into the theme of "glory," which he concludes is beyond the occasion. He leaves it up to the reader to find out why Ben Jonson is the best.

As if on second thought, he follows "Upon Ben Jonson" with a second poem about Jonson, "An Ode for Him." As epigram gives way to ode, we enter the "world" of the sons of Ben: the "lyric feasts" held at various taverns; the friendly competition among poets; and the grief that the source of their inspiration is gone. Yet

not quite gone. The poem ends with a prayer to the spirit of Jonson to "teach" the remnant to not squander the legacy, Jonson's "wits great over- plus." What may appear to us to be originality in the fusion of genres—ending the ode with a prayer—is something Herrick would have learned from Horace, Jonson, and other writers of odes. Originality was not a value for Herrick as it would become for the Romantics. On the other hand, in a time of change when prayers to saints may raise official hackles and had been proscribed, Herrick's "secular" prayer had real edge.

But as we suggested earlier, Herrick's attachment to Jonson was qualified by his attitude toward himself. Herrick is no Jonson: no "centered self" lashing out at fools from behind the shield of an impregnable facade. On the contrary, Herrick's self, as portrayed in the many epigrams on "himself," is the Christian pilgrim, split open by desire, at odds with his several wills, subject to melancholy yet always willing to seize the day, always aware of his folly, always already dying. While his imagined community includes Ben Jonson, it is bigger, more complex, more refined and nuanced, than the world of Jonson's poems and plays.

UPPER AND LOWER REACHES IN *HESPERIDES*

In a poem titled "Another," a quatrain rhyming *aabb,* the world of *Hesperides* is broadened in an unforeseen direction:

> WHo with thy leaves shall wipe (at need)
> The place, where swelling *Piles* do breed:
> May every ill, that bites, or smarts,
> Perplexe him in his hinder-parts.
>
> (p. 13)

Like the poem following it (and many others in the book), this is a curse poem, and reminds us how the epigram was used to reinvent old literary genres and cultural practices. Herrick devotes much art to these four lines: the over-precise parenthesis, and elegant rhyme that results; the sharpness of the verbs ("bites" and "smarts"); the going-away rush of the final line. It is an excellent epigram, and its excellence is in its specificity, for the genre valued clarity in its close-ups of small things just as it tended to miniaturize large things. Herrick's world is of a piece: his art embraces the whole range of creation, a range marked by difference. Such poems in their vulgarity may complicate our sense of sacral loci but add an important dimension to the world of *Hesperides*. For us, a poem about "piles," or hemorrhoids, creates dissonance; for Herrick, it would seem, resonance. There is a bottom to his world, and it is as real as the upper reaches are supernatural.

Herrick's *"saeculum"* includes bodily functions just as it includes cursing and the gnashing of teeth. His world is the "real" world. It is real by virtue of the hierarchy that allows for the fact of "piles" on the same page as the "shy virgin." The depth of this world is often contested by those who think of Herrick as a poetic "goldsmith" working at filigree and fiddling away the time as city and country were engulfed in civil war.

Such a judgment may be reinforced, temporarily, by a quick reading of the ninth poem, "Upon Julias Recovery," which is the first of many poems to and about his "mistress" named Julia, who is often associated with roses.

> DRoop, droop no more, or hang the head
> Ye *Roses* almost withered;
> Now strength, and newer Purple get,
> Each here declining *Violet*.
> O *Primroses*! let this day be
> A Resurrection unto ye;
> And to all flowers ally'd in blood,
> Or sworn to that sweet Sister-hood:
> For Health on *Julia's* cheek hath shed
> Clarret, and Creame commingled.
> And those her lips doe now appeare
> As beames of *Corrall,* but more cleare.
>
> (p. 14)

Notice first the imperative mood of the verbs: Herrick is instructing his reader, via others in the audience (roses, violets, primroses), to respond appropriately to the news of Julia's return to health. As we return strength and color to the "flowers" we experience a day of "resurrection." It is a moment of renewal.

The logic underlying the poem, which provides its rational basis (that the higher embodiments of love are participated in by the lower), was under severe strain during Herrick's time, but not so severe as to make his world collapse in on itself. Totter, yes—he makes much of its fragility—but not implode from absurdity. The world of *Hesperides* is sufficiently varied that we recognize it, even now: we find ourselves, whatever our degree of participation, part of his imagined community of flowers, shy virgins, and festering bums.

The traditional community imagined in *Hesperides* depends on harmony between high and low. Nowhere is this more true than in the very economy of the village. In "The Hock-cart, or Harvest Home," Herrick addresses three realms: labor, management, and church. Each have their roles in the community. A century earlier, in the first attack by Henry VIII's regime on traditional observances in the parishes, all feast days falling in harvest, from the first of July to late September, were abolished. This policy was difficult to maintain. In any event, Herrick's imagined harvest festival is more holiday than holy day, as much classical as English. In the sense that we have come to understand, it is imaginary. Which does not mean fantastical. The lord of the estate must participate by witnessing the blessing of the decorated cart and he must throw a feast. Rural traditions, some probably pre-Christian (the kissing of the sheaves), some clearly classical, fuse with Christian practice and culminate in the feast at the "Lords Hearth, / Glitt'ring with fire." Herrick does not allow the poetry to create unreal schema or pleasant fantasies of sentimental order. For example, he realizes that the lord may not offer wine to the workers, but there will be plenty of beer.

The poem abounds in speeches and toasts. And as so often in *Hesperides,* it imitates the event by instructing the participants. At the end of the poem, the poet addresses the "boys," encouraging them to "Feed, and grow fat." Soon they must return, with the oxen, to the fields.

> And, you must know, your Lords word's true,
> Feed him ye must, whose food fils you.
> And that this pleasure is like raine,
> Not sent ye for to drowne your paine,
> But for to make it spring againe.

(p. 142)

Herrick's candor here about pain and gain reserves him a place among the champions of the people. The pun on "spring" suggests that without the pain of the laborers, even the progress of the seasons will break down. The imagery of the poem recalls the Flemish painter Pieter Brueghel's peopled landscapes, whose peasants provoke both pathos and derision ("While other Rusticks, lesse attent / To Prayers, then to Merryment, / Run after with their breeches rent"). But, because of the linear nature of poetry, and the unfolding nature of poetic experience, Herrick's view becomes more nuanced than that comparison with painting suggests. The poem initiates the reader into the community. To read "The Hock-cart, or Harvest Home" is to take different roles in the community, from that of the son of summer, to the lord, to the stage-managing vicar of Christ, in that (ascending?) order. The harvest-home festivity ranks high among the sacral loci from which the community of *Hesperides* springs again.

A CALL FOR PARTICIPATION

One of Herrick's most popular poems provides a good test of Herrick's world. "Corinna's Going a Maying" is based on a stock scene in Roman elegiac poetry: the poet tries to rouse a girl who is reluctant to "seize the day." But it is more. It may even be a sacral locus which helps define the imagined community of *Hesperides.*

In poem after poem, Herrick gives directions with imperative verbs that would, if followed, lead to participation in his Christian community. Corinna is a reluctant listener; in fact, she seems to be asleep. The poet repeats the command with rising irritation: "Get up, get up for shame . . . Get up, sweet- slug-a-bed." The sequence of commands is as follows: "Rise . . . Wash, dresse, be brief in praying . . . Come, my *Corinna,* come, and coming, marke / How each field turns a street . . . see how / Devotion gives each house a Bough, / . . . Come, we'll abroad; and let's obay / The Proclamation made for May: / . . . come, let's go a Maying. / . . . Come, let us goe, while we are in our prime; / And take the harmlesse follie of the time. / Come, my *Corinna,* come, let's goe a Maying" (pp. 98–100).

If Corinna seems to ignore her poet's urgent demands, she may represent an oblivion resulting from years of suppression of maypoles and wassails. The reinvention of the carpe diem theme in Herrick's seventeenth-century England is no mere literary event. The "proclamation" (*The Book of Sports*) Archbishop Laud referred to had the strength of the king behind it. So such commands were not inappropriate, in this symbolic setting, for the vicar of Devon. In this poem, "shame" and "sin" refer to a reluctance to participate in the community, and the community includes "the blooming morn," "Aurora," "the dew-bespangled herb and tree." The birds say matins and sing "thankful hymns." Corinna is asked to be part of something big, to be a witness to "how each field turns a street; each street a park / Made green, and trimmed with trees." She is asked to see how others in the community have followed such practices, practices that could be understood to reach back into Old Testament times.

Yet as the poem broadens its scope, there is no indication that Corinna has agreed to go a Maying. The speaker seems to grow more urgent; the imagery becomes more sexual; finally, the argument turns toward the mortality of the speaker and Corinna. "Our life is short;

and our dayes run / As fast away as do's the Sunne: / And as a vapour, or a drop of raine, / Once lost, can ne'r be found againe." Partly because of the elaborate play of rhyme against syntax, the onward thrust of the poem creates a passionate music.

> So when or you or I are made
> A fable, song, or fleeting shade;
> All love, all liking, all delight
> Lies drown'd with us in endlesse night.
> Then while time serves, and we are but decaying;
> Come, my *Corinna,* come, let's goe a Maying.
>
> (p. 100)

"All love, all liking, all delight": that is surely a great burden to place on a groggy girl. Perhaps she refuses to rise to the occasion out of self-defense. Or perhaps the sequence of topics suggests that she is taking it all in. The poem simply doesn't say.

The formality of the poem reminds one of the role of art in pastoral. Pastoral art does not resolve the tensions created by violent conflict in nature and society and the loss of unity and order. Nor does art resolve the paradox of desire. Corinna resists the vicar's call for her to join his community just as the reader may resist, through a refusal of the imagination, to participate in the sacral loci of *Hesperides. Hesperides* assumes such resistance. The failure of the argument to persuade does not point to a weakness in the argument but to the strength of the opposition. Corinna is being awakened out of "sloth" into her existence as a member of the imagined community of *Hesperides.* Or at least her vicar would hope so.

For Herrick, the vicar of Devon, the poem was an act of resistance against almost a hundred years of radical suppression of the old religion. Things are slipping away; Corinna's melancholy refusal to get up is getting to him. He feels his age. He admits it:

> A deale of Youth, ere this, is come
> Back, and with *White-thorn* laden home.

> Some have dispatcht their Cakes and Creame,
> Before that we have left to dreame:
> And some have wept, and woo'd, and plighted
>   Troth,
> And chose their Priest, ere we can cast off sloth . .
> .
>
> (p. 99)

Marriage becomes the symbol of the old community at its most festive and meaningful. But it all seems like a dream now. We don't always know who is dreaming, Corinna or the poet.

Hesperides is full of women like Corinna. Herrick calls some of them his "mistresses." Frequently the object of ocular eroticism, his mistresses are not trivial. They are not fantasies in the modern sense. In "Delight in Disorder" Herrick's concept of nature and art luminously reveals details of a woman's dress: a shoulder wrap, a "Crimson Stomacher," a cuff, a bit of petticoat, a shoelace. These details, animated by the imagination, reveal a principle, the principle of "wilde civility." Like many principles of the tradition, this principle must be stated paradoxically. Yet "wilde civility" is precise, just as the opening phrase is precise: "A Sweet disorder . . ." Far from mere objectification, these details can become sacral loci, or sites where the holy intersects time. They are framed in a sturdy aesthetic of nature's order (which may seem disorderly to mere mortals).

Throughout the volume, the poet gives his mistresses instructions to follow after he is dead. Very soon after the opening of the book, in "To Perilla," he gives Perilla a number of instructions which, if followed, will keep his ghost from wandering, keep it "Still in the coole, and silent shades of sleep." Once again a brief lyric touches on a hot issue, this time purgatory. Lacking the terror of many seventeenth- century visions of purgatory, "To Perilla" nevertheless captures a major theme: neglect of the dead by the living. This small epigrammatic lyric produces a little spark (we recall the little stars of the title *Hesperides*). Like many of its fellow lyrics, "To Perilla" engages the tradition in such a way—this imitation of ritual, this imaginative participation—that the poem becomes one of many sacral loci revealing a transcendent principle that informs the community of the living and the dead.

HESPERIDES AS A WORK OF MELANCHOLY

The imagery of light and glorious verse in "When He Would Have His Verses Read" recalls *Hesperides'* prefatory poem to Prince Charles. In that poem Herrick prays that, under the protection of the prince, his book may "come forth like Publique Day." Once into *Hesperides,* according to "When He Would Have His Verses Read," these "Enchantments" must be reserved for the more festive moods of evening.

Behind Herrick's mirth lurks melancholy. By the time he was settled at Dean Prior, he had seen the times trans- shift more than once. His childhood joy was tempered by paternal absence; his father had died when Herrick was only a baby, after falling from (or possibly jumping out of) a window. As a child, Herrick witnessed the plague in London. He had tried, for six of his ten years as an apprentice, to learn the trade of goldsmith, and failed. He had gone to Cambridge University, yes, but he had had to transfer from St. John's College, which he could not afford, to the less glamorous Trinity Hall and the study of law. He did not become a lawyer; instead he was ordained a deacon in the Church of England. As a chaplain, on an ill-fated expedition under the duke of Buckingham, he had seen the English slaughtered by the French, then drowned, in large numbers, during a storm that capsized some of the smaller ships. The storm was the last indignity of an enterprise—the duke's private war with France—doomed from the start. Not long after he returned home the duke, the king's favorite, was murdered by a soldier with a tenpenny knife. Throughout his years at Dean Prior, he

saw King Charles gradually succumb to personal weaknesses, undermine the royalist cause, and lead the realm into civil war—this king who had civilized the English court, patronized artists and architects, and collected the treasures of the past, a record that must have gladdened Herrick's heart, even in sorrow.

Irresistible context for *Hesperides* comes from Robert Burton's 1621 text *The Anatomy of Melancholy.* In one of the few contemporary works that compares, in scope and tone, with *Hesperides,* Burton writes:

> To expel grief, and procure pleasance, sweet smells, good diet, touch, taste, embracing, singing, dancing, sports, plays, and above the rest, exquisite beauties, *quibus oculi jucunde moventur et animi* [which take the eye and charm the mind], are the most powerful means, *obvia forma,* to meet or see a fair maid pass by, or to be in company with her.
> (Vol. 2, p. 120)

Hesperides assumes melancholy. Over against the "times trans-shifting," *Hesperides* provides a map of a world of participation in all orders of being, natural, social, historical, and divine; furthermore, it provides a witnessing self— Herrick's persona—that, participating in these orders, nevertheless refuses to take itself as the origin of order, preferring to remain open to the influx of order, and beauty, from beyond itself. Herrick's irony protects the living, differentiating principle from solipsism and narcissism and other dualisms. His openness to order beyond himself resists the Puritan alienation of pure from popular religion. His resistance to self-assertive autonomy would have seemed craven to those who removed him from Dean Prior and beheaded King Charles. The silence that falls on Herrick's world after the publication of *Hesperides* is more or less complete. As we have seen, a few months later the king was dead.

ORDERS WITHIN ORDERS IN *HESPERIDES*

The meaning of *Hesperides* depends on orders within orders. We have discussed the reference in the title to an island at the edge of the world, where Hercules had to gather apples as one of his labors. Hesperides, as a place of overflowing, reaches back to medieval song and to the biblical Eden.

Yet an allusion to neglected European song may take us farther afield than a common reference to classical mythology. European lyric is an area of Herrick studies that deserves more attention. For example, in the collection titled the Harley Lyrics, we find a song titled "Mosti ryden by Rybbesdale," and in this song we find this Herrickian description intimating celestial power in erotic images: "Hyre tyttes aren anvnder bis / as apples two of parays" (these apples confer immortality to the possessor). Behind this imagery is a pattern of ideas described by Peter Dronke in *Medieval Latin and the Rise of European Love- Lyric* (1968): "a pattern in which a lover can win the fulfillment of his own destiny in so far as he surrenders it to his beloved, and in which she is able to bring this about inasmuch as it is not she, but the heavenly one in her" (p. 122).

We have seen how Herrick embodies such a pattern, makes it stick given his very own situation in Devonshire. "The heavenly one" is part of the community. In this economy, hierarchy does not mean alienation, and each real thing participates in reality through analogies of being. The ground of Herrick's "candor" and clarity, even of what some have called his miniaturization, may well be his respect for the kinds (genus) of things, and his intuitive understanding of kinds as related not as qualifications of being but through analogy. Herrick had an immense appetite for particularity—the precise way that a thing reveals itself. The world of *Hesperides* is clamorous with difference.

Unless such order within orders is grasped, it is easy to think of *Hesperides* as a fantasy rather than a mode of participation, structured by desire and loss, in an imagined community. Early in *Hesperides*, in the anthology favorite "To Live Merrily, and to Trust to Good Verses," Herrick connects the classical notion of art and his own sense of "now." The poem begins:

> NOw is the time for mirth,
>   Nor cheek, or tongue be dumbe:
> For with the flowrie earth,
>   The golden pomp is come.

And ends:

> Trust to good Verses then;
>   They onely will aspire,
> When Pyramids, as men,
>   Are lost, i'th'funerall fire.

> And when all Bodies meet
>   In *Lethe* to be drown'd;
> Then onely Numbers sweet,
>   With endless life are crown'd.

(pp. 113, 115)

The "now" of the calendar gives way to the eternal now of art. In the world of *Hesperides*, this Ovidian vision of the immortality of art—think how Shakespeare used the notion in his sonnets—is just one version of a great theme. The vision is repeated at the end of the first part of *Hesperides*, before we turn the page and enter the world of the smaller, plainer, more intense second part. Before we come to the end of the first part, we have felt the world darken. In the final two "centuries" (the name traditionally given to one hundred epigrams), there are poems on disorder, maladies, impotence, rapine, martyrdom, homelessness. Over all, a valedictory mood prevails. Something has gone down. Far from being a loose collection of lyrics, an "anthology," *Hesperides* is a structured universe, with its moments of despair and happiness, rage and exquisite pleasure; and yet, as a work of art, it has an undeniable drift away from itself and toward the unknown.

The sense of "drifting away" includes a disintegration of one of its orders in a changing attitude toward the king. As Anne Baynes Coiro suggests in her study of *Hesperides* as a book of epigrams, *Hesperides* comprises a chronicle of King Charles's bungling of the cause. Herrick uses the tradition of epigram to mark the devolution of order. Very late in the book we read: "If Kings and kingdomes, once distracted be, / The sword of war must trie the Soveraignty" (p. 437). That couplet is titled "Warre." It is followed by "A King and No King," which is presented by Herrick in italics: "*That Prince, who may doe nothing but what's just, / Rules but by leave, and takes his Crowne on trust.*" And this bit of Machiavellian commentary is followed by a couplet on plots and one on flattery.

These rapier thrusts at the current regime follow a couplet of a different kind. Titled "The Voice and Violl," it reminds us of Herrick's long devotion to music. "Rare is the voice it selfe; but when we sing / To'th Lute or Violl, then 'tis ravishing" (p. 437). Several of Herrick's songs had been put to music by the finest composers of the day, and some had been performed before King Charles. Herrick's carol that begins "What sweeter music can we bring" (p. 481), which was part of a New Year's Day masque set to music by William Laws, prompted a modern master of sacred music, John Rutter, to write in his liner notes for his CD *The John Rutter Christmas Album*, that it "seems to sum up the whole ethos of the carol genre as many composers and poets have understood it." For Herrick not only songs but also singing provided countless sacral loci by which the eternal is rediscovered in the real. The process of maintaining the community goes on despite worsening conditions, as if the process were an end in itself.

Yet not the only end: there is an end to the story of *Hesperides*, and it is not of this world.

"HIS NOBLE NUMBERS"

The second part of *Hesperides*, "His Noble Numbers: or, His Pious Pieces," is sometimes considered an afterthought. The poems seem colorless, stiff; mirth seems to have gone out of them. Some readers call the second part a "palinode," or retraction. Indeed, in "His Noble Numbers" Herrick refers to *Hesperides* with regret. There is no reason to believe that he felt "His Noble Numbers" inferior. Yet he could have suppressed the first part and just published "His Noble Numbers." The trade in divinity would perhaps have been more welcoming to such a work than it was to *Hesperides*. On the other hand, we are glad he did not suppress the first part and publish only the second. For reasons we will try to learn, Herrick wanted it both ways.

The title page reads: *His Noble Numbers: or, His Pious Pieces, Wherein (amonst other things), he sings the Birth of his Christ: and sighs for his Saviours saffering on the Crosse.* The use of "noble" is suggestive. As *Hesperides* shows, the political realm is only one among many sacral loci that connect the community to divinity; it may be the least trustworthy. Certainly, the behavior of the king was disappointing. So the glossing of nobility by piety in the title is no mere formality. It captures the tension that defines this threshold moment in the life of *Hesperides*.

As noted previously, the title page for "His Noble Numbers" is dated 1647, a year before the date on the first title page. As if to deepen the confusion, the epigraph is from Hesiod, in Greek, and untranslated. We will translate it here: "We know how to say many things that bear the guise of truth, and we also know when we intend to state the truth."

This text from Hesiod is one of the great literary paradoxes from archaic Greece, indeed of the Western literary tradition. Hesiod pictured himself as a rustic farmer thrown into confusion by a visit from the muses. As if to forestall any onset of hubris, they tell him: you are just the vehicle of our words. You won't know when what we tell you is the real thing or just the appearance of the real thing. We can give you the one as easily as the other.

This raises issues of truth and falsehood, of appearance and being, which lay just outside the world of *Hesperides*. The luminous, dreamlike intensity of that world is in contrast to the harsh backlit world of "His Noble Numbers." Hesiod's paradox, at this point between the two parts, suggests a continuity in difference. The kind of certainty sought by the Protestants, along with the new science, lay outside the tradition Herrick sought to remember in his book. He was happy to be the muses' fool. To repeat what was already quoted from Milbank: "Once, there was no 'secular.' . . . The *saeculum,* in the medieval era, was not a space, a domain, but a time—the interval between fall and *eschaton.*" Between the first and second parts of *Hesperides,* we turn to face the *eschaton*—the last things, the end. No wonder Hesiod's muses greet us with skepticism.

"His Noble Numbers" opens with "His Confession":

> LOok how our foule Dayes do exceed our faire;
> And as our bad, more then our good Works are:
> Ev'n so those Lines, pen'd by my wanton Wit,
> Treble the number of these good I've writ.
> Things precious are least num'rous: Men are
>   prone
> To do ten Bad, for one Good Action.
>
> (p. 450)

It is a professional job, if disingenuous. *Hesperides,* first part, contains over four times as many poems as "His Noble Numbers," not three times. In addition, many of the poems in the first part would serve as a pious piece. But the point is made. We have put the world of *Hesperides* behind us.

A second poem speaks of his "unbaptized Rhimes, / Writ in my wild unhallowed Times." It could be that Herrick had fallen foul of the Laudian censor before he became a victim of the change of regimes. *Hesperides* cannot be reduced to a blueprint for an ideological community: its order depends on "wild civility." The first poems in "His Noble Numbers" stress the unknowabity of God. "What God Is": "GOD is above the sphere of our esteem, / And is the best known, not defining Him" (p. 451). That said, the style becomes plain, the subject matter often doctrinal, as if clarity were a virtue. There is his pious piece on one of his favorite Hesperidian themes, titled "Mirth": "True mirth resides not in the smiling skin: / The sweetest solace is to act no sin" (p. 453).

"His Noble Numbers" includes beautiful carols and songlike lyrics. "His Letanie, to the Holy Spirit" reminds one of a Tudor lyric, were it not for his light touch. The poem contains one opening stanza setting the theme—"In the houre of my distress"—and eleven stanzas beginning "When" and varying the theme. It is a virtuoso performance. There are strokes of realism quite in keeping with the drift of the book as a whole:

> When the tapers now burne blew,
> And the comforters are few,
> And that number more then true;
>   Sweet spirit, comfort me!
>
> (p. 461)

One noble number is an anthology favorite: "A Thanksgiving to God, for His House." A remarkable stanza (a four-beat line followed by a two-beat line, and rhyming) creates a rocking motion that conveys something of the tedium as well as the bliss of life in this house. The irony reminds the reader of Horace on the small pleasures of his Sabine villa. "Lord, I confesse too, when I dine, / The Pulse is Thine . . ." (p. 464).

In *Hesperides* proper, Julia and Perilla and Corinna may be understood as sacral loci where erotic energies orient the community toward transcendence. In "His Noble Numbers," eros becomes *caritas* (charity) in two large poems, both dirges addressed to women of the Bible. Erotic spirituality, a well-known feature of medieval art, marks these poems by Herrick as boundaries of communal experience.

The first is "The Dirge of Jephthahs Daughter: Sung by the Virgins." Nearly a hundred years earlier, the great Scottish humanist George Buchanan had turned to the Old Testament story of Jephthah's daughter for a play that combined Greek tragedy and biblical story to explore questions of God's attitude toward evil. Jephthah is remembered as a great military leader who, in exchange for victory, promised to offer as a burnt offering to Yahweh whom or whatever greets him first on his return. As it turns out, the greeter is his daughter, an only child. After a month of mourning her maidenhood, she is sacrificed.

In the structure of *Hesperides*, Herrick's "Jephthah's Daughter" recapitulates the erotic sacred energies of the earlier poems and contains them. The story, as Herrick retells it, is feminist. Herrick's lines are candid about the quid pro quo:

> Thy Father brought with him along
> The Olive branch, and Victors Song:
> He slew the Ammonites, we know,
> But to thy woe;
> And in the purchase of our Peace,
> The Cure was worse than the Disease.
>
> (p. 476)

Herrick's priorities are clear. In the thematic flow of *Hesperides*, the connection between politics and the sacred was fragile; but without political order, other sacral loci were at risk. In thirteen rather grand stanzas combining long and short lines in compellingly musical shapes, Herrick's chorus of Virgins regret his sensuous themes—flowers, laces, frankincense—but not in shame. They sacrifice their "Maiden-pleasures" to "the wonder of all Maids":

> No, no; our Maiden-pleasures be
> Wrapt in the winding-sheet, with thee:
> 'Tis we are dead, though not I'th grave:
> Or, if we have
> One seed of life left, 'tis to keep
> A Lent for thee, to fast and weep.
>
> (p. 477)

The concluding stanza extends the moment into the future, the monument/tomb/poem becoming a sacred site for the community of *Hesperides*:

> May all shie Maids, at wonted hours,
> Come forth, to strew thy Tombe with flow'rs:
> May Virgins, when they come to mourn,
> Male-Incense burn
> Upon thine Altar! Then return,
> And leave thee sleeping in thy Urn.
>
> (p. 478)

The pun on "Male-Incense" (an allusion to Virgil but also to another poem earlier in *Hesperides*) neatly summarizes the ritual action of the poem. At its most resonant, "His Noble Numbers" does not renounce the world of *Hesperides*, it hallows it through sacrifice.

The second dirge is for Dorcas, a figure from the New Testament (Acts 9:36). "The Widdowes Teares: or, Dirge of Dorcas," like "The Dirge of Jephthahs Daugher: Sung by the Virgins," releases by containing the erotic spirituality of *Hesperides* as a whole. In the Bible, Dorcas, a "widow" known for acts of charity, was raised from the dead by Peter. Not so in Herrick's retelling. Like Jephthah's daughter, Dorcas is more erotic in death than in life.

> How wise wast thou in all thy waies!
> How worthy of respect and praise!
> How Matron-like didst thou go drest!
> How soberly above the rest
> Of those that prank it with their Plumes;
> And yet it with their choice purfumes.
>   *Chor.* Thy vestures were not flowing:
>   Nor did the street
>   Accuse thy feet
>   Of mincing in their going.
> And though thou here li'st dead, we see
> A deale of beauty yet in thee.
> How sweetly shewes thy smiling face,
> Thy lips with all diffused grace!
> Thy hands (though cold) yet spotlesse, white,
> And comely as the Chrysolite.

Chor. Thy belly like a hill is,
> Or as a neat
> Cleane heap of wheat,
All set about with Lillies.

(p. 495)

Herrick's mastery of line and syntax (note how he uses the short lines to focus up close on a telling image), his copious inventiveness, the ways he finds to make these rather formal pieces embody the overflowing energies that animate *Hesperides* as a whole: for these and other reasons, these poems on biblical women deserve to be better known. Even a brief consideration of them indicates how deeply considered was their place in Herrick's book.

HESPERIDES AND SACRED HISTORY

Trumping the darkening of *Hesperides*, "His Noble Numbers" concludes with several poems on Christ's passion. Before that sequence, there are two (in *Hesperides* there are many) more epigrams titled *To God*. The first asks for forgiveness of any faults: "Correct my errors gently with Thy Rod." The second one comes as something of a shock:

> THe work is done; now let my *Lawrell* be
> Given by none, but by Thy selfe, to me:
> That done, with Honour Thou dost me create
> Thy *Poet*, and Thy *Prophet Lawreat.*

(p. 529)

This "let" echoes down the volume: it is one of Herrick's most common verbs of instruction. Here it is said not to a mistress, fictive or otherwise, or to a prince, but to God. But if, as we have seen, *Hesperides* is an imagined Christian community that depends on its readers for fulfillment, the maker of such a world may indeed have prophetic status. His prayers may be heard. He may himself be among the community's sacral loci.

One of the greatest of Herrick's poems comes near the very end: "Good Friday: Rex Tragicus,

or Christ Going to His Crosse." The reinvention of Good Friday as a tragedy seems to have been original to Herrick. As a humanist trope, it was especially bold. It may have been a strike against the Puritan antitheatrical movement. It completes the removal of the Christian mystery from state institutions (including the church) into the realm of imaginative literature. Christ is an actor; we, his witnesses, observe his fidelity to the rules of the stage and respond accordingly (with sighs and tears).

As we have come to expect, the poem is a set of instructions: this time, to Christ. "Put off Thy Robe of *Purple*, then go on / To the sad place of execution" (p. 529). Thus it opens: and it could be about King Charles if it weren't about Christ; and it is surely about both, as if Herrick had a presentiment of the execution of the king.

Soon the poem explodes in derisive scorn against the "unpurged [note the allusion to tragic catharsis] Multitude" who can't wait to see Christ drag his cross across the stage of history. The poet urges Christ to ignore the rabble.

> Not as a thief, shalt Thou ascend the mount,
> But like a Person of some high account:
> The *Crosse* shall be Thy *Stage*; and Thou shalt there
> The spacious field have for Thy *Theater.*
> Thou art that *Roscius,* and that markt-out man,
> That must this day act the Tragedian,
> To wonder and afrightment . . .

(p. 529)

After identifying Christ with a Roman actor, Herrick suggests the parallel between king and Christ in terms of the "flux of Nations" that comes to see their execution. Not from those who come to gawk, "No, No, this *Scene* from Thee takes life and sense, / and soule and spirit[,] plot, and excellence" (p. 529). Here the sacral locus of Christ is the transcendent source of the very structures of tragic art.

The last four poems focus on sacral loci crucial to Christian community: the cross and the sepulchre. The energy, spiritually erotic, is also personal. "His Offering, with the Rest, at the Sepulcher" takes the "cleanly *Wantonnesse*" of the "The Argument of His Book" and raises it exponentially according to sacred decorum of "devotion":

> TO joyn with them, who here confer
> Gifts to my Saviours Sepulcher;
> Devotion bids me hither bring
> Somewhat for my Thank-Offering.
> Loe! Thus I give a Virgin-Flower,
> To dresse my Maiden-Saviour.
>
> (p. 533)

"His Noble Numbers," and thus *Hesperides,* ends with a scene at Christ's empty tomb. Herrick reinvents the Gospel story. The speaker is one of those who sealed Christ in this tomb. He asks the "white Angell,"

> Is He, from hence, gone to the shades beneath,
> To vanquish Hell, as here He conquered Death?
> If so; I'le thither follow, without feare;
> And live in Hell, if that my *Christ* stayes there.
>
> (p, 534)

Attaching a nonbiblical story onto a Gospel scene, Herrick again provides a further horizon for the community of *Hesperides*: hell. But this is not Dante's hell: Christ is there. This is Herrick's *eschaton*: the end. The logical delicacy of the hypothesis in Herrick's Christian imagination is notable: "if" Christ is in hell, I will follow him; I'll even live with him there, if he stays. One can't help but smile.

Herrick conceived *Hesperides* in the spirit of resistance to "*Times trans-shifting.*" The mode is pastoral, the ultimate hero is the great pastor, Christ, the resistance that of art, but art conceived as response to the sacral loci of a tradition that is passing. "His Noble Numbers" recapitulates and extends these principles directly into sacred history. "His Noble Numbers" creates a horizon for the human community continually rebuilding itself in *Hesperides*. To interpret a given poem in light of Herrick's intention as a poet, this unity must be acknowledged. Which is not to detract from Herrick's other excellences: his mastery of epigram; his profound grasp of the principles of pastoral; his unique capacity for song; his luminous imagery; the coherence and range of his Christian world; and so on. But what makes these worth praising in the end is the purpose that animates them, and that is Herrick's creation in *Hesperides,* of an imaginary Christian community with the capacity, even now, to move attentive readers to participation.

Selected Bibliography

EDITIONS

The Complete Poetry of Robert Herrick. Edited by J. Max Patrick. Garden City, N.Y.: Doubleday, 1963. Page citations herein refer to this edition.

The Poetical Works of Robert Herrick. Edited by L. C. Martin. Oxford: Clarendon Press, 1956.

SECONDARY WORKS

Alpers, Paul. *What Is Pastoral?* Chicago: University of Chicago Press, 1996.

Bednarz, James P. *Shakespeare and the Poets' War.* New York: Columbia University Press, 2001.

Bouwsma, William J. *The Waning of the Renaissance, 1550–1640.* New Haven, Conn.: Yale University Press, 2000.

Burton, Robert. *The Anatomy of Melancholy.* Edited by Holbrook Jackson. New York: New York Review Books, 2001. New introduction by William H. Gass.

Chute, Marchette. *Two Gentle Men: The Lives of George Herbert and Robert Herrick.* New York: Dutton, 1959.

Coiro, Anne Baynes. *Robert Herrick's Hesperides and the Epigram Book Tradition.* Baltimore: Johns Hopkins University Press, 1988.

Dronke, Peter. *Medieval Latin and the Rise of European Love-Lyric.* 2d ed. Oxford, U.K.: Oxford University Press, 1968.

Duffy, Eamon. *The Stripping of the Altars: Traditional Religion in England, c. 1400–c. 1580.* New Haven, Conn.: Yale University Press, 1992.

Eden, Kathy. *Hermeneutics and the Rhetorical Tradition: Chapters in the Ancient Legacy and Its Humanist Reception.* New Haven, Conn.: Yale University Press, 1997.

Eliot, T. S., "What Is Minor Poetry?" *Sewanee Review* 54 (1946), 1-18. Cited in Corns, *English Poetry: Donne to Marvell.*

Empson, William. *Some Versions of Pastoral.* New York: New Directions, 1974.

Fowler, Alastair. *A History of English Literature.* Cambridge, Mass.: Harvard University Press, 1987.

Hageman, Elizabeth H. *Robert Herrick: A Reference Guide.* Boston: G. K. Hall, 1983. Contains an extensive bibliography.

Hill, Christopher. *The World Turned Upside Down: Radical Ideas During the English Revolution.* (1972; reprint, New York: Penguin Books, 1991.)

Jonson, Ben. *Poems.* Edited by Ian Donaldson. New York: Oxford University Press, 1975.

Leavis, F. R. *Revaluation: Tradition and Development in English Poetry.* London: Chatto and Windus, 1936. Cited by Marcus in Corns, *English Poetry: Donne to Marvell.*

Marcus, Leah S. *The Politics of Mirth: Jonson, Herrick, Milton, Marvell, and the Defense of Old Holiday Pastimes.* Chicago: University of Chicago Press, 1986.

———. "Robert Herrick." In *The Cambridge Companion to English Poetry, Donne to Marvell,* edited by Thomas N. Corns. Cambridge and New York: Cambridge University Press, 1993. Pp. 171–182.

Milbank, John. *Theology and Social Theory: Beyond Secular Reason.* Oxford, U.K., and Cambridge, Mass.: Blackwell, 1991.

Norbrook, David. *Poetry and Politics in the English Renaissance.* Rev. ed. Oxford and New York: Oxford University Press, 2002.

Rollin, Roger B. *Robert Herrick.* Rev. ed. New York: Twayne, 1992.

Russell, Daniel. "The Genres of Epigram and Emblem." In *The Cambridge History of Literary Criticism.* Vol. 3, *The Renaisance,* edited by Glyn P. Norton. Cambridge, U.K., and New York: Cambridge University Press, 1999. Pp. 278–283.

Shuger, Deborah Kuller. *The Renaissance Bible: Scholarship, Sacrifice, and Subjectivity.* Berkeley: University of California Press, 1994.

———. *Habits of Thought in the English Renaissance: Religion, Politics, and the Dominant Culture.* (Berkeley: University of California Press, 1990; Toronto: University of Toronto Press, 1997.)

———. "'Society Supernatural': The Imagined Community of Hooker's Laws." In *Religion and Culture in Renaissance England,* edited by Claire McEachern and Debora Shuger. Cambridge, U.K., and New York: Cambridge University Press, 1997. Pp. 116–141.

———. *Political Theologies in Shakespeare's England: The Sacred and the State in "Measure for Measure."* New York: Palgrave, 2001.

Simpson, James. *Reform and Cultural Revolution,* volume 2 of *The Oxford English Literary History.* Oxford: Oxford University Press, 2002.

Vickers, Brian, ed. *English Renaissance Literary Criticism.* Oxford, U.K., and New York: Oxford University Press, 1999.

Welsh, Frank. *The Four Nations: A History of the United Kingdom.* New Haven and London: Yale University Press, 2003.

Woolrych, Austin. *Britain in Revolution, 1625–1660.* Oxford, U.K., and New York: Oxford University Press, 2002.

Charlotte Brontë's
Jane Eyre

~≈~

SANDIE BYRNE

CHARLOTTE BRONTË'S FATHER, the Reverend Patrick Brontë, was born to an Irish farm laborer and would have remained in County Down, probably in the profession to which he was apprenticed, blacksmith, had it not been for his intelligence, his studious habits, and the notice of a patron, which he attracted after becoming village schoolmaster. Sent to St John's College in 1802, he read Theology and Classics, and changed his name from "Brunty" to "Brontë," possibly in honor of Admiral Horatio Nelson, who had been made Duke of Bronti (in Sicily) in 1799. Patrick Brontë was ordained in 1806 and held curacies in a number of places including Hartshead, in West Yorkshire, where he met his wife, Maria Branwell, who had come north from her home in Penzance, Cornwall, to be a companion to a cousin. They were married in 1812 and their eldest children, Maria and Elizabeth, were born in 1814 and 1815 respectively.

In the year of Elizabeth's birth the family moved to a curacy in Thornton, near Bradford, where Charlotte was born in 1816, followed by Branwell in 1817, Emily Jane in 1818, and Anne in 1820. That year Patrick Brontë was made Perpetual Curate of Haworth, in the north of England. One of Charlotte's biographers, Lyndall Gordon, points out that the village had two drawbacks apart from its remoteness: "There was a strong body of Dissenters in the parish, and more serious, the village was excessively unhealthy, even by the unsanitary standards of the day, with no sewers and polluted water. The average age of death in Haworth was twenty-five" (*Charlotte Brontë: A Passionate Life* (p. 9). Haworth was not, however, an entirely isolated moorland village, but home to a number of mills and other manufactories. Mrs. Brontë was still weak from the birth of her last child, then four months old, when the family moved into the parsonage, and by early the following year she was suffering from cancer of the stomach. She died in September 1821. Her elder sister Elizabeth came from Cornwall to nurse her during her illness and remained afterwards to keep the house and care for the children. Elizabeth Branwell was a devout Wesleyan and, Gordon suggests, somewhat joyless. An efficient housekeeper, she saw to the children's material needs but did not offer them love; the place of a mother was taken by the precociously intelligent seven-year-old Maria. Patrick Brontë protected himself from the noise of small children and did not much concern himself with his daughters' early upbringing, though he took a keen interest in the intellectual development of his son.

In July 1824 Maria and Elizabeth were sent to the Clergy Daughters' School at Cowan Bridge, near Kirby Lonsdale, Lancashire, a charity school for the daughters of poor clergymen who nonetheless had to find £14 per year for each child, plus a further £3 for the accomplishments of French, music or drawing which would be indispensable for a governess. This represented a large part of Patrick Brontë's income, which, without his late wife's annuity, never passed £200 per year. Charlotte followed the next month and Emily in November. Said to be a model for Lowood School in *Jane Eyre,* Cowan Bridge was unsanitary, cold, and unhealthy; the food was meager and poor, and the teachers not always kind. Maria Brontë in particular was persecuted by a Miss Andrews. Tuberculosis was rife in the school, and in 1825 there was an epidemic of typhus. Maria was sent home to Howarth suffering from neglected tuberculosis in February 1825 and died there in May. The same month the next sister, Elizabeth, was sent home with the same condition, and died the following month, at the beginning of which Patrick Brontë finally brought away Charlotte and Emily.

From 1825 to 1831 the remaining three sisters were at home. Although they had little formal schooling, they did have access to books and periodicals, including *Blackwood's Magazine,* on which they modeled their own journal. Their nurses having been dismissed when they went away to school, they were cared for by an older woman, Tabitha Ackroyd (Tabby), whose kitchen became a domestic center. In 1826 Patrick Brontë gave Branwell a box of toy soldiers, one of which each child adopted and named. They began to invent stories about the exploits of these characters, which they wrote down as plays. The plays became sagas of exploration, warfare, and adventure in strange lands, which ultimately developed into an entire imaginative world of Glasstown or Verdopolis,

CHRONOLOGY

1816	April: Born in Thornton, near Bradford, West Yorkshire to the Reverend Patrick Brontë and Maria Branwell.
1820	April: The Brontë family moves to Haworth, West Yorkshire.
1821	Maria Brontë increasingly unwell. Her elder sister Elizabeth Branwell arrives from Cornwall to nurse her.
1821	September: Death of Maria Brontë.
1824	July: Older sisters Maria and Elizabeth Brontë enter the Clergy Daughters' School at Cowan Bridge, Lancashire.
1824	August: Charlotte enters the school.
1824	November: Emily enters the school.
1825	February: Maria Brontë sent home from the school with neglected tuberculosis.
1825	May: Maria dies; Elizabeth sent home with neglected tuberculosis.
1825	June: Charlotte and Emily brought home from school. Elizabeth dies.
1826	Patrick Brontë brings home a box of toy soldiers for Branwell.
1831	January: Charlotte enters Roe Head School near Huddersfield.
1832	Summer: Leaves Roe Head.
1832–1835	Remains at Haworth; she and Branwell write episodes of the Angrian saga.
1835–1838	Returns to Roe Head as a teacher as Anne returns as pupil.
1839	May–June: Works for the Sidwick family at Stonegappe near Skipton, Yorkshire.
1840	Back at Haworth, writing and housekeeping.
1841	March: Goes to work for the White family of Upperwood House, near Bradford.
1841	December: Leaves Upperwood.
1842	At Pensionnat Heger, Brussels, with Emily.
1842	December: Death of Aunt Elizabeth. Emily and Charlotte return to Haworth.
1843	Charlotte goes back to Brussels without Emily.
1844–1845	In Haworth, correspondence with M. Heger; Branwell Brontë degenerating.

1845	Charlotte discovers Emily's poems and plans a joint collection of the three sisters' work.
1846	*Poems* by Currer, Ellis, and Acton Bell published. *The Professor* rejected by six publishers.
1846	August–September: Patrick Brontë operated on for cataracts in Manchester. While staying with him Charlotte begins *Jane Eyre*.
1847	Smith, Elder and Co. accept *Jane Eyre* and publish in October. It receives good reviews. *Wuthering Heights*, published in December, is misinterpreted and condemned by some critics.
1848	Anne Brontë's *Tenant of Wildfell Hall* published. Charlotte and Anne visit Smith, Elder and Co. in London to prove that the sisters are not one person.
1848	September: Branwell dies. Emily falls ill.
1848	December: Emily dies. Anne falls ill.
1849	May: Charlotte and Anne in Scarborough. Anne dies.
1849	June: Charlotte completes *Shirley*. She visits London again. Edits second edition of her sisters' novels, includes a "Biographical Notice."
1851	Begins *Villette*. Close friendship with George Smith of Smith, Elder, stays with his family in May–June. Friendship ends in the autumn and Charlotte becomes ill.
1853	Last visit to London.
1854	March: Becomes engaged to Arthur Bell Nicholls, marries in June.
1855	Tabitha Ackroyd contracts digestive tract infection and dies in February, Charlotte possibly takes the infection from her (and may be pregnant), dies on 31 March.

which became Angria. These juvenilia, written in a minute hand on tiny pieces of paper, have been collected by Christine Alexander as *An Edition of the Early Writings of Charlotte Brontë, Vol. I, The Glass-Town Saga* (1987). While Charlotte was back at school in 1831, Emily and Anne developed their own saga, set in a place they called Gondal.

Charlotte's godmother Frances Atkinson offered to pay her fees at Roe Head School at Mirfield, near Huddersfield. Charlotte entered at the age of fourteen in January 1831, and remained as a pupil for eighteen months. She then had three years at home, keeping house and helping her sisters with their studies, before returning to Roe Head as a teacher in 1835. Charlotte's position entitled a sister to a free education at the school, and Emily returned with her in July 1835. Emily was intensely homesick, hated the lack of privacy and the constraints on her imagination and intellect, and became so ill that after less than three months Charlotte feared she would die. A substitution was made, and Anne came to Roe Head at the end of 1835, aged sixteen, and remained there until she fell ill and returned home at the end of 1837. After the Christmas vacation of 1837–1838, Charlotte returned briefly to the school, which had moved to Dewsbury Moor, but left for good in May 1838. While school was less unendurable for Charlotte than for Emily, she found the life of a schoolteacher, with its long hours, constant demands, little time for writing, and almost no privacy for indulging the imagination apart from the girls' evening prep hour, demoralizing and exhausting. During that Christmas vacation Charlotte and Branwell had both sent their poems to eminent poets, Branwell to Wordsworth, Charlotte to Southey. Though Charlotte's letter is lost, we know from Southey's quoting her words back to her that she told him of her ambition "to be forever known." His reply (the following March) was clearly designed to depress pretension: "Literature cannot be the business of a woman's life, and it ought not to be. The more she is engaged in her proper duties, the less leisure she will have for it, even as an accomplishment and a recreation. To those duties you have not yet been called, and when you are you will be less eager for celebrity" (p. 166) The desire for fame was considered improper, vainglorious, and unwomanly. In her reply Charlotte adopts a tone of submission and proper humility, which may have been heavily ironic, and duly received a less censorious (and more prompt) letter of condescending approval. She continued to write, but both rationed and hid her resort to the imaginative and creative aspects of her personality.

Having decided that school life was intolerable, Charlotte tried the profession of governess, first with the Sidgwick family at Stonegappe House (the original of Gateshead in *Jane Eyre*) near Skipton, where she was employed for two months from May 1839, and in March 1841 with the White family at Upperwood House, Rawdon, near Bradford. This proved no more congenial, and a letter from her friend Mary Taylor, who had just finished her education in Brussels, decided Charlotte on furthering her experience and intellectual pursuits abroad. Having induced her Aunt Elizabeth to fund the project as an investment which would lead to better paid employment, Charlotte and Emily left for the Pensionnat Heger in Brussels in February 1842.

Constantin Heger, the original of Paul Emmanuel in *Villette*, was Professor of Logic at the Athénée Royale, but gave some classes at his wife's school for girls. A brilliant and inspiring teacher and a voluble and volatile personality, he raged at and hectored but also encouraged Charlotte, in her studies and as a writer. The *devoirs* or essays written by the sisters at the Pensionnat Heger have been published as *Charlotte Brontë and Emily Brontë: The Belgian Essays* (1996). The sisters remained at the Pensionnat for six months as pupils and were then offered the post of pupil-teachers. The death of Aunt Branwell took them home at the end of 1842, and Charlotte returned to Brussels alone the following year, leaving Emily as house-keeper in their aunt's place. Charlotte's place at the Pensionnat was privileged. She was invited to sit with the Hegers in their private parlor, she had individual lessons with M. Heger, and reciprocated by teaching him English, but the developing friendship was abruptly terminated in April. It is possible that either M. Heger or

his wife had realized that Charlotte's feelings for him were more than respect and gratitude. Friendship was withdrawn, and Charlotte was left lonely amid pupils and teachers with whom she felt no affinity. After an abortive attempt to drag herself away at the beginning of the new school year, she finally left on 1 January 1844, and was escorted to Ostend by Mme. Heger. Missing M. Heger desperately, she at first wrote to him every fortnight but was subsequently restricted by his wife to twice a year. M. Heger was slow to reply or did not reply at all, and Charlotte finally relinquished the friendship in a letter of November 1845. Even during this low point of her life, Charlotte continued to fill exercise books with fragments of fiction, poems, and plans for fiction. By the middle of 1845 she had begun *The Master*, which includes a lightly fictionalized account of her relationship with Constantin Heger.

Charlotte was to record that in the autumn of 1845 she came upon her sister Emily's collection of poems (mostly connected with Gondal), was impressed by their originality and power, and undertook the hard task of persuading Emily to allow their publication in a collection with others of her own and Anne's. *Poems* by Currer, Ellis, and Acton Bell was published by Aylott and Jones at the sisters' expense in May 1846 but sold only two copies, though it did receive a favorable review in *The Critic* of 4 July 1846. Anne had returned from her time as a governess at Thorpe Green Hall with a large part of a novel, *Agnes Grey*, based on her experiences. Emily had written *Wuthering Heights*, and Charlotte had completed *The Master*, now titled *The Professor*. She again suggested that they seek publication. *Agnes Grey* and *Wuthering Heights*, together constituting the usual novel length, were sent out together at the same time as Charlotte sent *The Professor*. *The Professor* went to six publishers in 1846–1847, only to be returned six times. The last, Smith, Elder and Co., however, sent more than a curt rejection; the reader who had been given *The Professor*, William Smith Williams, had seen some potential. Smith, Elder and Co. intimated that a longer work, of the customary three volumes, would be given careful consideration. Charlotte sent them *Jane Eyre* in August 1847; it was immediately accepted, and published the following October. Three months later, she told her father that she had written a book. Soon after, Emily's *Wuthering Heights* and Anne's *Agnes Grey,* which had been accepted before *Jane Eyre,* were published by the slower-moving and less scrupulous Thomas Newby, who attempted to profit from the success of *Jane Eyre* by allowing it to be thought that all three Bells were the same author, and who offered Anne's second novel, *The Tenant of Wildfell Hall,* to an American publisher as the production of Currer Bell. To counter this, Charlotte and Anne arrived unannounced at the offices of Smith, Elder and Co., in July 1848 and made themselves known. They refused to be introduced to society or literary circles, and insisted on anonymity throughout their three- day stay in town.

Back in Haworth, Charlotte started work on *Shirley,* (1849) which was to make a statement about "the condition of woman question." In September 1848, after a protracted decline, Branwell died. By October Emily was gravely ill, and she died of tuberculosis in December. Anne's illness showed itself the following month, and she died in May during a last visit to Scarborough, on the Yorkshire coast.

A series of visits to London led to Charlotte's identity becoming an open secret, but she refused to be lionized. She met a number of the literary celebrities of the day, including Thackeray, G.H. Lewes, Harriet Martineau, and Elizabeth Gaskell, who was to become a confidante and biographer.

Shirley contains satirical portraits of Patrick Brontë's curates, but one of them is described with approval and even warmth. "Mr Macarthy" was based on Arthur Bell Nicholls, who began to court Charlotte Brontë in 1852. Charlotte had already declined two offers of marriage and frozen out another that, Gordon

suggests, James Taylor planned to make before his departure for India (p. 232). It is also suggested that George Smith either proposed or came close to proposing to Charlotte during a visit to London, but then was immediately so swallowed up by business difficulties that nothing came of it (p. 236). Charlotte's consequent collapse delayed composition of *Villette,* but the novel was finally completed in November 1852. Arthur Nicholls proposed in December 1852, but Charlotte resisted him for a year, at least partly because her father professed himself outraged that his curate should aspire to the hand of his daughter. Nicholls left Haworth but continued to pursue Charlotte through letters. In May 1854, soon after George Smith's marriage, they became engaged, and on 29 June they were married.

Arthur Nicholls was a conventional Victorian husband who expected Charlotte to subordinate her life and interests to his and to be a conventional Victorian wife. Charlotte gave up on "Emma," the novel she had been writing, and even submitted to having her correspondence examined. In December 1854 Tabitha Ackroyd became seriously ill, and soon afterwards Charlotte exhibited the same symptoms, which she initially attributed to pregnancy. Tabitha died in February 1855, Charlotte in March.

JANE EYRE: COMPOSITION AND SOURCES

Much of *Jane Eyre* was written when Charlotte Brontë accompanied her father to Manchester in August 1846, where he had an operation to remove cataracts from his eyes. The experience must have been appalling, both for Patrick Brontë, who endured it stoically, without anaesthetic, and Charlotte, who, at his insistence, stayed in the room throughout and nursed him during his prolonged recovery in a darkened room. Lyndall Gordon tells of events which happened near the Yorkshire city of Leeds at the time Charlotte was teaching at Roe Head, and may have inspired *Jane Eyre*. "A certain governess had married a gentleman employed by the family in which she held her post. A year after her marriage, by which time she had given birth to a child, it was discovered that her husband had another wife. This wife was said to be mad, which was the husband's excuse for bigamy" (*A Passionate Life*, p. 143).

The story of the madwoman in the attic has achieved iconic status, and was archetypal before publication of *Jane Eyre*, but there may be source stories for this manifestation. Charlotte had visited North Lees Hall Farm, home of the Eyre family, and knew the legend of the mistress of the house who had become insane and been confined to a padded room, and had died in a fire, and Norton Conyers, among other Yorkshire houses, had a "madwoman's room" in its attics.

Charlotte had drawn on her experiences at school for fragments of fiction before she wrote *Jane Eyre*, and had produced a number of heroines who were lightly disguised self-portraits and in some ways ancestors of Jane Eyre's, but Jane's character is blended from several sources. Her stoicism and powers of endurance may owe more to her younger sister Anne, who, with Emily, is depicted in the Rivers sisters, Diana and Mary. Maria Brontë was the model for the saintly and forbearing Helen Burns, and her tormentor Miss Andrews for Miss Scratcherd.

STRUCTURE AND THEMES

The title page of *Jane Eyre* describes it as an autobiography, and the story is narrated in the first-person past tense as a recollection in chronological order. It is not represented as a direct access to Jane's memories, however; an autobiography is a composition, and Brontë never attempts to suppress our awareness that we are reading a text. Jane addresses us directly as "Reader," reminding us that she is narrating and thus manipulating the material, and

preventing us from too prolonged a vicarious experience of her life. Jane appears to want her readers to sympathize and even empathize with her, but she discourages us from identifying with and substituting ourselves for her. With little subplot and no authorial (as opposed to protagonist's narratorial) interjections, the story is entirely focused on Jane and her concerns, though through her imaginative projections Jane sometimes gives us an insight into the feelings and motivations of other characters.

The book is a Bildungsroman in that it follows its protagonist from childhood to maturity, but it is also a spiritual autobiography. The physical journey that Jane makes from Gateshead to Thornfield (and Ferndean) and through physical ordeals from the age of ten to the age of twenty (the ten years which elapse between the reunion of Jane and Rochester and the end of the novel are summarized briefly) is also a spiritual journey through moral trials. Jane is a kind of Pilgrim, and her journey is in a sense as allegorical as the journey described in John Bunyan's *Pilgrim's Progress*, (1678) a text known to almost all literate Christians in mid-nineteenth-century Britain. Her goal is not Pilgrim's Celestial City (Heaven) but an earthly paradise, independence and union with an equal partner. Like Pilgrim, Jane is tested, and must prove her resolve, her moral strength, and her truth to herself. The emblematic nature of locations and people in the novel is indicated by their names: Gateshead (the gates of life, the beginning); Lowood (a low spot in Jane's fortunes); Thornfield (the thorny field of temptation). Characters divide into tempters or hinderers and potential models or helpers. The Reeds (broken Reeds) are hinderers, but they test Jane and she survives to move on to the next stage of her pilgrimage. Helen Burns, significantly reading Dr. Johnson's *Rasselas*, embodiment of Augustan ideals, is one version of what Jane might choose to be—stoic, resigned, Christian. Miss Temple (a temple of faith) is another; Jane could set aside her passion and her burning desire for freedom, suppress part of her nature and do good as a maidenly schoolmistress. Rochester tempts the opposite part of Jane's nature, her passionate side, which, if it were not for her powerful sense of morality, might declare the world and its conventions well lost for love, and Bertha Mason could be an awful warning of what giving free rein to that aspect would make her. St. John Rivers (always associated with cold imagery, the white marble pillar to Brocklehurst's black marble) perhaps appeals to her vanity or her half-buried desire for martyrdom, demanding of rather than offering her a vocation in which she is to work herself to death.

Although *Pilgrim's Progress* is a structural model, its ethos of Christian forbearance and altruism is not the overwhelming message of the novel but is in tension with the Romantic ethos of a self-centered drive for self-fulfilment, just as Jane's Romantic ethos of passion and the validity of desire is in tension with her rationality, self-abnegation, and self control. The heroine must reconcile these aspects of her character and temper passion with control, feeling with reason.

THE SUPERNATURAL

Though the burning candle, the strange low laughter, and Jane's visions of a bestial dark figure turn out to have a plausible explanation, a "madwoman in the attic" who is real and living and not a Gothic specter, there are supernatural and uncanny occurrences in *Jane Eyre* which we might call Gothic elements, though it is not a Gothic novel. Jane's imagination is Gothic; the images with which she avidly feeds it come from a sublime landscape of ice, storm, graveyard, and ruin. Her own paintings are Gothic and she insists on the Romantic idea that the shadow is as important as the light. In the Red Room Jane experiences the Sublime, and is duly overcome, but the phenomena she encounters are projections from her own mind. The narrative voice never suggests that Mr. Reed does haunt the

room, or that the light Jane sees in the garden is anything but the gardener's lantern. However plausibly explained, the effect of the incidents on the person experiencing them and on the reader remains powerful; the atmosphere becomes suffused with paralyzing terror.

The adult Jane's first encounter with Rochester is set up as a Gothic episode; the landscape darkening, misty and indeterminate, the large shaggy dog evoking memories of Betsy's tales of country superstitions (p. 112). The horse, rider, and dog, however, are soon shown to be corporeal, and it is Jane who is thereafter associated by Rochester with the other world, of which he says she has a look (p. 121).

> "When you came on me in Hay Lane last night, I thought unaccountably of fairy tales, and had half a mind to demand whether you had bewitched my horse: I am not sure yet. Who are your parents?"
>
> "I have none."
>
> "Nor ever had, I suppose: do you remember them?"
>
> "No."
>
> "I thought not. And so you were waiting for your people when you sat on that stile?"
>
> "For whom, sir?"
>
> "For the men in green: it was a proper moonlight evening for them. Did I break through one of your rings, that you spread that damned ice on the causeway?"
>
> (p. 122)

Although she is Christian, Jane is frequently compared to a fairy, a pixie, an elf, a witch, a sorceress, a genii, a spirit, and a changeling. On her return from her visit to Lowood, her walking to Thornfield from Millcote goads Mr. Rochester into remarking, "Yes—just one of your tricks: not to send for a carriage, and come clattering over street and road like a common mortal, but to steal into the vicinage of your home along with twilight, just as if you were a dream or a shade" (pp. 244–245). When, answering his question about what she has been doing for a month, Jane replies that she has been with her aunt, who is dead, Rochester exclaims: "A true Janian reply! Good angels be my guard! She comes from the other world—from the abode of people who are dead; and tells me so when she meets me alone here in the gloaming! If I dared, I'd touch you, to see if you are substance to shadow, you elf!" (p. 245).

Though it is Mr. Rochester who is the more given to fancy, and to extended fanciful stories woven around Jane, it is Jane who hears him calling her across hundreds of miles when she is at Moor House (p. 419), and Jane who has prophetic and symbolic dreams such as those of the infant she has on seven consecutive nights after helping Mr. Rochester with the wounded Richard Mason (p. 220).

The night before Jane leaves Thornfield, she has a dream of the moon, which becomes a human figure who says: "My daughter, flee temptation!" (p. 319). The mother seems to be the Great Mother, nature, with which Jane is intimately connected. Later, wandering starving and destitute, she thinks of casting herself into a hollow of a hill as on to the body of a mother, and reflects that she would rather die in the open than on a street (p. 330). The importance of the moon as symbol in Jane Eyre is traced by Robert B. Heilman in "Charlotte Brontë, Reason, and the Moon."

CONFINEMENT

Throughout the novel Jane Eyre is alternately constrained and liberated. Her initial confinement, behind the red curtains in the chill breakfast room at Gateshead, is a refuge, but her removal from it leads to a worse confinement in the Red Room. Removal from Gateshead and the Reed family is another liberation, but again the subsequent confinement is in some ways worse, the starvation and repression of Lowood School. Education liberates Jane from domestic servitude, but liberation from Lowood is to another kind of servitude, that of governess, and at Thornfield Jane experiences a sense of confinement and the desire for greater freedom. Liberation comes in the form of Mr. Rochester and the relationship that could elevate her to equal status, but this is thwarted, and Jane escapes again. The liberation of life in the open is soon shown to be only liberation into probable death, and benign captivity is provided by the Rivers. Liberated from the sickbed by returning health, Jane is subsequently liberated from poverty and her isolated state by the inheritance of wealth and discovery of her relations. She leaves the latter behind, however, refusing a new confinement and servitude as missionary, and voluntarily takes on a loving servitude and confinement with the blind Rochester, from which after the birth of her child she is partially released by his returning sight. Jane willingly accepts the yokes of nurse and of wife rather than remain an independent woman. As Sally Shuttleworth shows in her introduction to the Oxford World's Classics edition of Jane Eyre, Jane, like her creator, is ambivalent about attaining the liberation demanded by feminism. Citing Brontë's reaction to an article on "The Emancipation of Women" in the Westminster Review of 1851, Shuttleworth writes:

> She concludes that the writer's head "is very good, but I feel disposed to scorn his heart" [Letter to Elizabeth Gaskell, 20 September 1851; reprint, T. J. Wise and J. A. Symington, eds., The Brontës: Their Lives, Friendships and Correspondence, 4 vols. Oxford, 1932; vol. III, pp. 227–228] [....] she fully accepts the sensible nature of the arguments for female emancipation, but her heart recoils, as if she is convicting herself of unfeminine behaviour in even listening to such ideas. Her judgement is as severe as any we could find in a domestic manual of female etiquette: "the writer forgets there is such a thing as self-sacrificing love and disinterested devotion" [Letter to Elizabeth Gaskell, Correspondence, p. 278]. This is clearly not the dominant spirit of Jane Eyre, yet it suggests the ways in which ideologies of Victorian

femininity could wind themselves round the emotions, in despite of the intellect.

(Oxford, 2000, pp. xvi–xvii)

Neither confinement nor servility can make Jane Eyre consider herself inferior to other characters in the novel, any more than her supposedly inferior social and gender position can. The Reed children and servants are made to think of her as less than the lowest housemaid, because she is dependent and does not earn her living:

"Master! How is he [John Reed] my master? Am I a servant?"

"No; you are less than a servant, for you do nothing for your keep."

(p. 12)

Nonetheless, Jane retains her sense of her superiority, stubbornly and proudly maintaining when Mrs. Reed tells her children that Jane is beneath their notice: "They are not fit to associate with me" (p. 27). Though she might be expected to envy Blanch Ingram her superior beauty, social standing, and wealth, and be jealous of her association with Rochester, Jane tells her reader that "Miss Ingram was a mark beneath jealousy: she was too inferior to excite the feeling" (p. 185). At Thornfield, Jane is conscious of her isolated state because Leah and Mrs. Fairfax (once it is established that she is not the mistress of the house) are beneath her. At Morton, Jane has to remind herself that her pupils, "coarsely-clad little peasants," are "as good as the scions of gentlest genealogy" (p. 359), and reflects that becoming a village schoolmistress has "degraded" her: "I had taken a step which sank instead of raising me in the scale of social existence" (p. 359). She is "nettled," "hurt," and "irritated" by Mrs. Fairfax's incredulity at the engagement (pp. 264–265). Although she calls Rochester "master," she never doubts that she is his equal.

THE WOMAN QUESTION AND FEMINISM

Jane Eyre is multiply disempowered: as woman, poor woman, undersized and perhaps frail woman, and governess. Governesses occupied a difficult, intermediate position in nineteenth-century society; they were socially (though not always financially) above the servants and would rarely mix with them, but were not members of the family that employed them. This could lead to isolation. With no sick pay, paid holidays, or pension except at the whim of their employers, their position was often precarious as well as lonely. Yet taking a post as governess or schoolteacher was one of the very few options available for the middle-class, educated but impoverished unmarried woman of the time. The main alternatives were domestic service, which meant a large step down the social ladder, or writing. The "governess question," like the "woman question," was much under discussion in the Victorian period.

Jane Eyre ends with the passionate rebel Jane becoming a well regulated wife and mother, and the passionate fiery man to whom she had been so attracted neutralized and symbolically castrated by fire into a more passive and submissive husband and father. The ending is not a rejection of the novel's ethos, however; Jane has found fulfilment with Rochester, and she has not been the mouthpiece of nineteenth-century feminism throughout the story. When St. John Rivers tries to turn her mind from her catalog of domestic activities necessary for the preparation of Moor House for his sisters' return, saying, "I trust that when the first flush of vivacity is over, you will look a little higher than domestic endearments and household joys," Jane replies, like the approved voice of Victorian womanhood: "The best things the world has!" (p. 390). St. John wishes "to restrain the disproportionate fervour with which you throw yourself into common place home pleasures," but Jane says that she has "adequate cause to be happy" (p. 391). Only the novelty of having a home to make comfortable for her newfound relatives, and funds to do it with, can help us to reconcile this contentment with the ambition and restlessness Jane shows in early parts of the novel. Walking on the leas of Thornfield, Jane "looked out afar over sequestered field and hill, and along dim skyline" and "longed for a power of vision which might overpass that limit" (p. 109). She asks:

> Who blames me? Many no doubt; and I shall be called discontented. I could not help it: the restlessness was in my nature; it agitated me to pain sometimes. Then my sole relief was to walk along the corridor of the third story, backwards and forwards, safe in the silence and solitude of the spot, and allow my mind's eye to dwell on whatever bright visions rose before it—and certainly they were many and glowing; to let my heart be heaved by the exultant movement which, while it swelled it in trouble, expanded it with life; and best of all, to open my inward ear to a tale that was never ended—a tale my imagination created, and narrated continuously; quickened with all of incident, life, fire, feeling, that I desired and had not in my actual existence.
>
> (p. 109)

This restlessness and burning desire for more leads to reflections from the particular to the general, from Jane's enforced narrow sphere of activity to the life of women and their supposed nature.

> It is in vain to say human beings ought to be satisfied with tranquillity: they must have action; and they will make it if they cannot find it. Millions are condemned to a stiller doom than mine, and millions are in silent revolt against their lot. Nobody knows how many rebellions besides political rebellions ferment in the masses of life which people earth. Women are supposed to be very calm generally: but women feel just as men feel; they need exercise for their faculties, and a field for their efforts as much as their brothers do; they suffer from too rigid a restraint, too absolute a stagnation, precisely as men would suffer; and it is narrow-minded in their more privileged fellow-creatures to say that they ought to confine themselves to making puddings and knitting stockings, to playing on the piano and embroidering bags. It is thoughtless to condemn them or to laugh

at them, if they seek to do more or to learn more than custom has pronounced necessary for their sex.

> (p. 109)

This is the passage which Adrienne Rich calls "Charlotte Brontë's feminist manifesto." As she points out, it is immediately followed by a laugh, that of the madwoman, Bertha Mason (p. 469).

RECEPTION

W. A. Craik suggests that *Jane Eyre* was once more acceptable to its readership than *Wuthering Heights* because of its apparently conventional form as courtship ordeal novel but has suffered a reverse: "This recognizable novel form—adventure ending in marriage—was one of the qualities which made *Jane Eyre* acceptable to the novel-reader of the 1840s when *Wuthering Heights* was not; it is also the quality which has swung critical opinion over the last forty years the other way, so that while *Wuthering Heights* is an accepted masterpiece, *Jane Eyre* has sunk in esteem" (p. 71). This is hard to quantify; certainly *Wuthering Heights* is perceived as the more daring, experimental, and original novel, but nonetheless, *Jane Eyre* is more than "an adventure ending in marriage." As Lucasta Miller shows, it has become a modern myth, and been disseminated into mass culture. She accounts for its popularity by "its ability to be broken down into the basic building blocks of a simple Cinderella story or bluebeard narrative." Yet Brontë's real achievement in the story is the creation of a different kind of myth: a positive concept of the emerging female self in a society whose predominant models of middle-class femininity were self-denying, dutiful and passion-free" (p. 14). Miller suggests that Brontë transformed her own life into a universal myth.

Many of those who praise *Jane Eyre* most highly almost damn it through the nature of the praise, which tends to be for its powers to produce sympathy and empathy rather than for its aesthetic qualities. In 1906 Mrs. Humphrey Ward asserted that people "still sit up into the night" with the novel (p. x). Virginia Woolf finds that so intense is our absorption in the novel "that if some one moves in the room the movement seems to take place not there but up in Yorkshire." Brontë "has us by the hand, forces us along her road, makes us see what she sees, never leaves us for a moment or allows us to forget her" (pp. 455–456). Adrienne Rich speaks of turning to the novel at different periods of her life in order to find the "nourishment" she needed (p. 89). Angela Carter finds that it remains "one of the most durable of melodramas, angry, sexy, a little crazy, a perennial bestseller," and refers to it as "a delirious romance," (p. 161), and asserts that "of all the great novels in the world *Jane Eyre* veers the closest towards trash" (p. 167). These comments add up to an impression of an absorbing, even compelling story with whose heroine we empathize and whose romantic adventures we vicariously experience. The appeal of a work in which we can simultaneously find ourselves (through identification with the heroine) and lose (immerse) ourselves is clearly powerful, but the presence of these qualities does not necessarily indicate the absence of literary value.

One of Charlotte Brontë's early admirers was William Makepeace Thackeray, which greatly gratified Brontë, since she had long admired his work. Thackeray wrote to William Smith Williams that he wished Williams had not sent him *Jane Eyre.* "It interested me so much that I have lost (or won if you like) a whole day in reading it," even though his printers were screaming for copy. The novel "exceedingly moved & pleased" him and some of the love passages made him cry (p.70). When Brontë dedicated the second edition of *Jane Eyre* to him, he declared it (in a letter to W. S. Williams of January 1848) the greatest compliment he had received in his life, but in fact it must have caused him some embarrassment, since it fuelled gossip about coincidental parallels between private life and the novel. He

had put away a wife who suffered from mental illness, and rumor made "Currer Bell" the pseudonym of his daughters' governess and Thackeray's mistress.

The two novelists met during one of Brontë's visits to her publisher in London, but Thackeray found her too unlike the Victorian ideal of womanhood, declaring: "There's a fire and fury raging in that little woman, a rage scorching her heart which doesn't suit me" (Letter to Mary Holmes, 25 February 1852, quoted in *A Passionate Life,* p. 237), and she was outraged by his revealing her identity by calling her "Currer Bell" at a party he gave in June 1850 and hailing her as "Jane Eyre" at one of his lectures she attended in June 1851.

Jane Eyre was the most popular of the Brontë sisters' novels during Charlotte Brontë's lifetime, but while it received a great deal of praise, the approval was not universal, and it was condemned as a "dangerous" and even "antichristian" book. *The Christian Remembrancer* of January 1848 detected that the novel was written by a female "and as certain provincialisms indicate, by one from the North of England," yet found that "a book more unfeminine, both in its excellences and defects, it would be hard to find in the annals of female authorship." The masculine power of the novel, the reviewer asserted, was "combined with masculine hardness, coarseness and freedom of expression." Currer Bell is accused of "moral Jacobinism" and of being full of hate. "'Unjust, unjust,' is the burden of every reflection upon the things and powers that be. All virtue is but well masked vice, all religious profession and conduct is but the whitening of the sepulchre, all self-denial is but deeper selfishness. In the preface to the second edition, this temper rises to the transcendental pitch." With Helen Burns the Christianity of *Jane Eyre* is said to live and die. While the reviewer hesitates to say that it is "positively immoral or antichristian," the novel "wears a questionable aspect." The author is advised to "be a little more trustful of the reality of human goodness, and a little less anxious to detect its alloy of evil" for she will "lose nothing in piquancy, and gain something in healthiness and truth" (pp. 57–61). More damning was a piece by Elizabeth Rigby (who soon after became Lady Eastlake) on *Jane Eyre* and *Vanity Fair* for *The Quarterly Review* of December 1848. Rigby denounced Rochester as consistent but "coarse and brutal," and finds his creator guilty of "that highest moral offence a novel writer can commit, that of making an unworthy character interesting in the eyes of the reader." The criticisms of Jane Eyre's character are more interesting, since she is described as having virtues and principles but offensive language and manners. She is also accused of being, from childhood, "of a nature to dwell upon and treasure up every slight and unkindness, real or fancied," and "such natures we know are surer than any others to meet with plenty of this sort of thing." As a woman she is "an uninteresting, sententious, pedantic thing; with no experience of the world, and yet with no simplicity or freshness in its stead." She has "the worst sin of our fallen nature—the sin of pride," and this leads to the worst fault of the book, its lesson against Christian doctrines of resignation to the will of God and gratitude to him.

> Jane Eyre is proud, and therefore she is ungrateful too. It pleased God to make her an orphan, friendless, and penniless—yet she thanks nobody, and least of all Him. . . . It is by her own talents, virtues, and courage that she is made to attain the summit of human happiness, and, as far as Jane Eyre's own statement is concerned, no one would think that she owed anything either to God above or to man below.

Therefore, this review does condemn the novel as antichristian, deplores its heroine's desire for equality, and brackets the author with the contemporary social revolutionaries who were then campaigning for employment and election law reform.

> There is throughout a murmuring against the comforts of the rich and against the privations of the poor, which, as far as each individual is concerned, is a murmuring against God's appointment—there is a proud and perpetual assertion of the rights of man, for which we find no authority either in God's word or in God's providence—there is that pervading tone of ungodly discontent which is at once the most prominent and the most subtle evil which the law and the pulpit, which all civilized society in fact has at the present day to contend with. We do not hesitate to say that the tone of mind and thought which has overthrown authority and violated every code human and divine abroad, and fostered Chartism and rebellion at home, is the same which has also written *Jane Eyre*.
>
> (pp. 67–73)

On the basis of certain details of *Jane Eyre*, Rigby declared that the author could not be a woman, other than a woman who had for long "forfeited the society of her own sex." This was insulting, as the kind of woman who had forfeited rather than shunned or not had available the company of respectable women from whom she would learn acceptable and established ways is likely to have been a "fallen woman," a prostitute or one guilty of sexual impropriety. Rigby turns her disapproving gaze even on the novel readers, declaring that the popularity of Jane Eyre proves how deeply "the love of illegitimate romance" is implanted in our nature (p. 70).

The antifeminist writer Sarah Stickney Ellis, herself the author of "improving" works, condemned *Jane Eyre* for not being improving or elevated enough, while admitting the force of the novel and its ability to draw in the reader (against her better nature), since is it is "as unhealthy as it is absorbing" (pp. 34–42).

Once the gender of the Bells became known, the criticisms became harsher and more centered on allegedly unfeminine and improper qualities in the work. G. H. Lewes, novelist, playwright, philosopher and critic, initially championed *Jane Eyre* and corresponded with Charlotte Brontë and produced numerous reviews, but these later called attention to what Lewes described as defects in her writing and, after disagreements with Brontë, became damning. Later Victorian novelists condemned the work's calls for equality (albeit by our standards equality in limited areas of life, since Jane never demands equality of working, legal, or voting rights) as downright revolutionary. The novelist Margaret Oliphant, writing in 1895, refers to the book's "grossness," which she says misled readers about the sex of the author, since they failed to see that this was grossness which only a woman could produce.

> Nobody perceived that it was the new generation nailing its colours to its mast. No one would understand that this furious love-making was but a wild declaration of the "Rights of Woman" in a new aspect. The old-fashioned deference and respect—the old-fashioned wooing—what were they but so many proofs of the inferior position of the woman, to whom the man condescended with the gracious courtliness of his loftier elevation! The honours paid to her in society—the pretty fictions of politeness, they were all degrading tokens of her subjection, if she were but sufficiently enlightened to see their true meaning.

In a review replete with essentialist assumptions about the capacity and nature of the genders, Oliphant suggests that *Jane Eyre* is a salvo in a sex war which is to rage in place of proper relations because such women as Brontë require equality (pp. 117–122).

Charlotte Brontë's public demeanor and her Autobiographical Notice and Preface to her sisters' work inaugurated the myth of the Brontës, and Elizabeth Gaskell's *The Life of Charlotte Brontë*, which Patrick Brontë invited her to produce, reinforced it. In her attempt to correct the image of her friend as a coarse, vulgar, and unfeminine woman, Elizabeth Gaskell produced a Charlotte Brontë more in keeping with Victorian taste and with Brontë's own public persona. The angry, rebellious, radical, passionate woman was replaced by a figure equally false, the trembling, self-effacing spinster. As with Jane Austen, whose work Brontë detested, critics marvelled that such a weak frame and so retired a life could produce

such powerful writing. Lucasta Miller finds that Charlotte Brontë was her own mythologizer, and invented two distinct and conflicting myths, the second to deflect attention from the first.

> One was the positive myth of female self-creation embodied by her autobiographical heroines Jane Eyre and Lucy Snowe, who forge their own sense of selfhood in conflict with their social environment. The other, which eventually inspired the saintly heroine of Elizabeth Gaskell's *The Life of Charlotte Brontë*, was a quiet and trembling creature, reared in total seclusion, a martyr to duty and a model of Victorian femininity, whose sins against convention, if she had unwittingly committed any, could be explained away by her isolated upbringing and the sufferings she had endured. Both had their elements of truth in aspects of Charlotte Brontë's private character, but both were imaginative constructs, consciously developed.
>
> (p. 2)

In spite of this, many Victorian readers, women and men neither feminists nor revolutionaries, read *Jane Eyre* and were not shocked by it—including Queen Victoria (see Allott, *"Jane Eyre" and "Villette,"* pp. 140–141). As the Brontë myth took hold, critics "forgave" Charlotte her "coarseness" and supposed lapses of taste on the grounds of her innocence and ignorance, and applauded the verisimilitude of her portrait of her supposedly miserable childhood. This strand, focusing on the autobiographical nature of the work and its capacity to evoke a sense of identification in the reader, bedevilled criticism of *Jane Eyre*.

Twentieth-century critics who praised Emily Brontë at the expense of Charlotte often did so on the basis of Charlotte's overly personal and unbalanced approach. Virginia Woolf speaks of the "rancour" which "contracts" Charlotte Brontë's novels "with a spasm of pain" (p. 68) and suggests that Brontë wrote about herself "where she should write of her characters," leaving her story "to which her entire devotion was due, to attend to some personal grievance" (pp. 65–68). She finds a narrowness, a preoccupation with the concerns of the self in Brontë. "She does not attempt to solve the problems of human life; she is even unaware that such problems exist; all her force, and it is the more tremendous for being constricted, goes into the assertion, "I love," "I hate," "I suffer" (p. 456). As a "self-centred and self-limited" writer, Brontë has a power denied "the more catholic and broad-minded." The impressions of the former are "close packed and strongly stamped between their narrow walls. Nothing issues from their mind which has not been marked with their own impress" (p. 456).

A few years later, in his *Early Victorian Novels: Essays in Revaluation* (1934), Lord David Cecil declares that Charlotte Brontë's range is narrow, comprising only "the world of her own inner life" (reprinted in Allott, *"Jane Eyre" and "Villette,"* p. 174). F. R. Leavis did not find in her work the moral seriousness he required in great literature and did find in *Wuthering Heights,* and he declared the interest one feels in Emily Brontë's elder sister to be of a minor kind (*The Great Tradition,* 1948; reprinted London, 1962, p. 37.)

In the 1950s to 1970s a new concentration on form brought a change of focus, to Brontë's remarkable and original use of language as much as on her plots and characterizations or the moral tone of the novels, and critics such as Doreen Roberts ("The Warped System of Things" and David Lodge's "Fire and Eyre: Charlotte Brontë's War of Earthly Elements" explored both the poetics of the surface structures and their deep structures of symbol and theme. Lodge traces the patterns of elemental symbolism which unify *Jane Eyre,* associating safety, comfort, and pleasure with fire, and discomfort, repression, or exclusion with cold—but also immorality, excess, and passions over-indulged with heat (especially tropical heat), and self-discipline and rationality with cold.

Critics also analyzed the relationship between the Brontës' mature work and their juvenilia,

finding much of Angria and Gondal in the novels and poems. Kathleen Tillotson finds that *Jane Eyre*'s triumph is the author's emancipation from Angria with its high-Romantic passions and tyrannies (pp. 183–193).

In the second half of the twentieth century some of the most productive analytical approaches to the novel were feminist. The alleged narrowness of Brontë's range and overly personal nature of her approach was revaluated by writers such as Inga-Stina Ewbank in *Their Proper Sphere: The Brontë Sisters as Early Victorian Novelists* (London, 1966); Helene Moglen, *Charlotte Brontë: The Self Conceived* (New York, 1976); and Ellen Moers, *Literary Women* (London, 1977). Elaine Showalter locates *Jane Eyre* within a tradition of women's writing, comparing it in particular to George Eliot's later *The Mill on the Floss,* (1860) and argues that it is a classic feminist text whose imagery and symbolism chart specifically female experience (*A Literature of their Own,* 1977; rev. ed.: London, Virago, 1999, p. 112). Showalter suggests that in her heroine, Brontë attempts to depict "a complete female identity," expressing her consciousness through a range of narrative devices.

> Psychological development and the dramas of the inner life are represented in dreams, hallucinations, visions, surrealistic paintings, and masquerades; the sexual experiences of the female body are expressed spatially through elaborate and rhythmically recurring images of rooms and houses. Jane's growth is further structured through a pattern of literary, biblical, and mythological allusion.
>
> (pp. 112–113)

Showalter finds that Brontë's greatest innovation is her division of the Victorian female psyche into the "extreme components of mind and body" which are externalized as Helen Burns and Bertha Mason, characters who operate at both realist and archetypal levels of the story (p. 113). Jane Eyre, then has three faces, and her choice of which persona to assume is resolved by the destruction of two, to "make way for the full strength and development of the central consciousness, for the integration of the spirit and the body. Thus Jane Eyre anticipates and indeed formulates the deadly combat between the Angel in the House and the devil in the flesh" (p. 113). The "bad animal" shut up in the Red Room is the menarchal woman, punished for moving towards development in full womanhood. If *Pilgrim's Progress* lies behind Jane's spiritual and moral journey, then *Gulliver's Travels* lies behind her more terrifying adventures in the world:

> Like Gulliver, Jane moves from the nursery world of Lilliput to an encounter with the threatening and Brobdingnagian Reverend Brocklehurst ("What a face he had, now that it was almost on a level with mine! what a great nose! And what a mouth! and what large, prominent teeth!"), and an increasingly Calvinistic awareness of the "vile body" that leads to the climactic encounter with Bertha, the female Yahoo in her foul den.
>
> (p. 115)

To come to self-fulfilment and maturity, Jane must escape both the confinement and repression of individuality represented by her treatment at Gateshead and Lowood, and the passionate, instinctive behavior, uncontrolled by reason, represented by Bertha.

Perhaps the most famous analysis of *Jane Eyre* as a specifically female text comes in Sandra M. Gilbert and Susan Gubar's *The Madwoman in the Attic* (1979). Jane's progress is described as that of a nineteenth-century Everywoman overcoming the repressions of patriarchal society, and her encounter with Bertha Mason as a "dialogue of self and soul" (p. 336): "not with her own sexuality but with what Matthew Arnold called her own imprisoned 'hunger, rebellion, and rage'" (p. 337). Rochester's secret wife is "in a sense her own secret self." Just above the corridor where Bertha is housed Jane looks out from the battlements, longing for freedom. "Heavily enigmatic, ancestral relics wall her in; inexplicable locked rooms guard a secret which may have something to do with *her*; distant vistas promise an inaccessible but enviable life" (p. 348). As Jane paces, yearning for freedom, for more, she often hears the uncanny laughter from below. "Despite Miss Temple's training, the 'bad animal' who was first locked up in the red-room is, we sense, still lurking somewhere, behind a dark door, waiting for a chance to get free." Bertha is "Jane's truest and darkest double: she is the angry aspect of the orphan child, the ferocious secret self Jane has been trying to repress ever since her days at Gateshead" (p. 360). Each of Bertha's appearances coincides with Jane's feeling and repressing anger.

> Jane's feelings of "hunger, rebellion, and rage" on the battlements, for instance, were accompanied by Bertha's "low, slow ha! Ha!" and "eccentric murmurs." Jane's apparently secure response to Rochester's apparently egalitarian sexual confidences was followed by Bertha's attempt to incinerate the master in his bed. Jane's unexpressed resentment at Rochester's manipulative gypsy-masquerade found expression in Bertha's terrible shriek and her even more terrible attack on Richard Mason. Jane's anxieties about her marriage, and in particular her fears of her own alien "robed and veiled" bridal image, were objectified by the image of Bertha in a "white and straight" dress, "whether gown, sheet, or shroud I cannot tell."
>
> (p. 360)

The suggestion is that in setting fire to Thornfield, Bertha enacts Jane's desire to destroy the symbol of Rochester's mastery and her own servitude. Bertha, of course, also destroys herself in the process, ridding Jane of the obstacle to her own marriage. "And finally, Jane's disguised hostility to Rochester, summarized in her terrifying prediction to herself that 'you shall, yourself, pluck out your right eye; yourself cut off your right hand' comes strangely true through the intervention of Bertha, whose melodramatic death causes Rochester to lose both eye and hand." (p. 360)

This runs counter to Adrienne Rich's suggestion that Bertha is a distorted mirror-image of Jane, a kind of warning and example of what she might have become: "her instinct for self-preservation saves her from earlier temptations, so it must save her from becoming this woman by curbing her imagination at the limits of what is bearable for a powerless woman in the England of the 1840s" ("Temptations of a Motherless Woman," in *Jane Eyre*, ed. Dunn, p. 469). Gilbert and Gubar's conclusion is that Bertha not only acts *for* Jane but also acts *like* Jane.

Historicist and politicized analyses provide another important strand of *Jane Eyre* criticism. Terry Eagleton, in his *Myths of Power: A Marxist Study of the Brontës* (1975), finds at the center of all Charlotte Brontë's novels a figure who has lost or cuts the bond of kinship and thus is free to be exploited and injured and to progress through the class structure, choosing and forging relationships which are not prescribed. But these are not precisely rags-to-riches stories; the social status which the characters achieve is both won by merit and effort and inherently and entirely proper. In marrying Mr. Rochester, a gentleman, Jane enters her rightful sphere. Eagleton notes that Jane is acutely aware of the nuances of class; she is furious at being miscast as a servant by the Reeds and, though herself poverty-stricken and attending charity school, remarks that she would not like to belong to poor people. When she is teaching at Morton school, she has to remind herself "that these coarsely-clad little peasants are of flesh and blood as good as the scions of the gentlest genealogy; and that the germs of native excellence, refinement, intelligence, kind feeling, are as likely to exist in their hearts as in those of the best born" (p. 359). Eagleton remarks that

> the demotic generosity of this is sharply qualified by that stern self-reminder; Jane's doctrine of spiritual equality stems logically from her own experience, but it has to fight hard against the social discriminations bred into an expensively clad child. . . . . Jane feels degraded by her role as

schoolmistress ("I had taken a step which sank instead of raising me in the scale of social existence"), but guiltily scorns the feeling as "idiotic"; and that tension deftly defines the petty-bourgeois consciousness which clings to real class-distinctions while spiritually rejecting them.

> (p. 82)

Even Jane's relationship with Rochester is "marked by these ambiguities of equality, servitude and independence," for while he speaks of their union in terms of his bride's equality and likeness to him, this spiritual equality, "far from offering a radically alternative ethic. . . .is what actually smoothes your progress through the class system; Rochester may be spiritually egalitarian but he is still socially eligible." Jane's relationship to Rochester is "a complex blend of independence (she comes to him on her own terms, financially self-sufficient), submissiveness, and control" (p. 83).

INFLUENCE

The enduring appeal and influence of Brontë's novel can be seen in the number of modern novels which use its pattern of younger woman in love with a Byronic man who has a dead or absent or confined, mad or bad wife, such as Daphne du Maurier's *Rebecca* (1938) and Doris Lessing's *The Four-Gated City* (1969). A more important rewriting of the novel which is not a homage, is a postcolonial "writing back" to what its author perceives as the imperialism of the source text. Jean Rhys's *Wide Sargasso Sea* (1966) gives a voice to Bertha, virtually inarticulate in *Jane Eyre,* and fills in her West Indies background, rendered in a couple of reductive and homogenizing sentences of dialogue, by taking us back to the time before her marriage, when she was the beautiful, sensual, and sane Antoinetta Mason. Rhys depicts Antoinetta as a victim, desired for her money and her looks, and commodified to the extent that her identity is erased and she becomes a blank which can be renamed by

Rochester, obliterated under the generic "madwoman," and finally lost entirely in fire. Gayatri Chakravorty Spivak draws on postcolonial theory to compare *Jane Eyre, Wide Sargasso Sea* and Mary Shelley's *Frankenstein* (1818). For Spivak, Bertha Mason is the Other of imperialism, the horrible opposite onto which can be projected fears about the self ("Three Women's Texts and a Critique of Imperialism," *Critical Enquiry* 12, 1985, p. 244).

In addition to the literary descendants of *Jane Eyre* there have been a number of television and film adaptations (as well as of the lives of the author and her sisters). Most of these are set in the period of *Jane Eyre*'s publication, the 1840s or 1850s, rather than in the period in which the novel is set (we can date the opening to about 1799–1800 from St. John Rivers's bringing to Jane a "new publication," Sir Walter Scott's *Marmion*, which was published in 1808, since Jane is ten when the story begins and eighteen when she goes to Thornfield). Most adaptations compress the episodes at Gateshead, Lowood, Moor House, Morton, and the first three months at Thornfield, in order to focus on the love story.

Selected Bibliography

EARLY EDITIONS AND MS

British Library Add. Mss 43474-6. Charlotte Brontë's fair copy, used to set the first edition.

First edition: *Jane Eyre, A Biography,* edited by Currer Bell. London: Smith, Elder, 1847.

Second edition: *Jane Eyre, A Biography,* edited by Currer Bell. London: Smith, Elder, 1848 (January). (This edition was corrected by Brontë and included a preface with a dedication to Thackeray.)

Third edition: *Jane Eyre, A Biography,* edited by Currer Bell. London: Smith, Elder, 1848 (April). This edition was slightly revised by Brontë and included a note which refuted the rumor that Currer Bell was the author of the other Bell novels.

Fourth edition: *Jane Eyre, A Biography,* edited by Currer Bell. London: Smith, Elder, 1850. Inexpensive edition produced at the publishers' insistence.

Fifth edition: *Jane Eyre, A Biography,* edited by Currer Bell. London: Smith, Elder, 1855. First posthumous edition, of 3,000 copies.

Jane Eyre, A Biography, edited by Currer Bell. London: Smith, Elder, 1857. Edition of 25,000 copies following the publication of Elizabeth Gaskell's *Life,* reprinted (10,000 copies) the following year.

The Life and Works of Charlotte Brontë and Her Sisters. 7 vols., ed. Mrs. Humphrey Ward. London: Smith, Elder, 1906, vol. I, *Jane Eyre.*

MODERN EDITIONS

Smith, Margaret, and Jane Jack, eds. Oxford: Clarendon Press, 1969. A definitive edition based on the first edition but collated throughout with the second and third editions.

————, eds. With an introduction and revised notes by Sally Shuttleworth. Oxford: Oxford World's Classics, 1969; rev. ed., 2000.

Leavis, Q. D., ed. Harmondsworth: Penguin,1966; reprinted 1984.

Dunn, Richard J., ed. New York: W. W. Norton, 1971; rev. ed., 1987.

BIOGRAPHY AND LETTERS

Barker, Juliet. *The Brontës*. London: Weidenfeld and Nicholson, 1994.

Gaskell, Elizabeth. *The Life of Charlotte Brontë* (1857); reprt, Oxford: Oxford University Press, 1974.

Gérin, Winifred. *Charlotte Brontë: The Evolution of Genius.* Oxford: Clarendon Pres, 1967.

Gordon, Lyndall. *Charlotte Brontë: A Passionate Life.* London: Chatto and Windus, 1984.

Miller, Lucasta. *The Brontë Myth* (2001); reprinted London: Vintage 2002.

Smith, Margaret. *The Letters of Charlotte Brontë,* vol. I 1829–1847; vol. II. Oxford: Clarendon Press, 1995.

Wise, T. J. and J. A. Symington, eds. *The Brontës: Their Lives, Friendships and Correspondence,* 4 vols. Oxford: Shakespeare Head, 1932.

ESSAYS AND JUVENILIA

Charlotte Brontë and Emily Brontë: The Belgian Essays, ed. and trans. Sue Lonoff. New Haven and London: Yale University Press, 1996.

An Edition of the Early Writings of Charlotte Brontë, Vol. I, *The Glass-Town Saga* , ed. Christine Alexander. Oxford, 1987.

CRITICISM

Adams, Maurianne. "*Jane Eyre*: Woman's Estate" in A. Diamond and Lee R. Edwards, eds., *The Authority of Experience: Essays in Feminist Criticism.* Amherst: University of Massachusetts Press, 1977.

Carter, Angela. "Charlotte Brontë's *Jane Eyre,*" in *Expletives Deleted.* London: Chatto and Windus, 1992.

Glen, Heather, ed. *Jane Eyre,* New Casebooks Series. Basingstoke: Macmillan, 1997.

Heilman, Robert B. "Charlotte Brontë's 'New' Gothic" in Robert Rathburn and Martin Steinman Jr., eds., *From Jane Austen to Joseph Conrad.* Minneapolis: University of Minnesota Press, 1958, pp. 118–132.

Meyer, Susan. "Colonialism and the Figurative Strategy of *Jane Eyre,*" *Victorian Studies* 33: 2 (Winter 1990) pp. 247–268; reprinted in *Imperialism at Home: Race in Victorian Women's Fiction.* Ithaca, N.Y.: Cornell University Press, 1996, pp. 60–95.

Rich, Adrienne. "Jane Eyre: The Temptations of a Motherless Woman" in *On Lies, Secrets, and Silence: Selected Prose 1966–1978.* New York: W. W. Norton, 1979, pp. 89–106.

Roberts, Doreen. "*Jane Eyre* and 'The Warped System of Things'" in Ian Gregor, ed., *Reading the Victorian Novel: Detail Into Form.* London: Vision, 1980 pp. 131–149.

Williams, Carolyn. "Closing the Book: The Intertextual End of *Jane Eyre*" in Jerome K. McGann, ed., *Victorian Connections.* Charlottesville, Va.:, 1989, pp. 60–85.

Woolf, Virginia. "The Continuing Appeal of *Jane Eyre*" in *The Common Reader,* First Series, London: Hogarth Press, 1925; reprinted in *Jane Eyre,* ed. Richard J. Dunn. New York: W. W. Norton, 1987, pp. 455–456.

Yaeger, Patricia. *Honey-mad Women: Emancipatory Strategies in Women's Writing.* New York: Columbia University Press, 1988.

ARTICLES

Beaty, Jerome. "*Jane Eyre* and Genre" *Genre* 10 (1977) pp. 619–654.

Bellis, Peter J. "In the Window-Seat: Vision and Power in *Jane Eyre*," *English Literary History* 54 (1987) pp. 639–652.

Clarke, Michael M. "Brontë's *Jane Eyre* and the Grimm's Cinderella," *SEL* (Studies in English Literature) 1500–1900 40, (Autumn 2000) pp. 695–710.

Gribble, Jennifer. "Jane Eyre's Imagination," *Nineteenth-Century Fiction* 23 (1968) pp. 279–293.

Hennelly Jr., Mark M. "*Jane Eyre*'s Reading Lesson," *English Literary History* 51 (1984) pp. 693–717.

Lee, Hermione. "Emblems and Enigmas in *Jane Eyre*," *English* 30 (Autumn 1981) pp. 233–255.

Caroline Levine, "'Harmless Pleasure': Gender, Suspense and *Jane Eyre*," *Victorian Literature and Culture* 28, 2 (2000) pp. 275–286.

Pell, Nancy. "Resistance, Rebellion and Marriage: The Economics of *Jane Eyre*," *Nineteenth- Century Fiction* 31 (1977) pp. 397–420.

Scargill, M. H. "'All Passion Spent': A Revaluation of *Jane Eyre*," *University of Toronto Quarterly* 10 (1956) pp. 120–125.

Thomas, Sue. "The Tropical Extravagance of Bertha Mason," *Victorian Literature and Culture* 27 (1999), pp. 1–17.

Berman, Carolyn Vellenga. "Undomesticating the Domestic Novel: Creole Madness in *Jane Eyre*," *Genre: Forms of Discourse and Culture* 32, 4 (Winter 1999) pp. 267–296.

Ward, Maryanne C. "The Gospel According to Jane Eyre: The Suttee and the Seraglio," *Journal of the Midwest Modern Languages Association* 35, 1 (Spring 2002) pp. 14–24.

Watson, Reginald. "Images of Blackness in the Works of Charlotte and Emily Brontë," *CLA Journal* 44, 4 (June 2001) pp. 451–470.

Yeazell, Ruth B. "More True Than Real: Jane Eyre's 'Mysterious Summons,'" *Nineteenth-Century Fiction* 29 (1974) pp. 127–143.

CONTAINING MATERIAL ON *JANE EYRE*

Alexander, Christine and Jane Sellars, *The Art of the Brontës.* Cambridge: Cambridge University Press, 1995.

Allott, Miriam, ed. *The Brontës: The Critical Heritage.* London: Routledge and Kegan Paul, 1974.

———. *Charlotte Brontë: "Jane Eyre" and "Villette",* Casebook Series. Basingstoke: Macmillan, 1973.

Bock, Carol. *Charlotte Brontë and the Storyteller's Audience.* Iowa City: University of Iowa Press, 1992.

Bronfen, Elizabeth. *Over Her Dead Body: Death, Femininity and the Aesthetic.* Manchester, U.K.: Manchester University Press, 1992.

Boumelha, Penny. *Charlotte Brontë.* Bloomington: Indiana University Press, 1990.

Cecil, Lord David. *Early Victorian Novelists.* London: Constable. 1934.

Chase, Karen. *Eros and Psyche: The Representation of Personality in Charlotte Brontë, Charles Dickens and George Eliot.* New York and London: Methuen, 1984.

Craik, W. A. *The Brontë Novels.* London: Methuen, 1968.

David, Deirdre. "The Governess of Empire: Jane Eyre Takes Care of India and Jamaica" in *Rule Britannia: Women, Empire and Victorian Writing.* Ithaca, N.Y.: Cornell University Press, 1995.

DeLamotte, Eugenia C. *Perils of the Night: A Feminist Study of Nineteenth-Century Gothic.* New York and London: Oxford University Press, 1989.

Eagleton, Terry. *Myths of Power: A Marxist Study of the Brontës.* London: Macmillan, 1975; rev. ed., 1987.

Ellis, Sarah Stickney. *The Morning Call: A Table Book of Literature and Art.* London, 1850–1852, vol I.

Inga-Stina Ewbank, *Their Proper Sphere: A Study of the Brontë Sisters as Early Victorian Novelists.* London: Edward Arnold, 1966.

Fraiman, Susan. *Unbecoming Women: British Women Writers and the Novel of Development.* New York: Columbia University Press,1993.

Gezari, Janet. *Charlotte Brontë and Defensive Conduct: The Author and the Body at Risk.* Philadelphia: University of Pennsylvania Press, 1992.

Gilbert, Sandra M., and Susan Gubar. *The Madwoman in the Attic: The Woman Writer and the Nineteenth-Century Literary Imagination* (1979); reprinted New Haven, Conn.: Yale University Press, 2000.

Homans, Margaret. *Bearing the Word: Language and Female Experience in Nineteenth-Century Women's Writing.* Chicago: University of Chicago Press, 1986.

Kucich, John. *Repression in Victorian Fiction: Charlotte Brontë, George Eliot, and Charles Dickens.* Berkeley: University of California Press, 1987.

Leavis, F. R. *The Great Tradition.* London: Chatto and Windus, 1948.

Leavis, Q. D. *Fiction and the Reading Public.* London: Chatto and Windus, 1932.

Martin, Robert B. *The Accents of Persuasion: Charlotte Brontë's Novels.* New York: W. W. Norton, 1966.

Massé, Michelle A. *In the Name of Love: Women, Masochism and the Gothic.* Ithaca, N.Y.: Cornell University Press, 1992.

Maynard, John. *Charlotte Brontë and Sexuality.* Cambridge: Cambridge University Press, 1984.

Moers, Ellen. *Literary Women.* London: The Women's Press, 1978.

Moglen, Helene. *Charlotte Brontë: The Self Conceived.* Madison: University of Wisconsin Press, 1976.

Peters, Margot. *Charlotte Brontë: Style in the Novel.* Madison: University of Wisconsin Press, 1973.

Pinion, Francis B. *A Brontë Companion.* London: Macmillan, 1975.

Poovey, Mary. *Uneven Developments: The Ideological Work of Gender in Mid-Victorian England.* Chicago: University of Chicago Press, 1988.

Qualls, Barry. *The Secular Pilgrims of Victorian Fiction.* Cambridge: Cambridge University Press, 1982.

Showalter, Elaine. *A Literature of Their Own: From Charlotte Brontë to Doris Lessing* (1977); rev. ed., London: Virago, 1999.

Shuttleworth, Sally. *Charlotte Brontë and Victorian Psychology.* Cambridge: Cambridge University Press, 1996.

Small, Helen. *Love's Madness: Medicine, the Novel and Female Insanity, 1800–1865.* Oxford: Clarendon Press,1996.

Stoneman, Patsy. *Brontë Transformations: The Cultural Dissemination of "Jane Eyre" and "Wuthering Heights."* Hemel Hempstead Prentice Hall/ Harvester Wheatsheaf, 1996.

Tromly, Annette. *The Cover of the Mask: The Autobiographers in Charlotte Brontë's Fiction.* Victoria, B.C.: University of Victoria, 1982.

Vicinus, Martha, ed. *Suffer and Be Still: Women in the Victorian Age.* London: Methuen, 1980.

Winnifrith, Tom. *The Brontës and Their Background: Romance and Reality.* London: Macmillan, 1973.

Van Ghent, Dorothy. *The English Novel: Form and Function.* London: Harper, 1961.

Woolf, Virginia. *A Room of One's Own* (1929); reprinted, ed. Hermione Lee, London: Hogarth, 1991.

Wyatt, Jean. *Reconstructing Desire: The Role of the Unconscious in Women's Reading and Writing.* Chapel Hill and London: University of North Carolina Press, 1990.

ARTICLES

Bock, Carol A. "Authorship, The Brontës, and *Fraser's Magazine*: 'Coming Forward' as an Author in Early Victorian England," *VLC* (*Victorian Literature and Culture*) 29, 2 (2001) pp. 241–266.

Heilman, Robert B. "Charlotte Brontë, Reason, and the Moon," *Nineteenth-Century Fiction* 14 (1960) pp. 283–302.

Lane, Christopher. "Charlotte Brontë on the Pleasure of Hating," *ELH* 69, 1 (Spring 2002) pp. 199–222.

Ohmann, Carol. "Historical Reality and 'Divine Appointment' in Charlotte Brontë's Fiction", *Signs* 2, 4 (1977) pp. 757–778.

Spivak, Gayatri Chakravorty. "Three Women's Texts and a Critique of Imperialism," *Critical Enquiry* 12 (1985) p. 244.

J. R. R. Tolkien's
The Lord of the Rings

PAUL BIBIRE

THE LORD OF the Rings, by J. R. R. Tolkien, is a work that is difficult to classify, but has been described as a long heroic romance. It remains much read and rather controversial half a century after its publication. Numbers are uncertain, due to pirated editions, but probably over 100 million copies have been sold worldwide. Many have attempted to imitate it with differing degrees of failure; an entire new genre of literature, loosely termed "fantasy," has emerged largely in and from that process.

J. R. R. TOLKIEN

John Ronald Reuel Tolkien was a scholar who spent most of his professional life working on the ancient languages of England, including that of the Vikings. He was born in late Victorian South Africa, but spent his childhood from the age of three in the West Midlands of England, where rural Warwickshire met the outskirts of industrial Birmingham. He was brought up as a devout Roman Catholic and never lost his faith. After graduating from the University of Oxford, he served on the Western Front in World War I but was invalided out of military service with trench fever in late 1916. He lost all but one of

his close friends in that war. In 1916 he also married his childhood sweetheart, Edith Bratt; their marriage was long and stable, and they had four children. He worked on the *Oxford English Dictionary* and then taught at the University of Leeds, before occupying three professorships of Old English and English Language, at Leeds and then at Oxford, for a total of thirty-four years. He died in 1973.

The Lord of the Rings is Tolkien's largest completed work. It was written largely during World War II, and completed and published during the Cold War. Much of it was written for Tolkien's youngest son, Christopher, and sent to him while he was on military service.

The Lord of the Rings can be analyzed with the usual tools of literary criticism, but it also demands another sort of understanding. It is not freestanding, and it requires some knowledge of its implicit background. The constant backward reference within the narrative is not illusory or mere literary device. Most of this half-glimpsed history, legend, and myth already existed when the text was written. Remaining narratives alluded to or implied within the text were subsequently composed or elaborated, often at very great length, in material that Tolkien never intended for publication in their surviving form. This material gives the text a far larger meaning, within its own world and within our own. Only one previously published story is its immediate precursor.

THE HOBBIT

In 1937 Tolkien had published a story that he had originally composed for his own young children, *The Hobbit*. This is an important work in its own right and changed children's fiction in English. It begins in comically paternal mode, introducing its hero, Bilbo Baggins, a "hobbit." He is an adult of a child-sized people who mostly live in underground burrows in an idealized, preindustrial English countryside. This hobbit lived in respectable, middle-age, rural gentility, until one day a wizard, Gandalf, comes to his front door. Gandalf organizes a quest for some dwarfs to regain their treasure from a dragon, a quest Bilbo is to join as specialist burglar, much against his and their better judgment. Most of the story is taken up by their adventures on the long journey east. Before ever encountering the dragon, they are captured by trolls, received by elves, captured by mountain goblins and wolves, rescued by eagles, received by a shape-shifting bear-man, and captured by forest spiders and by hostile wood elves before being received by men. Only then in the distant east do they reach the Lonely Mountain, the ancient dwelling of the dwarfs, which is now dragon-haunted. There is a remarkable development of tone and content during these adventures, each of which becomes progressively more testing, more dangerous, and more significant. Each of them functions as a rite of passage, in which Bilbo himself grows up, until the final war over the dragon's treasure. By that stage he and his companions have become heroes of legendary stature comparable with Beowulf or Siegfried. The narrative itself comes to be worthy of any Viking legendary saga and is told in prose that is elegant, economical, and disconcertingly understated.

CHRONOLOGY

1892	3 January: John Ronald Reuel Tolkien is born in South Africa.
1895	His mother takes him and his younger brother back to England, where they settle on the outskirts of Birmingham in the West Midlands.
1896	Death of Tolkien's father.
1904	Death of Tolkien's mother, aged thirty-four.
1908	Tolkien meets Edith Bratt, then nineteen years old.
1911	Tolkien goes up to Exeter College, Oxford.
1914–1918	World War I.
1915	Tolkien graduates with first-class honors from Oxford. He joins the Lancashire Fusiliers.
1916	Tolkien marries Edith Bratt on 22 March. In June he is sent to the Somme. In November he is invalided back to England with trench fever.
1917	Much of this year is spent in the hospital; he occupies himself with writing. His eldest son, John, is born in November.
1918	After the Armistice, Tolkien joins the staff of the *Oxford English Dictionary*.
1920	Tolkien is appointed reader in English Language at the University of Leeds. His second son, Michael, is born.
1924	Tolkien is appointed professor of English Language at the University of Leeds. His third son, Christopher, is born.
1925	Tolkien is elected Rawlinson and Bosworth Professor of Anglo-Saxon at Oxford.
1929	Birth of Tolkien's daughter, Priscilla.
1930	Tolkien begins to write *The Hobbit*, but abandons it incomplete.
1936	At his publisher's suggestion, Tolkien completes *The Hobbit*.
1937	*The Hobbit* is published; his publisher requests a sequel, which Tolkien begins.
1939	Tolkien delivers the Andrew Lang lecture, *On Fairy-Stories*, at the University of St. Andrews.
1939–1945	World War II.

1945	Tolkien is elected Merton Professor of English Language and Literature at the University of Oxford.
1949	Tolkien completes a draft of *The Lord of the Rings*.
1954	Publication of the first two volumes of *The Lord of the Rings: The Fellowship of the Ring* and *The Two Towers*.
1955	Publication of the third and final volume of *The Lord of the Rings: The Return of the King*.
1959	Tolkien retires from his academic position.
1965	First American (unauthorized) publication of *The Lord of the Rings*.
1966	Second, revised edition of *The Lord of the Rings* (N.B. All references are to this edition, the last approved by Tolkein himself, cited by volume and page number).
1971	Death of Edith Tolkien, aged eighty-two.
1973	2 September, death of J. R. R. Tolkien, aged eighty-one.

The Hobbit seems in intention and inception to have been meant as a self-contained story; it contains very few overt external references and leaves very few loose threads. At beginning and end Gandalf mentions a figure of power and fear, the Necromancer. At their first visit to the elvish refuge of Rivendell, its master, Elrond, is said to be a descendant both of elves and ancient heroes of the North. He identifies their troll-won swords, including Bilbo's Sting, as from the elf city of Gondolin that fell in legendary wars long ago. Most importantly, however, after escaping from the mountain goblins Bilbo becomes briefly lost in their caves, and there he meets a strange creature called Gollum. By chance he finds Gollum's great treasure. This is a gold ring that makes its wearer invisible: unsurprisingly very useful later in the adventure.

THE HISTORY OF MIDDLE-EARTH

When Elrond mentioned Gondolin, *The Hobbit* was inextricably linked with Tolkien's own private body of myth and legend: the history of Middle-earth. He evidently started to compose this before the outbreak of World War I, though it first achieved coherent form in notebooks written in the trenches of World War I and during his convalescence back in England. He continuously elaborated and developed it, often at great length, and was still working on it at his death more than half a century later.

In the earliest versions of this work, literary influences can trivially be traced: Tolkien owed visible but insignificant debts to writers such as William Morris and Rider Haggard. Much more importantly, he had read and assimilated the legends that survive in the languages of Old English, Old Norse, Middle Welsh, Middle Irish, and Finnish, and the literary texts in which they were transmitted, as well as the earliest histories of these peoples. The Finnish folk epic *Kalevala*, or the Icelandic sagas, are far more important sources and models for Tolkien than any he needed or could find in his own time. In this he was not unusual: many of his predecessors and near-contemporaries had done the same. A romantic German tradition that goes back at least to the Brothers Grimm and culminated in Richard Wagner had its Anglophone parallels in Walter Scott and William Morris. More than any of these, however, Tolkien knew and understood the original texts in their original languages, and the cultures that had produced them. More, also, than any romanticizing antiquarian, Tolkien was prepared to create anew: he did not merely translate, or traduce, medieval texts, but created imagined analogues for the medieval traditions that he studied in his own professional life. Only occasionally, as in the legend of the tragic hero Túrin, is it possible to see direct influence from a specific and acknowledged source: in this case the story of Kullervo in the *Kalevala*, who kills himself after unwitting incest with his own sister.

Tolkien himself claimed that his own work arose from language. Languages, including those that he invented and developed from boyhood onward, presuppose their sentient speakers, and the world and worldviews within which they speak. Exploration of this world in all its dimensions, as these speakers move through it, then provided a compositional, narrative vehicle not only for his linguistic interests but for his personal philosophical and theological thought.

In conception, scope, and largely also in execution, this material is far larger a work, or body of works, than *The Lord of the Rings* itself. Tolkien's son Christopher published a rationalized and reworked summary of this material as *The Silmarillion* in 1977. Most but not all of the texts on which this was based were subsequently also published by Christopher in *Unfinished Tales* in 1980, and more fully, with the drafts of *The Lord of the Rings* and other material, in a twelve-volume series, The History of Middle-earth, 1983–1996. *The Hobbit* and *The Lord of the Rings,* in some senses, are simply narrative pendants to this far older and more complex material. A short, synthesized account of it is given here.

The imagined world was formed as and within the music that angelic beings created for Eru, the One, who gave actuality to its imagined perception. Some of these angelic beings descended into Creation as incarnate demiurgic powers, to bring to fulfillment the beauty that they had perceived in their music. These beings are the Valar, the Powers that order and maintain the world; men called them gods. But the greatest of them, Melkor, rebelled, seeking to create for himself, to order the world according to his own will and power, seeking therefore to dominate and devour everything that was not his own, and ultimately in nihilistic anger to destroy all other than himself. Some he seduced, who fell with him, many barely less great than himself, others became demons subject to him. He set his will and power in the physical substance of the world, so that all things might turn to malevolence. He appeared as a dark lord, described in terms of a volcano clad in ice yet burning with dark fire. So there was primordial war in the world, and its order and beauty were broken. But they were not destroyed, and the Valar restrained Melkor for a while. They set aside a continent, far to the West across an impassable ocean and guarded by unscalable mountains, for their own dwelling. This realm, Valinor, was long unstained by Melkor's malice, and remained as an image of what the world might have been.

Into the world at the center of things, Middle-earth, came the Children of the One. The Valar did not make them and cannot master them, and the gods both love and fear them. They are the Elder Children, the undying elves, and the Aftercomers, mortal mankind. The Valar summoned the first elves to Valinor, where some of them went. Melkor, now named Morgoth, the "Black Foe," partly succeeded in corrupting both elves and men, but although he could kill them, he could not wholly subject them to himself. There were also other "speaking peoples": Aulë the Smith of the Valar made dwarfs in anticipation of the Children of the One. When Aulë humbled himself they were adopted by the One and given their own being independent of their maker's will. Tolkien seems to have considered that Ents, the Shepherds of the Trees, were similarly creatures of Aulë's consort, Yavanna, patron of all growing things. Morgoth made trolls and dragons: they were effectively machines controlled by his will, and when that was withdrawn they went mad or ceased to exist; in Tolkien's earliest version of the legends dragons are described as semimechanical. Orcs, the goblins of *The Hobbit,* presented Tolkien with ethical problems. He tended to the view that they were elves that had been corrupted by Morgoth, though later he decided that they must have been corrupted men. He usually, however, described them as if partly reduced to biological automata, governed by Morgoth's will, so that they no longer possessed free will of their own and were incapable of turning to good; they were left only their anger and hatred for their master and themselves. Yet other beings, eagles and wargs, seem to have been spirits given the form of bird or wolf by that one of the Valar who ruled them.

Much is easily recognizable in this cosmogony and cosmology, and it can be directly related to Tolkien's own religious beliefs. The cosmology also integrates mono- theistic and polytheistic religion, including the medieval Christian view that polytheism is in some aspects devil worship, since one of the "gods" has become demonic. It is extended in that angelic beings mediate the act of Creation; they enter the nature of the created world, taking its physical substance in order to shape and control its physical being. Satan and the other archangels were physically present in the world; Hell was a place on earth.

The elves bear rather little relation, at least in Tolkien's later thought, to any antecedents bearing that name. They are more similar to the Tuatha dé Danaan of Irish myth, who are immortal, older, greater, and more beautiful than the human inhabitants of Ireland and have an undying Otherworld west across Ocean. This Otherworld was identified by early Irish Christians with the Earthly Paradise: a place on earth untainted by the Fall. Certainly Tolkien was aware that his own Elvish languages had Celtic affinities; he also produced verse paraphrases of some of the early Christian Irish tales of the Otherworld across the westward sea, specifically tales of the voyage of St. Brendan.

The notion of creative art, the angelic music of Tolkien's mythology, as "sub-creation" within God's greater Creation is equally applicable to literary creation, including his own. Tolkien pursued this argument in his Andrew Lang lecture *On Fairy-Stories,* given in St. Andrews in the spring of 1939, where he states most clearly his artistic creed. Human beings, as God's children and creatures, follow their Father in creating art; God, by grace, can give this "sub-creation" reality in its own right.

Some of the elves in Valinor achieved great feats of creation. Fëanor made the Silmarils, three gems that caught and preserved the light of the Two Trees that then illuminated the world. But Morgoth slew the trees and stole the Silmarils. In bitter rebellion against the Valar, Fëanor and his people left Valinor and returned to Middle-earth in exile, seeking vengeance against Morgoth. These Exiles, supported by the first men to come into the West of Middle-earth, fought a long and hopeless war against Morgoth, defeated as much by malice and treachery among themselves as by his open power. This war took up most of the First Age of the history of Middle-earth, rather more than three thousand years. Heroic legends, of Húrin and his son Túrin, of Tuor and Idril, of Beren and Lúthien, are woven into these tales of war. Gondolin was one of the cities of the exiled High Elves, and the legend of its fall is a continuous narrative strand throughout the whole of Tolkien's imaginative life. Only at the final and complete defeat of the Exiles did the Valar intervene, defeating and expelling Morgoth; in that conflict the world was much broken and the entire western part of Middle-earth was drowned beneath the sea. One of the Silmarils was set in the sky as the Evening and Morning Star, but the other two were lost, one in volcanic fire and one in the sea. The remaining High Elves were permitted to sail back to Valinor across the westward seas, but not all yet accepted this. So ended the First Age of the world.

Evil, however, was not ended. Morgoth was expelled from the world, but his will remained within it, and some of his former servants hid themselves and were not found. Chief among these was Sauron, himself of angelic origin but corrupted by Morgoth, who now set himself up as a divine king of benighted men. Some of the elves that remained in Middle-earth in their turn became great craftsmen, creating things of power with which to order and control the world around them. The ring-smiths made elven rings with the assistance of Sauron, who wished to seduce them. They made nine rings that Sauron gave to Númenorean lords of men, seven to the kings of dwarfs, and three that he never touched nor corrupted for the High Elves. But Sauron himself forged the One Ring in volcanic fire, a Ring that had power of command over all the other rings, those who wore them, and everything done with them. So he betrayed the elves and, in numerological blasphemy against Eru the One, claimed divine lordship over Middle-earth. Meanwhile the Valar, to reward those men who had fought against Morgoth, had created a new land for them, out in Ocean and within far sight of the Undying Lands of Valinor: that was Númenor, Westernesse. Following the new star, men sailed westward there and set up a kingdom of power and beauty. But although the span of their lives was much lengthened, the Valar could not take the gift, or curse, of mortality from them. As the centuries passed, so fear of death fell on the Númenoreans, and they began to envy and fear the Valar rather than love them. They built great fleets and sailed around the seas, returning to Middle-earth to aid the elves in their wars against Sauron. But this power brought desire for dominion, and the Númenoreans established increasingly cruel empires in Middle-earth. Only a few, the Faithful, kept their love for the Valar. Finally, in pride and power, the last king of Númenor resolved to challenge Sauron himself for the kingship of the world. But Sauron with cunning did not resist him, and in pretended submission was taken to Númenor. There he set up a new religion, worshipping the darkness and sacrificing all that opposed him. So he beguiled the Númenoreans until in fear of death their king resolved to assault the gods themselves, to gain the immortality of Valinor. At this Eru the One changed the world and bent the seas, so that the world thereafter was round and men could not come to Valinor. Númenor was lost in the abyss, but nine ships of the Faithful were spared, storm-driven back to Middle-earth. Here these exiled men of the West, led by Elendil and his two sons, Isildur and Anárion, set up two kingdoms: in the North, Arnor; in the South, Gondor, near Mordor, Sauron's "Black Land." Although Sauron's physical form was destroyed in the fall of Númenor, he too re-turned to Middle-earth and, reincarnated, made war on these kingdoms. Elendil, in alliance with the remaining king of the High Elves, defeated Sauron, though they themselves fell in the final battle. Isildur cut the One Ring from Sauron's hand, but he was seduced by its desire and took it for himself. He was ambushed and killed on his journey home; the Ring fell into the Great River and was lost. So ended the Second Age of the world.

Few of the High Elves now remained, and they were concerned only to preserve the memory of past beauty and glory using the Three Rings. So the Third Age is largely the tale of the two kingdoms of the men of the West. As the centuries passed, Arnor fell into division and ruin, though the line of its kings descended from Isildur remained unbroken; the North and West became desolate. But into these empty wastes came a small people, hitherto unmentioned: hobbits. In a corner of the Northwest they set up a little land where they farmed and grew prosperous, the Shire of Bilbo Baggins. In the South, Gondor grew great and for a while established wide power. But Sauron, though defeated and maimed by the loss of his Ring, was not destroyed; after about a thousand years he began to reestablish himself as a shadow of fear and began the search to regain his Ring. Very gradually his power grew, and he stirred up his ancient worshippers, men from the East and South, to attack Gondor. There the line of the kings had ceased, and the now diminishing kingdom was ruled by hereditary stewards. Attacked from the East, Gondor called for help from wild horsemen of the North and in gratitude gave them lands for their kingdom of Rohan. The Valar, meanwhile, had not forgotten Middle-earth, but feared to try to exercise power or dominion over men. About the same time as Sauron first reappeared, therefore, there also appeared five "wizards," sent to oppose him by persuasion and inspiration. Northern men named the two chief of these Gandalf and Saruman. The Third Age ended with the narratives of Tolkien's two published books. The One Ring was found by Gollum, and then by Bilbo Baggins as told in *The Hobbit*. This led to the events told in *The*

Lord of the Rings: the war in which Sauron sought final and total dominion of the world but was at last himself wholly defeated when the Ring was destroyed in the fire of the volcano where it had first been made.

The Lord of the Rings forms the culmination and end of the body of legend that defines its world. It does not merely depict a world of deep history and wide geography. It depicts multiple cultures within that world, as the hobbits explore them sequentially in their long quest. These include the hobbits themselves and the villagers of Bree, the High Elves of Rivendell, the ancient dwarf realm of Moria, the forest elves of Lothlórien, the quasi-barbarian Riders of Rohan, the almost Byzantine antiquity of Gondor. Each of these inhabits its own landscape with its own fully realized languages and cultural artifacts. Human and nonhuman peoples are presented each with their own understanding of the world, whether it be the immortal elves of Lothlórien, withdrawn into near-timeless enchantment from the unceasing flux of the world outside, or Ents, Shepherds of the Trees, in their own slow decay, or orcs in their anger and violence.

Much of this material existed in some written form before the composition of *The Lord of the Rings*, and some of the First Age legends survive in multiple versions of great length, in prose and verse, from all periods of Tolkien's creative life. The corpus is comparable with that of Arthurian legend, narrowly defined, though far greater in scope and driven by far more powerful ethical concerns. The immediate comparison that was made for *The Silmarillion* is with the Old Testament of the Bible, and that parallel is illuminating. Middle- earth is not, in any normal sense, fictional: it is a world created within a reinterpretation of fully believed Biblical and Christian myth and is underpinned by actual belief. It has its own long history, in which the narrative consequences of these myths are explored on a huge scale and in minute detail.

This world has its own ethics. These are certainly compatible with Christianity but are above all concerned with power, the desire for power, and treasured objects as the embodiment of such power. Its personages have to confront not merely mortality but immortality: neither the Valar nor the undying elves can shake off responsibility for the past, nor set aside the overwhelming burden of unending memory. They do not escape, as men do in death, and their immortality endures as long as the world exists. The elves indeed are to "fade" as the ages of the world pass; their physical bodies become faint with the intensity of their inner, spiritual life and become barely visible to men, shimmering twilight shadows, such as yet may be glimpsed in the wild places of the world. So finally Tolkien associates his imagined world with the awareness of present-day folklore.

THE RINGS

Into this world of ancient and tragic tales stepped the most unlikely person imaginable: Bilbo Baggins the hobbit, who found the One Ring. This Ring is now given not merely narrative explanation but narrative effect: it motivates the action of *The Lord of the Rings.* The powers of the Ring, as in part discussed by Gandalf, were subtle and far-reaching. Its simple ability to make its wearer invisible was now a sort of immediate physical "fading," a sort of undeath while remaining in this world. It accordingly conferred a sort of unnatural, quasi-elven immortality to a mortal bearer, since the undead do not die. Gollum had lived for many centuries in his caves after finding it, and Bilbo just did not grow any older over the seventy or so years after his own adventure. This immortality was not new life, since no one in this world, not even the Valar, can give true immortality to mortals. It was merely an indefinite stretching out of present life, "like butter that has been scraped over too much bread," as Bilbo put it (I 41). This "preservative" power was shared, for better or worse, by the Three and Nine Rings, so eventually a mortal ring bearer "faded" permanently to a wraith. This fate had befallen the nine lords of men to whom Sauron the Necromancer had given the Nine Rings: they had become undead Ring-wraiths, Nazgûl. They had gained power of command, through fear, over the wills of others, but had lost their own free will and were under the complete domination of the Rings to which they had given themselves. The Seven Rings of the dwarfs also gave power over the wills of others, but through proud and angry desire, gold lust. The dwarfs were made, however, steadfastly to resist any domination and could not be reduced to shadows, nor could their lives be affected by any ring. Similarly, the Three Rings gave the Elves power indefinitely to preserve the past in timeless beauty, but not to become or do anything new beyond it. Above all, however, the One Ring gave the power of command to those who already had strength of will. It was the focus and fulcrum of that strength, externalized from its maker and user so that it could itself be employed as a tool. Its purpose was to subject others to the ordering power of its user's will—domination of other wills through fear. The desire of this power was greatest for those who already potentially had the strength of will to dominate others. That domination was even more destructive for them, because they would be corrupted by this power and would eventually themselves become demonic. When he lost the One Ring, Sauron's power was made less effective because he could not directly employ this external leverage over others, but that leverage was not gone, merely inaccessible to him.

All the rings derived all their attributes from a power of ordering and control that could lock even the flux of time into an endless loop, that could control things seen and unseen, that could master the wills of others. They were made for the ordering of the world, for better or worse, and their power was apparently tied into their own hierarchical and numerological ordering of the Nine, Seven, Three, and One. This would be shattered at the destruction of the One controlling Ring, and the other rings would also lose their powers. If the One Ring were destroyed,

its ordering power would seem to be catastrophically released into the chaotic disorder of freedom; that power would not return to Sauron, its source, who would thereby be permanently disabled. The One Ring was not Sauron's "external soul" and did not embody Sauron's "life force": such notions are alien to Tolkien's understanding of personality. So the Ring did not work in quite the same way as the life-egg of folktale figures like the Russian King Kastchei, who hid his life in an external object and could not be killed until that object was broken.

The Ring clearly has no exact and direct external correlate in our own world; for us it embodies an abstraction, in part that of the ordering power of command. It has, however, often been interpreted relative to World War II in terms of nuclear weapons. Tolkien's world does not lend itself, however, to such exact allegorizations, and he specifically rejected this reading; indeed, he sketched out the alternative narrative that would have been needed to fulfill such an interpretation. In the foreword to the second edition (1966) of *The Lord of the Rings*, he wrote that:

> certainly the Ring would have been seized and used against Sauron; he would not have been annihilated but enslaved, and Barad-dûr [the Dark Tower, Sauron's fortress] would not have been destroyed but occupied. Saruman, failing to get possession of the Ring, would in the confusion and treacheries of the time have found in Mordor the missing links in his own researches into Ring-lore, and before long he would have made a Great Ring of his own with which to challenge the self-styled Ruler of Middle-earth. In that conflict both sides would have held hobbits in hatred and contempt: they would not long have survived even as slaves.
>
> (I 7)

However, the ease with which Tolkien was able to construct such an alternative narrative suggests that some degree of applicability, to use his own preferred term, is appropriate. Tolkien experienced the industrial and social devastation of much of the England that he loved; he witnessed the wage enslavement of tens of thousands of workers, treated as if they were mindless biological automata, on the industrial production lines of Longbridge in Birmingham and Cowley in Oxford. He fought in World War I; his career spanned the enslavement of Europe under Lenin and Stalin, Salazar and Franco, Mussolini and Hitler. He wrote *The Lord of the Rings* mostly during World War II, in which his son fought, and he completed it under the imminent threat of nuclear war between East and West. It deals directly with most of the major issues of these times, political, social, and environmental. Above all, however, it describes and analyzes world war, even though that world and its wars are presented as if they were legend.

STRUCTURE

Each of the numbered "books" of *The Lord of the Rings* has its own dramatic structure. Like *The Hobbit*, the text as a whole is picaresque, depicting a journey or journeys that explore an episodic sequence of inhabited landscapes. Each chapter usually recounts one such episode. Each book contains ten chapters, apart from the very last, which now only has nine, like the fingers of Frodo's hands: much of the substance of an intended tenth chapter was relegated to appendices at a very late stage of composition. Each narrative usually rises to a climax, but through differing structural developments.

The first of the three named volumes as originally published, *The Fellowship of the Ring*, contains the first two books. Frodo Baggins, Bilbo's cousin and heir, is now the Ring bearer; his journey to Rivendell with his three hobbit companions, Sam, Merry and Pippin, is told in Book One. It has a cyclic series of contrasting encounters that become progressively more serious: in this it echoes, sometimes overtly, the structure of *The Hobbit*. Book Two tells of the

southward journey of the companions, now nine; it seems to be structured by a balanced opposition of episodes, most obviously the thematic contrast of Moria and Lothlórien at its center, either side of which are long hazardous journeys, and at beginning and end the making and breaking of the Fellowship of the Ring. The second volume, *The Two Towers*, contains the third and fourth books. Book Three shows interlacing of the two narratives dealing with war in Rohan and the defeat of Saruman, one with an overt climax at the battle of Helm's Deep and another with an implicit climax at the fall of Saruman's fortress of Isengard. Book Four is relatively simple: sequential episodes of increasing narrative tension on Frodo and Sam's journey to Mordor, up to Frodo's capture by orcs. Books Five and Six were published in the third original volume, *The Return of the King*. Book Five shows interlacing of three narratives associated with the narrative viewpoints of Pippin, Merry, and the dwarf Gimli respectively, all of which come together in Gondor at the single climax of the Battle of the Pelennor Fields. Book Six falls into two sharply divided halves: the simple narrative of Frodo and Sam's journey through Mordor to the volcano, rising to its climax at the destruction of the Ring; and then the second half, which acts as a coda for the entire text.

The text is very highly structured, often using cyclic narrative patterns. Some of these repeat patterns already established in *The Hobbit*—the passage through hills or mountains by inhabited underground passages, usually involving fire. In both texts the object of the quest is a single mountain, entered by a passage, with treasure-associated fire at its heart. Even the Barrow-wights participate in this pattern, as had Bilbo's trolls: in both cases the hobbits acquire their swords from these early opponents. In both texts the passage of the Misty Mountains involved complex underground journeys, encountering more than one foe, and ambivalent fire: the Mines of Moria have a double conflict with orcs and a troll, and then the Balrog. Gandalf sets his own white flame against the red fire of the Balrog. Gollum recurs. The Paths of the Dead represent a similar pattern, if much abbreviated; treasure and fire are trivially present, and the inhabitants of the underground passages are the wraiths of the dead. The tunnel of Cirith Ungol lacks treasure, and the opposed flames are those of Shelob's eyes and Galadriel's phial, both described in terms of fire. The passage of inhabited forests is similarly cyclic: the Old Forest and Bombadil, Lothlórien and Galadriel, Fangorn and Treebeard, Drúadan forest and the Wild Men; this pattern is echoed when the Ring bearers are captured by Faramir in the woods of Ithilien. Such cyclic repetition is less obvious than in *The Hobbit* only in that it is more varied and on a larger scale. Also, as in *The Hobbit*, character development has a structural function, as each of the persons of the story develops toward the climax of his or her own narrative line. Much of this was not foreseen: when first composing the scene in the inn at Bree, for instance, Tolkien had no more idea than the hobbits of who the shadowy stranger might be; Strider underwent his own development, mostly through the decisions that he himself took.

Narrative viewpoint shifts during the text. The events of most of the first two books are seen through Frodo's eyes, as if he were almost a third-person narrator. Thereafter the journey to Mordor is told mostly from Sam's viewpoint. This is overtly rationalized within the text: we are told that Frodo wrote the earlier parts of the history of the War of the Ring, but that it was completed by Sam. Events in which neither Frodo nor Sam participated are narrated from the viewpoints of Merry and Pippin, or of Gimli the dwarf. It has become a truism of Tolkien criticism that the hobbits "mediate" the great events of world war, of wizards and heroes, relating them to an essentially "ordinary" viewpoint, and this is accurate enough as far as it goes. But it does not go far enough; it obscures the changes in the hobbits themselves, and there are many other sorts of "mediation" that can be seen in the text. Above all there is a continuous

relation of events to the physical experience of air, earth, water, grass, tree, stone—an insistence upon the sensory reality of the setting. This linkage operates in both directions: the narrative is tied to physical reality, but the substance of physical reality also accordingly acquires mythic status. The very trees can wake up and walk.

STYLE

Tolkien employs a very large variety of styles. There is no single, "unmarked" narrative style in *The Lord of the Rings;* as in *The Hobbit*, the narrative tone shifts during the story, partly according to location. This location always receives close and specific sensory description, always highly visualized but also frequently involving other senses. Accordingly the narrative is often dense with adjectives, but these are rarely static and usually imply some development of experience, whether following the eye movement of the implied percipient, the character from whose viewpoint the narrative is currently being observed, or some extension of his perception and understanding. Indirectly, therefore, they characterize the percipient himself as well as the scene described. As with *The Hobbit*, narrative, description, and dialogue are designed to be spoken; Tolkien almost certainly composed aloud, and the text always seems to be intended for performance. The different varieties of English employed correspond in function to the different languages represented in the text: each implies distinct worldviews. Each personage is characterized by a distinct prose style, a separate voice, and several of the major characters have several styles available to them. Obvious instances are Gandalf and the sequential personae of Aragorn (as Strider, Aragorn, and Elessar the king). For some characters and situations, Tolkien is prepared to use several very formal "high styles." For this he has been criticized as though this were ornate Victorian Gothic archaism. It is not so; Tolkien's high styles at this stage in his writings are very bare and simple. They avoid Latinatepolysyllabic vocabulary and syntax; they echo the prose of seventeenth-century writers such as John Bunyan, and are only in that sense archaic.

There is much verse in the text. The hobbits recite comic verse, sometimes at comically inappropriate moments, and some of this is of high quality. The intricate metrical games of Sam's troll song, for instance, are entertaining in themselves, while its content parodies the hobbits' own adventure. Other hobbit songs include bath songs, drinking songs, and walking songs. This hobbit verse shifts into heroic legend in Bilbo's lay of Eärendil, sung at Rivendell, maintaining metrical complexity but allowing the content to go beyond the merely picturesque. The scrap of the legend of Beren and Lúthien recited by Aragorn, although thematically important, is sub-Tennysonian and sentimental. The Riders of Rohan are given some rather good poetry modeled on the strong, slow rhythms of Old English. Probably the best poetry in the text, however, is not in English at all. Some fragments of elvish poetry are performed in their own languages, both at Rivendell and in Lothlórien, in particular Galadriel's farewell. This is extraordinarily fine, both in the euphony of its original language and in its terse and poignant English translation.

CHARACTERS

Middle-earth itself participates in the narrative, so much so that it has been claimed as a character in the story, even its most important character. This is not so. Both Middle-earth and the Ring can be seen as to some extent "animate." In the case of the Ring, this is fairly simply explained: as an embodiment of will, it can to some extent have a will of its own. It is nonetheless an artifact, even itself a work of art, a tool for other wills. Middle-earth is in origin also a work of art. Although it to some extent has the will of Morgoth set within it and is to that extent potentially malevolent, it is neither originally nor wholly so. Further, it bears and represents

the depth of memory of all its history; it embodies the consciousness of its own past. Every stone has meaning. Nonetheless it cannot usually act of itself; only those set within it may do so.

The hobbits provide not only a narrative link to Tolkien's earlier published work but a literary link to the fatherly narrative voice of *The Hobbit*, effectively Tolkien's own voice as he told the stories to his children. The hobbits themselves, therefore, start off as almost childlike: innocent, passive figures to whom adventures happen. The wizard Gandalf acts as a father figure for them within the text, both protective and initiatory. He himself sees his function for them as educational: that they need to "grow up." For Frodo Baggins, Bilbo's heir in both literal and literary senses, this process is almost entirely destructive. He is the Ring bearer, who is to lose everything in this world, including in some senses his humanity, in his erosive experience of the narrative. He begins with the innocent wish to follow Bilbo in having an adventure, and also to save his beloved Shire from incomprehensible fears. At Rivendell he chooses his quest for the second time, now understanding the meaning of his choice but not its means. At this point he seems motivated by duty. At the breaking of the Fellowship he chooses, for a third time, to leave his companions and go to Mordor. His motivation here is analyzed in some detail. Duty has become nearly compulsion, but he is also driven by fear of his companions and for them. He makes this choice in full knowledge of the cost to himself and others. He knows the terror that awaits him and how the lust of the Ring corrupted Boromir. Thereafter his burden gradually consumes him until the climax of the narrative, when nothing is left of him but the conscious will to bear the Ring. Sam Gamgee is quite different. He starts off simply as the faithful gardener and friend, characterized mostly by dogged loyalty. As Frodo remarks, however, he rapidly becomes much more than this: "First he was a conspirator, now he's a jester. He'll end up by becoming a wizard—or a warrior!" "I hope not," said Sam. "I don't want to be neither!" (I 220) Naturally both prophecies are fulfilled: Sam indeed becomes a fearsome warrior, an almost elvish hero. He takes the Ring to guard it when Frodo has been stung by the spider Shelob and captured by orcs, and it tempts him by a vision of power, the power of a gardener extended across the world to bring it into flower and fruit. His rather reductive good sense, his unwillingness, enables him to resist. So at the end of the story, through power given to him by Galadriel, his role as a gardener extends to heal and renew the entire Shire. Merry, Meriadoc Brandybuck, and Pippin, Peregrin Took, are young hobbit aristocrats, as playful as Tolkien's own Oxford undergraduates, who may be affectionately reflected here. Pippin in particular causes much direct harm, especially for Gandalf, through his irresponsibility, both in Moria and when he steals the seeing-stone of Orthanc. Both grow up; both become active rather than passive figures, causing rather than undergoing the action of the narrative. They precipitate the action of the Ents against Saruman; it is Merry who saves Éowyn in battle against the Lord of the Ring-wraiths, just as Pippin saves Faramir from death at the hands of his own father, Denethor. So at the end it is they who can cleanse the Shire from political oppression and enforced industrialization.

Gollum receives narrative explanation. He too was once a hobbit, but one corrupted long since by the Ring; Bilbo Baggins as he might have become, had he chosen otherwise. Tolkien presents Gollum very clearly as a split personality, known by his original name, Sméagol, and his new one, Gollum—"Slinker" and "Stinker" as Sam ungenerously calls them. (Sam thoroughly and rather jealously dislikes Gollum.) Gollum even refers to himself with the plural pronoun "we," and his two personalities debate with each other in pain and anger. Sam's jealous distrust proves decisive at the crucial moment at which Gollum nearly repents. He finds the two hobbits asleep on the mountain path into Mordor, and almost in entreaty reaches

out tremulously to touch Frodo. Sam awakes and accuses him of "sneaking," at which Gollum retreats into his malice and pain. Gollum's dual personalities reflect the doublet he forms with Frodo. Gollum too is simplified and denuded of his humanity by the narrative, until at the end all that is left of him is his desire for the Ring, and he is destroyed with it.

The strictly human characters of *The Lord of the Rings* begin with almost hobbit-like rustics such as the innkeeper at Bree, caught up in events too great for him, but not patronized nor dismissed. He "thinks less than he talks, and slower; yet he can see through a brick wall in time (as they say in Bree)" (I 233).

The Riders of Rohan are almost Anglo-Saxons, the early English as they might have been had they settled an open prairie-like land adjacent to and in friendship with a far older and greater civilization such as that of Rome or Byzantium. Similarly their language is effectively an unattested dialect of Old English, and their poetry echoes that of the Anglo-Saxons. They are noble and naive barbarians, brave and impetuous, and with awareness of other things older and greater than themselves. Their elderly king, Théoden, has fallen prey to melancholy at the death of his only son and the promptings of his corrupt counselor, Wormtongue. Théoden nonetheless has the strength, when aroused, to face his fate and ride singing to his death. For Théoden, Wormtongue functions as his own inner voice always prompting to doubt, mistrust, and despair, the dark shadow of the will, often expressed in Old English poetry. This despair is shared on her own terms by the king's niece, Éowyn. Wormtongue is enslaved to Saruman's will and voice, and when Gandalf expels him, Wormtongue returns to Saruman. His power to subvert the wills of others lies in the subversion of his own free will by Saruman. In mutual dependency and hatred they "gnaw one another with words" (II 189). His need for his master is matched only by Saruman's increasingly desperate need to dominate, and Wormtongue is himself destroyed when he finally kills his master. This is almost comparable with the relationship that develops between Frodo and Gollum. Éomer, Théoden's nephew, shows the noble naïveté of his people, but he is forced to question himself and his own position when confronted by Aragorn and responds with a proud love not dissimilar to that of his sister Éowyn.

The Númenoreans are a people under the shadow of an almost supernaturally great past, from which they fell through pride. Strider in the inn at Bree is almost as dark and disquieting a figure as the Black Riders, the Ring-wraiths pursuing the hobbits, who were once themselves corrupted Númenoreans; he has considerable power against them. At Rivendell much of the history of their people is told, and Strider is identified as Aragorn, Isildur's heir; he commits himself to helping Frodo in order to make good Isildur's fault. After Gandalf's fall in Moria he leads the Fellowship. He is consumed with self-doubt when it breaks, and thinks that he has completely failed in his duty. At this turning point he chooses what seems the less important task: to rescue Merry and Pippin from Saruman's orcs. This brings him into the wars of Rohan, and so into contact with Éomer and Éowyn. Another turning point is reached when he looks into the seeing-stone of Orthanc and for the first time makes a decision of action independent of other events and persons, to fulfill his role as Isildur's heir over the dead and the living. So he comes to battle claiming the kingship of Gondor. He reaches fulfillment at his crowning as Elessar the king and his wedding to Arwen, daughter of Elrond; at this stage he is now the iconic archetype of the King of Men, the completement and culmination of the legendary dynasties behind him. It is no small achievement that this development seems credible, natural and inevitable.

Earlier in the narrative, Aragorn is contrasted with Boromir; later there is some contrast with Boromir's father, Denethor, steward of Gondor. Denethor, however, is primarily parallel with Théoden, both elderly rulers facing despair.

Théoden accepts healing from Gandalf to do what has to be done, and dies heroically in battle. Denethor, in contrast, will accept no such duty. Instead, in despair, he resolves rather to kill himself and his son Faramir than accept any defeat of his own pride. His suicide is described in horrible detail—like Gollum, he is devoured by fire. Tolkien does not spare his readers here: the wages of pride is death. The brothers Boromir and Faramir also form a doublet. Boromir is proud and impetuous, and largely lacking self-knowledge; Faramir is gentler, quieter, more understanding. Boromir's suicidal defense of the two younger hobbits, Merry and Pippin, allows him narrative redemption for his fault in falling to the lust of the Ring. As he dies he confesses to Aragorn what he had done, and in final self-awareness admits his own failure. Aragorn contradicts him: he had triumphed as few have done, for he had overcome his own fault. Faramir is different. He is active where action is needed, but not driven by pride in himself or in Gondor but by love of it. This saves him when he is tested by desire of the Ring, since he does not seek his own power. Like Éowyn he is saved from death by a hobbit, Pippin. Like Éomer, he then also faces Aragorn and responds with love: not the proud love of a warrior for his comrade, but love for the healer, the renewer, the king.

The other peoples of Middle-earth are also represented. Of the elves, only Legolas plays an active role in the narrative. His only major development is an awaking of the sea-longing when he hears the cry of the gulls, a longing to leave the endless mutability of Middle-earth, despite his love for the trees of his home. The dwarf Gimli, however, develops considerably. The simple, gruff, and direct figure whom we first meet at Rivendell experiences grief for his own people and their lost pomp in Moria, and then love, received and given, in Lothlórien, when he commits himself to Galadriel. This love is reflected in the strong bond that then develops between himself and Legolas. Then, on the Paths of the Dead, he is put to shame by his own barely mastered fear. So he learns grief, love, and self-knowledge. He ends the main text as a dwarf-lord in his own right, yet bound in generous friendship with elves and men. His story, however, is continued in a brief appendix: after Aragorn's death many years later, Legolas built a ship to sail west, and for their friendship Gimli the dwarf went with him. So Gimli, alone of his people, went to the undying lands of the gods.

Treebeard and the Ents, the Shepherds of the Trees, are associated with another group of themes. In particular, Treebeard is changed by his own anger: the long, slow patience of the forest is broken, and the Ents awake and find that they are strong. Their anger is at the devastation that Saruman causes—"he has a mind of metal and wheels" (II 76)—and his orcs fell the forest in wanton destructiveness, polluting and poisoning earth, air, and water. The trees rebel and take their revenge.

The two wizards, Saruman and Gandalf, are contrasted figures who change and are changed by the events of the narrative. They both have power over the minds of others, to inspire, persuade, or daunt. Saruman had long since begun to be corrupted by the desire for the power to order and organize; he shows the process whereby Sauron had himself been seduced. Increasingly this power had become political, industrial, and military: he is in this sense the technocrat. Correspondingly he had studied the lore of the rings and fallen under the desire of the One Ring and, consequentially, under the will of Sauron. His desire for power made him the unwitting puppet of a greater power. After his defeat and the fall of his fortress of Isengard, he comes to the Shire and in revenge attempts to set himself up as ruler of a police state, and to impose industrialization. But hobbits in stubborn passive resistance are hard to daunt, and Merry and Pippin, those agents of the destruction of Isengard, have grown too great for his powers. Frodo, in remote and understanding mercy, dismisses him. His end comes as he taunts Wormtongue, his one remaining slave, who finally turns upon him.

Gandalf appears as an old gray wanderer, always the catalyst of action, never the actor. He is present at but does not participate in human battles; his foes are demonic beings such as the Balrog and Ring-wraiths. He uses his power to kindle hearts and minds, not to daunt but to inspire. His element is fire: flame that kindles, enlightens, sustains, and cleanses. So in Moria he claims to wield the Sun's flame against the Balrog's hellfire. But he is oddly vulnerable, and his weakness, mocked by Saruman, is his pity, care, and affection for the hobbits. They can hurt him, and he is hurt when they are hurt. That is the temptation of the Ring for him: to take it in order to protect them. He knows this, and this self-knowledge saves him from the Ring. He is also accordingly prepared to face physical death in conflict against the Balrog in order to save his companions; he returns disembodied to those who sent him, whether they be the Valar or even Eru himself. He is sent back into Middle-earth, but he is transfigured by his self-sacrifice. He is now an iconic figure, white and shining, his angelic being barely concealed from those who know and love him.

Sauron, the actual Lord of the Rings, is never directly encountered. He is seen from afar only as a blazing eye: the emblem of dominant will. Isildur had cut the One Ring from Sauron's hand in battle at the volcano, so as Gollum notes he has only nine fingers. At the moment when Frodo claims lordship of the Ring at the volcano, Gollum bites off his ring finger, so that Frodo also has only nine fingers—an alarming equivalence of power and weakness at the very heart of the narrative.

Tolkien's female characters in *The Lord of the Rings* are often dismissed or disregarded. Unlike *The Hobbit,* which contains no female characters whatsoever, *The Lord of the Rings* is sometimes dismissed as sexist. Certainly most of its personages are masculine, though the hobbits are sometimes portrayed as almost sexless children. But there are several important female characters whose gender is central to the narrative. The most powerful figure whom we meet in the politics of Middle-earth is Galadriel, the Lady of Lothlórien. She is for the most part beautiful, remote, and inaccessible, a figure of awe and ancientry. She seems, perhaps, as a mother might be seen by a small child in love and fear. She must be encountered, but she must also be left; the children must go out into the world in order to grow up, and she sends them out with gifts. There is a striking mirror symmetry here with Shelob. She also is presented as a monstrous mother, the parent and incestuous mate of the forest spiders who once caught Bilbo in their webs in Mirkwood. She seeks to capture and devour all, including her own offspring. Frodo and Sam challenge her with the starlight of Galadriel's phial, thus establishing a direct link between the two figures. She stings Frodo into unconsciousness. Sam is caught right beneath her body, and as she tries to crush him he fends off her belly with Bilbo's sword, Sting, and pierces her. The sexual imagery adds an almost incestuous passion to the scene. The two opposed aspects of the dominant mother, in beauty and horror, generosity and greed, are explored here. This must be associated with Frodo's offer of the Ring to Galadriel, a gift that would corrupt her and make her into her opposite, a Dark Lady who would devour the world. She finds the strength to resist: "I will diminish, and go into the West, and remain Galadriel." In this at last she repents of the pride and desire for power that had caused her to rebel against the Valar three ages ago. It trivializes this scene to see it merely or mostly in sexual terms, but such implications are probably present, as also when Boromir attempts almost to rape Frodo for the Ring.

Arwen daughter of Elrond, although her narrative role is very small, is given some complexity. She has much symbolic importance within the body of legends, since her marriage to Aragorn forms the third and last union between mortal men and the High Elves. The previous two marriages, Beren and Lúthien, and Tuor and Idril of Gondolin, took place in the legendary past of the First Age; their descendants included Elrond Halfelven and his mortal brother Elros, first king of Númenor, from whom Aragorn himself is ultimately descended. Arwen must choose between the two sides of her own nature, immortality and mortality, between her father and her husband, and both choices are cruel. But her story is continued after the War of the Ring, and she is not allowed to escape the consequences of her choice: she must not only lose her immortal father as he departs into the undying West, but must also lose her mortal husband in death. And at the last she experiences the bitterness of man's mortality.

Éowyn is the most complex of the female characters. She comes from a royal and heroic background, a princess of the royal house of Rohan brought up by her uncle the king, and she is shamed and embittered by Théoden's decline into impotent weakness. There are also sexual implications here: she is ice-cold and untouchable, her frustrated and imprisoned embitterment partly brought about by Wormtongue, who desires her. His power to induce despair is not limited to Théoden. When Aragorn comes to Rohan, she sees a figure of free and heroic nobility, and loves him, but as Faramir is to point out to her, this love is as much hero-worship as sexual attraction. Aragorn rejects her, as she sees it, by not allowing her to accompany him on his quest. This rejection is both sexual and heroic. Théoden, now recovered, sets her as regent in his absence in the East, but she refuses the responsibility of this non-heroic role and disguises herself as a young man to follow her uncle and brother into war. At the battle of the Pelennor Fields she achieves the felling of the Lord of the Ring-wraiths, predestined not to fall at a man's hands. But there is more to this than the fulfillment of an ancient and arbitrary prophecy. Éowyn is possessed by personal despair, and only accordingly can face the despair of the Ring-wraith: he cannot master her through fear. It is here that Merry is relevant, for the hobbit's unquenchable and glad will to life enables Éowyn to achieve her feat. She faces her despair and fells it. But Éowyn has nothing more left in her life at this point. It is only when she can turn from war to Faramir, who has been through comparable experiences of his own, that she can become a woman. In the new light she mocks her own former status as a shield-maiden, an Amazon of the North. Unlike the hobbits, Éowyn must in a sense grow down, not up, from iconic status to humanity.

ETHICS

The ethics of the narrative are continually explored: there is constant ethical debate, centered always upon the Ring, of the rights and wrongs of wisdom and folly, of power and weakness, of action and inaction, of war and peace. "Good" and "evil" are terms largely avoided in this discussion, as they are in *The Lord of the Rings* itself. They presuppose some certainty over who or what is good or evil, a certitude that is rarely present even for the "best" and "worst" characters. Each of the persons in the story has his or her own moral decisions to make, decisions that are rarely simple or easy, and they are allowed to make them on their own differing terms. Each also bears the individual responsibility for the consequences of every choice; there are no excuses, and each character is changed, developed, or diminished by each choice. Saruman and Gollum have the chance to change their minds, to repent, and both nearly take it. Even orcs are sometimes given ethical status. Uglúk, leader of Saruman's orcs, is shown as an efficient and effective commander and is allowed a heroic death in single combat against Éomer. Both Gandalf and Galadriel are seriously tempted by the Ring, at Frodo's active doing, and at the very heart of the narrative Frodo himself finally fails. He refuses his quest at the very point of its fulfillment. It is indeed fulfilled, but by Gollum.

No character, therefore, is a fixed type. Some become archetypes, but that process only takes place through making their own choices and living with the consequences. This is not merely a matter of Tolkien's view of personality. The text was largely composed in this way, and the early drafts show that little of the story was predetermined by narrative necessity; rather, it took its shape from the unforeseen inner development of individual characters through the choices that they made. They "grow up" and fulfill previously hidden potential, and each always has alternative courses of action and development that are clearly demonstrated within the text. The clearest and most important example of all is Frodo and his relationship with Gollum. As each of them is devoured by the Ring, they become alter egos, opposed aspects of each other, until at the last Gollum the Ring-bearer falls into the fire. At this Frodo is permanently maimed and loses the capability for action. Similar relationships may clearly be seen between, for instance, the two wizards Gandalf and Saruman, the two human heroes Aragorn and Boromir, the two human rulers Théoden and Denethor. These symmetrical oppositions define dimensions of ethical debate. Such a reading of course oversimplifies and must not be allowed to obscure the individuality of each character in his or her own right and the particularity of each scene. Some characters, perhaps most obviously Sam, do not usually seem to participate in such obvious narrative dualism. He fulfills many functions, but one of these is of the "ordinary man" caught up in great events, and much of the later parts of the narrative are seen through his eyes. On this basis he can form a stable center within some of the ethical paradigms.

The Lord of the Rings is much concerned with what are now called environmental issues. This appears largely aesthetic but is underpinned ethically. On first reading a concern with natural beauty, whether of the tamed and humanized agricultural landscape of the Shire, or of the wild world of mountain and forest, seems simply and uncritically romantic. Similarly its obverse, the condemnation of Saruman's military industrialization, or of the postindustrial wastelands around Mordor, seems equally simpleminded, even naive. The Shire is idealized: a rustic idyll that never existed in English history. In particular it lacks effective government: it is largely a self-regulating cooperative of free farmers, uncontrolled by any ruler until Saruman, as "Sharkey," tries to take it over. This vision of an idealized rural society is clearly related to the sort of anarchic socialism preached and to some extent practiced by William Morris and his associates. However, Tolkien's view of it is complex. On its own terms hobbit society is meritorious, but it is petty, even silly, and in order to "grow up" the hobbits must leave it. Further, the Shire can only exist under protection of which it must itself remain unaware. The world is too dangerous for such childlike innocence to survive unguarded. Hobbits are protected in part by their own insignificance: they can survive while they are disregarded. They are also, however, actively guarded, in large part by the wizard Gandalf. Aragorn, speaking at the Council of Elrond, makes this point explicitly about the villagers of Bree: "If simple folk are free from care and fear, simple they will be, and we must be secret to keep them so" (I 261). The naïveté of the Shire is the childlike innocence of its inhabitants: something beautiful in its own right, but which must be outgrown.

The beauty of the wild world correlates in part with its danger. The mountains above Moria are beautiful and perilous; their peril is in part malevolent and is sufficient to defeat Gandalf as he attempts to guide the Fellowship of the Ring across them. The woods of Lothlórien, and their elvish ruler, the Lady Galadriel, are also beautiful beyond natural measure, but that beauty itself constitutes a peril for anyone who enters. Here the danger is not of itself malevolent; evil is within the stranger. So Boromir here first realizes his own lust for the Ring which is nearly to destroy him. Gimli the dwarf is nearly seduced from the quest by the beauty of Galadriel, but this experience opens to him a moral awareness of other beauties than those of things made by skill; it gives him the friendship of Legolas and a driving motivation

for his further deeds. Frodo the Ring-bearer brings about the full realization of Galadriel's peril, not least for the character herself. She tests him through the visions of the Mirror, but he tests her more terribly, almost to destruction, by the temptation of the desire of the Ring. Ithilien, beneath the mountains of Mordor, is shown as a garden now deserted, once domestic and now wild: its danger is straightforwardly as a war zone, both literally and between control and chaos.

Saruman's hideous industrialization of his fortress, Isengard, is entirely based upon his desire for power. That power is in this instance military, but when he finally comes to the Shire as "Sharkey," he seeks economic and political power by industrialization enforced through a puppet police state. He reduces his servants to the status of orcs. Tolkien's attitude here subverts the military-industrial complex of modern "developed" nations. With apposite irony, Saruman's military power was destroyed by the very trees that he used to fuel his furnaces. He had forgotten the wild wood, the Ents, or regarded them and their trees as without value in themselves. For him they were merely things to use for his own purposes, just as Sauron used him in his turn. Because he did not value them, he took no account of them, and could not resist when at last they rebelled. Saruman himself is reduced from his former nobility to a thing both contemptible and pitiable, slain by his own slave. His desire for power, both in motivation and consequence, destroys whatever it touches, and above all himself. It is remedied not by Wormtongue's final, murderous and suicidal rebellion, but by Merry and Pippin's reassertion of the older values of personal freedom, and above all by Frodo's almost metaphysical pity.

The devastation of Isengard, however, is childish in comparison with Mordor. That is partly and trivially industrial: the slag heaps at its entrance, the Black Gate, are artificial and intentionally created. Mordor itself, however, is devastated by the volcano: it is a desert of lava and ash, poisoned by volcanic fumes. It is a fundamental expression of diabolically determined malevolence, inherent within the natural world itself. This supersedes any romantic view of natural beauty, or any social commentary on industrialization, presented within *The Lord of the Rings.*

Since it deals with the politics of its world, *The Lord of the Rings* must partly be read in political terms. As such it is subversive of most of the political ideologies that it seems to depict. For the political Left, Tolkien is a romantic reactionary; for the Right, an opponent of industrial capitalism; for the feminist or libertarian, a supporter of hierarchical, masculine hereditary monarchy; for the authoritarian, an anarchic opponent of political power. All these, and others, miss the point. All his examples, of success or failure or merely muddling through, are based upon the personal ethics of those who succeed or fail, developed through the choices that they make. Tolkien propounds no single or simple political ideology but only personal ethics: all else follows from that.

COMEDY

The Lord of the Rings is not strictly speaking a comedy, in that it does not have a particularly happy ending. Certainly the war was won for this time, the king was crowned, the Shire restored. These have value because in all cases the cost is counted. That cost is very great and is borne by several of the central characters. Part of the price is the loss of former innocence and beauty, both for the hobbits and the elves. Elrond departs bereaved of his daughter Arwen. Galadriel too departs in grief at the beauty of Middle-earth now lost. Frodo pays a higher price: a sort of death-in-life. He can find nothing more in this world and must leave it. Even beyond these, there is a continuing awareness of transience. Aragorn has become Elessar the king, and he will rule Gondor in glory for a while. But he is a mortal man and shall die, and his glory shall pass. The story ends in twilight.

The text largely lacks the wit of *The Hobbit,* where verbal registers are contrasted to comic effect, though actual or implicit hobbit narration often has ironic lightness of tone. Social comedy, mostly associated with the hobbits, is found in *The Lord of the Rings,* but the mode itself is subverted. Hobbits are admirable only insofar as they can transcend it. Lobelia Sackville-Baggins, for instance, is an unpleasant elderly cousin, snobbish and greedy. But she is finally allowed her brief moment of comic heroism when, armed only with her old umbrella, she attacks a bullying ruffian twice her size. The ruffians imprison her, but when rescued weeks later she insists on hobbling out, still clutching her umbrella, to great applause—she had never been popular before. But she is broken by the news of her son's death, and when she dies the next spring, she leaves her money to help hobbits made homeless in the troubles. The character is allowed to transcend her type, and the essentially trivial game of social stereotypes is disrupted by contact with the reality of death. She achieves her own small narrative redemption.

There is other comedy at times in *The Lord of the Rings.* Tolkien sometimes mocks himself, and the entire scholarly apparatus erected behind the narrative is certainly presented as comic in, for instance, the prologue. Gandalf is short-tempered and sometimes professorially irritable. Treebeard plays professorial word games with the younger hobbits, and once also with Gandalf; similarly, Merry launches into a mock-academic history of tobacco at a quite inappropriate moment. Gimli's sentimental infatuation with Galadriel is presented as comic, though also as accurate recognition of beauty and nobility. Inappropriate clashes of register and narrative level take place when, for instance, Sam offers Gollum the prospect of the traditional British working-class dish fried fish and chips, but Gollum grumpily refuses: "Spoiling nice fish, scorching it. Give me fish *now,* and keep nassty chips" (II 263). At one of its darkest moments, as Frodo and Sam climb the mountains into Mordor, they talk about their own story, in a sort of wry meta-textuality, as a tale that will be told, or rather read out of a book, and in the darkness they laugh about the bored child who will not want to hear any more of it (II 322).

CONCLUSION

The Lord of the Rings could hardly be more different from the bourgeois social comedy that has been the dominant mode of the English novel for nearly two centuries. This has not proved competent to deal with the historical, emotional, and ethical issues raised during the last hundred years, and mainstream British novelists mostly dealt with these by omission. The world wars make no appearance in the novels of such writers as Forster, Woolf, Joyce, or Lawrence.

The Lord of the Rings is fantasy, a word and concept that Tolkien discussed at length in his St. Andrews lecture of 1939. Trivially it contains monsters and marvels, wizards and heroes. Those who cannot cope with these presumably cannot deal with the *Odyssey* or *The Tempest*, let alone the history of the last hundred years. That century, if the words "scientist" and "soldier" be substituted for "wizard" and "hero," has given us actual monsters and marvels, and heroism, beyond the fear and imagination of previous ages. Far more importantly, *The Lord of the Rings* exemplifies φαντασια, the liberating power of the imagination to make things of its own, things previously not seen or thought of, and the "elvish" ability to make these visible to the conscious mind as if real and actually present. The relevance of *The Lord of the Rings* to our own world in our own time is great and immediate, simply because it tackles some of the great issues of our time. But, beyond that, it asserts the power of the mind to transcend these merely particular matters and be set free.

Selected Bibliography

EDITIONS

The Hobbit. London: George Allen and Unwin, 1937; 2d edition, revised, 1954.

The Fellowship of the Ring. London: George Allen and Unwin, 1954; 2nd edition, revised, 1966.

The Two Towers. London: George Allen and Unwin, 1954; 2d edition, revised, 1966.

The Return of the King. London: George Allen and Unwin, 1955; 2d edition, revised, 1966.

J. R. R. TOLKIEN'S WORKS AS PUBLISHED AND EDITED BY HIS SON, CHRISTOPHER TOLKIEN

The Silmarillion. London and Boston: George Allen and Unwin, 1977.

Unfinished Tales. London and Boston: George Allen and Unwin, 1980.

The Monsters and the Critics, and Other Essays. London and Boston: George Allen and Unwin, 1983. (*On Fairy-Stories*, pp. 109–161.)

The Book of Lost Tales I (The History of Middle-earth 1). London and Boston: George Allen and Unwin, 1983.

The Book of Lost Tales II (The History of Middle-earth 2). London and Boston: George Allen and Unwin, 1984.

The Lays of Beleriand (The History of Middle- earth 3). London and Boston: George Allen and Unwin, 1985.

The Shaping of Middle-earth (The History of Middle-earth 4). London: George Allen and Unwin, and Boston: Houghton Mifflin, 1986.

The Lost Road and Other Writings (The History of Middle-earth 5). London: Unwin Hyman, and Boston: Houghton Mifflin, 1987.

The Return of the Shadow: The History of The Lord of the Rings *Part One* (The History of Middle-earth 6). London: Unwin Hyman and Boston: Houghton Mifflin, 1988.

The Treason of Isengard (The History of Middle- earth 7). London: Unwin Hyman, and Boston: Houghton Mifflin, 1989.

The War of the Ring (The History of Middle- earth 8). London; Unwin Hyman, and Boston: Houghton Mifflin, 1990.

Sauron Defeated (The History of Middle-earth 9). London: Unwin Hyman, and Boston: Houghton Mifflin, 1992.

Morgoth's Ring (The History of Middle- earth 10). (London: Unwin Hyman, and Boston: Houghton Mifflin, 1993.

The War of the Jewels (The History of Middle- earth 11). London: HarperCollins, and Boston: Houghton Mifflin, 1994.

The Peoples of Middle-earth (The History of Middle-earth 12). London: HarperCollins, and Boston: Houghton Mifflin, 1996.

BIOGRAPHY AND LETTERS

Carpenter, Humphrey. *J. R. R. Tolkien: A Biography.* London: George Allen and Unwin, 1977.

Carpenter, Humphrey, and Christopher Tolkien, eds. *The Letters of J. R. R. Tolkien.* London and Boston: Allen and Unwin, 1981.

TOLKIEN BIBLIOGRAPHIES

Jönsson, Åke. *En Tolkienbibliografi 1911–1980.* Tredje uplagan. Uppsala: HarperCollins, 1986.

West, Richard C. *Tolkien Criticism: An Annotated Checklist.* Revised edition. Kent, Ohio: Kent State University, 1981.

Hammond, Wayne G., and Douglas A. Anderson. *J. R. R. Tolkien: A Descriptive Bibliography.* Winchester, U.K.: St. Paul's Bibliographies, and New Castle, Del.: Oak Knoll, 1993.

Arda. The occasional publication of the Forodrim, Stockholms Tolkiensällskap. Online at http://www.forodrim.org/arda/tbchron.html

SECONDARY WORKS

Bibire, P. "*Sægde se þe cuþe:* J. R. R. Tolkien as Anglo-Saxonist." In *Scholarship and Fantasy.* Edited by K. J. Battarbee. Turku, Finland, 1993. Pp. 111–131.

Foster, Robert. *The Complete Guide to Middle-Earth: From* The Hobbit *to* The Silmaril-lion. London: George Allen and Unwin, 1978.

Shippey, T. A. *The Road to Middle-earth: How J. R. R. Tolkien Created a New Mythology.* London: George Allen and Unwin, and Boston: Houghton Mifflin, 1982.

———. *J. R. R. Tolkien: Author of the Century.* London: HarperCollins, and Boston: Houghton Mifflin, 2000.

Thomas Hardy's
The Mayor of Casterbridge

NEIL POWELL

THOMAS HARDY IS the only writer in the history of English literature to have achieved indisputable greatness both as a novelist and as a poet; that he pursued these two careers sequentially rather than simultaneously, and that one belongs to the nineteenth and the other to the twentieth century, is more extraordinary still. The retrospective time scale of novels such as *The Mayor of Casterbridge*, whose opening chapters are set well before their author was born, makes his long creative life appear even longer: his is the distinctive, authoritative voice of rural England during a century of change.

Hardy's background, though far from literary, provided an ideal preparation for a writer. Born in 1840, in the Dorset hamlet of Higher Bockhampton, he grew up in a landscape richly populated with memorably eccentric relatives; although later he added imaginary grandness to his past (inventing a "pedigree" to prove his descent from "the Le Hardys of Jersey"), his family circumstances were sufficiently humble for him to conceal them from his first wife, Emma Gifford. His education, local and rudimentary, was significantly enhanced by his friendship with Horace Moule, son of the vicar

of Fordington, who extended his reading and encouraged his writing. At the age of sixteen, Hardy was apprenticed to a Dorchester architect, John Hicks: architecture would supply his passport to London and hence to the literary world, and it would become a recurrent motif for his fiction—*The Mayor of Casterbridge* in particular.

Success as a writer came to Hardy neither immediately nor consistently. His first novel, *The Poor Man and the Lady,* was rejected on the advice of George Meredith in 1868 by Alexander Macmillan, who many years later became his publisher. His early fiction appeared to mixed receptions, often initially in serial form, from the more populist firm of Tinsley Brothers. Characteristics we are now likely to find admirable—his interest in rural working people rather than fashionable socialites, his unflinching honesty about his characters' emotional lives—were often at odds with Victorian taste. He was more justly criticized for improbable twists of plot, a habit that affects even his finest work—for example, Lucetta's chance first meeting with Elizabeth-Jane or Newson's uncanny reappearances in *The Mayor of Casterbridge.* It was (as Robert Gittings persuasively argues in

Young Thomas Hardy, pp. 258–264) the suicide of Horace Moule in 1873 that transformed his writing: Hardy modified the character of Farmer Boldwood in his then work-in- progress *Far from the Madding Crowd,* hitherto conceived as a light comedy, striking for the first time that note of tragic grandeur that distinguishes his greatest novels. After his marriage in the following year to Emma Gifford, Hardy and his wife moved back and forth between London and Dorset until, following a serious illness, he decided to build his own home in Dorchester. Work began on this house, Max Gate, in 1883; the Hardys, meanwhile, rented the gloomy and forbidding Shire-Hall Place (a name closely echoed in Casterbridge's High-Place Hall).

This permanent return to his roots—or to their closest urban equivalent—was of immense significance for Hardy the novelist. It enabled him to realize the physical setting of *The Mayor of Casterbridge* with the special immediacy of one who could literally tread the streets and touch the fabric of the place he was describing. He carefully researched his local history, drawing especially on the files of the *Dorset County Chronicle* for the late 1820s: "Wife-selling, living with a second 'husband,' the dinner at the King's Arms, Henchard's honourable conduct at his bankruptcy, his oath to abstain from drink, even the shaming of Abel Whittle, can all be found in these files" (Gittings, *The Older Hardy,* p. 66). It was vital too that the book's time scale should embrace the unpredictable harvests and erratic grain prices that preceded the repeal of the Corn Laws in 1846: this provides an absolutely plausible background for Henchard's business difficulties, although it also involves Hardy in some pardonable chronological blurring. (Prince Albert's visit to Dorchester, which supplies the pretext for chapter 37, took place in 1849, while the railway, which Hardy says had not yet reached Casterbridge, had actually arrived in Dorchester in 1847.) In practice, this combination of an exactly realized topographical setting with a helpfully fudged chronology provides a perfect context for the novel.

CHRONOLOGY

1840	2 June: Thomas Hardy born, Higher Bockhampton, Dorset. First child of Thomas (a master mason) and Jemima Hardy (née Hand).
1848–1856	Educated at Lower Bockhampton and subsequently at Dorchester. Reading encouraged and influenced by Horace Moule.
1856–1862	Articled to John Hicks, a Dorchester architect.
1862–1867	Moves to London, working for church architect Arthur Blomfield; awarded architectural prize in 1863.
1867	Returns to Dorset and employment with John Hicks, who dies in 1869.
1870	While working on church restoration at St. Juliot, Cornwall, meets Emma Lavinia Gifford.
1871	First published novel, *Desperate Remedies.*
1872	*Under the Greenwood Tree* published.
1873	*A Pair of Blue Eyes* published. Suicide of Horace Moule.
1874	*Far from the Madding Crowd* published. Marries Emma Gifford.
1876	*The Hand of Ethelberta* published. The Hardys move to Sturminster Newton.
1878	*The Return of the Native* published. The Hardys return to London.
1880	*The Trumpet-Major* published. Hardy becomes ill; decides he must return to Dorchester and build a house there.
1881	*A Laodicean* published.
1882	*Two on a Tower* published.
1885	The Hardys move to Max Gate, Dorchester.
1886	*The Mayor of Casterbridge* published.
1887	*The Woodlanders* published. The Hardys travel in France and Italy.
1888	*Wessex Tales* published.
1891	*Tess of the d'Urbervilles* published.
1895	*Jude the Obscure* published.
1897	*The Well-Beloved* published in book form (serialized in 1892).

1898	Publishes *Wessex Poems,* his first volume of verse; it is to be followed by a further seven collections, ending with *Winter Words* (1928).
1905	Meets Florence Emily Dugdale.
1912	Death of Emma Hardy.
1914	Marries Florence Dugdale.
1928	11 January: Hardy dies. His ashes are buried in Westminster Abbey, his heart in Emma's grave at Stinsford. *The Early Life of Thomas Hardy* is published, followed in 1930 by *The Later Years of Thomas Hardy.*

In any case, Hardy seems to have correctly sensed that his great tragic hero Michael Henchard needed to be placed in an unusually solid and authentic setting. Casterbridge was, moreover, the most important town in the steadily evolving fictional area of "Wessex," which would eventually comprise not only Dorset but its adjacent counties: "The result," as Simon Gatrell has pointed out, "is that *The Mayor of Casterbridge* becomes the focus of a circle of previous fictions, stories as well as novels, through Boldwood and Everdene and Darton, through Egdon Heath and Port-Bredy and Overcombe" (*The Cambridge Companion to Thomas Hardy,* p. 25). It is thus Hardy's pivotal novel, the one in which his imaginary world locates and explores its true center. *The Mayor of Casterbridge* first appeared in serial form, simultaneously in the *Graphic* and in *Harper's Weekly* between January and May 1886. When it was published in volume form later the same year, it received almost unanimously favorable reviews, and, despite the special qualities of Hardy's last two major novels, *Tess of the d'Urbervilles* (1891) and *Jude the Obscure* (1895), it retains a strong claim to be considered his most perfectly balanced and accomplished book.

Hardy's subsequent literary career—including his reinvention of himself as a major poet—need not concern us here. But it is worth noting that this change of direction, which has often

been attributed to the hostile reception of *Jude,* almost certainly sprang from a deeper sense that his major fictional work was done. It is noteworthy too, and perhaps a key to Hardy's creative character, that his poetry was transformed by a personal crisis, just as his fiction had been: in 1912, Emma Hardy died, and the poems memorializing her ("Poems of 1912–13: *Veteris vestigia flammae*") are among the finest in twentieth-century English poetry. In 1914, Hardy married Florence Emily Dugdale, with whom he collaborated on two not wholly reliable volumes of autobiography. He died in 1928.

A DISPLACED PROLOGUE

Thomas Hardy, as the outline of his career suggests, was not a careful or a consistent writer: it is hard to think of another major novelist whose output includes so large a proportion of unsatisfactory works. Consequently *The Mayor of Casterbridge* is all the more noteworthy for its meticulous construction and (despite a few spectacular lapses) controlled writing. The novel's form is, of course, partly imposed by the necessities of serial publication—there are some cliff-hanging conclusions, such as that of chapter 22, that might make a soap-opera author blush—but its underlying structure is based on an older and grander model. We know that Shakespearian tragedy was much in Hardy's mind while he was working on the book, and Michael Henchard is certainly among the relatively few characters in English fiction to attain genuinely tragic status. Moreover, the disposition of the central figures in the novel is strikingly reminiscent of classical tragedy: five main characters—Henchard, his wife Susan, his stepdaughter Elizabeth-Jane, his former mistress Lucetta, and his rival Donald Farfrae—act out their destiny against the sour comments and meddlesome interventions of a rustic chorus. To this rather severe formula Hardy adds descriptive passages of extraordinary detail and subtlety, based on his intimate knowledge of Dorchester and its surrounding countryside. It is the tension between the sternness of Hardy's central theme and the richness of his local evocation that gives *The Mayor of Casterbridge* its unique texture.

Before reaching even the first chapter, we should attend to the title and the subtitle. The novel is *not* called—in the tradition of *Tom Jones* or *David Copperfield* or *Silas Marner*—by the name of its protagonist, Michael Henchard, but by the position he holds for a single year in which many of the book's pivotal events take place. The effect of this is twofold: it defines him by his office, just as *King Lear* is defined by his, and it accords equal priority to the place that both creates and destroys him. Thus, *The Life and Death of the Mayor of Casterbridge*, to give it its full title, joins that distinguished company of English novels (*Mansfield Park, Bleak House, Howards End*) in which the values and pressures of the named location dominate the action that takes place within it. Hardy's subtitle, "A Story of a Man of Character," might in these circumstances seem almost superfluous, yet it at once refocuses our attention on that central tragic figure and reminds any doubting reader that Henchard, for all his faults, is a man we are to admire.

The book begins with apparent artlessness, in the traditional storyteller's fashion: "One evening of late summer, before the nineteenth century had reached one-third of its span, a young man and woman, the latter carrying a child, were approaching the large village of Weydon-Priors, in Upper Wessex, on foot" (p. 35). Although this opening sentence could hardly be plainer, it is full of information: it introduces three of the five main characters; it sets both a geographical and a chronological starting point (the first two chapters take place some seventy years before the book's publication); and it establishes a predominant season—for, as we shall see, this is a novel richly colored by late summer and autumn, the time of harvest. Everything about this scene is autumnal: it is the end of the day, the annual fair is packing up, and when Henchard inquires about the pos-

sibility of renting a newly built cottage, he is firmly told: "Pulling down is more the nater of Weydon" (p. 37). Seeking refreshment, the couple deliberates between two tents:

> One was formed of new, milk-hued canvas, and bore red flags on its summit. It announced "Good Home-brewed Beer, Ale, and Cyder." The other was less new: a little iron stove-pipe came out of it at the back, and in front appeared the placard, "Good Furmity Sold Hear." The man mentally weighed the two inscriptions, and inclined to the former tent.
>
> "No—no—the other one," said the woman. "I always like furmity; and so does Elizabeth-Jane; and so will you. It is nourishing after a long hard day."
>
> "I've never tasted it," said the man. However, he gave way to her representations, and they entered the furmity booth forthwith.
>
> (p. 38)

This is the choice upon which everything else in the novel depends, so it warrants careful attention. The crucial point to notice—in a narrative so catastrophically determined by Henchard's own failings—is that it is Susan, not Michael, who makes the fateful decision, and that she does so in a way that betrays a culpable lack of candor on her part. She suspects that her hot-tempered husband will drink too much, but instead of gently cautioning him against this before entering the more prosperous and inviting tent, she produces her spurious commendation of furmity, a porridgelike concoction that Hardy unappetizingly describes as an "anti-quated slop." She is both timid and disingenuous, and that is a fatal combination.

The scene that now unfolds within the tent, despite its displacement in both time and place from the main action of the novel, forms the template for much that is to follow. Henchard, his furmity laced with rum, becomes impetuous and rash; the intervention of a calm-mannered stranger proves decisive; and a chorus of bystanders provides a sardonic commentary.

When, having sold his wife and daughter to the sailor for five guineas (an arrangement that only a woman as gullible as Susan would believe to be legally binding), Henchard looks out of the tent, the rough local scene expands into one of tragic grandeur:

> Outside the fair, in the valleys and woods, all was quiet. The sun had recently set, and the west heaven was hung with rosy cloud, which seemed permanent, yet slowly changed. To watch it was like looking at some grand feat of stagery from a darkened auditorium.
>
> (p. 45)

Variations on this theatrical motif will recur throughout the novel: in, for example, Henchard's reunion with Susan at the Roman amphitheater; in Farfrae's tented ballroom; in the market square "like the regulation Open Place in spectacular dramas" (p. 192); and in the pageantry of the royal visit to Casterbridge and its grotesque sequel of the skimmity ride, during which effigies of Henchard and Lucetta are paraded through the town. When Henchard awakes the morning after the scene in the tent it is as if he is the solitary remnant of a departed circus—"A warm glow pervaded the whole atmosphere of the marquee, and a single big blue fly buzzed musically round and round it" (p. 47)—and this sense of an absent audience is reaffirmed by a small dog, who "barked as a matter of principle" and "was the only positive spectator of the hay-trusser's exit from the Weydon Fair-field" (p. 48). Entering the village church, another place of ceremony and enactment, Henchard solemnly vows to "avoid all strong liquors for the space of twenty-one years to come, being a year for every year I have lived" (p. 49). While we respect his seriousness, we shouldn't overlook the fatal flaw of the self-imposed time limit.

One further point needs to be made about this prologue, and this concerns Hardy's clarity of focus. The characters of Michael Henchard and his wife are fully conveyed through their actions and reactions. The contrast between them is neatly suggested by Henchard himself, just before he takes his vow of abstinence: " 'Tis like Susan to show some idiotic simplicity. Meek—that meekness has done me more harm than the bitterest temper!" (p. 49). However, two other characters—the haggish furmity seller and the amiable sailor—remain mere cyphers: both will reappear, with devastating results, but Hardy has no interest in developing them any further than their function in the plot demands. In resisting the temptation to embellish minor roles with more detail than they need, he further demonstrates the secure grasp of dramatic structure that typifies *The Mayor of Casterbridge*.

STRANGERS IN TOWN

If Hardy had presented this drama in the form of a play, the opening stage direction for chapter 3 might have read: *"The same; twenty years later."* Instead of taking us directly to Casterbridge, he wants us to discover it in the company of Susan Henchard and her daughter; to do this, we must first travel with them to Weydon-Priors in search of information and there once again meet the furmity seller, "now tentless, dirty, owning no tables or benches, and having scarce any customers" (p. 53). Elizabeth-Jane finds her mother's association with this disreputable character inexplicable—for she is that recurrent figure in nineteenth- century fiction, a sensitive and intelligent but undereducated young woman in search of education and "improvement." Dorothea Brooke, in *Middlemarch*, is the outstanding example of this phenomenon, and Hardy's description of Elizabeth-Jane strikes comparable notes:

> The desire—sober and repressed—of Elizabeth-Jane's heart was indeed to see, to hear, and to understand. How could she become a woman of wider knowledge, higher repute—"better," as she termed it—this was her constant inquiry of her mother. She sought further into things than other

girls in her position ever did, and her mother groaned as she felt she could not aid in the search.

(p. 58)

Dorothea has, of course, the advantage of social position over Elizabeth-Jane, but their intellectual ambitions are similar; in their respective novels, they also find themselves ultimately allied with modernizing outsiders (Will Ladislaw and Donald Farfrae) in conservative country towns.

Seeing Casterbridge initially through Elizabeth-Jane's eyes enables Hardy to emphasize exactly this aspect of the town: "What an old-fashioned place it seems to be!" says the daughter, as they look down on it from an adjacent hill. She thinks it resembles a plot of garden surrounded by a box hedge, an idea Hardy hastens to elaborate:

Its squareness was, indeed, the characteristic which most struck the eye in this antiquated borough, the borough of Casterbridge—at that time, recent as it was, untouched by the faintest sprinkle of modernism. It was compact as a box of dominoes. It had no suburbs—in the ordinary sense. Country and town met at a mathematical line.

To birds of the more soaring sort Casterbridge must have appeared on this fine evening as a mosaic-work of subdued reds, browns, greys, and crystals, held together by a rectangular frame of deep green. To the level eye of humanity it stood as an indistinct mass behind a dense stockade of limes and chestnuts, set in the midst of miles of rotund down and concave field. The mass became gradually dissected by the vision into towers, gables, chimneys, and casements, the highest glazings shining bleared and bloodshot with the coppery fire they caught from the belt of sunlit cloud in the west.

(p. 59)

Although Casterbridge is thus painted in the autumnal evening colors that are so characteristic of this book, these are soon complicated by more somber notes. As we follow the newly arrived pair into the town, we pass old houses and shops selling agricultural implements before we come to "a grizzled church": the clock in its tower strikes eight, the hour of curfew, and other clocks follow in so ramshackle a way that "chronologists of the advanced school were appreciably on their way to the next hour before the whole business of the old one was satisfactorily wound up" (p. 61). Casterbridge is not merely old-fashioned; it is a place where time is, in Hamlet's words, "out of joint."

Meanwhile, the Casterbridge chorus, which is to play a decisive role in the novel, has made its first appearance: it is from them that the strangers first hear the name of Henchard, before learning that he is both the mayor and the corn merchant responsible for their bad bread. This juxtaposition of high office and blundering carelessness is typical of the man whom they now see, framed by the window of the King's Arms, presiding at the head of the table but with his wine glasses empty and unfilled: "He scorns all tempting liquors; never touches nothing," one of the bystanders explains. "O yes, he've strong qualities that way. I have heard tell that he sware a gospel oath in by-gone times, and has bode by it ever since" (p. 66). And that too is a key to Henchard: whenever his integrity is put to the test—at the furmity seller's trial, at his bankruptcy hearing, in the pathetic dignity of his will—he proves more than equal to the challenge.

By now, a third stranger has joined the crowd outside the window: he is about to make as quietly decisive an intervention in Henchard's life as the sailor at the entrance to the furmity tent. Donald Farfrae's Scottishness, which Hardy conveys with extravagant phonetic representation, both defines him as an outsider and makes him classless: his "foreign" accent allows him to float free of the stratified Casterbridge society. He is a traveler without baggage, whose past is defined only by the sentimental songs he sings about a country to which he has no intention of returning. His airy mobility challenges the old-fashioned rootedness of the town that will be his adopted home, and although he will prove both honorable and just, his generosity is entirely without warmth. Farfrae is a good man—of a modern, successful, and unencumbered sort—but he is a lesser man than Henchard. This is a point Hardy is at pains to emphasize: Farfrae's inability to notice Elizabeth-Jane either at the Three Mariners or when she calls at Henchard's office, his uncomprehending naïveté in the face of Henchard's moral dilemmas, and his priggish puzzlement at the messiness of others' lives all suggest a deficiency of human imagination.

However, Elizabeth-Jane (and this is a symptom both of her innocence and of her inner moral strength) is immediately impressed by Farfrae:

> She admired the serious light in which he looked at serious things. He had seen no jest in ambiguities and rogueries, as the Casterbridge toss-pots had done; and rightly not—there was none. She disliked those wretched humours of Christopher Coney and his tribe; and he did not appreciate them. He seemed to feel exactly as she felt about life and its surroundings—that they were a tragical rather than a comical thing; that though one could be gay on occasion, moments of gaiety were interludes and no part of the actual drama. It was extraordinary how similar their views were.
>
> (pp. 85–86)

The reader will notice here a shrewd anticipation of the novel's closing words: by that time, both she and her eventual husband will have learned from experience. But for now their "similar" views, however morally admirable they may be, are inimical to passion and spontaneity, and that is fair warning that both will fall out with Henchard. He, in his cumbersome way, is determined to behave properly by marrying (or in fact remarrying) the unattractive widow Susan Newson, to the mocking astonishment of the Casterbridge chorus. But his good intentions are to be thwarted by her death, by his rash discovery of Elizabeth-Jane's true

parentage, by his inevitable jealous quarrel with Farfrae, and—above all—by the arrival of a fourth stranger.

If this meticulously constructed novel has a weak point, it is Lucetta. Hardy's problem is one familiar to writers of serial fiction: he needs to introduce a previously unanticipated character as a catalyst without seeming to cheat the reader by altering events that have already taken place. Here, curiously, the unsteady point of view in *The Mayor of Casterbridge*, which will finally settle down as Elizabeth-Jane's, comes to his rescue: because the narration is only patchily omniscient, we do not have a full interior sense of Henchard, and so we can accept the external retrospective discovery of his affair with a woman from Jersey (a mild ancestral joke on Hardy's part). But that is not quite the end of the difficulty. In a novel where the interaction of the other main characters is extremely subtle, Lucetta fails to come to life: it is almost as if the woman who decides to be "the cherry-coloured person at all hazards" (p. 193), Hardy's sly equivalent of a scarlet woman, is little more than the cherry-colored effigy in the skimmity ride that precipitates her death. Despite Lucetta's showy vulgarity, the normally level-headed Elizabeth-Jane is instantly enchanted, and both Henchard and Farfrae are ludicrously smitten by a woman who has little in common with either of them. Hardy clearly views the situation as absurd, and for a moment the novel lurches most uncharacteristically into drawing-room comedy:

> "More bread-and-butter?" said Lucetta to Henchard and Farfrae equally, holding out between them a plateful of long slices. Henchard took a slice by one end and Donald by the other; each feeling certain he was the man meant; neither let go, and the slice came in two.
>
> "Oh—I am so sorry!" cried Lucetta, with a nervous titter. Farfrae tried to laugh; but he was too much in love to see the incident in any but a tragic light.

"How ridiculous of all three of them!" said Elizabeth to herself.

(p. 207)

Though incongruous, this is surprisingly effective: it is appropriate that Lucetta, whose arrival so disrupts the lives of Henchard and Farfrae, should also disrupt the tone of the novel. Yet this must imply that, crucial as the love triangle is to its plot, the heart of *The Mayor of Casterbridge* lies elsewhere.

THE WORKING WORLD

Hardy's Wessex is a relatively small geographical area, within which distances are correspondingly exaggerated; as can still be the case in country areas, a village thirty miles away may remain unvisited for years or even for a lifetime. And although some rural trades in this world are casual and peripatetic, most characters—like the chorus of Casterbridge worthies—remain rooted in their place of birth. When we first meet Michael Henchard, he is an itinerant hay trusser, and that too is how he ends his days in the novel's closing chapters. In one sense, then, his settled spell as corn factor and mayor of Casterbridge is an aberration that runs counter to his deeper nature: he might echo Macbeth's "Why do you dress me / In borrowed robes?" This, indeed, is precisely the idea that underpins the novel's pivotal turning point, the moment at which Henchard publicly rejects his former office and its "borrowed robes." The occasion is one of the book's great theatrical set pieces, the visit of a "Royal Personage" to Casterbridge. All the inhabitants are arrayed in their finery, including "the Corporation in their robes," when Henchard makes his appearance. Hardy's account is unambiguous in its emphasis:

He was not only a journeyman, unable to appear as formerly he had appeared, but he disdained to appear as well as he might. Everybody else, from the Mayor to the washerwoman, shone in new vesture according to means; but Henchard had doggedly retained the fretted and weather-beaten garments of bygone years. . . .

There were a few clear yards in front of the Royal carriage, sanded; and into this space a man stepped before any one could prevent him. It was Henchard. He had unrolled his private flag, and removing his hat he staggered to the side of the slowing vehicle, waving the Union Jack to and fro with his left hand, while he blandly held out his right to the Illustrious Personage.

(p. 288)

Henchard's existential gesture unmakes him as a pillar of Casterbridge society as surely as his vow in Weydon-Pryors church (the term of which has, at this point, just expired) set him on the road to worldly success. He had invented a self that he now relinquishes, and if this seems to us a strikingly modern concept, we should remember that it is also a fundamentally Shakespearian one. Hardy, however, casts this self-definition specifically in terms of *work*.

Work, in *The Mayor of Casterbridge,* shapes human destiny to a far greater extent than is usual in fiction. Henchard makes the fateful transition from casual laborer, an impoverished life but one that suits his temperament, to small-town entrepreneur, a role for which his fiery intuitive nature is unsuited; Farfrae, meanwhile, having decided to "see the warrld" in search of his fortune, is canny and resourceful, a born manager where Henchard is a born blunderer. While Farfrae's rational, progressive attitude to his work is epitomized by his introduction of "the new-fashioned agricultural implement called a horse-drill" (p. 193)—which Henchard scornfully dismisses (" 'tis impossible it should act") and Lucetta idiotically describes as "a sort of agricultural piano"—Henchard's instinctive, superstitious approach is symbolized by his visit to the "weather-prophet" of "curious repute," Mr. Fall: "By the sun, moon, and stars, by the clouds, the winds, the trees, and grass, the candleflame and swallows, the smell of the herbs; likewise by the cats' eyes, the ravens, the leeches, the spiders, and the dungmixen, the last fortnight in August will be—rain and tempest" (p. 212). The sensible reader can hardly deny that Farfrae is right, but the sympathetic reader will feel for Henchard: an ideal reader, being both sensible and sympathetic, will find his or her loyalties divided exactly as Hardy intends.

The shifting relationship between the two men is continually defined and redefined in these terms. When Henchard first persuades Farfare to remain in Casterbridge as his manager, he utters an oblique prophecy of the trouble to come. "You can see that it isn't all selfishness that makes me press 'ee," he says, "for my business is not quite so scientific as to require an intellect entirely out of the common" (p. 94): recognizing that Farfrae's cast of mind differs incomprehensibly from his own, he is yet unable to turn this useful potentiality to his own advantage. He is all instinct ("when a man takes my fancy he takes it strong"), and it is this warmth that Farfrae finds equally incomprehensible and irresistible, even going so far as to thank "Providence" for bringing him to Casterbridge, which in so rational a man strikes an ominous note. Each is entranced by what he least resembles and understands in the other, which may produce a lively friendship but seems a dangerous basis for a stable business partnership. Farfare's ascendancy is swift and inevitable. In the teasing, seesawing chapter 15, Elizabeth-Jane observes from a window her stepfather's "impetuous cordiality" and her future husband's "genial modesty"; "Friendship between man and man," she innocently reflects, "what a rugged strength there was in it, as evinced by these two" (p. 126).

Yet this view is immediately qualified by two subtly interlinked incidents that close the chapter. In the first, Henchard humiliates his chronically oversleeping workman, Abel Whittle, by marching into his house and sending him off to work half-dressed, only to have his orders countermanded by Farfrae:

> "Get back home and slip on your breeches, and come to wark like a man! If ye go not, you'll ha'e your death standing there!"
>
> "I'm afeard I mustn't! Mr Henchard said—"
>
> "I don't care what Mr Henchard said, nor anybody else! 'Tis simple foolishness to do this. Go and dress yourself instantly, Whittle."
>
> "Hullo, hullo!" said Henchard, coming up behind. "Who's sending him back?"
>
> All the men looked toward Farfrae.
>
> "I am," said Donald. "I say this joke has been carried far enough."
>
> "And I say it hasn't! Get up in the waggon, Whittle."
>
> "Not if I am manager," said Farfrae. "He either goes home, or I march out of this yard for good."
>
> (pp. 128–129)

Farfrae, although he is obviously right, fails to win the reader's unequivocal support: his chilly and remote justness contrasts unfavorably with the human warmth that underlies Henchard's rough treatment of his employee. Henchard's is the authentic manner of rural Wessex, Farfrae's the reasonable though unengaged style of the outsider. When Henchard, a few paragraphs later, is asked to make a simple managerial decision, he replies with grim irony, "Ask Mr. Farfrae. He's master here!" Hardy comments: "Morally he was; there could be no doubt of it." But there are times when moral authority runs counter to the human spirit, and in the second of these two incidents Hardy reemphasizes the distinction between Henchard's emotional complexity and Farfrae's superficially attractive simplicity.

A child, sent as a messenger summoning Farfrae to value a haystack, instead encounters Henchard, who offers to go instead. But the child is insistent that Farfrae should do the job "because they like him so," whereupon Henchard bitterly suggests that this is "because he's cleverer than Mr Henchard, and because he knows more; and in short, Mr Henchard can't hold a candle to him." Bribed with sixpence, the child is more than happy to elaborate on this theme:

" 'And he's better-tempered, and Henchard's a fool to him,' they say.

And when some of the women were a-walking home they said, 'He's a diment—he's a chap o' wax—he's the best—he's the horse for my money,' says they. And they said, 'He's the most understanding man o' them two by long chalks. I wish he was the master instead of Henchard,' they said."

"They'll talk any nonsense," Henchard replied with covered gloom. "Well, you can go now. And *I* am coming to value the hay, d'ye hear?—I."

The boy departed, and Henchard murmured, "Wish he were master here, do they?"

(p. 130)

This, of course, is the idea that will eat away at Henchard and, disastrously for him, ends the two men's business partnership; but it should be noted that he himself, not the child, proposes it and that the child—hardly a reliable or impartial witness—merely embroiders what Henchard has put into his head. Moreover, the reader (unlike Henchard) will note that Farfrae is praised more for his charm than for his substance. At the end of the chapter, the two men are temporarily reconciled—Henchard apologizing with his characteristic warmth ("I have been hearing things that vexed me. . . . 'Twas that made me short in my manner—made me overlook what you really are") and Farfrae "forbearing to ask Henchard for meanings that were not very plain to him" (p. 131).

The occurrences that precipitate an irreparable breach between the two men swiftly follow. Hardy rather coyly refers to "a national event," possibly the tenth anniversary of Queen Victoria's accession, which requires appropriate celebration in Casterbridge: as soon as Farfrae offers to organize one, Henchard realizes that this should be his responsibility as mayor. Two rival celebrations take place, each neatly symbolizing its sponsor's character. Henchard's entertainment, in a large open space, is as full of traditional rural generosity as the man himself: it includes "greasy-poles for climbing, with smoked hams and local cheeses at the top," "hurdles in rows for jumping over," "a slippery pole [across the river], with a live pig of the neighbourhood tied at the other end, to become the property of the man who could walk over and get it," "wheelbarrows for racing, donkeys for the same, a stage for boxing, wrestling, and drawing blood generally," "sacks for jumping in," and "a mammoth tea, of which everybody who lived in the borough was invited to partake without payment" (p. 133). Farfrae, however, is busy arranging a covered area of rick cloths in the West Walk, a markedly inferior enterprise. But it rains. Not for the last time, Henchard is undone by the weather: "The hams at the top of the poles dripped watered smoke in the form of a brown liquor, the pig shivered in the wind, the grain of the deal tables showed through the sticking tablecloths . . ." (p. 134). This transformation of a benign rustic scene into a malevolent one, so characteristic of Hardy's poetry, is among his finest effects. Meanwhile, in his impromptu covered ballroom, Farfrae is dancing to a Scottish tune with Elizabeth-Jane. For Henchard, arriving and overhearing yet more extravagant praise of Farfrae, it is the last straw. When the wonderfully tactless Alderman Tubber remarks, "He'll be top-sawyer soon of you two, and carry all afore him," Henchard's reply is inevitable: "He won't be that, because he's shortly going to leave me. . . . Mr Farfrae's time as my manager is drawing to a close—isn't it, Farfrae?" (p. 137).

Hardy knows that men are made and destroyed by mundane events. Of Henchard's tragic flaws, it is not his hotheaded (and at the beginning and end of the book, drunken) impetuousness that ruins him, but his simple inability to accept that his happiness and prosperity would be assured by embracing Farfrae in the dual role of business partner and son-in-law. When his business fails, it is because of his simple misjudgment in first seeking and then mistrusting the weather prophet's advice on the eve of harvest. Hardy also knows that his tragic hero is too great a character to be interested in mere happiness and prosperity: astonishingly, as Henchard declines, his sheer physical and emotional size seems to increase. Among Farfrae's well-meaning but curiously souless acts of restitution to his bankrupt former employer is the scheme to set him up in a "little retail seed and grain shop, not much larger than a cupboard" (p. 324). The shop, managed by father and stepdaughter, is successful for a while, but its scale has the ludicrous *Alice in Wonderland* incongruity of Alice crammed into the White Rabbit's house. His domestic confinement in two rooms rented from Joshua Jopp, the wholly unreliable scoundrel who was passed over in favor of Farfrae and who brings trouble to everything he touches, seems hardly less impossible. Henchard's departure from Casterbridge is prompted by the reappearance of Newson, Elizabeth-Jane's true father, but at a deeper level it seems inevitable simply in terms of the man's need for space. It takes place, of course, in autumn: Henchard returns to Weydon-Priors and eventually finds "employment at his own occupation of hay- trusser, work of that sort being in demand at this autumn- time." The phrase "his own occupation" is telling and exact: this is the work for which he is naturally fitted. "And thus," Hardy adds, "Henchard found himself again on the precise standing which he had occupied a quarter of a century earlier" (p. 340). He is undeniably a failure, yet this failure is underpinned by a paradoxical sense of triumph. And the reason is plain: Henchard, in returning to his honest countryman's trade, is doing something that would have been quite beyond the more clever but less physical and intuitive Farfrae. He has become himself once more.

GENIUS LOCI

When Susan and Elizabeth-Jane first arrive in Casterbridge, the spirit of the place—the genius loci—immediately makes itself felt, as we have already seen, and it remains pervasive throughout the novel. Casterbridge is, of course, Dorchester: a town that Hardy, as a local boy

and a trained architect, knew almost brick by brick. Its surrounding landmarks also play significant roles in the book—for instance, Henchard meets his former wife at "the Ring on the Budmouth road" (p. 99), which is based on Maumbury Ring, and his ill-fated entertainment takes place at "an elevated green spot surrounded by an ancient square earthwork" (p. 133). But Hardy's particular interest is in the resonances of more urban architecture. Sometimes this is used to suggest nuances of social class: both the King's Arms and the Three Mariners are described in exact, affectionate detail, which reinforces our sense that the former, appropriate for a mayoral occasion, is (in Susan's words) "too good for us—we can't meet it" (p. 75), whereas the latter, though respectable, is no place for a mayor's wife to have stayed, nor for her daughter to have paid their way by helping out, "not for charity but for hire; and at a public-house in this town," as Nance Mockridge triumphantly declares (p. 159). But Hardy's more distinctive use of architectural description is to imply deeper, and bleaker, psychological aspects of his characters.

An outstanding example of this is his account of High- Place Hall, the house to which Lucetta is about to move when she chooses Elizabeth-Jane as her companion. Based on Colliton House, Dorchester, it sounds grandly imposing, and this is Elizabeth-Jane's innocent first impression:

> The Hall, with its grey *façade* and parapet, was the only residence of its sort so near the centre of the town. It had, in the first place, the characteristics of a country mansion—birds' nests in its chimneys, damp nooks where fungi grew, and irregularities of surface direct from Nature's trowel. At night, the forms of passengers were patterned by the lamps in black shadows upon the pale walls.
>
> This evening motes of straw lay around, and other signs of the premises having been in that lawless condition which accompanies the entry of a new tenant. The house was entirely of stone, and

formed an example of dignity without great size. It was not altogether aristocratic, still less consequential, yet the old-fashioned stranger instinctively said, "Blood built it, and Wealth enjoys it," however vague his opinions of those accessories might be.

(p. 167)

Yet already the effect of solid prosperity is qualified by Hardy's uncanny knack of turning an obvious fact into a menacing one: of course passersby at night cast shadows on the wall (and would be the more alarming if they didn't), but here they already hint at clandestine nocturnal visitors—notably Henchard, when he extracts his fruitless promise of marriage from Lucetta.

Hardy now devotes two paragraphs to precise architectural detail before returning to elaborate on the sinister peculiarities of High-Place Hall:

Elizabeth trotted through the open door in the dusk, but becoming alarmed at her own temerity she went quickly out again by another which stood open in the lofty wall of the back court. To her surprise she found herself in one of the little-used alleys of the town. Looking round at the door which had given her egress, by the light of the solitary lamp fixed in the alley, she saw that it was arched and old—older even than the house itself. The door was studded, and the keystone of the arch was a mask. Originally the mask had exhibited a comic leer, as could still be discerned; but generations of Casterbridge boys had thrown stones at the mask, aiming at its open mouth; and the blows thereon had chipped off the lips and jaws as if they had been eaten away by disease. The appearance was so ghastly by the weakly lamp-glimmer that she could not bear to look at it—the first unpleasant feature of her visit.

The position of the queer old door and the odd presence of the leering mask suggested one thing above all others as appertaining to the mansion's past history—intrigue. By the alley it had been possible to come unseen from all sorts of quarters in the town—the old play- house, the old bull-stake, the old cock-pit, the pool wherein nameless

infants had been used to disappear. High-Place Hall could boast of its conveniences undoubtedly.

(pp. 168–169)

This is Hardy at his best and at his worst. The meticulous description of the mask (it is to be seen in Timothy O'Sullivan's *Thomas Hardy: An Illustrated Biography*, p. 103, and can be found in the Dorset County Museum) and the menacing list of the house's "conveniences" work to wonderfully macabre effect, but the overexplicit references to "the first unpleasant feature of her visit" and "the mansion's past history—intrigue" are glaring instances of an author telling when he ought to be showing. Henry James would have known better.

More completely successful is Hardy's emblematic use of the two bridges in chapter 32:

Two bridges stood near the lower part of Casterbridge town. The first, of weather-stained brick, was immediately at the end of High Street, where a diverging branch from that thoroughfare ran round to the low-lying Durnover lanes; so that the precincts of the bridge formed the merging point of respectability and indigence. The second bridge, of stone, was further out on the highway—in fact, fairly in the meadows, though still within the town boundary.

These bridges had speaking countenances. Every projection in each was worn down to obtuseness partly by weather, more by friction from generations of loungers, whose toes and heels had from year to year made restless movements as they had stood there meditating on the aspect of affairs. In the case of the more friable bricks and stones even the flat faces were worn into hollows by the same mixed mechanism. The masonry of the top was clamped with iron at each joint; since it had been no uncommon thing for desperate men to wrench the coping off and throw it down the river, in reckless defiance of the magistrates.

For to this pair of bridges gravitated all the failures of the town; those who had failed in business, in love, in sobriety, in crime.

(p. 247)

Hardy develops the "speaking countenances" of the two bridges—respectively, Swan Bridge and

Grey's Bridge in Dorchester—as images for two distinct classes of "failures." Those who had never been notably respectable, even in the days of their success, choose the brick bridge, nearer the town, for "they did not mind the glare of the public eye"; others, "of a politer stamp," gravitate to the stone bridge:

> They included bankrupts, hypochondriacs, persons who were what is called "out of a situation" from fault of lucklessness, the inefficient of the professional class—shabby-genteel men, who did not know how to get rid of the weary time between breakfast and dinner, and the yet more weary time between dinner and dark. The eyes of this species were mostly directed over the parapet upon the running water below. A man seen there looking thus fixedly into the river was pretty sure to be one whom the world did not treat kindly for some reason or other. While one in straits on the townward bridge did not mind who saw him so, and kept his back to the parapet to survey the passers-by, one in straits on this never faced the road, never turned his head at coming footsteps, but, sensitive to his own condition, watched the current whenever a stranger approached, as if some strange fish interested him, though every finned thing had been poached out of the river years before.
>
> There and thus they would muse; if their grief were the grief of oppression they would wish themselves kings; if their grief were poverty, wish themselves millionaires; if sin, they would wish they were saints or angels; if despised love, that they were some much-courted Adonis of county fame. Some had been known to stand and think so long with this fixed gaze downward that eventually they had allowed their poor carcases to follow that gaze; and they were discovered the next morning out of reach of their troubles, either here or in the deep pool called Blackwater, a little higher up the river.
>
> (p. 248)

This, of course, is the bridge to which Henchard is drawn, not simply because of his outward circumstances but because, as Hardy so shrewdly suggests, his broodingly melancholic character is at one with the bridge. Nor is that

the only subtle feature of this passage: Hardy's description of the suicides who drown themselves at the bridge exactly prefigures what we might almost call the virtual suicide of Henchard himself. For on the day after the fateful skimmity ride, he walks from the stone bridge to "the weir-hole where the water was at its deepest," in which he intends to drown himself, and there makes out "a something floating in the circular pool formed by the wash of centuries":

> In the circular current imparted by the central flow the form was brought forward, till it passed under his eyes; and then he perceived with a sense of horror that it was *himself*. Not a man somewhat resembling him, but one in all respects his counterpart, his actual double, was floating as if dead in Ten Hatches Hole.
>
> (pp. 318–319)

It is his discarded effigy. Hardy's clear implication is that, just as Lucetta's sight of her "living" effigy kills her, Henchard's discovery of his "dead" effigy spares him the necessity of actual death: it is an audaciously Shakespearian symmetry; indeed, the book's chronologically staggered double tragic closure is almost a mirror image of that in *Antony and Cleopatra*.

MICHAEL HENCHARD'S WILL

Nineteenth-century English novels conventionally conclude with a tying-up of loose ends, however cursory, or an epilogue that dutifully records what happened to the main characters beyond the chronological span of the narrative. Hardy allows us no such comfort: the ending of *The Mayor of Casterbridge* is more complex, more subtle, and more truthful. For a while it seems as if we may have, outrageously, an oblique version of Shakespearian comedy: Henchard, like Malvolio or Jacques, is self-exiled, while the lovers celebrate their marriage and all is well. But it is not to be quite like that. The wedding of Farfrae and Elizabeth-Jane is a low-key affair—its "gaiety," we are glumly informed, was "of [Newson's] making rather than of the married couple's" (p. 348)—and it is moreover overshadowed by Henchard's reappearance as "a humble old friend" (p. 344) bearing a caged goldfinch as a wedding gift. The point at which Elizabeth-Jane recognizes and addresses him with icy formality as "Mr. Henchard" is perhaps the most shocking moment in the novel:

> "What; Elizabeth?" he cried, as he seized her hand. "What do you say?—*Mr* Henchard? Don't, don't scourge me like that! Call me worthless old Henchard—anything—but don't 'ee be so cold as this! O my maid—I see you have another—a real father in my place. Then you know all; but don't give all your thought to him! Do ye save a little room for me!"
>
> (p. 346)

She cannot forgive him: for all her qualities, she still lacks greatness of character. But that is just what Henchard himself displays when he replies to her understandably bitter attack:

> Waiving, therefore, his privilege of self-defence, he regarded only her discomposure. "Don't ye distress yourself on my account," he said, with proud superiority. "I would not wish it—at such a time, too, as this. I have done wrong in coming to 'ee—I see my error. But it is only for once, so forgive it. I'll never trouble 'ee again, Elizabeth-Jane—no, not to my dying day! Good-night. Good-bye!"
>
> (pp. 346–347)

This is a speech of heroic stoicism, and Hardy is careful to insist on its honorable motivation: Henchard "regarded only her discomposure."

The caged bird—a rather awkward symbol, fitting neither Henchard, who is unhappy but free, nor Elizabeth-Jane, who is constrained but happy—brought by "that farmer's man who called on the evening of the wedding" is eventually found dead. It is this that prompts Elizabeth-Jane's remorseful search for her stepfather. Instead she discovers Abel Whittle, who remembers only his former employer's kindness in supplying coal for his mother and

from whom she learns of Henchard's death. His will, which the illiterate Abel cannot read, is pinned to his bed:

> Michael Henchard's Will
>
> That Elizabeth-Jane Farfrae be not told of my
>   death, or made to grieve on account of me.
> & that I be not bury'd in consecrated ground.
> & that no sexton be asked to toll the bell.
> & that nobody is wished to see my dead body.
> & that no murners walk behind me at my funeral.
> & that no flours be planted on my grave.
> & that no man remember me.
> To this I put my name.
>
> Michael Henchard
>
> (p. 353)

This time, Elizabeth-Jane gets it right: "She knew the directions to be a piece of the same stuff that his whole life was made of, and hence were not to be tampered with to give herself a mournful pleasure, or her husband credit for large-heartedness." Thus, on the novel's penultimate page, she finally grows into the maturity Hardy has always seemed to promise for her, by at last understanding her stepfather. She is rewarded with the rare combination of good fortune and self-knowledge: "And in being forced to class herself among the fortunate she did not cease to wonder at the persistence of the unforeseen, when the one to whom such unbroken tranquility had been accorded in the adult stage was she whose youth had seemed to teach that happiness was but the occasional episode in a general drama of pain" (p. 354). As final sentences go, it is a hedged and qualified one, and rightly so. Hardy knows that Elizabeth-Jane's happiness is a fine thing, but that Henchard's greatness is finer still.

IMPORTANCE AND INFLUENCE

The Mayor of Casterbridge is a book that triumphantly passes the simplest and the sternest test of literary greatness: it continues to surprise and impress on each rereading. Because Hardy's literary career overlapped the rise of twentieth-century modernism—it is odd and salutary to reflect that Eliot's "The Love Song of J. Alfred Prufrock" was finished in 1911, the year before Hardy began his elegiac "Poems of 1912–13"—he is often regarded as a conservative writer, but *The Mayor of Casterbridge* is far from being a conservative novel. Its single-strand narrative and relentless focus on its central character are quite different from the busy complexity of much nineteenth-century English fiction. To come to *The Mayor of Casterbridge* after the tortuous plots of Dickens or the clerical manipulations of Trollope is to enter a world of deeper roots, bolder emotions, and fresher air. Its concentration on a figure of almost mythic proportions has less in common with the English or European mainstream than with another deeply unconventional nineteenth-century novel, Emily Brontë's *Wuthering Heights,* and with the work of American writers such as Nathaniel Hawthorne and Herman Melville. If we borrow Richard Chase's useful rough-and-ready distinction (from *The American Novel and Its Tradition*) between the European "novel" and the American "romance," then it becomes clear that Henchard is, at the very least, a character poised on the brink of a transatlantic leap.

Yet in another sense *The Mayor of Casterbridge* seems to form the central panel in a triptych of great novels about social change in nineteenth-century rural England. On one side of it stands George Eliot's *Middlemarch* (1871); on the other is D. H. Lawrence's *The Rainbow* (1915). Each of these books deals with a part of provincial England intimately known to its author, and each explores the catalytic effects of strangers—new people with modern ideas—on a traditional community. Will Ladislaw and Dr. Lidgate disrupt the settled ways of Middlemarch; Anna Lensky and Anton Skrebensky completely alter the lives of two generations of Brangwens; while the changes in Casterbridge are triggered not by Henchard himself but by two interlopers from outside Wessex, Donald Farfrae and Lucetta. All three writers treat these changes judiciously, although it is probably fair to say that George Eliot is the most sympathetic (Ladislaw's iconoclastic approach to provincial life becomes Dorothea's means of self-fulfillment) and Lawrence the least (for him, modernization is inextricably linked with the evils of industrial capitalism). Hardy's approach is the most finely balanced of all three: commercial progress, as represented by Farfrae, may be less picturesque than traditional farming but it is inescapably necessary, for without it the rural economy would collapse; irresponsible emotional meddling, as represented by the dubiously cosmopolitan Lucetta, is on the other hand wholly to be deplored. *The Mayor of Casterbridge* is firmly yet not at all sententiously a moral novel.

Hardy's influence on subsequent writers was to be far more evident among poets—one thinks of Edward Thomas, Robert Graves, W. H. Auden, and, above all, Philip Larkin—than among novelists, although Graham Swift's *Waterland* (1983) may stand as an eloquent example of a novel grounded in historical change within a rural community: not surprisingly, the only one of Swift's characters to approach the scale of a Michael Henchard is a nineteenth-century rather than a more modern figure. Otherwise, Hardy's legacy is most familiar to British audiences in the form of a long-running radio soap opera, *The Archers,* whose semifictional setting of Borsetshire is based on the West Midlands in much the same way as Hardy's Wessex is derived from Southwest England. Hardy, many of whose novels were initially popular serials aimed at a broadly comparable audience, would perhaps not have minded this as much as might at first be supposed.

In the end, we read and reread *The Mayor of Casterbridge* for Henchard. His incomparable tragic stature; his ability to command every scene in the book (whether or not he is physically present); his grand, complex mixture of folly and integrity: these are very rare qualities in prose fiction of any period. He is simply too large a character to survive in the Farfraes' more egalitarian, fairer but duller modern world, and that, of course, is why we so seldom meet his like in more recent novels. For this reader, at any rate, Michael Henchard remains Thomas Hardy's most impressive fictional creation and one of the handful of truly heroic figures in the English novel.

Selected Bibliography

EDITIONS

The Mayor of Casterbridge. London: Smith, Elder, 1886.

The Mayor of Casterbridge. London: Sampson Low, Marston, 1887.

The Mayor of Casterbridge. The Wessex Edition. London: Macmillan, 1912.

The Mayor of Casterbridge. The New Wessex Edition. P. N. Furbank, general editor. London: Macmillan, 1974. Page references are to this edition.

The Mayor of Casterbridge. Norton Critical Edition. 2d edition. Edited by Philip Mallett. New York: Norton, 2001.

SECONDARY WORKS

Bayley, John. *An Essay on Hardy.* Cambridge and New York: Cambridge University Press, 1978.

Brown, Douglas. *Thomas Hardy: "The Mayor of Casterbridge."* London: Edward Arnold, 1962.

Cox, R. G., ed. *Thomas Hardy: The Critical Heritage.* London: Routledge and Kegan Paul, 1970.

Draper, R. P., ed. *Hardy: The Tragic Novels.* Rev. ed. London: Macmillan, 1991.

Gatrell, Simon. *Hardy the Creator: A Textual Biography.* Oxford and New York: Clarendon Press, 1988.

Gibson, James. *Thomas Hardy: A Literary Life.* London: Macmillan, 1996.

Gittings, Robert. *Young Thomas Hardy.* London: Heinemann, 1975; Harmondsworth, U.K.: Penguin, 1978.

———.*The Older Hardy.* London: Heinemann, 1978; Harmondsworth, U.K.: Penguin, 1980.

Gregor, Ian. *The Great Web: The Form of Hardy's Major Fiction.* London: Faber, 1974.

Howe, Irving. *Thomas Hardy.* New York: Macmillan, 1967.

Kramer, Dale, ed. *The Cambridge Companion to Thomas Hardy.* Cambridge and New York: Cambridge University Press, 1999.

Langbaum, Robert. *Thomas Hardy in Our Time.* London: Macmillan, 1995.

Millgate, Michael. *Thomas Hardy: His Career As a Novelist.* London: Bodley Head, 1971.

———. *Thomas Hardy: A Biography.* Oxford and New York: Oxford University Press, 1982.

Millgate, Michael, ed. *The Life and Work of Thomas Hardy by Thomas Hardy.* London: Macmillan, 1984.

O'Sullivan, Timothy. *Thomas Hardy: An Illustrated Biography.* London: Macmillan, 1975.

Page, Norman. *Thomas Hardy.* London: Routledge and Kegan Paul, 1977.

Pinion, F. B. *A Hardy Companion.* London: Macmillan, 1968.

Purdy, Richard Little. *Thomas Hardy: A Bibliographical Study.* Oxford and New York: Clarendon Press, 1954.

Turner, Paul: *The Life of Thomas Hardy.* Oxford, U.K.: Blackwell, 1998.

Virginia Woolf's
Mrs. Dalloway

PETER FILKINS

PUBLISHED IN 1925, *Mrs. Dalloway* marks Virginia Woolf's first critical and popular success as a novelist. Along with James Joyce's *Ulysses,* T. S. Eliot's *The Waste Land,* and Marcel Proust's *Remembrance of Things Past,* it remains one of the central literary works of the modernist movement. Though for many years *The Waste Land* and *Ulysses* were considered more important by literary critics in how they affected the way literature was written and read, Woolf's work has become more influential for the subject matter she chose to write about, her complex depiction of human identity, and her exploration of female consciousness. Both *Mrs. Dalloway* and *To The Lighthouse,* her next novel, represent the apex of her achievement as a writer who helped to change the way we think about how human beings think and feel, as well as how we think about the nature and meaning of history and society in Western civilization.

In "Mr. Bennett and Mrs. Brown," an essay she wrote right at the time she was beginning work on *Mrs. Dalloway,* Woolf declared audaciously that "in or about December, 1910, human character changed" (*Collected Essays,* vol. 1, p. 320). While such a statement strikes

one as a bit pompous and typical of the gathering of writers, critics, and intellectuals that came to be known as the Bloomsbury group, the observation still seems trenchant to this day. Woolf goes on to explain that at the heart of this change was a gradual dismantling of political and social hierarchies, "those between masters and servants, husbands and wives, parents and children" (p. 321). With this came a greater and more complex valuation of the individual. Maids or housewives no longer felt compelled to "stay in their place" but rather, with the rise of travel and automation, the expansion of education, and the increase in middle-class affluence, society became more fluid in its evolution and makeup. The people who "mattered" were no longer just the aristocrats and politicians but also the common everyday individuals whose increasing numbers and power began to shape the society in which they lived.

The Mrs. Brown of Woolf's essay is an anonymous, wizened old lady she observes sitting across from her in a train. But rather than write about her as a stock character by simply describing her house or street as the novelist Arnold Bennett would, Woolf calls for writers to "come down off their plinths and pedestals" and detail the inner life and thoughts of Mrs. Brown. "You should insist that she is an old lady of unlimited capacity and infinite variety," writes Woolf, "capable of appearing in any place; wearing any dress; saying anything and doing heaven knows what. But the things she says and the things she does and her eyes and her nose and her speech and her silence have an overwhelming fascination, for she is, of course, the spirit we live by, life itself" (pp. 336–337).

The result of this insistence is *Mrs. Dalloway.* There Woolf would further the experimentation she began with the publication of *Jacob's Room* in 1922. While Woolf's third novel represents an important breakthrough in her depiction of character through a description of objects and events that surround the character, it would not be until *Mrs. Dalloway* that Woolf was able to refine her method and create a more cohesive whole. How she accomplished this was by "tunneling" into her characters in order to reveal the inner workings of their thoughts and feelings, and how these both shaped and interpreted the life around them. "The writer must get in touch with the reader," wrote Woolf in advocating the importance of "Mrs. Brown," and that meant "putting before him something which he recognizes, which therefore stimulates his imagination, and makes him willing to cooperate in the far more difficult business of intimacy" (p. 331).

The "far more difficult business of intimacy" is at the heart of what Woolf meant by the change in human nature "in or about December, 1910." Her genius, in fact, was to see and appreciate the social, political, and historical dimensions of this challenge, not only for writers interested in creating engaging characters but also for how people lived and worked. As our understanding of consciousness and psychology became more complex after Freud (whose work the Woolfs published in English translation at The Hogarth Press), so too did our difficulty in appreciating the motivations and desires circulating within ourselves and each other. Perhaps more than any writer of her generation,

CHRONOLOGY

1882	Virginia Stephen is born on 25 January in London.
1895	Her mother, Julia Stephen, dies. Virginia suffers her first mental breakdown.
1897	Studies Greek and history at King's College, London. Begins her first diary.
1904	Her father, Leslie Stephen, dies. Suffers second mental breakdown. Publishes first book review. Moves with siblings to Bloomsbury neighborhood of London.
1906	Brother Thoby Stephens dies of typhoid.
1907	Sister Vanessa marries the art critic Clive Bell. Begins work on what would become her first novel, *The Voyage Out.*
1910	First Postimpressionist exhibition organized by her friend Roger Fry.
1912	Marries Leonard Woolf.
1913	Third mental breakdown after completion of *The Voyage Out.* Attempts suicide.
1914	World War I begins.
1915	*The Voyage Out* is published.
1917	With husband Leonard, founds The Hogarth Press. Begins the diary she keeps for the rest of her life.
1918	World War I ends in November 1918. Spanish influenza epidemic strikes worldwide, killing 25 million people.
1919	*Night and Day,* her second novel, is published.
1922	Publishes *Jacob's Room.* Begins to expand her short story "Mrs. Dalloway in Bond Street" into a novel.
1925	Publishes *Mrs. Dalloway* and *The Common Reader,* a collection of reviews and essays.
1927	Publishes *To the Lighthouse.*
1928	Publishes *Orlando.* Lectures on "Women and Fiction" at Newnham and Girton Colleges, Cambridge. Awarded the Prix Femina for *To the Lighthouse.*
1929	Publishes *A Room of One's Own,* a feminist tract developed from her "Women and Fiction" lectures.
1931	Publishes *The Waves.*
1937	Publishes *The Years.*
1939	World War II begins.

1941   Fearing the approach of another mental breakdown, drowns herself in the river Ouse in Sussex County on 28 March. *Between the Acts,* her ninth and final novel, is published posthumously.

Woolf saw the difficulty inherent in the negotiation of who we are on the inside and what we are expected to be on the outside, as well as how the nexus of those two questions is at the very heart of what we call "reality." For it was now possible to divorce "reality" from "history," or at least the history that had previously consisted only of the lives of kings and momentous battles. Instead, the "reality" perceived within individual and collective consciousness could itself be seen as a new and legitimate form of "history." This then makes momentous not only World War I and the 10 million lives lost in it, but also the unspoken thoughts and feelings of a fifty-two-year-old woman walking through London in search of flowers for the party she will host that evening.

LIFE AND DEATH

The action of *Mrs. Dalloway* takes place on a Wednesday in June 1923. Like Joyce's *Ulysses,* the novel's plot focuses on two principle characters as they follow their separate paths through a modern European city. Unlike *Ulysses,* however, *Mrs. Dalloway* does not contain an elaborate array of literary styles, but uses interior monologue to record the thoughts and feelings of its characters, each of them struggling to square present hopes with past disappointments as they reflect on the sensory experience immediately around them.

Clarissa Dalloway and Septimus Warren Smith are the novel's two main characters. Though they do not know each other and never meet, in the foreword to the Modern Library edition of the book Woolf even went so far as to describe Smith as Mrs. Dalloway's "double," a comment that has been a point of debate among

critics ever since. On the one hand, such a notion provides a clear framework for the novel as a struggle between Septimus's madness and eventual suicide versus Mrs. Dalloway's life force as she brings her family and friends together for her party. On the other hand, numerous critics have also pointed out the emptiness of Clarissa's existence, her lack of self-confidence, and her constant fear that her life has meant nothing. Though she survives, her horror at hearing about Septimus's suicide at the novel's end also represents "her disaster—her disgrace," for even she feels that it is "her punishment to see sink and disappear here a man, there a woman, in this profound darkness, and she forced to stand here in her evening dress" (p. 282).

To understand how it is possible to arrive at such different readings, it is important to appreciate the historical context in which the novel was written and in which its characters live. Clarissa herself notes early on, "The late age of the world's experience had bred in them all, all men and women, a well of tears" (p. 13). This refers of course to the cataclysm of World War I. We also learn that Clarissa suffers from a heart condition brought on by a bout with influenza, thus linking her with the worldwide Spanish influenza epidemic that killed another 25 million people right after the war. Add to this the rapid rise of industrialization, the coming collapse of the British Empire already foreshadowed in *Mrs. Dalloway* by Peter Walsh's return from India, the residue of suffering manifested in countless shell-shock victims such as Septimus, and the London of 1923 seems a precarious place, one haunted by death and nervous about its future.

In the face of such deep anxiety, Clarissa's sense of affirmation can be read as both an inner desperation and a powerful life force. However, it would be a mistake to dismiss it as the meaningless worries of an upper-class housewife. Rather, as she makes her "plunge" (p. 3) into the street in search of flowers for her party, what passes through her mind is no less than a metaphysical debate on the meaning of human society in the face of quotidian despair.

> Such fools we are, she thought, crossing Victoria Street. For Heaven only knows why one loves it so, how one sees it so, making it up, building it round one, tumbling it, creating it every moment afresh; but the veriest frumps, the most dejected of miseries sitting on doorsteps (drink their downfall) do the same; can't be dealt with, she felt positive, by Acts of Parliament for that very reason: they love life. In people's eyes, in the swing, tramp, and trudge; in the bellow and the uproar; the carriages, motor cars, omnibuses, vans, sandwich men shuffling and swinging; brass bands; barrel organs; in the triumph and the jingle and the strange high singing of some aeroplane overhead was what she loved; life; London; this moment in June.
>
> (p. 5)

Before we let ourselves get too quickly swept up in the ringing affirmation that Clarissa comes to, it is important to note that the impetus that leads her to ask "why one loves it so" also contains the buried possibility that life is unbearable and the fact that "one loves it so" is an absurdity in itself. Recalled in the "tramp, and trudge; in the bellow and uproar" that Clarissa celebrates amid the bustle of Victoria Street is the melancholy march of soldiers toward the trenches and the bombardment that awaited them. Also, those "most dejected of miseries sitting on doorsteps" call to mind the poverty and stratification that will come to plague the modern welfare state, just as the notion that they "can't be dealt with . . . by Acts of Parliament" introduces the tension between individual lives, particularly women, and the political institutions that seek to control them. In short, Clarissa may be affirming "this moment in June" and her ability to "plunge" into it, but as Woolf would describe in her diary, such a moment is no more than "a little strip of pavement over an abyss" (*A Writer's Diary*, p. 29).

The abyss that threatens to swallow up the buoyant Clarissa has already consumed Septimus. As Clarissa enters a shop and hears the backfire of a motor car carrying the prime minister down Bond Street, the same sound most likely reminds Septimus of the shelling that has broken his health. Whereas Clarissa finds herself caught up by "this moment in June," Septimus experiences "this gradual drawing together of everything to one centre before his eyes, as if some horror had come almost to the surface and was about to burst into flames" (p. 21). Interestingly, he too is immersed in the day, but whereas Clarissa rides on "the ebb and flow of things" (p. 12), Septimus has curiously lost the power to "feel" and thinks "it might be possible that the world itself is without meaning" (p. 133). Despite the devotion and care of his wife, Rezia, he has come to distrust "human nature" and feels "that human beings have neither kindness, nor faith, nor charity beyond what serves to increase the pleasure of the moment" (p. 135).

Septimus, however, is no villain, nor is he the simplified victim. Instead Woolf is careful to humanize his suffering and to create a deeply sympathetic portrait of him as "the most exalted of mankind; the criminal who faced his judges; the victim exposed on the heights; the fugitive; the drowned sailor; the poet of the immortal ode; the Lord who had gone from life to death" (p. 147). In fact, he is more closely linked with Woolf herself than is Clarissa. Whereas Clarissa laments that she "could not think, write, or even play the piano" (p. 185), Septimus reads both Shakespeare and Dante and at least attempts to write by recording the mad insights that plague him. And when an airplane writes an advertisement for toffee in the sky above London, it is Septimus who most identifies with the act of writing:

> So, thought Septimus, looking up, they are signalling me. Not indeed in actual words; that is, he could not read the language yet; but it was plain enough, this beauty, this exquisite beauty, and tears filled his eyes as he looked at the smoke words languishing and melting in the sky and bestowing upon him in their inexhaustible charity and laughing goodness one shape after another of unimaginable beauty and signaling their intention to provide

him, for nothing, for ever, for looking merely, with beauty, more beauty!

(p. 31)

Poignant as it is mad, the passage reminds us of how close Woolf was to such experience given the several crippling breakdowns she suffered in her life. She too felt that words were a lifeline to the world, and that for all of her fascination with Mrs. Brown's "silence" and her valuation of Mrs. Dalloway's ability to make an "offering for the sake of offering" (p. 185), Septimus Smith lives more by the values and practices of the writer than any character in the book.

CHARACTER AND CONSCIOUSNESS

Though in her diary Woolf characterizes *Mrs. Dalloway* as "a study of insanity and suicide; the world seen by the sane and the insane side by side" (*A Writer's Diary,* p. 52), the way human character is depicted in her fiction argues against assigning such rigid categories. While it might have been useful in the writing of the novel to think of Septimus and Clarissa as counterparts, all of the characters in *Mrs. Dalloway* seem to share in each other's experience, be it Peter Walsh passing Septimus and his wife as they quarrel in Regent's Park, or the way Peter and Clarissa notice the ringing of Big Ben and St. Margaret's at different hours and different parts of the city, or Clarissa's own anxiety over learning secondhand at her party about Septimus's death. In this way Woolf's ideas on the nature of identity mirror closely Clarissa's notion, as reported to us by Peter, that "to know her or any one, one must seek out the people who completed them; even the places" (p. 231).

To know and understand Clarissa is in some ways to know and understand Septimus, and vice versa. It is also to establish a third entity, call it Clarissa-Septimus, that stands outside of each individual and yet is part of the fabric from which each is made. The critic Jeremy Hawthorn argues that such a quasi-relation only masks the alienation that individuals experience in modern capitalist societies, while even Clarissa agrees that it is unsatisfactory "how little one knew people" (p. 231). On the other hand, very early on Clarissa announces that she will not "say of any one in the world now that they were this or were that" (p. 11). Woolf also refuses to reduce any character to a single trait or entity, but rather has each function as the locus through which a series of connections to people and places pass. In trying to know a person by seeking out "the people who completed them," Clarissa arrives at

> a transcendental theory which, with her horror of death, allowed her to believe, or say that she believed (for all her scepticism), that since our apparitions, the part of us which appears, are so momentary compared with the other, the unseen part of us, which spreads wide, the unseen might survive, be recovered somehow attached to this person or that, or even haunting certain places after death . . . perhaps—perhaps.
>
> (pp. 231–232)

One could argue that this is mere wishful thinking on Clarissa's part as a modern woman with no ties to a structured religion that can provide her with a viable model for the afterlife. On the other hand, Woolf shrewdly manipulates plot and events within her novel as proof of the validity of such a framework by allowing her characters to think parallel thoughts and observe parallel events without any notion of their shared experience. This then turns the reader's awareness of the ties between them into a kind of spiritual residue that outlasts their own creation. In the case of Clarissa, it is what leads to a powerful sense of her as a character who is everywhere and nowhere at once, turning her into a kind of aura that permeates the entire novel, even when she is not present.

The key to this achievement lies not only in the way Woolf constructs her characters, but also in the way that process stands for her conception of how fiction should mirror and shape reality. While writing *Mrs. Dalloway*, she describes this process in her diary as "my discovery: how I dig out beautiful caves behind my characters: I think that gives exactly what I want; humanity, humor, depth. The idea is that the caves shall connect and each comes to daylight at the present moment" (*A Writer's Diary*, p. 60). Elsewhere in the diary she names this her "tunnelling process, by which I tell the past by instalments" (p. 61). In *Mrs. Dalloway* this approach is manifested through the many repeated patterns and phrases that connect one character to another, one moment to another, though in real time neither would be contiguous. By "tunnelling" out each character and revealing the corpus of memory and experience that surrounds them, Woolf enlarges the space around each until, inevitably, one cave breaks through to another in the present.

Peter Walsh is an excellent example of Woolf's technique. "One of the triumphs of civilization" (p. 227) he thinks to himself as he hears an ambulance ring its alarm bell and marvels at the organization and cooperation involved in the rescue. What he does not know, of course, is that inside the ambulance is the lifeless body of Septimus Smith, whom he had passed in Regent's Park only hours before. Thus the past is brought into the present, but if this were the extent of Woolf's technique it would amount to no more than a series of convenient plot twists. However, Peter's thoughts press on as he reflects on his own emotional difficulties.

> It had been his undoing—this susceptibility—in Anglo-Indian society; not weeping at the right time, or laughing either. I have that in me, he thought standing by the pillar-box, which could now dissolve into tears. Why, Heaven knows. Beauty of some sort probably, and the weight of the day, which beginning with that visit to Clarissa had exhausted him with its heat, its intensity, and the drip, drip, of one impression after another down into that cellar where they stood, deep, dark, and no one would ever know. Partly for that reason, its secrecy, complete and inviolable, he had found life like an unknown garden, full of turns and corners, surprising, yes; really it took one's breath away, these moments; there coming to him by the pillar-box opposite the British Museum one of them, a moment, in which things came together; this ambulance; and life and death.

> (p. 230)

Like Clarissa, Peter finds himself caught up in "this moment in June," one that has also brought them together after many years apart. He too suffers from self-doubt that often transforms itself into a kind of stoic resignation, such as when Clarissa thinks, "So on a summer's day waves collect, overbalance, and fall; collect and fall; and the whole world seems to be saying 'that is all' " (p. 58). Clarissa also shares a certain amount of pride in "civilization" when she later is pleased to have the prime minister attend her party, and the evocation of "beauty . . . life and death" here shows that the two characters both feel enthralled by and victim to the transitory nature of life itself.

But to set up a binary connection exclusively between Peter and Clarissa is to miss the depth and complexity of Woolf's "tunnelling process," for another presence that haunts this passage is that of Septimus. Earlier in Regent's Park, suffering from his own madness, it is he who tries to open his eyes to the beauty of the world around him.

> He had only to open his eyes; but a weight was on them; a fear. He strained; he pushed; he looked; he saw Regent's Park before him. Long streamers of sunlight fawned at his feet. The trees waved, brandished. We welcome, the world seemed to say; we accept; we create. Beauty, the world seemed to say. . . . Up in the sky swallows swooping, swerving, flinging themselves, round and round, yet always with perfect control as if elastics held them; and the flies rising and falling; and the sun spotting now this leaf, now that, in mockery, dazzling it with soft gold in pure good temper; and now and again some chime (it might be a motor horn) tinkling divinely on the grass stalks—all of this, calm and reasonable as it was, made out of

ordinary things as it was, was the truth now; beauty, that was the truth now. Beauty was everywhere.

(p. 105)

Like Septimus, Peter finds himself overcome with emotion, "not weeping at the right time, or laughing either." The difference between the two, however, is that Peter's difficulty in controlling his emotions falls within parameters acceptable to "civilization." Each hears a "chime" in the sound of a "motor horn" or the "light high bell" of the ambulance. Septimus, however, hears it "tinkling divinely on the grass stalks," a degree of perception more intense and hypersensitive than Peter marveling at the way the carts and carriages pull to the side in unison to let the ambulance pass. Later, on the way to Clarissa's party, Peter anticipates the "beauty" he will experience there as "[a]bsorbing, mysterious, of infinite richness" (p. 248), which would seem to correspond with Septimus's appreciation for the richness inherent in "ordinary things." But at the very next moment, through the branches of the trees that seem so beautiful, Septimus sees his friend Evans, killed in the war, "raising his hand like some colossal figure who has lamented the fate of man for ages in the desert alone" (pp. 105–106). The beauty that Peter perceives, meanwhile, rests in the more "civilized" locus of the party, "the windows lit up, a piano, a gramophone sounding; a sense of pleasure-making hidden" (p. 248) among the men and women enjoying each other's company.

Concepts such as "civilization" and "beauty" then are matters of degree, and so too the nature and essence of character. To map the patterns and gradations of thought within any single character is to explore the nature of consciousness itself rather than simply assign reductive traits. In *Mrs. Dalloway,* such mapping also quickly turns the appreciation of one character into the connection with several. In the passage quoted above, Peter's thoughts are of Clarissa, but how he thinks about her and the beauty of the day going by strongly echoes the inner life

of Septimus. In turn, on the very next page Peter reports how Clarissa "felt herself everywhere; not 'here, here, here' " (p. 231), after which she then shares her "transcendental theory." Within a matter of three pages, the reader experiences Peter thinking of Clarissa, but in a manner akin to Septimus, and also reporting a memory of Clarissa so vividly that we hear her in the present. In this way character bleeds into character, thus creating a consciousness that supersedes them all.

Though each individual consciousness may be different in shape and degree, none can claim exclusivity over another, for consciousness itself is not self-contained but instead shared, fragmentary, and continually evolving. In other words, Septimus and Peter and Clarissa may lead very different lives, but there is also a way in which they share one life within the "moment" of the society in which they live. This is not to deny their separateness and uniqueness, for though Peter may think like Septimus, he does not think for him. It is only when one separate consciousness "tunnels into" another and discovers a shared "moment" that a collective consciousness or experience is had. For the most part this happens invisibly, without the characters even knowing their links to one another. When such links occur more openly, such as when Clarissa thinks about the old woman in the flat across from her or Peter experiences his revelation of the meaning of Clarissa's presence at the novel's end, something "beautiful" and "civilizing" transpires as the characters or "caves . . . connect and each comes to daylight at the present moment."

A FEMINIST AESTHETIC

Woolf's urge to change the way character is shaped in fiction is not merely a question of aesthetics, it is also a question of the social and political consequences attached to various constructs of the self, particularly for women, and how those play out in real life. In the novel, Clarissa is most aware of the stakes involved in how she is perceived, for it is she who has "the oddest sense of being herself invisible; unseen; unknown; there being no more marrying, no more having of children now, but only this astonishing and rather solemn progress with the rest of them; up Bond Street, this being Mrs. Dalloway; not even Clarissa any more; this being Mrs. Richard Dalloway" (p. 14). As a woman born in the Victorian age, she is forced into various roles assigned to her as wife, mother, and host. With little formal education and as wife to a member of Parliament, there is little leeway in her life to shape her own role and function. Within that role, however, she can at least take solace in her ability to bring people together, to make "an offering; to combine, to create" by giving her parties. Staring into a mirror while doing her makeup, she thinks, "That was her self when some effort, some call on her to be her self, drew the parts together . . . and made a meeting-point, a radiancy no doubt in some dull lives, a refuge for the lonely, perhaps . . ." (p. 55).

But even Clarissa is aware of the potential emptiness of such an existence. In the face of Peter's disdain she feels criticized for giving foolish parties, and though her husband, Richard, brings her flowers, theirs is a marriage often devoid of feeling. The connection with her daughter also is threatened when Elizabeth is drawn away by her tutor Miss Kilman, a born-again Christian who detests Clarissa for having "trifled [her] life away" (p. 189). However, in the face of such vehemence and the expectations that have limited her reach as a woman, Clarissa feels that "love and religion would destroy that, whatever it was, the privacy of the soul" (p. 192). This causes her to long for the anonymity and lack of restraints enjoyed by the old woman looking out the window opposite, "quite unconscious she was being watched" (p. 192). Clarissa, however, feels continually watched, if not by Peter or Richard or Miss Kilman, then by the artificial rigors imposed by her class and social role.

The pressure of constructs and categorizations is something also felt by Septimus.

Interestingly it is Woolf herself who goes on the attack against the medical profession when, as narrator, she describes Sir William Bradshaw alone in his office after just having treated Septimus. "Proportion, divine proportion" is the goddess that Sir William worships, for in "[w]orshipping proportion, Sir William not only prospered himself but made England prosper, secluded her lunatics, forbade childbirth, penalised despair, made it impossible for the unfit to propagate their views until they, too, shared his sense of proportion" (p. 150). This is a passage where Woolf herself appears to step up to the microphone. When she proclaims "this is madness, this sense; in fact, his sense of proportion" (p. 151), it is clear that she vents her own hatred for the tidy categories into which medicine places suffering in order to manage it.

In going further to explain that "Proportion has a sister, less smiling, more formidable" and that "Conversion is her name" (p. 151), Woolf takes a clear feminist stance in her disdain for the expectations and social roles that force woman to "convert" their own lives into that of their husbands. We learn that Conversion also has "her dwelling in Sir William's heart, though concealed, as she mostly is, under some plausible disguise; some venerable name; love, duty, self sacrifice" (pp. 151–152). That Rezia "divine[s]" that Sir William worships the goddess Conversion shows at least some breakthrough in consciousness, though this does little for Lady Bradshaw, who "long ago . . . had caught salmon freely" but is now "quick to minister to the craving which lit her husband's eye so oilily for dominion" (p. 152).

As a novelist Woolf questions and subverts the roles of "Proportion" and "Conversion" in the shaping of character. Rather than give us a "balanced" portrait of the material lives of her characters by describing their houses, jobs, and forms of dress in detail, Woolf tips the scales vastly towards an exploration of their inner lives. For Clarissa, this is important because only through the "tunnelling process" do we get to experience a life that is led largely inside herself, thus reversing the process of "Conversion" which she has no doubt succumbed to as well. The same holds true for Septimus, though unlike Clarissa, he can find no means or grounds on which to maintain his own inner life without destroying it. In the end, it seems no accident that when he dies Woolf makes clear that he "would not recover consciousness" (p. 227).

Woolf's aesthetic plan is also her way of creating the conditions under which she can write "what [she] chose, not what [she] must," as she outlined in her 1919 essay "Modern Fiction" (*Collected Essays,* vol. 2, p. 106). There as well she takes up arms against Edwardian realist writers such as John Galsworthy and Arnold Bennett, claiming that in shaping characters only through external details, "the enormous labour of proving the solidity, the likeness to life, of the story is not merely labour thrown away but labour misplaced" (p. 106). To this approach Woolf counters:

> Examine for a moment an ordinary mind on an ordinary day. The mind receives myriad impressions—trivial, fantastic, evanescent, or engraved with the sharpness of steel. From all sides they come, an incessant shower of innumerable atoms; and as they fall, as they shape themselves into the life of Monday or Tuesday, the accent falls differently from of old; the moment of importance came not here but there; so that if a writer were a free man and not a slave, if he could write what he chose, not what he must, if he could base his work upon his own feeling and not upon convention, there would be no plot, no comedy, no tragedy, no love interest or catastrophe in the accepted style, and perhaps not a single button sewn on as the Bond Street tailors would have it. Life is not a series of gig-lamps symmetrically arranged; life is a luminous halo, a semi-transparent envelope surrounding us from the beginning of consciousness to the end.
>
> (p. 106)

More than in any of her other novels, *Mrs. Dalloway* seeks to examine "an ordinary mind on an ordinary day" and the "myriad impressions" that pass through it. Six years later in *A Room of One's Own* she would name the specific conditions of £500 a year and a room of one's own as necessary for women to write fiction, but in important ways *Mrs. Dalloway* provided her the narrative "space" needed to explore female consciousness outside of the literary tropes handed to her by the past. Of all of her books it is the one most singularly focused on the inner life of a woman. Lily Briscoe in *To the Lighthouse* is perhaps Woolf's most fully realized heroine, but it is a novel much more about Lily's struggle with her father and her art than *Mrs. Dalloway* is about Clarissa's struggle to validate within herself and for others "that extraordinary gift, that woman's gift, of making a world of her own wherever she happened to be" (p. 114).

SELF AND SELVES

The question that has haunted Woolf's work, however, has always been the degree to which she succeeds at creating characters rather than merely weaving together voices in interesting ways. Coupled with this is the question of whether or not her "tunneling process" uncovers what occurs in real life. This is a central point of debate not only in Woolf studies but also in modern thought. Each of us has experienced the uncanny way in which we find ourselves thinking the same thoughts as another, or discovering that we have been in the same place or had the same experience as someone else without our knowing it. In addition, the density of the modern age, both in population and the speed at which information travels, can often make it seem that a good deal of our thinking is formulated for us by the society in which we live. Add to this Marxist notions about the way in which political and economic structures foster and shape individual consciousness, and the notion of the individual as a unique entity can seem a very flawed one indeed.

If Woolf is saying ironically that the real "triumph of civilization" is the hidden way in which, at a given moment, Peter thinks of

Clarissa while thinking like Septimus in order to report Clarissa's transcendental theory as if Clarissa were standing right next to Peter, it's also true that the reader is the only one to know this outside of Woolf. Perhaps I and a friend, or a total stranger, might think one and the same thing, as well as maintain our individual makeups and memories, but in real life no one can know that for sure. In *Mrs. Dalloway* all of this is possible because Woolf is writing a work of fiction. Whether and how the model of consciousness Woolf traces in her work corresponds to the way in which people actually think and live is in some ways the crux of her entire work.

Despite the thorough portrait of her thinking that Woolf left behind in several volumes of diaries, letters, and essays, there is a curious way in which, like Clarissa Dalloway, Woolf seems everywhere present and nowhere in particular at one and the same time. In her biography, Hermione Lee devotes an entire chapter to the notion of "selves" in Woolf's life and writing, and quotes Woolf's playful biography of *Orlando* in order to point out that "she had a great variety of selves to call upon" (p. 529). As the daughter of a renowned literary journalist; the sister of a painter; friend to poets, novelists, critics, and thinkers; husband to Leonard and cofounder of The Hogarth Press; Vita Sackville-West's lover; diarist and letter writer; critic and biographer; and finally, at times victim to severe mental illness, no doubt Woolf had many different selves to draw on at any given time. However, which of these selves is most predominant or influential in her work can be awfully difficult to pin down. Furthermore, despite the extensive record she left behind of her private thoughts and feelings, quite often she can say one thing in a letter and the very opposite thing in a diary entry. Thus to fix on Woolf's own "character" can be as difficult as getting to the heart of those she created.

Clarissa too has "a great variety of selves to call upon." We have already discussed the many roles she must fulfill as wife, mother, and socialite. In addition we learn early on that she

and Peter were once in love, and that her choice of Richard over him haunts her to this day. Thoughts of their past often mix with those of Bourton, her childhood home in the countryside where her sister Sylvia was killed by a falling tree. It was also at Bourton that her friend Sally Seton used to come to stay and with whom Clarissa also fell in love. Even now she realizes that the "strange thing, on looking back, was the purity, the integrity, of her feeling for Sally" (p. 50) and that "the most exquisite moment of her whole life" was when Sally kissed her on the lips (p. 52). This moment is shattered when Peter happens along and Clarissa feels "how Sally was being mauled already, maltreated; she felt his hostility; his jealousy; his determination to break into their companionship" (p. 53). Whether or not this is true, the moment and feeling stays with her, despite the fact that she remains friends with Peter, chooses to marry Richard, and Sally herself goes on to marry a rich man and have five boys as Lady Rosseter.

When Sally happens to be passing through London and arrives at Clarissa's party unannounced, it is as if Clarissa's many selves begin to converge in a single moment. Sally enters and the two embrace after not having seen one another for many years, but then the prime minister arrives, and Clarissa is forced to tear herself away in order to greet him and show him around the house with Richard. As can be expected, several of the characters note the prime minister's presence, each of them feeling "to the marrow of their bones, this majesty passing; this symbol of what they all stood for, English society" (p. 262). Standing in the corner, Peter despises the "snobbery of the English" (p. 262) and in particular the presence of Hugh Whitbread, the epitome of the privilege and corruption Peter sees as so much a part of the English gentry. Unable to show mercy, he cannot help but feel that "Villans there must be, and God knows the rascals who get hanged for battering the brains of a girl out in a train do less harm on the whole than Hugh Whitbread and his kindness" (p. 263).

The reference to "battering the brains of a girl out" seems a very pointed one on Woolf's part given Clarissa's experience of Peter's hostility toward Sally many years before. At the moment, however, how Peter perceives her in action is quite interesting: "And now Clarissa escorted her Prime Minister down the room, prancing, sparkling, with the stateliness of her grey hair. She wore ear- rings, and a silver-green mermaid's dress. Lolloping on the waves and braiding her tresses she seemed, having that gift still; to be; to exist" (p. 264). That she is a "mermaid" turns her into an exotic creature able to live and breathe in two worlds, just as her knack for "lolloping on the waves" marks her ability, in Peter's eyes, to maneuver the dangerous seas of high society. Noting that there is "a breath of tenderness" in her presence, he admits to himself that "her severity, her prudery, her woodenness were all warmed through now, and she had about her . . . an exquisite cordiality" (pp. 264–265), even though he makes sure to note, at least parenthetically, that "he was not in love" (p. 265).

Clarissa's thoughts on the very same moment, however, are quite different. Though she is aware of her success in entertaining her guests and achieving "that dilation of the nerves of the heart itself till it seemed to quiver, steeped, upright," she realizes,

> yes, but after all it was what other people felt, that; for, though she loved it and felt it tingle and sting, still these semblances, these triumphs (dear old Peter, for example, thinking her so brilliant), had a hollowness; at arm's length they were, not in the heart; and it might be that she was growing old but they satisfied her no longer as they used. . . .
>
> (p. 265)

In the contrast between Peter's admiration for Clarissa's "exquisite cordiality" and her own inner self-doubt about its worth Woolf mimics the way in which Clarissa must also negotiate her public image and her various inner selves. Interestingly, just when Sally Seton shows up, it is the prime minister's arrival that calls Clarissa away. Early on in the novel, it was also the prime minister's car that caused such a stir in Bond Street, thus representing the demands made upon Clarissa's "public" version of herself as wife to Richard and host of her party. Clarissa's most intimate life, namely her love for Sally, as well as her youthful love for Peter, remains on the inside of her, just as she must also keep her own self-doubt about the masquerade of the party to herself since the party provides her only means of public identity.

The degree to which this dilemma represents a tragedy or simply the run of life for all of its paradox and beauty is central to *Mrs. Dalloway*. To think Clarissa is not a standard heroic character who commits deeply memorable action misses the point of what Woolf is saying about the very nature of human character itself. Each of us is a bundle of various memories, experiences, and past lives, and how those elements are woven together into both our own present perception of the world and the perception of ourselves by others makes up a large part of the day-to-day life we live. To dwell too inwardly on the paradoxes of our many selves risks becoming narcissistic, or at the very worst, like Septimus, we can become cut off from the reality of the world around us. On the other hand, if the public self we live by is constructed for us, our own true natures are never allowed to see the light of day. The needed balance lies somewhere between. In the end, *Mrs. Dalloway* is only a novel, but one that models the process by which each of us must close the book and think more deeply and intricately about our own stance and value in the scheme of things.

To do this requires a complex act of "reading" that mirrors the way we are asked to "read" and put together the fragmentary thoughts and feelings of the characters that people Woolf's novel. Though in some profound way we never wholly perceive the single self that ties together all of Clarissa's many different selves, Woolf's consciousness in creating the patterns of the novel provides the "self" that contains and unites the various parts. Thus the novel is titled *Mrs. Dalloway*, as if that outward attribute were the sum of its many parts, whether those belong to Clarissa or Peter or Septimus. As David Dowling points out in his conclusion, "In considering Clarissa standing there as hostess . . . the reader is situated precisely at the point where Woolf's debate pivots, between judgement and endorsement," and that this debate is also important to the difficulty of living within any society. Rather than say of people simply that "they were this or were that," as Clarissa and Woolf refuse to do, Dowling emphasizes that "what must be preserved within [any] community is the individual's right to interpret and to *read* for himself and herself" (p. 126). *Mrs. Dalloway* not only seeks to preserve such a right, but demands this action from us if we are to comprehend the interplay of its characters and the narrative strategy that creates them. Only then can Woolf succeed at fulfilling the challenge she sets for herself in *A Room of One's Own* when she asks:

> What is meant by "reality"? It would seem to be something very erratic, very undependable—now to be found in a dusty road, now in a scrap of newspaper in the street, now in a daffodil in the sun. It lights up a group in a room and stamps some casual saying. It overwhelms one walking home beneath the stars and makes the silent world more real than the world of speech—and then there it is again in an omnibus in the uproar of Piccadilly. Sometimes, too, it seems to dwell in shapes too far away for us to discern what their nature is. But whatever it touches, it fixes and makes permanent. That is what remains over when the skin of the day has been cast into the hedge; that is what is left of past time and of our loves and hates. Now the writer, as I think, has the chance to live more than other people in the presence of this reality. It is his business to find it and collect it and communicate it to the rest of us.
>
> (pp. 191–192)

IMPORTANCE AND INFLUENCE

There are few books that actually help to change the way novels are written or read. *Mrs. Dalloway* is just such a book. Even though Joyce's *Ulysses* was three years ahead of it in telling the story of the meandering thoughts and feelings of Stephen Dedalus and Leopold and Molly Bloom on a single June day, *Mrs. Dalloway* granted legitimacy to everyday women as both a serious subject for fiction and as authors in their own right. Before Woolf there was Jane Austen, the Brontës, and George Eliot, but few others. Woolf's work as a novelist and critic, as well as her prominent role in the Bloomsbury gatherings, established her as an intellectual able to go toe to toe with the best of her generation and beyond. Before her there were "men" of letters; after her it became acceptable to think of writers as male and female alike.

Yet stylistically Woolf's influence has been more diffuse than direct, for despite the way in which *Mrs. Dalloway* opened up new subject matter for the novel, there have been few writers who have actually mimicked its fragmentary use of inner monologue. In fact, many would argue that Woolf has been more influential as a figure than she actually has as a novelist. While she helped pioneer the importance of common lives and their interior makeup, in general, fiction still remains bound more by nineteenth-century realism than the modernist mosaic that writers like Joyce and Woolf forwarded. We expect now for novels to be about the common man or woman struggling to find meaning amid diminished lives, unlike nineteenth-century novels such as *War and Peace* or *The Brothers Karamazov* that explore complex philosophical ideas on a large canvas. This change in emphasis clearly owes a great deal to *Mrs. Dalloway*. But all too often the prose style utilized to create contemporary characters often focuses on the material outer reality of their jobs, homes, and clothing rather than the ineffable nature of their inner feelings. Life may indeed be "a luminous halo, a semi-transparent envelope surrounding us from the beginning of consciousness to the end," but in most novels of the twentieth-century it is not.

There are of course exceptions, both within Woolf's lifetime and after. Woolf herself was partially influenced by Katherine Mansfield, and one cannot help wonder what their friendly rivalry would have brought each of them if Mansfield had not died so young. Woolf herself served as a mentor and friend to Rosamond Lehman and Elizabeth Bowen, both of whom went on to long and successful careers. As her work came to be more widely known in England and America, as well as the world, one can see her influence, whether direct or indirect, on writers as diverse as Eudora Welty, Ingeborg Bachmann, Elizabeth Hardwick, and Jamaica Kincaid, all of whom remain committed to exploring female consciousness by formulating character through everyday speech and inner monologue. Other writers such as Grace Paley, Marilynne Robinson, and Alice Mattison also owe a debt to Woolf and the permission she gave them to write about everyday women caught in seemingly epic struggles amid mundane circumstances. Beyond this, the rise in feminist studies that began to champion Woolf in the 1960s and 1970s also helped open the door to a wide array of women novelists, short-story writers, and essayists who, though they do not always sound like Woolf, no doubt owe a great deal to her for the barriers she broke down before them.

Interestingly, the two novelists who recently have most closely mimicked her style are men. Though his earlier work is more gothic and edgy, Ian McEwan's 2002 novel *Atonement* clearly echoes Woolf's ability to capture the inner workings of a family and set of friends as well as how the consciousness of individuals overlaps with one another, especially as portrayed in *To the Lighthouse*. However, Michael Cunningham's 1998 novel *The Hours* goes a step further. Not only does it take Woolf's working title for *Mrs. Dalloway* as its own, it purposefully mirrors the plot line of Woolf's novel when a woman named Clarissa Vaughan buys flowers and plans a party for her friend Richard, an ailing poet who has just won a major prize but is dying of AIDS in contemporary New York. Interspliced with this narrative is the story of Laura Brown, a single mother who is trying to raise her son Richie in

California in 1949, and who happens to be reading Woolf's *Mrs. Dalloway*. Eventually the two characters are brought together by quite tragic circumstances at the end of the novel, Laura Brown representing the "Mrs. Brown" whom Woolf writes of as "life itself" in her essay, as well as the old woman that Clarissa watches and envies at the end of *Mrs. Dalloway*. Cunningham's novel also ends on a wrenching note when Richard throws himself out of his apartment window, unable to face the party that his friend Clarissa wishes to give him or his imminent end. This of course mirrors the death of Septimus, the difference being that Clarissa and Richard know each other directly, and the loss is felt by both Clarissa and the reader as more personal and jarring. Nonetheless, Cunningham does an ingenious job of tapping Woolf's use of inner monologue and the description of characters whose paths cross unawares amid an urban setting and across time. Both a critical and popular success worldwide, *The Hours* won the Pulitzer Prize in 1999, again reigniting interest in Woolf and *Mrs. Dalloway*. In 2002, the book was made into a major motion picture starring Nicole Kidman, Julianne Moore, and Meryl Streep. It, too, was a critical success and earned Kidman her first Oscar for her portrayal of Woolf.

But in the end there is no one who writes or thinks quite like Woolf, and given the importance of the individual to her, that is perhaps as it should be. Early on Clarissa wonders whether or not it matters "that she must inevitably cease completely; . . . or did it become consoling to believe that death ended absolutely?" (p. 12) This is the question that drives the characters to muse upon the worth of their existence and their connection to one another, just as it most certainly was the lingering doubt that propelled Woolf to capture "this moment in June" in all its headlong flight. Nonetheless, Clarissa is convinced that "here, there, she survived, . . . laid out like mist between people she knew best, who lifted her on their branches as she had seen the trees lift the mist, but it spread ever so far, her life, herself" (p. 12). If nothing else, Woolf's novel proves this to be true. Despite Septimus's despair, Clarissa survives as a presence in the lives around her, whether it be the characters of the novel or ourselves as readers. Before *Mrs. Dalloway,* human beings had never been described in quite this way, and thus Clarissa's survival also marks that of Woolf and our very own in the imagination's power and ability to give shape and nuance to inner being. As E. M. Forster put

it in his Rede Lecture given at Cambridge shortly after the death of his dear friend Virginia, "Our debt to her is in part this: she reminds us of the importance of sensation in an age which practices brutality and recommends ideals" (p. 27). While sadly this still seems true, *Mrs. Dalloway* is there to help us as a fictive model for the self whose various realities and fictions it is our lifelong purpose to know and understand as best we can amid the chaos and beauty that is a moment or a day.

Selected Bibliography

EDITIONS

Mrs. Dalloway. London: Hogarth Press, and New York: Harcourt Brace, 1925. The Harvest Paperback published by Harcourt Brace Jovanovich in 1985 is cited in this essay.

OTHER WORKS

Jacob's Room. London: Hogarth Press, 1922; New York: Harcourt Brace, 1923.

To the Lighthouse. London: Hogarth Press, and New York: Harcourt Brace, 1927.

A Room of One's Own. London: Hogarth Press, and New York: Harcourt Brace, 1929. The latter edition is cited in this essay.

Collected Essays. 4 vols. London: Hogarth Press, and New York: Harcourt Brace, 1967. The latter edition is cited in this essay.

A Writer's Diary. Edited by Leonard Woolf. London: Hogarth Press, 1953; New York: Harcourt Brace, 1954. A useful selection from Woolf's diary which was later edited by Anne Oliver Bell and published in five volumes by The Hogarth Press between 1977 and 1984.

Mrs. Dalloway's Party. Edited by Stella McNichol. London: Hogarth Press, 1973. This volume collects the stories from which Woolf generated *Mrs. Dalloway.*

SECONDARY WORKS

Abel, Elizabeth. *Virginia Woolf and the Fictions of Psychoanalysis.* Chicago: University of Chicago Press, 1989. Explores how *Mrs. Dalloway* both mirrors and alters Freud's theories on female development.

Barrett, Eileen, and Patricia Cramer, eds. *Virginia Woolf: Lesbian Readings.* New York: New York University Press, 1997.

Bell, Quentin. *Virginia Woolf, A Biography.* 2 vols. London: Hogarth Press, and New York: Harcourt Brace Jovanovich, 1972. The first substantive biography of Woolf, written by her nephew.

Beja, Morris, ed. *Critical Essays on Virginia Woolf.* Boston: G. K. Hall, 1985.

Bloom, Harold, ed. *Modern Critical Interpretations of Virginia Woolf's "Mrs. Dalloway."* New York: Chelsea House, 1988. A valuable collection of recent criticism that includes articles by Abel, DiBattista, Lee, McLaurin, Ruotolo, Zwerdling, and others.

————, ed. *Modern Critical Views of Virginia Woolf.* New York: Chelsea House, 1986.

Clements, Patricia, and Isobel Grundy. *Virginia Woolf: New Critical Essays.* London and Totowa, N.J.: Vision Press and Barnes and Noble, 1983. Includes essays by Maria DiBattista on "Joyce, Woolf and the Modern Mind" and Susan Dick on "The Tunneling Process: Virginia Woolf's Use of Memory and the Past."

DeSalvo, Louise A. *Virginia Woolf: The Impact of Childhood Sexual Abuse on Her Life and Work.* London: Women's Press, and Boston: Beacon Press, 1989. A highly controversial view of Woolf's life and writing.

DiBattista, Maria. *Virginia Woolf's Major Novels.* New Haven: Yale University Press, 1980. A chapter on *Mrs. Dalloway* discusses the importance of time and space in the novel.

Dowling, David. *Mrs. Dalloway: Mapping Streams of Consciousness.* Boston: Twayne, 1991. Provides a very good overview of the novel's critical reception and detailed charts and maps of when and where the characters walk through London.

Fleishman, Avrom. *Virginia Woolf: A Critical Reading.* Baltimore and London: Johns Hopkins University Press, 1975. Provides a thorough reading of the novel's themes and symbols.

Forster, E. M. *Virginia Woolf.* Cambridge: Cambridge University Press, and New York: Harcourt Brace, 1942. Reprinted in *Two Cheers for Democracy,* New York: Harcourt Brace Jovanovich, 1970.

Harper, Howard. *Between Language and Silence: The Novels of Virginia Woolf.* Baton Rouge and London: Louisiana State University Press, 1982. Discusses varying levels of consciousness in the characters and the narrative consciousness that encompasses them.

Hawthorn, Jeremy. *Virginia Woolf's Mrs. Dalloway: A Study in Alienation.* Sussex, U.K.: Sussex University Press, 1975. Forwards a Marxist reading of the novel.

Hussey, Mark. *Virginia Woolf A to Z.* London and New York: Oxford University Press, 1996.

Kirkpatrick, B. J., and Stuart N. Clarke, eds. *A Bibliography of Virginia Woolf* 4th ed. London and New York: Oxford University Press, 1997.

Latham, Jacqueline E. M., ed. *Critics on Virgina Woolf.* Coral Gables, Fla.: Miami University Press, 1970. Contains important early essays by David Daiches, Joan Bennett, John Graham, and others.

Lee, Hermione. *Virginia Woolf.* London: Chatto and Windus, 1996; New York: Knopf, 1997; New York: Vintage, 1999. Considered by many to be the best biography of Woolf currently available.

Love, Jean O. *Worlds in Consciousness: Mythopoetic Thought in the Novels of Virginia Woolf.* Berkeley, Los Angeles, and London: University of California Press, 1970. Discusses the role of a unified collective consciousness in the novel.

Marcus, Jane, ed. *New Feminist Essays on Virginia Woolf.* Lincoln: University of Nebraska Press, 1983. Collects Suzette A. Henke's article "*Mrs. Dalloway:* The Communion of Saints," which discusses Clarissa as a feminine life force pitted against patriarchy.

———, ed. *Virginia Woolf: A Feminist Slant.* Lincoln: University of Nebraska Press, 1983. Contains Emily Jensen's article on "Clarissa Dalloway's Respectable Suicide," which argues that Clarissa's acceptance of a conventional life is a form of suicide.

Marsh, Nicholas. *Virginia Woolf: The Novels.* New York: St. Martin's Press, 1998. Broad overview of the themes, styles, and development of Woolf's novels.

Maze, John R. *Virginia Woolf: Feminism, Creativity, and the Unconscious.* Westport, Conn.: Greenwood Press, 1997. Argues that Woolf identifies more closely with Septimus than with Clarissa and that his suicide foreshadows her own.

McNees, Eleanor, ed. *Virgina Woolf: Critical Assessments.* 4 vols. Sussex: Helm, 1994. Collects critical assessments of Woolf's work from the time it was published to the present day.

Minow-Pinkney, Makiko. *Virginia Woolf and the Problem of the Subject.* New Brunswick, N.J.: Rutgers University Press, 1987. Argues that Woolf's urge to disrupt narrative linearity corresponds to her rejection of masculine discourse.

Naremore, James. *The World Without a Self: Virginia Woolf and the Novel.* New Haven: Yale University Press, 1973. Focuses on stylistic concerns and Woolf's use of interior monologue.

Nicolson, Nigel. *Virginia Woolf.* New York: Viking, 2000. Breezy, short biography written by Vita Sackville- West's son, who knew Woolf personally.

Roe, Sue, and Susan Sellers, eds. *The Cambridge Companion to Virginia Woolf.* Cambridge and New York: Cambridge University Press, 2000. Contains essays by current leading scholars on Woolf, including DiBattista, Dick, Lee, Marcus, and Roe.

Rosenman, Ellen Bayuk. *The Invisible Presence: Virginia Woolf and the Mother-Daughter Relationship.* Baton Rouge: Louisiana State University Press, 1986. Argues that Clarissa's role as hostess mirrors Woolf's urge as a novelist to preserve and unify consciousness.

Ruotolo, Lucio P. *The Interrupted Moment: A View of Virginia Woolf's Novels.* Stanford, Calif.: Stanford University Press, 1986. Explores how moments and characters connect and disconnect with one another over the course of the novel.

Sprague, Claire. *Virginia Woolf: A Collection of Critical Essays.* Englewood Cliffs, N.J.: Prentice-Hall, 1971. Collects important early essays by Erich Auerbach, Reuben Brower, Forster, Jean Guignet, and others.

Warner, Eric. *Virginia Woolf: A Centenary Perspective.* London: Macmillan, and New York: St. Martin's, 1984. Contains two very lively panel discussions of Woolf's influence as a writer.

Zwerdling, Alex. *Virginia Woolf and the Real World.* Berkeley and Los Angeles: University of California Press, 1986. Discusses Woolf's response to historical and political events of her day, and how *Mrs. Dalloway* illustrates her critique of the class system.

FILM

Mrs. Dalloway. Directed by Marleen Gorris. With Vanessa Redgrave and Rupert Graves. Fox Lorber, 1997. A surprisingly passable version of the novel that uses flashbacks and voice-over narration to render Woolf's narrative technique.

The Hours. Directed by Stephen Daldry. With Nicole Kidman, Julianne Moore, and Meryl Streep. Miramax, 2002. An excellent film of Michael Cunningham's novel in which Nicole Kidman convincingly portrays Woolf's intensity while writing *Mrs. Dalloway.*

Oscar Wilde's
The Picture of Dorian Gray

THOMAS WRIGHT

WHEN OSCAR WILDE died in poverty and disgrace in Paris in 1900, some of his obituarists predicted that nothing that he wrote would endure. Yet a century after his death, he has become a sort of literary superstar. As well as being the subject of countless conferences and critical studies, he frequently appears in novels and comics, and is often quoted in films and TV shows. His writings too are more popular and resonant than ever. They have been translated into every major language, and their place in the canon of Western literature is secure.

There are many reasons why Wilde's name is, to use his own phrase, "musical in the mouth of fame." The romantic story of his life continues to exercise a powerful fascination over us; it has indeed achieved the status of a modern myth. The irrepressible humor and the Mozartean lightness of his writing have acted as agents of preservation, making his works accessible to a general as well as a scholarly audience. Another factor is the inherent ambiguity of his works, which invites endless rereading and reinterpretation and ensures that they can never be entirely explained away.

All of these attributes are embodied in *The Picture of Dorian Gray*, a typical Wildean production in a number of other respects. It is utterly pervaded by Wilde's marvelous personality and informed by his characteristic concerns. It also bears out his claim to have stood in "symbolic relations" to the art and culture of his age, as the political, scientific, and cultural concerns of the 1890s all find expression in its pages. This may help explain the novel's enormous appeal: along with the play *The Importance of Being Earnest,* it is the most popular of Wilde's writings. Currently one of the best-selling titles in the prestigious English Penguin Classic paperback series, *Dorian Gray* also receives more critical attention than any of Wilde's other works. Annotated scholarly editions of the novel have been published as well as book-length study guides and detailed commentaries on the various stages of its composition.

Dorian Gray's popularity cannot however solely be attributed to the fact that it offers us, as it were, the perfect entrée into Wilde's society. It is also remains perennially relevant because of its mythical qualities. Like the numerous legends and myths from which it derives, its central narrative, of a man who is granted his wish that his portrait ages while his body remains young, strikes a chord very deep within us. The story is so powerful that many of those who have not read Wilde's novel are familiar with it. Like the tales of Faust or Don Quixote, it has, in other words, become a permanent part of the landscape of the Western imagination.

Like all myths, the story of Dorian Gray fascinates us because it expresses a poetic truth about life, a truth that can be endlessly adapted to the particular concerns of its readers. It has been read as a thinly veiled apologia for homosexuality, a study of psychological collapse, and as a parable of the war between the mind and the body. The novel's malleability is also attested to by the fact that it has been translated into countless languages and numerous media. There have been films, operas, ballets, and plays based on the novel; there has also been a Dorian Gray musical. The number and variety of these adaptations suggest that the novel's basic plot retains its potency even when it is transformed into other media.

Dorian Gray is thus a quintessentially Wildean narration of a beguiling myth; it is also one of the few novels that offers readers (and particularly the young) a genuine Socratic experience. It wakes up such readers intellectually and challenges their vision of the world; it also provides a vicarious life experience. So charming and seductive is it that to read it for the first time is, for many, to begin a lifelong romance.

EARLY LIFE

Oscar Fingal O'Flahertie Wills Wilde was born at 21 Westland Row, Dublin, on 16 October 1854 ("Fingal" and "Oscar" were the names of the father and son of Ossian, the great hero of Celtic mythology—fitting appellations for a man who would become a legend). Wilde's father, Sir William, was a brilliant eye and ear surgeon, a leading Irish antiquarian, and one of the country's first folklorists. Wilde's mother, Jane Francesca Elgee, was a passionate and

CHRONOLOGY	
1854	16 October: Oscar Wilde born in Dublin.
1864	Enters Portora Royal School.
1871–1874	Studies at Trinity College, Dublin.
1874–1878	Studies at Magdalen College, Oxford.
1881	*Poems* published.
1882	Lecture tour of America as apostle of aestheticism.
1884	Marries Constance Lloyd.
1886	First homosexual experience, with lifelong friend Robert Ross.
1888	*The Happy Prince and Other Tales* published.
1890	*The Picture of Dorian Gray* published in *Lippincott's Magazine*.
1891	*Dorian Gray* published in book form. First meets Lord Alfred "Bosie" Douglas.
1892	Performance of his first social comedy, *Lady Windermere's Fan*.
1895	*The Importance of Being Earnest* first performed. Failure of action against Bosie's father, the marquess of Queensberry, for libel. Wilde is placed on trial and sentenced to two years' hard labor after having been found guilty of "gross indecency."
1897	Writes *De Profundis* in Reading Gaol. Is released from prison and settles in France.
1898	*The Ballad of Reading Gaol* published.
1900	30 November. Wilde dies, having spent the last three years of his life wandering the Continent, an impoverished and broken man.
1908	*Collected Works* published.
2000	Public monuments, speeches, performances, readings, and exhibitions mark the centenary of Wilde's death.

patriotic poetess; her son inherited from her his intense theatricality and his hatred of all things respectable and commonplace.

As a child, Wilde educated himself in his father's vast library and in the family drawing room, where he would converse with the intellectual elite of Dublin. He attended Portora Royal, a boarding school in Enniskillen, then entered Trinity College, Dublin, in 1871. In his four years at Trinity he established himself as a brilliant classicist and developed his aesthetic doctrines and his striking personality. He was to perfect both of these at Magdalen College, Oxford, where he matriculated in 1874. He went down from Magdalen in 1878 with the prestigious Newdigate poetry prize and a double first in "greats" (*literae humaniores*). At Oxford he encountered John Ruskin and Walter Pater, two writers who have been regarded as formative influences on him and whose ideas inform a number of passages in *Dorian Gray*.

During his student years Wilde wrote a great deal of verse, some of which he published in a single volume entitled *Poems* in 1881. This book, and the various public pronouncements Wilde made at this time, established him as the popular spokesman for aestheticism. The aesthetic movement emphasized the autonomy of art and encouraged people to surround themselves with objects of beauty in their daily lives. It was as the spokesman of aestheticism that Wilde lectured throughout America in 1882, a tour that made him a household name in America and England.

On his return to London, Wilde succeeded in making a splash in society with his dandified clothes, his extravagant public gestures, his marvelous conversation, and his brilliant after-dinner stories. His early writings, however, were ostentatious failures. He wrote two unexceptional plays entitled *Vera* (c. 1879–1880) and *The Duchess of Padua* (1883); *Vera* ran for only three weeks in New York, and he failed to get *The Duchess* produced until 1891. Wilde settled into a rather conventional Victorian life of journalism, lecturing, and quiet domesticity with his wife, Constance (whom he had married in 1884), and his two young boys. During the early years of his marriage Wilde seems to have been happy; after a while, however, married life started to bore him. In around 1886 he also discovered his attraction to men. The discovery was a momentous one; it certainly coincided

with, and according to some, occasioned, his emergence as a writer of genius.

At the end of the 1880s, Wilde composed the fairy tales and short stories that would eventually be published in three collections: *The Happy Prince and Other Tales* (1888), *A House of Pomegranates,* and *Lord Arthur Savile's Crime and Other Stories* (both 1891). In writing these, Wilde discovered a medium that suited his particular genius. Having been brought up on Irish folk tales and fantastic Gothic stories, he was instinctively drawn to strong and marvelous narratives. From anecdotal evidence it is clear that his mind characteristically moved from concept to story. To one friend he remarked that his ideas never came "naked" into the world: "I can think," he said, "in no other way save in stories."

Wilde was the greatest storyteller of his age, and he had an inexhaustible fund of stories that he would narrate and embellish at dinner parties or in the company of friends. Nearly all of his works began life as spoken tales: in writing them down he was simply transcribing what he had already written on the air. At the end of the 1880s, Wilde also wrote a number of brilliant and strikingly original critical pieces, including the "Platonic" dialogues, "The Decay of Lying," and "The True Function of Criticism" (later called "The Critic As Artist"), which would appear in his collection *Intentions* (1891).

ORIGINS AND COMPOSITION OF *DORIAN GRAY*

Wilde's only novel is informed by, and in a sense embodies, the ideas expressed in his critical writings. It also bears many thematic and stylistic similarities to his short stories. Wilde actually referred to *Dorian Gray* as a long short story, and its plot is essentially that of a fairy tale. In the novel Wilde reused ideas and scenes from stories of his such as "Lord Arthur Savile's Crime" and "The Young King," and it is no coincidence that it was written immediately after

"The Fisherman and His Soul," a fairy tale that it resembles in a number of respects.

The genesis of *Dorian Gray* is also similar to that of Wilde's short stories. Years before composing it, Wilde told fantastic variations on its basic plot (which may have been inspired by his experience of having his own portrait painted in 1884). One of his friends recorded an incredible strand of the narrative that Wilde chose to omit when he came to write it down, which involved the discovery of Christ's body in a forgotten tomb near Jerusalem. The subplot involving Sybil Vane also derived from a spoken story about an actress who loses her great talent when she falls in love.

Wilde seems to have been aware of the special value of his story because he expressly asked one of his listeners not to use the plot. This suggests that Wilde always intended to commit it to paper (however, it should be noted that countless other projected works remained unwritten at his death). The fact that he actually came to write it in 1889–1890 is largely due to J. M. Stoddart, a publisher from Philadelphia who managed *Lippincott's Monthly Magazine.* Stoddart, whom Wilde had met on his American lecture tour, came to London in 1889 to commission short novels for *Lippincott's.* He invited Wilde and Arthur Conan Doyle to a dinner, after which Conan Doyle promised to write for him the second Sherlock Holmes story, which became *The Sign of Four.* Wilde, who needed the money and who was keen to establish himself as a major author, also agreed to send Stoddart a tale.

From Wilde's letters it is clear that his original intention was to offer Stoddart "The Fisherman and His Soul"—a long fairy tale concerning a man who magically divides his body from his soul so that he may go and live among the sea people. Perhaps because he was unable to stretch the story out to the required length of 100,000 words ("There are not," Wilde wrote facetiously to Stoddart, "100,000 beautiful words in the English language." Ellmann, *Oscar Wilde,* p.

296), he decided to begin a new story, which became *Dorian Gray,* around December 1889. Wilde later boasted that he completed the entire story in a few weeks (adding that he did so as a result of a bet). Although he did compose it quickly, it is likely that it took him three or four months. By May 1890 the story had been revised at least twice and Wilde sent it off to Stoddart to proofread and edit. It was published on 20 June, in the July issue of *Lippincott's.*

PUBLICATION OF *DORIAN GRAY*

Like *Blackwood's Magazine* and the various periodicals in which Edgar Allan Poe published his arabesque tales, *Lippincott's Monthly* favored sensational stories that would appeal to the tastes of the magazine-reading public. It was particularly important that stories displayed a variety of atmosphere and action, not only because of the limited attention span of magazine readers but also as a strategy to appeal to as wide an audience as possible. Conan Doyle's *The Sign of Four,* an exotic tale of treasure, betrayal, murder, and miraculous detection set in India and London, obviously met these criteria.

The same can be said of *Dorian Gray,* a novel that, despite its apparent lack of action and its abundance of talk, is crowded with sensational incident. It contains two suicides (three if we include Dorian's death), a murder, an accidental death, a terrifying account of a stalker's pursuit of the hero, and a supernatural picture. It also displays a dazzling variety of moods, styles, themes, and influences and, within it, Wilde promiscuously blends several genres and traditions of literature.

Like *The Sign of Four,* Wilde's novel can be described as a brilliant example of popular Victorian literature. As we shall see, it drew upon and extended a number of popular contemporary literary traditions. Wilde was thoroughly familiar with these traditions and with the tastes of the magazine-reading public from his experiences as a journalist in the early 1880s. He had reviewed countless popular novels, published several stories in English magazines, and actually edited a periodical called *The Woman's World.*

It is important to understand the context in which the novel first appeared, as this clearly exercised a significant influence over its style and content. The most obvious demonstration of this is Stoddart's own contribution to the tale. He introduced a number of important revisions to the text that Wilde accepted; others are likely to have been made without Wilde's permission. We should also recall that but for Stoddart the story might never have been written in the first place.

In a letter to an unidentified publisher in May 1890, Wilde expressed the desire to bring out *Dorian Gray* in book form when, after three months, the copyright of the story reverted to him. The reason for this was probably financial: having been paid a fixed fee for his story, Wilde did not receive any royalties on sales of *Lippincott's,* which, given the critical controversy that followed its publication, must have been considerable.

In his letter Wilde proposed to write two new chapters to pad out his story to novel length. In the event he added six chapters, which appear in the 1891 version as numbers 3, 5, 15, 16, 17, 18, and a preface in which he responded to his critics and set out the tenets of his aesthetic creed. This additional material, which amounted to over a quarter of the book's length, fundamentally altered the nature of the story. In fact, such is the difference between the 1890 and 1891 versions of *Dorian Gray* that they have been published together in critical editions, and certain scholars have treated them as separate and distinct entities.

Wilde's publishers, Ward, Lock and Company (also the publishers of *Lippincott's*), and the book's designer, Charles Ricketts, did their utmost to distinguish the novel from the original version by producing a book that bore no

physical resemblance whatsoever to *Lippincott's Magazine.* According to the book historian Nicholas Frankel, the magazine adhered fairly strictly to the normal practices of Victorian publishing in terms of its type and the rather poor quality of its paper. In contrast, the book that Ward, Lock and Company issued in April 1891 was strikingly unconventional in format and appearance. Ricketts devised a cover of ash-gray paper on which he placed several golden butterfly designs; he was also responsible for the fanciful shapes on the novel's dust jacket (*Dorian Gray* was one of the first novels to be issued with a jacket) and the idiosyncratic title page, which employs curious lettering.

The book's appearance is sumptuous, arresting, and mysterious. It is a wonderful product of an age that believed in the book not simply as a receptacle for its text but also as an object of artistic value in its own right. Pioneers of the so-called "book beautiful," such as William Morris and Walter Crane, were reacting against the kind of cheap, mass-produced publications (of which *Lippincott's Magazine* was a good example) that had been made possible by new technology. Wilde, who knew both men, and whose earlier book *The Happy Prince* had been illustrated by Crane, had much sympathy with their cause and took a great deal of interest in the design and production of his books.

The book's design complimented the text of *Dorian Gray,* as it is the kind of beautiful object frequently handled and alluded to by Wilde's characters. It is a physical emblem of their world of luxury and impeccable taste: an object from their fictional world that has magically materialized in the hands of the reader. Wilde and his publishers were obviously trying to remove the story from its original magazine context, which Wilde regarded (or affected to regard when it suited him) as cheap and vulgar. A thing of great aesthetic beauty written for all time would, it was hoped, replace a conventional story composed hurriedly for money on the request of a magazine editor. In the first words of his preface Wilde introduces himself as "the artist" (rather than the literary journalist); Ricketts produced a book that justified and amplified that claim.

The book was designed with the idea of appealing to a more select group than a general audience of magazine readers. It was issued in an edition of 1,000 copies priced at 6 shillings, and there was a 21-shilling "large paper" edition of 250 signed and numbered copies. This deluxe edition was clearly aimed at wealthy readers who appreciated the book as an aesthetic object. It was for this kind of audience that some of Wilde's later books, such as *The Sphinx* (1894), were exclusively produced.

Wilde's attempt to appeal to two distinct audiences with the same book is entirely characteristic; it is also of a piece with a story that can be read in different ways by different types of readers. Wilde always wanted to have it both ways as an author: he aspired to the status of an artistic genius but at the same time craved popularity and wanted to make a lot of money from his pen. One of the secrets of Wilde's enduring appeal surely lies in his success in this context. His writing is at once popular and elitist, exoteric and esoteric, accessible and arcane. As a result, he is able to convince his millions of readers that they are part of a select group.

STORY OF *DORIAN GRAY*

The basic plot of Wilde's novel (unless stated otherwise, references are to the 1891 version, with page citations from *The Writings of Oscar Wilde*, 1989) is a retelling of the myth of Faust: the eponymous hero exchanges his soul for eternal youth. Wilde's particular contribution to the Faust legend was to have Dorian Gray's soul incarnated in a portrait that ages and bears the traces of his sins. The picture is a visible emblem of the corruption of Dorian's soul and also a symbol of his conscience. The heterogeneous stylistic and thematic elements of the novel are held together by this central narrative idea and by the story of Dorian's relationship with the

portrait. At the denouement, Dorian decides to destroy the picture, but in killing his soul and conscience, he inadvertently kills himself.

The novel is a full-length portrait of the hero or, as Wilde put it, the "story of a soul." As such it can be compared to Walter Pater's *Marius the Epicurean* (1885) and to J.-K. Huysmans's *À Rebours* (1884), both of which chart the progress of their hero's spiritual history. Dorian is beautiful, passionate, and extremely spoiled; after uttering the fatal wish concerning his portrait, he embarks on a life of intellectual and sensual experimentation. He treats his life in the spirit of art and makes it his mission to "give form to every feeling, expression to every thought, reality to every dream" (p. 61). To this end he adopts a variety of exotic doctrines, pastimes, and pleasures that include drug-taking and sexual promiscuity. Wilde generally obscures his protagonist's sins with an air of vagueness and mystery, however, so that, as he put it, "each man sees his own sin in Dorian Gray" (*Complete Letters,* p. 439). Dorian's antinomianism degenerates into amoral self-indulgence, and he eventually looks upon evil merely "as a mode through which he could realize his conception of the beautiful" (p. 157).

Dorian is not naturally disposed to evil. At the beginning of the tale his personality is a blank sheet on which the novel's two other main characters sketch their images of what he might become. Basil Hallward, the artist who paints Dorian's portrait, is intense, romantic, and rather earnest. He is obviously in love with Dorian, whom he regards as a muselike figure. "He is," Basil remarks, with a nod to Shakespeare, "all my art to me now" (p. 55). Basil tries to exercise what he regards as a positive influence over Dorian by exhorting him to leave the path of sin and sensual ease. He thus plays the role of the Faustian good angel in the novel who struggles for the mastery of Dorian's soul with the bad angel, Lord Henry Wotton.

Languid, witty, and utterly marvelous, Lord Henry is a prince of paradox who sums up the world in fabulous phrases and cuts life to pieces with his cynical epigrams. "Men marry because they are tired," he characteristically remarks at one point; "women because they are curious: both are disappointed" (p. 83). Lord Henry is always flinging himself onto sofas, saying dangerous, unexpected things and waving opium- tainted cigarettes around in his lilylike hands. He becomes Dorian's Mephistophelian corrupter, filling him with the desire to yield to every temptation and to realize his youth while it lasts.

Lord Henry provides the Socratic charge and intellectual frisson of the book. His Nietzschean creed of embracing the life of the senses, and of rejecting the claims of Christian and middle-class morality, is convincing and utterly seductive. Younger readers are especially affected by his homilies on hedonism and his paeans to pleasure: like Dorian, they sit, as it were, at Lord Henry's feet "open-eyed and wondering" (p. 65). Yet Lord Henry himself is more a sinner in word than in deed, a spectator or "critic" of life where Dorian is an "artist." By the end of the novel it is obvious that he is, psychologically speaking, out of his depth so far as Dorian is concerned and utterly unable to understand the consequences of his hedonistic creed when it is put into practice.

Other characters in the novel include Sybil Vane, the actress who falls in love with Dorian and commits suicide when he spurns her, and her brother James, who pursues Dorian in an attempt to avenge Sybil's death. It is, however, the unholy trinity of Dorian, Basil, and Lord Henry that dominates Wilde's book and the triangle of their interrelationships that provides its emotional focus. Basil loves Dorian, who comes to despise and eventually murder him; Dorian regards Henry as his spiritual and intellectual mentor. Henry is indifferent to Basil but fond of Dorian, whom he thinks of as his protégé or Frankensteinian creation.

The world of Wilde's three characters is luxurious and alluring, fashioned with the aim of affording them the maximum amount of pleasure. It is made up of delicate food, fine wine, beautifully fashioned books, paintings, artifacts, and drugs, the best of conversation and the best of cigarettes. It is an artificial utopia in which style rather than sincerity is essential and in which the dandies and the exquisites rule. Mundane realities are banished with a fine phrase or the wave of a hand; everyday considerations are rarely allowed to intrude.

Their world is not unlike that of Edward Bulwer- Lytton's or Benjamin Disraeli's dandy novels, or the all-male and exclusively aristocratic society of Oxford undergraduates. Women and the middle classes are conspicuous by their absence, and the working class appears only as servants or as objects of aristocratic desire. In both its themes and its style the novel can (and was) read as an assault on middle-class values and taste, despite the fact that it originally appeared in a popular magazine. Toward the end of the novel Lord Henry openly criticizes the English middle classes as materialistic, ignorant, and hypocritical: "Beer, the Bible, and the seven deadly virtues," he remarks, "have made our England what she is" (p. 192). One of his favorite linguistic tricks is turning Victorian orthodoxies on their head: he thus recasts the proverb "procrastination is the thief of time" as the paradox "punctuality is the thief of time."

Wilde draws us into this dazzling and seductive world with his brilliant dialogue and his luxurious—and occasionally syrupy—prose. The opening lines immediately transport the reader. "The studio was filled with the rich odour of roses. . . . From the corner of the divan of Persian saddlebags on which he was lying, smoking, as was his custom, innumerable cigarettes, Lord Henry Wotton could just catch the gleam of the honey-sweet and honey-coloured blossoms of a laburnum. . . ." (p. 49). It is exquisite, dandified, and wonderfully evocative prose that induces in the reader a sort of "malady of reverie."

SOURCES

Like a medieval author, Wilde believed that it was largely through the original combination and treatment of existing works that the best literature could be produced. "It is only the unimaginative," he commented in one of his reviews, "who ever invents. The true artist is known by the use he makes of what he annexes, and he annexes everything" (*A Critic in Pall Mall*, p. 195). The foremost artist of the decadent movement, Aubrey Beardsley, drew a mischievous portrait of Wilde that brilliantly captures this aspect of his authorship. In *Oscar Wilde at Work* we see a number of books, such as the Bible, Swinburne's poems, and Flaubert's *Trois Contes*, either open or piled up on Wilde's desk as he scribbles away.

Beardsley's picture playfully suggests that Wilde was a plagiarist, a charge that was made by many critics of his writings and also by reviewers of *Dorian Gray*. While there is material in the novel that Wilde clearly plundered from other books (notoriously, in chapter 11, he copied out entire paragraphs from works on embroidery and precious stones) the accusation is largely unwarranted. It derives in part from a misunderstanding of Wilde's medieval conception of authorship; it also comes from a failure to appreciate his deliberately allusive style. When Lord Henry echoes Walter Pater, the Bible or Shakespeare, for instance, the reader is obviously intended to recognize a reference that is an essential part of the sentence's meaning.

Wilde makes it clear that his novel is a patchwork of allusions and quotations. Lord Henry often begins a speech with a phrase such as "As Browning says somewhere," and the novel has a palpable air of bookishness about it. Books are frequently handled, read, and referred to, and sometimes people are compared to them. One woman resembles "the edition de luxe of a bad French novel"; another is like "a badly bound hymn book." It is surely no coincidence either that much of the book's action (or inaction) takes place in libraries. The novel can itself be compared to a library full of the author's most cherished volumes. It is hardly surprising that a large scholarly literature has developed concerning *Dorian Gray*'s sources and

influences. Even a cursory look at the notes of any annotated edition of the novel reveals the vast number of influences that have been identified; a few of these will be mentioned here and classified according to their genre.

Dorian Gray exhibits many characteristics of the Gothic novel, particularly in the sections that deal with Dorian's murder of Basil, his Faustian bargain with an invisible devil, and his relationship to the supernatural portrait. Horace Walpole's *The Castle of Otranto* (1764) and *Melmoth the Wanderer* (1820), written by Wilde's ancestor Charles Maturin, both contain magical pictures that might be said to lie beneath the portrait of *Dorian Gray*. Maturin's hero (whose name Wilde adopted after his release from prison) also sold his soul for eternal youth. The tales of Edgar Allan Poe (in particular, "The Oval Portrait" and "William Wilson") should also be mentioned in this context.

A number of passages in Wilde's novel (for example, chapters 5 and 16) draw upon the tradition of "lowlife" writing about London. Charles Dickens, Thomas De Quincey, and James Thomson probably influenced Wilde, although it is difficult to identify specific sources. This becomes far easier when we turn to the decadent sections of the novel, such as chapter 11, in which Dorian's delight in such artistic pleasures as music, perfumes, embroidery, jewels, and stones is related. Théophile Gautier, who is alluded to on several occasions, was clearly an important influence on these. Wilde's most significant precursor was, however, J.-K. Huysmans, whose novel *À Rebours* chronicles the history of the reclusive hedonist Des Esseintes. *À Rebours* influenced the subject and the style of *Dorian Gray*, especially its jeweled and purple passages. Huysmans's novel actually makes a cameo appearance in *Dorian Gray* as the unnamed book that "poisons" Dorian. In an early typescript version of the story, Wilde called that book "Le Secret de Raoul par [by] Catulle Sarrazin," but it is clear that Huysmans's novel had suggested it.

The episode in which Dorian reads the decadent book in turn suggests other sources. This is typical of *Dorian Gray*, where, on several occasions, Wilde does not so much imitate a single source as fuse together a number of influences. Books exercise a powerful hold over the heroes of Walter Pater's *Marius the Epicurean* (1885) and his unfinished *Gaston de Latour*. The influence of Pater's *Studies in the History of the Renaissance* (1873) should also be noted. Lord Henry repeatedly (mis)quotes it, and it is the chief inspiration of his epicurean creed. Other important influences were Disraeli and Bulwer-Lytton—authors of stylish dandy novels in which young men sit around saying marvelous things—along with Restoration comedy and certain nineteenth-century society novels, such as those of Ouida.

The most interesting critical work in this area is that of Kerry Powell, who has identified two traditions of popular Victorian fiction that significantly influenced *Dorian Gray*. In one sense his findings should not surprise us, as Wilde's story first appeared in a popular magazine. However, as most critical attention has been directed toward the influence of literary classics such as *À Rebours*, Powell's findings are fascinating and original.

The first of these popular traditions was the so-called magic-picture tradition that flourished throughout the nineteenth century. It was established and developed not only by important writers such as Poe, Nathaniel Hawthorne, Henry James, and Nikolay Gogol, but also by hundreds of now forgotten minor authors. According to Powell, a typical magic-picture story included the following narrative elements. A beautiful model inspires a great work in an artist; the completed picture (which often has magical properties) then exercises an important influence over its subject, acting either as a good or a bad angel. Finally the model's relationship with the picture becomes so fraught that the model is driven to destroy it, an act that often leads to his or her death.

The plot of *Dorian Gray* includes all of these elements. Indeed, Powell suggests that part of the novel's originality and force derives from the fact that it combines more commonplaces of the tradition than any other magic-picture novel. It differs, however, from such novels in a number of respects: few of them are, for example, informed by the aesthetic debate that is conducted in the pages of Wilde's novel; Powell also argues that in aesthetic terms, *Dorian Gray* is infinitely superior. The other popular tradition identified by Powell is that of the "mesmeric novel," in which one character (in this case Lord Henry) exercises a remarkable hold over another. Once again, Powell suggests that Wilde turned the base metal of this tradition into gold in his novel, altering many of its conventional features to create something striking and original.

Powell argues that Wilde achieved his best work when he "stooped to mine the worn-out veins of popular literature" ("The Mesmerizing of Dorian Gray," p. 20) and cites *The Importance of Being Earnest*, which draws upon the popular tradition of farce, as a further example. This suggestion may throw some light on Wilde's remarkable ability to appeal to both general and select audiences today. He raised popular literary traditions to the level of art, just as he made complex and rarified ideas and genres popular.

Scholars have also tended to overlook another source of inspiration for Wilde: that of folktales, legends, and myths. Here we could mention the legends of Faust and Don Juan, or the myth of Narcissus. In the book's opening pages Lord Henry compares Dorian to Narcissus, and the outline of Dorian's life is not unlike that of the Greek hero. In one of the versions of the myth, Narcissus angers the gods by rejecting the love of Echo. His punishment is to fall in love with his reflection and to pine away in contemplation of his own beauty. Throughout his life Wilde was fascinated by this story, alluding to it on several occasions in his works and inventing fantastic variations on it in his prose poems and spoken stories.

Wilde was strongly influenced too by the Irish tales and legends that his mother and father had told him as a child. His parents were among the first folklorists of Ireland, and his mother published a number of Irish folktales in two anthologies around the time that Wilde wrote his novel. David Upchurch has identified a number of specifically Celtic elements in *Dorian Gray;* here we can briefly note the novel's resemblance to two traditional Irish tales, which may have suggested its conclusion.

In "The Priest's Soul," a story that appeared in the first of Lady Wilde's anthologies, a priest who denies the existence of the soul redeems himself at the last when he is stabbed in the heart by a little boy. His soul then becomes miraculously beautiful as it flies from his body. The other tale (or group of tales) concerns Tir-na-n-Og, or the Country of the Young. People visiting that magical place enjoy eternal life, but as soon as they return to the world of mortals the years that have passed fall upon them and they die instantly. Wilde was evidently drawn to this collection of stories: he gives them special praise in his review of Yeats's *Fairy and Folk Tales of the Irish Peasantry,* written in the same year that he commenced *Dorian Gray.*

Dorian Gray is itself rather like a folktale. Its traditional narrative was evidently suited to oral narration (as we have seen, Wilde told the story years before he came to set it down), its characterization is limited in terms of psychological depth, and much of the writing has a distinctly oral flavor. Walter Pater remarked upon this in his review of the novel: "there is always something of an excellent talker," he commented, apropos of the dialogue, "about the writing of Mr. Oscar Wilde." He also perceptively noted that the narrative was handled with the "ease and fluidity withal of one telling a story by word of mouth" (Lawler, ed., *The Picture of Dorian Gray,* pp. 352, 354). It is surely no coincidence either that spoken words are so important in *Dorian Gray.* Lord Henry's words fill Dorian with a desire to know everything about life and directly inspire him to utter his fatal wish regarding the portrait—itself a typical episode in many folktales.

Wilde's novel is thus at once extremely bookish and intensely oral in terms of both its sources and its style. If Beardsley's picture of Wilde at work serves as one symbol of his allusive and "intertextual" authorship, another emblem must be that of Wilde the traditional storyteller, enchanting a group of friends with his tales. These two aspects of his authorship come together to great effect in the novel.

RECEPTION OF *DORIAN GRAY*

Dorian Gray caused a great sensation with its publication in *Lippincott's Magazine.* Although the critical response was generally (and often violently) hostile, Wilde understood the value of every kind of publicity and no doubt delighted in the book's succès de scandale. It gave him the kind of exposure he had enjoyed in his aesthetic phase in the early 1880s and turned him into a symbol of the decadent movement in art and literature.

A review that appeared in the *Daily Chronicle* of 30 June 1890 is fairly representative in its distaste for novel's "immorality." It called the book "unclean" and "pestilent" and expressed horror about its hints concerning "secret and unspeakable vice." The reviewer was not alone in alluding to the "homosexual" subtext of the novel; other critics rather chillingly and prophetically suggested that the author ought to be prosecuted by the government on account of it. The piece was also typical in its criticism of Wilde's "garish vulgarity" and "cheap scholarship"; unlike other articles, however, it generally refrained from attacking the book's construction and style (in Lawler, ed., *The Picture of Dorian Gray,* pp. 342–344).

Much of the criticism was extremely personal, and Wilde must take at least some of the blame for this. He included a number of autobiographical elements in the novel, and its pages are utterly saturated with his views and stylistic idiosyncrasies. Everything he wrote was a kind of personal performance, and both he and his publishers to some extent marketed it as such. It is hardly surprising then that after its publication Wilde became inextricably linked with the novel in the public imagination. He came to be regarded as the antithesis (or "other") of all things middle-class, and by the time of his trials in 1895 the public evidently saw him as a Lord Henry Wotton–type corrupter of young men. This is clear from Robert Hichens's satirical novel *The Green Carnation* (1894), in which Esmé Amarinth, a thinly veiled caricature of Wilde, is the twin or double of Lord Henry.

At his trials, Wilde (like Flaubert before him) was cross-examined on the "immorality" of his novel. The prosecution rehearsed many of the criticisms made by *Dorian Gray*'s first reviewers; in his defense Wilde echoed some of the newspaper letters he had written in 1890 in response to his critics. These letters, which can be found in the *Complete Letters,* constitute a spirited riposte to the reviewers and a general statement of Wilde's aesthetic creed.

Wilde chastised his reviewers for dismissing his characters as unrealistic. "If they existed," he commented, "they would not be worth writing about. The function of the artist is to invent, not to chronicle" (*Complete Letters,* p. 430). Taking his cue from Basil Hallward, he also criticized the critics for confusing the artist with his subject matter by interpreting the novel in an autobiographical light. The main thrust of his response concerned the charges of immorality brought against his novel, and here he was characteristically inconsistent. Rather like Baudelaire when he was preparing to publicly defend his poetry, Wilde oscillated between two apparently contradictory positions. On the one hand he argued that it was ludicrous to criticize art from a moral standpoint: "The sphere of art and the sphere of ethics," he wrote, "are absolutely distinct and separate" (p. 428). On

the other, he claimed that *Dorian Gray* was a distinctly, even excessively, moral novel, the moral being that "all excess, as well as all renunciation, brings its punishment" (p. 435). "Having led a life of mere sensation and pleasure," he added, "[Dorian] tries to kill conscience and at that moment kills himself" (p. 430).

Wilde's response to his critics did not end with these letters. In "The Soul of Man under Socialism," a polemical essay published in 1891, he continued the debate. He criticized the tyranny of the press and any form of government censorship over the arts. At one point he made a direct reference to the criticism of his novel: "what the public call an unhealthy novel," he commented, "is always a beautiful and healthy work of art" (in Ellmann, *The Artist As Critic,* p. 275). The preface to *Dorian Gray,* which was first published in the *Fortnightly Review* in March 1891 and then in the book, is written in exactly the same vein. It is composed of a page of brilliant aphorisms, succinctly expressing Wilde's intentions and aesthetic aims. "There is no such thing as a moral or an immoral book" reads one of the most famous. "Books are well written, or badly written. That is all" (*Writings,* p. 48).

In these imperious and oracular pronouncements it is noticeable that Wilde refers to himself as "the artist." This suggests something of the confidence that the publication of his novel gave him. At last he could stand before the public as an artist rather than as a lecturer or journalist who popularized the ideas of others. He suddenly became as famous and relevant as he had been ten years previously, but his celebrity came at a price. The critics pigeonholed him as a decadent and immoral writer, and many members of society began to shun his company.

THE TWO VERSIONS OF *DORIAN GRAY*

It has sometimes been suggested that the criticism of the *Lippincott's* version of *Dorian Gray* influenced Wilde when he came to revise the story in 1891. If anything, Donald Lawler's excellent study of the changes Wilde made to the tale suggests that the opposite is the case. Most of the alterations were stylistic: Wilde introduced hundreds of minor improvements throughout. These give the lie to the popular idea of Wilde as a lazy writer and suggest that he was far more of a diligent craftsman than he pretended to be. "Who am I? To tamper with a masterpiece," he once loftily remarked when asked to rewrite an early work.

In response to critics who complained that there was not enough action in the story, Wilde diluted the action yet further by adding six chapters that contribute very little to the overall narrative. They mostly contain society scenes made up of witty dialogue along with melodramatic evocations of the working- class life of Sybil Vane and her family. Wilde's introduction of these chapters alters the structure and pace of the novel considerably: it seems less crowded with incident, less like a rather breathless Gothic short story. The tone of the book is also dramatically altered: the comic and melodramatic passages provide an excellent contrast to the heavier Gothic scenes, and the story becomes lighter and more various. Wilde believed in continually blending incongruous styles and moods, a technique Dickens referred to as the "streaky-bacon effect." "Never be afraid," Wilde once commented on the subject, "that by raising a laugh you destroy tragedy. On the contrary, you intensify it" (*Complete Letters*, p. 204).

Charged with "immorality," Wilde set about making the moral of his story even less apparent, as he had promised in one of his newspaper letters. The new chapters draw the reader's attention away from the central moral of the tale, and the conclusion is altered in a significant way. It is possible for the reader of the *Lippincott's* version to interpret the final scene in which Dorian stabs his portrait as a form of repentance for his wicked past. The magical return of the picture to its original beauty may then represent the purification of his soul. In the 1891 version, however, Wilde makes it clear that Dorian's desire to repent is mere hypocrisy. Consequently the possibility of Christian redemption is denied him.

In one respect, however, Wilde may well have been influenced by the critics. There is evidence to suggest that he toned down the "homoerotic" elements of the story. As we have seen, reviewers commented upon the "secret and unspeakable vice" hinted at in the story, and one of them alluded to a recent notorious "homosexual" affair known as the "Cleveland Street scandal." This concerned the discovery of a male brothel in West End London, frequented by a number of prominent social figures.

Even at the very early stages of composition, Wilde was conscious of the need to keep the homoerotic element of the novel vague and implicit. In the manuscript of the *Lippincott's* version he deleted several references to physical contact between Basil and Dorian and also cut a line in which Basil commented on the ardor that he had poured into his portrait of the young man. "Where there is merely love," Basil remarks, "they [the public] would see something evil. Where there is spiritual passion, they would suggest something vile" (in Lawler, ed., p. 181). Similar deletions occur throughout the typescript, and Wilde's editor, J. M. Stoddart, continued the pruning process before the story was printed. Thus he silently removed the following line from Basil's cross-examination of Dorian: "why is it that every young man that you take up . . . seems to go to the bad at once? . . . it is quite sufficient to say of a young man that he goes to stay at Selby Royal [Dorian's country house], for people to sneer and titter" (in Lawler, ed., p. 258).

When Wilde revised the *Lippincott's* version he removed other hints that had slipped through Stoddart's net. Further references to physical contact between Basil and Dorian were omitted, and Basil's description of his passion for the young man became less explicit and ecstatic. At

Wilde's trials, the prosecution referred to the 1891 *Dorian Gray* as the "purged edition." While this is an exaggeration, Wilde conceded that he had altered parts of the story that were "liable to misconstruction."

"HOMOSEXUALITY" IN *DORIAN GRAY*

The prosecution at Wilde's trials suggested that *Dorian Gray* described and advocated "the relations, intimacies, and passions of certain persons of sodomitical and unnatural habits, tastes and practices" (Sinfield, p. 104). After the trials (and in particular, in our own post-Stonewall period) it has become almost impossible, as Alan Sinfield has suggested, to disagree with this assertion. We should, however, be cautious before we describe *Dorian Gray* as a "gay" novel, chiefly because terms such as "gay" and "homosexual" are anachronistic in this context.

Sinfield has argued that the modern idea of the "homosexual" was created at the time of Wilde's trials in order to explain and classify Wilde's tastes and identity. It was at this point that various medical, legal, and cultural languages came together to define the "homosexual" as a type with a particular case history. Prior to that, people who performed "homosexual" acts were not therefore classified as "homosexuals." It would thus be wrong to think of Wilde as a "gay" man or as a "gay" writer in the modern sense: he certainly did not, and could not possibly have thought of himself in these terms. Consequently when we turn to Wilde's works we should tread carefully. As Sinfield comments with regard to Dorian Gray's mysterious "vices," "[they] should not be viewed as the cunning-masking of an already-known queerness, but as reaching out towards formulations of same-sex experience that were . . . as yet nameless" (pp 102–103).

There can be no doubt that in writing *Dorian Gray* Wilde was attempting to introduce elements of same-sex passion and desire into the English novel. However, in doing so, he did not so much look forward to twentieth-century forms of homosexual relations as look back to ancient types of male friendship that derived from Plato and writers of the Renaissance. At one point in the novel Dorian reflects that the "love [Basil] bore him . . . had nothing in it that was not noble and intellectual. . . . It was such love as Michael Angelo had known, and Montaigne . . . and Shakespeare himself" (p. 136). These words echo a section of the extended version of "The Portrait of Mr. W. H.," a brilliant essay-story in which Wilde explores Shakespeare's love for a young boy actor. They also anticipate Wilde's famous and spirited defense of the "love that dare not speak its name" at his trials.

According to Linda Dowling, author of *Hellenism and Homosexuality in Victorian Oxford* (1994), these and other comments by Wilde on same-sex passion are characteristic examples of the kind of "homosexual" writing that flourished at late-nineteenth-century Oxford. Dowling also places the writings of Walter Pater and John Addington Symonds within this tradition, which was inspired by the university's renewed interest in Greek culture and in particular in Plato's dialogues.

The spokesman and representative of "Oxford Hellenism" in *Dorian Gray* is the artist Basil Hallward, the only character who is a recognizable 1890s "homosexual" type. Basil's intense and idealistic worship of Dorian, and his fear of expressing his adoration physically, reminds one of certain passages in John Addington Symonds's posthumously published memoirs. It is interesting that Symonds regarded Wilde's novel as "unwholesome" (Basil would surely have agreed), perhaps because the novel suggests that Dorian gave physical expression to what, in Symonds's eyes, ought to have remained a purely spiritual and Platonic ideal of male friendship. Symonds and men like him agonized over their physical urges and tried desperately to sublimate them in art, philosophy, and intellectual comradeship. It is a measure of the distance between our culture and the culture of the 1890s that we regard such men as frustrated and pathetic figures.

As well as making one of his main characters a recognizable "homosexual" type, Wilde scatters a number of "homosexual" hints and allusions throughout his novel. He mentions Piers Gaveston, minion to King Edward II, and a holiday that Dorian and Lord Henry take together in Algiers, one of the most popular destinations for "homosexual" tourists. The name "Dorian" itself derives from the inhabitants of the Greek city of Doris, who were widely believed to practice Greek love. These allusions were evidently meant to be understood by certain readers, such as Wilde's "gay" friends. Wilde's lover, John Gray, who adopted the name "Dorian," clearly read between the lines, as did Wilde's acquaintance Lionel Johnson, who wrote a Latin poem in praise of the novel that includes the phrase "here are the apples of Sodom."

Wilde's writings are often classified according to their intended audience. "The Happy Prince and Other Tales" was clearly aimed at a popular readership, while the expensively produced and ostentatiously obscure poem *The Sphinx* was intended for a group Wilde referred to as "the elect." Wilde's best works (and *Dorian Gray* is certainly one of these) succeed in appealing to two or more audiences simultaneously. Thus, while general readers and many reviewers failed to identify the "homosexual" allusions, Wilde's immediate circle understood them.

THE DOUBLE

Dorian Gray is a classic doppelgänger (or double) story that explores the division and antagonistic relationship between two elements of its hero's personality: his body and his soul. Gothic writers such as E. T. A. Hoffmann established the genre at the end of the eighteenth century, and it flourished throughout the nineteenth, appealing to the imaginations of such authors as James Hogg, Mary Shelley, Hawthorne, and Dostoyevsky.

Doppelgänger stories usually include elements of the supernatural; they also tend to chronicle the psychological collapse of their heroes. The popularity of the genre in the Victorian period has indeed been attributed to the breakdown and separation of the traditional self as a consequence of urbanization, secularization, and the rise of science. Another factor may have been the growing gulf between the public and the private self in the period, a result of the Victorian emphasis on public propriety. This idea seems to inform Robert Louis Stevenson's tale of *Doctor Jekyll and Mr. Hyde* (1886); in *Dorian Gray* too we are told that the wicked hero feels "keenly the terrible pleasure of a double life" (p. 178) when he goes into society.

It is hardly surprising that Wilde was attracted to the genre. As an Irishman who enjoyed a number of "homosexual" affairs, he too must often have felt the terrible pleasure of a double life in London. Many of his works, such as "The Fisherman and His Soul" and *The Importance of Being Earnest*, revolve around the idea of the double. In his writings he is also fascinated by the notion of the divided (or multiplied) self. In *Dorian Gray* he writes: "Is insincerity such a terrible thing? I think not. It is merely a method by which we can multiply our personalities" (p. 154). The novel can in fact be read as a debate between the various facets of its author's personality. "It contains much of me in it," Wilde remarked to a friend. "Basil Hallward is what I think I am: Lord Henry what the world thinks me: Dorian what I would like to be—in other ages, perhaps" (*Complete Letters*, p. 585).

Dorian Gray belongs to a particular variety of doppelgänger tale in which the hero's double is a projection of his conscience. Stevenson's "Markheim" is an exemplar of this tradition. In it the eponymous hero is confronted by his conscience-double after committing murder in a pawnbroker's shop. Edgar Allan Poe's famous tale "William Wilson," which undoubtedly influenced Wilde, can also be mentioned. In Poe's story, Wilson is pursued by his conscience-double throughout his life of debauchery and

THE PICTURE OF DORIAN GRAY

crime. At the denouement, Wilson kills his double but in doing so kills all hope of redemption.

The idea of the double is also central to *Dorian Gray* insofar as it is a novel that is built out of a number of oppositions. We have already noted the dialectic between its popular and elitist, comic and Gothic, and oral and written stylistic elements; we could also mention its continual shifts between aristocratic and working-class scenes and locations. This is what makes the novel such a wonderful evocation of late Victorian London: Wilde takes us on a tour of the East as well as the West End; in the space of a few pages we walk from Mayfair to the Euston Road and back again.

In thematic terms, we can also discern an ongoing struggle between paganism and Christianity within the book. Inspired by Lord Henry Wotton to "return to the Hellenic ideal" (p. 61) of living out his life completely, Dorian embraces a "new hedonism" (p. 65). Basil Hallward, who quotes the Bible on a number of occasions, warns him that by living selfishly, and amorally, he will one day have to pay in "remorse, in suffering [and] the consciousness of degradation" (p. 106). Many of Wilde's works contain a similar dialogue. In the fairy tale "The Young King," for instance, the hero renounces his life of pleasure to kneel before the Cross. We also discern this dialectic developing across the works of Wilde's oeuvre; *De Profundis* is thus a Christian reply to the thoroughly pagan essay, "The Soul of Man under Socialism."

DORIAN GRAY AS "AN ESSAY ON DECORATIVE ART"

Wilde's description of *Dorian Gray* as "an essay on decorative art" alerts us to the fact that it belongs to that most un-English fictional category, the "novel of ideas." It has in consequence often been called the first "French novel" in the English language. From the outset we are aware that a debate about art and artistic

creation is being played out in its pages. Basil tells Lord Henry that "every portrait that is painted with feeling is a portrait of the artist, not of the sitter" (p. 52), and only a few paragraphs later he seems to contradict this when he declares that "An artist should create beautiful things, but should put nothing of his own life into them" (p. 56). The characters in Wilde's critical dialogues discuss exactly this kind of issue in exactly the same language. The setting of the dialogues and the opening of the novel are also similar: two men lounge around smoking cigarettes and playing gracefully with ideas.

Dorian Gray is not only a continuation of Wilde's critical dialogues, it is also an embodiment of the ideas they contain. Thus the notion that, at bottom, all the arts are one, finds expression in a novel in which painting, music, and many other arts are discussed endlessly. *Dorian Gray* is also consistent with the antirealistic principles laid down in the dialogues. While it could never be described, in Lord Henry's phrase, as a novel that is as unreal as a Persian carpet, it is nevertheless an utterly theatrical, artificial, and self-conscious production. Many of its scenes are melodramatic (or, to use a modern expression, "camp"), and most of the minor characters are funny caricatures.

Wilde also dramatizes the ideas of his dialogues in the character of Dorian Gray, who, as Richard Ellmann commented, is an exemplary figure for the aesthetic movement. Dorian tries to live life as a form of art and to attain what a character in "The Critic As Artist" describes as "the perfection of those to whom sin is impossible . . . because they can do everything they wish without hurt to the soul" (*Writings*, p. 296). Dorian's failure to achieve this blessed state has something heroic and even tragic about it, despite his wickedness and irresponsibility. Ellmann is surely correct in this context to read Wilde's novel as both a manifesto for and a cautionary tale about aestheticism. This thematic ambiguity, or doubleness, is typical of Wilde: in Ellmann's phrase, he characteristically offers his readers not a single doctrine but a debate between doctrines.

WILDE'S LATER LIFE

In the years following the publication of *Dorian Gray*, Wilde's biography reads like a continuation of his novel. This is, of course, entirely fitting for a man who expounded the theory that life imitates art. At around the time of the publication of the 1891 version, Wilde met Lord Alfred Douglas, known as "Bosie," a young man who would be his grand passion and nemesis. Soon after their first meeting Wilde gave Bosie a copy of the novel; Bosie read it again and again and proceeded to use it as a manual for living. He became a sort of real-life version of Dorian Gray, and rather like Basil, Wilde worshipped him with a fatal passion.

Wilde was to pay an enormous price for his association with Bosie when he foolishly became involved in a long-standing quarrel between Bosie and his father, the marquess of Queensberry. Queensberry, who was evidently insane, hated his son's indolent lifestyle and in particular his relationship with Wilde. As part of his campaign against Bosie he publicly insulted Wilde by leaving a card at his club with the words "To Oscar Wilde posing Somdomite [sic]" written on them. Egged on by Bosie, Wilde prosecuted Queensberry for libel. Wilde lost his case, was arrested, and then was twice tried for "gross indecency" under the Criminal Law Amendment Act of 1885. After having been found guilty he was sentenced to two years' hard labor. He served out the full sentence in a number of English prisons. Released in 1897, he spent his final years wandering the Continent, a physically and mentally broken man. In 1900 he died in Paris—which, as Doctor Chasuble remarks prophetically in *Earnest*, "hardly points to a serious state of mind at the last."

If *Dorian Gray* influenced Wilde's life, it had an even more profound influence on his art. As we have noted, the critical furor it caused inspired Wilde to write his preface to the novel and essays such as "The Soul of Man under Socialism." More generally it may have encouraged the more radical and subversive elements of his work. In the composition of his novel Wilde also discovered his great gift for comic dialogue, a skill that he exploited to brilliant effect in the four social comedies he wrote between 1891 and 1895 and upon which his fame largely rests. Many of these borrow lines from *Dorian Gray*, and Lord Illingworth, the dandy in *A Woman of No Importance*, is a reincarnation of Lord Henry Wotton. In *Dorian Gray*, Wilde thus not only announced his arrival as an artist of genius and great relevance, he also found his voice.

THE NOVEL'S AFTERLIFE

It is appropriate that a novel that is itself the retelling of many myths and stories should have been retold on a number of occasions. The first adaptation of *Dorian Gray* was Max Beerbohm's short novel *The Happy Hypocrite* (1897); the most recent is Will Self's *Dorian: An Imitation* (2002). Between the publication of these two novels, countless stories, plays, musicals, films, and operas have been inspired by Wilde's novel. One book worthy of particular mention is Patrick Süskind's *Perfume* (English translation, 1986). Although the novel's setting and narrative are quite different from *Dorian Gray*, Wilde's influence on its style and themes is pervasive.

The reasons for *Dorian Gray*'s fascination for writers are probably similar to the reasons for its popularity. In the book, Wilde narrates a brilliant variation on a powerful myth in his own inimitable way. It is also a novel that is hospitable to continual adaptation and interpretation because of its inherent ambiguity and indeterminacy. In *Dorian Gray*, Wilde brings together a variety of apparently contradictory themes, styles, moods, settings, sources, and audiences and holds them together in perfect balance. In this sense, it may be said to display the artistic quality Keats referred to as "negative capability." And this, in the final reckoning, may be the great secret of its power: writers, readers, and critics will never exhaust its range of possible meanings and will go on reinterpreting and re-creating it endlessly.

Selected Bibliography

EDITIONS

"The Picture of Dorian Gray." *Lippincott's Monthly Magazine* 46 (July 1890).

The Picture of Dorian Gray. London: Ward, Lock and Company, 1891.

The Picture of Dorian Gray. Edited by Donald L. Lawler. New York: Norton, 1988. Annotated.

The Writings of Oscar Wilde. Edited by Isobel Murray. Oxford, U.K.: Oxford University Press, 1989. Annotated.

LETTERS

Selected Letters of Oscar Wilde. Edited by Rupert Hart-Davis. London, 1979.

The Complete Letters of Oscar Wilde. Edited by Merlin Holland and Rupert Hart-Davis. London: 2000.

CRITICAL WORK BY WILDE

The Artist as Critic; Critical Writings of Oscar Wilde. Edited by Richard Ellmann. New York: Random House, 1969. Chicago: University of Chicago Press, 1982.

SECONDARY WORKS

Ackroyd, Peter. *The Last Testament of Oscar Wilde.* London: H. Hamilton, 1983; New York: Harper and Row, 1983.

Beckson, Karl. *The Oscar Wilde Encyclopedia.* New York: AMS Press, 1998.

Beckson, Karl, ed. *Oscar Wilde: The Critical Heritage.* London: Routledge and Kegan Paul, 1970; New York: Barnes and Noble, 1970.

Dowling, Linda. *Hellenism and Homosexuality in Victorian Oxford.* Ithaca, N.Y.: Cornell University Press, 1994.

Ellmann, Richard. *Oscar Wilde.* London: H. Hamilton, 1987; New York: Knopf, 1988.

Ellmann, Richard, ed. *Oscar Wilde: A Collection of Critical Essays.* Englewood Cliffs, N.J.: Prentice-Hall, 1969.

Frankel, Nicholas. *Oscar Wilde's Decorated Books.* Ann Arbor, Mich.: University of Michigan Press, 2000.

Freedman, Jonathan, ed. *Oscar Wilde: A Collection of Critical Essays.* Upper Saddle River, N.J.: Prentice-Hall, 1996.

Gagnier, Reginia. *Idylls of the Marketplace: Oscar Wilde and the Victorian Public.* Stanford, Calif: Stanford University Press, 1986.

Guy, Josephine M., and Ian Small. *Oscar Wilde's Profession: Writing and the Culture Industry in the Late Nineteenth Century.* Oxford: Oxford University Press, 2000.

Hichens, Robert Smythe. *The Green Carnation.* London: William Heinemann, 1894; New York: D. Appleton, 1894.

Holloway, C. Robert. *The Unauthorized Letters of Oscar Wilde.* Princeton, N.J.: XLibris, 1997.

Lawler, Donald L. *An Inquiry into Oscar Wilde's Revisions of The Picture of Dorian Gray.* New York and London: Garland, 1988.

Mikhail, E. H. *Oscar Wilde: An Annotated Bibliography of Criticism.* London: Macmillan, 1978. Comprehensive bibliography.

Mikhail, E. H., ed. *Oscar Wilde: Interviews and Recollections.* 2 vols. London: Macmillan, 1979: New York: Barnes and Noble, 1979.

Miyoshi, Masco. *The Divided Self.* New York: New York University Press, 1969.

Pearson, Hesketh. *The Life of Oscar Wilde.* London: Methuen, 1946.

Powell, Kerry. "Tom, Dick and Dorian Gray: Magic- Picture Mania in Late Victorian Fiction." *Philological Quarterly* 62 (1983): 147–166.

———. "The Mesmerizing of Dorian Gray." *Victorian Newsletter* 65 (1984): 10–17.

Raby, Peter. *Oscar Wilde.* Cambridge and New York: Cambridge University Press, 1988.

Raby, Peter, ed. *The Cambridge Companion to Oscar Wilde.* Cambridge: Cambridge University Press, 1997.

Ransome, Arthur. *Oscar Wilde. A Critical Study.* London: M. Secker, 1912.

Shewan, Rodney. *Oscar Wilde: Art and Egotism.* London: Macmillan, 1977; New York: Barnes and Noble, 1977.

Sandulescu, C. George, ed. *Rediscovering Oscar Wilde.* Gerrards Cross, U.K.: C. Smyth, 1994.

Sinfield, Alan. *The Wilde Century.* New York: Columbia University Press, 1994; London: Cassell, 1994.

Small, Ian. *Oscar Wilde Revalued.* Greensboro N.C.: ELT Press, 1993. Collects recent works of Wilde criticism.

———. *Oscar Wilde: Recent Research.* Greensboro N.C.: ELT Press, 1999.

Upchurch, David A. *Wilde's Use of Irish Celtic Elements in "The Picture of Dorian Gray."* New York: Peter Lang, 1992.

Wright, Thomas, ed. *Table Talk/Oscar Wilde.* London: 2000. Wilde's spoken stories.

Rudyard Kipling's
Plain Tales from the Hills

∽

PHILLIP MALLETT

IT WAS RUDYARD Kipling's fate to win a reputation as a young man, essentially as the first great English writer to take as his subject the story of the British in India, and to have it diminish in the later years of his life, as attitudes to empire, and to the role of the British in the world, began to change in the aftermath of World War I (1914–1918). Kipling's own son, John, died in the war, at the battle of Loos in 1915, only six weeks after his eighteenth birthday, and those who knew him said that Kipling was thereafter a changed man: harder, less willing to make new friends, politically further to the Right. Yet in these late years, until his death in 1936, he continued to develop the short story form and to take it in new and more complex directions, as he explored themes which might be seen as the balance to his anger: healing, forgiveness, the supernatural. But despite his Nobel Prize for literature, and the activities of the young Kipling Society (founded in 1927), among the pallbearers at his funeral in Westminster Abbey, who included a prime minister, a field marshal, and an admiral, there were no novelists or poets. Literature, it seemed, had lost interest in Kipling.

In fact, the critical debate about his work was just beginning. In 1941 T. S. Eliot brought out his *A Choice of Kipling's Verse,* with a long introductory essay touching on the stories as well as the poems. Eliot's essay prompted a reply from George Orwell, who argued that while Kipling's work was often "morally offensive and aesthetically disgusting," he had "at least tried to imagine what action and responsibility are like," as, according to Orwell, his detractors had never dared to do (Rutherford, ed., pp. 70–84). In the United States Edmund Wilson produced a brilliant piece of speculative biography entitled "The Kipling That Nobody Read," drawing attention especially to the later stories, the "fragments," as it seemed to Wilson, of a man badly hurt as a child and emotionally damaged by the Great War, but at last "losing his hatred" (Rutherford, ed., p. 66). In 1943 Lionel Trilling wrote disparagingly about Kipling's Tory politics as mean-spirited and intellectually impoverished (pp. 85–94); in the same year W. H. Auden, more sympathetically, wrote about Kipling and "The Poetry of the Encirclement." In 1948 C. S. Lewis added his voice to the debate, concluding that Kipling was, whatever his faults, a "very great writer" (p. 117). That critics of such distinction, on both sides of the Atlantic, felt impelled to write about Kipling's work, even in the years of trial produced by

World War II (a war which Kipling had long predicted), is a measure of his stature. The debate continues into the twenty-first century, and has in some respects widened with the emergence of "postcolonialism" as a critical notion, but its starting point is now likely to be, as English poet and critic Craig Raine puts it in the introduction to his *A Choice of Kipling's Prose* (1987), that Kipling is "our greatest short-story writer" (p. 1). This, at least, is one of the starting points of the present essay.

Consideration of Kipling's life naturally begins with his own piece of autobiographical writing, *Something of Myself,* published a year after his death in a version edited by his American wife, Carrie. The title flaunts the author's reticence, and "something of myself" has usually been taken to mean "not much of myself." There is no reference to his early, unhappy love affair with Florence Garrard, which ended, in her mind at least, when he left England for India in September 1882; or to his friendship with the American literary agent Wolcott Balestier, whose sudden death precipitated his marriage to Carrie, Wolcott's sister. His marriage is reported in a single sentence: "and then to London to be married in January '92 in the thick of an influenza epidemic, when the undertakers had run out of black horses and the dead had to be content with brown ones" (p. 63). He records the birth of his daughter Josephine, but not her name, nor the fact that his 1902 collection, *Just So Stories for Little Children,* were originally written for her. He is silent about her death from pneumonia in 1899, at the age of six, at a time when he was himself so ill from pneumonia that the news of her death had to be kept from him until the doctors were sure he was out of danger. There is no mention of the death of his parents, nor of the death of his son John. Yet, with a characteristic last flash of writerly cunning, he manages to end, as logically all autobiographies should end, with the words "my death."

But for all its reticence, *Something of Myself* is written with the same economy of means and

CHRONOLOGY

1865	30 December: Kipling born in Bombay, India, the first child of Lockwood and Alice Kipling; a sister, also named Alice but known as Trix, born in 1868.
1871	Both Kipling children left at Lorne Lodge (the "House of Desolation"), in England, under the care of Pryse and Sarah Holloway.
1877	Alice Kipling returns to England to rejoin her children.
1878	January: Kipling enters the United Services College, in Devon, England, where he remains until July 1882.
1882	September: Kipling sails to India, to work as assistant editor on the *Civil and Military Gazette* in Lahore.
1884	September: Kipling publishes "The Gate of the Hundred Sorrows," the first of the stories that would be collected as *Plain Tales from the Hills.*
1887	E. Kay Robinson takes over as editor of the *Civil and Military Gazette,* and encourages Kipling's fiction. In November, Kipling moves to a larger paper, the *Pioneer* in Allahabad, where he edits, and provides most of the fictions for a supplement called the *Week's News.*
1889	March: Kipling leaves India, to return to London via the Far East and the United States, arriving in England in October.
1888	The first edition of *Plain Tales from the Hills* is published in Calcutta by Thacker, Spink.
1890	The first English edition of *Plain Tales from the Hills* is published. In March Kipling is the subject of an admiring leading article in the *Times* (London).
1891	Kipling makes a final visit to India, but is called back by the news that his friend Wolcott Balestier has died.
1892	January: Kipling marries Carrie (Caroline) Balestier. They settle in Brattleboro, Vermont, where their daughter Josephine is born in December; a second daughter, Elsie, is born in February 1896.

1896	The family returns to England following a bitter quarrel with Carrie's brother Beatty.
1897	August: John Kipling born.
1899	Josephine dies in New York, while Rudyard is seriously ill. He never returns to America. The Boer War breaks out in October; Kipling becomes deeply involved in South African and U.K. politics.
1901	The novel *Kim*, perhaps Kipling's finest work, is published.
1902	The Kiplings buy Bateman's, a Jacobean house in Sussex, England, where they remain for the rest of their lives.
1907	Kipling awarded the Nobel Prize for literature.
1915	John Kipling missing in action at battle of Loos (27 September) during World War I. Kipling later serves on the Imperial War Graves Commission, set up to look after the graves of those who died in the Great War.
1918	11 November: the armistice is signed, marking the end of the war; Kipling is among those who think the terms imposed on Germany were too generous, and from now on he anticipates the coming of another major European war.
1924	Elsie, Kipling's surviving child, marries; Bateman's now seems empty, and both Kipling and Carrie are increasingly troubled with poor health.
1932	Kipling's last collection of stories, *Limits and Renewals,* is published.
1936	January 18: Kipling dies, with Carrie beside him; it is his forty-fourth wedding anniversary. King George V, who had become a friend, dies two days later; it is reported in the press that the king has died, and taken his trumpeter with him.

and with his earliest memories, of "golden and purple fruits" in the market, the sound of night winds heard through palm leaves, the song of the tree frogs. Here he lived at the center of the world around him, or rather of two worlds: the world of the servants, where he spoke Hindi and ruled as an unquestioned despot, and that of his parents, where he was allowed to play with lumps of wet clay in his father's studio, and where "the Mother sang wonderful songs at a black piano" (p. 4) when he and his younger sister Alice—known as Trix—were allowed to join the adults in the dining room. But it was the custom for British parents in India to send their children "home" to be educated, and just before his sixth birthday Kipling and his sister were deposited at Lorne Lodge on the English south coast, "a new small house smelling of aridity and emptiness" (p. 5), as the paying guests of Pryse Holloway, his wife, Sarah, and their eleven-year-old son, Harry.

For whatever reason, Alice and Lockwood Kipling had done nothing to prepare their children for this sudden exile into a strange, cold world, and Rudyard took it hard. He was not an easy child to manage—he was stubborn, clumsy, and demanding—and Mrs. Holloway evidently disliked him and treated him harshly. From being the center of attention, he became marginalized; instead of having servants he could order about, he found himself liable to be beaten, and worse than that, beaten by a woman: a terrible blow to his sense of caste. Lorne Lodge, in his memory, was always "the House of Desolation."

But both in *Something of Myself* and in the 1888 autobiographical story "Baa Baa, Black Sheep," he insisted that the experience of these years was the making of him as a writer. Once he had learned to read, he would sit on the floor of his basement room behind a piece of packing case "which kept off any other world. Thus fenced about, everything inside the fence was quite real, but mixed with the smell of damp cupboards. If the bit of board fell, I had to begin the magic all over again. . . . The magic, you see,

richness of implication as the stories Kipling had been writing for fifty years. Nowhere is this more true than in the opening chapter, Kipling's portrait of the artist as a young boy. It opens with his childhood in Bombay, where his father taught architectural sculpture to Indian students, lies in the ring or fence that you take refuge in" (*Something of Myself*, p. 8). As reading became a means of retreat, he also learned to lie, and to plot imagined acts of revenge against Mrs. Holloway. The telling of lies, and the need to make them plausible, was, he came to feel, "the foundation of literary effort," while life at Lorne Lodge taught him "constant wariness, the habit of observation, and attendance on moods and tempers" (*Something of Myself*, p. 11). This was all good training for a writer, and it is easy to see here the basis of Kipling's habitual wariness, and of his acute sense of the need to be effective with respect to his chosen audience.

His unhappiness was not unbroken, since there were occasional escapes to the home of his aunt Georgiana, where he found laughter, affection, and the company of other children, but it took its toll on his health. In 1876, at the age of ten, he had some sort of nervous breakdown, which led him to see "shadows and things that were not there" (p. 12); he was in fact so nearsighted as to be almost blind, but the condition had gone undiagnosed. In March 1877 his mother was summoned home, and he was released from his exile; according to one story, when she came to kiss him goodnight he reached up his arm to ward off the expected blow. From this time on, as he himself put it, it would often happen that "the night got into my head" (*Something of Myself*, p. 13), and he would wander about until daybreak. Something like it happens to many of his characters, from Morrowbie Jukes on a manic ride across country in a story written when Kipling was only twenty ("The Strange Ride of Morrowbie Jukes," collected in *The Phantom 'Rickshaw*, 1888), to the shell-shocked John Marden in his last collection, *Limits and Renewals* (1932). If it is easy to see signs of the precocious, watchful child in Kipling's stories, and of his desire to prove himself as a member of a group, it is necessary too to recognize his no less powerful fascination with the haunted and the obsessed. It is in the driving single emotion, or the solitary driven character, that he often finds his subject. He

gave his conscious loyalty to the pack, group, or tribe, but his imagination was stirred by loneliness.

Kipling was fortunate that he came to love and admire the parents he had not seen for more than five years. His father, John Lockwood Kipling, had left school at fourteen to work in the ceramics trade in Staffordshire, and to study at the School of Art in Stoke. It was through his connections as a Methodist that he met Alice Macdonald, the daughter of a Methodist minister. Three of Alice's sisters married remarkable men: Georgiana married the painter Edward Burne-Jones, Agnes another painter, Edward Poynter, and Louisa a wealthy ironmaster, Alfred Baldwin, whose son Stanley (Kipling's cousin) served three times as prime minister in the 1920s and 1930s. Alice Macdonald had already been engaged at least three times before she met her eventual husband, but the marriage, by all indications, was a successful one. It was not quite a union of opposites, though Lockwood was a quiet and unassuming man, while Alice was usually described as "witty"—often, in Victorian usage, a code word for clever when used of women, but it was appropriate for Alice in both senses. Both she and Lockwood were intelligent, cultivated people, whose friends included some of the leading artists of their time; over the years a shared interest in literature held the family together, and Rudyard turned willingly to them for advice. His allegiance to what he called the "Family Square," made up of himself and the Father, Mother, and Maiden (Trix), is the prototype of his many determined efforts to write for and belong to a group, often with the overinsistence suggested by the initial capital letters he used for these designations.

Kipling began his schooling in January 1878, shortly after his twelfth birthday, at the United Services College on the North Devon coast near Bideford. The subject of the USC was one on which he could always be drawn throughout his life, perhaps because it was at school that he began to recognize the caste to which he was to belong; school was to him what class has been to other writers. The USC had been set up in 1874 primarily to serve the needs of boys born overseas into army families, in particular to prepare them for the army entrance examinations, and to do so economically. As a new foundation, it was less burdened with traditions than its British public school competitors—there was no school corps, or compulsory military drill, and no organized fagging, by which younger boys were obliged to act as servants to senior ones—and perhaps its chief advantage to Kipling, though not one he liked to play up in later years, was precisely that it did not knock off the rough edges of its less conformist members. That it did not do so owed much to the personality of its headmaster, Cormell Price, who soon recognized that the best service he could do for his young pupil was to give him the free run of his own library, and to ask him to revive and edit the school magazine. But the USC could not offer Kipling a route into university education, and in September 1882, three months before his seventeenth birthday, he left for India, to take up a post as assistant editor of the *Civil and Military Gazette* in Lahore, the capital of the Punjab. It was there that he would find himself as a writer.

KIPLING'S INDIA

The British had established an economic foothold in India by the end of the sixteenth century, when Elizabeth I granted a royal charter to the East India Company. To secure its position, both against other traders—the Dutch, the Portuguese, and especially the French—and against those Indian states which refused to trade on satisfactory terms, the company had its own soldiers, forts and garrisons, and by the 1830s it was effectively an arm of British government. There continued a process of piecemeal annexation, sometimes by law, sometimes by force—the Punjab, where Kipling was to work, had been taken from the Sikhs as recently as 1849—until, in May 1876, Queen Victoria was declared Empress of India. Thenceforth the country was ruled on her behalf by a viceroy rather than a governor, with even the "Native States," though officially autonomous, subject to British control. The Raj, as British rule in India was generally known, was to last until independence was granted in 1947. Until that time, the security of India, in particular against the perceived threat from Russia, remained a central concern in British foreign policy. It was not quite true, though it was sometimes said, that the British had conquered half the world in a fit of absence of mind; it was true that they had not set out to become an imperial power. But now they had an empire, they had no wish to let it go.

On his arrival in Lahore, Kipling was elected to the Punjab Club, among some seventy white civilians, all "picked men at their definite work," and each "talking his own shop." These men, together with the officers stationed at the nearby fort and in the military cantonment—altogether only a few hundred in number—were, in the most immediate sense, his audience, as the readers of the *Civil and Military Gazette*. From the first, what was impressed upon him was the need for solidarity. Anglo-Indians, as the British in India were known, were suspicious of the government at home, and deeply opposed to metropolitan notions of progress and reform. They insisted on the absolute superiority of the British, and had their own views on the task of ruling India. In the first half of the nineteenth century that task had been debated in terms of the Evangelical program to regenerate Indian society by reforming its morality, and the Utilitarian program to improve its morality by reforming its social structure, but the principles underpinning both approaches had been shaken by the events of 1857—the Mutiny, as the British called it, or the Great Rebellion, as it is more often described by Indian historians, when the sepoys, or native soldiers, turned on their officers, and for a time threatened the British hold on the area around Delhi. Increasingly it was argued that the "evils" of Indian society were the inevitable expression of an unchanging Indian character. There was and would remain, Kipling wrote in a letter of 1885, an "immeasurable gulf" between the English and "the peoples of the land." British codes might be imposed, but they would never be accepted; despite the best efforts of those who governed the country, native life would continue "wholly untouched and unaffected . . . dark and crooked and fantastic." The government of India could never safely be taken out of British hands: "if we didn't hold the land in six months it would be one big cock pit of conflicting princelets" (*Letters* [British edition], vol. 1, pp. 98–99). The task facing the British was to rule India, not to reform it.

Kipling never consciously changed his view about India, the Indians, and the responsibilities of the British, though (as will become clear) even in his early stories, including those in *Plain Tales from the Hills,* he was never quite content with this confident distinction between the whites and the right, on the one hand, and the natives and the "dark and crooked" on the other. His first duty, however, was his work for the *Civil and Military Gazette,* which required him to make digests of official publications, and to sift through various local and specialist journals, extracting whatever "scraps" could be used. When the editor, Stephen Wheeler, fell ill, it was Kipling's responsibility to make sure that the paper continued to appear daily, keeping himself going with an occasional peg of whisky and soda as the office thermometer hovered around the one-hundred-degrees mark. It was exciting enough work for a young man still in his teens. But he was also busy writing for himself, and in 1884 he and his sister appeared as the coauthors of a volume of verse parodies and imitations, *Echoes, By Two Writers,* published in an edition of 150 copies. These were well received, but much more significant was the publication in the *Civil and Military Gazette* in September 1884 of "The Gate of the Hundred Sorrows," the earliest of the stories later collected as *Plain Tales from the Hills.*

Wheeler's editorship had done little to encourage Kipling's talent as a creative writer. When in the summer of 1886 ill health obliged Wheeler to return to England, Edward Kay Robinson was brought in to revamp and brighten up the *Gazette.* Robinson quickly recognized that the best way to do so was to give Kipling a free hand. They soon established an effective and at times furiously productive working relationship, despite an office which was home to three fox terriers and a tame crow named Obadiah. In the summer of 1887 they bought new type for the paper and changed its format, in part to make room for Kipling's work. In the new layout, the right-hand column of the front page was to be used for original contributions, often running over into the first column of the second page. These were known as "turnovers," and many of Kipling's stories were first published in this form. As this suggests, Kipling was expected to make his stories fit the space available, which typically meant that he had to introduce, develop, and round off each tale in around two thousand words. One of the fascinations of the *Plain Tales* lies in the study of Kipling's resourcefulness in working within these limits.

Only two of the *Plain Tales* had appeared in four years during Wheeler's regime, but under Robinson's more relaxed guidance Kipling was soon writing a new story almost every week. But if Wheeler had shown little imagination in keeping Kipling to the hard grind of journalism, Kipling's work as a reporter did allow him to discover what India meant to him, and how to write about it. One example must suffice. In "Typhoid at Home," an investigation into the milk supply in Lahore, Kipling adopts the tone and stance of the novelists and reformers who had explored the slums of Manchester and London in mid-Victorian England (*Kipling's India: Uncollected Sketches, 1884–88,* pp. 69–77). The entry into unmappable areas ("high walled clefts," "dark courtyards"), the assault on the senses ("rainbow hues of putrescence," "fetid stench"), the claim that what is uncovered breaches the limits of linguistic decency ("unutterable abominations")—all these can be found in the industrial novels of Dickens, Elizabeth Gaskell, and Charles Kingsley. So too can the governing shape of the narrative: on the one hand, the study of how to manage a local problem by exercising "efficient and intelligent control"; on the other, the horrified sense of strangeness and danger, with "the tide of unclean humanity" threatening at any moment to "burst through its dam of rotten brickwork and filth-smeared wood." In the newspaper essay, the tension between the apparent confidence of the reporting voice, and a world felt to be unknowable, affords only a frustrated recognition of the inevitable outcome, in the form of "preventable disease leading to death." But in a number of the early Indian stories the gulf which opens up here becomes one of Kipling's most powerful and unsettling effects. The desire for "efficient and intelligent control," and the appalled awareness of "the tide of unclean humanity," mark the boundaries of the *Plain Tales* stories "In the House of Suddhoo" and "The Gate of the Hundred Sorrows" as well as those of "Typhoid at Home." The disciplines of journalism shaped Kipling's imagination, and taught him to write sentences in which every word is made to count.

PLAIN TALES FROM THE HILLS

Between November 1886 and June 1887, Kipling issued thirty- nine stories in the *Civil and Military Gazette* under the title "Plain Tales from the Hills." Initially they were unattributed, and at least one had been written by his sister Trix, but in January 1888 he revised and collected twenty-nine of them, and added eleven others, for publication in Calcutta under the same title. Of the eleven, three—"The Gate of the Hundred Sorrows," "In the House of Suddhoo," and "The Story of Muhammad Din"—had appeared in the *Civil and Military Gazette*; the remaining eight were now published for the first time. Most of the stories concentrate on Anglo-Indian life, civilian and military,

including four featuring Kipling's soldier trio, made up of the characters Terence Mulvaney, John Learoyd, and Stanley Ortheris. Only six out of the forty deal directly with native Indian or Eurasian life, but these include the best stories in the collection.

Kipling revised *Plain Tales from the Hills* for a number of later editions, particularly for the first English edition, published by Macmillan in 1890, where most of the changes were designed to clarify the Indian background for English readers: thus, "anna" becomes "penny," "this country" becomes "India," "you know" becomes "every household in India knows." A new paragraph inserted in "Wressley of the Foreign Office" explains to the English reader that India (unlike England) is a place "where every one knows every one else." The overall effect of these changes, often simple in themselves, is to shift the relation between narrator and reader. By needing to be explained, such references act as the markers of a world which is remote and unfamiliar, to which the narrator does and the reader does not belong. The "very scenes are strange," wrote Andrew Lang in a review originally published, unsigned, in the 2 November 1889 *Daily News* and included in *Kipling: The Critical Heritage*, and the reader is "baffled by *jhairuns*, and *khitmatgars*, and the rest of it." Rather than stories of "out here," written from and addressed to a shared experience, they become tales of "out there," beyond the reader's range (*Kipling: The Critical Heritage*, pp. 47–48).

The sense of being introduced to a strange new world was an important part of the response to Kipling's work among English readers. Reading *Plain Tales from the Hills*, wrote Oscar Wilde, "one feels as if one were seated under a palm-tree reading life by superb flashes of vulgarity. The jaded, second-rate Anglo-Indians are in exquisite incongruity with their surroundings. The mere lack of style in the story-teller gives an odd journalistic realism to what he tells us" (from "The True Function of Criticism," in *Kipling: The Critical Heritage*, p. 104). The version of the essay published in *Intentions* (1891) added the suggestion that Kipling had "seen marvellous things through keyholes" (from "The Critic As Artist" in *Intentions,* p. 208). Wilde's essay was one of a number which located Kipling at the meeting point of two kinds of literature, evoking simultaneously an exotic world of palm trees and summer lightning, and the familiar terrain of keyholes and journalistic realism. Victorian England was often uneasy about "realism" in literature, especially where it required the reader to enter into the darker sides of human nature, whether sexual or violent. Kipling managed, for the most part, to escape censure, and censorship, because he dealt with a world with which his English readers had little direct contact. India, like the past, was another country.

In the *Civil and Military Gazette,* the significant division in the *Plain Tales* is not between Anglo-India and "Home," but between the Indian world and that of the Anglo-Indians—not least because Indians generally appear only as part of the mass of humanity. The epigraph begins, "In the House of Suddhoo," one of the earliest of the stories,

A stone's throw out on either hand
From that well-ordered road we tread,
And all the world is wild and strange.

The pattern in many of Kipling's Indian stories, in *Plain Tales from the Hills* and in later collections, is to enter this "wild and strange" world for a few pages, and then return, often with an emphasis that seems designed to foster the doubts it pretends to dismiss, to the "well-ordered road"—the world of the Punjab Club and the officers' mess, with their reassuring if sometimes stuffy rituals, and their entire confidence in the superior wisdom of the English. In 1886 Kipling wrote that he would happily forgo a literary career in London in order to write about India; Lahore was his "own place," where he could find "heat and smells of oil and spices, and puffs of temple incense, and

sweat, and darkness, and dirt and lust and cruelty, and, above all, things wonderful and fascinating innumerable" (*Letters* [British edition], vol. 1, p. 127). But in the stories he was writing at the same time, the narrator is not always so securely in control. Even where the *Plain Tales* most powerfully command our assent, we may not be sure what it is we are assenting to.

"Beyond the Pale" may be taken as an example. It is the story of a secret interracial liaison between the Englishman Trejago and the young Hindu widow Bisesa, which ends with Trejago stabbed in the groin and Bisesa mutilated. Like many of the stories, it has an epigraph, which is left for the reader to make of it what he or she may. In this case it is identified by Kipling as a Hindu proverb, and reads: "Love heeds not caste nor sleep a broken bed. I went in search of love and lost myself" (p. 162). If this is Hindu wisdom, the reader might reflect, it seems to echo many of the great love stories of the Western world: Dido and Aeneas, Tristan and Isolde, Romeo and Juliet. It is not a view we can easily set aside, yet this is what we are asked to do by the first sentence of the story proper, in the voice of the Anglo-Indian narrator: "A man should, whatever happens, keep to his own caste, race, and breed." The second paragraph announces that we are about to be told "the story of a man who wilfully stepped beyond the safe limits of decent everyday society, and paid for it heavily" (p. 162). This proves to be true, but in settling for the safe and the everyday, the narrative voice, we might feel, seems smaller, more timid, than that of the proverb.

These irreconcilable voices provide the first of many oppositions in this story of a "double life": daytime and nighttime, English and Indian words (*bustee, dhak, bhusa*), the respectable "calling-clothes" Trejago wears for his usual social visits and the foul-smelling *boorka* that he wears to visit Bisesa, the familiar routines of work and the "madness" of the affair, all leading toward the opposition of Bisesa's "roseleaf hands" and the "funny little gestures" which

Trejago finds so appealing, and the nearly healed "stumps" (p. 165) she holds out to him after their affair has been discovered. What is left at the end is the renewed doubleness of Trejago's existence: outwardly "a very decent sort of man," (p. 166) who pays his calls regularly, but inwardly a man haunted by his loss, who wakes in the night to wonder what had happened to Bisesa.

The narrator occupies an ambiguous position in this story. First, he appears to know more about what has happened than we can imagine Trejago confiding to anyone but a close friend, yet his tone is wholly lacking in affection or intimacy ("his" tone, because the narrative voice in all these stories is evidently male), to the point where it has seemed to some readers that we should imagine the story as told by Trejago himself, using the third-person form because he now feels so profoundly alienated from the man he had once been. This view would explain the otherwise paradoxical manner in which the narrator rebukes Trejago for knowing too much ("No Englishman should be able to translate object-letters" [p. 163]), when of course his authority as a storyteller depends on his own possession of such knowledge. It would also invite us to interpret the opening paragraphs of the story, with their injunction to keep to one's race and caste, not as the merely conventional view of the Anglo-Indian community, but as the outcome of bitter personal experience. It is perhaps some support for this reading that Kipling does indeed use precisely this means to suggest the character Peachey's disturbed state of mind in one of the best-known of the Indian stories, "The Man Who Would Be King" (included in his 1888 collection *The Phantom 'Rickshaw*).

But whoever we suppose to be speaking, there is a further puzzle about this voice. It is a mark of Kipling's extraordinary confidence, even so early in his career (the story was written when he was twenty-two), that we so willingly believe in the existence of the "object-letter"—a broken glass bangle, a blood-red flower, a pinch of cattle food, and eleven cardamoms—which initiates the liaison. Yet we might find something odd in the readiness to translate this set of signs, spread out on the lid of Trejago's office-box, while the stumps of Bisesa's arms, thrust out toward him in the moonlight, are the signs of a story the narrator cannot or will not fully interpret. Whether Bisesa confessed the affair, or whether it was discovered, and how, are questions to which we have no answer. The discrepancy between what is so confidently known, and the impossibility of complete knowledge, is finally the most significant of all the oppositions in the story. The narrative voice is drawn toward the sensational on the one level (Bisesa's mutilation, and the wound which symbolically castrates her lover), and the exemplary on the other (the instruction to keep to one's own caste and creed), but neither voice is adequate to the experience of Trejago and Bisesa. The voice that might have reached their story is heard momentarily in the second sentence of the epigraph—"I went in search of love and lost myself"—but is then silenced by the narrator's resolute insistence on race separateness, and the "safe limits" of the everyday (p. 162).

Kipling returns to the theme of interracial relationships in several of the *Plain Tales,* typically with some unease. "Kidnapped" provides a brutal example. Here a group of friends engineer the kidnapping of a colleague who is about to make what in Anglo-Indian terms is an obviously unsuitable marriage. Miss Castries has "what innocent people at Home call a 'Spanish' complexion" (in the *Civil and Military Gazette* version, the text refers to "innocent people at Home" simply as "they"); the "opal-tinted onyx at the base of her finger-nails" reveals to the less innocent "as plainly as print" that she is Eurasian, that is, of mixed blood. It follows that marriage between her and Peythroppe of the Indian civil service would be "impossible" (p. 136). The quotes around this word are Kipling's, but if they subject the general view to a measure of irony, they do not signify his dissent from it; Miss Castries is the only person in the story to behave with dignity, but nobody doubts that Peythroppe's friends are right to prevent the marriage.

Even so the tone of the story is hard to read. The narrator begins with a paragraph defending the Hindu system of arranged marriages— "How can a man who has never married, who cannot be trusted to pick up at sight a moderately sound horse . . . go about the choosing of a wife?"—which, he insists, always work well: "As everybody knows" (p. 133). But of course his Anglo-Indian readers, and still more his English ones, do not "know" this at all, and if they did would not admit to it; even where marriages were arranged, it was still the custom to present them as love matches. The narrator's overcertainty has the paradoxical effect of making the reader mistrustful. At the same time, however, the story allows the reader no other point of view: Miss Castries later makes a successful marriage with someone within her own racial group, her father reveals himself as the coarse and unpleasant man Peythroppe's friends had suspected, and the would-be bridegroom's career and reputation are saved.

Rather like Peythroppe himself, the reader might feel that he or she has been "kidnapped" by the story, and coerced into supporting views which go wholly against the grain. It is essentially an extended anecdote, in the original sense of a secret story known only to the members of a select group. But Kipling's pretended unawareness of those outside the group is so flagrant as to be provocative; we are driven to question his values, and the sensibility to which they bear witness, just where he himself seems most determined to dismiss such questions. This is the effect of a number of the *Plain Tales*, sometimes of the story as a whole, sometimes of a sentence or a paragraph. Again, one further example will suffice. Bronckhorst, in "The Bronkhorst Divorce-Case," is an unpleasant man, possibly of mixed ancestry; according to rumor, there is "a touch of country-blood in him" (p. 216). He habitually treats his wife badly, and then brings an unfounded charge

against her of adultery with a man called Biel. Biel's friends rally around him, and are able to discredit the witnesses Bronckhorst had bribed to support his accusation. The case is dismissed, and a whip is dropped by Strickland, a friend of Biel's, in the veranda outside the court: "Ten minutes later, Biel was cutting Bronckhorst into ribbons behind the old Court cells, quietly and without scandal. What was left of Bronckhorst was sent home in a carriage; and his wife wept over it and nursed it into a man again" (p. 218).

There is a good deal here which is (to recall Orwell's words) "morally offensive and aesthetically disgusting," including the use of the pronoun "it" for a human being and, especially, the word "quietly" with reference to how the beating was undertaken. The sentence itself is manifestly not quiet, but calculated to make us declare ourselves: Do we, or do we not, agree that there is no reason to protest when Biel flogs the man who had insulted him? We are, in effect, being asked to align ourselves with the group or caste Kipling addresses, or to admit either that we want no part in it, or that we do not have the courage to defend it, and its values, against men like Bronckhorst. Wherever we choose to stand, Kipling, emphatically, is "in."

"Lispeth" treats the story of an interracial liaison more sympathetically than "Kidnapped." Lispeth is a "Hill-woman," a woman from the hill region in northern India, brought up from childhood by missionaries, who wants to marry an Englishman whose life she has saved after a fall. In the version published in the *Civil and Military Gazette*, the chaplain's wife tells Lispeth that it is "wrong and improper" (p. 36) of her to have such hopes. The quotation marks around these words in Kipling's text suggest an irony at the expense of those who assert the racial boundary, all the more so, we might suppose, since the chaplain's wife has earlier told the Englishman that Lispeth "is but a child, you know, and, I fear, at heart a heathen" (p. 36): a conclusion which hardly reflects well on the missionary work she and her husband are in India to do. When he came to revise the story,

Kipling removed the quotation marks: possibly because he was now more confident that the irony would be detected by his readers, perhaps because he was no longer sure that it ought to be present. It is the narrator who says of Lispeth's willingness to trust the Englishman that "being a savage by birth, she took no trouble to hide her feelings" (p. 35), but it is left to the reader to decide how much weight to give to the rest of what is implied here, that the English, being civilized, have a greater ability to lie. Kipling admired the work of Jane Austen, and the reader may recall that Austen's novel *Sense and Sensibility* uses similar narrative material—a fall, a rescue, love at first sight, and a subsequent betrayal. If so, it is surely relevant that in Austen's work the heroine is similarly unable to hide her feelings, but she is a well-bred English girl, not a "savage"; and while the novel shows that she has been foolish, there is no doubt that the man who deceives her is to be seen as weak and heartless. In contrast to "Kidnapped," the story of "Lispeth" leaves the reader to find his or her own bearings. Kipling placed it first in the volume edition of *Plain Tales,* and it has a claim to be one of the best stories in the collection.

THE SOLDIER STORIES

Four of the *Plain Tales* concern Kipling's trio of soldiers, Mulvaney, Ortheris, and Learoyd. They were to feature in some eighteen of his stories, and his touch became increasingly sure, especially in the handling of dialect. "The Three Musketeers" is hardly more than an anecdote, in which the three arrange the fake abduction of a visiting nobleman who has caused them to be turned out on parade once too often. "The Taking of Lungtungpen" elaborates a report Kipling had written for the *Civil and Military Gazette* by the fairly simple device of employing a narrator. Writing as a civilian and a journalist, Kipling had been limited to routine reflections on the bravery of the British soldier, under the generic name of Private Thomas Atkins; retold in Mulvaney's stage Irish, the story becomes an

illustration of Mulvaney's paradoxical theory that an inexperienced soldier is the best to work with, "on account of the surpassin' innocence av the choild" (p. 122). "The Daughter of the Regiment" is a sentimental piece, superficially toughened up by Mulvaney's brogue, in which army wives come to the aid of their men when the camp is stricken with cholera. Much the best of the soldier stories, at least in *Plain Tales,* is "The Madness of Private Ortheris," in which Ortheris, the Cockney, goes mad with homesickness and a longing for the smells of the London streets—"orange-peel and hasphalt an' gas comin' in over Vaux'all Bridge"—and is ready to desert (p. 245). But once he has changed into civilian clothes, he undergoes a kind of collapse, and his friends find him "dripping with perspiration, and trembling like a startled horse" (p. 248). Back in uniform, he hands his belt over to Mulvaney, and invites him to thrash him with it, to bring him back to his senses.

This is one of a number of attempts Kipling made to write of the tedium of army life. There had been a number of army reforms during the 1870s, including the abolition of peacetime flogging as a punishment, but living conditions for the lower ranks were still harsh and sometimes squalid, with very little allowance made for married men; the pay was poor, and the feeling was widespread that only the reckless or the criminal would choose to enlist. Kipling recognized the brutality of army life, but he also understood that the way of life which allowed the middle classes at home the luxury of looking down on the soldier depended on the employment throughout the empire of "either blackguards or gentlemen, or, best of all, blackguards commanded by gentlemen, to do butchers' work with efficiency and dispatch" ("The Drums of the Fore and Aft"). As several commentators have pointed out, the ordinary soldier is almost entirely absent from English fiction before Kipling—indeed, from English literature, with the exception of some scenes in Shakespeare's *Henry V*—and the life of Private Thomas Atkins, like that of the men of the Indian civil service, was another subject that Kipling made his own, not least because both in India, and later, during the Boer War of 1899–1902, he took pains to meet the lower ranks as well as their commanding officers.

He was to return to the subject of Thomas Atkins in his collection *Barrack-Room Ballads*, published to huge acclaim in 1890 and in print ever since. What the early stories about his "Soldiers Three" suggest is that they are often drunk, impatient of routine, inclined to theft and occasional outbreaks of violence, but also unfailingly committed to their task as soldiers, though their loyalty is to each other and to the army first, and to the queen and the empire second. Their rebellions are temporary, a necessary release from the boredom and frustration of their lives; at the end of the day they not only fall into line, but compel their fellows in the barracks to do so as well. In every sense, they belong to the army; it is the "rasp" (p. 248) of his gray army shirt, and the squeak of his boots, that brings Ortheris to himself. In this story, as in most of the others, the role of the narrator is ambiguous. He is both a friend and an irrelevance, a journalist who buys their stories for the price of some beer, but who cannot "come to any conclusion of any kind whatever" about the nature of their world and their inner troubles. The attempt to do so, however, was to produce two of Kipling's finest stories, "On Greenhow Hill" (*Life's Handicap*, 1891) and "'Love-o'-Women'" (*Many Inventions*, 1893).

TALES OF ANGLO-INDIA

Of the *Plain Tales* that deal with official Anglo-Indian life, a majority turn on confusions, mistaken identities, and missed meetings, suggesting a world where social life is as little under control as the Indian landscape and weather. In his journalism, and in his letters home, Kipling warned of danger and inefficiency if Indians were allowed to govern themselves, but the stories in *Plain Tales from the Hills* reveal what

he describes in "Bitters Neat" as "the hopelessness and tangle—the waste and muddle" of life in the Anglo- English community (p. 61). Some are bitter, others broadly comic, though the laughter is often clouded with pain, as in "False Dawn," where Saumarez proposes to the wrong sister in the darkness and confusion of a sudden dust storm, or "The Arrest of Lieutenant Golightly," whose identity is washed away by the rain so that he is mistaken for a deserting private. The refusal to look deeper in these stories is justified, as stated in "The Conversion of Aurelian McGoggin," by the claim that "in India, where you really see humanity—raw, brown, naked humanity—with nothing between it and the blazing sky," only the foolish and the conceited look beyond the immediate tasks of the day, or ponder the final meaning of things (p. 118). McGoggin, the central character in this story, is both conceited and foolish, has read books and has theories, but he is properly punished by an attack of aphasia, which silences him when his colleagues at the Club have been unable to do so. The main character in "Wressley of the Foreign Office" is an expert on the Central Indian States, who comes to believe that his knowledge is "absolutely and imperatively necessary to the stability of India." But when he falls in love with a girl who has no interest in his work, he is "broken, smashed," and sinks every copy he can find of the book he has spent years researching into a pool of water (p. 264). Like McGoggin, he has made the mistake of taking himself, and life, too seriously.

There is a complex double bluff behind the apparent anti-intellectualism of these stories. McGoggin's ideas are dismissed with the explanation that life in India is not long enough to expend on theories:

The Deputy is above the Assistant, the Commissioner above the Deputy, the Lieutenant-Governor above the Commissioner, and the Viceroy above all four, under the orders of the Secretary of State, who is responsible to the Empress. If the Empress be not responsible to her Maker—if there is no Maker for her to be responsible to—the entire system of Our administration must be wrong. Which is manifestly impossible.

(p. 118)

The suggestion is that sensible men recognize the possibility that there is no Maker, and therefore no final authority to appeal to in order to justify their own lives, or the purpose of the empire; but rather than become paralyzed by questions about purpose and authority, they turn to the hard work of government, or to their preferred forms of play—polo, dances, amateur theatricals, practical jokes. Doubt is not addressed, but silenced: not so much faced, as faced down.

Kipling's stance here has some affinities with the work of one of the most influential of Victorian writers, Thomas Carlyle, whom he could almost be quoting in "His Private Honour" (*Many Inventions,* 1893), another of the soldier stories: "First a man must suffer, then he must learn his work, and the self-respect that knowledge brings." India, in Kipling's view, was full of men who had suffered and learned in this way, and no doubt many of them had read and admired Carlyle. The significant comparison, however, is with Joseph Conrad, Kipling's near contemporary. Marlow, Conrad's narrator in *Heart of Darkness* (1899), sees work much as Kipling does, as a means to find "your own reality." But he also sees it as the performance of "monkey-tricks," a way of attending to "the mere incidents of the surface" in order avoid the "inner truth" of human frailty and corruption, and of the futility of our notions of efficiency and progress. In the *Plain Tales,* Kipling refuses to admit such ambiguities, or rather, he affects a toughness of manner which suggests that he and his fellow Anglo-Indians—with the exception of men like Aurelian McGoggin—have dealt with them once and for all. "Mr. Kipling has the wisdom of the passing generations," Conrad wrote to his friend Cunninghame Graham. "He squints with the rest of his excellent sort. It is a beautiful squint; it is an useful squint" (*The Letters of Joseph Conrad,* pp. 422–423). But every artist squints, or has his own angle of vision. The limitation on Kipling's greatness, in the early stories at least, is not that his vision is partial, but that he seems so anxious to present it as a whole and sufficient one, and anyone who does not share it as morally as well as intellectually inadequate.

Some of the stories do push further, to show that what was confidently supposed in England to be a process of initiation, a way of life and work which turned boys into men, might as often be the means of their destruction, as it is for Dicky Hatt in "In the Pride of His Youth," tired of life before he reaches his twenty-third birthday, and the hero-victim of "Thrown Away," a young man who is named simply as "The Boy," and who commits suicide because he supposes that he has disgraced himself. The Boy has lived a sheltered life at home, until he arrives in India, where he has "no one to fall back on in time of trouble except himself," and no one to tell him that India is a place "where one must not take things too seriously": that flirtation, good work, bad work, amusements, sickness, none of them matter, since "the memory of his performances would wither away in one hot weather" (p. 43–44). But The Boy takes things seriously, and commits suicide because he supposes that he has disgraced himself. Together with the Major, the narrator destroys The Boy's letters of confession to his family and "a girl at Home," and concocts a story that he has died of cholera, though without pain; lying, the narrator declares, is his profession, and "it was no time for little lies, you will understand" (p. 67). As he writes, he is aware that The Boy has been changed into "the poor Thing on the bed" (p. 67); the contrast makes him "choke" with pity, but at the same time laugh at "the grotesqueness of the affair." The letter is sent off to The Boy's family, with a lock of the Major's hair, since The Boy had shot himself, and "there were reasons why we could not find a lock fit to send" (p. 68). The story ends with a sardonic comment from the narrator, when The Boy's mother, still believing that her son had died of cholera, writes to express her sense of obligation for the kindness they had shown him: "All things considered, she was under an obligation, but not exactly as she meant" (p. 50).

The title of the story, "Thrown Away," has a double meaning: not just that The Boy's life was wasted, but also that the tale itself is something to throw off, since it is, the narrator admits, "as old as the Hills" (p. 63). It is the kind of story at which wise men weep, then laugh, then dismiss, or (as the narrator does) reduce to an illustration to prove the failings of "the 'sheltered life system'" of education. Taken as a whole, the *Plain Tales* suggest a world where men must be broken in to their work, like colts, or break down in the effort to do it. They can look to no long-term purpose, since they know or believe that the end of their work will be its own destruction, when India demands to go its own way, and fails in attempting to do so (this was Kipling's own view of the moves toward an independent India). In the meantime their daily lives will be harsh, their pleasures few, and their attempts to establish any sense of permanency constantly undermined by the physical facts of the landscape; as one of Kipling's later stories, "The Education of Otis Yeere," has it, "we are only little bits of dirt on the hillside—here one day and blown down the *khud* [cliff] the next" (*Wee Willie Winkie*).

It is often suggested that the stories of Anglo-Indians at work can be seen as extended metaphors for some more radical trial of the spirit, that the burdens carried by Kipling's junior officers and civil servants are not essentially different from those found in Thomas Hardy, or the poems of W. E. Henley and A. E. Housman. In such readings, India stands as the sign of the eternal insufficiency of the rational mind, or of the enduringness of the physical world against which human life pales into insignificance, or as a testing ground in which men can prove themselves as men. There is some justice in this, but to see Kipling's India in this way is to push into the background the political

realities of the British presence. Kipling, inconsiderately, keeps more than half an eye on these realities. The soldier stories, evenly distributed through the volume, provide one clear reminder, in keeping with what the narrator tells us in "His Chance in Life," that "unless the outward and visible signs of Our Authority are always before a native he is as incapable as a child of understanding what authority means, or where is the danger of disobeying it" (p. 93). The reader too is never allowed to forget "Our Authority"—the authority, that is, that "we," the Anglo-Indians, exercise on the ground in India, on behalf of "you" in England who so easily fail to appreciate it.

"THE STORY OF MUHAMMAD DIN"

Michele D'Cruze, in "His Chance in Life," is able to put down a riot because of the "White drop" in his veins (he is seven parts native, but one-eighth English). To be "White," on this account, is to be strong (p. 95). But in "Beyond the Pale," and in a number of other stories, an Englishman loses or comes near to losing his identity. The shifts and uncertainties within these stories, and the incompleteness of the explanations they offer, challenge the implicit claim of the narrative to derive from a position of knowledge and to be in control of its material. In "The Gate of the Hundred Sorrows," the narrator insists that what follows is "no work of mine," merely a record of what was said on the night of his death by "My friend, Gabriel Misquitta, the half-caste" (p. 236), but Kipling was clearly fascinated by the attempt to trace the disintegration of a man addicted to opium; he himself had taken opium, to help get through a period of fever, and he had already been through at least one nervous breakdown (he was to undergo several more during his twenties). McIntosh, in "To Be Filed for Reference," is an Oxford-educated sahib who has "gone native," but he too makes a friend of the narrator, as if recognizing a kindred spirit, who shares the impulse to step beyond the boundary separating

English and Indian life. The narrator of "In the House of Suddhoo" congratulates himself on his friendship with Suddhoo, and on his understanding of Janoo, the prostitute who is one of Suddhoo's tenants; but as the story unfolds he finds that despite his Western education he is implicated in a chain of events that will conclude in a murder he is powerless to prevent. "Knowledge," in these stories, is not enabling, but rather the reverse. In another of the early tales, the title story of *The Phantom 'Rickshaw*, the narrator offers as an "explanation" for the breakdown of an Englishman named Pansay that "there was a crack in Pansay's head and a little bit of the Dark World came through and pressed him to death." Something like this seems to happen to a number of Kipling's characters, just as it had happened to Kipling himself as a child at Lorne Lodge. The authority of the narrative voice, like "Our Authority" over the Indian population, is constantly asserted, but never entirely secure.

In at least one of the *Plain Tales*, however, "The Story of Muhammad Din," Kipling shows that he was not hopelessly bound to such a stance. In this, the shortest and arguably the best of the stories, the unnamed English narrator becomes aware of the existence in his household of young Muhammad Din, the son of Imam Din, the narrator's servant. Imam Din asks the narrator if he can give an old polo ball, discovered in the course of housecleaning, to his son, for him to play with. The narrator consents, and the child uses the ball as the centerpiece of a design in the garden—the ball, with "six shrivelled old marigold flowers in a circle round it" (p. 251), surrounded by a square of broken brick and glass. When the narrator inadvertently tramples over one such design, he is genuinely sorry, and leaves out odds and ends that Muhammad might find useful. Noting the boy's absence for a day or two, he makes inquiries; discovering that the boy is ill, he calls a doctor, but is too late: "They have no stamina, these brats," says the doctor. The story ends as follows: "A week later, though I would have given much to have avoided it, I

met on the road to the Mussulman burying-ground Imam Din, accompanied by one other friend, carrying in his arms, wrapped in a white cloth, all that was left of little Muhammad Din" (p. 253).

This is a moving story, as that eloquent final sentence testifies, and it also hints at parable. The narrator's courtesy to Muhammad—ensuring "that my salutation might not be slurred over or given unseemly" (p. 251)—comes from a position of superiority: the adult on a horse, the child in the dust. The relation between the two suggests in miniature a familiar view of that between the Anglo-Indian and the Indian communities. The narrator has no wish to destroy the child's handiwork, yet his tolerance of it, as "only the play of a baby" (p. 252), mimics conventional Anglo-Indian views of Indian art and architecture, as his patronage of this play, by dropping "a gaily-spotted sea-shell" (p. 252) for Muhammad to use, echoes the conviction that Anglo-Indians could guide native Indians to a better understanding of their own culture—as, indeed, Kipling's father, Lockwood, sought to do in his work as a teacher and as curator of a museum of Indian artifacts.

But the narrator, well-intentioned though he is, fails in his role as pseudo-parent: Muhammad dies. Wrapped in its white cloth, the child's body is not the image of an inherently unknowable India, but of the inadequacy of the narrator's uncritical assumption that he can indeed tell "the story of Muhammad Din." The authority he takes for granted is called into question by the epigraph: "Who is the happy man? He that sees, in his own house at home, little children crowned with dust, leaping and falling and crying" (p. 250). Neither Imam Din nor the narrator is "in his own house at home"; each is denied the pleasure of children; they are linked by a sorrow they cannot share. Yet the boundary between the two men appears to be impassable. Politically it was; only in the fiction, in the wider view which encompasses and goes beyond that of the narrator, is there any possibility of reaching across it. In the best of the *Plain Tales*—in this story, in "Lispeth," and in "Beyond the Pale"—Kipling is patrolling the boundary not merely to defend it, but also to discover its weak point, and push against it.

Plain Tales from the Hills was Kipling's first collection of stories. It is in many respects apprentice work, in which we see an author finding his voice (or one of his voices), and learning how to work within the constraints of the space available. Some of the techniques he developed at this early stage were to remain with him through his career. The use of an epigraph was developed in his later work, where a story is often accompanied by one and sometimes two poems, to suggest, as do the epigraphs to "Beyond the Pale" and "The Story of Muhammad Din," a different perspective on the story. Similarly, later stories continue to experiment with the relation between the voice of the narrator and the narrative itself, so that in tales otherwise as unlike each other as "Thrown Away" and "In the House of Suddhoo" we have both the story, that is, the narrative proper, and what we might call "the story of the story." Thematically, also, the later work is foreshadowed in the *Plain Tales*: the interest in the supernatural, or at least in what lies beyond our immediate understanding, forms a main concern of the stories Kipling wrote after World War I, when he also began to examine more deeply the implications of the hoax, or revenge plot, in which one character sets out to entrap another, which gave him the raw material for the *Plain Tales* stories "Pig," "A Friend's Friend," and "The Watches of the Night." But if the *Plain Tales* belong to the category of early work by a major writer, at least two of the stories, "Beyond the Pale" and "The Story of Muhammad Din," deserve to stand at the front of any anthology of Kipling's prose; and if they deserve to stand there, they have a claim to a place in any anthology of great short stories by English writers.

Selected Bibliography

EDITION

Plain Tales from the Hills. Edited by H. R. Woodhuysen, with an introduction and notes by David Trotter. Harmondsworth, U.K.: Penguin Books, 1987; New York: Viking Penguin, 1987. The most useful edition of the text; page references herein are to this edition.

OTHER WORKS BY KIPLING

The Complete Barrack-Room Ballads of Rudyard Kipling. Edited by Charles Carrington. London: Methuen, 1973.

Kipling's India: Uncollected Sketches, 1884–88. Edited by Thomas Pinney. Basingstoke, Hampshire, U.K.: Macmillan, 1986; New York: Schocken Books, 1986.

A Choice of Kipling's Prose. Edited by Craig Raine. London: Faber and Faber, 1987. The best anthology of Kipling's stories.

Just So Stories. Edited by Peter Levi. Harmondsworth: Penguin Books, 1987.

Kim. Edited by Edward Said. Harmondsworth: Penguin Books, 1987.

Limits and Renewals. Edited by Phillip Mallet. Harmondsworth: Penguin Books, 1987.

Wee Willie Winkie. Edited by Hugh Haughton. Harmondsworth: Penguin Books, 1987.

Rudyard Kipling: Something of Myself, and Other Autobiographical Writings. Edited by Thomas Pinney. Cambridge, U.K., and New York: Cambridge University Press, 1990.

The Letters of Rudyard Kipling. 4 Vols. Edited by Thomas Pinney. London: Macmillan, 1990; Iowa City: University of Iowa Press, 1990–1999.

SECONDARY WORKS

Birkenhead, Frederick. *Rudyard Kipling.* London: Weidenfeld and Nicolson, 1978; New York: Random House, 1978.

Bodelsen, C. A. *Aspects of Kipling's Art.* New York: Barnes and Noble, 1964.

Carrington, Charles. *Rudyard Kipling: His Life and Work.* London: Macmillan, 1955.

Cornell, Louis L. *Kipling in India.* London, Macmillan, 1966; New York: St. Martin's Press, 1966.

Davies, Lawrence, and Frederick B. Karl. *The Letters of Joseph Conrad, Vol. I: 1861–97.* Cambridge, U.K.: 1983.

Dobrée, Bonamy. *Rudyard Kipling: Realist and Fabulist.* London and New York, Oxford University Press, 1967.

Eliot, T. S. Introduction to his *A Choice of Kipling's Verse.* London: Faber and Faber, 1941; New York: Scribners, 1943.

Gilbert, Elliott L. *The Good Kipling: Studies in the Short Story.* Athens: Ohio University Press, 1971.

Gilbert, Elliott L., ed. *Kipling and the Critics.* New York: New York University Press, 1965.

Gilmour, David. *The Long Recessional: The Imperial Life of Rudyard Kipling.* London: John Murray, 2002; New York: Farrar, Straus and Giroux, 2002.

Green, Roger Lancelyn, ed., *Kipling: The Critical Heritage.* London: Routledge and Paul, 1971; New York: Barnes and Noble, 1971.

Harbord, Reginald Engledow, ed., *The Reader's Guide to Rudyard Kipling's Work.* 8 Vols. Canterbury, U.K.: Mssrs. Gibbs and Sons, 1961–1972. Provides a mass of useful material.

Islam, Shamsul. *Kipling's "Law": A Study of His Philosophy of Life.* London: Macmillan, 1975; New York: St. Martin's, 1975.

Kemp, Sandra. *Kipling's Hidden Narratives.* Oxford, U.K., and New York: B. Blackwell, 1988.

Le Gallienne, Richard. *Rudyard Kipling: A Criticism.* London and New York: John Lane, 1900.

Lycett, Andrew. *Rudyard Kipling.* London: Weidenfeld and Nicolson, 1999.

Mallett, Phillip. *Rudyard Kipling: A Literary Life.* London: Palgrave Macmillan, 2003.

Mallett, Phillip, ed. *Kipling Considered.* London: Macmillan, 1989; New York: St. Martin's, 1989.

Mason, Philip. *Kipling: The Glass, the Shadow, and the Fire.* London: J. Cape, 1975; New York: Harper and Row, 1975.

McClure, John A. *Kipling and Conrad: The Colonial Fiction.* Cambridge, Mass.: Harvard University Press, 1981.

Moore-Gilbert, B. J. *Kipling and "Orientalism."* London: Croom Helm, 1986; New York: St. Martin's, 1986.

Orel, Harold. *A Kipling Chronology.* Houndsmills, U.K.: Macmillan, 1990; Boston: G. K. Hall, 1990.

Orel, Harold, ed. *Critical Essays on Rudyard Kipling.* Boston: G. K. Hall, 1989.

Paffard, Mark. *Kipling's Indian Fiction.* London: Macmillan,1989; New York: St. Martin's, 1989.

Page, Norman. *A Kipling Companion.* London: Macmillan, 1984.

Rao, K. Bhaskara. *Rudyard Kipling's India.* Norman: University of Oklahoma Press, 1967.

Ricketts, Harry. *The Unforgiving Minute: A Life of Rudyard Kipling.* London: Chatto and Windus, 1999.

Rutherford, Andrew, ed. *Kipling's Mind and Art: Selected Critical Essays.* Edinburgh and London: Oliver and Boyd, 1964; Stanford, Calif.: Stanford University Press, 1964. Includes Orwell's essay "Rudyard Kipling" and Wilson's essay "The Wound and the Bow."

Sandison, Alan. *The Wheel of Empire: A Study of the Imperial Idea in Some Late Nineteenth and Early Twentieth Century Fiction.* New York: St. Martin's, 1967.

Seymour-Smith, Martin. *Rudyard Kipling.* London: Macdonald/Queen Anne Press, 1989.

Stewart, James McG. *Rudyard Kipling: A Bibliographical Catalogue.* Edited by A. W. Yeats. Toronto: Dalhousie University Press, 1959.

Sullivan, Zohreh T. *Narratives of Empire: The Fictions of Rudyard Kipling.* Cambridge, U.K., and New York: Cambridge University Press, 1993.

Tompkins, J. M. S. *The Art of Rudyard Kipling.* 2d ed. London: Methuen, 1965; Lincoln: University of Nebraska Press, 1965.

Wilde, Oscar. *Intentions.*

Wilson, Angus. *The Strange Ride of Rudyard Kipling: His Life and Works.* London: Secker and Warburg, 1977.

Wilson, Edmund. *The Wound and the Bow: Seven Studies in Literature.* Boston: Houghton Mifflin, 1941.

Wurgaft, Lewis D. *The Imperial Imagination: Magic and Myth in Kipling's India.* Middletown, Conn.: Wesleyan University Press, 1983.

A. S. Byatt's
Possession

AMY EDWARDS

POSSESSION: A ROMANCE was first published in Britain in 1990, and marked a turning point in A. S. Byatt's career. Byatt had been writing for almost three decades, and had published four novels and one collection of short stories, but while her highly literary and intelligent style was well regarded in academic circles, Byatt did not have a wide readership. Before *Possession,* she was perhaps most famous simply for being the older sister of Margaret Drabble, a novelist whose style of social realism had been popular in Britain during the 1960s and 1970s. However, Byatt's reputation was assured when *Possession* won Britain's most prestigious literary prize, the Booker Prize, as well as the high-profile *Irish Times*/Aer Lingus International Fiction Prize. The resulting publicity made *Possession* a bestseller, a critical and commercial success on both sides of the Atlantic.

A. S. Byatt was born on 24 August 1936 in Sheffield, England, as Susan Drabble. (Antonia was a name she adopted as a teenager.) Byatt was educated in a Quaker school in Yorkshire, and went on to read English literature at Cambridge University. It is perhaps unsurprising that the young Byatt was a keen scholar, as she came from an academic family; both her parents had studied at Cambridge (at a time when female graduates were extremely rare), and could recite large sections of Shakespeare, Keats, and Browning from memory.

After graduating from Cambridge in 1957, Byatt did a year of postgraduate study at Bryn Mawr College in Pennsylvania, and then began a doctorate at Oxford University, which she abandoned shortly before her first marriage in 1959. Byatt has said that she left university because she wanted to concentrate on her creative writing, but marriage must have been a considerable obstacle to her academic career—at this time any female student who got married almost certainly lost their funding as a result. The description of the literary scholar Beatrice Nest's nun-like existence in *Possession* provides some indication of how women fared in academia at this time. Byatt started writing her first novel, *The Shadow of a Sun* (1964), while studying at Cambridge, but it was not completed until a decade later. Likewise, her second novel, *The Game* (1967), was begun in the 1950s but only finally published in the late 1960s. This fairly slow output was partially due to Byatt's perfectionism, and her early habit of drafting and redrafting her work; but becoming a mother in 1960 must have further frustrated her progress. The problems faced by women attempting to fulfill their role as a mother as well as their own personal ambitions is a perennial theme in Byatt's fiction, and particularly well-explored in her novels *Still Life* (1985) and *Babel Tower* (1996).

The middle part of Byatt's career is dominated by her work as a teacher and critic of English literature—in the introduction to her essays *Passions of the Mind* (1991), Byatt explains that reading and writing are "points on a circle" for her, and that her pleasure in reading and studying literature has always inspired her to write. In the late 1960s Byatt wrote two book-length critical studies: *Degrees of Freedom* (1965), a study of the novels of Iris Murdoch, and *Wordsworth and Coleridge in Their Time* (1970). During this period, Byatt also taught adult-education classes in English literature, and occasionally appeared as a literary critic on various television and radio programs for the BBC. After her divorce and remarriage to Peter Duffy in 1969, Byatt obtained a full-time teaching job in the English Department of University College London, a post she retained until 1983. She left UCL in order to be able to concentrate full-time on her creative writing, and since *Possession* her creative output seems to have increased considerably. Between 1990 and 2003 she has published three novels, two novellas, three collections of short fiction, and two volumes of critical essays. In 1990 she was appointed a CBE (Commander of the Order of the British Empire) and in 1999 a DBE (Dame Commander of the Order of the British Empire).

Apart from *Possession*, Byatt's major works have been characterized by a narrative mode which she has described as "self-conscious realism," a style that is particularly noticeable in her four-book "tetralogy," *The Virgin in the Garden* (1978), *Still Life* (1985), *Babel Tower* (1996), and *A Whistling Woman* (2002). Realism is often associated with the nineteenth-

CHRONOLOGY

1936	Born 24 August in Sheffield, England, as Susan Drabble. (Adopts the first name "Antonia" as a teenager.)
1954–1957	Studies at Newnham College, Cambridge University. Graduates with first-class-honors degree in English Literature.
1957–1958	Attends Bryn Mawr College, Pennsylvania.
1958–1959	Pursues a doctorate in Renaissance poetry at Somerville College, Oxford University.
1959	Abandons studies at Oxford; marries Ian Byatt.
1960	Daughter Antonia is born.
1961	Son Charles is born.
1962–1971	Works as part-time teacher in the extramural department of the University of London.
1964	Publishes first novel, *The Shadow of a Sun*.
1965–1969	Works as part-time lecturer in liberal studies at the Central School of Art and Design, London.
1965	Publishes *Degrees of Freedom*, a critical study of the early novels of Iris Murdoch.
1967	Publishes second novel, *The Game*.
1967–1979	Makes frequent appearances as a literary critic on BBC radio.
1969	Divorces Ian Byatt. Marries Peter Duffy.
1970	Daughter Isabel is born. Publishes *Wordsworth and Coleridge in Their Time*.
1972	Son Charles dies in a car accident.
1972–1983	Works as lecturer in English literature at University College, London.
1973	Daughter Miranda is born.
1978	Publishes *The Virgin in the Garden* (volume one of tetralogy).
1980	Serves as British Council lecturer in Germany, Australia, Hong Kong, China, and Korea.
1985	Publishes *Still Life* (second volume of tetralogy).
1986	Receives Silver Pen Award for *Still Life*.
1987	Publishes *Sugar and Other Stories*.
1990	Publishes *Possession. Possession* wins Booker Prize. Awarded a CBE

	(Commander of the Order of the British Empire).
1991	Publishes *Passions of the Mind.*
1992	Publishes *Angels and Insects: Two Novellas.*
1993	Publishes *The Matisse Stories.*
1994	Publishes *The Djinn in the Nightingale's Eye: Five Fairy Stories.*
1996	Publishes *Babel Tower* (third volume of tetralogy).
1998	Publishes *Elementals: Stories of Fire and Ice.*
1999	Awarded a DBE (Dame Commander of the Order of the British Empire).
2000	Publishes *The Biographer's Tale,* and *On Histories and Stories.*
2002	Publishes *A Whistling Woman* (final volume of tetralogy).

century novel, and Byatt has acknowledged the influence of the Victorian novelist George Eliot on her fiction; however, Byatt's version of realism is absolutely contemporary, as these novels display an acute awareness of twentieth-century literary theories about the artificiality of language and the nature of fictional representation. The books making up the tetralogy are dense novels of ideas, bursting with references to philosophy, science, and literature. Indeed, *The Virgin in the Garden* and its successors have given Byatt a reputation for intellectualism which has not always been appreciated by some of her readers—some critics have even complained that Byatt's fiction is simply "too clever" to be enjoyable. *Possession* represents a change of style for Byatt, and an opportunity to silence the critics. It is noticeably more playful than her earlier work, and clearly aims to please the reader with its compelling, detective-novel-style plot; however, it retains the intelligence and play of ideas that have become Byatt's trademark. The complexity of the narrative in *Possession* makes it difficult to analyze chapter by chapter, and so it seems best to discuss the novel thematically.

THE DETECTIVE-STORY PLOT

In her essay "Choices: On the Writing of *Possession*," A. S. Byatt proclaimed, "Art does not exist for politics, or for instruction—it exists primarily for pleasure . . . and the pleasure of fiction is narrative discovery." In *Possession* the reader's feeling of pleasure in narrative discovery is mirrored by the characters, all of whom are eager readers, who are motivated by a burning desire to know what happened next. Byatt's use of a detective-story plot exploits this instinctive human appetite for narrative, teasing with partial disclosures and revelations before finally satisfying the reader with a full, rewarding conclusion.

In *Possession*, reading and detective work are shown to be closely related activities for the novel's protagonists Roland Michell and Maud Bailey. Roland's first discovery comes about while he is reading, in the London Library, a book that once belonged to the Victorian poet Randolph Henry Ash. The drafts of two intimate letters to an unnamed woman spark off Roland's narrative curiosity, and "seized by a strange and uncharacteristic impulse" (p. 8), he sets off to discover the story that this tantalizing narrative opening will lead him to. By cross-referencing the letter with the diaries of one of Ash's contemporaries, Crabb Robinson, Roland is able to identify the unnamed woman as the poet Christabel LaMotte, but his unfamiliarity with LaMotte's work leads him to turn to the feminist scholar Maud Bailey for help. Many of the subsequent discoveries made by the two literary scholars come about as a result of interpreting texts. Crucial clues include LaMotte's poem beginning "Dolly keeps a secret" (p. 82), which leads Maud to discover further letters hidden underneath the mattress of a doll's cot in LaMotte's old home, Seal Court. The letters themselves confirm that Ash and La-Motte enjoyed a brief love affair in 1859, and hint that some sort of elopement took place in the summer of that year. When Maud and Roland travel to the North of England to look for more evidence, they again fruitfully employ their reading skills: as Maud comments, "literary critics make natural detectives" (p. 237). It is references to the Yorkshire landscape in LaMotte's poem *Melusina* that finally convince these literary critics that Ash must have been accompanied by his lover when he traveled to Yorkshire on a natural history expedition in the summer of 1859. Later on, entries in a diary written by LaMotte's niece Sabine de Kercoz reveal that she fled to Brittany after the affair, pregnant with Ash's child. After this, the textual trail becomes hard to decipher, as further poems by LaMotte hint that the child was stillborn.

By now, information about the letters has been leaked to rival academics, including Mortimer Cropper, James Blackadder, and Leonora Stern. Cropper detects that the final piece of the puzzle can be found in a diary written by Ash's wife, Ellen, who has recorded the fact that she buried a mysterious box with her husband's coffin. Cropper is so eager to discover the contents of this box—the secrets deliberately buried by Ash's wife—that he plots to illegally exhume Ash's grave. The other scholars find out about his plans, although in the interests of textual criticism, and their own personal curiosity, they decide to let Cropper retrieve the letters before they catch him. The dramatic conclusion to *Possession* takes place in a theatrical gothic graveyard scene, on a stormy autumn night, when the literary detectives close in on the lawbreaking professor. After Cropper has been caught red-handed, the academics gather together in a local country hotel (in true Agatha Christie style) to hear the conclusion of the story. The contents of the buried box include a letter from LaMotte to Ash which Ellen Ash never delivered to her husband, and a fine braid of blond hair. The purloined letter reveals that Ash and La Motte's daughter was Maud Bailey's great grandmother; an ironic and fitting conclusion to the story, as it transpires that what Maud has been seeking all along is the truth of her own family origins.

The narrative of *Possession* makes full use of uncanny repetitions and unlikely coincidences, and ends partly in the manner of the classic detective story and partly in the manner of a Shakespearean comedy—with characters like Leonora Stern and James Blackadder pairing up in the most unlikely combinations. Every mystery raised in the course of the novel has been solved, except for one final fact which cannot be gleaned from the scholars' textual analysis, and is instead supplied by a third-person narrator in the book's epilogue, "Postscript 1868." Maud and Roland mistakenly assume that Ash had no knowledge of his child, but the postscript tells us that Ash briefly met his daughter during the summer of 1868, taking away a lock of her hair as a keepsake.

Some reviewers criticized the ending of *Possession* for being a little too neat and unrealistic. However, Byatt has said that this artificiality is deliberate. It seems that Byatt intended the novel's clean summation as a reaction against the trend in postwar literature for open-ended narratives, which can be seen, for example, in the French *nouveau roman* which employed a deliberately shapeless narrative form in imitation of the randomness of real life; or in avant-garde postwar novels such as *The French Lieutenant's Woman* (1969) by John Fowles, which offered the reader a choice of three alternate endings. In *The French Lieutenant's Woman*, Fowles told the story of a love affair in Victorian England, but deliberately disrupted the story line and frustrated his readers' expectations because he believed that it was not possible or desirable to write realist narrative in the late twentieth century. Byatt's more traditional happy ending is no less self-conscious than Fowles's was, but importantly, it recognizes the pleasure that the reader finds in reaching a conclusion.

The postscript of *Possession*, which is provided specifically to satisfy the reader's narrative expectations, at first sight looks as if it would not be out of place at the end of a Victorian realist novel. However, on closer inspection, this last episode seems to have a somewhat hallucinogenic quality about it. The grass is so green it seems "enamelled," the butterflies are so plentiful they form "a cloud" around the poet as he walks through the meadow, and "all the summer flowers" are blooming in "great abundance" (p. 508). However, most of the flowers mentioned here only blossom in the warmer months of June or July, and we are told that it is only May. This is not a mistake on Byatt's part; rather, this English meadow is a knowingly artificial paradise, conveyed in the mannered style of a medieval romance. It reminds the reader that fiction is not so much an imitation of life as an enhanced, perfected version of life. Endings, conclusions, and indeed any narrative shapes are always artificial, yet they are exactly what literature can provide us with and real life can't—and here lies the true pleasure of reading.

REALISM AND ROMANCE

At first glance, the most prominent narrative mode of *Possession* is realism, mainly because Byatt is adept at creating a sense of the physical world, but does this mean that we can call *Possession* a realist novel? Like many abstract literary terms, *realism* is extremely tricky to define. While it has sometimes been described as a naive narrative mode, which attempts to use language in an entirely neutral way in order to provide a window on reality; in the context of *Possession*, realism can be seen as an imaginative re-creation of experiences, images, sensations, tastes, and smells that the reader will be able to relate to his or her own experience of life. A passage of third-person commentary in chapter 26 draws the reader's attention to the peculiar illusion created by the text, which is essentially "papery and dry," and unconnected to the physical world; and yet "It is possible for a writer to make, or remake at least, for a reader, the primary pleasures of eating, or drinking, or looking on, or sex" (p. 470).

Possession aims to remake several such "primary pleasures" for the reader. Many of the

scenes described in the book are intended to be visually striking; such as the glittering waterfall seen by Maud and Roland in Yorkshire, where refracted light creates "flames of white light" along the cavern walls (p. 265); or Roland's first impressions of Maud Bailey in her crisp green-and-white clothing and peacock-colored silk turban (p. 38). Maud's association with the color green (she also has a green car and a "chill green glassy" bathroom in her Lincoln home) is so insistent that it does invite some kind of symbolic explanation; it both hints at a brightness and boldness of character, and links her to the mythical mermaid created by her ancestor Christabel LaMotte. However, there is also a sense in which such details are employed purely for the aesthetic enjoyment of the reader. Byatt often employs a painterly vocabulary in the attempt to evoke precise shades of color, such as in the rocks at Boggle Hole, "a soot-black, a sulfur-gold, a chalky grey," or Christabel LaMotte's eyes, "green, glass-green, malachite green" (p. 277).

Other "primary pleasures" can be found in Byatt's descriptions of food, which are plentiful and gratuitous: for example, the meal Maud offers to Roland when he visits Lincoln is precisely described, "potted shrimps, omelette and green salad, some Bleu de Bresse and a bowl of sharp apples" (p. 52), as is the pale, chilled pudding that Roland becomes "addicted" to when he and Maud are searching for clues in France, "a white island of foam floating in a creamy yellow pool of vanilla custard, haunted by the ghost, no more, of sweetness" (p. 425). Such descriptive passages invite the reader to imagine a physical sensation, such as the taste of a dessert that melts on the tongue; or a bowl of apples that are distinctly sharp and green, not sweet and red. Byatt's writing is consistently sensuous, even when she is describing unpleasant things, such as the olfactory oppressiveness of the British Museum basement, where "the air smelt of metal, dust, metal-dust and burning plastic" (p. 299), and Roland's impressions of his unappealing home:

The Putney basement was silent, sensuously entangled with the BM [British Museum] basement by its feline reek. Winter was darkly coming, and dark stains and some sort of slow form of creeping life had appeared on the walls. It was hard to heat. There was no central heating, and Roland and Val had supplemented their one gas fire with paraffin stoves, so that the smell of petrol mingled with the smells of cat and mild mould.

(p. 123)

The portions of narrative involving Roland and his live-in girlfriend, Val, are treated in a style that might be described as "gritty realism" or perhaps even "tragicomedy"; their soured relationship, drab lifestyle, and nasty accommodation, are described by Byatt with an eye for detail and comic irony. We are told that the couple met "at a Freshers' tea party" at university, and have "never not been together" since this time; facts which suggest that the relationship is fulfilled and contented. But this is not so—it soon becomes clear that Roland and Val have long outgrown each other's company, and continue to live together out of habit more than anything else. Their domestic discord is described in exact and often humorous detail. As the main breadwinner, Val feels taken for granted by Roland, and takes revenge by making emasculating and scornful remarks about his career prospects. On his part, Roland no longer feels any passion for his girlfriend, and can only get sexually aroused by imagining Ellen Ash "voluminously clothed" in her Victorian bodice and skirts (p. 126). Far from being jealous when other men pay attention to his girlfriend, he secretly wishes that somebody else would step in and take her off his hands. If *Possession* was a realist novel, this depressing scenario would be unlikely to change except, perhaps, for the worst. But, as is clearly stated in the novel's subtitle, *Possession* is intended to be "A Romance." But what exactly is a romance, and how might we expect it to differ from a realist novel?

Byatt indicates what she might mean by the label romance in one of the novel's epigraphs, a quotation from Nathaniel Hawthorne's *The House of the Seven Gables* (1851): "When a writer calls his work a Romance, it need hardly be observed that he wishes to claim a certain latitude, both as to its fashion and material, which he would not have felt himself entitled to assume, had he professed to be writing a Novel." This epigraph makes explicit the fact that *Possession* is no realist novel, governed by the laws of probability, but a tale in which nothing is impossible, in which anything can happen.

As with realism, it is difficult to provide a comprehensive definition of *romance*. Most English-speaking people would probably associate the term with a lowbrow literature of the Harlequin variety. This is correct, but the pulp romance is only one manifestation of what is in fact a very wide and elastic genre, which finds its origins in the medieval chivalric romance. The chivalric romance typically depicts a knight errant embarking on a quest to find a holy grail, and encountering marvelous challenges and adventures on the way. Modern-day variants of the romance include the gothic horror novel, the detective thriller, and the science fiction novel, as well as the familiar formulaic love story. (A comprehensive account of the romance can be found in Gillian Beer's 1970 study, *The Romance*). All these types of fiction tend to incorporate a large element of fantasy: the romance mirrors our inner desires rather than our experience of "real life," and hence has considerable escapist value for the reader.

In *Possession*, Byatt explores many different aspects of this multifaceted genre. Most obviously, the novel imitates the traditional love romance with its depiction of the passionate affair between the Victorian poets. In addition, *Possession* features a modern-day variation on the chivalric quest plot in which the hero Roland Michell (who has a medieval namesake in the Childe Roland of legend) is engaged in "the tiresome and bewitching endlessness of the quest for knowledge" (p. 7). At points this quest seems to get sidetracked into the episodic, wandering narrative form typical of the medieval romance, such as the episode in which the characters travel to Brittany in France and get distracted from their tasks by the pleasant scenery and the good food. Being a literary type of person, Roland himself is not unaware of these parallels between his story and the romance, and often muses about their significance:

> He was in a Romance, a vulgar and a high Romance simultaneously; a Romance was one of the systems that controlled him, as the expectations of Romance control almost everyone in the Western world, for better or worse, at some point or another.
>
> He supposed the Romance must give way to social realism, even if the aesthetic temper of the time was against it.
>
> (p. 425)

Roland holds a down-to-earth, slightly pessimistic attitude toward his fate: when things are going well he expects them to go wrong again. Indeed, the traditional realist novel often has this sort of narrative shape, which demonstrates how reality fails to live up to people's hopes and expectations (a classic example would be Gustave Flaubert's 1857 novel *Madame Bovary*). Realistically, Roland has no hope of winning the heart of a woman like Maud:

> Maud was a beautiful woman such as he had no claim to possess. She had a secure job and an international reputation. Moreover, in some dark and outdated English social system of class, which he did not believe in, but felt obscurely working and gripping him, Maud was County, and he was urban lower-middle- class, in some places more, in some places less acceptable than Maud, but in almost all incompatible.
>
> (p. 425)

Roland is intellectually suspicious of romance, regarding it as a set of narrative conventions, or even as a controlling ideological "system," which tricks people into hoping for the impossible. In the contemporary world, no one seems to believe in romance any more: compared with their passionate and spontaneous Victorian counterparts, Roland and Maud's attitude toward relationships seems cold and calculating. Both are primarily obsessed with safeguarding their own personal space, are keen on the idea of "celibacy as the new volupté" (p. 271), and enjoy imagining the rather sterile image of "a clean empty bed in a clean empty room" (p. 267) The problem with Roland and Maud is that they are too cerebral and knowing for their own good; they seem to have killed passion with theoretical analysis: "They were children of a time and culture which mistrusted love, 'in love,' romantic love, romance *in toto*, and which nevertheless in revenge proliferated sexual language, linguistic sexuality, analysis, dissection, deconstruction, exposure" (p. 423).

Roland and Maud can't believe in romance, because they view the world through a web of twentieth-century theories which undermine traditional concepts of romantic love. Their first obstacle is psychoanalytic theory, which seems to have robbed sexual love of its mystique. Both Maud and Roland feel slightly battered by the relentless discourse of sex and sexual symbolism that surrounds them, and Maud's ex-lover Fergus Wollf seems to have put her off sex entirely with his fondness for quoting psychoanalytic theory: "He used to quote Freud at me at six in the morning. *Analysis Terminable and Interminable.* He got up very early. He used to *prance around* the flat—with nothing on—quoting Freud saying that 'at no point in one's analytic work does one suffer more from a suspicion that one has been preaching to the winds than when one is trying to persuade a woman to abandon her wish for a penis'" (p. 271).

Another threat to romantic love comes from poststructuralist theories which question traditional notions of the self. The work of French theorists like Michel Foucault and Jacques Derrida describe the human subject as a construction of the larger social and linguistic structures in which they operate, without essence or soul. But if the self is merely "a crossing-place for a number of systems, all loosely connected" (p. 424), as Roland tends to believe, if people have no essential "character," then how is love possible?

Maud and Roland deal with their ambivalent feelings about love by not talking about it, and trying to ignore the hints that indicate that their working relationship is developing into a romance. When they bump into each other at the bathroom door at Seal Court they experience the "kick galvanic" of physical attraction (p. 147), but remain silent. Later on, their fact-finding missions to Yorkshire and Brittany are arranged with the secrecy of lovers' trysts, but they avoid taking up the romantic opportunities these provide, determined to avoid the cliché of "falling in love" (p. 422). When the couple do eventually spend the night together in Brittany, Roland merely curls up to sleep against Maud's back, a picture of innocence. Eventually, this being a romance, both must succumb to their fate—but even the consummation of their love is described in a slightly ironic, mannered way which seems to reflect their feelings that love is an outmoded concept: "very slowly and with infinite gentle delays and delicate diversions and variations of indirect assault Roland finally, to use an outdated phrase, entered and took possession of all her white coolness" (p. 507). But love still has the power to solve and satisfy, despite the current cultural climate. The climax of Byatt's novel, describing the calm after the storm, reveals that *Possession*, like the grail myth of medieval romance, is essentially a celebration of fertility and the endless recycling of life: "In the morning, the whole world had a strange new smell. It was the smell of the aftermath, a green smell, a smell of shredded leaves and oozing resin, of crushed wood and splashed sap, a tart smell, which bore some relation to the smell of bitten apples. It was the smell of death and destruction and it smelled fresh and lively and hopeful" (p. 507).

HISTORY AND NATURAL HISTORY

History is clearly a major theme of *Possession*, and in this respect it closely resembles much other British fiction of the 1980s and 1990s. These decades saw the publication of a number of novels concerned with the nature of history, and how we come to know about it; such texts have been described as "historiographic" by critics. Examples of this type of novel include *Chatterton* (1987) by Peter Ackroyd, *Flaubert's Parrot* (1984) by Julian Barnes, and *Waterland* (1983) by Graham Swift. Such novels suggest that our knowledge of historical events (both our personal history and history in general) is only ever partial and indefinite, and that we tend to create fictions to fill the gaps in our knowledge. Seen from this angle, history seems less like a solid and objective record of fact, and more like a collection of stories of dubious provenance and uncertain authenticity. A useful discussion about this distinctly postmodern representation of history in contemporary fiction can be found in Linda Hutcheon's *A Poetics of Postmodernism: History, Theory, Fiction* (1988).

This postmodernist concept of history also informs the plot of *Possession*. To the reader, it often seems as if nothing is certain or solid about history—after all, despite their careful research, Roland and Maud never find out the complete facts about Ash and LaMotte. They wrongly assume that Ash never knew of his child, and that the lock of hair buried with the poet belonged to Christabel LaMotte, when it actually belonged to her daughter Maia. Historical facts are similarly misinterpreted throughout the novel. Feminist scholars have deduced that LaMotte must have been a lesbian, because she lived in an unusual domestic arrangement with her female friend Blanche Glover. However, the truth of the situation was clearly more complex than this; so perhaps this is a case of modern academics fictionalizing history, by inaccurately imposing their twentieth-century ideas and ideologies onto the past.

Mortimer Cropper is guilty of a similar twentieth-century complacency. He has written the definitive biography of Randolph Henry Ash, called *The Great Ventriloquist*. As part of Cropper's scrupulous biographical research, he has retraced all of Ash's journeys so that he could experience what Ash experienced and discover minor facts that might otherwise have escaped his attention. As a result, the extracts of Cropper's biography which appear in *Possession* are written in a confident, authoritative tone, and are often convincingly detailed. For example, Cropper seems to have access to the most intimate moments of the Ashes' honeymoon in Southern France, even describing a "charming gesture" in which Ash lifted his new wife onto a rock in the middle of the stream at the Fontaine de Vaucluse: "We may imagine her sitting there, smiling demurely under her bonnet, holding her skirts away from the wet, whilst Randolph contemplated his possession, so unlike Petrach's, of the lady he had worshipped from afar" (p. 109). But what seems to be a true and complete picture of the couple's marriage turns out to be flawed: Ash is not quite the gallant knight described by Cropper, content to sublimate his libido into pure poetry; and later on in the novel we discover that Ellen was not actually "smiling demurely" during this episode, as Cropper had guessed, but was feeling uncomfortable and "afraid" of the rushing water (p. 449). Despite his rigorous scholarship, Cropper has not managed to grasp what was really important to Ash and Ellen; it seems that discovering the whole truth about a person's life is more difficult than he imagines. It is Maud Bailey's opinion that, in a biography, "you will always get a sense that there's something missing" (p. 89), a comment that the author of *Possession* appears to agree with.

However, while expressing some postmodern doubts about history's epistemological uncertainties, *Possession* appears to refute more extreme theories which suggest that history is a mere textual construct. There are three points in *Possession* where an omniscient third-person narrator steps in to reveal information that was never recorded, and thus cannot be known by the twentieth-century scholars. The first is in chapter 15, which describes the experiences of the Victorian lovers in Yorkshire; the second is in chapter 25, when Ellen Ash's version of events is conveyed; and the third is in the postscript, which describes the meeting of Ash and his daughter Maia. This third-person narrator tells us that "there are things that happen and leave no discernible trace, are not spoken or written of, though it would be very wrong to say that subsequent events go on indifferently, all the same, as though such things had never been" (p. 508). Those readers familiar with George Eliot might notice a turn of phrase here similar to the ending of *Middlemarch* (1871–1872), where the narrator comments that "the growing good of the world is partly dependent on unhistoric acts; and that things are not so ill with you and me as they might have been, is half owing to the number who lived faithfully a hidden life, and rest in unvisited tombs." Like *Middlemarch*, *Possession* takes an interest in the unrecorded part of history: what was not said and not written, but can be imaginatively re-created through fiction.

This sort of unspoken history is illustrated by Ellen Ash's mysterious diary. Beatrice Nest's slow progress in editing the diary has become legendary in academic circles. A footnote to Cropper's 1967 biography, *The Great Ventriloquist* that says the journal will be published "shortly," is a small hint that the project is currently running two decades late. But it gradually becomes apparent that Beatrice is not merely incompetent, but befuddled by Ellen's deliberate evasiveness; Beatrice has become swallowed up in her labyrinthine riddles. Ellen has not been honest or open in her diaries, intending them to act like a "smoke screen" to conceal painful domestic truths from the prying eyes of future biographers. In chapter 25 of *Possession*, Ellen's motives become a little clearer to the reader. It seems that her diaries are true to character; as in life Ellen's nature "was profoundly implicated in not knowing, in silence, in avoidance" (p. 494). Rather than confront her husband when Blanche Glover reveals information about his affair, Ellen keeps quiet and resolves in her diary to maintain a facade of normality (p.232). Even when Ash makes a confession to his wife, she avoids discussing the topic, preferring to tolerate her husband's misdemeanors in silence: "Let us not talk of it again" (p. 455).

Ellen's extraordinary silence is tied up with feelings of shame and guilt so overwhelming that she cannot articulate them, even to herself. We are told that she remembers her honeymoon as a series of images: "She did not remember it in words. There were no words attached to it, that was part of the horror. She had never spoken of it to anyone, not even to Randolph, precisely not to Randolph" (p. 458). These images suggest that the honeymoon was fraught with tension, and that the marriage to Ash was never consummated. Ellen has made herself into the perfect, dutiful wife in an attempt to alleviate the guilt she feels over her sexual inadequacies, and in the process has effectively erased her real self from history. Ellen's true voice is never heard until the narrator of *Possession* steps in to retrieve it.

Ellen likes to compare her secret life to the crystalline formations described by the Victorian geologist Charles Lyell: "these hard, crystalline things, which were formed in intense heat, beneath the 'habitable surface' of the earth, and were not primeval monuments but 'part of the living language of nature'" (p. 458). Such events, though unrecorded and unnoticed, are still real, and form the foundations of everyday life. Ellen's metaphor is one of "natural history," a concept which was current in the Victorian age: during the nineteenth century, scientific theories of the sort which fascinated Randolph Henry Ash provided exciting new accounts of the earth's prerecorded history. For example, Charles Darwin's *On the Origin of Species* (1859) described the theory of evolution by natural selection, and Lyell's *Principles of Geology* (1830–1833) argued that the layers of rock which form the earth's crust were gradually formed over millions of years. It seems that in *Possession* this idea of a rock-solid natural history is set against the history of textual interpretations that concerns the postmodern theorists. Another version of natural history which is explored in the novel, albeit one unknown to the Victorians, is the genetic history of living creatures. While Ellen Ash has attempted to bury the textual history of Ash and LaMotte, it still lives on in the world, inscribed in Maud Bailey's DNA: Maud incorporates the physical features of both of her famous ancestors—LaMotte's blond hair and Ash's width of brow. Such natural histories exist—and are real—regardless of any human ability to read and understand them.

Another paradigm of history which *Possession* considers is the idea of history as circular. Significantly, the book in which Roland finds the letters that begin his quest is Giambattista Vico's *New Science*. Vico was an Italian philosopher of the eighteenth century, who believed that civilizations rose and fell in evolutionary cycles. Instead of seeing history as a linear progression, with humans attaining ever higher degrees of civilization, this work described history as cyclical and repetitive. Likewise, in *Possession* history is shown to repeat itself in various ways. The love affair of Maud and Roland is like an echo (although a paler imitation perhaps) of that enjoyed by Ash and LaMotte. The idea of circular history also helps explain some ironic coincidences in the novel's plot—it is when Maud and Roland decide to take a day off from their investigations in Yorkshire that they actually get closest to Ash and LaMotte, as it later transpires that the Victorian couple had made an identical but unrecorded trip to Boggle Hole in the summer of 1859. The jet brooch which Maud uses to fasten her turban is most likely a brooch given by Ash to LaMotte during their trip to Whitby. Such repetitions and echoes of the past add to the novel's sense of a living history; it seems as if the past is never dead, but continues to live on in the present.

PASTICHE

Perhaps the most striking stylistic feature in *Possession* is Byatt's frequent use of pastiche—texts which imitate the style of Victorian poems, letters, and diaries, or works of contemporary biography and criticism. Most of the chapters begin with a suggestive extract from one of the works of Ash or LaMotte, which introduce or echo narrative themes and present clues, or sometimes even red herrings, about the Victorian past. These capture the nineteenth-century idiom so well that it is sometimes easy to forget that Ash and LaMotte are characters created by Byatt, and not real Victorian poets. However, it is possible to detect some historical figures that Byatt may have used as models for her fictional authors.

Ash, with his vast range of intellectual interests and remarkable creative energy, clearly resembles the poet Robert Browning, and like Browning, Ash is fond of writing dramatic monologues—poems spoken in the first-person voice of an imagined character. There are also hints of Alfred, Lord Tennyson in the diction and rhythms of some of Ash's mythic poetry. LaMotte's reclusive lifestyle, and her domestic themes, echo those of the poet Christina Rossetti; while her fiercer, more passionate poems, punctuated by dashes and exclamations, are reminiscent of the work of Emily Dickinson. In addition, some parts of her epic poem *The Fairy Melusina* echo the romantic imaginings of Keats in "The Eve of Saint Agnes."

In one sense these poems are like a patchwork of voices from the past; and yet they are equally Byatt's original creations. In *Possession*, Randolph Henry Ash is described as "The Great Ventriloquist" because of his fondness for the dramatic monologue—a description that might equally apply to A. S. Byatt herself. Byatt has described the process of writing the poems as being like method acting, and has said that she had to put herself "in character" in order to write them.

Byatt's Victorian poems and letters cannot be described as parodies, as they have no satirical intent; but neither are they shallow imitations, whose purpose is merely to add a little historical color to the story. They represent an attempt both to revive the rhythms of Victorian language, and to fully engage with the intellectual history of the period.

This might be illustrated by looking at the Ash-LaMotte correspondence which is presented at length in chapter 10. While the letters fulfill a useful narrative function, relating the story of the developing relationship in the style of an epistolary novel, they also provide a fascinating insight into some of the ideas and issues that preoccupied the Victorians. Readers interested in finding out more about these topics will find many of the references elucidated in Byatt's essay "Robert Browning: Fact, Fiction, Lies, Incarnation and Art" in her book *Passions of the Mind* (1991).

The poets share many common interests, including literature, mythology, science, and nature. Popular science was greeted with both enthusiasm and alarm by the Victorians, as it undermined the traditional belief structures of Christian society. LaMotte has written some poems about insect life (p. 157), and Ash himself plans to write a poem on the Dutch biologist Jan Swammerdam, "who discovered in Holland the optic glass which revealed to us the endless reaches and ceaseless turmoil of the infinitely small just as the great Galileo turned his optic tube on the majestic motions of the planets and beyond them the silent spheres of the infinitely great" (p. 158). Such an interest in insect life and minute organisms highlights a growing sense in this era that life was more complex and polymorphous than had been previously assumed, and that human beings were not necessarily at the center of creation, as the Bible taught. In an extract from "Swammerdam," Ash explicitly invokes this anxious sense of Man being displaced "from the just centre of the sum of things" (p. 209). The biblical world order was dealt a further blow by Darwin's theory of natural selection, which painted a disturbing new picture of nature as an evolving, autonomous, and often destructive force. It is this uncomfortable sense of life as chaotic and random that seems to inform Ash's "atheistic and diabolically despairing" poem *Ragnarök* (p. 9). *Ragnarök* is based on an episode from Norse mythology, describing the battle at the end of the world in which the giants and gods are destroyed and the natural order consumed by chaos. This could indeed be seen as a metaphor for current intellectual developments.

The poets' interest in mythology is another faithful reflection of the period, as it was a popular area of academic inquiry in the nineteenth century. While Ash has shown an interest in Norse mythology, Christabel writes about her plans for a "Fairy Epic" based on ancient French folklore. It seems that her choice of topic has been influenced by her father, Isodore LaMotte, who has gathered and recorded the oral tales of Brittany, rather like the Brothers Grimm did in Germany. At this time it was thought that collecting the ancient tales of folklore was both a way of preserving oral culture and of charting the origins of European culture and racial character. However, the new scientific approach toward mythology also came to be applied to the Bible, leading some scholars to question its factual basis. The German materialist philosopher Ludwig Feuerbach (whose work is to be found on Ash's bookshelf) shocked contemporary readers by reinterpreting the Bible as an elaborate folk myth, and suggesting that God was a projection of man's desires.

Naturally enough, the poets touch on the growing crisis of religious faith in this era. LaMotte tells Ash, "Your great poem *Ragnarök* was the occasion of quite the worst crisis in the life of my simple religious faith," having detected parallels drawn between the Bible and Norse myth: "It seemed to me you made Holy Scripture no more than another Wonder Tale" (p. 160). Ash himself is ambivalent about his religious beliefs, and admits that he does not know whether, when he writes on biblical topics, he is "lending life to truth with my fiction—or verisimilitude to a colossal Lie" (p. 168).

Related to this crisis in faith was a growing interest in spiritualism in the nineteenth century. In one of her letters, LaMotte mentions that she has attended some séances with her friend Blanche Glover, and appears to be receptive to the idea of psychic phenomenon. In her essay on Robert Browning, Byatt suggests that spiritualism was the religion of a materialist age; with the traditional foundations of faith seeming increasingly insecure, Victorians wanted to touch and see physical evidence for the spirit world. *Possession* contains an extract from the autobiography of the fictional Victorian medium Hella Lees called *The Shadowy Portal*, which describes a séance disrupted by Randolph Henry Ash. The reader may deduce that the unnamed lady whom Ash upsets is Christabel LaMotte, attempting to come to terms with Blanche's suicide: although it seems as if Ash has mistakenly assumed that LaMotte is trying to make contact with their dead child. Ash's mistrust of spiritualism is later documented in his letter to Priscilla Penn Cropper (pp. 103–105) and in his poem "Mummy Possest" (pp. 418–429), another pastiche monologue which is similar in style and theme to Robert Browning's "Mr. Sludge."

FAIRY TALES

Among its various pastiche narratives, *Possession* contains several examples of the folk or fairy tale; two are written by Christabel La-Motte, and one is supposedly a transcription of an oral tale told by Sabine de Kercoz's nurse-maid Gode. Clearly, LaMotte's children's book *Tales Told in November* is an extension of her interest in Breton myth; but these tales, as well as giving us a sense of LaMotte's dry humor, also seem to be saying things about the nature of narrative.

"The Glass Coffin," which Roland reads during his stay with Maud in Lincoln, is not a traditional fairy tale, but has been invented by Byatt using some of the recurring themes that characterize such tales; such as the forest setting, the system of rewards for good behavior, the shape-shifting animals and magical gifts, and the tasks that must be successfully completed by the resourceful hero in order to achieve a happy ending. However, the tale is clearly too self-conscious of itself as a tale to be taken for the genuine article: it is characterized by a twentieth-century metafictional tone. For example, when the man of the forest offers the little tailor three items to choose from, the tailor knows that the purse and pot are likely to have magical properties because he has heard fairy tales before and understands their narrative conventions. Often in fairy tales, the gift with the least obvious value turns out to be that with the most benefit, and so it is here: the glass key takes the tailor on an adventure, which leads to him rescuing an enchanted princess asleep in a glass coffin, another typical scenario. However, the convention that the princess will marry her rescuer is treated in a very ironic fashion. Instead of taking his reward for granted, the little tailor remarks, "Why you should have me, simply because I opened the glass case, is less clear to me altogether, and when, and if, you are restored to your rightful place, and your home and lands and people are again your own, I trust you will feel free to reconsider the matter, and remain, if you will, alone and unwed" (p. 66). LaMotte's story of the glass coffin turns out to have a feminist twist that is rather before its time. It is like one of Angela Carter's twentieth-century feminist rewritings of fairy tales, such as can be found in *The Bloody Chamber* (1979), which delight in bending the rules of the tale and foiling the reader's expectations. It is easy to see why LaMotte, whose life as a Victorian woman is as governed by conventions and prohibitions as the plot of a fairy tale, might be attracted to this sort of imaginative rule-breaking.

By drawing attention to the narrative conventions of the fairy tale, Byatt also encourages the reader to detect similar narrative patterns within the main text of the novel. Shortly after Roland reads "The Glass Coffin," he is involved in a fairy tale adventure of his own. While visiting Christabel LaMotte's grave the next day, Roland comes across an elderly lady whose wheelchair has slipped from the path, and helps her back to safety. As in a fairy tale, this act of kindness is rewarded by a positive turn of fate, as the damsel in distress turns out to be Lady Joan Bailey, one of the "Lincolnshire Baileys" that Maud's branch of the Bailey family have little contact with. This chance introduction gives Maud and Roland access to Seal Court, which would have been otherwise unobtainable, and thus enables the equally serendipitous discovery of the letters in the doll's cot. Certainly, the plot of *Possession* often creates a feeling of inevitability or necessity that is very like the operation of fate in a fairy tale.

Roland himself is a small, nimble, and resourceful hero, rather like the little tailor in "The Glass Coffin," and his fate leads him to a similarly happy ending. Roland's good fortune is threefold, echoing the three wishes commonly granted in fairy tales. First, he wins the heart of Maud, who, in working at the top of a white-tiled tower in Lincoln University, somewhat resembles a princess in an ivory tower—especially to Roland, who thinks of her as out of his class and untouchable. (At other times it seems that Maud is a reluctant Rapunzel, although she does finally let down her hair at Roland's request.) Roland's life is transformed in two more ways: while he does not get to edit the Ash-LaMotte correspondence, his career is unexpectedly boosted by three job offers, from universities in Amsterdam, Barcelona, and Hong Kong. And finally, after years of uninspiring academic hack work and stifling literary theory,

Roland finds that he has magically gained the ability to write poetry.

LANGUAGE AND METAPHOR

Like most of Byatt's fiction, *Possession* is shaped by recurring metaphors that thread their way through the text, linking disparate objects and events into a whole system of meaning. One example of this technique can be illustrated by a consideration of the different possible interpretations of the novel's title. Possession could describe the effect of narrative curiosity which impels Roland to steal the letters he finds in Ash's book. Possession also clearly has a sexual connotation, as the lovers are seized by the demonic possession of love and long to possess the object of their desire. Ash insists that he respects his lover's freedom; "He *knew* her, he believed. He would teach her that she was not his possession, he would show her she was free" (p. 279), but ends up chasing LaMotte to Brittany, and to the fateful séance with Mrs. Lees, in a manner which suggests he is not prepared to let her slip from his grasp. Similarly, Fergus Wolff is jealous of Maud's new relationship with Roland because, he says, "I have an interest in Maud" (p. 302).

Obviously, possession can also be understood as the acquisition and ownership of material objects. The issue of who owns the letters, and who they should belong to, is a theme which runs throughout the novel, complicated by issues of patriotism, propriety, and legal technicalities (as the lawyer Toby Byng explains, under British law the ownership of the physical manuscripts and the ownership of the copyrights are in different hands). The most acquisitive character in the novel is Mortimer Cropper, who intends to buy the letters for his Stant Collection, based in New Mexico. In his spectacular "hi-tech" lecture, Cropper argues that in the electronic age the physical possession of the letters is unimportant: he presents a hologram image of a snuffbox in The Stant Collection, claiming that "Everything can be everywhere,

our culture can be, is, worldwide" (p. 386). However, his comments seem disingenuous in the light of his mania for collecting Ash memorabilia. Cropper is so keen to possess letters written by Ash that he has invented a portable photocopying machine to make illicit copies of those that cannot by acquired by legal means. In chapter 6, Cropper visits the home of an elderly lady named Daisy Wapshott, and makes secret copies of a letter in her bathroom. The comic image of Cropper sitting on the toilet undermines the air of refinement created by his silk pajamas and velvet slippers, and hints that his acquisitiveness is "anal retentive" in a Freudian sense.

The frequent references to the Victorian craze for spiritualism and séances in the novel further suggest the idea of spiritual possession, or of the dead speaking through the living. Roland Michell, Mortimer Cropper, and James Blackadder could all be said to be possessed by the dead poet to whom they devote their working lives: at times these scholars seem to be so absorbed by their research, they almost seem to be living vicariously though Ash. Cropper surrounds himself with Ash's effects; "Mortimer Cropper was in the habit of drawing Randolph Henry Ash's large gold watch from an inner fob pocket, and arranging his time by Ash's timepiece" (p. 23). Blackadder thinks his mind is "primed" with Ash's thought, to the extent that he cannot have any original ideas for himself—we are told that, in a rare moment of creative inspiration, Blackadder has considered writing a poem which uses owl-pellets as a metaphor for history, only to find that the polymath Ash has already written such a poem (p. 29). Roland defines himself in terms of his work at the "Ash Factory," a research group dedicated to producing a definitive edition of the poet's work. Roland has pictures of Randolph Henry Ash on his desk at home, rather than photos of his family or girlfriend as one might expect. In the London library, his search through Ash's copy of Vico is described as "recuperating a dead man's reading." (Indeed, Vico's idea that history repeats itself is hovering around the margins of this scene, providing an ironic comment on Roland's activities.) The laborious drudgery of academic research does not seem to be at all fulfilling for Ash's disciples: the novel suggests that these characters, in compulsively pursuing a ghostly version of Ash's life, are not really fulfilling their own.

Thus a range of different narrative strands and themes are all tied up together through the pervasive metaphor of "possession." This is a highly contrived conceptual scheme, of the sort that Byatt seems to delight in creating in her fiction, and which sometimes provokes a hostile response from her critics. However, in *Possession*, Byatt implicitly argues the legitimacy of this approach, by showing the reader how human beings naturally and inevitably use metaphor as a way of understanding the world.

This way of thinking is particularly apparent in the pastiches of contemporary academic language that Byatt inserts into her text. Leonora Stern's interpretations of LaMotte's poetry, for example, are saturated with Freudian metaphor, and every detail of landscape is perceived to be a sexual symbol (p. 245). Although this critical obsession with sex seems to exasperate Byatt, and is to some extent the target of her satire, there is a sense that, like it or not, in the post- Freudian age such sexual metaphors cannot be ignored. There is no such thing as a purely objective observation of the world, it seems, as human beings are a product of their time and historical mindset: "Roland laid aside Leonora Stern with a small sigh. He had a vision of the land they were to explore, covered with sucking human orifices and knotted human body-hair. He did not like this vision, and yet, a child of his time, found it compelling, somehow guaranteed to be significant, as a geological survey of the oolite would not be. Sexuality was like thick smoked glass; everything took on the same blurred tint through it" (p. 246). At Filey Brigg, a discussion with Maud involving verbal play on the image of gloves, provokes an exasperated outburst from Roland:

> Do you never have the sense that our metaphors *eat up* our world? I mean of course everything connects and connects—all the time—and I suppose one studies—I study—literature because all these connections seem both endlessly exciting and then in some sense dangerously powerful—as though we held a clue to the true nature of things? I mean, all those gloves, a minute ago, we were playing a professional game of hooks and eyes—mediaeval gloves, giants' gloves, Blanche Glover, Balzac's gloves, the sea-anemone's ovaries—and it all reduced like boiling jam to—human sexuality. Just as Leonora Stern makes the whole earth read as the female body—and language—all language. And all vegetation is pubic hair.
>
> (p. 253)

However, as Roland realizes, making analogies is part of the academic game, and is not just a feature of twentieth-century thought—even Ash used the metaphor of a glove to try and understand the way in which sea anemones function. It seems as if the human mind instinctively creates metaphors in order to understand the world, and people of all eras impose their own matrix of meaning onto the diverse and chaotic phenomena that surrounds them.

WOMEN AND FEMINISM

On the surface of things, Byatt does not appear to be sympathetic toward feminism. In *Possession*, feminist theory is frequently satirized, and feminist characters like Leonora Stern are presented with a large splash of caricature. In the Women's Studies block at Lincoln University, the language of feminism is rather archly imitated in the posters on the walls: "Come and see the Sorcieres, the Vamps, the daughters of Kali and the Fatae Morganae. We'll make your blood run cold and make you laugh on the Sinister side of your face at Women's Wit and Wickedness" (p. 48). The way that Byatt flatly inserts these portentous boasts into the text without quotation marks creates an effect of deadpan irony, which makes the comic potential of these "Daughters of Kali" seem highly suspect. There is a sense that these hard-line feminists take themselves too seriously and overstate their politics; and that feminist theory, in its more extreme forms, borders on self-parody. Leonora Stern's book *Motif and Matrix in the Poems of LaMotte* is a pastiche of the "gynocentric" criticism of feminist theorists like Hélène Cixous, who argue that women "write from the body":

> This may all be read as a symbol of female language, which is partly suppressed, partly self-communing, dumb before the intrusive male and not able to speak out. The male fountain spurts and springs. Mélusine's fountain has a *female* wetness, trickling out from its pool rather than rising confidently, thus mirroring those female secretions which are not inscribed in our daily use of language (*langue,* tongue)—the sputum, mucus, milk and bodily fluids of women who are silent for dryness.
>
> (p. 245)

Byatt gently pokes fun at the whole idea of *écriture feminine,* or feminist criticism, as such theories seem to reinforce historical gender stereotypes, which describe men as essentially cerebral and women as more earthy and fleshy creatures. In her letters to Ash, we can see that Christabel LaMotte is an intellectual person, who finds great satisfaction in the life of the mind—as Byatt herself does.

However, despite the occasional dig at women's studies and feminist theory in *Possession,* the novel's deep concern with historical inequality, the problem of women's expression, and their fulfillment as individuals, creates a feminist ethos. Underlying the novel's surface exuberance is a recurring theme of disappointed women, thwarted ambitions, and restricted lives. The portions of narrative set in the Victorian era reveal the very limited range of lifestyle choices open to women at this time. Beatrice Nest's critical study of Ellen Ash and Jane Carlyle, entitled

Helpmeets, typifies the role of women in Victorian society: regardless of their own personal talents or personalities, the wives of great men are only defined in terms of their helpfulness to their husband. Ellen Ash's inferiority complex and hero-worship of her husband preclude any possibility of their marriage being an equal partnership, and yet one senses that this situation has not been brought about by Ash himself, but rather by the complex web of social convention that governed people's lives at this time. In her diary, Ellen Ash writes about how her role as Ash's helpmate has thwarted her own moderate poetic ambitions:

> But I now think—it might have been better, might it not, to have held on to the desire to be a Poet? I could *never* write as well as Randolph, but then no one can or could, and so it was perhaps not worth considering as an objection to doing something.
>
> Perhaps if I had made his life more difficult, he would have written less, or less freely. I cannot claim to be the midwife to genius, but if I have not *facilitated,* I have at least not, as many women might have done, *prevented.* This is a very small virtue to claim, a very negative achievement to hang my whole life on.
>
> (p. 122)

The twentieth-century editor of Ellen's diaries, Beatrice Nest, feels similarly thwarted in her career. Although not encumbered by the rigid conventions of the nineteenth century, she has arrived in academia a little too early to benefit from the women's liberation movement. We are told that Beatrice embarked on a scholarly career after she "fell in love with Randolph Henry Ash" at university, but that her real passions and interests were promptly sidelined by the academic establishment. Instead of studying Ash, she finds herself editing his wife's journals, a "modestly useful" undertaking suitable for a woman (p. 144). Beatrice is marginalized by the men in her department at Prince Albert College, and when she ages into the role of a confirmed spinster, by the women too: "Those girls in the 1950s and 1960s had thought of her as motherly. Later generations had assumed she was lesbian, even, ideologically, that she was a repressed and unregenerate lesbian" (pp. 116). As she ages, Beatrice feels a growing sense of "irrelevance" and isolation: "When she was past a certain age, what had been read as benign was read, equally arbitrarily, as threatening and repressive" (p. 117). Indeed, Roland, Blackadder, and Cropper all seem to regard Beatrice primarily as a nuisance. Other women of Beatrice's generation are similarly frustrated: we are told that Roland's mother was "a disappointed English graduate," who couldn't fulfill her own personal ambitions, and so displaced them on to her son (p. 10). Val's mother, too, is bitterly disappointed with her lot, and drowns her sorrows with alcohol (p. 13).

The all-female community established by Christabel LaMotte and Blanche Glover represents an attempt to escape from the restrictions imposed on women by society. In the past, both women have been discouraged from taking themselves seriously as artists: LaMotte tells how her ambitions were discouraged by a great poet, who told her that her poems "would do well enough to give me an interest in life until I had—I quote him exactly—'sweeter and weightier responsibilities'" (p. 180). Blanche has tried to present her religious paintings to a local church, but they have been rejected, because she is a woman (p. 217). The all-female community that Christabel and Blanche have established creates a space in which they can be who they want to be: It is a fragile environment, which depends on their abstention from contact with the outside world: "It is pointed out to me, quite rightly—that if I am jealous of my freedom to live as I do—and manage my own affairs—and work my work—I must be *more than usually careful* to remain sufficiently respectable in the eyes of the world and his wife" (p. 184). The household is also economically insecure, and barely sustained by Christabel's modest financial resources: when Christabel disappears to Brittany to have her child in secrecy, Blanche is

unable to continue without her assistance, and the household implodes.

Christabel's relationship with Ash upsets this state of independence, although, being a man, Ash never quite fully appreciates its importance. In a riddle she includes in one of her letters, Christabel warns Ash to keep his distance, an implicit request to the importunate poet to leave her alone: "Shattering an Egg is unworthy of you, no Pass time for men. Think what you would have in your hand if you put forth your Giant strength and crushed the solid stone. Something slippery and cold and unthinkingly disagreeable" (p. 137).

LaMotte does not want to fall in love, and describes it as a necessary evil rather than a pleasant or liberating experience. Her letters to Ash describe the poet as a "salamander" or "Firedrake" (p. 195) whose burning passion will ultimately destroy her. Love diminishes her, threatens her independence and therefore her creativity. Ash breaks into her refuge, and as a result she is forced to reassume the roles that society allocates to women; firstly as a fallen woman with an illegitimate child, and later, after she has given the child to her sister Sophie to raise as her own, as "the spinster aunt who is not loved" (p. 502), a hated and feared "old witch in a turret" (p. 500). At the end of her life, Christabel muses, "I wonder—if I had kept to my closed castle, behind my motte-and-bailey defences—should I have been a great poet—as you are?" (p. 502). There is no way of answering this question, but LaMotte's reputation certainly never reaches the heights obtained by Randolph Henry Ash, and she remains a marginal figure in the history of English literature.

It is only in the contemporary world described by the novel that women are beginning to realize their full creative potential. Maud Bailey shares her ancestor's love of solitude, but enjoys a freedom and autonomy that LaMotte could never experience. In fact, Leonora and Maud are both portrayed as strong and independent women, in control of their own destiny, regardless of their relationship to men, and this happy ending could not have been reached without the feminist movements of the twentieth century. It has been said by some critics that *Possession* is a conservative text (as romances tend to be) that reinforces the traditional idea that all women secretly desire is to be swept off their feet by a handsome man. It has also been said that Byatt favors the Victorian age over the present, and expresses a yearning for its ideals and values. However, such claims should be treated with caution. In *Possession* there is no misty-eyed nostalgia for an age that treated unnamed and unnoticed women like Christabel LaMotte, Blanche Glover, and Ellen Ash so unjustly. As a celebration of female expression, and an attempt to give a voice to those historical women who have not been heard, *Possession* is very much attached to the twentieth century.

Selected Bibliography

A full bibliography of works by and about A. S. Byatt can be found on her official Web site, www.asbyatt.com.

EDITION

Possession: A Romance. London: Chatto and Windus, 1990; New York: Random House, 1990. Page references are to the Chatto and Windus edition. First paperback edition, London: Vintage: 1991; New York: Vintage Books, 1991 (First Vintage International edition).

OTHER WORKS

Shadow of a Sun. London: Chatto and Windus, 1964; New York: Harcourt, Brace, 1964.

Degrees of Freedom: The Early Novels of Iris Murdoch. London: Chatto and Windus, 1965; New York: Barnes and Noble, 1965.

The Game. London: Chatto and Windus, 1967; New York: Scribners, 1968.

Wordsworth and Coleridge in Their Time. London: Nelson, 1970; New York: Crane, Russak, 1973.

The Virgin in the Garden. London: Chatto and Windus, 1978; New York: Knopf, 1979.

Still Life. London: Chatto and Windus, 1985: New York: Scribners, 1985.

Sugar and Other Stories. London: Chatto and Windus, 1987; New York: Scribners, 1987.

"Choices: On the Writing of *Possession*." On the A. S. Byatt official Web site. http://www.asbyatt.com/Posses.htm. 24 September 1999. Originally delivered as a lecture at the Tate Gallery, London, 3 February 1995. Also published as "In the Grip of Possession," *Independent*, 2 February 1995, p. 26. Also published as "Choices: The Writing of Possession." In *Threepenny Review* (Fall 1995), p. 17.

Passions of the Mind: Selected Writings. London: Chatto and Windus, 1991; New York: Turtle Bay Books, 1992.

Angels and Insects. London: Chatto and Windus, 1992; New York: Random House, 1993.

The Matisse Stories. London: Chatto and Windus, 1994; New York: Random House, 1995.

The Djinn in the Nightingale's Eye: Five Fairy Stories. London: Chatto and Windus, 1994; New York: Random House, 1997.

Babel Tower. London: Chatto and Windus, 1996; New York: Random House, 1996.

Elementals: Stories of Fire and Ice. London: Chatto and Windus, 1998; New York: Random House, 1999.

The Biographer's Tale. London: Chatto and Windus, 2000; New York: Knopf, 2001.

On Histories and Stories. London: Chatto and Windus, 2000; Cambridge, Mass.: Harvard University Press, 2000.

A Whistling Woman. London: Chatto and Windus, 2002; New York: Knopf, 2003.

INTERVIEWS

Chisholm, Anne. "A Withering Look at the Scavengers." *Sunday Telegraph* (London), 25 February 1990, Review section p. 54.

Kenyon, Olga. "A. S. Byatt." In *The Writer's Imagination.* Bradford, U.K.: University of Bradford, 1992, pp. 9–21.

Tredell, Nicholas. "A. S. Byatt." In his *Conversations with Critics.* Manchester, U.K.: Carcanet, 1994; Riverdale-on-Hudson, N.Y.: Sheep Meadow Press, 1994.

SECONDARY WORKS

Beer, Gillian. *The Romance.* London: Methuen, 1970.

Brink, André. "Possessed by Language: A. S. Byatt: *Possession.*" In his *The Novel: Language and Narrative from Cervantes to Calvino.* New York: New York University Press, 1998, pp. 288–308.

Buxton, Jackie. "'What's Love Got to Do with It?' Postmodernism and *Possession.*" In Alexa Alfa and M. J. Noble, eds., *Essays on the Fiction of A. S. Byatt: Imagining the Real.* Westport, Conn.: Greenwood Press, 2001, pp. 89–104.

Chevalier, Jean-Louis. "Conclusion in *Possession.*" In Alexa Alfa and M. J. Noble, eds., *Essays on the Fiction of A. S. Byatt: Imagining the Real.* Westport, Conn.: Greenwood Press, 2001, pp. 89–104.

Coe, Jonathan. "Byatt's Pendulum." Review of *Possession. Guardian* (London), 1 March 1990, p. 23.

Franken, Christien. *A. S. Byatt: Art, Authorship, Creativity.* Houndsmills, U.K.: Palgrave, 2001.

Hutcheon, Linda. *A Poetics of Postmodernism: History, Theory, Fiction.* London and New York: Routledge, 1988.

Jameson, Fredric. *Postmodernism, or, The Cultural Logic of Late Capitalism,* London: Verso, 1991; Durham, N.C.: Duke University Press, 1991.

Jenkyns, Richard. "Disinterring Buried Lives." Review of *Possession. Times Literary Supplement* (London) 4535 (2–8 March 1990): 213–214.

McAleer, John. "Satirizing the Academy." Review of *Possession. Chicago Tribune,* 18 November 1990, p.14.

Neville, Jill. "Passionately Literary, Dazzlingly Highbrow." Review of *Possession. Independent* (London), 18 October 1990, p. 25.

Parini, Jay. "Unearthing the Secret Lover." Review of *Possession. New York Times Book Review,* 21 October 1990, pp. 9, 11.

Shuttleworth, Sally. "Natural History: The Retro- Victorian Novel." In Elinor S. Shaffer, ed., *The Third Culture: Literature and Science.* New York: W. de Gruyter, 1998, pp. 253–268.

Sutherland, John. "A. S. Byatt: *Possession.*" In *Was Rebecca Shot?* London: Phoenix, 1999.

Todd, Richard. *Consuming Fictions: The Booker Prize and Fiction in Britain Today.* London: Bloomsbury, 1996.

Robert Browning's
The Ring and the Book

N. S. THOMPSON

IN THE DRAMATIC monologue "How It Strikes a Contemporary" (in *Men and Women*, 1855), Robert Browning has his speaker portray a poet who, as a simple observer of mankind, unassuming in his habits, is the exact opposite of the popular image of the flamboyant Romantic poet. Although the city is Valladolid in Spain, it could very well be Browning's adopted city of Florence, Italy, in the middle years of the nineteenth century, especially as captured by the pioneering photographic firm of Alinari, and many readers have taken the monologue to depict Browning himself as he strolled about those colorful streets:

He stood and watched the cobbler at his trade,
The man who slices lemons into drink,
The coffee-roaster's brazier, and the boys
That volunteer to help him turn its winch.
He glanced o'er books on stall with half an eye,
And fly-leaf ballads on the vendor's string,
And broad-edge bold-print posters by the wall.
He took such cognizance of men and things. . . .

(lines 23–30)

It was while rummaging through a bookstall in Florence's Piazza San Lorenzo one June day in 1860 that Browning discovered the seventeenth-century vellum-bound volume that inspired him to create what was to be his greatest sustained work in *The Ring and the Book* (1868–1869). This "Old Yellow Book" as Browning called it (it was later translated and published under this title) consists of two hundred and sixty-two pages, comprising nineteen printed pamphlets and three manuscript letters concerning a 1698 Roman murder trial which was the sensation of its day. These materials were collected and bound by a Florentine lawyer named Francesco Cencini, who had an interest in the case.

As Browning describes the find in the opening lines of *The Ring and the Book*, the discovery was not merely fortuitous but touched by the hand of God:

I found this book,
Gave a *lira* for it, eightpence English just,
(Mark the predestination!) when a Hand,
Always above my shoulder, pushed me once,
One day still fierce 'mid many a day struck calm,
Across a Square in Florence, crammed with booths,
Buzzing and ablaze, noontide and market-time. . . .

(book 1, lines 38–44)

267

As soon as he had purchased the volume that "memorable day," Browning began reading and continued to read as he walked all the way south across the River Arno to his first-floor apartment in the Palazzo Guidi, absorbing the details of his "Romana Homicidiorum," whose title page he translates as follows:

> A Roman murder-case:
> Position of the entire criminal cause
> Of Guido Franceschini, nobleman,
> With certain Four the cutthroats in his pay,
> Tried, all five, and found guilty and put to death
> By heading or hanging as befitted ranks,
> At Rome February Twenty Two,
> Since our salvation Sixteen Ninety Eight:
> Wherein it is disputed if, and when,
> Husbands may kill adulterous wives, yet 'scape
> The customary forfeit.
>
> (book 1, lines 121–131)

At first glance, these grisly and macabre details, and the sensational story that the documents reveal, of a count who murders his teenage wife, Pompilia, and her parents, believing that his wife had been unfaithful to him, are not what one would expect a poet to find fruitful material, especially for a work that, as one critic has written, will become "the epitome of all his thought and artistic habits" (DeVane, 1955, p. 346). While Browning certainly shared the Victorian taste for contemporary murder stories as they appeared in the newspapers, he went further in re-creating historical scenes of murder in poems as early as "Porphyria's Lover," "In a Gondola," and "My Last Duchess" (in *Dramatic Lyrics,* 1842). His interest with the Old Yellow Book was to broaden his scope and bring all of its events back to life via the testimony of selected participants and observers.

Although Browning says he conceived of the work that became *The Ring and the Book* immediately after taking possession of the Old Yellow Book, he was not able to begin writing for another four years, as events in his own life became dramatic. He and his wife, the poet

CHRONOLOGY

1812	7 May: Robert Browning born in Camberwell (near London) to Robert Browning, Sr., a bank clerk and avid book collector, and Sarah Anna Browning (née Wiedemann). Sister, Sarianna, born in 1814.
1820–1826	Attends Peckham School as weekly boarder.
1826–1829	Education continues at home with private tutors. For a time becomes atheist and vegetarian, emulating Percy Bysshe Shelley, whose works he had read. Attends newly founded London University from October 1828 to May 1829, studying classics and German. Further private studies.
1833	March: Having persuaded his parents to support his career of poet, publishes *Pauline* anonymously. No sales or reviews.
1834	March–June: Visits Russia as unpaid secretary to a representative of Rothschild's. Tries unsuccessfully for diplomatic service. Begins work on both *Sordello* and *Paracelsus.*
1835	August: *Paracelsus* published, favorably received by London's literary community, including Elizabeth Barrett. Makes contacts in the theatrical world.
1837	1 May: Publishes the play *Strafford,* which has five performances at Covent Garden but receives poor reviews. Returns to work on *Sordello.*
1838	April–July: First trip to Italy. Visits Venice and towns in the Veneto, including Asolo.
1840	March: Publication of *Sordello,* which damages his reputation for many years with the charge of needless obscurity.
1841	April: Publication of *Pippa Passes,* set in Asolo, first in a series of eight pamphlets titled *Bells and Pomegranates,* paid for by his father.
1846	12 September: Marriage to Elizabeth Barrett, after a courtship of nearly two years. Given the opposition of Elizabeth's father, the couple leaves clandestinely for

	France, then Italy. Elizabeth and her father are never reconciled.
1848	May: Robert and Elizabeth take permanent residence in Casa Guidi, an apartment near Pitti Palace, Florence, but take extended periods of travel, including Paris (1851–1852).
1849	Robert's two-volume *Poems* published by Elizabeth's publisher Chapman and Hall. 8 March: birth of Robert Wiedemann Barrett, the couple's only child.
1855	Publication of *Men and Women,* containing many of Browning's greatest dramatic monologues, but sales and reviews are poor.
1861	29 June: Elizabeth dies at Casa Guidi. Browning returns to London.
1864	Publication of *Dramatis Personae* restores Browning's reputation. Begins work on *The Ring and the Book.*
1868–1869	Publication of *The Ring and the Book* to generally favorable reviews and sales. From this point on, critical interest is high, studies appear, and Browning is awarded many honors.
1881	Foundation of the Browning Society, the first literary society devoted to a living poet.
1889	12 December: dies in Venice on the same day as the publication of his last collection of lyrics, *Asolando,* which sells out on the first day.

Elizabeth Barrett Browning, spent the winter of 1860–1861 in Rome and traveled to Arezzo, which figures in the murder story, so that Browning could make researches into the case, but Elizabeth, whose health had always been fragile, died on 29 June 1861. Browning felt that he could no longer live in Italy and eventually settled in London with his young son Robert ("Pen"). Once there he became busy with the publication of Elizabeth's *Last Poems* (1862), a collection of her essays, and his own three-volume *Poetical Works* (1863), containing all his previously published poetry. He was also writing the poems he published in *Dramatis*

Personae (1864). In the meantime, with the help of a friend, in 1862 Browning was sent another contemporary pamphlet known as the "secondary source," which gave further details about the case. Work finally began while Browning was on holiday in France in the summer of 1864. Four years later *The Ring and the Book* was ready for publication; it was issued in four volumes, in 1868 on 21 November and 26 December, and in 1869 on 30 January and 27 February.

The work had a mixed reception at first, some reviewers of the first two volumes finding the subject offensive to Victorian sensibilities, but enthusiastic notices in journals such as the *Athenaeum,* the *London Quarterly,* and the *Fortnightly Review* (see Litzinger and Knickerbocker, 1965) ensured good sales and a second edition was issued in 1872. It has to be said that not all readers have accepted Browning's noble reworking of the narrative to show Pompilia's purity and God's agency working through Pope Innocent XII, and many have been put off by its grotesque surfaces—if not also by a length of 21,116 lines—but it is still generally considered to be Browning's most adventurous artistic enterprise and one of the great monuments of nineteenth century poetry.

BROWNING'S ARRANGEMENT OF MATERIAL

The twenty-two items of the Old Yellow Book were translated in 1908 by C. W. Hodell; they are as follows: two anonymous pamphlets in Italian, issued during the course of the trial to influence public opinion; five prosecution pleadings, seven defense pleadings, and two summaries in Latin; three papers dealing with Pompilia; and three letters to the lawyer Francesco Cencini. The plan of *The Ring and the Book* probably had its genesis in the range of depositions and pleadings collected in the Old Yellow Book, but would also have suggested itself to a poet who had virtually invented the dramatic monologue or, at least, made it his own as a poetic vehicle, especially in the psychological confessions of *Dramatic Lyrics* and *Dramatic Romances and Lyrics* (1845).

The Ring and the Book is made up of twelve monologues. Book 1, an introductory monologue in the voice of the poet, is followed by ten monologues representing different speakers at the time of the case, the concluding book being a collage of voices introduced again by the poet. Strictly speaking, some of the monologues are soliloquies (Browning himself, the lawyers, the pope) as there is no auditor present to hear the speech, but Browning's typically extrovert monologue style is vibrantly in place.

The twelve books are as follows: 1, "The Ring and the Book" (1,416 lines); 2, "Half-Rome" (1,547 lines); 3, "The Other Half-Rome" (1,694 lines); 4, "Tertium Quid" (1,640 lines); 5, "Count Guido Franceschini" (2,058 lines); 6, "Giuseppe Caponsacchi" (2,105 lines); 7, "Pompilia" (1,845 lines); 8, "Dominus Hyacinthus de Archangelis" (1,805 lines); 9, "Juris Doctor Johannes-Baptista Bottinius" (1,577 lines); 10, "The Pope" (2,134 lines); 11, "Guido" (2,425 lines); 12, "The Book and the Ring" (870 lines).

A SUMMARY OF THE MURDER STORY, FROM THE SOURCES

The narrative to be deduced from the materials of the Old Yellow Book and the secondary source is not strictly necessary to a reading of the poem, but the exercise is useful for introducing characters and events.

The story begins with a ruse by Violante Comparini, a woman who, past childbearing age, attempts to secure a permanent legacy for her and her husband, Pietro, which they can only inherit on the condition that they have a child. Without Pietro's knowledge, Violante feigns a pregnancy, but the child she eventually produces is that of a poor local prostitute, which she duly passes off as her own, and has the child

baptized as her daughter. Once the child, Francesca Pompilia, is thirteen, the couple's aspirations are to marry her to a suitable nobleman. It happens that Abate Paolo Franceschini is looking for an heiress for his elder brother, Count Guido Franceschini of Arezzo, who lived in Rome for many years in the hope of patronage and preferment, but returned in poverty to the family seat—a fact that the abate does not disclose.

Once the wedding takes place in 1693, Pompilia and her parents go to live in the family seat in Arezzo, only to discover the count's true circumstances. After intense friction, Violante and Pietro return to Rome in March of the following year, declare Pompilia is illegitimate, and initiate proceedings for the return of the dowry. Outraged by this revelation, Guido vents his anger on Pompilia, accusing her of infidelity, while she sues for divorce and tries to escape the household on many occasions, after pleading with the bishop and governor of Arezzo to intervene, which neither are inclined to do. Matters come to a head in April 1697, when she finally takes flight in the company of a young canon, Giuseppe Caponsacchi, and the two head south for Rome so that Pompilia may join Pietro and Violante. The youthful couple are pursued and overtaken by Guido as they stay overnight in Castelnuovo, some fifteen miles from Rome, and the count has them both arrested for the flight and adultery, after first having to disarm Pompilia, who makes a spirited attempt at defense with a sword. Although the couple denies any wrongdoing, Guido produces love letters between the two in which details of the elopement are discussed, which again the defendants insist are forgeries, Pompilia even going so far as to declare she is illiterate (see addendum in Altick edition, pp. 634–635).

Pompilia and Caponsacchi are tried by an ecclesiastical court, which "relegates" (exiles) Caponsacchi for three years to a monastery at Civita Vecchia, "for complicity in the flight, and the seduction of Francesca Pompilia and for carnal knowledge of her," which both parties denied. Curiously, Pompilia is not formally charged with adultery, but is still sent off to a convent to do penance. When the nuns find out that she is pregnant, however, they apply to the court that she be allowed to return to live with her parents and on 18 December she gives birth to a baby boy she names Gaetano, who is quickly passed on to neighbors for his safety. Soon after the birth (2 January), Guido arrives with four men from his estate, gains entrance to the Comparini household by pretending to bear a message from Caponsacchi, and the five men duly massacre Violante and Pietro, leaving Pompilia for dead with twenty-two wounds. Guido and his hired band are soon captured as they make their way back on foot to Arezzo, Guido having forgotten that he needed a special passport to acquire post horses to leave the Papal State of Rome. Pompilia dies after four days (on 6 January) and, given her testimony, especially her deathbed last confession, Guido and his men are put on trial for murder. Guido produces a confession, and the facts of the case are barely contestable. The center of attention thus becomes his claim, as put forward by his defense, that the murders were justified on the grounds of *honoris causa* (for the sake of honor).

The problem with this defense is the lapse of time from the original flight, which occurred in April, coupled with the horrific nature of the massacre of the Comparini and Pompilia some eight months later. Although the court had pronounced Caponsacchi guilty, because the couple had denied they were lovers, question of whether any intimate relations had occurred between the young couple was again raised. Despite all the pleadings, for and against, Guido and his men were found guilty and, on 18 February, the count was sentenced to beheading and his men to hanging. Since Guido was able to appeal his sentence because he had taken minor orders and could claim privilege of clergy, the case went to Pope Innocent XII. The pope swiftly turned down the appeal and the sentences were carried out in public on 22 February 1698. In the subsequent court case over Pompilia's estate, to which the Convertite nuns (who automatically inherited the estates of fallen women) laid claim, Pompilia was declared innocent of adultery and her son Gaetano pronounced the legal heir.

As a collection of legal documents and popular pamphlets, the Old Yellow Book is not a straight narrative of events; it contains much biased information, and leaves many questions unanswered. A good many further documents on the case have come to light since Browning's death, but they only partially clarify matters. It is highly probable from the evidence that Pompilia was literate enough to have exchanged letters with Caponsacchi, and, furthermore, that they were lovers. The reader is referred to Beatrice Corrigan, *Curious Annals* (1956) for an excellent summary (pp. xix–xl) of this material. Thus, despite Browning's asseverations of adhering faithfully to his sources, and while they will be referred to, it must be borne in mind that *The Ring and the Book* is essentially a work of the poet's imagination and should be treated on its own terms as an independent work of literature.

A READING OF THE MONOLOGUES

After book 1 introduces the case in the poet's own voice, the reader is taken behind the outward facts into a dramatic re-creation of the thoughts and feelings of both the Roman public and the protagonists at the time of the trial, thus showing different interpretations and varying motivations of the various speakers. The suspense of inner revelation is therefore substituted for that of formal narrative sequence as different aspects of the narrative are emphasized. The trial brought crucial issues of class and gender into play, which is why it became a cause célèbre over and above its gory details, and it was this that allowed Browning to create so many monologues without undue repetition as each voice looks on the events from a different, and often very biased, point of view. Nevertheless, they do not appear randomly and are organized into a series of three triads. The first comprises views by the Roman public (Half- Rome, the Other Half-Rome, Tertium Quid), the second by the major protagonists (Guido, Caponsacchi, Pompilia), and finally by those making up the legal side, the two lawyers and the pope. These triads have the appearance of a Hegelian dialectic, but the resolution offered by the third speaker is not a synthesis of the preceding opposing views, but a move away from them into a different perspective.

BOOK 1: "THE RING AND THE BOOK"

Browning introduces his artistic method with a trope that has caused some confusion. He refers to the process whereby a copy of an Etruscan ring was made for his wife, Elizabeth: to the pure gold an alloy had to be added so that the metal could be worked. When the ring was fashioned, it was then treated with acid and the surface alloy "burned" away. The analogy the poet pursues is that the Old Yellow Book is "pure crude fact" (book 1, line 86), "absolutely truth, / Fanciless fact" (book 1, lines 143–144), to which the poet adds the alloy of his "fancy with those facts" (book 1, line 679):

> . . . such alloy,
> Such substance of me interfused the gold
> Which, wrought into a shapely ring therewith,
> Hammered and filed, fingered and favoured, last
> Lay ready for the renovating wash. . . .
>
> (book 1, lines 681–685)

The trouble with the trope is in considering the Old Yellow Book as fact, when it is patently a series of opinions; furthermore, in writing the work, the poet declares, "I disappeared" (book 1, line 687), which is true in that he voices events through a series of nine people, but only as he directs them, so the alloy analogy is not strictly true, and of course the poet returns with a conclusion in the last book where he unequivocally supports the pope's decision, as he intimates here in book 1.

But the real interest, as Browning says, is to "Let this old woe step on the stage again!" (book 1, line 824), thus creating a courtroom drama. This takes place not in the courtroom itself, but the effect emerges for the reader throughout the succeeding monologues. Many voices pick up the dramatic metaphor to remind the reader that what is heard might indeed be a "performance," and nothing else, as Browning creates a gallery of reliable and unreliable narrators for the reader to negotiate. Finally, after detailing what is to come with a series of brief sketches of characters and their points of view, the poet ends his introduction with an intensely-felt dedication to the memory of Elizabeth as his "lyric Love" (book 1, line 1391).

BOOK 2: "HALF-ROME"

The voice of Half-Rome opens the first triad of public opinion. The designation "Half-Rome" and its counterpart "the Other Half-Rome" stand for two anonymous speakers representing for Browning the two sides to the public debate: those who are in favor of Guido and those who support Pompilia (whether they see her as blameless or not). Half- Rome meets an acquaintance and informs him of "the facts" on the day after the murders (3 January) while the bodies of Pietro and Violante Comparini are laid out in the church of San Lorenzo nearby and Pompilia lies dying of her wounds in the hospital of Santa Anna. The voice has a basis in the anonymous eleventh pamphlet of the Old Yellow Book, published in Italian to sway the general public in Guido's favor. Browning gives the force of an individual personality to this point of view and indeed the weight of personal feeling. He also introduces the reader to another aspect of the work's ambiguous view of language, namely the metaphorical play around the main protagonists, where the same metaphors are often used in an ironic or reversed manner. For Half-Rome, the three main protagonists form a love triangle played out as the tragedy of the Fall, but seen in ludicrously comic terms:

The gallant, Caponsacchi, Lucifer
I' the garden where Pompilia, Eve-like, lured
Her Adam Guido to his fault and fall.

(book 2, lines 167–169)

The same metaphor is then applied to the lure and deception by Violante (Eve) of Pietro (Adam) in their "cabbage- plot" (book 2, line 254) over the deception of Pompilia's birth. He then uses the metaphor of angling to show both the Comparini and Guido and his clerical brothers casting about in the world for their own ends, where the unfortunate Pompilia is the "bait" (book 2, line 323) that Violante throws to the brothers Franceschini. Similarly, although he uses terms such as "the perfect cavalier" (book 2, line 1000) for Caponsacchi, his figurative reading of the flight as Paris's abduction of Helen of Troy is seen in satiric terms:

Pompilia, soon looked Helen to the life,
Recumbent upstairs in her pink and white,
So, in the inn-yard, bold as 't were Troy-town,
There strutted Paris in correct costume,
Cloak, cap and feather, no appointment missed,
Even to the wicked-looking sword at side,
He seemed to find and feel familiar at.

(book 2, lines 1003–1009)

It will be seen from this brief examination of Half- Rome's language that, for all his support of Guido, he sees the world in tawdry terms, a cynical snarl on his face as he relates the tragicomic machinations of both families. Indeed, such is Half-Rome's cynicism that he has no faith in the law as arbiter and sees the first judgment on the flight, where in effect the defendants receive extremely light sentences of exile and the nunnery, as a travesty, recommending that the only rightful path is "the old way trod when men were men!" (book 2, line 1524), that is, taking the law into one's own hands as Guido has done. Thus, for this speaker, Guido has set a good example for all husbands keen to assert patriarchal authority in the home by any possible means, including violence:

The better for you and me and all the world,
Husbands of wives, especially in Rome.
The thing is put right, in the old place, —ay,
The rod hangs on its nail behind the door,
Fresh from the brine: a matter I commend
To the notice, during Carnival that's near,
Of a certain what's-his-name and jackanapes
Somewhat too civil of eves with lute and song
About a house here, where I keep a wife.
(You, being his cousin, may go tell him so.)

(book 2, lines 1538–1547)

The final lines reveal the speaker to have a vested interest in maintaining order in his own home, but the manner in which he does so shows Half-Rome's view of a savage dog-eat- dog world where it is up to each individual to take care of his own.

BOOK 3: "THE OTHER HALF-ROME"

This speaker is in Piazza Barberini near Santa Anna, where Pompilia is dying, and is obviously profoundly moved by the circumstances to express his support for the young victim. His monologue is loosely based on the Old Yellow Book's anonymous sixteenth pamphlet, but again the personality is Browning's own invention. As a romantically inclined bachelor, this character has an altogether lighter touch than Half- Rome, his language depicting Pompilia in a range of simple diminutives and adjectives, but we see the same play of language and allusion to other narrative episodes that gives rise to complex responses and alerts the reader to the speaker's partiality.

On the one hand he imagines Pompilia's speech in her defense in terms of salvation. He envisions her as making the following claim:

Earth was made hell to me who did no harm:
I only could emerge one way from hell
By catching at the one hand held me, so
I caught at it and thereby stepped to heaven.

(book 3, lines 1344–1347)

On the other hand, he undercuts this elevated, if desperate view, when he refers to Guido as a comic figure, contemplating the flight as a tale out of Boccaccio's *Decameron,* when Guido

> Found the world's face an universal grin
> At this last best of the Hundred Merry Tales
> Of how a young and spritely clerk devised
> To carry off a spouse that moped too much,
> And cured her of the vapours in a trice.
>
> (book 3, lines 1445–1449)

Indeed, the Other Half-Rome seems to have difficulty in not taking the romantic view that Pompilia and Caponsacchi were truly lovers:

> Pompilia penned him letters, passionate prayers,
> If not love, then so simulating love
> That he, no novice to the taste of thyme,
> Turned from such over-luscious honey-clot
> At end o' the flower, and would not lend his lip
> Till . . . but the tale here frankly outsoars faith:
> There must be falsehood somewhere.
>
> (book 3, lines 901–907)

But then he remembers that Pompilia cannot write and thrashes out these and other problems of fact without arriving at any satisfactory conclusion. He wants to believe in Pompilia as the romantic heroine and wishes to see Caponsacchi more as man than priest, appealing to the idea of masculinity in a completely different way than Half-Rome has:

> Men are men: why then need I say one word
> More than this, that our man the Canon here
> Saw, pitied, loved Pompilia?
>
> (book 3, lines 880–882)

Finally, unsure of the canon's role, finding that the whole business of truth eludes him, the Other Half-Rome decides to put his trust in faith and simply believe that the couple arranged their flight on an impromptu basis "As in romance- books" (book 3, line 922) without letters, and concludes that if they were not lovers, then "It were improbable; / [but] So is the legend of my patron-saint" (book 3, lines 1050–1051).

As for Guido, the speaker picks up on book 1's image of him and his men as wolves in sheep's clothing and will not excuse him on the grounds of an injured man taking the law into his own hands, especially as the speaker has had his own problems with the count over an inheritance case, but has abided by the legal process (book 3, lines 1674–1694). If this speaker is also revealed as partisan, his world is a law- abiding one, even if he is antagonistic to the count.

BOOK 4: "TERTIUM QUID"

Tertium Quid is a minor aristocrat holding forth at a soirée to a "Highness" (a prince) and an "Excellency" (a cardinal) to whom he appears to defer for final judgment after trying to present the case as judiciously as he can. He sets himself up against the common gossiping herd, "this rabble's-brabble of dolts and fools / Who make up reasonless unreasoning Rome" (book 4, lines 10–11), but his high-minded view is simply to ingratiate himself with his more elevated audience. One feels that the role of commentator is somehow forced upon him, as an inferior, to explain inferior matters and, perhaps, also to entertain his superiors with details of what he scorns as a puppet show (book 4, line 1282ff.).

If he affects aristocratic disdain for the whole business, indeed flaunting his disinterestedness throughout, he is at the same time trying to keep his audience captive with the spicy story:

> . . . this is an episode
> In burgess-life, —why seek to aggrandize,
> Idealize, denaturalize the class?
> People talk just as if they had to do
> With a noble pair that . . . Excellency, your ear!
> Stoop to me, Highness, —listen and look
>   yourselves!
>
> (book 4, lines 64–69)

Naturally, he does exhibit a class bias toward Guido as an aristocrat, but also sees the count as having sullied himself by mingling with the lower orders, especially once the truth of Pompilia's birth is known. Although he also utilizes the Adam/Eve and priest/knight paradigms, together with the hunting and snaring metaphors that other speakers use, his exquisite distaste for the unequal marriage is given by a startling culinary metaphor about the married couple:

> How evolve happiness from such a match?
> 'T were hard to serve up a congenial dish
> Out of these ill-agreeing morsels, Duke,
> By the best exercise of the cook's craft,
> Best interspersion of spice, salt and sweet!
> But let two ghastly scullions concoct mess
> With brimstone, pitch, vitriol and devil's-dung—
>
> (book 4, lines 725–731)

As with the other two speakers, this voice's sophisticated performance ends with the ironic comment that he feels he has not "advanced himself" after his "teaching the two idiots here" (book 4, lines 1639–1640), while they have enjoyed the game of cards.

BOOK 5: "COUNT GUIDO FRANCESCHINI"

After hearing the previous three speakers, it is with some relief that the reader comes to one of the three major players in the case. In the Roman law courts of the day, pleas were not delivered and heard in court but entered as printed documents intended for circulation. Hence, although Browning has drawn on the advocates' defenses, there is no such speech in the Old Yellow Book's pamphlets. Witnesses could be examined by the judges, however, and Guido is speaking to them in a private chamber some days after the crime, but without any conclusive mention of Pompilia's death (in book 5 at lines 936 and 978 she is given as dead, but at lines 1687–1688 she is alive). Whatever the cause of this inconsistency, the fact that Pompilia is not categorically dead at this point allows his testimony to be seen in perhaps less harsh a light.

Indeed, there is initial sympathy for Guido when he is portrayed as having come fresh from the rack; such judicial torture was still legitimate for extracting a confession, although there is some question as to whether it was inflicted on members of the nobility. Ruefully rubbing his limbs, the count presents himself as a hearty fellow, one who has almost cheerfully undergone torture as a test of manhood and will now willingly relate all his troubles: his struggle as an impoverished nobleman, his dignified attempts to find a patron in Rome, and finally the desperate tricks played on him, first by the Comparini, then by his adulterous young wife. His monologue takes the form of a classical oration, complete with references to virtuous examples in literature, and is a measured performance from a mature figure, nine years older than the historical Guido (forty-nine instead of forty). If he is potentially the comic cuckold, Guido does little to detract from this, emphasizing his awkwardness and his difficulties. But, as a social critic, he is also keen to point out how the structures into which he was born have failed him and how he has been wronged. He boasts, "I am representative of a great line" (book 5, line 140), but then we learn of how he feels betrayed by a system that allows social climbers to ascend above him:

> I waited thirty years, may it please the Court:
> Saw meanwhile many a denizen o' the dung
> Hop, skip, jump o'er my shoulder, make him
>   wings
> And fly aloft, —succeed, in the usual phrase.
> Everyone soon or late comes round by Rome:
> Stand still here, you'll see all in turn succeed.
> Why, look you, so and so, the physician here,
> My father's lacquey's son we sent to school,
> Doctored and dosed this Eminence and that . . .
>
> (book 5, lines 292–300)

This may solicit the reader's sympathy for Guido's view of the world, but a Victorian reader would most certainly have also questioned it and considered the fact that the physician referred to in this speech deserved to succeed after his efforts. As will be seen, when the pope comes to measure Guido's character, the fact that the count has been a passive player in life comes to stand out, and his attempt at gaining sympathy as a victim himself is seen merely as an impotent whine. As has already been stated, given the incontrovertibility of the facts and confessions, the only recourse Guido has is to plead mitigating circumstances.

In sum, Guido's persuasive monologue is aimed at a knowing male aristocratic audience which, albeit clerical, is assumed to share a common understanding about the ways of men in ensuring dominance and family honor. If it were not for the horrific details of the murders (which Guido conveniently sidesteps), it is almost as if he were in a smoking room, relating how he had "taught the little woman what is what." It is this gross insensitivity to the fact that he has mercilessly butchered three defenseless people that condemns him most of all, but the full revelation of his motivation comes only in book 11.

BOOK 6: "GIUSEPPE CAPONSACCHI"

The canon is also shown speaking before the judges while Pompilia is still alive, but his monologue could not be in greater contrast to the count's. It is based loosely on the Old Yellow Book's eighth pamphlet, his deposition at the *processus fugae* (the trial of the flight), but this is a matter-of-fact statement without hint of emotional involvement, and contradicts Pompilia's evidence at several points, such as the time of arrival at the Castelnuovo inn and the question of her literacy. Browning's portrait is of a paradoxical young man in clerical orders, noble by birth, who only becomes truly noble and Christian when he assumes the role of courtly lover to Pompilia. While he was able to dress up for the role literally as a cavalier, and metaphorically in his language, his role as a saintly knight in the imagined romance only

leads to ignoble tragedy. Thus for all his fine words, and despite his brief role as a man of action, Caponsacchi ends by being yet one more of Browning's contemplative studies in failure (such as "Andrea del Sarto" in *Men and Women*).

Nevertheless, on an equal footing with his noble cleric judges, he is able to round on them immediately for the comic role they forced upon him by the judgment of the *processus fugae,* where they saw him playing the not-so-gallant swain in Guido's cuckolding. He opens with a blistering attack on the smugness he sees there and likens their levity to that of the soldiers who diced at the Crucifixion, reminding them of "an old book, you should con" (book 6, line 49), a barbed comment on how distant he sees the Bible has become for these men. He then begins to relate his personal history and relives the events of the flight, speaking as:

> . . . the hot-headed youth
> Who lets his soul show, through transparent words,
> The mundane love that's sin and scandal too!
>
> (book 6, lines 128–130)

The canon is at great pains to show that, although he loved Pompilia, his action was "Consistent with [his] priesthood" (book 6, line 139), and his true sorrow is that, although he was able to help her take flight, he was not able to save her from attack. Naturally, he blames the judges for relegating him to the monastery at Civita Vecchia. If his role in the young woman's life has been questionable, his final reasoning is that a priest who truly understands the human heart is more fitted for his vocation:

> . . . but priests
> Should study passion; how else cure mankind,
> Who come for help in passionate extremes?
> I do but play with an imagined life
> Of who, unfettered by a vow, unblessed

By the higher call,—since you will have it so,—
Leads it companioned by the woman there.

(book 6, lines 2078–84)

Ultimately, it is the safety of Caponsacchi's position that makes his position in the drama less effective. He can be construed as simply "playing" a role, and could not be a real hero as his clerical status prevents him from attacking Guido. His life was therefore never in any real danger and he suffers only a temporary loss of reputation. In the end, he was simply "relegated"—as the documents say—to a different town, his youthful foible soon to be forgotten by a Church used to such things. Concentrating on the flight and the events leading up to it, the canon confesses his youthful poetic frivolity as a young deacon lost in the stifling social provincial round of Arezzo, but attests to more serious and reflective yearnings:

...'t is but poor work this—
Counting one's fingers till the sonnet's
    crowned. . . .
    . . .
'T is more amusing to go pace at eve
I' the Duomo, —watch the day's last gleam
    outside
Turn, as into a skirt of God's own robe,
Those lancet-windows' jewelled miracle, —
Than go eat the Archbishop's ortolans,
Digest his jokes.

(book 6, lines 455–456; 459–464)

Into this small world, Pompilia eventually breaks as a "sunbeam thro' shut eyes" (book 6, line 435) and, although the practicalities whereby the tryst is arranged are obfuscated (the original evidence over letters exchanged is conflicting), it too is associated with light as Caponsacchi considers the noble duty he has accepted:

Dawn broke, noon broadened, I —
I sat stone-still, let time run over me.
The sun slanted into my room, had reached
The west. I opened book, —Aquinas blazed

With one black name only on the white page.
I looked up, saw the sunset: vespers rang:
"She counts the minutes till I keep my word
And come say all is ready. I am a priest.
Duty to God is duty to her" . . .

(book 6, lines 1022–1030)

But he realizes that his role could be otherwise construed: "The officious priest would personate Saint George / For a mock Princess in undragoned days" (book 6, lines 1771–2). Indeed, as he is a priest, he is prohibited from taking personal revenge against Guido, much though his manhood told him to (book 6, line 1894 ff), so his role as hero and savior is very much a frustrated one. He is caught between the comic role assigned him at the *processus fugae* and the tragic outcome of the triple murder, and in the end can only feel sorry for himself with his final exclamation of "Miserable me!" (book 6, line 2105).

BOOK 7: "POMPILIA"

For the portrait of his idealized heroine, Browning utilized the historical evidence of her deposition during the *processus fugae* (pamphlet eight) but especially the attestation by Fra Celestino, the friar who hears her deathbed testimony and last confession (pamphlet five). As victim of a cruel world, Pompilia elicits all the tragedy and pathos of a Dickensian heroine, such as Little Nell or Little Dorrit, by means of a serenity and maturity far beyond her seventeen years. It is true that Browning was not able to create as effective an idiolect for her as he had for his male characters, especially the lawyers, but with her simplicity of expression and tranquillity Pompilia's words are devoid of bathos as she makes what is her dying speech in the hospital on 6 January.

Pompilia concentrates on her childhood, the flight, and on her present state of acceptance as she approaches death. She has pardoned Guido and his gang and makes no mention of the violent marriage, but rather condones her parents for arranging it because she thinks that they were acting in good faith. She masks her feelings (and also evades any of the questions over her actions) by referring to events as if in a dream, thus distancing herself from brutal reality:

> All since is one blank,
> Over and ended; a terrific dream.
> It is the good of dreams—so soon they go!
> Wake in a horror of heart-beats, you may—
> Cry, "The dread thing will never from my
>   thoughts!"
> . . .
> And when you rub your eyes awake and wide,
> Where is the harm o' the horror? Gone! So here.
> I know I wake, —but from what? Blank, I say!
>
> (book 7, lines 583–588; 592–594)

Thus Pompilia offers no sordid revelations of the past, only quietly offers to the reader her current transcendent state. She uses imagery of light for the canon, whose "white light, blazed the truth" (book 7, line 922) and also for her escape (book 7, lines 622–625; 1224–1226). Apart from this, she praises Caponsacchi as her "soldier-saint" (book 7, line 1786), and expresses her sense of fulfillment in giving birth at Christmas in terms of a Marian figure:

> I never realized God's birth before—
> How he grew likest God in being born.
> This time I felt like Mary, had my babe
> Lying a little on my breast like hers.
>
> (book 7, lines 1690–1693)

Obviously, we are to understand that the child has a biological father in Guido (and not the canon, as the defense insisted), but if there is a convenient blur over the child's paternity in her testimony, it is because she wishes her son to be considered a child "born of love not hate," therefore she argues that he is hers alone (book 7, lines 1762–1763). Elsewhere, she repeats the words and opinions of others in a dramatic ploy

not entirely credible for someone about to die. Finally, as she approaches the point for her soul to rise, she meditates on marriage and Caponsacchi, reminding herself that he could not marry, but concluding:

> I think he would not marry if he could.
> Marriage on earth seems such a counterfeit,
> Mere imitation of the inimitable . . .
>
> (book 7, lines 1823–1825)

Having thus put everything into perspective from the eternal point of view, which would have even mortal happiness as a "mere imitation," she passes on to meet her maker, a Madonna figure as Caponsacchi has depicted her.

BOOK 8: "DOMINUS HYACINTHUS DE ARCHANGELIS"

Nothing could make the reader more aware of the precarious state of earthly justice than the pleas of the "two buffoon" lawyers, as Browning called them in a letter to his friend Julia Wedgwood (19 November 1868). In book 1, the poet comments scathingly on the law as a "patent truth-extracting process" (book 1, line 1114), a machine that produces simply "flowery foam" (book 1, line 1113) to "teach our common sense its helplessness" (book 1, line 1107). After we have heard the two partisan halves of Rome, followed by a ludicrously neutral third, then come the two conflicting male testimonies concerned with the worldly outcome, followed by Pompilia's otherworldly concerns. The two lawyers then begin a third triad, laying out the views of the defense and prosecution, resolved beyond the scope of the judicial system by the pope. Although both characters are based on the pleas in the Old Yellow Book, their personalities and interests are Browning's invention. In giving the lawyers latinized titles, Browning reminds us of legal pomposity, but they will be referred to here—as in the texts—by their Italian surnames Arcangeli and Bottini. It should be said, too, that an earlier commentator on the work, John Marshall Gest, an eminent jurist and expert on the Italian law of the day, found nothing procedurally or professionally lacking in either attorney from the evidence of the Old Yellow Book.

Browning's portrait is a comic masterpiece of the mildly grotesque, reminiscent of "Soliloquy of the Spanish Cloister" (*Dramatic Lyrics*), where—as with the voices of Rome—pettiness in the face of large events shows how small and self-interested a community can be. Here Arcangeli is depicted writing notes for his first deposition to the judges, where he wishes to impress them with his learning and outdo his rival prosecutor, but he also ruminates on the upcoming birthday feast for his young son and matters regarding his education and future. His speech is larded with references to food and with Latin phrases from his plea, which he translates as he goes along, but with some sly twists and transpositions added by Browning (which notes in the standard edition make clear) in order to satirize him.

It is perhaps easy to condemn Arcangeli for his personal faults, but he is after all defending a man who has confessed (albeit under duress) and against whom there is overwhelming and incontrovertible evidence. Arcangeli is forced to make the best of a difficult task and offer the defense of *honoris causa*: "Honour is the supreme good" (book 8, line 583). He proceeds by appeals to a variety of authorities, from the example of nature (book 8, lines 531–540) to a range of saints and biblical authorities (book 8, lines 578–655), to words he attributes to Christ: "'*Honorem meum nemini dabo!*' 'No, / My honour I to nobody will give!'" (book 8, lines 664–665), where the text is actually Isaiah 62:8 in the Vulgate Bible. But Arcangeli is not above a low appeal to manhood as well as a source for law and order:

> For if wronged husband raise not hue and cry,
> *Quod si maritus de adulterio non*
> *Conquereretur,* he's presumed a—foh!
>
> (book 8, lines 753–755)

Although he sees them as secondary to his defense, Arcangeli sets himself the task of explaining six points which he anticipates Bottini will take up: the defendants constituted an illegal armed band; used prohibited weapons; attacked victims in their own house; used disguise; attacked a ward of court; interfered in a matter already sub judice. Most of all he has to convince the court that Guido's outrage at his honor is not undercut by his long procrastination in taking the law into his own hands (book 8, line 1031ff.). To this he says that once honor has been offended, the slur remains until honor has been satisfied and, regarding the exaggerated violence of the attack, merely asks is it not right that "All means are lawful to a lawful end?" (book 8, line 1315). If indeed Guido's response was exaggerated, he says, then exaggeration is not a sin. After such a chilling argument, this counsel ends on a comic note, contemplating (via a distortion of Horace) the purchase of a set of pearls for his wife's ample bosom, presumably his reward for securing Guido a favorable verdict.

BOOK 9: "JURIS DOCTOR JOHANNES-BAPTISTA BOTTINIUS"

Bottini is in complete contrast again to his judicial adversary. A bachelor, unmoved by the delights of home life, he is evidently attracted and repelled at the same time by the opposite sex, and very suspicious of their nature. If Arcangeli has to present the best he can of an unfortunate case, he takes as much pride as he can in doing it, whereas Bottini is patently unhappy with his job. He has written a final summing up (based on pamphlet thirteen) which is about to be printed and delivered to the court, but wishes to test its skill and reads it aloud as a soliloquy. Instead of roundly condemning the count—in many ways that has been achieved by Arcangeli—Bottini decides that Guido's guilt can best be demonstrated through Pompilia's innocence, in the hope that "by painting saintship I depicture sin" (book 9, line 1409). But he gives so many concessions to Pompilia's youth and attractiveness, and the charms of young women in general, that he undermines his own case. After other speakers' positive views of Pompilia as an innocent lamb and a maiden after the Virgin Mary, the lawyer uses the same images satirically:

> Know one, you know all
> Manners of maidenhood: mere maiden she.
> And since all lambs are like in more than fleece,
> Prepare to find that, lamb-like, she too frisks . . .
>
> (book 9, lines 221–224)

One of the more unseemly of his fantasies is to imagine Caponsacchi making love to Pompilia as she sleeps, exhausted, in the inn (book 9, lines 730–766), which resolves his own particular problem of "How so much beauty is compatible / With so much innocence!" (book 9, lines 765–766).

He is equally ambivalent about the priest's worthiness and ends his rather shoddy prosecution on a different kind of cynical note that reveals his self-interest: "Still, it pays" (book 9, line 1577).

BOOK 10: "THE POPE"

In the Old Yellow Book, three letters written to Francesco Cencini relate that after Guido appealed his guilty verdict to the pope, citing privilege of clergy, the appeal was quickly dismissed and Guido's sentence carried out on 22 February. The brief outline of the circumstances surrounding the pope's rejection of the appeal gave Browning a free hand in fashioning the moral center of the work as he created his portrait of Pope Innocent XII (1615–1700), deliberating the rights and wrongs of the case. Although he researched accounts of the pope's life, Browning made him his own character, depicting him by means of an inner debate which has little reference to the theology of the day. Knowing that he is nearing death himself,

Innocent XII considers his fallibility both as pope and as a human being, anxious to make the right decisions in life before he passes on to a higher judgment. Papal infallibility was much discussed in the 1860s, leading to its incorporation in doctrine in 1870, but it would not have been an issue for Innocent XII. His belief in an unknowable God who must be taken purely on faith harks back to the affective piety of the late medieval period, as well as recalling Browning's own evangelical leanings. But what ultimately motivates the pope's decision over Guido is a reading of his character. Here inaction and inertia are heavily criticized:

> This is why Guido is found reprobate.
> I see him furnished forth for his career,
> On starting for the life-chance in our world,
> With nearly all we count sufficient help:
> Body and mind in balance, a sound frame,
> A solid intellect: the wit to seek,
> Wisdom to choose, and courage wherewithal
> To deal with whatsoever circumstance
> Should minister to man, make life succeed.
>
> (book 10, lines 398–406)

In the pope's view, Guido turned from his natural gifts to a perverted kind of self-interest. Where his doctrine should have been "Man is born nowise to content himself / But please God" (book 10, lines 434–435), instead he felt the stirrings of "unseemly greed and grasp undue" (book 10, line 421), his taking minor orders simply a move for protection and advantage, in the same way as his marriage was for gain alone (book 10, lines 531–571). These faults are compounded by his cowardice and his fraudulence, especially in gaining entrance to the Comparini house, and committing the murders during the celebration of Christ's birth. Albeit within the bounds of seemliness, Guido is described in the course of this examination by means of a whole range of unappealing animal traits. In short, the pope does not consider the facts of the case from a legal point of view, but from his understanding of Guido Franceschini as a man and a Christian, and finds him wanting in the extreme. After a fervent prayer in which the pope appeals to God, he concludes:

> Beyond the tale, I reach into the dark,
> Feel what I cannot see, and still faith stands:
> I can believe this dread machinery
> Of sin and sorrow, would confound me else . . .
>
> (book 10, lines 1372–1375)

If the pope is decisive, it is only after due consideration of the *honoris causa* plea, with its argument that the fabric of society is served by male dominance (book 10, lines 1983–2097); he ultimately dismisses the plea, by reference to the divine intervention he feels "a voice other than yours / Quickens my spirit" (book 10, lines 2098–2099). He also appeals to his own conscience: "And how should I dare die, this man let live?" (book 10, line 2133). Although God is seen taking a hand in the decision through the pope's humble faith, Guido is condemned in the reader's eyes more by the depiction of his flawed character.

BOOK 11: "GUIDO"

After the pope's climactic judgment, it may seem superfluous that Guido be allowed another say, yet he is given the work's longest monologue, and his dramatic shift in perspective attests to the work's interest in the tenuous fabric of words. Informed that there will be no reprieve from the pope, the count is attended by a family friend, Cardinal Acciaiuoli, and by Abate Panciatichi, a friend from boyhood, for spiritual guidance before he is collected at dawn for execution by the Company of Death. With no reverence for the churchmen beside him, Guido launches into a defiant justification of his life and deeds, still claiming that he is innocent in that he was addressing an insult to his honor, and reminding his listeners that he had support among the public for the action he took against a wayward wife:

> All honest Rome approved my part;
> Whoever owned wife, sister, daughter, —nay,

> Mistress, —had any shadow of any right
> That looks like right, and, all the more resolved,
> Held it with tooth and nail, —these manly men
> Approved!
>
> (book 11, lines 39–44)

He reminds his audience of a time when a nobleman could defend his honor with impunity, such as when his own grandfather stabbed a "knave" for throwing a gibe at him (book 11, lines 103–106), then likens his own crime to such a "prank" (book 11, line 111). As representatives of "civilisation and society," the cardinal and abate are his enemies and he will "cross blades" (book 11, line 485) verbally with them. He accuses them of being there not for his soul's sake, but to encourage a confession of guilt so that the pope's decision will be validated and no untoward gossip will follow his death. Given this supposed provocation, Guido decides to reveal his true nature as the wolf beneath sheep's clothing (book 11, lines 434–444)—an image alluded to in preceding monologues—to which he returns time and again (book 11, lines 821–830; 1174–1190; 2302–2309). As he dissociates himself entirely from Christianity (book 11, lines 515–763; 1914–1915; 2286–2287) and declares himself a "primitive religionist" (book 11, line 1917), he is revealed as a man of appetites, who will have what he desires no matter how much he has to cheat to obtain them. Naturally, the people whom he feels have cheated him in turn—the Comparini, Pompilia—come in for the greatest contumely, with animal imagery well to the fore. Perhaps the most damning revelation is of Guido's arrogance, reminiscent of that of the extremist duke in "My Last Duchess," who has his wife killed because she was not haughty enough for his name and title. Guido taunts the cardinal and abate about the commonly accepted practice of killing pesky insects; he questions why he should be punished simply for doing away with something that annoyed him:

> Does memory haunt your pillow? Not a whit.
> God wills you never pace your garden-path

One appetizing hour ere dinner-time
But your intrusion there treads out of life
An universe of happy innocent things:
Feel you remorse about that damsel-fly
Which buzzed so near your mouth and flapped
    your face,
You blotted it from being at a blow?
It was a fly, you were a man, and more,
Lord of created things, so took your course.
Manliness, mind, —these are things fit to save,
Fit to brush fly from: why, because I take
My course, must needs the Pope kill me?

            (book 11, lines 2240–2252)

In believing himself to be a "lord of created things" who can kill at will without a twinge of remorse, and in seeing human life on the same level as he does a fly, Guido is revealed not only as arrogant but as insane, especially in his invective against the Comparini and Pompilia (book 11, lines 2398–2404). But if his last appeal is to live and die a man (book 11, line 2410), his final terrifying cry once the Company of Death come for him is only that of a vile coward seeking escape from the justice coming to him:

Abate, —Cardinal, —Christ, —Maria,
—God, . . .
Pompilia, will you let them murder me?

            (book 11, lines 2424–2425)

BOOK 12: "THE BOOK AND THE RING"

Inverting the title of book 1 brings Browning back full circle, as it were, having thus created his ring from the "gold" of the Old Yellow Book. But before it ends on the theme of art, the last book breaks up into a variety of voices that offer views on the execution and the way Guido and his henchmen died. Again the three letters to Francesco Cencini and the secondary source were used, but Browning creates a wider range of voices. The first is the letter of a Venetian visitor to Rome, who comments on the holiday atmosphere of the end of Carnival and remarks on the execution as the most sensational of several contemporary events. The second is a letter from Arcangeli to Cencini (as in the Old Yellow Book), in which the Roman lawyer commiserates with himself on his legal defeat as "the fate of war" (book 12, line 284), but reports that Guido died a good death, begging God's forgiveness (book 12, lines 275–276). Third, Bottini writes to an unknown correspondent and reveals that he is now to represent the convent of the Convertites in their case to claim Pompilia's estate, which will involve him in proving that she was unchaste and therefore merited being sent there. The sermon preached by Fra Celestino, Pompilia's confessor and supporter, outrages him and he encloses a printed version for his correspondent. The friar reminds his audience of the legal system's many failings, then says that the pope's decision was "God's hand" (book 12, line 592), while admitting that what other people might call "the true instinct of the good old man" (book 12, lines 592–593) could also be construed as merely chance. He then delivers his startling claim that all human testimony is flawed:

            —I demand assent
To the enunciation of my text
In face of one proof more that "God is true
And every man a liar"—that who trusts
To human testimony for a fact
Gets this sole fact—himself is proved a fool . . .

            (book 12, lines 598–603)

Thus the tenuous web of language revealed throughout the monologues is again emphasized, at the same time as a good case has been made that the fabric can also be pierced by divine intervention. When Browning returns in his own voice, he is happy to report that the Convertites lost their case for Pompilia's estate and that her memory was vindicated. He too takes up the friar's lesson "that our human speech is naught" (book 12, line 834) and questions what art may achieve; his reply is a major statement on artistic method:

But Art, —wherein man no wise speaks to men,
Only to mankind, —Art may tell a truth
Obliquely, do the thing shall breed the thought,
Nor wrong the thought, missing the mediate
    word.
So may you paint your picture, twice show truth,
Beyond mere imagery on the wall, —
So, note by note, bring music from your mind,
Deeper than ever the Andante dived, —
So write a book shall mean, beyond the facts,
Suffice the eye and save the soul beside.

                (book 12, lines 854–863)

This final explanation of his technique reveals how much the reader has to be involved in the work and has to read between the fallible lines in order to perceive the truth. If it is remarkably similar to what Emily Dickinson was writing at the same time ("Tell all the truth but tell it slant"), it gives a more precise explanation of how "Truth must dazzle gradually / Or every man be blind" (11.7–8). Art can breed a truth by suggestion rather than overt statement and without the danger of relying on a mediating language that rings false. If this demands a good deal of the reader, there are enough pointers in the work to ensure that its true moral center can be discerned.

THE TRAGEDY AND COMEDY OF *THE RING AND THE BOOK*

If Browning intended his masterpiece to be a revelation of divine providence, that revelation was set very much on a dangerous edge in the fallen world. In a famous letter to John Ruskin (10 December 1855, quoted in Woolford and Karlin, 1996), Browning observed that "all poetry" was a "putting [of] the infinite within the finite" (pp. 256–259). Although a paradox, this view of poetry is perhaps the only way of proceeding with respect to *The Ring and the Book,* where human life is shown as bound very much into the finite, and human expression inevitably locked into a fallible language, rife

with ambiguity. As Browning says in the opening book, language is the primary instrument we have: "For how else know we save by worth of word?" (book 1, line 837), but in presenting humanity's faults and flaws by its use of fallible language, he hoped at the same time to depict how the transcendental plane could penetrate and illuminate false witness. In doing so, he also had to negotiate a critical balance between tragedy and comedy.

The petty squabbles and not-so-petty outcome of the trial let the reader into a world of reduced circumstances and imperfect institutions, where individual effort seems to produce no improvement in life and any advancement at all is achieved only by the ability to manipulate and fawn upon one's superiors. The prime example here is Guido's younger brother, Abate Paolo, who came to Rome with the express purpose of making a career in the Church, in which he has succeeded in good measure. Guido himself took minor orders, but despite years of attempting to ingratiate himself with influential clerics and nobility, his efforts came to nothing. Similarly with his other brother, Canon Girolamo, who lives with him in Arezzo during the time of his marriage. As a straitened member of the minor nobility, Guido is therefore a disappointment and a failure. The deposition of a serving woman in the Old Yellow Book details the meanness and frugality with which the family lived at the time the Comparini endured their four months' stay, and Browning gives a skillful rendering of the penny-pinching.

On the other hand, the Comparini seem blessed with an independent income, but fear it will revert to another beneficiary if they have no child to inherit it. Violante adopts the stratagem of purchasing the child of a local prostitute and passing it off as her own not only to the authorities, but even to her own husband. As a mother, she is a ruthless social climber who wants to secure Pompilia's marriage to a wealthy nobleman, but finds only a disillusioned and desperate older man attracted more by a substantial dowry than a pretty young wife.

In any other treatment, this material would be the stuff of comedy, if of a rather cruel kind, but wholly in accord with Victorian taste. The deception over wealth reminds one of the newly married Lammles in Charles Dickens's *Our Mutual Friend* (1864–1865), the older couple who, "both deceiving, both deceived," are at daggers drawn after discovering that neither possesses the income which the other believed they had. Thus the Comparini-Franceschini machinations depict a world of petty deception that is basically comic in its disruption of normality. In the reality of the Old Yellow Book documents, this view is barely sustained, but in the poem the speakers have great fun at the expense of this pettiness, mocking the protagonists, their pretensions and deceptions.

When both parties to the marriage discover the other's deception, the Comparini turn to the law and sue for the return of the dowry by admitting that Pompilia is not their biological daughter, while Guido opposes with a counterclaim and Pompilia then sues for divorce, after appealing to the local authorities, who are unwilling to help. But as neither the law nor the Church provides a resolution, Pompilia assumes the role of romantic heroine with her cavalier priest, and escapes. This again has its comic aspects when Guido overtakes the couple in a single room in the Castelnuovo inn and has them arrested. The governor's tribunal merely sends the canon away to a different seat and Pompilia to a convent. It is this court's interpretation of events as a comedy that ultimately leads to the tragedy.

Pompilia suffers a violent death because of the wiles of her family and instituted authority's failure to save her from the outrage of an embittered husband; her parents also suffer unwarranted slaughter. Moreover, Guido's second monologue (Book 11) reveals a man of desperate inhumanity against which society seems to be impotent: neither the law nor the Church are seen to prevent the terrible climax of events, while opinion after the tragedy is seen to be merely self-interested or mocking. And if the young canon is dissatisfied with the court's earlier interpretation of him as a lover, then he has only himself to blame given his self-admitted reputation for frivolity.

In many ways, the world portrayed is random and capricious, the forces of law and order in Roman society and the Church portrayed in a state of comic disruption. Guido and his henchmen are captured not for the murder but because of a failure to follow municipal procedures. While Pietro and Violante Comparini die immediately as a result of their injuries, Pompilia miraculously survives her twenty-two wounds and is able to identify the murderers. If it is part of Browning's dramatic method to plunge his readers into the precariousness of such a world, there is relief in a young canon who achieves enlightenment and identity in his heroic—but thwarted—attempt at rescue, and there is some resolution as the young heroine/victim achieves self- understanding and fulfillment as a mother before dying with forgiveness for the people who have sinned against her. The whole narrative serves as a cautionary tale where the rigorous example of the pope is a fortuitous, but redeeming, feature in a chaotic world.

If it is by the example of this dreadful series of low domestic events that Browning shows the chance workings of the highest, of the infinite in the finite, he importantly shows the necessity for individuals to find a true order in themselves as a sure path between the extremes of comedy and tragedy that he depicts.

CONCLUSION

Although ultimately he need not have worried, Browning was wary of what readers and reviewers would make of *The Ring and the Book*. In his opening monologue he adopts a jocular tone toward the "British Public, ye who like me not, / (God love you!)" (book 1, lines 410–411), but modulates this more hopefully in the last book to "So, British Public, who may like me yet, / (Marry and amen!)" (book 12, lines 831–832).

As it was, the many positive reviews attested to his "genius" and made favorable comparison with Shakespeare, heralding the work as the "opus magnum of our generation" (*Athenaeum*, 20 March 1869). Such praise was continued by later critics, with G. K. Chesterton in 1903 calling it the "great epic of the age" (Chesterson, 1957, p. 317), and serious evaluations by Henry James and George Santayana led to the first major scholarly studies of the twentieth century, which have continued to produce valuable insights into this complex and superbly crafted work.

For Chesterton, the work was also "typical" of its time in that it was "the enormous multiplication of a small theme" (1957, p. 167);

in this respect it foreshadowed the later modernist scope of James Joyce's *Ulysses* (1922). The same ironic tension between epic stretch and sordid detail is seen in the smaller compass of T. S. Eliot's *The Waste Land* (1922). Many early reviewers commented on *The Ring and the Book* as being like a painting; indeed, it bears comparison with the art of the Pre-Raphaelites, whose precision and workmanship leave the viewer absorbed by the colorful detail rather than the grand design. But the intricate weave of metaphor, allusion, and reference to alternative points of view is ultimately the most captivating aspect of a work that was well before its time in technique, if almost touchingly medieval in its surety of faith.

Selected Bibliography

EDITIONS

The Ring and the Book. Edited by Richard D. Altick. New Haven and London: Yale University Press, 1971. Standard edition of the text.

The Complete Works of Robert Browning. Edited by Roma A. King Jr. et al. 10 vols. Athens: Ohio University Press, 1969–2001. *The Ring and the Book* is in vols. 8 and 9 of this set.

OTHER WORKS BY BROWNING

Dramatic Lyrics. London: Moxon, 1842.

Dramatic Romances and Lyrics. London: Moxon, 1845.

Men and Women. 2 vols. London: Chapman and Hall, 1855.

The Poetical Works of Robert Browning. 6 vols. London: Smith, Elder, 1868.

Robert Browning. Poetical Works, 1833–1864. Edited by Ian Jack. London: Oxford University Press, 1970.

Robert Browning. The Poems. 2 vols. Edited by John Pettigrew, supplemented and completed by Thomas J. Collins. New Haven and London: Yale University Press, 1981.

The Poetical Works of Robert Browning. Edited by Ian Jack. Oxford: Clarendon Press, 1983.

SECONDARY WORKS

Altick, Richard D., and James F. Loucks II. *Browning's Roman Murder Story: A Reading of* The Ring and the Book. Chicago and London: University of Chicago Press, 1968.

Anderson, Vincent P. *Robert Browning as a Religious Poet: An Annotated Bibliography of the Criticism.* Troy, N.Y.: Whitston, 1983.

Bailey, Suzanne. "Somatic Wisdom: Refiguring Bodies in *The Ring and the Book.*" *Victorian Studies* 41 (1998): 567–591.

Baker, Lee C. R. "The Diamond Necklace and the Golden Ring: Historical Imagination in Carlyle and Browning." *Victorian Poetry* 24 (1986): 31–46.

Brady, Ann P. *A Feminist Reading of Robert Browning's* The Ring and the Book. Athens, Ohio: 1988.

Broughton, Leslie N., and Benjamin F. Stelter. *A Concordance to the Poems of Robert Browning.* Repr. 4 vols. New York: Haskell, 1970.

Broughton, Leslie N., Clark S. Northup, and Robert B. Pearsall. *Robert Browning: A Bibliography 1830–1950.* New York: B. Franklin, 1970.

Buckler, William E. *Poetry and Truth in Robert Browning's* The Ring and the Book. New York: New York University Press, 1985.

Chesterton, G. K. *Robert Browning.* New York: St. Martin's Press, 1903.

Cook, A. K. *A Commentary upon Browning's* The Ring and the Book. London and New York: Oxford University Press, 1920.

Corrigan, Beatrice. *Curious Annals: New Documents Relating to Browning's Roman Murder Story.* Toronto: University of Toronto Press, 1956.

Cundiff, Paul A. *Browning's Ring Metaphor and Truth.* Metuchen, N.J.: Scarecrow, 1972.

Curle, Richard, ed. *Robert Browning and Julia Wedgwood: A Broken Friendship as Revealed by Their Letters.* London and New York: F. A. Stokes, 1937. Contains an interesting correspondence on *The Ring and the Book.*

DeVane, William C. *A Browning Handbook.* 2d ed. New York: Appleton-Century-Crofts, 1955.

Drew, Philip. *The Poetry of Robert Browning: A Critical Introduction.* London: Methuen, 1970.

———. *An Annotated Critical Bibliography of Robert Browning.* New York and London: Harvester Wheatsheaf, 1990.

Findlay, L. M. "Taking the Measure of Difference: Deconstruction and *The Ring and the Book.*" *Victorian Poetry* 29 (1991): 401–414.

Gest, John Marshall. *The Old Yellow Book: Source of Browning's* The Ring and the Book. Boston: Chipman Law, 1925.

Griffiths, Eric. *The Printed Voice of Victorian Poetry.* Oxford, U.K., and New York: Oxford University Press, 1989.

Hodell, C. W. *The Old Yellow Book.* Washington, D.C.: Carnegie Institution of Washington., 1908; second edition, 1915.

Honan, Park. *Browning's Characters: A Study in Poetic Technique.* New Haven: Yale University Press, 1961.

Irvine, William, and Park Honan. *The Book, the Ring, and the Poet: A Biography of Robert Browning.* London: Bodley Head, 1975.

James, Henry. *Notes on Novelists with Some Other Notes.* London: J. M. Dent, 1914.

Karlin, Daniel. *Browning's Hatreds.* Oxford, U.K., and New York: Oxford University Press, 1993.

Langbaum, Robert. *The Poetry of Experience: The Dramatic Monologue in Modern Literary Tradition.* New York and Chicago: University of Chicago Press, 1985.

———. "Is Guido Saved? The Meaning of Browning's Conclusion to *The Ring and the Book.*" *Victorian Poetry* 10 (1972): 289–305.

Litzinger, Boyd, and K. L. Knickerbocker, eds. *The Browning Critics.* Lexington: University of Kentucky Press, 1965.

O'Connor, Lisa. "The Construction of a Self: Guido and Metaphor in Book XI of *The Ring and the Book.*" *Australian Universities Modern Language Association* 71 (1989): 139–158.

Pearsall, Cornelia D. J. "Browning and the Poetics of the Sepulchural Body." *Victorian Poetry* 30 (1992): 43–61.

Peckham, Morse. "Historiography and *The Ring and the Book.*" *Victorian Poetry* 6 (1968): 243–257.

Pettit, Alexander. "Place, Time and Parody in *The Ring and the Book.*" *Victorian Poetry* 31 (1993): 95–106.

Raymond, William O. *The Infinite Moment, and Other Essays in Robert Browning.* 2d ed. Toronto: University of Toronto Press, 1965.

Rigg, Patricia Diane. *Robert Browning's Romantic Irony in* The Ring and the Book. Madison, N.J.: Fairleigh Dickinson University Press, 1999.

Rundle, Vivienne J. "'Will You Let Them Murder Me?' Guido and the Reader in *The Ring and the Book.*" *Victorian Poetry* 27 (1989): 99–114.

Ryals, Clyde de L. *The Life of Robert Browning: A Critical Biography.* Oxford, U.K., and Cambridge, Mass.: Blackwell, 1993.

Santayana, George. *Interpretations of Poetry and Religion,* New York: Harper, 1957.

Shaw, David W. "Browning's Murder Mystery: *The Ring and the Book* and Modern Theory." *Victorian Poetry* 27 (1989): 79–98.

Slinn, E. Warwick. *Browning and the Fictions of Identity.* Totowa, N.J.: Barnes and Noble, 1982.

———. "Language and Truth in *The Ring and the Book.*" *Victorian Poetry* 27 (1989): 115–133.

Sullivan, Mary Rose. *Browning's Voices in* The Ring and the Book: *A Study of Method and Meaning.* Toronto: University of Toronto Press, 1969.

Swingle, L. J. "Truth and *The Ring and the Book*: A Negative View." *Victorian Poetry* 6 (1968): 353–365.

Treves, Sir Frederick. *The Country of* The Ring and the Book. London and New York: Cassell, 1913.

Tucker, Herbert F. Jr. *Browning's Beginnings: The Art of Disclosure.* Minneapolis: University of Minnesota Press, 1980.

Ward, Maisie. *Robert Browning and His World.* 2 vols. London: Cassell, 1968–1999.

Wood, Sarah. *Robert Browning: A Literary Life.* Houndsmills, U.K., and New York: Palgrave, 2001.

Woolford, John. *Browning the Revisionary.* New York: St. Martin's, 1988.

Woolford, John, and D. Karlin. *Robert Browning.* New York: Longman, 1996.

Zietlow, Paul. "The Ascending Concerns of *The Ring and the Book*: Reality, Moral Vision and Salvation." *Studies in Philology* 84 (1987): 194–218.

Chinua Achebe's
Things Fall Apart

GARETH CORNWELL

CHINUA ACHEBE WOULD no doubt be pleased by the recognition accorded his first and most famous novel by its inclusion in a series entitled *British Writers Classics.* He would also be affected—wryly amused, perhaps dismayed—by this new evidence of Western culture's powers of cooptation. For *Things Fall Apart* was conceived and written in deliberate reaction against the dominant British tradition of writing about Africa and Africans. Achebe has on numerous occasions recounted how, as a student in the early 1950s, his encounter with Joyce Cary's novel set in West Africa, *Mister Johnson,* convinced him that "the story we had to tell could not be told for us by anyone else no matter how gifted or well intentioned" (*Hopes and Impediments,* p. 38). That realization has proved to be a founding moment for modern African writing, for the publication of *Things Fall Apart* marked the arrival in world literature of an entirely new idiom and field of representation. It was not that there were no other novels by native Africans in existence —fellow Nigerians Amos Tutuola and Cyprian Ekwensi had published books before Achebe—but that *Things Fall Apart* introduced as if from nowhere (for there is no obvious literary precedent for this novel) a fully developed, defiantly non-European style, perspective, and tradition-in-the-making. Ever since, *Things Fall Apart* has remained the very paradigm of African fiction, influencing scores of writers and providing millions of readers around the world with a vivid impression of precolonial African life and its demise.

THINGS FALL APART AS A TRAGEDY

Things Fall Apart is a historical novel set in Igboland, southeastern Nigeria, in the latter part of the nineteenth century. It portrays the consequences for the inhabitants of an Igbo village of the advent of Christian missionaries and British civil administration. The novel is with justice often described as a tragedy, and it makes sense to begin by asking what sort of tragedy it is.

The book's title is taken from W. B. Yeats's poem "The Second Coming," a celebrated evocation of the social and cultural entropy that the poet, writing between the two twentieth-century World Wars, associated with modernity. Achebe employs an extract from the poem as epigraph to his novel:

Turning and turning in the widening gyre
The falcon cannot hear the falconer;
Things fall apart; the center cannot hold;
Mere anarchy is loosed upon the world.

The "widening gyre" of dissolution is in this novel a consequence primarily of the impact of Christianity. Converts to the new religion no longer recognize the authority of the village's time-honored social, cultural, and religious institutions. As the character Obierika recognizes, communal consensus is essential for the survival of the Umuofian community:

> The white man is very clever. He came quietly and peaceably with his religion. We were amused at his foolishness and allowed him to stay. Now he has won our brothers, and our clan can no longer act like one. He has put a knife on the things that held us together and we have fallen apart.
>
> (p. 176)

Without unity, Umuofians can mount no cohesive resistance to the British colonial forces that follow in the missionaries' wake; this in turn means that their traditional way of life is doomed to perish.

This narrative appears to be focused or embodied in the tragic story of Okonkwo, an exemplary representative of the Umuofian people, driven to murder and then suicide by British colonial intrusion. Obierika unequivocally apportions blame for these events when he remonstrates with the District Commissioner: "That man was one of the greatest men in Umuofia. You drove him to kill himself; and now he will be buried like a dog. . . ." (p. 208; suicide is considered by the Igbo an abomination, an offense against the earth precluding ceremonial burial for the deceased). Now in classical tragedy, it will be remembered, the audience witnessed the fate of a man "neither great nor wicked" (in Aristotle's words) brought low by the inscrutable will of the gods. The experience effected a purging or catharsis of the emotions of pity and terror so as to reconcile the audience anew to the flagrant caprice of destiny.

CHRONOLOGY

1600s	Trade between West Africa and Europe commences, initially almost entirely in slaves.
1841	Anglican Church sends its first missionaries to the region.
c.1880–1910	Era in which *Things Fall Apart* is set.
1900	Royal Niger Company's administrative charter is revoked and British Government assumes direct control of the Company's territories.
1920s	Era in which *Arrow of God* is set.
1930	Chinua Achebe born on 16 November in Ogidi, a small town near Onitsha, Nigeria.
1948–1953	Attends University College, Ibadan; graduates with B.A. (London) 1953.
1954	Joins the Nigerian Broadcasting Corporation.
1955–1957	Writes *Things Fall Apart*.
1958	*Things Fall Apart* published; wins the Margaret Wrong Memorial Prize for African Literature the following year.
1960	*No Longer at Ease* published. Nigeria attains independence from Britain.
1962	Achebe appointed founding editor of the hugely influential Heinemann African Writers Series.
1964	*Arrow of God* published.
1966	*A Man of the People* and *Chike and the River* (Achebe's first book for children) published. *Arrow of God* receives the Jock Campbell-*New Statesman* Award for Literature.

Amid widespread dissatisfaction with government corruption, Nigeria experiences its first military coup on January 15, its second on July 29. Achebe's novel *A Man of the People* is credited with having anticipated these developments.

Apart from a brief interlude in the early 1980s, the country will be ruled by a series of military dictators for the next thirty years. Territorial and ethnic discord will prevail as the various nations

	comprising Nigeria seek political and economic accommodations with each other.
1967–1970	The oil-rich southeastern region, homeland of the Igbo people, declares its independence from Nigeria under the name of Biafra. The subsequent civil war, which lasts for three years and sees the deaths of over two million people, culminates in defeat for the secessionists. During these years Achebe travels widely in Africa and abroad, lobbying support for the Biafran cause.
1971	*Beware, Soul Brother* published. Wins the first Commonwealth Poetry Prize the following year.
1972	*Girls at War and Other Stories* published.
1973	Appointed Professor of English, University of Nigeria, Nsukka.
1975	*Morning Yet on Creation Day: Essays* published.
1981	Takes early retirement from the University of Nigeria; in subsequent years accepts a number of positions as visiting professor at institutions abroad, mainly in the United States, where he eventually makes his home.
1983	*The Trouble with Nigeria* published.
1987	*Anthills of the Savannah*—Achebe's fifth novel and first for over two decades—published and short-listed for the Booker Prize.
1988	*Hopes and Impediments* (essays) published.
1999	Nigeria returns to civilian rule: former General Olusegun Obasanjo elected President of the Third Republic of Nigeria.
2000	*Home and Exile* published.

Modern realist narratives deserving of the epithet "tragic" differ in that they historicize and politicize this formula: our feelings of pity and terror are not purged but converted into resentment or anger against the circumstances responsible for the hero's downfall, circumstances seen not as "fate" but in historical terms as the result of human agency. So-called "protest writing" is an extreme manifestation of this tendency, which is visible (as we have seen) in *Things Fall Apart* to the extent that we can blame the British colonizers for the sad end of Okonkwo. Let us, for convenience's sake, label this reading of the novel A.

Since Shakespeare, however, we have become accustomed to a variation on the classic model of tragedy in which greater emphasis is laid on the character of the tragic hero, in such a way as to render him responsible—at least in part—for his tragic fate. In plays such as *Macbeth* or *King Lear* the protagonist is destroyed by a combination of circumstances and a particular flaw or weakness in his make-up, this latter being a moralized version of what Aristotle referred to as *hamartia*. If we apply this modified template to the narrative of Okonkwo, two other possible stories present themselves. In one, Okonkwo is no longer a representative of the clan but an exception, a man whose unfortunate end seems directly accountable to his unique character and temperament (reading B). In the other, Okonkwo remains representative of Umuofia, but his tragic demise now serves to dramatize failings common to the clan as a whole, failings which render its social order brittle and unusually vulnerable to fragmentation (reading C). (In practice, it is virtually impossible to separate B from C: Okonkwo both is and is not "typical," in that he embodies in a relatively extreme fashion certain patterns of thought and behavior characteristic of the community as a whole. Perhaps we should dub this conflated reading B-C.) In any event, I would suggest that none of these readings is on its own correct, but rather that the sympathetic reader must be prepared to countenance all four (and more, of course) in order to gain secure purchase on Achebe's complex and ambivalent representation of the colonial encounter.

In the discussion that follows, I wish to explore two other features of the text which bear strongly upon Okonkwo's story in *Things Fall Apart,* and which—I shall argue—can be in certain ways aligned with the readings or interpretations distinguished above. The first is the question of mode of representation, and the second, the important symbolic role played by gender differentiation.

REPRESENTATION, GENDER, AND THEME

The novel opens in such a way as to set the scene for the first kind of tragic story adumbrated above (reading A):

> As a young man of eighteen [Okonkwo] had brought honor to his village by throwing Ama- linze the Cat. Amalinze was the great wrestler who for seven years was unbeaten, from Umuofia to Mbaino. He was called the Cat because his back would never touch the earth. It was this man that Okonkwo threw in a fight which the old men agreed was one of the fiercest since the founder of their town engaged a spirit of the wild for seven days and seven nights. . . . That was many years ago, twenty years or more, and during this time Okonkwo's fame had grown like a bush-fire in the harmattan. He was tall and huge, and his bushy eyebrows and wide nose gave him a very severe look. He breathed heavily, and it was said that, when he slept, his wives and children in their houses could hear him breathe.
>
> (p. 3–4)

Okonkwo is thus introduced on the first page of the novel as a man of great prowess and achieve- ment, with a reputation that is already the stuff of legend. In the next few pages the elevated folkloric idiom will be sustained as Achebe elaborates this portrait of an archetypal hero figure, offering Okonkwo's hapless father, Unoko, as a comic contrastive foil. The reader appears to have embarked on an epic narrative in which qualities such as strength and weak- ness, and good and evil, promise to be both clearly differentiated and fully externalized through embodiment in human conduct or performance (as opposed to the inner realm of thought or emotion). In such a narrative, Okonkwo will become a tragic figure through

innocent victimhood at the hands of the interloping missionaries and imperial officials.

Then, in the second section of chapter 2, a different kind of story about Okonkwo emerges. This story explains his behavior not in terms of mythic patterns or heroic values but according to the conventions of psychological realism. (It is, of course, a generalized sort of psychological realism, a cursory interiority, far removed from the minute discriminations of consciousness characteristic of the European Modernist novel, and not inconsistent with the oral epic register of the novel as a whole.) Okonkwo's strength, we are told, is actually a weakness, the expres- sion of a chronic fear:

> Okonkwo ruled his household with a heavy hand. His wives, especially the youngest, lived in perpetual fear of his fiery temper, and so did his little children. Perhaps down in his heart Okonkwo was not a cruel man. But his whole life was dominated by fear, the fear of failure and weakness. . . . Okonkwo's fear . . . was not external but lay deep within himself. It was the fear of himself, lest he should be found to resemble his father. Even as a little boy he had resented his father's failure and weakness, and even now he still remembered how he had suffered when a playmate had told him that his father was *agbala*.
>
> (p. 13)

If we pursue this story through the novel, a dif- ferent sort of tragedy emerges. Through overcompensating for his fear of being thought weak, Okonkwo commits some serious errors. First he beats his wife Ojuigo during the Week of Peace; then, he not only joins the party of men charged with the sacrifice of Ikemefuna but actually does the deed himself, cutting down the child who has for years lived in his home as an adopted son. (The narrator tells us that Okonkwo is at that moment "dazed with fear . . . of being thought weak" [61]; we might rather be inclined to interpret this "fear" as blind panic occasioned by the horror of the situation.) Nevertheless, these excesses culminate in the unintentional slaying of a kinsman, for which

Okonkwo is banished from the village for seven years. When he returns, he is unable to regain his position in the community because the world of Umuofia has changed: the Christians have established themselves and the clan's autonomy is being challenged by the new British colonial administration. Unable to adapt owing to the inflexibility of his temperament, he seals his own fate through one further rash, inappropriate and excessive deed. Acting on impulse, he kills the messenger sent by the District Commissioner to break up a meeting of the clan's elders. It is the desperate act of a man whose very sense of identity is collapsing in the shame of surrender and submission: it seems that Okonkwo cannot survive *as Okonkwo* in the new dispensation. But neither he nor his conduct is representative of the Umuofian community: as much as they respect him, the other men do not act as he does, and the reader has long been aware that Obierika is often disapproving of his arrogant, impulsive friend. Thus we might say that while Okonkwo's doom is precipitated by colonial incursion, it remains essentially his affair alone (reading B).

At the same time, although the others do not act as he does, Okonkwo undoubtedly embodies the values of the traditional warrior code and remains the paragon whom Umuofian men aspire to emulate: it is only their cowardice, abetted by an acquired habit of passive acceptance, that restrains them from doing so. Thus, in as much as Okonkwo remains representative of Umuofia and Igbo society more generally, his fate is consequent on a characteristic intemperance and unwillingness to adapt which together render the Umuofian community especially susceptible to influence and injury by external forces (reading C). There is considerable evidence to support this interpretation, most of which will be led when we come to consider the significance of gender identifications in the novel. Here I wish to point out a feature of Igbo social organization that is not necessarily apparent to the reader, but which Achebe has in recent years been at pains to stress.

In the first of three lectures delivered at Harvard University in 1998 and published as *Home and Exile,* Achebe drew attention to some salient features of traditional Igbo culture. First, delving into the history of his hometown of Ogidi, he tells the story of how a new clan moving into the vicinity asked to be shown how to worship the gods of Ogidi. The people of Ogidi were unwilling to oblige until an appropriate compromise was reached—the new neighbors' gods would be called the sons and daughters of their gods! From "the reluctance of an Igbo town to foist its religious beliefs and practices on a neighbour across the road, even when it was invited to do so," Achebe concludes that "such a people could not have had any notion of the psychology of religious imperialism. And that innocence would have placed them at a great disadvantage later when they came to deal with European evangelism" (*Home and Exile,* p. 12–13).

Secondly, Achebe ponders the fact that the Igbo had no kings or central government, but chose rather to live in a multitude of independent village communities or clans. He concludes:

> those hundreds of autonomous Igbo villages and towns, so deeply suspicious of political amalgamation, would be stretched to the limit should they ever face an enemy able to wield the resources of a centralized military power, acting directly or through local surrogates. They would need every fortification to be found in their histories and creation myths. The threat of anarchy, always attendant on the Igbo choice of political organization, crept closer and closer to realization as the devastation of the Atlantic slave trade reached further and further into their heartland.
>
> (p. 17–18)

He goes on to speak of "the cosmological fear of anarchy that burdened the characters in [*Things Fall Apart*]" (p. 19).

These observations help to explain the precariousness of Umuofian society: traditional beliefs and practices are adhered to with a dedication and tenacity proportional to the tenuousness of the people's sense of stability and community, their fear of things falling apart. The basic problem for the Igbo is that the communality on which their sense of group identity must be founded is undermined ab initio by an overwhelming cultural emphasis on the importance of the *individual*:

> This insistence on separate and individual creations of towns chimed perfectly with [the Igbos'] belief that every single human being was a unique creation of chi, Chukwu's agent, assigned exclusively to that individual throughout his or her life. . . . (p. 14) To assert the worth of the individual by making him not the product of some ongoing, generic creativity but rather of a particular once-and-for-all divine activity is about as far as human imagination can go on the road of uniqueness.
>
> (*Home and Exile*, pp. 14, 16)

The concept of the *chi* or personal god is crucial to the way in which the characters in Achebe's novel negotiate the tension between their community's healthy respect for individual achievement and their shared religious sense of helpless equality before the inscrutable authority of the gods. The blame for the manifold failure of Unoka, Okonkwo's father, is thus explained: "Unoka was an ill-fated man. He had a bad *chi* or personal god, and evil fortune followed him to the grave, or rather to his death, for he had no grave. He died of the swelling which was an abomination to the earth goddess" (p. 18). In the case of Okonkwo, on the other hand:

> Anyone who knew his grim struggle against poverty and misfortune could not say he had been lucky. If ever a man deserved his success, that man was Okonkwo. At an early age he had achieved fame as the greatest wrestler in all the land. That was not luck. At the most one could say that his *chi* or personal god was good. But the Ibo people have a proverb that when a man says yes his *chi* says yes also. Okonkwo said yes very strongly; so

his *chi* agreed. And not only his *chi* but his clan too, because it judged a man by the work of his hands.

> (p. 27)

The suggestion here is that it is the individual and not Chukwu, working through his *chi*, who fashions his destiny. But the proverb quoted above is contradicted by another, invoked by the villagers when Okonkwo beats his wife Ojiugo during the Week of Peace: "people said he had no respect for the gods of the clan. His enemies said his good fortune had gone to his head. They called him the little bird *nza* who so far forgot himself after a heavy meal that he challenged his *chi*" (p. 31). And it is to this viewpoint that Okonkwo himself turns for bitter consolation after his return from exile:

> His life had been ruled by a great passion—to become one of the lords of the clan. That had been his life- spring. And he had all but achieved it. Then everything had been broken. He had been cast out of his clan like a fish onto a dry, sandy beach, panting. Clearly his personal god or *chi* was not made for great things. A man could not rise beyond the destiny of his *chi*. The saying of the elders was not true—that if a man said yea his *chi* also affirmed. Here was a man whose *chi* said nay despite his own affirmation.
>
> (p. 131)

The unresolved—irresolvable—tension between individual endeavor and the whims of the *chi* not only touches on timeless and universal questions of free will but also appears specifically to embody the ambivalence with which Achebe approaches traditional Igbo beliefs in this novel. What is more, it is an ambivalence that the contradictory Umuofian wisdom on the subject of *chi* suggests is inscribed in the very belief system of the Igbo people. In a poem called "Misunderstanding," Achebe recalls his father's favorite saying—"Wherever Something / stands, he'd say, there also Something / Else will stand" (*Beware, Soul Brother*, p. 33)—and provides the following gloss:

The Igbo people have a firm belief in the duality of things. Nothing is by itself, nothing is absolute. . . . Igbo proverbs bring out this duality of existence very well. Take any proverb that puts forward a point of view or a "truth" and you can always find another that contradicts it or at least puts a limitation on the absoluteness of its validity.
(*Beware, Soul Brother*, pp. 65–66)

For souls in search of certainty, the suspensive subtlety of the concept of *chi*—existing in the form of an ongoing, unfinishable conversation—would clearly be no match for the hearty dogma of a revealed religion like Christianity, with its fixed creeds and litanies. (Achebe returns to the whole question of the nature, power, and function of traditional religious beliefs in his third novel, the superb *Arrow of God* [1964].)

I wish now to return to a comparative consideration of the three readings of *Things Fall Apart* identified above as A, B, and C, by examining their gendered associations within the novel. This step is mandated both by the novel's insistence that masculinity and femininity are key concepts in the Igbo people's symbolic coding of reality, and by the fact that Achebe uses this to create a major imagistic and interpretive motif in the novel.

In the first place, Umuofia is quite obviously a patriarchal society. Masculine values are universally paramount: men dominate their womenfolk; men make the decisions affecting the tribe as a whole; men dispense justice; only men may join the secret order of the *egwugwu* and assume the guise of the ancestral spirits. Okonkwo himself is practically a caricature of the values of masculinity: his strength, his courage, his ferocity and prowess in war, his unbending will and severe (self-)discipline. In the eyes of a man like Okonkwo, manliness is actually defined in terms of domination over women:

[Okonkwo] was always happy when he heard [Nowoye] grumbling about women. That showed that in time he would be able to control his women-folk. No matter how prosperous a man was, if he was unable to rule his women and his

children (and especially his women) he was not really a man.

(p. 53)

On the other hand, clustered about the opposite pole of femininity are several qualities associated with Okonkwo's father, Unoka. These qualities are despised by Okonkwo as symptomatic of failure, though they need not necessarily be so regarded: gentleness, idleness (an interest in music and culture, the arts of peace rather than war), love of conversation (contrast Okonkwo's characteristic silence), and sociableness (contrast, again, Okonkwo's solitariness).

Now what is interesting to note at this point is that, right from the beginning of the novel, everything associated with the dominant male principle in the tribe is shadowed or underpinned by something with female associations. The war-medicine for which Umuofia is famous, ensuring the tribe's success in war, is named *agadi-uwayi* or "old woman." The clan's Oracle seems to embody a male principle of absolute authority (evoking unquestioning obedience), and yet its name is *Agbala*, which means woman, and its priestess or interpreter is a woman named Chielo. What is more, the supreme deity in the Igbo pantheon is Ani, "the earth goddess and source of all fertility" (p. 36). All aberrations execrated by the clan as "abominations" are designated thus because of the offense they cause to Ani, which means that the ultimate arbiter of what is good, proper and natural is female. Finally, when Okonkwo is driven into exile it is to his mother's kinsfolk in Mbanta that he flees, a fact of which his aged uncle Uchendo is at pains to remind him. Pointing out that a name frequently given to children is Nneka, meaning "Mother is Supreme," he goes on:

It's true that a child belongs to its father. But when a father beats his child, it seeks sympathy in its mother's hut. A man belongs to his fatherland when things are good and life is sweet. But when there is sorrow and bitterness he finds refuge in his motherland. Your mother is there to protect you. She is buried there. And that is why we say that mother is supreme.

(p. 134)

The overarching importance thus symbolically afforded to "female" values by the clan suggests that Okonkwo's attitudes and behavior, far from being exemplary or even typical, are in fact eccentric and unbalanced. The narrator emphasizes Okonkwo's pride and "brusqueness in dealing with less successful men" (p. 26), noting how the entire company at a kindred meeting turns against him when he insults an untitled man by impugning his masculinity (p. 26). One might also mention his seemingly excessively harsh treatment of his son Nwoye; his wife-beating, even in the Week of Peace (pp. 29–30); and of course—and despite a direct warning to the contrary from one of the clan's most respected elders, Ezeudu (p. 57)—his hand in the death of Ikemefuna. Whatever his motive for joining the group charged with the killing, and however involuntary the actual blow, Okonkwo's conduct here compromises the sympathy of even the most indulgent reader and seems to set in motion the fateful sequence of events that culminate in his suicide. The discrepancy between Okonkwo's exaggerated machismo and the behavior of a reasonable or typical Umuofian man emerges clearly in the conversation he has with Obierika afterwards:

Whenever the thought of his father's weakness and failure troubled him he expelled it by thinking about his own strength and success. And so he did now. His mind went to his latest show of manliness.

"I cannot understand why you refused to come with us to kill that boy," he asked Obierika.

"Because I did not want to," Obierika replied sharply. "I had something better to do."

"You sound as if you question the authority and the decision of the Oracle, who said he should die."

"I do not. Why should I? But the Oracle did not ask me to carry out its decision."

"But someone had to do it. If we were all afraid of blood, it would not be done. And what do you think the Oracle would do then?"

"You know very well, Okonkwo, that I am not afraid of blood; and if anyone tells you that I am, he is telling a lie. And let me tell you one thing, my friend. If I were you I would have stayed at home. What you have done will not please the Earth. It is the kind of action for which the goddess wipes out whole families."

"The Earth cannot punish me for obeying her messenger," Okonkwo said. "A child's fingers are not scalded by a piece of hot yam which a mother puts into its palm."

"That is true," Obierika agreed. "But if the Oracle said that my son should be killed I would neither dispute it nor be the one to do it."

(pp. 66–67)

This is a revealing exchange. Okonkwo defends himself by appealing simultaneously to a standard public discourse on bravery and the necessity of obedience to the Oracle. His attitude exhibits an absolute or unquestioning respect for authority that in the symbolic schema of the novel we are encouraged to regard as quintessentially masculine. Obierika's response, on the other hand, is marked by compassion and common sense and evinces a capacity for flexibility or adaptability conspicuously absent in Okonkwo's discourse. That we are prompted to interpret this as feminine thinking is underscored by Obierika's prescient invocation of the authority of the Earth goddess. There is a parallel passage a few pages later:

"Sometimes I wish I had not taken the *ozo* title," said Obierika. "It wounds my heart to see these young men killing palm trees in the name of tapping."

"It is so indeed," Okonkwo agreed. "But the law of the land must be obeyed."

"I don't know how we got that law," said Obierika. "In many other clans a man of title is not forbidden to climb the palm tree. Here we say he cannot climb the tall tree but he can tap the short ones standing on the ground. It is like

Dimaragana, who would not lend his knife for cutting up dogmeat because the dog was taboo to him, but offered to use his teeth."

"I think it is good that our clan holds the *ozo* title in high esteem," said Okonkwo.

(pp. 69–70)

Here Okonkwo is again insisting on blind obedience to the law of the land, while Obierika's perspective is considerably less dogmatic and more open-minded, even to the point of entertaining what we today recognize as cultural relativism. Obierika, "a man who thought about things" (p. 125), brings the same questioning point of view to bear on matters such as Okonkwo's excessive punishment for an inadvertent offense and the treatment of twins in the village (p. 125).

Nwoye, like his grandfather, is associated from the beginning with female rather than male values. As a boy he far prefers his mother's whimsical animal stories to the fierce narratives of battle told by his father (Okonkwo of course regards all women's stories as "silly" (p. 75). Nwoye's reaction to the killing of Ikemefuna is a revulsion so strong and integral to his character that, in order to capture its intensity, the narrator seems obliged to resort to metaphor: "something seemed to give way inside him, like the snapping of a tightened bow" (p. 61). It is an emotional pain that Nwoye had experienced once before, when hearing the pitiful cries of infant twins abandoned to die in the forest. It is thus through the feelings of the sensitive and compassionate Nwoye, as well as in the questionings of the thoughtful Obierika, that the novel's reservations about certain traditional Ibo customs are registered. In the terms of the narrative, it is the "feminine" aspects of Nwoye's personality—his gentleness and kindness, his imaginative sympathy, his love for stories and music—that make him a natural convert to Christianity.

It was not the mad logic of the Trinity that captivated him. He did not understand it. It was

the poetry of the new religion, something felt in the marrow. The hymn about brothers who sat in darkness and in fear seemed to answer a vague and persistent question that haunted his young soul— the question of the twins crying in the bush and the question of Ikemefuna who was killed. He felt a relief within as the hymn poured into his parched soul.

(p. 147)

Now Christians are consistently perceived as "effeminate" (153) and "womanly" (p. 159) by Okonkwo, who blames the religion for making Umuofian men "soft like women" (p. 183). He even dismisses Nowoye as "a woman" for joining the Christians (p. 172). It is as if the "feminine" values of Christianity appeal to a keen but repressed need in Igbo society, a need denied or effaced by the dominant patriarchal discourse. It is a need for greater recognition and indulgence not only of the qualities of "softness" associated in the Western tradition with femininity—tolerance, compassion, gentleness, selflessness—but also other values that attach themselves to the female principle in *Things Fall Apart*, most strikingly (and, for the Western reader, counter-intuitively), common sense or rationality. This can be seen at work in Obierika's musings, in Ekwefi's insistence on following the priestess Chielo in her wanderings with Enzinma, and in the attitude of the "effeminate" Christians towards the sacred python or the untouchable *osu*, who find full acceptance in the Christian congregation for the first time in their lives (pp. 155–157). This flouting of the "superstitious" aspects of Umuofian tradition is the exact opposite of Okonkwo's masculine discourse of absolute authority and obedience.

It makes sense to speak, then, of two contrasting, "gendered" perspectives on the narrative of *Things Fall Apart*, generating two stories which correspond essentially to readings A and B-C distinguished above. The first point to be made is that the stories unfold in two different modes of discourse. The first story inhabits the realm of legend. It posits heroic masculine values as supreme and construes the community's customs and values as fixed and unchanging, existing, as it were, outside of history. Into this changeless, perfectly functioning society come intruders from abroad, who ridicule the local customs and values and impose new ones. The sad fate of Okonkwo bears exemplary witness to this tragic course of events. We might call this the masculine narrative embedded in *Things Fall Apart.*

The other, "feminine" narrative portrays, on the contrary, a dynamic society already in the process of disintegrating as a result of its own internal contradictions. We are often reminded of ways in which the customs and practices of the clan have changed over time (pp. 22, 31, 137, 166–167); and one of the most memorable proverbs in the novel recognizes the necessity of adaptation to changed circumstances: "Eneke the bird says that since men have learned to shoot without missing, he has learned to fly without perching" (p. 22). A wise man like Obierika finds it difficult to reconcile certain traditions of the tribe with his own ideas of what is good or right—traditions such as the abandonment of twins, obedience to the Oracle even when it demands the sacrifice of an innocent youth, the harsh punishment of people for accidental offenses, or the cruel and irrational treatment of those designated *osu*. Sensitive souls like Nwoye have similar misgivings about these things. In terms of this communal story, Okonkwo not only embodies a damaging repression of feminine values and qualities; he has also failed to understand the nature of his own society, misreading any sign of flexibility or openness as divisive weakness. In this "feminine" perspective, the demise of traditional Umuofia is in some ways tragic and regrettable, yet in other ways inevitable and even to be welcomed.

Reminding ourselves that these two stories are merely aspects of the same complex narrative, we can conclude that Achebe has presented a finely balanced picture of early colonial encounter in Igboland. And there is no doubt that one's sense of the narrator's generous even-handedness is what makes the concluding paragraph of the novel so strikingly effective:

> The Commissioner went away, taking three or four of the soldiers with him. In the many years in which he had toiled to bring civilization to different parts of Africa he had learned a number of things. One of them was that a District Commissioner must never attend to such undignified details as cutting a hanged man from the tree. Such attention would give the natives a poor opinion of him. In the book which he planned to write he would stress that point. As he walked back to the court he thought about that book. Every day brought him some new material. The story of this man who had killed a messenger and hanged himself would make interesting reading. One could almost write a whole chapter on him. Perhaps not a whole chapter but a reasonable paragraph, at any rate. There was so much else to include, and one must be firm in cutting out details. He had already chosen the title of the book, after much thought: *The Pacification of the Primitive Tribes of the Lower Niger.*
>
> (pp. 208–209)

In a narrative hitherto innocent of knowing authorial irony, this brief sardonic glimpse into the mind of the complacent British official is simply devastating. The entire novel now functions to show up this character's stupid self-importance and self-delusion. The irony at his expense builds, sentence by sentence, until—already outraged at the trivializing of Okonkwo's story to a "reasonable paragraph" of "interesting reading" by this ignorant expert on Africa—the reader experiences each word of the book title which concludes the novel as a hammer blow of social and political protest. Moreover, one's anger and pity is sharpened by the chill terror of recognition that the paragraph one has just read accurately enacts the way in which the story of African colonization has up to this point typically been inscribed in European history. The effect is shocking, and was doubtless intended to be. Perhaps it is time we returned to our point of departure, in order to gain both a clearer sense of Achebe's purpose in writing and some understanding of the means he employed to achieve it.

THINGS FALL APART: CONTEXT AND SIGNIFICANCE

Things Fall Apart may be a direct retort to what Achebe regarded as the caricature of Africans in *Mister Johnson*, but its significance is more clearly discernible in juxtaposition with the most celebrated literary evocation of Africa in the European tradition, Conrad's *Heart of Darkness* (1902). In an essay published in 1977, "An Image of Africa," Achebe offered a trenchant critique of Conrad's famous novel which served to expose a text long celebrated for its searing indictment of Western hypocrisy as in fact perpetuating some of the West's most derogatory and insulting stereotypes of Africa and Africans. The customary defense of *Heart of Darkness* in the face of Achebe's attack is to say that, while the book carries the inevitable imprint of the ideas on race current in the late nineteenth century, it is not ultimately *about* Africa or race or colonialism. On the contrary, the novel has a *universal* theme: it reveals, say, the fragility of civilization and the savagery that lurks in the innermost heart of every human being. But this is what Achebe has said on the subject of "universality":

> I should like to see the word "universal" banned altogether from discussions of African literature until such a time as people cease to use it as a synonym for the narrow, self-serving parochialism of Europe, until their horizon extends to include all the world.
>
> ("Colonialist Criticism," *Hope and Impediments* p. 76).

According to Achebe, the West uses the rubric of the "universal" to impose upon others the point of view and values which it regards as "natural," "reasonable," "logical," etc. The concept of the universal thus glosses over historical and cultural specificity, it reduces

difference to the same, it assimilates the other to the self. The first task of non-Western literature, as—like *Things Fall Apart*—it impinges on Western consciousness as an aesthetic artifact fashioned in a Western form and language, is therefore to assert its difference, to insist on its otherness, to refuse facile assimilation. In so doing it draws attention to the contingency of ways of seeing and speaking which, for its Western audience especially, have hitherto seemed inevitable or natural; in so doing it demonstrates the extent to which these ways of seeing and speaking have formed or deformed an entire conception of the world and pre-empted the meaning of cultural difference. As an assertion of otherness, post- coloniality comes into being with the recognition of colonialism as discourse, and the business of post-coloniality becomes the deconstruction of the world as it has been constructed by colonial discourse.

Thus it is that many critics date the appearance of postcolonial literature to 1958, almost twenty years before Achebe's essay on Conrad: the year in which *Things Fall Apart* first appeared. To compare the two novels is to appreciate the extent to which Achebe's novel is a response to Conrad's, a singular instance of "the Empire writing back to the Centre," in Salman Rushdie's famous phrase. The differences between the two novels are legion, but they can be reduced to a single phrase—point of view—and point of view makes all the difference in the world. It probably goes without saying that it is not necessarily the case that any African who writes a novel will automatically write from an African perspective. For a writer like Achebe, mission-educated and taught as a young Christian to despise the unconverted "heathen" or "people of nothing" ("Named for Victoria, Queen of England," *Hopes and Impediments*, p. 30) and all their ways, such a point of view may be the achievement of years of concerted "unlearning" or self re-education. In his essay "Named for Victoria, Queen of England," Achebe writes: "I now know that my first book, *Things Fall Apart*, was an act of atonement with my past, the ritual return and homage of a prodigal son" (p. 38). This experience of what Ngugi wa Thiong'o has called "homecoming" is something that Achebe shared with an entire generation of African intellectuals who came to repudiate the cultural assumptions of the system in which they were educated, and to revaluate pre-colonial African culture. It must be added, though, that Achebe has remained a political moderate in his willingness to embrace a syncretic identity in which elements of African and Western culture are blended. While Ngugi and others have abandoned English as a literary medium in favor of indigenous African languages, Achebe has consistently defended his use of English, arguing that his work helps to Africanize the language, to domesticate it for African use as a lingua franca.

How this Africanization proceeds can be illustrated by returning to the comparison with *Heart of Darkness*. This is one of the narrator Marlow's more memorable (but patently dehumanizing) descriptions of the Africans he encounters on his journey:

> But suddenly, as we struggled round a bend, there would be a glimpse of rush walls, of peaked grass roofs, a burst of yells, a whirl of black limbs, a mass of hands clapping, of feet stamping, of bodies swaying, of eyes rolling, under the droop of heavy and motionless foliage. The steamer toiled along slowly on the edge of a black and incomprehensible frenzy. The prehistoric man was cursing us, praying to us, welcoming us—who could tell?
>
> (p. 37)

In *Things Fall Apart* Africans of the same historical era appear as the Igbo inhabitants of the village of Umuofia: a civilized, agrarian community, distinguished by a high standard of personal and public morality and a great respect for the law; a community with a democratic system of government and great respect for the rights of the individual; a community in which social interaction is marked by elaborate courtesy, and speech is characterized by vivid,

concrete imagery and wise proverbs. When Marlow hears distant drums beating as he journeys up the river, he generously allows the sound a purpose—"whether it meant war, peace or prayer, we could not tell" (p. 37)—but it does not occur to him that the drums might merely be calling people to watch a wrestling match (as they are at the beginning of *Things Fall Apart*). The objection that the comparison with Conrad is unfair because it is anachronistic has already been answered by Achebe. Discussing his objections to Joyce Cary's novel *Mister Johnson*, which was published to great critical acclaim in 1952, just a couple of years before he began work on *Things Fall Apart*, Achebe writes:

> There is a certain undertow of uncharitableness just below the surface on which [Cary's] narrative moves and from where, at the slightest chance, a contagion of distaste, hatred and mockery breaks through to poison his tale. Here is a short excerpt from his description of a fairly innocent party given by Johnson to his friends: "The demonic appearance of the naked dancers, grinning, shrieking, scowling, or with faces which seemed entirely dislocated, senseless and unhuman, like twisted bags of lard, or burst bladders." Haven't I encountered this crowd before? Perhaps, in *Heart of Darkness*, in the Congo. But Cary is writing about my home, Nigeria, isn't he?
>
> (*Home and Exile*, p. 24)

To recognize that Achebe's novel effectively inhabits a different world of discourse from Conrad's and Cary's is not to deny the intertextuality between them: as I have said, there is a real sense in which Achebe writes back to Conrad. We might for instance compare Kurtz's report for the Society for the Suppression of Savage Customs in *Heart of Darkness* with the book the District Commissioner intends to write in *Things Fall Apart, The Pacification of the Primitive Tribes of the Lower Niger*—the irony attaching to the words "savage" and "primitive" is similarly created and directed. There are even echoes of the discourse on Africa that *Heart of Darkness* engages in Achebe's famous description of his role as a writer:

Here then is an adequate revolution for me to espouse—to help my society regain belief in itself and put away the complexes of the years of denigration and self abasement. And it is essentially a question of education, in the best sense of that word. Here, I think, my aims and the deepest aspirations of my society meet. . . . I would be quite satisfied if my novels (especially the ones I set in the past) did no more than teach my readers that their past—with all its imperfections—was not one long night of savagery from which the first Europeans acting on God's behalf delivered them. Perhaps what I write is applied art as distinct from pure. But who cares? Art is important, but so is education of the kind I have in mind. And I don't see that the two need be mutually exclusive.

("The Novelist as Teacher," *Hopes and Impediments*, pp. 44, 45)

Here, then, is the *difference* of *Things Fall Apart* as a postcolonial novel. It is a book that seeks to educate and to rehabilitate by waging discursive warfare against the lingering effects of "the years of denigration and self-abasement." What is so remarkable about it is that its appeal is not confined to any particular audience. In a characteristic display of cultural arrogance, early European reviewers accused Achebe of vitiating his work's artistic integrity by providing lashings of anthropological information for Western consumption. Achebe's rejoinder that he was not in the first instance writing for a Western audience is supported by the novel's reception in Nigeria and the rest of Africa, where it remains a best seller and *the* canonical modern African novel. (On the question of anthropological description, Achebe has on several occasions insisted that he did no research for his novel but drew on childhood memories of village life and the ways and sayings of his "heathen" neighbors and relatives.)

Is it only with regard to point of view that *Things Fall Apart* differs from Western novels? How is this difference manifested? Is there anything else specifically African about Achebe's book? Or is it simply a typical example of that Western genre we call the novel that just happens to be set in Africa and to feature African characters?

Before I proceed to address these questions I would like to anticipate the objection that they are irrelevant because good art is "universal." I would reply that to make such a statement is to perpetuate specifically Western assumptions about the nature of art and what it is that makes it good. Like any other kind of value, aesthetic values are culture-specific, and their specificity deserves particular respect when they are deliberately embodied in the text—as, I will argue, they are in *Things Fall Apart*.

Let us begin by returning to Achebe's description of his enterprise as "applied" art rather than "pure" art. The latter term refers us back to a notion first formulated in Europe in the early nineteenth century—*l'art pour l'art*—meaning (in this context) that fictional mimesis or representation is self-validating and requires no additional justification.

Now, as has often been pointed out, a conception of art as an expression of an individual's vision of the world that is an end in itself is utterly foreign to African tradition. Before colonialism and literacy, African art was functional and communal in nature. The plastic arts and crafts that were produced consisted of, on the one hand, useful (however embellished) artifacts, like drinking vessels and weapons; and on the other hand, items with ritual, religious, and symbolic significance, like spirit masks. Verbal art was oral. Through stories, myths, epic poems, and proverbs, oral tradition sought to preserve the history of the community and to codify and memorialize its core values, thus fostering unity and identity. Similarly, Achebe's novel, although it features a central protagonist, is in fact a tale which commemorates a whole community or society at a crucial time of dislocation in its history; moreover, *Things Fall Apart* serves a communal purpose in the present in that it speaks on behalf of Igbo people (and beyond them,

Nigerians and Africans in general), addressing present psychological, emotional and political needs.

One of the most important indicators of this identity and function is the oral quality of the narrative. If one compares a page of *Things Fall Apart* with a page from virtually any twentieth-century British novel, a number of differences become evident (in their groundbreaking study *Towards the Decolonization of African Literature,* Chinweizu and Madubuike and Madubuike compare the first page of Achebe's book with the first page of Cary's *Mister Johnson*). One notes in Achebe's text an absence or at least paucity of highly detailed descriptions of people, places, emotions, etc.: there are, for instance, no "set-piece" descriptions of landscape conventionally found in the scene-setting portions of a narrative. I would suggest that the main reason for this is that *Things Fall Apart*'s narrative style retains traces of orality, of the oral tradition of narrative in Igbo culture. Oral narrative is governed by a temporal rather than spatial dynamic: one can't go back and re-read spoken discourse, and one can't pause or linger for too long lest one loses one's audience. In the novel's oral narrative economy, descriptive detail of the kind customary in Western fiction is redundant. Although the story is realistic, what Roland Barthes has called "the reality effect" (the inclusion of authenticating, unmotivated detail) is largely absent. What is narrated is simply what needs to be narrated in order for the narrative's meaning or "point" to be made clear; it consists of no more nor less than what is necessary in order for the "message" or "lesson" to be made clear to the listeners or readers. This does not mean that the narrative unfolds in a straightforwardly linear way: there is plenty of prolepsis (for instance, the "ill-fated" Ikemefuna is first mentioned in chapter 1) and digression (e.g., bride price negotiations, new yam festivals, the activities of the Christians). Perhaps linearity itself is a western narrative convention: Ngugi wa Thiong'o, for instance, has described "the linear/biographical

unfolding of a story" as "removed from [the] actual social practice" of storytelling (*Decolonizing the Mind,* p. 76).

Another striking feature of *Things Fall Apart* is the meagerness of interiority: that is, very little narrative time is devoted to the revelation of characters' innermost thoughts and feelings. The emphasis throughout is on *action*, on human conduct. In this world, what matters about people is the way they behave; the truth about them is visible in their conduct, not hidden away in the part of them which is private and invisible to others (how different from the assumptions informing Western modernist texts like *To the Lighthouse* or *The Sound and the Fury*!). This is because a heroic, pre-modern society is being represented largely according to the conventions of what Ian Watt in *The Rise of the Novel* called the "high mimetic" or heroic narrative mode, as distinct from the "low mimetic mode" of the bourgeois novel.

Thirdly, narrative authority in *Things Fall Apart* is not neutral or detached. The narrator is not an omniscient, unseen, infallible mediator whose presence is all but effaced. Achebe's narrator rather seems to derive his authority from the views of the represented community. A character will often be introduced via his or her reputation in the tribe, or via, say, his or her parents' or friends' opinions about him or her; or as he or she is seen through the eyes of others. The narrator thus seems for the most part to speak representatively and sympathetically, for the community. Only very occasionally is a sense of distance between the narrator and the characters in the presented world made explicit—for instance, when he remarks that "Among the Ibo the art of conversation is regarded very highly . . ." (p. 7). For by far the greater part of the text, what is evoked by the narrative strategy is a kind of communal point of view, importantly, a point of view that is not *judged* by the implied author. This seeming neutrality on the part of the narrator allows him to report on practices, customs, and events which may be new or strange or incredible to the reader, in such a way as to get them to appear *normal* or natural and unexceptional. For example, the belief that that Okonkwo and other elders dressed up in raffia masks become *egwugwu* or ancestral spirits, or that Ezinma is an *ogbanje*—"one of those wicked children who, when they died, entered their mothers' wombs to be born again" (p. 77)—these are simply reported without comment. Possibly the most memorable instance of this is the description in chapter 9 of the discovery of Ezinma's *ogbange* charm, her *iyi-uwa*. While most readers will assume that the fetish is planted by Okagbue, the man who digs for it, Achebe declines to comment on this possibility and asks us to witness the event at face value, as it is witnessed, indeed, by the characters present. One might compare Achebe's narrative strategy here with that of magic realism, a mode which allows what to the modern Western mind appear to be fantastic events and situations to be represented from the point of view of characters who accept them as real. "Irrational" beliefs and "superstitions" are thus represented without judgment or condemnation, and a community or culture appears in its coherent totality, not censored or deformed through subjection to normative Western rationalism.

Perhaps one of the strongest indicators of orality in the novel (here the term indicates specifically the oral nature of the society portrayed) is the conversational idiom of both the characters and the narrator. Spoken discourse as represented in the novel is highly formal, often ritualized. And just as elaborate courtesies, such as the breaking of kola nut, mark all but the most casual social encounters, so conversation itself is thoroughly stylized through the frequent use of proverbs. The narrator acknowledges this in the opening pages of the novel, remarking: "Among the Ibo the art of conversation is regarded very highly, and proverbs are the palm oil with which words are eaten" (p. 7).

Among the Igbo, then, conversation is seen as something more than an instrument for transmitting information: it is a means of adding quality to life, of making reality more palatable. The use of proverbs is also vital to the establishment and regulation of relationship among the Igbo people, for their collective human experience—their traditions, values and hard-won wisdom—is codified and preserved in these memorable, seemingly simple but often frustratingly opaque sayings (the importance of the principle of doubleness, of ambiguity and ambivalence in Igbo culture, has been discussed above). If the novel depicts the tragedy of a community falling apart, then what had hitherto held it together was strong social consensus, a shared and largely unquestioning knowledge of and belief in its values, customs and institutions. And this consensus is pre- eminently embodied in the highest currency of verbal exchange, the proverb. Handed down by parents to their children, proverbs come cloaked in the authority of the elders and, beyond them, of the ancestors. And insofar as proverbs characterize the standard public discourse that prevails in exchanges between individuals, their use serves to make the private public, the personal, communal.

These arguments for the *Africanness* of *Things Fall Apart* pay tribute to the ways in which Achebe has appropriated the English language and the genre of the novel in order to represent previously unrepresented experience. Perhaps in closing we should briefly countenance the views of those like Ngugi who argue that it is impossible to render African experience in a European language. Further than being a carrier of cultural values, a language —the argument goes—is a discourse, permitting only certain things to be said: the things that cannot be said remain unknowable through the medium of that language. In this sense, Achebe can make no serious claim to have produced an authentic portrait of the Igbo people (quite apart from the issues raised by the matter of historical distance).

This kind of argument deserves firm rebuttal: it leads directly into the cul-de-sac of radical cultural relativism that would deny the validity of translation in any form. It implies also that human experience is wholly incommensurable and that communication between human beings impossible. The pleasure of reading *Things Fall Apart* and responding to its overwhelmingly convincing portrait of a vanished way of life, for millions of Africans as well as readers all around the world, is surely the most eloquent refutation of such a position.

Selected Bibliography

EDITIONS

Things Fall Apart. New York: Anchor Books, 1994. The standard U.S. paperback edition cited in this essay.

Things Fall Apart. London: Heinemann, 1996. Classics in Context edition. The best available edition, with an introduction by Simon Gikandi, an essay on "Igbo Culture and History" by Don Ohadike, the original African Writers Series illustrations by Uche Okeke, and Suggestions for Further Reading.

OTHER WORKS BY ACHEBE (SELECTED)

No Longer at Ease. 1960. New York: Anchor Books, 1994.

Arrow of God. 1964. New York: Anchor Books, 1969.

A Man of the People. 1966. New York: Anchor Books, 1989.

Beware, Soul Brother: Poems. 1971. London: Heinemann, 1972.

Girls at War and Other Stories. 1972. New York: Anchor Books, 1991.

Anthills of the Savannah. 1987. New York: Anchor Books, 1989.

Hopes and Impediments: Selected Essays. 1988. New York: Anchor Books, 1990.

Home and Exile. 2000. New York: Anchor Books, 2001.

SECONDARY WORKS

Achebe's own essays in *Hopes and Impediments* and *Home and Exile* are the best source of contextual material relating to his fiction, and the interested reader is urged to begin there.

In addition to the works listed below, there are dozens of study guides to *Things Fall Apart.* Some of these are of decidedly indifferent quality, and the reader is advised to exercise caution.

Begam, Richard. "Achebe's Sense of an Ending: History and Tragedy in *Things Fall Apart.*" *Studies in the Novel* 29.3 (1997): 396–411.

Carroll, David. *Chinua Achebe.* 2nd ed. New York: St. Martin's Press, 1980.

Chinweizu, Onwucheka Jemie, and Ihechukwu Madubuike. *Toward the Decolonization of African Literature.* Volume 1: African Fiction and Poetry and Their Critics. Washington DC: Howard University Press, 1983.

Conrad, Joseph. *Heart of Darkness.* Ed. Robert Kimbrough. 3rd ed. New York: W.W. Norton, 1988.

Contemporary Literary Criticism. This periodical features extracts from scores of critical essays on Achebe's work. For material on *Things Fall Apart,* see volumes 1, 3, 5, 7, 11, 26, 51, 75, 127.

Ezenwa-Ohaeto. *Chinua Achebe: A Biography.* London: James Currey, 1997.

Gikandi, Simon. *Reading Chinua Achebe: Language and Ideology in Fiction.* London: Heinemann, 1991.

Innes, C.L., and Bernth Lindfors, eds. *Critical Perspectives on Chinua Achebe.* Washington, D.C.: Three Continents Press, 1978.

JanMohamed, Abdul R. "Sophisticated Primitivism: The Syncretism of Oral and Literate Modes in Achebe's *Things Fall Apart.*" *ARIEL: A Review of International English Literature* 15.4 (1984): 19–39.

Lindfors, Bernth, ed. *Approaches to Teaching Achebe's "Things Fall Apart."* New York: Modern Language Association of America, 1991.

———. *Conversations with Chinua Achebe.* Jackson: University Press of Mississippi, 1997. Invaluable collection of interviews with Achebe, 1962–1995.

Literary Griot: International Journal of Black Expressive Cultural Studies 10.2 (1998). Contains five essays in "40th Anniversary Symposium on *Things Fall Apart.*"

Lott, Sandra Ward, Maureen S.G. Hawkins, and Norman McMillan, eds. *Global Perspectives on Teaching Literature: Shared Visions and Distinctive Visions.* Urbana, Ill.: National Council of Teachers of English, 1993. Contains five essays in section entitled "Approaches to Chinua Achebe's *Things Fall Apart.*"

McCarthy, B. Eugene. "Rhythm and Narrative Method in Achebe's *Things Fall Apart.*" *Novel: A Forum on Fiction* 18.3 (1985): 243- 256.

Moore, Gerald. "Chinua Achebe: Unless Tomorrow." *Twelve African Writers.* London: Hutchinson, 1980. Pages 123–145.

Ngugi wa Thiong'o. *Decolonizing the Mind: The Politics of Language in African Literature.* London: James Currey, 1986.

Obiechina, Emmanuel. "Narrative Proverbs in the African Novel." *Research in African Literatures* 24.4 (1994): 123–140.

Onweme, Michael C. "Limits of Transliteration: Nigerian Writers' Endeavors toward a National Literary Language." *PMLA* 114.5 (1999): 1055–1066.

Quayson, Ato. "Realism, Criticism, and the Disguises of Both: A Reading of Chinua Achebe's *Things Fall Apart* with an Evaluation of the Criticism Relating to It." *Research in African Literatures* 25.4 (1994): 117-136.

Rutherford, Anna, and Kirsten Holst Petersen, eds. *Chinua Achebe: A Celebration.* London: Heinemann, 1991.

Wren, Robert M. *Achebe's World: The Historical and Cultural Context of the Novels of Chinua Achebe.* London: Longman, 1980.

———. *Chinua Achebe: "Things Fall Apart."* London: Longman, 1980.

William Makepeace Thackeray's
Vanity Fair

SANDIE BYRNE

BORN INTO THE upper middle class, Thackeray could have followed the conventional route through public school, Cambridge, travel, and legal training to an assured and a comfortable future furnished by a professional and private income. Instead he lost most of the inheritance that would have provided his unearned income and quickly gave up the studies that would have provided the earned.

William Makepeace Thackeray was named for his grandfather, whose middle name came from an ancestor said to have been a Protestant martyred in the reign of Mary Tudor. The family was made up of wealthy professionals: doctors, lawyers, and civil servants, many of whom served in the powerful East India Company or Indian civil service. The clan was large, with tentacles in India, Bengal, and Ireland, as well as England, so Thackeray could find relations wherever he went.

John Carey, in *Thackeray: Prodigal Genius* (1980), suggests that Thackeray's life reads like fiction (p. 11). An extraordinary event of his childhood resembles an implausible episode from a romantic novel. As a young girl in England, Thackeray's mother had been in love with Henry Carmichael-Smyth, then a lieutenant,

but the match was considered unsuitable, and she had been given a false report of his death from fever. Years later, her husband, Richmond Thackeray, brought home an officer from the Bengal Engineers as a dinner guest, Carmichael-Smyth. Anne Thackeray married him after the death of her husband.

Bereft of his mother from the ages of five to nine, Thackeray suffered miseries at school in Southampton but was happier with Dr. Turner in Chiswick. His mother and stepfather returned from India in 1820 and the following year Carmichael-Smyth purchased his promotion and settled in Surrey, where he taught at the local military academy. Thackeray was sent to the public school Charterhouse, near London, then an unpleasant place with poor scholastic standards and a brutal regime. He had his nose broken in a fight, did little work, and developed his gift for dashing off comic and satiric sketches. In 1824 the major resigned his position and, living on his half-pay pension, moved the family home to a Devon farm where Thackeray subsequently spent his vacations.

At Trinity College, Cambridge, Thackeray seems to have done little work but made many friends. During the vacation he took a trip to

France and in Paris discovered his passion for the theater, opera (and opera dancers), and, disastrously, gambling. He also met "Mlle. Pauline," who became his mistress and may have given him gonorrhea. Leaving Cambridge without taking a degree, he traveled and wrote in France and Germany for some time before returning to settle in London. Having run through most of his fortune and lost the rest through unsuccessful newspaper ventures and the failure of Indian banks, he was forced to undertake a great deal of hack journalism to support himself and, following his marriage to Isabella Shawe, his wife and daughters. His wife seems to have suffered from postnatal depression following the birth of their third daughter, and this developed into langor, "melancholy," and finally insanity. En route to Ireland in September 1840 she threw herself into the sea but was buoyed up by air trapped in her voluminous crinolines and rescued. The family remained in Cork while Isabella's health fluctuated between convalescence and ravings, then returned home to London, where she seemed to improve, and finally to Paris and the assistance of Thackeray's mother and stepfather. Isabella's condition worsened, and in December she was confined for some months to the Maison de Santé at Ivry, just outside Paris. Following a period back with her family, early in 1842 she was treated at an asylum in Chaillot, where she remained until Thackeray placed her with a private keeper in Camberwell, southeast London, in October 1845. Thackeray returned to London in May. The hand-to-mouth existence continued for some time, but commissions from the new periodical *Punch* provided a regular income from the mid-1840s and made his name as a writer. He continued to work for others, such as *Fraser's* magazine, in which *Barry Lyndon* was serialized in 1844, but *Punch* became his principle source of income.

In 1847 he established a home for himself, his daughters, whom he brought back from their grandparents, and a succession of governesses in Kensington. When Charlotte Brontë dedicated

CHRONOLOGY

1811	William Makepeace Thackeray born 18 July in Calcutta, India, to Richmond Thackeray and Anne Becher.
1815	Death of Richmond Thackeray.
1816	Thackeray sent home to England.
1817	Mrs. Thackeray marries Henry Carmichael-Smyth. Thackeray arrives in England and enters school in Southampton, then moves to Dr. Turner's academy in Chiswick, London.
1822–1828	Attends Charterhouse School.
1829	Matriculates into Trinity College, Cambridge.
1830	Leaves Cambridge without taking a degree; travels in Germany.
1831	Enters the Middle Temple (legal chambers).
1832–1833	Lives mostly in Paris, studying art. Begins to contribute articles to periodicals.
1833	Back in England; most of Thackeray's fortune lost through gambling. Purchases the *National Standard,* a literary periodical. Thackeray and his stepfather lose money following failure of Indian banks.
1836	Marries Isabella Shawe in August.
1837	The Thackerays settle in Albion Street, London. Thackeray continues to publish journalism and fiction pseudonymously, mostly for *Fraser's Magazine* and *Punch.* In July the *Constitutional,* which Thackeray had purchased, fails. Birth of Anne Thackeray in June.
1838	In May, first installment of Thackeray's first novel, *Catherine,* appears in *Fraser's Magazine.* Birth of Jane Thackeray in July; she dies the following March.
1840	Publication of first full-length work, *Paris Sketch Book,* by "M. A. Titmarsh." Birth of Harriet Thackeray in May; in August Isabella shows signs of mental illness.
1844	Publication of *Barry Lyndon;* journey to the East August–November.
1845	Isabella Thackeray declared incurably insane and placed in care.

1846	Thackeray and his daughters move to Young Street, Kensington.
1847–1848	Publication of *Vanity Fair* (by W. M. Thackeray) in twenty monthly episodes.
1848–1850	Publication of *Pendennis* in monthly episodes.
1851	Elected to the Atheneum Club. Gives series of lectures on "The English Humorists" in London; resigns from *Punch* magazine.
1852	Publication of *Henry Esmond* in three volumes.
1852–1853	Gives series of lectures on "The English Humorists" in the United States.
1853–1855	*The Newcomes* published in monthly episodes.
1854	Publication of *The Rose and the Ring*.
1855–1856	Lectures on "The Four Georges" in the United States.
1856–1857	Lectures in England.
1857	Stands as Independent Liberal candidate for the city of Oxford but is unsuccessful.
1857–1859	*The Virginians* published in monthly episodes.
1858	Quarrel with Edmund Yates and Charles Dickens becomes a public scandal.
1859	Becomes editor of the *Cornhill Magazine* in which he publishes *Lovel the Widower* (1860), *Roundabout Papers* (1860–1863), *Philip* (1861–1862).
1862	Moves to Palace Green, Kensington; resigns editorship of *Cornhill Magazine*.
1863	Begins *Denis Duval* in May. On 24 December dies of a stroke and is buried in Kensal Green Cemetery, London.
1864	*Denis Duval* published in *Cornhill Magazine*.

the second edition of her *Jane Eyre* to Thackeray in 1848 it fueled speculation that he was the original of Mr. Rochester, who confines his mad wife to an attic, and even that the novel had been written by a governess of the Thackerays. The embarrassment the dedication caused Thackeray was unintentional on the part of Brontë, whose life in Haworth was distant from such gossip. None of Thackeray's biographers give credence to the rumors and agree that the love of his life was Jane, wife of his close friend William Brookfield.

Publication of *Vanity Fair* brought a measure of prosperity, increased commissions, lionization, and an even busier social life than Thackeray had enjoyed before. His career in some ways paralleled that of Charles Dickens, both publishing journalism, satire, and fiction in installments and both enjoying popularity, Dickens's considerably greater than Thackeray's. The relationship between them was uneasy and in 1858 developed into a feud, the "Garrick Club Affair." Like the rest of literary London, Thackeray had heard of Dickens's estrangement from his wife, Catherine, and his relationship with a young actress, Ellen Ternan. When another member of his club, the Garrick, repeated a rumor that Dickens was seeing Thackeray's sister-in-law, Thackeray corrected him. Dickens heard of this, or interpreted it, in the form of Thackeray's discussing and criticizing his private life. Shortly afterward, on the same day that Dickens's public defense of himself and denigration of his wife appeared in *Household Words*, a profile of Thackeray appeared in *Town Talk* that portrayed him as a toadying hypocrite. Its author was Edmund Yates, then close to Dickens and also a member of the club. Thackeray asked the committee to revoke Yates's membership, thus causing a split in the club between his own supporters and those of Dickens. The committee voted in favor of Thackeray, and Dickens, furious, advised Yates to seek legal advice. A court case proved too expensive, but Yates kept up his attacks in spoof articles and a pamphlet, to which Thackeray riposted in satirical portraits in his fiction. The affair was widely satirized in the press, which lampooned and caricatured the protagonists mercilessly.

Thackeray's editorship of the new *Cornhill Magazine* was a success. The paper sold well and attracted contributors of promise such as Anthony Trollope. Thackeray's financial situation improved, and he was able to buy a larger house on Kensington Palace Green.

Thackeray's nature seems to have been protean, and he left widely different impressions on the relatives, friends, colleagues, and acquaintances he encountered in different periods of his life. He was mercurial and volatile, or composed of contradictory traits: voluble and taciturn, affable and haughty, forthcoming and shy, a rampant snob and a professed Bohemian, loved and detested.

COMPOSITION AND FIRST PUBLICATION OF *VANITY FAIR*

Part of *Vanity Fair*, without its final title and referred to by Thackeray as his "Novel without a Hero," may have been offered to the *New Monthly Magazine* in about 1845 and rejected by its then publisher, Henry Colburn, or its subsequent proprietor, Harrison Ainsworth, both of whom Thackeray satirized in later novels. Thackeray was later to say that the story had been rejected by three or four publishers before it was finally accepted by Bradbury and Evans, publishers of *Punch* magazine. Bradbury and Evans agreed to publish the novel in the form made popular by Charles Dickens, monthly parts, which would be illustrated with sketches drawn by Thackeray himself. The terms of the contract required Thackeray to provide sufficient matter for at least two printed sheets with two etchings on steel and a number of drawings on wood each month. That meant about sixteen pages of print and a variety of illustrative material, from pictorial capitals to elaborate illustrations of key characters and scenes. For this he was paid £60 per number (John Sutherland, "Thackeray as Illustrator," p. xliv). The etchings and woodcuts sometimes illustrated the text and sometimes provided an ironic counterpoint. One of the last etchings illustrates the point in the text at which Dobbin "besought Jos to fly at once—to go back to India, whither Mrs. Crawley could not follow him; to do anything to break off a connexion which might have the most fatal consequences to him" (p. 874). Jos replies that he will go back

but he cannot yet and begs Dobbin to say nothing to Becky, since: "she'd—she'd kill me if she knew it." The illustration shows the reader that Becky does know it; she is hidden behind a curtain, and the caption is "Becky's second appearance in the character of Clytemnestra" [who killed her husband, the Greek king Menelaus] (p. 875). Her first appearance in the role was in a charade, during which she acted the stabbing of her husband, Rawdon, playing Menelaus.

Though initially scheduled for May 1846, the first part appeared in January 1847. Subsequent parts appeared each month, and two appeared in July 1848.

The first collected edition of the monthly parts, now subtitled "A Novel without a Hero," was published by Bradbury and Evans in 1848 and included a prefatory "Before the Curtain." Thackeray revised his text for a non- illustrated edition in 1853. Other editions followed, and in 1908 George Saintsbury attempted to produce an authoritative text for the Oxford Complete Thackeray series. Paperback editions include the Oxford World's Classics edition, edited by John Sutherland (Oxford, 1998), from which quotations below are taken.

TITLE

The novel's title comes from an episode in John Bunyan's allegorical *Pilgrim's Progress* (1678–1684), in which the hero, Pilgrim, passes through a town called Vanity, where Apollyon, Beelzebub, and Legion have set up a fair where they sell houses, honors, kingdoms, and other delights. Pilgrim manages to continue his journey toward the Celestial City, but Faithful is burned to death in Vanity Fair. Thackeray said that it came to him in the middle of the night, but critics have suggested that he was influenced by Thomas Carlyle's 1832 essay on J. W. Crocker's edition of Boswell's *Life of Samuel Johnson* (1791). In his *Thackeray* (1968; reprinted in Pollard, ed., *Thackeray*, Vanity Fair: *Critical Essays*, 1986), Ioan M. Williams asserts that the passage from Carlyle quoted below suggests the intention that Thackeray had in writing *Vanity Fair:*

> while others hovered and swam along in the grand Vanity Fair of the world, blinded by the mere Shows of things, these saw into the Things themselves, and could walk as men having an eternal lode star and with their feet on sure paths. Thus was there a Reality in their existence; something of a perennial character; in virtue of which indeed it is that the memory of them is perennial. Whoso belongs only to his own age, and reverences only its gilt Popinjays or soot-smeared Mumbo jumbos, must needs die with it: though he have been crowned seven times in the Capitol.
>
> (p. 186)

The narrative voice directs us to remember that "this history has 'Vanity Fair' for a title, and that Vanity Fair is a very vain, wicked, foolish place, full of all sorts of humbugs and falsenesses and pretensions" (p. 95), but does not exclude itself from the humbuggers, deceivers, and pretentious inhabitants, but is one of the "congregation" to whom he is shown preaching in one of the illustrations. For Williams,

> "Vanity" in this novel is not to be taken as having simply a biblical reference such as that which we see in Bunyan's *Pilgrim's Progress* where the idea of the Fair originated. The word refers to that which is involved in the passage from Carlyle—it suggests that those who seek it are fundamentally godless and are living their lives without directing their energies in a fruitful way. According to Carlyle's interpretation of life, Amelia would be a creature who was seeking after Vanity because she worshipped something unreal, and Dobbin would be so because he sought for happiness and expected to find it by means of another human being.
>
> (in Pollard, ed., p. 186)

Thus Thackeray refers to his creations as "puppets" rather than as men and women because "according to the attitude of life which his reading of Carlyle had helped him to, none of the characters acquire the status of human beings; all are puppets in a very real sense, driven by their own desires rather than purposefully seeking an object worthy of the devotion of complete men and women" (p. 186).

THE NOVEL

Vanity Fair is one of the most exuberant, ironic, and sheerly funny novels of the nineteenth century. It is also possibly the novel that most calls attention to its own fictionality, with a narrator whose showmanship and deviousness are without equal. In spite of even more frequent narratorial interventions and assertions of opinion than can be found in the works of Thackeray's literary predecessor and model Henry Fielding, the reader can never be sure of the narrator's attitude to the characters. How much does he condemn and how much sympathetically condone their actions? Who is he, anyway? The omniscient and omnipotent "Manager of the Performance" of the "Before the Curtain" section? The puppet master suggested by the closing lines? Or the less confident man in later sections of the novel who has merely been an audience and conduit for the story?

The theatrical register of the prologue is appropriate to *Vanity Fair*. Though Thackeray exploits the possibilities provided by the novel form, such as glimpses into the minds of characters and commentary on the action, many scenes are theatrical; there are revelations, posturings, speeches, and tableaux. *Vanity Fair* is, among other things, a historical novel, since it is set at the time of the Regency, opening in 1814, thirty years before its composition. The historical detail is rich, accurate, and vivid. It is also satirical; Thackeray's subtitle for his original publication, in monthly parts, was "Pen and Pencil Sketches of English Society." Society is satirized and its popular reading material parodied, though much of the parodic sting is lost on the modern reader who may not have encountered the "silver fork novels," "Newgate novels," "Waterloo novels," and mid-nineteenth-century romances whose styles Thackeray mimics. Some of the satire is personal and in the form of caricature, such as that of Thackeray's mother-in-law, Mrs. Shawe, who provided material for a number of Irish matrons all depicted as coarse, overbearing, and conforming to racial stereotypes.

Vanity Fair is as tantalizing and frustrating as it is pleasurable to read. Often the reader is carried to the brink of an exciting event or revelation, or to the threshold of a magnificent location or presence of an important character, only to find the narrative veer away. Sometimes the narrator's tone becomes arch, as when he modestly protests his inadequacy to the task which "it does not become such a feeble and inexperienced pen as mine to attempt to relate" (p. 608). Since the task is to describe the person of the Prince Regent (the future George IV), a corpulent, extravagant dandy whom Thackeray despised, the intent is presumably irony, but whether directed at royalty in the contemporary flesh or in contemporary fiction it is hard to say.

> The dazzled eyes close before that Magnificent Idea. Loyal respect and decency tell even the imagination not to look too keenly and audaciously about the sacred audience-chamber, but to back away rapidly, silently, and respectfully, making profound bows out of the August Presence.
>
> (p. 604)

A similarly ignominious description of the ostensibly sublime is employed in the entrance into the novel of the duke of Wellington. The hero of Waterloo and England's Savior does not appear in his own right; we hear only indirectly of his presence (in a group including Becky Sharp) as they ride past Amelia's carriage, because the comic character Mrs. O'Dowd is keen to stress her (probably imagined) relationship to the Wellesley family.

> "Sure it's the juke himself," cried Mrs. Major O'Dowd to Jos, who began to blush violently;

> "and that's Lord Uxbridge on the bay. How elegant he looks! Me brother, Molloy Moloney, is as like him as two peas. . . ."
>
> "How well the juke looked," Mrs. O'Dowd remarked. "The Wellesleys and Moloneys are related, but, of course, poor *I* would never dream of introjuicing myself unless his Grace thought proper to remember our family- tie."
>
> (pp. 347–348)

The Brussels section of the novel builds inexorably toward the climax of the Battle of Waterloo (1815), but the narrator refuses to take us to the scene of the fighting. Perhaps the point is that the important battles of *Vanity Fair* are those fought in Becky's social campaign and on the battleground of Amelia's prolonged mourning. More puzzling perhaps is the choice of the register of a naval engagement for an infantry battle. Thackeray metaphorically projects the battle from inland to the sea, perhaps to an air of mock-grandeur to his comments. Chapter 30 opens:

> We do not claim to rank among the military novelists. Our place is with the non-combatants. When the decks are cleared for action we go below and wait meekly. We should only be in the way of the manoeuvres that the gallant fellows are performing overhead. We shall go no farther with the —th than to the city gate: and, leaving Major O'Dowd to his duty, come back to the major's wife, and the ladies and the baggage.
>
> (p. 361)

The significance allotted to events and characters, real and imagined, in *Vanity Fair* is not the significance retrospectively awarded by history, nor always the significance that seems to be demanded by the narrative. As John Sutherland notes in his introduction to the Oxford World's Classics edition of the novel, a major narrative event (the marriage of two of the main characters) is overshadowed by history (the changing life of London and the coming Battle of Waterloo), while a real event of major importance (the European crisis of 1813–1814) is made insignificant in proportion to Amelia's anxieties about the worthless George (p. xix). Though this is a historical novel, and a pen-and-pencil sketch of society, it is history and society seen through a magnifying glass placed over one small section: Rebecca (Becky) Sharp, Amelia Sedley, William Dobbin, Rawdon Crawley, and Jos Sedley are at once characters made distinct and individual and types made wonderfully recognizable. Their perspective and their scale of values apply, which is why it is appropriate for Wellington, the Prince Regent, and other dignitaries to remain offstage or have mere walk-on parts.

A "NOVEL WITHOUT A HERO"—OR A HEROINE?

If *Vanity Fair* is, among other things, an anti-romance, then we should expect that its central male protagonist should be the antithesis of heroic. In appearance and manner this is true of Dobbin, who is plain, ungainly, and awkward: "the quietest, the clumsiest, and, as it seemed, the dullest of all Dr. Swishtail's young gentlemen" (p. 48). Nor is Dobbin's background that of a hero. Neither well born and wealthy nor of mysterious, obscure, and possibly exalted origin, he is, prosaically, the son of a grocer. Through the inhabitants of Dobbin's school we are reminded that "the selling of goods by retail is a shameful and infamous practice, meriting the contempt and scorn of all real gentlemen" (pp. 48–49). Though endowed with the admirable qualities of loyalty, steadfastness, patience, and kindness, Dobbin seems to lack the passion and drive of a true hero. He also, like Amelia, has one major failing: he is entirely bedazzled by the gratuitous charms of George Osborne, whose adoring slave he becomes after George fights the school bully on his behalf. If Thackeray wished to make a point about the truly heroic virtues and replace the aristocratic hare with a mercantile tortoise, or a natural as opposed to a genetic gentleman, he did not give Dobbin the conventional reward of the hero—the heroine—

until very late in the novel and the relationship, and it is doubtful whether Amelia *is* a heroine or worth Dobbin's having. The description of Amelia on the day she leaves Miss Pinkerton's academy is just the catalog of virtues and accomplishments appropriate to the pattern-card heroine of a novel such as Fielding's *Tom Jones* or novel of sentiment such as Richardson's *Clarissa:*

> For she could not only sing like a lark, or a Mrs. Billington, and dance like Hillisberg or Parisot; and embroider beautifully; and spell as well as the Dixionary itself; but she had such a kindly, smiling, tender, gentle, generous heart of her own as won the love of everybody who came near her.
>
> (pp. 6–7)

However, the narrative voice almost immediately explicitly denies Amelia heroine status:

> she was a dear little creature; and a great mercy it is, both in life and in novels, which (and the latter especially) abound in villains of the most sombre sort, that we are to have for a constant companion so guileless and good-natured a person. As she is not a heroine, there is no need to describe her person.
>
> (p. 7)

Furthermore, "Jones," the reader imagined by the narrative voice ensconced in his wing chair at the club, is warned that if he seeks the great and the heroic he should look elsewhere (p. 8). The ironic tone may nonetheless fool us into looking for contradiction, especially since, having said that there is no need to describe her person, the narrator immediately does and a few pages later refers to Amelia as "the heroine of this work" (p. 15). The only "heroical act" so far in the story has, however, been performed by Becky, who has taken the copy of Dr. Johnson's *Dictionary* presented to her by Miss Jemima and thrown it out of the coach window (p. 13). It is soon evident that Amelia is a goose—silly, naive, narrow-minded, and deluded—but that she is good. Becky is her antithesis: she is as sharp as her name, where Amelia's wits are duller and more slow; she is also worldly, clear-sighted, opportunistic, ambitious, and thoroughly self-centered. She is of course thoroughly wicked, and much more lively and entertaining than Amelia. Even Amelia, the conventionally infantilized and sentimentalized heroine, is not as straightforward as she might seem. No one escapes taint in *Vanity Fair*, and Amelia seems to be infected by the general principle of selfishness. Though she is a devoted wife and mother (very important in a Victorian heroine) in contrast to the neglect and abuse Becky showers on her son (the worst of her crimes, for a Victorian readership), Amelia is entirely self-centered in her treatment of Dobbin.

> Amelia stood scared and silent as William thus suddenly broke the chain by which she had held him, and declared his independence and superiority. He had placed himself at her feet so long that the poor little woman had been accustomed to trample upon him. She didn't wish to marry him but she wished to keep him. She wished to give him nothing, but that he should give her all.
>
> (p. 853)

The word "hero" becomes yet more ambivalent when applied to George Osborne (p. 57), but as it is used by Amelia, who worships him and is blind to the vanity, self-centeredness, and shallowness of his nature, it is evident that heroism in *Vanity Fair* is a relative term and largely in the eye of the beholder.

Amelia's romantic delusions about George are never punctured, but Dobbin's illusions about her are. Having lured the reader, perhaps against his or her better judgment, into willing the union of Amelia and Dobbin as the climax of the novel, the narrator gives an anticlimax in which, following more than fifteen years of hopeless devotion, Dobbin gains Amelia only after realizing that she is not worthy of him, and when, for the first time, he seems to gain a sense of his own worth.

> I know what your heart is capable of: it can cling faithfully to a recollection and cherish a fancy; but

it can't feel such an attachment as mine deserves to mate with, and such as I would have won from a woman more generous than you. No, you are not worthy of the love which I have devoted to you. I knew all along that the prize I had set my life on was not worth the winning; that I was a fool, with fond fancies, too, bartering away my all of truth and ardour against your little feeble remnant of love.

> (pp. 852–853)

Dobbin reflects on his wasted years of unrequited ardour and has a moment of clarity and insight into the truth of his relationship with Amelia that robs their union of the anticipated romance.

> No, William thought again and again, "It was myself I deluded and persisted in cajoling; had she been worthy of the love I gave her, she would have returned it long ago. It was a fond mistake. Isn't the whole course of life made up of such? And suppose I had won her, should I not have been disenchanted the day after my victory? Why pine, or be ashamed of my defeat?" The more he thought of this long passage of his life, the more clearly he saw his deception. "I'll go into harness again," he said, "and do my duty in that state of life in which it has pleased Heaven to place me."
>
> (pp. 862–863)

The marriage of Dobbin and Amelia is not the story's denouement: after a brief summation of the intervening years, the novel depicts an unromantic future of stolid country-gentry married life for them and solidly entrenched bourgeois respectability for Becky. The closing words show Dobbin's continued goodness, his integrity, his kindness; he will always take care to behave well toward Amelia, but she is aware that he is fonder of her daughter than he is of her, and we suspect that he finds his "History of the Punjaub" more interesting than he does the former love of his life. Just as Faithful dies in Bunyan's Vanity Fair, perhaps Vanity Fair has killed the faithful Dobbin's love.

Where Dobbin's appearance and lack of dash debar him from the position of conventional hero, Rawdon Crawley's past as a rake and a gambler as well as his lack of intelligence and impercipience would seem to debar him. Rawdon is one of the few characters in the novel to change, however. He matures and displays unexpected attributes of courage and decision that become less surprising when we reflect that he is a long-serving soldier with moral strength, courage, and decency. His status depends upon Becky's feelings about him and the reader's reaction to her feeling. Initially he is an object of desire and fantasy as Becky pursues him as a potential husband, and we see him as nothing more than a callow young man who will be her means of entry into an old family. Once married to him, Becky clearly no longer desires Rawdon. When she realizes that she could have become Lady Pitt, had she not so greedily and impatiently grasped the son, Rawdon becomes positively undesirable, an impediment to her schemes. During their marriage, as Becky cheats and deceives him, and is perhaps unfaithful to him, the reader may share some of her contempt for Rawdon, but we are also becoming aware of his more admirable qualities, such as his steadfastness to the undeserving Becky and his fond care of his son, for which Becky despises him:

> Becky's contempt for her husband grew greater every day. "Do what you like—dine where you please—go and have ginger-beer and sawdust at Astley's or psalm- singing with Lady Jane—only don't expect me to busy myself with the boy."
>
> (p. 662)

When Rawdon finds Becky in an adulterous liaison with Steyne, we see him revealed as a man after all, a man of action, heroic in his refusal to strike Becky and his determination to return Steyne's money. Interestingly it is at this point, when Rawdon is cuckolded and in debt and of least use to Becky materially, that she comes to admire him as the reader does and perhaps desires him for his true self. Becky and Steyne have gone through their charade of protested innocence and grotesque grinning:

> But Rawdon Crawley, springing out, seized him by the neckcloth, until Steyne, almost strangled, writhed and bent under his arm. "You lie, you dog!" said Rawdon. "You lie, you coward and villain!" and he struck the peer twice over the face with his open hand, and flung him bleeding to the ground. It was all done before Rebecca could interpose. She stood there trembling before him. She admired her husband, strong, brave, and victorious.
>
> (p. 676)

In some ways Becky Sharp could be seen as the real hero of the novel. She is the heroine of (the allegorical place) Vanity Fair, having assimilated its morality of self-interest and perfected its methods of ruthless opportunism. She is the most active of the characters, decisive and confident where Amelia is feeble and dependent. She is also an effective, if not a good, wife and mother. While Amelia can do nothing to improve George Osborne's financial situation, Becky takes a feckless gambling rake, comes to terms with his creditors, shows him how to live on "nothing a year," reconciles him with his relations, and makes his career so that he ends up as governor of Coventry Island. Of course she is also unfaithful to him, conceals her ill-gotten gains from him, and leaves him in debtors prison. Amelia dotes on her son, young George, but gives him up to his grandfather, and he grows up spoiled and cowardly. Becky ignores and beats her son, young Rawdon, but he grows up strong and brave.

Thackeray ends the novel on a note of *vanitas vanitatum,* but it is Dobbin, the good character, who feels the hollowness of his long-desired prize; Becky is smugly happy with her lot. Like Heathcliff in *Wuthering Heights,* she has beaten the class system, which might be admirable and even denote heroic qualities of perseverance and determination, but she has no intention of changing that system for the benefit of others; once at the top she will simply stay there. But here again *Vanity Fair* is ambivalent. How content will Becky be with dull respectability in Bath and Cheltenham, where she "chiefly hangs about" (p. 877)? We have been told that Becky is at the apex of society, but will she not be hankering for the capital, the court, and aristocratic circles? She is at the apex of respectability now—a genteel lifestyle, but not a gaily fashionable one. What do her smile and demurely downcast eyes conceal? (Revealingly, at the end of the novel it is in London that the Dobbins encounter her behind a charity stall.) Yet when she was at the height of her social success, Becky was bored.

> "I wish I were out of it," she said to herself. "I would rather be a parson's wife, and teach a Sunday school than this; or a sergeant's lady and ride in the regimental wagon; or, oh, how much gayer it would be to wear spangles and trousers and dance before a booth at a fair."
>
> (pp. 637–638)

The tone of *Vanity Fair* is often described as cynical, and we should perhaps pay attention to the penultimate sentences of the novel: "Which of us is happy in this world? Which of us has his desire? Or, having it, is satisfied?" (p. 878).

Becky performs a moral and heroic (because selfless) deed when she reveals to Amelia the worthlessness of Amelia's late husband, George, that "selfish humbug, that low-bred Cockney dandy, that padded booby, who had neither wit, nor manners, nor heart, and was no more to be compared to your friend with the bamboo-cane than you are to Queen Elizabeth!" (p. 866). She produces the note George had written to her, secreted in a nosegay of flowers, and thus opens the way for Amelia to accept Dobbin.

> "Why, the man was weary of you, and would have jilted you, but that Dobbin forced him to keep his word. He owned it to me. He never cared for you. He used to sneer about you to me, time after time; and made love to me the week after he married you."
>
> "It's false! It's false! Rebecca," cried out Amelia, starting up.
>
> "Look there, you little fool," Becky said, still with her provoking good humour, and taking a little paper out of her belt, she opened it and flung it into Emmy's lap. "You know his handwriting."
>
> (p. 866)

But is this a selfless act, or merely the last act in Becky's carefully staged revenge on George for having opposed her marriage to Jos? Certainly she ends vindictively: " 'He wrote that to me—wanted me to run away with him—gave it me under your nose, the day before he was shot—and served him right!' Becky repeated" (p. 866). Thackeray does not allow the reader much time for any grateful or softer feelings we do have towards Becky: we immediately learn that her revelation is not responsible for the reunion, for Amelia has already sent for Dobbin.

More importantly perhaps than any single action of Becky's that might redeem her from villain status is the sympathetic understanding the narrator shows for her attitude to life. From the opening of the novel, Becky is despised for her poverty, by Miss Pinkerton, by the servants at the Sedleys' house, at Sir Pitt's. The narrator frequently reminds the reader that it is not difficult to be philanthropic and altruistic if one has a large income but that anyone might stoop to steal bread or behave like Becky if deprived of income. As Becky reflects, "I think I could be a good woman if I had five thousand a year" (p. 532).

CLASS

Members of the mercantile, middle-class gentry and aristocratic classes are all satirized in *Vanity Fair*. The worst villains of the story, such as the marquis of Steyne, have the highest social position, and the worst toadies are the rising merchants. John Osborne, we're told, pronounced the names of peers "with the greatest gusto," and whenever he met "a great man he grovelled before him, and my-lorded him . . . introduced his name into his daily conversation [and] bragged about his Lordship to his daughters. He fell down and basked in him" (p. 152). When Amelia writes to her parents about the rudeness of her aristocratic guests, who will not know her and go out of their way to make her uncomfortable, her mother "was mightily pleased nevertheless, and talked about Emmy's friend, the Countess of Bareacres, with such assiduity that the news how his son was entertaining peers and peeresses actually came to Osborne's ears in the City" (p. 342). In spite of this satire, however, *Vanity Fair* is not a Victorian social problem novel, and it does not depict the sufferings of the laboring classes whose toil upholds the system that produces the unearned income of Steyne and Pitt Crawley or the returns on capital of Osborne. Nor does it precisely criticize those characters whose incomes are unearned. After retiring from the army Dobbin adopts the life of a country squire, we assume, on the interest of Osborne's money. There is never any suggestion that George Osborne, reared as he has been, is capable of earning a living, or even of managing on his "pittance" of £2000 (p. 295), which he calculates would be worth £100 per annum; Amelia's attempt to turn to profit her small skill at the genteel craft of screen-painting is made pitiful and ludicrous (p. 622). These characters are as incapable of earning money as they are of living without it. To be poor is to descend the social ladder, but to work is to lose their hold on it entirely, which is why characters such as Rawdon Crawley contrive to live on nothing.

If Becky is the Pilgrim of *Pilgrim's Progress*, her journey is a material rather than spiritual one, and her apotheosis is the Temple of Mammon (and the charity stall) rather than the Celestial City. Although her journey begins while "the present century was in its teens" (p. 3), it continues into a past within the lifetime of the novel's older readers. Thus, though much is blamed on earlier, coarser, and more corrupt times (and monarchs), the satire is also of the present day of the reader. As wealthy industrialists retired to build or buy great houses in the nineteenth century, and the merchant class

intermarried with the gentry and aristocracy, the ethos of hard work and self-help of Thomas Carlyle and Samuel Smiles was seen to have undesirable side effects. Becky, acme of social climbers and self-helpers, is a sign of Victorian unease about increased materialism (manifest in visible consumption) and crumbling social barriers. If the daughter of an impoverished and drunken artist and an opera dancer could move in the first circles, be presented at court, and style herself "Lady Crawley" (though she has no right to the title), the fabric of society was at risk. The narrator does not warn society against such interlopers or hold up his hands in horror at their successful invasion; *Vanity Fair* suggests that society has only itself to blame. The reader is reminded that Becky is not the only social climber in Vanity Fair; Mrs. Sedley's and George Osborne's objections to Becky as a wife for Jos are all the more vehement for the fact that the Sedley and Osborne families have only recently ascended to middle-class status.

STRUCTURE

Much of the structure of *Vanity Fair* is based on binaries. Becky and Amelia are each the focus of a major plot, their lives are intimately entwined in the opening and closing chapters of the novel, and they are one another's antithesis: Amelia the good fool, Becky the clever opportunist. George and Dobbin similarly meet at school, remain friends into adulthood, and are antithetical in that George is handsome, dashing, and feckless while Dobbin is good, noble, and unprepossessing. The lives of Becky and Dobbin are also parallel, since they both have unpropitious beginnings and are underdogs at their respective schools, but both go far in life through their own efforts. Becky's suitors (or victims) and their parents also come in pairs. Mr. Sedley and Jos contrast with Sir Pitt Crawley and Rawdon and with John and George Osborne. There is also a chain of parallels in partners' illusions and disillusionment. Just as Amelia begins by cherishing powerful illusions about George but is shown his weaknesses, so Dobbin begins by cherishing illusions about Amelia but later learns that she is not the idol he set her up to be, and Rawdon receives dramatic proof that he has been a blind dupe where Becky is concerned. Only Becky, the most critical and jaundiced social observer of all, is never jolted out of a rosy-colored dream into the reality of another's flawed character. Her jolt comes when she realizes that she has underestimated and undervalued Rawdon, just as she loses him.

AFTERLIVES

The duke of Devonshire was clearly a fan of *Vanity Fair* and enquired about the fates of Becky Sharp and the rest after the novel's ending. A playful letter from Thackeray of 1 May 1848 gives news of them.

> My Lord Duke,—Mrs. Rawdon Crawley, whom I saw last week, and whom I informed of your Grace's desire to have her portrait, was good enough to permit me to copy a little drawing made of her "in happier days," she said with a sigh, by Smee, the Royal Academician.
>
> Mrs. Crawley now lives in a small but very pretty little house in Belgravia, and is conspicuous for her numerous charities, which always get into the newspapers, and her unaffected pieties. Many of the most exalted and spotless of her own sex visit her, and are of the opinion that she is a *most injured woman.* There is no *sort of truth* in the stories regarding Mrs. Crawley and the late Lord Steyne. The licentious character of that nobleman alone gave rise to reports from which, alas! the most spotless life and reputation cannot always defend themselves. The present Sir Rawdon Crawley (who succeeded his late uncle, Sir Pitt, 1832; Sir Pitt died on the passing of the Reform Bill) does not see his mother, and his undutifulnesss is a cause of the deepest grief to that admirable lady. "If it were not for *higher things,*" she says, how could she have borne up against the world's calumny, a wicked husband's cruelty and falseness, and the thanklessness (sharper than a serpent's tooth) of an adored child? But she has been preserved, mercifully preserved, to bear all these griefs, and awaits her reward *elsewhere.* The italics are Mrs. Crawley's own.
>
> She took the style and title of Lady Crawley for some time after Sir Pitt's death in 1832; but it turned out that Colonel Crawley, Governor of Coventry Island, had died of fever three months before his brother, whereupon Mrs. Rawdon Crawley was obliged to lay down the title which she had prematurely assumed.
>
> The late Jos. Sedley, Esq., of the Bengal Service, left her two lakhs of rupees, on the interest of which the widow lives in the practices of piety and benevolence before mentioned. She has lost what little good looks she once possessed, and wears false hair and teeth (the latter give her rather a ghostly look when she smiles), and—for a pious woman—is the best-crinolined lady in Knightsbridge district. . . .
>
> I think these are the latest particulars relating to a number of persons about whom your Grace was good enough to express some interest. I am very glad to be enabled to give this information, and am—
>
> Your Grace's very much obliged servant,
>
> W. M. Thackeray
>
> (in Pollard, ed., pp. 34–35)

RECEPTION

By the fourth part, *Vanity Fair* was established as a popular success, and Thackeray was made as a novelist. Charlotte Brontë was an early fan of *Vanity Fair,* as she was of all Thackeray's works until some time after their meeting. In a letter to her publisher, W. S. Williams, she refers to Thackeray as a "Titan" and "unique" and writes of his strength, power, simplicity, self-control, and genius (letter of 29 March 1848, *Life and Letters of Charlotte Brontë,* 1932, p. 200). An early review in the *Examiner* of 22 July 1848 was mostly admiring, but R. S. Rintoul, writing in the *Spectator* of the same date, found Thackeray lacking in imagination. *Fraser's Magazine* (September 1848) found the characters in *Vanity Fair* too unredeemably wicked. Conversely,

Elizabeth Rigby, Lady Eastlake, reviewing for the *Quarterly Review* in December of the same year, found that the characters were too like our everyday selves to provide the reader with a moral. Where modern readers admire the panoply of life and wealth of everyday detail in *Vanity Fair*, she deplored it, asking

> what are all these personages in *Vanity Fair* but feigned names for our beloved friends and acquaintances, seen under such a puzzling cross-light of good in evil, and evil in good, of sins and sinnings against, of little to be praised virtues, and much to be excused vices, that we cannot presume to moralise upon them—not even to judge them. . . . Every actor on the crowded stage of *Vanity Fair* represents some type of that perverse mixture of humanity in which there is ever something not wholly to approve or to condemn.
>
> (in Pollard, ed., pp. 30–31)

A younger Victorian writer, Anthony Trollope (*Thackeray*, 1879), after playfully describing assumed "faults" such as Amelia's failure of beauty and Dobbin's of heroic appearance, goes on to find *Vanity Fair* flawless. "Though the story is vague and wandering, clearly commenced without any idea of an ending, yet there is something in the telling which makes every portion of it perfect in itself" (in Pollard, ed., p. 43.)

Lack of planned structure, or formlessness, was a criticism leveled at *Vanity Fair* by a number of twentieth-century critics, who assumed that Thackeray had written each number at speed to a deadline, veering from episode to episode without much idea of the overall shape of the story. In 1930, G. K. Chesterton pointed out that

> *Vanity Fair* might have appeared somewhat formless to some of the old supporters of the classical unities; it might again have appeared somewhat formless to the exact artistry of the school and generation of Stevenson; but even if it were much more formless than it is, it could hardly reach the superb ecstasy of formlessness, which is admired

in many of the long realistic novels of today. As a matter of fact it is far less formless than it looks.

> (in Pollard, ed., p. 57)

The structure of gossip, according to Chesterton, provided the structure of *Vanity Fair*, and seemingly irrelevant material was crucial. Whereas in other novels it is essential to know what characters think of one another, in *Vanity Fair*,

> it is very necessary that we should also know what the World thinks of the character; for indeed in *Vanity Fair* the chief character is the World. It would be an exaggeration to say that the World is the villain of the piece; but it may well be said that in this sense it is a novel without a hero. The theme is what the old comic dramatist called *The Way of the World*; and a sort of satiric but not too severe judgment on it. . . . For this purpose it is necessary that the club of Thackeray, like the island of Prospero [in *The Tempest*], should be "full of voices"; and that we should get a general sense of much that is mere talk, or even mere echoes.
>
> (in Pollard, ed., p. 58)

By the 1930s Thackeray's popularity had declined and was to decline further during the 1940s and 1950s, in spite of the earlier centenary publications of 1911 and Gordon N. Ray's impressive 1945–1946 edition of Thackeray's correspondence and private papers and later studies. George Orwell's essay "Oysters and Brown Stout" (*Tribune*, 22 December 1944) argued that Thackeray's best and most representative writing was not to be found in the long fiction but in his burlesques and other contributions to periodicals. Lord David Cecil's section on Thackeray in his *Early Victorian Novelists* (1934) suggested that Thackeray failed to fulfill his ambitious scheme for *Vanity Fair*. J. Y. T. Grieg's *Thackeray, A Reconsideration* (1950) was not entirely sympathetic. Dorothy Van Ghent, in a section on novelists' use of the omniscient author convention in her *The English Novel: Form and Function* (1953), wrote that although almost exactly a century separates *Tom Jones* from *Vanity Fair*, so far as technical developments in the novel are concerned, it is as if there had been none. We are in the story telling convention of the "omniscient author" sanctioned by Fielding's great example, but with a damaging difference that is due, not so much to an inherent inadequacy of that convention itself, as the spiritual incoherency of another age.

(p. 139)

Most studies of Victorian or nineteenth-century fiction during the 1950s and 1960s included a section on Thackeray, including Arnold Kettle's *Introduction to the English Novel* (1951), which treated *Vanity Fair* as Thackeray's vision of bourgeois society. Some full-length scholarly studies of his fiction also appeared, notably Geoffrey Tillotson's *Thackeray the Novelist* (1954), but his work was relatively neglected in comparison with that of Charles Dickens, Anthony Trollope, and the other Victorian high realists, and far less popular. Some modern critics have suggested that Thackeray's best writing lies in the early journalism, no longer much read, and that his style and themes began to degenerate after *Vanity Fair.* Carey (*Thackeray: Prodigal Genius*) refers to a "disastrous collapse" into "gentlemanliness and cordiality" (p. 11) and finds the later novels insipid (p. 20), the art emasculated. Robert Colby disagreed with this estimation and D. J. Taylor's concurrence with it in Taylor's 1999 biography of Thackeray. A BBC serialization in 1998 may have brought the novel to a wider audience.

Though its targets are mid-nineteenth-century and its settings early nineteenth-century, *Vanity Fair* seems less remote than many Victorian novels to a twenty-first-century reader. Its characters are not patterns of perfection but flawed, deceived, even ridiculous; they are not of exalted social rank but from the huge, many-tentacled and busy middle class which dominated Victorian affairs. Thackeray's social snapshots, like those of the later novelist John Galsworthy (author of *The Forsyte Chronicles*), repudiated the prevailing Carlyle-influenced view that great men are the forces of social change, and the idea that literature should be about the ideal rather than the material. In *Vanity Fair* there are no Titans shaping history on the battlefields or in the debating chamber. There is no one of conventional heroic stature and no one overly concerned with honor, duty, patriotism, religion, or philanthropy. The characters are mostly materialists, and those who cherish the ideal and the immaterial are usually found to be self-deceived. Even Dobbin ends as a comfortable country squire on inherited income. The representation of an unheroic society populated by unheroic people pursuing unheroic ends gives *Vanity Fair* a modern feel and an enduring appeal.

Selected Bibliography

EDITIONS

Vanity Fair: Pen and Pencil Sketches of English Society. In *Punch* (London). Twenty monthly numbers, January 1847–July 1848.

Vanity Fair: A Novel without a Hero. London: Bradbury and Evans, 1848.

The Oxford Thackeray. 17 vols. Edited by George Saintsbury. London: Oxford University Press, 1908.

Vanity Fair. Edited by Geoffrey Tillotson and Kathleen Tillotson. New York: Norton, 1963.

Vanity Fair. Edited by Catherine Peters. London: Dent, Everyman's Library, 1991.

Vanity Fair. Edited by Peter Shillingsburg. New York: Norton, 1994.

Vanity Fair. Edited by John Sutherland. Oxford: Oxford World's Classics, 1998.

Vanity Fair. Edited by John Carey. Harmondsworth, U.K.: Penguin Classics, 2001.

LETTERS AND MEMOIRS

The Letters and Private Papers of William Makepeace Thackeray. 4 vols. Edited by Gordon N. Ray. London: Oxford University Press, 1945–1946; Cambridge, Mass.: Harvard University Press, 1945–1946.

Thackeray: Interviews and Recollections. Edited by Philip Collins. London: Macmillan, 1983; New York: St. Martin's Press, 1983.

SECONDARY WORKS

Carey, John. *Thackeray: Prodigal Genius.* London: Faber and Faber, 1977; repr. London: Faber and Faber, 1980.

Cecil, David, Lord. "Thackeray." In his *Early Victorian Novelists.* London: Constable, 1934; Indianapolis, In.: Bobbs-Merrill, 1935.

Clarke, Michael M. *Thackeray and Women.* De Kalb: Northern Illinois University Press, 1995.

Colby, Robert A. *Thackeray's Canvass of Humanity: An Author and His Public.* Columbus: Ohio State University Press, 1979.

Dyson, A. E. "An Irony Against Heroes." In *The Crazy Fabric: Essays in Irony.* New York: St. Martin's Press, 1965; London: Macmillan, 1966. Pp. 76–95. Repr. in Arthur Pollard, ed., *Thackeray:* Vanity Fair, *A Selection of Critical Essays.* Basingstoke, U.K.: Macmillan, 1986.

Ennis, Lambert. *Thackeray, the Sentimental Cynic.* Evanston, Ill.: Northwestern University Press, 1950.

Flamm, Dudley. *Thackeray's Critics: An Annotated Bibliography of British and American Criticism, 1836–1900.* Chapel Hill: University of North Carolina Press, 1966.

Gilmour, Robin. *Thackeray:* Vanity Fair. London: Edward Arnold, 1982.

Grieg, J. Y. T. *Thackeray, A Reconsideration.* London and New York: Oxford University Press, 1950.

Harden, Edgar F. *The Emergence of Thackeray's Serial Fiction.* Athens: University of Georgia Press, 1979.

———. *Thackeray the Writer: From Journalism to* Vanity Fair. Basingstoke, U.K.: Macmillan, 1998; New York: St. Martin's Press, 1998.

———. *Thackeray the Writer:* Pendennis *to* Denis Duval. Basingstoke, U.K.: Macmillan, 2000.

Hardy, Barbara. *The Exposure of Luxury: Radical Themes in Thackeray.* London: Owen, 1972; Pittsburgh: University of Pittsburgh Press, 1972.

Kettle, Arnold. "Thackeray: *Vanity Fair.*" In his *Introduction to the English Novel.* London: Hutchinson, 1951.

Loufbourow, John. *Thackeray and the Form of Fiction.* Princeton, N.J.: Princeton University Press, 1963.

McMaster, Juliet. *Thackeray: The Major Novels.* Manchester, U.K.: Manchester University Press, 1971; Toronto: Toronto University Press, 1971.

Mandel, Oscar. *Annotations to* Vanity Fair. Washington, D.C.: University Press of America, 1981.

Olmsted, John C. *Thackeray and His Twentieth- Century Critics.* New York: Garland, 1977.

Orwell, George. "Oysters and Brown Stout" (1944). In Peter Davidson, ed., *George Orwell: The Complete Works.* Vol. 16: *I Have Tried to Tell the Truth.* London: Secker and Warburg, 1998. Pp. 498–501.

Peters, Catherine. *Thackeray's Universe: Shifting Worlds of Imagination and Reality.* London and Boston: Faber and Faber, 1987.

———. *Thackeray: A Writer's Life.* Stroud, U.K.: Sutton, 1999.

Pollard, Arthur, ed. *Thackeray:* Vanity Fair: *A Selection of Critical Essays.* Basingstoke, U.K.: Macmillan, 1986.

Ray, Gordon N. *Thackeray: The Uses of Adversity, 1811–1846.* London: Oxford University Press, 1955.

———. *Thackeray: The Age of Wisdom, 1847–1863.* London: Oxford University Press, 1958.

———. "*Vanity Fair*: One Version of the Novelist's Responsibility." In *Essays by Divers Hands: Being Transactions of the Royal Society of Literature in the United Kingdom.* New Series 25. Oxford, 1950. Pp. 342–356.

Stevenson, Lionel. *The Showman of Vanity Fair.* London: Chapman, 1947; New York: Scribners, 1947.

Sutherland, J. A. *Thackeray at Work.* London: Athlone Press, 1974.

Taylor, D. J. *Thackeray.* London: Chatto and Windus, 1999; repr. London: Pimlico, 2000.

Tillotson, Geoffrey. *Thackeray the Novelist.* London: Methuen, 1954.

Tillotson, Geoffrey, and Donald Hawes, eds. *Thackeray: The Critical Heritage.* London: Routledge and Kegan Paul, 1968; New York: Barnes and Noble, 1968.

Tillotson, Kathleen. "The Debatable Land between Middle Classes and Aristocracy." In her *Novels of the Eighteen-Forties.* Oxford: Clarendon Press, 1954. Pp. 234–256.

Van Ghent, Dorothy. *The English Novel, Form and Function.* New York: Rinehart, 1953.

Wheatley, J. H. *Patterns in Thackeray's Fiction.* Cambridge, Mass.: MIT Press, 1969.

Williams, Ioan M. *Thackeray.* London: Evans, 1968; New York: Arco, 1969.

Samuel Beckett's
Waiting For Godot

SOPHIE RATCLIFFE

IN A SMALL Parisian apartment in the winter of 1948, a little-known Irish novelist was suffering from writer's block. Having reached what he felt was an "impasse" with his prose works, he opened a notebook and began to work on something new. After four months, he reached the final line. The result was *En Attendant Godot,* a play for a cast of five, which he later translated into the two-act tragicomedy *Waiting for Godot.* Beckett himself once joked that it was a mess. The public felt differently, and the impact of this drama, which shatters conventional expectations of form and meaning, is still being felt today. While *Godot* has been praised for its control and linguistic beauty, readers and critics agree that the play, like much of his work, is difficult. Its vision of life appears, at first, to be both depressing and harsh. Interpreting the text can be confusing, and inconclusive.

A TIMELESS CLASSIC?

Some have dwelt on its confused textual history. While *En Attendant Godot* was published in 1952, American audiences had to wait two years for their *Godot,* translated by Beckett himself, while an unexpurgated version only reached British bookshelves in 1965. Although his mother-tongue was English, Beckett often chose to write in French. He then put himself through what he termed the "wastes and wilds of self-translation." The existence of two different, but equally valid, versions of the same work creates multiple difficulties for readers. Others have been perplexed by the plot of the play itself. Is this tale of two men waiting for an appointment with a mysterious Mr. Godot meant to symbolize something—a parable, or metaphor perhaps, for the condition of mankind? Does the road they wait on stand for the journey of life?

Not so long before the first production, Beckett and his partner Suzanne endured their own life on the road, as they escaped from the gestapo, on their way to Vichy France. Knowing this, one can pick up on elements within the play which reflect an atmosphere of world at war. Characters endure long waits, crossed wires, and low resources. Strange, tyrannous figures appear. There is even a brief mention of Vaucluse, the region in which Beckett and Suzanne waited for the liberation of Nazi-occupied France. A simplistic biographical reading of the play is near impossible, however, as well as unrewarding. Beckett carefully preserved the anonymity of his tramps. Their provenance is never made clear, and the play seems to take place in an indefinite location.

Indeed, the fact that Beckett does not, in this or any work, appear directly to address historical and political concerns led critics such as Georg Lukács to feel that his work is escapist. Beckett's purported failure to use the theater as a tool for social change—together with the agonizing positions that he puts his characters in—has attracted the charge that his theater is uninteresting, or even inhumane.

Such accusations certainly bear no relation to Beckett's life. Born on Good Friday, 13 April 1906, this brilliant student was destined for a great academic career. After spending a year teaching in Paris, however, he rejected the secure life of academia for a precarious existence reviewing, writing, and traveling in Europe. He eventually settled in Paris—and, when the Germans invaded, began to work for the French resistance, narrowly escaping capture. His work during the war led to his being awarded the Croix de Guerre in 1945, and he went on to work for the Irish Red Cross in Normandy.

A careful viewing or reading of *Waiting for Godot* reveals Beckett's sense for the devastations of his time that he had witnessed, which he referred to as a vision of "humanity in ruins." Beckett was as wary of claims for artistic power as he was of political tyranny, however, and he was elliptical when asked to comment about the conflicts of his time. He is, perhaps, not concerned with saying things. Instead, he tackles the more difficult question of whether anything can be expressed at all.

EMPTYING THE THEATER

Beckett didn't mind if his productions flopped. He decided to ask Roger Blin to take on the first production of *Godot* partly because the French actor-director's previous productions had been

CHRONOLOGY	
1906	April 13: Samuel Beckett born in Foxrock, near Dublin, Ireland.
1923–1927	Beckett studies for a degree in Modern Languages at Trinity College, Dublin.
1928–1930	Beckett moves to Paris, where he works as a lecteur, at the École Normale Supérieure. He meets James Joyce.
1930–1931	Beckett returns to Dublin, as an assistant lecturer at Trinity College, and his first piece of literary criticism, a book on Proust, is published.
1932–1937	Beckett resigns his lecturing post and returns to Paris. After much travelling, he settles there for good.
1938	Beckett begins a lifelong relationship with Suzanne Descheveaux-Dumesnil. His first novel, *Murphy,* is published.
1940–1942	Hitler invades France; Beckett joins the French resistance, and moves from Paris to the South of France in 1942 to escape the gestapo.
1946–1953	Back in Paris, Beckett writes his trilogy of novels—*Molloy, Malone Dies, The Unnameable*—and *Waiting for Godot.*
1953	*Waiting for Godot* premieres in Paris.
1954–1988	Beckett continues to write plays and novels in both French and English, including *Happy Days, Worstward Ho,* and *Ill Seen Ill Said.*
1969	He is awarded the Nobel Prize for Literature.
1989	22 December, Beckett dies.

commercially unsuccessful. The theater was nearly empty every night; the cast was forced gave out free tickets to passers-by. Blin may not have been crowd-pleasing, but for Beckett, a director who would not sacrifice artistic integrity for audience numbers was a find. Blin had to wait three years to get the funds together, and *En Attendant Godot* was first performed at the Théatre de Babylone, Paris, on 5 January 1953. The reaction was mixed. One of the original cast claims that the first night was "the theatre event of the world." Nevertheless, the cast had to put up with criticism. At one performance, the curtain even had to be dropped early, as the audience hooted and whistled their way through Lucky's extraordinary, incomprehensible monologue. Soon, however, murmurs of approval spread, and with the public's appetite for controversy, Beckett's play became the must-see show of the Left Bank, spawning versions in Spanish and German in the same year. Concerned that somebody would soon attempt a poor English translation, Beckett quickly set about the job himself, but getting *Waiting for Godot* onto an English stage was tricky. Along with difficulties finding the right directors and cast, the British Laws of Censorship demanded that a number of passages be cut. This issue also delayed the publication of the play, which was finally issued by New York's Grove Press in 1954.

Nevertheless, Peter Hall's production opened in London in August 1955. Although two reviewers found it exceptional, the play was not well received. As Peter Bull, the actor who played Pozzo, describes: "Waves of hostility came whirling over the footlights, and the mass exodus, which was to form such a feature of the run of the piece, started quite soon after the curtain had risen. The audible groans were also fairly disconcerting." Audiences in America were equally difficult to please. Director Alan Schneider wrote to Beckett to apologize for his disastrous production in Miami, in which a large number of the audience walked out. Beckett told Schneider that he was not disappointed. Failure, it seems, was part of the way in which he thought about art. He had, he admitted, "breathed deep" of its "vivifying air" for his entire career.

Waiting for Godot investigates the ways in which such failures can be brought to life. The plot itself seems to set out to disappoint the audience. Two men sit under a tree on a country road, waiting for an appointment with a Mr. Godot. They are Estragon and Vladimir, though they refer to each other by the diminutives "Gogo" and "Didi." At the end of both the first and the second act, a small boy arrives to let them know that Mr. Godot will not come. Though they are interrupted, twice, by a man named Pozzo, who is accompanied by his servant, Lucky, nothing of great significance appears to happen. At the end of each act they decide to leave, but do not move from the stage. Through this curious situation, Beckett offers a theater that is empty of easy meanings. Watching *Godot* involves the audience in the drama of what it is like not to be certain about reality, truth, or meaning. *Godot* is, Beckett notes, "a play which was striving all the time to avoid definition."

Beckett's *Godot* has been aligned with works by group of playwrights writing in Europe just after World War II, such as Eugene Ionesco, Antonin Artaud, and Jean Paul Sartre. Their work, which collectively became known as the "Theater of the Absurd," might be said to share a common disillusionment with the times in which they lived, and an anxiety about the nature of religion, politics, identity, responsibility, and language. Sartre was also a philosopher, and much absurdist drama is related to the concerns of the existentialist philosophy that he espoused. For the existentialists, individuals are trapped in a dilemma in which they are forced to act without a secure sense of the external world, reality, universally accepted moral criteria, or any omnipotent being such as God. The playwrights who were influenced by this philosophy set about using theatrical form to examine the idea that existence itself was futile and senseless, characteristically playing with theatrical conventions and offering dreamless, nonsensical, reflexive dramas.

While Beckett's dramatic world, envisaging life "Astride a grave and a difficult birth," seems to share features of absurdism, it is wrong to place him in any such category. As he noted himself, his drama is "not about philosophy, but about situations," while Blin, his chosen director, claimed to have "no ideas—no theories—on theatre at all." There is still a remnant of coherence about existentialist philosophy evident in the very fact that it can even be characterized as a "philosophy." Sartre held on to the possibility that individuals could force their own philosophical meaning out of a situation of meaninglessness. This is reflected in his drama, in which characters hold philosophical positions, and seem to urge the audience to reconsider, act, and take responsibility. While Beckett read many philosophers with great depth, including Descartes, Pascal, Schopenhauer, and Kierkegaard, his texts consider the idea of taking up a philosophical stance with scepticism, and continually parody the condition that might be seen as existential Angst. As the critic Theodor Adorno notes, in Beckett's world, philosophy itself seems to have become bankrupt.

One must perhaps look further afield in the attempt to define Beckett's *Godot*. While he wrote in postwar Paris, the play clearly shows his Irish heritage. The tramps on the roadside echo the tinkers and beggars inhabiting Synge's turn-of-the-century Irish tragedies, which Beckett had seen in the Abbey Theatre in Dublin. Meanwhile, the play adapts and draws on numerous other literary models. The Greek tragedians, Shakespeare, and Racine are all woven into its complex texture. The thoughts of Wittgenstein, Heidegger, Saussure, and Derrida jostle among these classic tones. Perhaps the best way of coming closer to understanding *Waiting for Godot* is to see a good production. This experience is not necessarily an easy one. Beckett was always careful to tell his directors that they should "bore the audience." The effect, and the influence, of the drama depend, primarily, on the experience of waiting, and of struggling with this emptiness.

The play itself begins begins with a struggle. As the curtain opens on a near-empty stage, we watch a man attempting to remove his boot with little success, pulling at it, panting, resting, resuming, only to balk again. But the failure is not his alone. As the man, Estragon, speaks, the audience members, too, are placed in difficulties. Who is he? Where is he? When he speaks the play's opening line—"Nothing to be done"—is

he referring to the state of his footwear, or is he making a more general comment on life? Vladimir's entrance promises some clarity at first, as he addresses his companion with an air of familiarity: "so there you are again." But Estragon's bewildered and cynical response "Am I?" jokes with the audience, plunging us into an unfamiliar world of philosophical confusion about the nature of being (p. 1). Does Estragon, in fact, exist at all? Our uncertainty is increased further as they begin to discuss the fact that Estragon has spent the night in a ditch, being beaten by a group of people.

Most audiences, of course, expect to be a little disoriented at the beginning of a dramatic production. They are perhaps used to being initially confused about the location, the relationship between the characters, and the plot. They expect, however, that all will soon be revealed, that their efforts will be rewarded by a story that makes sense. In this manner, *Waiting for Godot* struck its first audiences as a scandalous dramatic outrage, a hoax of a play in which nothing happened. Many of his audience in the 1950s, and many readers today, still expect what is known as a "well-made play"—one which will quickly set up the relationships and the story so far, offering a climax, a denouement, and, most importantly, a moral. This may be what tradition demands, but, as Vladimir remarks at the end of the play, "habit is a great deadener" (p. 83). If we are to adopt Shakespeare's idea that the play holds up a mirror to nature, then a "well-made play" implies that reality is, in some ways, well-made. It suggests that the world, like the play, has a plot, has a moral, and is shaped according to some design. In playing with the Bard's thoughts on dramatic mimesis, Beckett offers his audience a new world, shaking them out of their habitual, deadened modes of thought. Though perfectly constructed, *Waiting for Godot* is revealed to defy our conventional expectations of theatergoing. Beckett claimed that if it was performed the way that he desired, *Godot* "would empty the theatre." It is a comment that can be read in two ways. Beckett suggests a drama so complex and difficult that it will make people want to leave the before the intermission. If they stay, however, they will be given the sense that the idea of theater itself has been hollowed out, emptied of its potency and of its gravitas. Emptied, perhaps, of everything but its humor.

DOUBLE ACTS: ESTRAGON AND VLADIMIR

Beckett's set is intentionally minimal. The road is the stage itself; its only ornaments are a leafless tree and a "low mound," which was changed, by Beckett, to a rectangular stone in later productions. Beckett also pares away the bare bones of characterization. Estragon and Vladimir seem oddly similar, both dressed like tramps, with matching bowler hats. They are, however, distinguished by their specific health complaints. Vladimir has been offstage because he has some sort of problem with his kidneys. With his weak bladder he becomes, quite literally, a running joke over the course of the play, frequently ducking toward the exit to relieve himself. Estragon, it transpires, is taking off his boots because he has problems with his feet. Pain, however, brings them into a strange kind of harmony.

> ESTRAGON: [*Feebly.*] Help me!
> VLADIMIR: It hurts?
> ESTRAGON: Hurts! He wants to know if it hurts!
> VLADIMIR: [*Angrily*] No one ever suffers but you. I don't count. I'd like to hear what you'd say if you had what I have.
> ESTRAGON: It hurts?
> VLADIMIR: Hurts! He wants to know if it hurts!
>
> (p. 2)

The circular rhythm of this exchange, as each echoes the other, is typical of the play, and has implications for our perception of characterization and meaning. Here, as at many points during the play, the characters appear to be not so much individual entities as elements in a larger

musical pattern. Questions such as "It hurts?" are asked, but they remain unanswered. Beckett was constantly pushing against the limits of language in his work, striving to express what he referred to as "a mocking attitude to the word through words." Throughout *Godot*, language seems to form part of a game, rather than functioning as a medium of communication. For many critics, this small example of dysfunctional dialogue points to larger implications in Beckett's work. It suggests the idea that language cannot bear relation to reality, that expression is impossible.

All these ideas may be fruitfully explored, but perhaps the key fact to bear in mind about Vladimir and Estragon's repetitive banter is that it is funny. While at University in Dublin, Beckett frequently attended vaudeville theater, and loved watching the films of Chaplin, Laurel and Hardy, and Harold Lloyd. The influence of their slapstick antics is clearly evident in *Godot*—even down to the bowler hats. Early audiences commented that Vladimir and Estragon's eschatological banterings resembled a weary, well-worn comic routine. Nevertheless, it is not the kind of laughter one usually expects in a theater. Beckett was much influenced by the French philosopher Henri Bergson, who suggested that laughter can provide something akin to a momentary anaesthesia of the heart. In *Waiting for Godot* laughter often coincides with pain, indignity, or obscenity. Take the combination of scatological and slapstick humor when Vladimir is told that his trouser fly is still undone, or Estragon's excitement when he hears that he might get an erection from hanging himself. Such moments jostle with more complex forms of verbal humor, as when Vladimir ponders why he waits until the last moment before going to the toilet:

> VLADIMIR: [*Musingly.*] The last moment . . . [*He meditates.*] Hope deferred maketh the something sick, who said that?
> ESTRAGON: Why don't you help me?

VLADIMIR: Sometimes I feel it coming all the same.
    Then I go all queer . . . How shall I say? . . .
    Relieved and at the same time . . . appalled.

(pp. 2–3)

Like most of Beckett's prose and dramatic works, the gags are learned. A subtle pun on the idea of physical relief (emptying the bladder) and emotional relief (getting offstage in time) is woven into a biblical reference. Here, Vladimir puts a comic twist to Proverbs 13:12, which says, "Hope deferred maketh the heart sick: but when desire cometh it is a tree of life." He continues in a biblical vein as he muses on the story of the two thieves who were, according to two of the Gospel writers (Luke 23:39–43 and Matthew 27:44) crucified alongside Jesus. Vladimir ponders the fact that, according to Luke's gospel, one of the "thieves was saved." For him, this is "a reasonable percentage" suggesting, perhaps, that he has a fifty-fifty chance of escaping Hell if God exists. He also goes on to point out, however, that the Gospels are as unreliable, and conflicting, as his memory of them.

Although he professed no religion, Beckett was brought up in a strict Protestant background, and the Bible would have been part of his everyday vocabulary. These are just the first of many references to the scriptures in the play. Here, by parodying the work of nineteenth-century Higher Critical scholars, who tried to prove or deny the existence of God by exegetically examining the tales of human witness, Vladimir seems to be suggesting that believing in things could be an enormous joke. The written word of the Bible, in Beckett's world, is, like all language, revealed to be unreliable, and infinitely forgettable. Elsewhere, we find the idea of the crucifixion reduces to a cliché—as Vladimir sententiously sighs, "To every man his little cross"—or to a parody, as when they take it in turns to "do" a yoga exercise called "the tree" (p. 53, p. 68). Elsewhere, the characters carry each other, paralleling images of Calvary and Christ's descent from the cross. Such sacred resonances invite one to read the play as if it were, in some sense, a religious allegory. Beckett resisted such readings, commenting simply that Christianity "is a mythology with which I am perfectly familiar, so naturally I use it." Like all the allusions in the play, references to the scripture set up echoes to our common memories, making us think about what we have lost.

WHO IS GODOT?

Estragon is not particularly impressed by Vladimir's scriptural analyses, and only manages to drum up an "*exaggerated enthusiasm*" for the theological problem (p. 5). In fact, while they keep engaging in this rhythmic exchange, they only seem to aggravate each other. Through one of their most repetitive refrains, we learn why they keep going on:

ESTRAGON: Let's go
VLADIMIR: We can't.
ESTRAGON: Why not?
VLADIMIR: We're waiting for Godot.
ESTRAGON: [*Despairingly.*] Ah!

(p. 6)

The identity of Godot is never made clear; Estragon claims that he would not know him if he saw him, nor can they remember what they asked him for. That said, the semantic richness of his name, along with the recollection that they have formerly addressed him with a "kind of prayer," invites various allegorical explanations (p. 10). In answer to the actor Jack MacGowran, Beckett was emphatic in denying the most popular theory: "Because Godot begins with g-o-d, people have got the idea that he's referring to God. But he categorically states that that is not the point at all, that it doesn't mean God at all." Nevertheless, Beckett tempts the religious interpretation, always emphasizing that the word should be pronounced with the stress on the first syllable. Later, he joked with the director Alan Schneider that the name derived from the French slang for various kinds of boots ("godillot" or "godasses"). Overall, Beckett encouraged a proliferation of interpretations of "Godot," but resisted explanation. When asked "Who or what does Godot mean?" he replied, "If I knew, I would have said so in the play." Perhaps the one thing that we can be certain about is that "Godot" offers the reader the same experience of not knowing, waiting, and questioning, that pervades the entire play.

Vladimir's famous line can also be read as a metadramatic comment. The actors cannot leave the stage because they are *Waiting for Godot*—they are the substance of the play's title. The situation for Estragon and Lucky is rather like that of one of Shakespeare's characters in *As You Like It* who commented that "all the word's a stage." While neither of these players seems sure what he is doing on this stage, they are agonizingly aware of a need to continue to perform, as when Vladimir urges Estragon to "return the ball" of their dialogue (p. 5). Sometimes, it seems, the performance becomes too much for them. When Estragon attempts to get him to tell a formulaic dirty story about an Englishman in a brothel, Vladimir's response is to shout for him to stop. The argument implies that the pair have been performing the same routine and telling the same jokes like two worn-out comedians in a run that never has a last night. While Vladimir tries to exit the stage, hurriedly, he soon returns. Rather like life, there is no exit, in this play, apart from suicide.

POZZO'S PERFORMANCE

Vladimir and Estragon muse upon what Sartre referred to as the only serious philosophical question—suicide—but gravity is a problem for them in both senses. They cannot quite work out how to hang themselves off the branch, without it breaking. Meanwhile, the reality of death seems rather too serious after all, and they decide to finish lunch rather than life. For the audience, at this point, Beckett is playing on the art of suspense; just when they think something will happen, the characters return to their usual activity (waiting), and their usual resigned rhythmic banter:

> VLADIMIR: Nothing you can do about it.
> ESTRAGON: No use struggling.
> VLADIMIR: One is what one is.
> ESTRAGON: No use wriggling.
> VLADIMIR: The essential doesn't change.
> ESTRAGON: Nothing to be done. [*He proffers the remains of the carrot to* Vladimir.] Like to finish it?

(p. 14)

The "terrible cry" that interrupts this impromptu snack marks the entrance of Pozzo and Lucky. It is typical of Beckett's brilliant structuring that only when the play appears to have come full circle, back to its opening line—"Nothing to be done"—does something happen. It seems as if the entire preceding action has been redundant. Quite different from the symbiotic pairing of Estragon and Vladimir, Pozzo appears to be the master to Lucky's slave. Lucky enters first, driven by Pozzo's whip and his cries of "On!"—a human who is forced to behave like a dog by a vicious master. Estragon and Vladimir are at first mystified by the relationship between the pair, then appalled, as they note the running sore around Lucky's neck, caused by the rope. Why, both they and the audience are forced to ask, would anyone continue to exist under such tyrannical command, and what will be done about it?

Pozzo and Lucky are Estragon and Vladimir's first visitors, and their encounter plays off conventions of manners and keeping up appearances—concerns that seem comically at odds with their degraded status. The exaggerated politeness also serves a more complex formal process, echoing back to Ancient Greece. It is the violation of the sacred guest-host relationship, known as *xenia*, that marks the beginning of Aeschylus's tragedy, *The Oresteia*. Things do not bode well in this case of hospitality either. Even the introduction seems confused as Vladimir and Estragon wonder, initially, if he is the long-awaited Godot, initiating a wrangle over names. The various confusions of "Bozzo," "Pozzo," and the figure of "Godot" (to whom Pozzo soon refers as "Godet . . . Godot . . . Godin") are not merely comic (p. 15, p. 22). They show the way in which the names, the most certain signifiers of self-definition, seem to be losing their meaning in this world. Soon, the idea of self-definitions becomes even more confusing, as Pozzo assures himself that Estragon and Vladimir are, at least, "human beings none the less" and "of the same species" as himself (p. 15).

Quite what species any of these characters are seems uncertain. While Pozzo sets about eating his chicken *"voraciously, throwing away the bones"* (p. 18), Vladimir and Estragon seem to be having trouble in classifying Lucky, as he stands, leash around his head, holding Pozzo's bags. While they settle on the possibility that "he's a cretin" or "a half-wit" (p. 18), his degraded state leaves Vladimir uncertain as to whether he is a "man" or not, as the hesitation in his outburst shows:

VLADIMIR: To treat a man . . . [*Gesture towards* LUCKY] . . . like that . . . I think that . . . no . . . a human being . . . no . . . it's a scandal!
ESTRAGON: [*Not to be outdone.*] A disgrace!
[*He resumes his gnawing*]

(p. 20)

Despite Pozzo's exaggerated politeness, his treatment of Lucky appears to lack the basic features of what Vladimir considers humanity. Pozzo himself soon admits that he is "not particularly human," in his revelation that he is about to sell Lucky at the fair (p. 24).

Indeed, as Lucky begins to cry, the audience might begin to wonder quite what species of drama we are watching—and Beckett's note that he is writing in the hybrid genre of tragic-comedy should be borne in mind. Estragon's attempts at compassion, going over to Lucky to wipe away his tears, suggests that we are in the realm of tragedy. As Lucky kicks him violently in the shins, however, Estragon picks up on

Pozzo's own brutality. This sudden switch from compassion to brutality seems both comic and disturbing—while one figure suffers in the play, it appears that another is enjoying himself. It was one of Beckett's great heroes, the eighteenth-century writer Samuel Johnson, who wrote of the way in which enjoyments and sufferings co-exist in the "real state of sublunary nature." Pozzo is certainly enjoying himself, beginning his own pompous rhapsody upon the world, in which for "each one who begins to weep, somewhere else another stops"—mixing Johnsonian syntax with the sweeping terms of a statistician (p. 25).

Though Estragon seems appalled by his guests, there are aspects of the relationship that echo his own friendship with Didi. Pozzo's brutality toward the man that he refers to as "pig" is tempered by a fondness for him, just as Estragon and Vladimir bicker, but embrace, and call each other by pet names. What is more, just like Estragon and Vladimir, Pozzo and Lucky appear to have a need to perform, and a consciousness of their staged existence. Pozzo's outburst, in which he claims that he is tormented by Lucky, is choreographed by Beckett to suggest that he is seeing himself in a dramatic light. He groans, clutches his head and collapses, and goes on to offer an account of the state of the sky that is complete with pauses and lyrical passages. Estragon's response to the tormented outburst—"It's terrible"—could be seen as a comment on Pozzo's unconvincing acting, as much as on his state of mind (p. 34). They soon go on to comment upon their adventure, like a pair of disgruntled critics:

ESTRAGON: It's awful.
VLADIMIR: Worse than the pantomime.
ESTRAGON: The circus.
VLADIMIR: The music-hall.
ESTRAGON: The circus.

(p. 28)

Conventionally, the playwright aims to get the audience to collaborate with him in what

Coleridge refers to as "a willing suspension of disbelief"; to forget that they are watching a play and to pretend, for the performance, that the world they are viewing is "real." Throughout *Waiting for Godot* the characters purposely sabotage the realism of their own play in this way. Here, Vladimir and Estragon draw attention to their theatrical environment, as when Estragon looks out at the "Inspiring prospects" of the audience (p. 6). His later comment—"Nobody comes, nobody goes. It's awful!"—could be taken as apposite commentary on the play itself. Indeed, the playwright Jean Anouilh adopted the phrase as a joyful summary of the 1953 premiere of the play. Estragon's lament invites a question, though. Why are the characters continuing to "act," if they are aware that their performance is so terribly shoddy? As with the play as a whole, there is no answer, but there is perhaps a hint, in the fact that all these figures are under another tyrannical command: they are following a script.

Those reading the text, rather than viewing it, will notice that the play contains numerous detailed, italicized commands. Beckett commented that he started to write *Waiting for Godot* because he wanted to work in a medium where he had "control of where people stood or moved." This control is evident throughout. When Lucky puts down Pozzo's bag or helps him off with his coat, or when Pozzo sits down and eats a chicken lunch, every action is carefully choreographed by Beckett. Such attention to detail is characteristic of Beckett's drama. As the Beckettian actress and critic Rosemary Pountney remarks, "no playwright has more exacting stage directions than Beckett" (1988, p. 169), and he was fierce with directors who tried to change *Godot*'s staging. If art is a mirror of life, then Beckett's mirror suggests that we live in a world in which we are forced to perform to a preordained script. Beckett's stage directions could be seen as the voice of a dictator, manipulating figures onto the stage, and commanding them to perform. These ideas are followed through and developed in the many of

Beckett's later plays, especially *Play* (1964) and *Catastrophe* (1982). In *Waiting for Godot,* some stage directions, such as the complex maneuverings between Lucky and Pozzo, are difficult for the actors to carry out. Others, such as the extraordinary stage direction in which Vladimir "[*uses his intelligence*]" (p. 10), are unperformable. It is tempting to see the artist's stage-directing voice as analogous to an indifferent higher power. To suggest, however, that Beckett's play is drawing direct parallels between the artist and God is to go against his own principles of interpretation. Nevertheless, the power of what Beckett termed his "cold eye" forces us to think, and thinking, as Lucky goes on to show, is a dangerous thing.

REMEMBERING LUCKY'S THINK

The character suffering under the most dramatic constraints is, of course, Pozzo's servant Lucky. In terms of the plot, Pozzo himself stages Lucky's entire existence. Meanwhile, the actor playing this part is required to memorize nearly two pages of incomprehensible monologue. The director of the first Dublin production remembers that his Lucky was nearly overwhelmed by the sheer magnitude of the task. The monologue in question is, of course, performed at Pozzo's command, forcing him to "think" for their entertainment. Beckett was reported to require that Lucky's speech be "like a phonograph record getting faster and faster and faster until it is out of control"—a feat of delivery that would ask a great deal of any actor.

When Pozzo suggests this brand of diversion, Estragon and Vladimir are taken aback:

Pozzo: [*He picks up the whip*]. What do you prefer? Shall we have him dance, or sing, or recite, or think, or—
Estragon: Who?
Pozzo: Who! You know how to think, you two?
Vladimir: He thinks?
Pozzo: Certainly. Aloud. He even used to think

very prettily once, I could listen to him for hours.

(p. 32)

The cause of Vladimir's surprise is left uncertain. Is he shocked that "thinking" is seen as a form of entertainment, that it can be performed on command, or is he surprised because thinking is an activity that Vladimir and Estragon have forgotten about? As Lucky begins his tirade of incomprehensible prose, Beckett draws his audience's attention to a paradox. For if one is "ordered" to "think," the suggestion is that one is obeying, rather than thinking.

The speech that follows, lacking in any punctuation or conventional grammar, was of great importance to Beckett. He chose it as the starting point when rehearsing the production in Berlin in 1975. Despite its apparent nonsensicality, Beckett claimed that it could be divided into three parts, and the second of these parts fell into two sections:

> The first part is about the indifference of heaven, about divine apathy. This part ends with "but not so fast. . . ." The second part starts off with "considering what is more," and is about man, who is shrinking—man who is dwindling. Not only the dwindling is important here, but the shrinking, too. These two points represent the two under sections of the second part. The theme of the third part is "the earth abode of stones" and starts with "considering what is more, much more grave."

(Pountney, 1981, p. 25)

Lucky begins by wondering about the existence of an idea of God, who has a white beard, and is compassionate, rather like Miranda, the heroine of Shakespeare's *The Tempest*. There is, however, something forgetful about this God. He suffers from "athambia," which denotes imperturbability about those around him, "aphasia," the loss of the ability to speak or write, and "apathia," which results in little concern for those around him. For "reasons unknown" to Lucky, he loves all of humanity

deeply "with some exceptions." At this point the speech dives down into the idea of what happens to those "exceptions" who are "plunged in torment," and consumed with fire and brimstone. He then moves on to the idea that despite the progress that man has made—what Lucky terms "the strides of alimentation and defecation"—and all the various activities man undertakes, we can be seen to "shrink and dwindle." He finishes with a morbid lament on the state of man, reflecting on the skull and the stones. One can tenuously link Lucky's reference to the skull with Golgotha, the site of Christ's crucifixion. Beckett, meanwhile, noted that the speech is "all about stones, about the world of stones," as if emphasizing that he was speaking about the most basic elements of existence.

At around the mid-point of Lucky's enigmatic speech, which he claims to give "in brief," Bishop Berkeley, an eighteenth-century churchman and philosopher, makes a brief appearance. George Berkeley wrote about the nature of existence, arguing that matter only exists if perceived, and the world exists because it is perceived by God. This thesis, contained in his most famous observation—"esse est percipi" (to be is to be perceived)—haunts much of Beckett's work, including *Waiting for Godot*. While Lucky's speech seems to be pondering such metaphysical questions, however, it is also a parody of such metaphysical thinking. In the style of an academic giving an account of his research, Lucky repeatedly alludes to imaginary texts and scholars to back up his points. Some, such as "Testew and Cunard" and "Fartov and Belcher," are crude puns. Elsewhere, Lucky makes joking references to concerns about man's existence. "Essy-in-Possy," for instance, the location of Lucky's fictional Academy, picks up on the Latin for "being" and "being able"— "esse" and "posse." While Lucky leans on the language of scholarly argument, especially its use of formal conjunctions such as "hereinafter" and "what is more," the sense of his own argument seems to be falling apart. The strange stammering of "quaquaquaqua," a failed attempt to say "quaversalis," meaning "in all directions at the same time," gives the impression that his speech has become stuck in a groove. Lucky's grip on language seems to be slipping, as he clings to the remnants of his argument, and finally finishes, "unfinished." In choosing to present the play's main "philosophical" argument in an incomprehensible, fragmentary, comic form, Beckett seems to be suggesting to his audience that metaphysical thought is beyond speech. Language cannot offer us a route to truth. As he wrote in a letter to his friend Axel Kaun a decade earlier, "my own language appears to me like a veil that must be torn apart in order to get at the things (or the Nothingness) behind it" (*Disjecta*, p. 171).

MEETING THE BOY

The other characters' reaction to this performance, as they groan, protest, and finally leap upon him to "put an end to his thinking," increases the comic aspect of Lucky's philosophizing. It also suggests, however, that hearing such ideas being articulated is deeply unpleasant, and after Pozzo and Lucky's protracted departure, Estragon and Vladimir return to their more routine use of language. "It's so we won't think," as Estragon later says (p. 53). Quite what they need to not think about becomes clear as a boy arrives with a message for Vladimir. Beckett noted that Lucky was called "Lucky" because he was "lucky to have no more expectations." Vladimir, meanwhile, is still waiting for Godot, and is once again disappointed, this time by the appearance of the messenger boy.

The "nuntius" or messenger is a familiar inhabitant of Greek and French classical tragedy, usually entering to narrate spectacular deaths or battles that occurred in another time or place. The genre dictated that the unities were not broken, and that no violent action took place on the stage. While Beckett still uses the convention of the messenger, as if to highlight the fragility and limits of human knowledge, he adapts it for comic purposes. Conventionally, the messenger's speech would be long and elaborate, but Beckett's boy is afraid to deliver his brief message, and has to rush his words.

Beckett also draws on scripture here. By making the boy a goat-herd and giving him a sheep-minding brother, he alludes to Matthew 25.31–46, in which God divides the sheep from the goats. It is a sly allusion, though. While the gospel claims that the "sheep" will be saved, and the "goats" condemned to a realm of everlasting fire, Beckett reverses the pattern. As the boy confesses, Mr. Godot beats the boy who minds the sheep, and not the one who minds the goats. This sense of arbitrary punishments and rewards echoes back to Vladimir's musings on the fate of the two thieves, increasing the layers of confusion in this neo-eschatological drama.

On hearing that good news has eluded them, and that Godot is not to arrive that day, the pair despondently return to thoughts of ending it all. Death has been on their lips ever since the beginning of the act, as they wait under their lifeless tree, but by their third return to this subject, it appears to be all talk and no action. Even language itself seems to have lost its animation. Death, as the critic Ruby Cohn argues, has been "robbed of its fatality; Estragon reacts to Vladimir's offstage urination: 'He'll be the death of me,' and he mock-warns Pozzo: 'you'll catch your death.' Vladimir sighs: 'We're bored to death'" (*Just Play*, pp. 7–8). As they reconsider hanging themselves, regretting the absence of a noose, the act draws to a close, with their decision to leave. Estragon suggests "Well, shall we go?"—but despite Vladimir's affirmative response "Yes, let's go," they appear to be blocked by Beckett's stage direction: "[*They do not move.*]" (p. 47).

ACT TWO: DA CAPO

The beginning of act 2 was a risky business when the play was first performed. In the first Paris production, a group of the audience made a sensation by exiting en masse when the curtain opened on the same scene of two men, waiting under a tree. This was a shame, because they were destined to miss a certain beauty in this replay. In *Proust*, his 1931 essay about ideas of perception in the novel *A La Recherche du Temps Perdu*, Beckett praised the novelistic technique of repetition, making a comparison with "the beautiful convention of the 'da capo'" in musical composition, in which a musician is directed to return to the beginning of a section of music, and repeat (*Proust*, p. 92).

While it may be pleasing when encountered on a small scale, Beckett's use of repetition in *Waiting for Godot* has a more powerful and disturbing effect. As Ihab Hassan points out in *The Literature of Silence*, it only takes two acts to suggest an infinite sequence of recurring, identical scenes (p. 176). The implication is that, perhaps, we are witnessing an excerpt from a play that has an infinite number of acts, each the same as the next. This sense of infinite repetition is heightened by Beckett's teasing introduction of an actual "da capo," Vladimir's Chinese-box song, which can be repeated for an eternity.

As they resume their discussion, Vladimir becomes increasingly alarmed that Estragon claims not to remember the actions of the previous act. Only under pressure does he recall Pozzo and Lucky, and he cannot remember when their last meeting took place. Estragon's forgetfulness is unsettling, but, perhaps, comprehensible. If the pair is being forced to repeat the same actions from day to day (like actors in an endless run), then perhaps it is better not to be conscious of the repetition. Indeed, as the pair's dialogue proceeds, they appear to fall into a purgatorial circular linguistic dynamic, playing off the "comedy of exhaustive enumeration" that Beckett felt was inaugurated by the vaudeville genre (*Proust*, p. 92). Sidekick to Vladimir's showman, Estragon can only repeat the word "leaves":

ESTRAGON: All the dead voices.
VLADIMIR: They make a noise like wings.
ESTRAGON: Like leaves.
VLADIMIR: Like sand.
ESTRAGON: Like leaves.

(p. 54)

The idea of life as an eternal repetition bears a relation to a famous essay of 1941 by the existential philosopher Albert Camus, which compares man's condition to the Greek myth of Sisyphus, who was condemned to perform the same action, of rolling a rock up a hill, only to have it to roll down again, eternally. The concept of repetition can be both comforting and terrifying. Small-scale refrains, like the lullaby that Vladimir later sings to Estragon or the habitual give-and-take of daily routine, can be comforting, helping us to confirm our identity. The idea of infinite repetition seems less easy. If life is simply played on repeat, one suspects that it may lose its authenticity or significance, like the historical events that Karl Marx famously said happen twice, first as tragedy, and then again as farce.

While Beckett's characters seem to be caught in the same plight as Sisyphus, Beckett's treatment is less tragic. It is lightened, in part, by his almost blasé opening stage direction—"*Next Day. Same Time. Same Place*"—which seems to suggest that the existential dilemma is, itself, a little old hat. What is more, as the second act reveals, there are subtle and mysterious differences in their environment—four or five leaves on the previously bare tree, and a different pair of boots beneath it.

POZZO NEEDS HELP

Once Vladimir and Estragon have established that today is, indeed, slightly different from yesterday, Estragon proceeds to try on the new pair of boots that have appeared under the tree. His discovery that they fit has echoes of the Cinderella fairy tale about it, but it also chimes with another proverbial commonplace—the old adage of a person putting himself in somebody else's shoes, of trying to understand what it is like to be to be another person.

Over the next few minutes, Estragon and Vladimir play with ideas of being other people. First they swap hats in a parodic vaudeville. Then they try "playing at being Pozzo and Lucky." While their posturings, echoing Pozzo's vicious nature and Lucky's bereft drooping, are mocking, it also shows the characters reaching toward a position of understanding. This same tonal ambivalence underlies their melodramatic calls for divine justice, as they both pretend to pray, and desperately plead for help:

ESTRAGON: [*Stopping, brandishing his fists, at the top of his voice.*] God have pity on me!
VLADIMIR: [*vexed*] And me?
ESTRAGON: On me! On me! Pity! On me!

(p. 69)

Pozzo, re-entering the stage, interrupts their outburst, and his blinded figure recalls the stuff of Greek tragedy. Like Sophocles's Oedipus, or Shakespeare's Gloucester in *King Lear*, he seems to ask for the audience's and the protagonists' pity, as he falls down on the stage and is unable to find his feet. His plight, however, is followed by a long debate between Vladimir and Estragon as to whether or not they should come to his aid. Questions of human solidarity, help, and sympathy run through this section of the play. Indeed, Beckett highlighted the idea of "Help" in his notebooks about the production of *Waiting for Godot*, noting that there are twenty-one instances in which one of his protagonists asks for help—and only fourteen are answered.

Understanding and compassion were not things that Beckett thought came easily to humanity. Pain, he commented in his essay on Proust, can "only be focussed at a distance" (p. 45). This view has led some critics to perceive his drama as inhumane. In fact, what he does show is how difficult it is for people to achieve a truly humane understanding of each other.

While Pozzo lies crying for help, Vladimir sets off on a tour de force of rhetorical flourishes and self-congratulation in an attempt to urge Estragon into some sort of action. While he claims that they should not "waste . . . time in idle discourse," this is precisely what he does:

It is not every day that we are needed. Not indeed that we personally are needed. Others would meet the case equally well, if not better. To all mankind they were addressed, those cries for help still ringing in our ears! But at this place, at this moment of time, all mankind is us, whether we like it or not. (p. 72)

Beckett picks up on the irony of Vladimir's pose. While he enjoys the idea of human solidarity, he is only considering it as a theoretical possibility, taking what T. S. Eliot refers to as the aesthetic rather than the moral attitude to life. Beckett slyly signposts Vladimir's speech for us, showing us that we are to take his compassion with a pinch of salt by giving him dramatic stage-directions and overly metaphorical language. He even turns him, for a moment, into a parodic tragic hero. Vladimir's "What are we doing here, *that* is the question" (p. 74) sends the audience back to that most famous of literary procrastinators—Hamlet the Dane.

VLADIMIR CAN'T GO ON

When they do finally help Pozzo, Vladimir and Estragon both end up on the stage floor as well. In making the idea of giving someone a helping hand so farcically difficult, Beckett once again suggests that helping people may not be as easy as convention dictates. What Beckett is mocking here is not the idea of human solidarity. He mocks those who try to make it sound easy. Beckett is also deeply aware of the human need that fuels the sentimental urges behind Vladimir's speech. Indeed, he cannot survive without his friend, waking Estragon as soon as he appears to drop off. This is one of the many times in the play when Vladimir will not let him sleep. The subsequent soliloquy, which explains a little of why Vladimir fears being alone, shows Beckett writing with such beauty that it cannot but rouse that sentiment he is so quick to parody—our compassion:

> VLADIMIR: Was I sleeping, while the others suf-
> fered? Am I sleeping now? Tomorrow, when I
> wake, or think I do, what shall I say of today?
> That with Estragon my friend, at this place
> until the fall of night, I waited for Godot? That
> Pozzo passed, with his carrier, and that he
> spoke to us? Probably. But in all that what truth
> will there be? . . . He'll know nothing. He'll tell
> me about the blows he received and I'll give
> him a carrot . . . Astride of a grave and a dif-
> ficult birth. Down in the hole, lingeringly, the
> gravedigger puts on the forceps. We have time
> to grow old. The air is full of our cries. [*He
> listens.*] But habit is a great deadener. [*He looks
> again at* ESTRAGON.] At me too someone is look-
> ing, of me too someone is saying, he is sleeping,
> he knows nothing, let him sleep on. [*Pause.*] I
> can't go on! [*Pause.*] What have I said?
>
> (p. 83)

As he watches Estragon doze off, Vladimir becomes entwined in the sort of dilemma posed by the philosopher René Descartes, some four hundred years earlier, and by Bishop George Berkeley. Is he merely dreaming the world he thinks that he is participating in? Has the entire play been merely a figment of his dreaming imagination? As he ponders this, and the idea that someone may be looking at him while he sleeps, he suddenly stops himself in horror. Logically, the next step of his philosophical mus-ing is that the person who is looking at Vladimir is, himself, also asleep. In which case Vladimir himself is merely the product of somebody else's dream world. This philosophical problem was one that haunted Beckett's work. Indeed, Vladimir's painful cry echoes back to the closing words of *L'Innomable*, the novel Beckett completed just before writing *Godot*, and translated into English as *The Unnameable* in 1958: "Where I am, I don't know, I'll never know, in the silence you don't know, you must

go on, I can't go on, I'll go on" (p. 418). In a dramatic sense, "I can't go on" implies a bad case of stage-fright, almost as if we have caught Vladimir trembling in the wings. His musing on self- disintegration comes to an abrupt conclu-sion, as he, too, seems to have lost his memory of what he has said. The entry of the boy, for the second time, serves to increase his anxiety.

THE CLIMAX

Anton Chekhov, another great writer of tragi-comedy, pointed up the way in which play-wrights conventionally structure their dramatic structure, noting that if there was a gun hanging on the wall in the first act, it must fire in the last. The ending of *Godot,* as with much of Chekhov, brings nothing so explosive. The boy returns, to inform them that Mr. Godot "won't come this evening" (p. 84). What is worse, he appears to have no recollection of Vladimir, or his previous visit, referring to him, again, as "Mr. Albert." In place of the classical scene of recognition, or anagnorisis, Vladimir meets a blank. Vladimir tries to make sense of the fact that the boy does not recognize him, suggesting, perhaps, that the boy has a brother who came the day before, but to no avail. Things are no easier for the audi-ence. As the cast list notes that there is only one "Boy," this figure is identical to the previous one. Why has he forgotten their last meeting? The conversation increases Vladimir's sense of anxiety about his tenuous existence:

> BOY: What am I to tell Mr Godot, sir?
> VLADIMIR: Tell him . . . [*He hesitates*]. . .tell him
> you saw me and that . . . [*He hesitates*] . . . that
> you saw me.
> [*Pause.* VLADIMIR *advances, the* Boy *recoils.*
> VLADIMIR *halts, the* BOY *halts. With sudden
> violence.*] You're sure you saw me, you won't
> come and tell me tomorrow that you never
> saw me!
>
> (p. 86)

Vladimir's need for confirmation that their meeting has taken place is entwined with the problem of whether one's existence is governed by being perceived. His appeal has a history: in act 1, Vladimir has asked the same boy whether he came the previous day, asking, "You did see us, didn't you?" (p. 45). One senses that this exchange has been going on for some time.

As the final act draws to its close, and Estragon and Vladimir contemplate what they are to do, and whether they should, at last, hang themselves, Beckett provides his audience with a final, brilliant, comic sadness. Lacking a noose to finish the job off, they wonder whether Estragon's belt will do the trick. "It might do at a pinch," Vladimir considers, "But is it strong enough?" (p. 86). As they each take an end of the cord and pull, the rope-belt breaks. Recovering from their tug-of war, *"They almost fall."* "Almost", like "perhaps," is a key word for Beckett. Estragon confesses to Vladimir that he, too, "can't go on like this"—but, while the two figures are in the depths of despair, they have not quite fallen. Perfecting the art of tragic bathos, the final descent is not of humanity, but of a pair of trousers.

Beckett was very particular about the trousers. He was concerned to hear that in the French premiere of the show, Estragon kept them halfway up, and wrote to Roger Blin to make sure that they fell completely around the character's ankles. Beckett admitted that such attention to detail must seem silly, but following Estragon's advice, he never neglects the "little things" (p. 2).

It is little things like the poetic reversal at the close of act 2 that give the play its power. Beckett's entrances and exits act, for the characters, and perhaps for the audience, as rehearsals of their final leave-taking. In this sense, *Waiting for Godot* offers a sensitivity to the simultaneous longing for closure and desire for continuance that haunt every life, and every good piece of art. This time, it is Vladimir, not Estragon, who suggests that they should go.

This time, Estragon agrees. Once again *"They do not move"* (p. 87). One cannot fail to be moved.

CRITICAL INTERPRETATIONS

Considering Beckett's sensitivity to endings, it is not surprising that echoes of *Waiting for Godot* persist throughout his writing life, creeping into his later works. The concerns of Vladimir and Estragon, Pozzo and Lucky, find themselves played out again and again in his later prose. But the play also finds what Beckett referred to in his novel *Mercier and Camier* as a "life of afterlife" elsewhere, influencing his contemporaries Edward Albee, Harold Pinter, and Sam Shepard as well as the next generation of writers for stage and screen, such as Sarah Kane, Tom Stoppard, David Mamet, and Quentin Tarantino.

Godot has also found itself consistently resurrected and rewritten away from the stage, in the world of academia. As William Hutchings notes in his essay on "*Waiting for Godot* and the Principle of Uncertainty," only Shakespeare's *Hamlet* can lay claim to a greater number and variety of critical readings (p. 27).

In some ways, *Waiting for Godot* can be seen as an example of the way in which modernist drama stands on the threshold of the postmodern. Rather than asking epistemological questions about how we interpret the world, the play seems to be concerned with ontological worries. Audiences are asked to consider multiple worlds, and to wonder whether the "world" of *Waiting for Godot* bears any relation to their own. The resulting text communicates (or fails to communicate) undecidability and openness, and sheds light on the ways in which language fails to match up to what we might term reality. Full of parody, it verges on what Fredric Jameson terms the Postmodern Condition, in which there is no "healthy linguistic normality" that remains to be mocked.

Beckett himself spoke of working with "impotence" and "ignorance" as an artist. With this in mind, negotiating a critical stance with which to approach *Waiting for Godot* is tricky. Whether one sees his work as offering a complete severance from, and destabilizing of, the very idea of reality, or as an engaged humanism that helps us to move closer toward the real world, Beckett directs us to treat any critical stance with a dose of scepticism. It is worth remembering that when he is exchanging insults with Vladimir, "Crritic!" is the worst insult that Estragon can summon.

Perhaps the best way to approach *Waiting for Godot* is to consider the impression it has made. Among the many anecdotes and tales about this play, one stands out. In 1957, a group of actors from San Francisco had visited the notoriously tough San Quentin State Prison. They had chosen to perform *Waiting for Godot,* in part, because it has no women in it, and was therefore suitable for the all-male confines of San Quentin. The cast was nervous as the curtain rose, but as the critic Martin Esslin notes, what "bewildered the sophisticated audiences of Paris, London and New York was immediately grasped by an audience of convicts" (*The Theatre of the Absurd,* p. 19). One among the audience, Rick Cluchey, went on to write himself, and later became close friends with Beckett. Even within a prison, it seems, *Waiting for Godot* managed to open doors.

Selected Bibliography

EDITION

Waiting for Godot. London: Faber, 1965.

OTHER WORKS BY SAMUEL BECKETT

Proust. London: Chatto and Windus, 1931. (Citations taken from *Proust and Three Dialogues.* With Georges Duthuit. London: John Calder, 1965).

Play: And Two Short Pieces For Radio. London: Faber, 1964.

The Unnameable. New York: Grove Press, 1958. (Citations are taken from *Molloy: Malone Dies: The Unnameable.* London: John Calder, 1994.)

Disjecta: Miscellaneous Writings and a Dramatic Fragment, ed. Ruby Cohn. London: John Calder, 1983.

Catastrophe (1982), in *Samuel Beckett: The Complete Dramatic Works.* London: Faber, 1986.

STUDIES OF *WAITING FOR GODOT*

Asmus, Walter. "Beckett Directs *Godot,*" *Theatre Quarterly,* 5 (September, November 1975), pp. 19–26.

Bloom, Harold, ed. *Samuel Beckett's Waiting for Godot: Modern Critical Interpretations.* New York: Chelsea House, 1987.

Busi, Frederick. *The Transformations of Godot.* Lexington: University Press of Kentucky, 1980.

Cohn, Ruby, ed. *Waiting for Godot: A Casebook.* London: Macmillan, 1987.

Connor, Steven, ed. *Waiting for Godot and Endgame.* London: Macmillan, 1992.

Fletcher, Beryl, et al. *A Student's Guide to the Plays of Samuel Beckett.* London: Chatto and Windus, 1967.

Graver, Lawrence. *Waiting for Godot.* Cambridge: Cambridge University Press, 1989.

Gordon, Lois. *Reading Godot.* New Haven and London: Yale University Press, 2002.

Hutchings, William. "*Waiting for Godot* and the Principle of Uncertainty," in *Approaches to Teaching Beckett's Waiting for Godot,* ed. June Schlueter and Enoch Brater. New York: The Modern Language Association of America, 1991.

Knowlson, James, ed. *The Theatrical Notebooks of Samuel Beckett, Volume 1: 'Waiting for Godot.'* London: Faber, 1992.

Martin, Jean. "Creating Godot," in *Beckett in Dublin.* Dublin: The Lilliput Press, 1992.

McMillan, Dougald, and Martha Fehsenfeld. *Beckett in the Theatre: The Author as Practical Playwright and Director: Volume 1: From 'Waiting for Godot' to 'Krapp's Last Tape.'* London: John Calder, 1988.

Pountney, Rosemary, and Nicholas Zurbrugg. *Waiting for Godot.* Longman: York Press, 1981.

Schlueter, June, and Enoch Brater, eds. *Approaches to Teaching Beckett's Waiting for Godot.* New York: The Modern Language Association of America, 1991.

States, Bert O. *The Shape of Paradox: An Essay on Waiting for Godot.* Berkeley and Los Angeles: University of California Press, 1978.

CRITICAL AND BIOGRAPHICAL STUDIES

Abbott, H. Porter. *Beckett Writing Beckett; the Author in the Autograph,* Ithaca, N.Y.: Cornell University Press, 1996.

Adorno, Theodor W. "Trying to Understand Endgame," in *Samuel Beckett's 'Endgame,'* ed. Harold Bloom. New York and New Haven: Chelsea House, 1988.

Andonian, Cathleen Culotta, ed. *The Critical Response to Samuel Beckett.* London: Greenwood Press, 1998.

Bair, Deirdre. *Samuel Beckett: A Biography.* London: Vintage, 1990.

Cohn, Ruby. *Just Play: Beckett's Theater* (Princeton, New Jersey: Princeton University Press, 1980).

Cohn, Ruby, ed. *Samuel Beckett: A Collection of Criticism.* New York: McGraw, 1975.

Driver, Tom. "Beckett by The Madelaine," *Columbia University Forum* IV, Summer 1961.

Esslin, Martin. *The Theater of the Absurd.* rev. edn., Harmondsworth: Penguin, 1968.

Harmon, Maurice, ed. *No Author Better Served: The Correspondence of Samuel Beckett and Alan Schneider.* Cambridge, Mass.: Harvard University Press, 1998.

Hassan, Ihab. *The Literature of Silence: Henry Miller and Samuel Beckett.* New York: Peter Smith, 1967.

Kenner, Hugh. *A Reader's Guide to Samuel Beckett.* London: Thames and Hudson, 1973.

Knowlson, James. *Damned to Fame: The Life of Samuel Beckett.* London: Bloomsbury, 1997.

Levy, Shimon. *Samuel Beckett's Self-Referential Drama: The Three I's.* New York: St Martin's Press, 1990.

McDonald, Ronan. *Tragedy and Irish Writing: Synge, O'Casey, Beckett.* Basingstoke, U.K.: Palgrave, 2002.

Mercier, Vivian. *Beckett/Beckett.* New York: Oxford University Press, 1977.

Pattie, David. *The Complete Critical Guide to Samuel Beckett.* London and New York: Routledge, 2000.

Pountney, Rosemary. *Theatre of Shadows: Samuel Beckett's Drama 1956–76.* Gerrards Cross, U.K.: Colin Smythe, 1988.

Reid, Alec. *All I Can Manage, More than I Could: An Approach to the Plays of Samuel Beckett.* Dublin: Dolmen Press, 1968.

Ricks, Christopher. *Beckett's Dying Words.* Oxford: Oxford University Press, 1993.

Schneider, Alan. *Entrances: An American Director's Journey.* New York: Viking, 1986.

Webb, Eugene. *The Plays of Samuel Beckett.* Seattle: University of Washington Press, 1972.

Worth, Katherine. *Samuel Beckett's Theatre: Life Journeys.* Oxford: Clarendon Press, 1999.

OTHER WORKS

Bergson, Henri. *Le Rire: essai sur la signification du comique.* Paris: F. Alcan, 1910.

Lukács, Georg. *The Meaning of Contemporary Realism*, trans. John and Necke Mander. London: Merlin, 1962.

Jameson, Fredric. *Postmodernism; or the Cultural Logic of Late Capitalism.* Durham, N.C.: Duke University Press, 1991.

Graham Swift's
Waterland

JOSEPH DEWEY

I T IS SPRING 1980. Tom Crick, only fifty-three years old, is unexpectedly nearing the end of a solid if unremarkable thirty-two-year career as a history teacher in a private Greenwich secondary school. His wife, Mary, in the grip of a menopausal delusion in which she believes God has spoken to her, has kidnapped an unwatched baby from a shopping cart at a neighborhood supermarket. Because of the ensuing public embarrassment—pending criminal charges, she has been committed for psychological evaluation—the school's headmaster, himself a science teacher with little patience for what he views as the dead-end pessimism and backward-looking triviality of historical study, has maneuvered Crick into early retirement and plans now to phase out the history department altogether.

Crick's life suddenly tilted precipitously toward chaos, he abandons the course syllabus (prepared lectures on the French Revolution) and enthralls the seventeen students in his upper-form European history class with tales of his own life, particularly his tumultuous adolescence in the forbidding Fens country of East England (his father was a lock-keeper, eeler, and part-time farmer along the River Leem).

More than forty years after the fact, Crick still wrestles with the implications of those distant events: principally, his sexual initiation with Mary, a farmer's daughter with a healthy eagerness for sexual experimentation, and the primitive abortion Mary subsequently endured that left her sterile. More problematically, he explores within the awkward public space of these classroom talks his culpability in both the callous murder of a friend, Freddie Parr, and the drowning-suicide of his retarded older half-brother, Dick, both deaths connected to Mary's pregnancy. Dick was in love with Mary and thought the baby could be his, although he was not entirely sure how conception worked. Mary, not wanting to tell him the difficult truth (that the baby was in fact his younger brother's), told him rather that it was Freddie's, whose shady reputation as a wartime black marketeer and notorious womanizer made him a viable candidate. Enraged, Dick got Freddie drunk, assaulted him with the empty beer bottle, and then pushed him into the murky Leem.

Unable to swim, Freddie drowned. His death, however, was summarily ruled an accident and no one ever suspected Dick's involvement. But Tom, who had noticed a yellowish bruise on

Freddie's temple, had later found the bottle in the river: it was a special ale, bottles of which only the Cricks kept, locked in a chest in their attic. When Mary then told him of her clumsy lie, he quickly pieced together what must have happened. Within days, Tom told Dick the truth about the baby's paternity and then revealed to Dick the far darker truth of Dick's own paternity, that he was the offspring of the illicit love between their mother and *her* father, Dick's grandfather. Confused, overwhelmed by the information, Dick drowned himself by leaping from the railing of a river dredger on which he worked.

Searching for some explanation for the pressing weight of the cumulative failure of his life since, Crick extends these classroom story hours to include ruminations about the forbidding beauty of the vast Fens low country itself, conjuring its green-gray monotony, its nuance and lines, its press and feel, its intricate ecosystem of flora and fauna, and the complicated man-made waterway system of locks and sluices that his family had helped maintain for more than a century. He offers as well extensive yarns about his own family, tales his mother had told him long ago when sleep would not come to him amid the forbidding Fens nightfall, riveting tales, stretching back three generations, of forbidden love, ruthless ambition, and episodes of near fairy-tale magic, including stories of the sweet unexpected intrusion of love at first sight and even of the inexplicable brush with the paranormal. In the process, Crick engages one of his brighter students, the skeptical Price, in a probing dispute on the relevance of history itself. Price, a leader of a school political activist group called the Holocaust Club, in which students contemplate the approaching nuclear apocalypse, argues passionately that all his generation has is the moment and that even that is in dire threat, that history is a dodge, its pretense at explanation a narcotic. "You know what your trouble is, sir? You're hooked on explanation. Explain, explain. Everything's got to have an explanation. . . ."

CHRONOLOGY

1949	4 May: Graham Swift born in South London, near Bermondsey. His father, a civil servant, served as a naval pilot during World War II. Swift is raised in the relative comforts of the middle-class postwar urban boom.
1960–1966	Attends Dulwich College, a prestigious prep school in London long dedicated to the "linguistic, mathematical, scientific, technical, spiritual, physical, cultural, creative, and social" development of its boys. Begins to write stories.
1967–1970	Completes B.A. and master's degrees in literature from Queen's College, Cambridge.
1970–1973	Works on but does not complete Ph.D. (York University) in the field of the nineteenth-century novel.
1973–1983	Teaches literature part time at various London colleges. Also works as a security guard and as an attendant at a mental hospital.
1980	Publishes first novel, *The Sweet-Shop Owner,* the life story of a small-business owner and his difficult relationship with his estranged daughter, the only child of a loveless and failed marriage. Records his thoughts, memories, and experiences during a single June day, his daughter's birthday and his last as he deliberately exacerbates a heart condition to cause a fatal attack.
1981	Publishes *Shuttlecock,* in which a grown son, a senior clerk and police archivist in the late 1970s, struggles with difficult revelations he uncovers in forgotten government files that raise questions about the distinguished World War II record of his father, a celebrated undercover agent now confined in a mental hospital, by suggesting he may actually have collaborated with the Nazis. Awarded the Geoffrey Faber Memorial Prize.
1982	Releases a collection of eleven previously published, largely experimental

short stories, *Learning to Swim and Other Stories.*

1983   Publishes *Waterland*, which receives enthusiastic reviews and draws comparisons to Hardy, Melville, and Marquez, and establishes Swift as a major talent. Short-listed for Britain's prestigious Booker Prize and receives the Geoffrey Faber Memorial Prize, the *Guardian* Fiction Prize, the Royal Society of Literature Winifred Holtby Award, and the Italian Premio Grinzane Cavour; his first novel to be made available in the United States and the subject of a 1992 film adaptation.

1985   An accomplished amateur fly fisherman, coedits (with writer David Profumo) *The Magic Wheel: An Anthology of Fishing in Literature,* a compilation of reflections on the sport from the ancients to contemporaries.

1988   Publishes *Out of This World,* a study of three generations of a family: an arms manufacturer and World War I hero whose record of valor may or may not be entirely accurate; his son, a war photographer who abruptly retires when his father is killed by IRA terrorists; and the photographer's estranged daughter, who struggles to accept her father's passion for photographing atrocities.

1992   Publishes *Ever After,* a novel that counterpoints the contemporary story of an academic struggling to understand the accidental death of his young wife with the journals and letters of a Victorian era ancestor who, as a surveyor for the national railway, must confront the shattering implications of Darwin's evolution thesis when he excavates dinosaur fossils. Awarded the French Prix du Meilleur Livre Étranger.

1996   Publishes *Last Orders,* a comic homage to both Faulkner's *As I Lay Dying* and Chaucer's *Canterbury Tales,* in which three close friends travel from Bermondsey to the dismal Kentish seaport at Margate to comply with the last request of a dead companion and war buddy, a

butcher, to dispose of his ashes; in the process, they reveal their own lives in chapters that move without authorial center from one character to another, offering a poignant cultural portrait of the World War II working-class generation. Awarded the James Tait Black Memorial Prize and the Booker Prize.

explaining's a way of avoiding facts while you pretend to get near them" (pp. 166–167). Crick thus finds himself examining the very purpose of history, its processes, and specifically the human need to explore events, to search out cause and effect, to make sense of what is otherwise the crude and often careless work of chance. Although Crick's unconventional classes manage to kindle unexpected enthusiasm among his students, the myopic headmaster moves forward with Crick's retirement, and Crick delivers a brief, powerfully understated farewell address on the fragility of civilization and, on Easter weekend, closes his life as a teacher.

Given such dramatic narrative action, *Waterland* appears at first approach a most singular event in contemporary narrative: a needful text, that is, a work of serious fiction that wants simply to be read, to be relished one turned page after another in a way that would recall the High Victorian grand narratives of master storytellers such as Thomas Hardy and Charles Dickens, both of whom serve as acknowledged influences and exert considerable stylistic and formal pressure on Swift's tale. The novel offers a reassuring commitment to mimesis, encouraging a reader's involvement with plot and sympathy toward a grand cast of vivid characters, poignantly human in their aspirations and imperfections. It is unapologetically indulgent of a plot- heavy narrative, where, within its 300-plus pages, unfolds the sensational mayhem of tempestuous love, incest, illicit offspring, a ghastly primitive abortion, the shadow-cut of madness, a daring daylight kidnapping, apocalyptic fires and biblical-size floods, dramatic suicides, religious ecstasies, the regular intrusion of ghosts, the terrible waste and pain of war, large-scale ambition and greed and the inevitable fall from such self-sustained sense of import, profound friendships and deep betrayal, and incidentally a dead body found floating in a river. To this is added the novel's rich Hardyesque evocation of the exotic East English Fens country, a swampy inland peopled by a primitive culture rich in folk traditions and unmoved by the contemporary "outside" world, and its ambitious scope—a tightly fashioned intricacy of events that spans two centuries and weaves a genealogy of two families: the visionary Atkinsons, who attempt to tame the Fens country by founding the district's largest brewery and then by channeling its difficult backwaters into navigable passageways; and the humble Cricks, who help maintain that riverway system. Finally, the novel's considerable catalog of resonant symbols appears to require, even encourage, the traditional interactive play of an interpretative reader—the uncontrollable riverways of the Fens, the mysterious eels that nestle in its miry bottom, the decrepit windmills that dot its swampy countryside. Given all this, *Waterland* begs just to be read—indeed, to be filmed. (It was, in fact, the subject of an uneven 1992 interpretation by director Stephen Gyllenhaal featuring Jeremy Irons as Tom Crick, a Britisher transplanted oddly to the dreary environs of Pittsburgh.) In an era when serious fiction had grown weary, even wary, of plot as a distraction and had downsized narratives into minimalist examinations that poked about the unsuspected poetry of the little lives that unfold in backyards and living rooms, here was a maximalist text that embraced scale and appeared to invite even those most swayed by the contemporary credo of "less is more" to relax into the traditional largesse of narrative.

Then why does *Waterland* itself not sustain such satisfaction? Although surely the intricacy of Crick's marvelously wrought generational narrative suggests the same sort of totalizing text reminiscent of the grand narratives of the High Age of realism (the Landow website actually tacks out Crick's genealogy back to the early Middle Ages, a testimony to Swift's meticulous design), something interdicts the casual seduction-by-narrative. *Waterland* is suspicious, indeed critical of the very need it engenders; suspicious of the refuge of fiction, the pleasure prison of narratives into which readers gladly withdraw, seeking in that retreat into a wholly symbolic landscape some respite from a chaotic world that stubbornly refuses to conform to the simplest logic assumed by a manufactured plot.

What skewers the reading experience here? There is the over-the-top element of the narrative action, a deliberate excess of plot, a plot so chock full of events that draw so generously on the stock conventions of gothic/romance/mystery novels (including, seriously, a dark family secret in a sealed letter that is actually locked in a chest kept in a web-thick attic) that the plot begins to undercut itself with a mocking irony. You name it, whatever behavior—quirky, eccentric, criminal, perverse—it has happened somewhere in the Crick lineage. And even that carnivalesque excess of action is filtered secondhand, told by an unassuming history teacher who, facing his own professional collapse, dispenses with history in favor of "his story." Thus, storytelling itself is moved to the center of the reading experience. *Waterland* is a novel told, spoken, in which the sole action in the narrative present is, well, a man talking, or more exactly an articulate, educated man telling stories, a man who in the interest of accessing a generally resistant audience (his bored history honors class) violates just about every convention of traditional narratology. He shifts freely into the interiors of his characters, male or female, young or old, contemporary or historical. At other times, he vividly re-creates scenes that he never actually witnessed, audaciously reanimating events and characters, times and places not even remotely within his own experience, indeed not even within his own era, or casually lopes off into odd, albeit fascinating, asides on esoteric topics including eel reproduction and ale brewing, medieval hagiography and plate tectonics. Amid such generous suppositions, unsponsored speculations, elaborate digressions, and creative conjurings, a needful reader coming only for the rich seclusion afforded by careful plot and consistent character, the sturdy shelter-space of a traditional grand novel, is surely invited in but then rudely treated.

The plot itself is rendered without regard to linear development, denied the traditional momentum of suspense: Crick's talks, mimicking the recursive, looping feedback of memory itself, circle back to salient points, repeat critical scenes, foreshadow other critical moments, tease with promises of elaboration later. At times he recasts entire episodes into the deliberately self-mocking voice-over of a fairy-tale raconteur, complete with the obligatory "Once upon a time." In addition, he is given to indulging, in a disquieting third person, provocative self-reflexive ruminations about the slow-motion crash and burn of his own life. More frustrating, the narrative, despite its generous scope and willingness to dwell on the finest details of landscape and character psychology, deliberately leaves numerous critical plot questions unresolved, revealing the alarming poverty of investigation itself as the whys remain not merely unaddressed but apparently unaddressable, thus mocking the very need for tidiness implicit in any reader's retreat to the shelter-space of a novel.

Indeed, *Waterland* begins as a straightforward murder mystery: Crick's narration of the morning that Freddie Parr's murdered corpse floated up among the detritus of the lock near the Crick cottage in July 1943, and his determination to solve the mystery of the unaccounted bruise on Freddie's temple. But Crick, narrating to his class more than forty years after Freddie's death, knows the circumstances of the crime and yet withholds that information from his audience/ class as he unfolds his tales of the Fens in a deliberate tease that necessarily foregrounds not tidy resolution (because even Crick's take on the murder is open to question) but rather the

intricate process of reanimating events via the imagination, a grand play designed solely to secure/enthrall a needful audience. Even as Crick, a failed schoolteacher, struggles to account for the implosion of his life events, struggles to find a context for explaining the turns of his experience by conducting within the public forum of his own classroom a decidedly personal historical inquiry, the tale he tells frustrates, even mocks that very imperative. He cannot talk himself into logic, cannot conjure sufficient context, cannot satisfyingly link a single slender cause to a single clear and evident effect, cannot even inadvertently stumble upon the traditional reward of realistic fiction: the illumination of an epiphany.

Thus Swift shatters his own intricate story line much as the curious would shatter a fancy watch to expose the intricacy of its workings, even though such exposure necessarily dooms its ability to function smoothly—indeed, at all. Swift deploys the familiar devices of conventional realism only to test, even contest them, to reveal them as devices, thus sustaining a tension between the story and its own telling. This may account for some initial criticism of the novel that found it cold, even dispassionate, its author too distanced from the characters who appear to be treated more as props or conveniences. But this shattering of the narrative causes the reader to acknowledge the provisional and fragile nature of narration itself and thus lends storytelling its nuance, its depth, and ultimately its heroic dimension. Shattering here affirms faith in what has been shattered, much as Tom Crick, surrounded by the stunning evidence of civilization's fragility amid the ruins of World War II Germany, professes to Price years later that such a moment triggered his epiphanic certainty of the need for civilization: an "artifice . . . but precious" (p. 240). As readers, we are given only Crick's voice, the resilient voice of the storyteller/conjurer, and the spell of the story itself rendered in Crick's high-caloric prose line that sounds a pitch-perfect aural event. In Tom Crick's resilient voice-over, Swift valorizes the sweet verbal suction of narrative itself. *Waterland* is not "about" the stories Tom Crick tells. For all their fascinating turns and poignant twists, they are merely an enthralling scrim, a distraction to the novel's truer imperative: the telling of those stories and the wider implications of why we crave such curious inventions in a contemporary world vulnerable, as the student Price despairs, to extinction at the slightest press of a button or two. It is a narrative that despite its considerable complexity draws as its formal model that most accessible of experiences: the soft comfort of a bedtime story, a tale told to calm the deepest fears against the onrush of the darkest sort of night. That it cannot hold back the night is evident; that it can make its approach endurable is heroic. *Waterland* then is a writer's inquiry into the imagination itself, the sole energy capable of the daunting project of creating order in the late-twentieth-century world; it is an anatomy of narrative itself, its reach and its daring, its limits and its vulnerabilities, a complex validation of storytelling that acknowledges its stubborn futility even as it extends its generous consolation.

A READING: THE POWER AND LIMITS OF THE IMAGINATION

Waterland thus has something of a disputed narrative center. Does that contested center belong to Tom Crick, history teacher, or to Graham Swift, the larger author-ity? Character and author, historian and writer, manifestly do not share the same agenda, indeed cannot. In his meandering confession, his jerry-rigged autobiography constructed via extemporaneous class lectures in the quietus of an imploding teaching career, Crick seeks explanation, a satisfying context to account for the persistent mysteries of his emotional life: a misbegotten older half-brother, the byproduct of incest, who may—or may not—have coldly (or clumsily) executed Freddie Parr and whose suicide by drowning still rests uneasily on Crick's

conscience for a part he may (or may not) have played; Crick's own child aborted in a bloody backwoods procedure when he was only sixteen; and most recently his wife's bizarre decision to kidnap a baby in broad daylight from a supermarket.

As in the endless rounds of toss and fetch he plays with his handsome golden retriever, Crick expects his inquiry to retrieve the telling evidence of logic. "To uncover the mysteries of cause and effect. To show that to every action there is a reaction. That Y is a consequence because X preceded. . . . To know that what we are is what we are because our past has determined it" (p. 107). He struggles mightily to touch the reassurance of explanation at the very moment of deepest crisis (a traditional ignition site for revelation in classic realism), to manage a single sturdy construct of sense out of his life story by tracking his ancestry through nearly two centuries. Although he finds stunning iterations of behavior among his ancestry, they are unprovoked; thus he moves no closer to explanation, despairing over the sheer inconsequence of the dozen or so lives he recounts, among them ultimately his own. Like the dark, restless Fens waters that frustrate every effort to dam and direct them, events frustrate Crick's earnest desire to channel them into the convincing elegance of explanation. Despite the seductive pull of his recollection narratives, the looking back is the source of Crick's agony—a "crick," after all, is the stabbing pain in the neck, the cutting muscle contraction caused by the head turning backward. The fragments Crick recollects cannot sustain the trick of coherence. Crick's very delivery, his overfondness for the fragment as a sentence construction, stringing eloquent and often lengthy fragments that cannot find their way to the simplest exertion of a complete sentence, reminds the reader of the deep difficulty of such an endeavor. A usurped mock sovereign (his class is being taken from him in ways that parody the grand coup d'état that triggered the French Revolution), a mock father being removed from his adopted children (he calls his students "children" and regrets their being forcibly taken from him), Crick as character cannot easily resist the bittersweet pull of poignancy.

But Crick is a textual event, a writer's conjuring. The patterns and iterations Crick supposedly recovers through his classroom perusal of his family's history are actually the inventions of a larger author-ity. Crick's anxieties are the stuff of Swift's consolation: knowledge is imperfect, facts shallow, solutions ironic, endings ultimately undercut. Clearly Swift, as writer-authority, understands the incipient threat of Crick's intention, how devastating it would be to the writer's craft if accountability and explanation were possible, how narratives since the *Iliad* have thrived only by virtue of the sheer inexplicability of human actions, the persistent mysteries of the needful heart amid the careless and chartless intrusion of chance and against ultimately the clumsy interference and necessary pressure of death. Tom Crick needs to understand—but the author Swift needs more to understand that need to understand and offers rather the investigation of curiosity itself, open-ended and sustained not by resolution but rather by the intrigue of investigation itself, the rush of reconstructing rather than solving events. If experience were as neat as Crick's history texts contend, tidying up as they do the horrific mischief of entire civilizations into the efficient neatness of chapters with attractive subtitles and answerable questions at the end that codify as "fact" a wholly invented system of causality and explanation; if revelation were workable and reliable; if order were indeed a realistic goal of experience itself, there would be no need for the libraries of narratives that have long wrestled with the whys. We do not write fiction (or read it for that matter) because understanding is possible; we participate in the interactive art of narrative exactly because understanding is impossible, the confidence the narrative's participants share that a narrative will ultimately, joyfully reveal its own inability to reveal. Bound to the evident glory of storytelling, Swift nevertheless suspects its futility. Even as Crick tells his-story, Swift un-tells it, exposes that narrative line and thus permits/compels the reader into a far different plot.

Despite then the difficult confessional narrative of Tom Crick, deposed history teacher, childless at midlife, his wife dispatched to an asylum, Graham Swift will not concede to the evident downward trajectory of his narrating center largely because such a collapsing life becomes the satisfying substance of his narrative play. Indeed the novel moves in the narrative present, unironically, toward Easter weekend despite the collapsing life possibilities of the narrative's hero. What finds revival here, what claims resurrection, is not faith in humanity or faith in the human heart (both traditional affirmations of the grand narratives of the nineteenth century) but rather faith in the act of storytelling itself. Storytelling alone enjoys unequivocal redemption in a novel that broadly parodies other moments when characters ironically evoke Christian analogues. For instance, Crick renders the sudden appearance of the kidnapped baby in his home in vocabulary that recalls the virgin birth and the familiar Nativity tableau. Elsewhere, Dick, perceived by his eccentric grandfather/father as a latter-day savior sent to redeem the world, the offspring of pure love (his) for pure beauty (ironically his own daughter), commits suicide but his body is never recovered, a game parody of the mystery of Good Friday, the passion and destruction of another innocent sent to redeem the world whose body is likewise never secured. Amid such parodies, *Waterland* celebrates the achievement, indeed the audacity, of the charged imagination, embattled and often neglected in the late-twentieth-century techno-wonderland that has made such a remarkable interior energy oddly antiquated amid a cultural geography now thickened with massive theme parks, tamed by the tentacled reach of home entertainment technologies, anesthetized by the irresistible pull of computer and television screens, and-mesmerized by big-budget special effects films projected in every multiplex.

The narrative tension then is not the historian's much-vaunted showdown between the present and the past. Time itself, Swift argues, is a convenience, an invention, a clever concoction to create the illusion of movement; day, hour, minute, second, each a mutually agreed upon fiction within a fallible measuring system that artificially creates distance and the handy premise of generations (underscored by Crick's residency in Greenwich, where the world's watches are, quite literally, set). As Crick explores his family's considerable archives, time is rendered more as a fluid continuum (like the great ecosystem of the Fens). The present is always informed, shaped, by the press of an ever-recycling past (suggested by Crick's signatory fluid verb tenses, moving effortlessly from past to present tense and back again). Current events manage to repeat the past in attractive (albeit meaningless) patternings, cycles of iterations that suggest the past and present are merely different words for the same moment. As Crick cautions, "It [history] goes in two directions at once. It goes backwards as it goes forwards. It loops. It takes detours. Do not fall into the illusion that history is a well-disciplined and unflagging column marching unswervingly into the future" (p. 135). Indeed the novel's most elaborate aside, about the mysterious, apparently global migratory habits of the common British river eel, is a grand, even staggering suggestion of nature's preference for the closed cycle that, in the case of the eels, can span open oceans and cross multiple decades.

But if past and present are not oppositional, Swift finds far more intriguing the clear opposition between the imagined and the real, between the rich poetry of the engaged imagination and the stark, unadorned immediate. The Fens itself is offered not merely as a vividly evoked narrative site, generously detailed and sensually reconceived, but also as an engrossing metaphor for the relationship between dreary reality (the dark monotony of the Fens waterways, a formless, empty vacancy) and the stories we tell (the reclaimed, dredged-up land bits, fragile and decidedly artificial assertions of stability and organization amid the shapeless vacuum of the river). Here the real, the "Here and Now," is comfortless and unpromising, suggested not only by the miles of brutal, unbroken peat-black flatness of the Fens but as well by the events rendered within Tom Crick's narrative, a grinding succession of smalltime tragedies, the familiar, banal cycle of expectation and disappointment compelled by the irresistible itch and scratch of the carnal appetites, all played out amid a larger yawning emptiness, a boredom of time within which these characters exist that is interrupted only by the occasional hammer blow of surprise, the cutting heat of chance, and ultimately by the clumsy, intrusive stroke of mortality. As Crick observes, "Reality does not reside in the sudden hallucination of events. Reality is uneventfulness, vacancy, flatness. Reality is that nothing happens. For each protagonist who once stepped on the stage of so-called historical events, there were thousands, millions, who never entered the theatre" (p. 40).

Recall that the great stretch of Crick's majority years (from his marriage to Mary in 1947 to her religious awakenings in 1980) is dismissed in a terse sentence or two, lost to the pulverizing grind of work and the routine lapse of minutes into hours into days, a generic sort of non-life ("regular habits and regular diversions," p. 123), lost because it is never examined by the imaginative impulse. Turn the considerable technology of narrative, the restless eye of curiosity and the lavish empowerment of tale-telling, on any family, on any geography, and the imagination will permit the meanest surface, the sparest life to sparkle with import. Swift argues for narrative's ability to elevate experience to the grand and the significant. (After all, *Hamlet,* without the telling, is a messy palace coup involving a dysfunctional family; the *Iliad,* without the telling, is a catch-bin of bulletins from a faraway war zone; *Don Quixote,* without the telling, is a thick-foldered case study in clinical paranoia and delusional neuroses.)

Without storytelling, how else might we negotiate such an unpromising medium, the vast stretches of the terrifying neutrality that define, for Swift, the unexamined life? Swift tracks a number of such alternative responses, other accommodations that characters test. There is alcohol, for one (the Atkinson brewery, known for producing an almost magic ale, becomes the regional purveyor of the happy nullity of excess drinking, a disastrous strategy of accommodation that Swift dismisses—much of the mayhem in the narrative occurs with characters under the considerable influence of the brewery's potent ale). There is the call of suicide and the erotic fascination with anticipating, even encouraging endings: Crick's grandfather shoots himself after his daughter/lover marries; a grieving Jack Parr, after the inquest rules his son's drowning death an accident, settles down onto the railroad tracks, bottle in hand, to await the death-hurl of the next train; slow-witted Dick, after learning who his true father is, dives off the dredger into elected oblivion; Price's Holocaust Club accepts the premise of impending nuclear extermination and anticipates downing suicide pills in a world of radioactive ash and burned rubble. But such extreme measures, Swift cautions, are themselves inelegant dodges, clumsy escapes from complication. Far more prosaically, there is the determined settling down to the hard busy-ness of a lifetime of routine, the curious sustenance of work, sleep, work, sleep at the expense of acknowledging the insidious emptiness of such dedication—the donkey endurance suggested both by Henry, Tom's father, who mans the intricate locks along the Leem with Sisyphean dedication, dutifully raising and lowering the river despite the riverway's regular flooding, and by Dick's daily dedication to the thankless (and equally pointless) work of dredging the same river, the raw stench of it clinging to him even after his dousing showers.

More darkly, there is the ironic blessing of madness, the mental shutdown of characters such as Henry himself, who manages to diminish his own brutal experiences amid the atrocities of World War I by returning home with a cloaking amnesia for which he is ultimately hospitalized. Crick recounts the tale from a generation earlier of his maternal grandmother, the young, beautiful Sarah Atkinson, reportedly assaulted by her elderly husband, who was enraged over imagined infidelities; a woman left with a grievous head wound who remains for more than a half- century unable to speak, unable to react, adrift within the cool comfort of her damaged sanctuarial interior. Tom's own wife, in the narrative present, conjures a conversational intimacy with the God of her Catholic upbringing to justify her determination to kidnap a random baby from a neighborhood supermarket and then claim it as God's gift. Both Sarah and Mary close out their stories/lives in the living death of an asylum. Perhaps less dramatic but equally disturbing is Mary's response, years before, to her bloody abortion, the fetus literally sucked out of her womb by the haggish Martha Clay, and to the reality that the clumsy work of that backwoods "abortionist" had rendered her unable to bear children. She retreats for three years into the protective enclosure of her father's isolated farm, self-elected withdrawal from any contact, where she struggles to touch the comforts of an abiding God who might render sense from such horrific events. Absent the storytelling impulse, these are all comfortless strategies for negotiating the reality of the Here and Now, each ultimately a dead end: leaden ennui, madness, hallucination, retreat (drugged or otherwise), the sweet illusion of religion, the relentless pull of the logic of self-destruction amid the emptying pointlessness of work. Ours is a singularly joyless world, as Henry explains one night to a ten-year-old Tom as they admire the splash of stars, which Henry observes, are actually "the silver-dust of God's blessings" (p. 1) that God sent down long ago but then withheld seeing the evident wickedness of his own creation.

But against such pressing emptiness, Swift offers the benediction of storytelling, the inexhaustible energy of probing curiosity (the "gong-beat of Whywhywhy," p. 283), the inexplicable hunger of those sensitive few (poets, dramatists, novelists) to relate tales of such pointlessness—pointlessness that, under the conjuring energy of the re-creating imagination, can ascend to the dignity of direction and even purpose. After all, absent Tom Crick's mesmerizing narrative, absent his resilient interrogating process that gives a sense of poignancy, even passionate tragedy, to the end of his family line (he and Mary are childless), the events he relates are the tawdry, tacky privacies of any number of families, events by themselves unspectacular, consigned to the cold obscurity of oblivion, but here elevated to the grand because they have been salvaged by the relentless dredging engine of Crick's imagination and, in turn, offered as subject of a story to a captive audience (Crick's bewildered class) and to a voluntary one (Swift's enthralled reader).

Thus, the dominant narrative braids—in 1943, Tom and Mary's adolescent affair that ends with the abortion and then Dick's suicide, and in 1980, Crick's inelegant shuttering off into forced retirement—move toward open rather than closed endings and confirm the search for, rather than the recovery of, truth. As Crick begins his valedictory address, a lone student, Price, shouts from the back of the auditorium, "Keep Crick. No cuts," a brave, if slender, call for the inquisitorial spirit to continue within an academic atmosphere that is about to drastically shift its priorities to the cool, end- oriented solution disciplines of mathematics and the sciences. (Price's Holocaust Club darkly chants "Fear is here" even as the headmaster introduces Crick.) And, decades earlier, as Crick and his father, horrified and stunned, gather on the deck of the dredger to confront the implications of Dick's dive, the dredger captain, confused and reeling after a night's drinking, demands, "Someone better explain" (p. 358). Given the circumstances (When does a suicide ever conform to expectations of logical explanation?), even that affirmation of curiosity is undercut by the unsettling reminder that resolution, even the simplest gesture of explanation, must be rendered ironic. Indeed, we are given (despite the narrative's premise of Crick's extemporaneous recollections to his class) extensive passages from the public inquest into the death of Freddie Parr, an inquest that appears to render reliable explanation by determining that death to be an accident, a finding that momentarily suspends the narrative action ("End of story," p. 109), threatened suddenly by tidiness, until Mary, who meets Tom that very afternoon, confides in him that in fact *they* are responsible for the death and tells him of her lie to Dick, thus beginning a new cycle of curiosity and complication, neatly fending off the impress of closure.

We are then left with untidy loose ends, unanswered and ultimately unanswerable: murder, suicide, abortion, kidnapping, the sort of dramatic human actions that necessarily beggar the reasoning premise itself, that leave themselves tauntingly unresolvable. The reader is teased not by the tantalizing premise of solution and epiphany but rather by the sustained act of narration itself—the "Whywhywhy"—keeping the story going rather than ending it, the pulsing push of curiosity itself, the restless interrogation of experience, the range, scope, breadth of the engaged imagination, the why that ranges through the narrative text like the pulsing waters of the Leem itself. Mystery haunts the narrative line. Who exactly was responsible for the devastating 1911 fire that destroys the Atkinson brewery and commences Ernest Atkinson's retreat from the world that would kindle his incestuous affair with his beautiful daughter, which would in turn produce the retarded Dick? No one is ever sure. The town is in the throes of a drunken celebration of the coronation of George V, a rowdy night compelled by an especially potent ale prepared under the care of Ernest himself, a darkling soul soured on his fellow humanity and determined in that single batch to give the rabble world what it most craved: oblivion. How did Sarah Atkinson, Ernest's tragic mother, come to sustain the head wound that rendered her so irreparably impaired for more than fifty years? What exactly are the circumstances of Freddie Parr's death—Crick's reconstruction of the events is, at best, likely. We must be sustained by conjecture.

Indeed, Crick's narratives are even touched by the paranormal: not only the mad Sarah Atkinson's eerie power of prophecy (in her half-century of otherwise damaged quiet, she is given to fits where she suddenly rants about a fire, long before the great brewery conflagration) but also her periodic appearances after her death. The night Ernest Atkinson commits suicide, the very night he sends to his daughter's cottage the sealed chest that contains his confession of Dick's paternity, Henry, newly married to Ernest's pregnant daughter/lover, is walking along the Fens and sees a will-o'-the-wisp, the eerie night glow that, according to folklore, predicts unavoidable disaster. If Tom Crick seeks in his rambling classroom stories to define his self at a moment of crisis, the normative urgency behind the autobiographical confession, the public act of exposure here is a performance that finally does not tidy up a life but, from the perspective of the ultimate authority (Swift himself) serves dramatically to create an audience (Crick's normally dull-eyed students) for storytelling itself.

Of course, tendering a good yarn as remedy for the late- twentieth-century wasteland world of malaise and unaccountable angst, that unshaped immediate that lurks just outside the neat designs of such narratives, may seem precious and necessarily ironic. But Swift tests other interactions with that selfsame immediate, other strategies for involvement, strategies for engaging the immediate—and each in turn proves disastrous, pointless, or massively destructive. There are those who seek to remedy the world through political activism—Crick's infrequent history lectures themselves focus on the cataclysmic naïveté of the French Revolution and its hapless collapse into the terror of the guillotine, a grim parody of its own idealism. Crick's grandfather, Ernest, attempted to mount a political career that foundered when his jeremiad of isolationism was mocked and misunderstood amid the heady jingoism of pre-World War I; World War II, in which Crick himself serves, offers irrefutable evidence of the horrors that political activism can justify. Then there are those who seek control of the immediate via the exertion of technology, the entrepreneurial savvy of progress and business, the cultivation of markets and industry, the taming of the natural world to serve humanity's needs. The grand rise and swift fall of the Atkinson brewery testifies to such misbegotten enterprises that, despite momentary success, here fall victim to biblical-size catastrophes of fire and water, the mysterious brewery conflagration and the subsequent massive flooding of the Fens lands that had given the brewery its envied ingredients of Norfolk barley and malting hops and had provided the brewery itself with a reliable transportation system—all lost in a fortnight. God? Surely a deity can render satisfying purpose. Yet a menopausal Mary Crick finds comfort in her delusional conversations with a God who apparently sanctions her scheme to kidnap a neighborhood baby. What about helping others, the determination to minister to the sick world one patient at a time? Tom's mother and his wife both tend to the sick (the mother to the walking dead who returned from World War I; Mary to the forgotten elderly through a civil service appointment) but both find within such ministrations small comfort—they tend to those who do not promise recovery, indeed are the incurables. Teaching? Surely the offer of instruction, a profession geared toward helping and sympathetic enlightenment, is rewarding—but the narrative begins with Crick being brusquely terminated after more than thirty years of service, his department in the process of being dismantled by a headmaster who believes that the sole purpose of education is not to challenge but rather to generate the false hope for an economic future in the minds of mediocre students doomed, he knows, to economic hardships. What about scientific investigation, the outreach of the mind to map the world into the known? Crick recounts with bemused irony the quest of more than five generations of scientific minds to render clear the mating habits of a simple river eel only to find such a modest natural phenomenon stubbornly inexplicable. We are given then a series of avenues to engage the immediate, each of which collapses of its own irony, its own futility.

Amid such evident failures, Swift brings the gift of narrative. But it is given with a caution—narratives cannot provide shelter or escape. As a brainy and shy child, the nerdy Crick uses books as a simple escape from the dreary rural life of drudgery all about him. Amid the difficult summer of Mary's abortion, Crick turns to the sweet escape of books, particularly the adventure tales of Robert Louis Stevenson and obscure Norman epics chronicling heroic feats of fearless warriors. He will be the first in his family's long history to be college educated, an ivory-tower sort of non-life, where he will pore over his own recondite historical research, happily oblivious to the great-bellied bombers that fly past overhead to the European theater. But if in such moments Crick appears weak and vulnerable, he will come ultimately to affirm storytelling as a method for negotiating rather than escaping from the immediate. Such thematic argument puts Dick in particularly tragic shadings because he alone of the characters has virtually no access to language, pulled from school at fourteen without mastering the ability to read or to write. Entirely disenfranchised from the magic of narrative, even his speech a clumsy chop of stutters, Dick is left, by Crick's own description, as pure body, pure physical form without the redeeming reach of the imagination. (To emphasize such sheer physicality, Swift endows Dick with great strength, a massive frame, and, as his name underscores, an enormous appendage—without recourse to the nuance and dimension of life

afforded by language.) Thus Dick wants people to act according to predictable rules, like automatons, and their failure to do so, the intrusion of surprise, leaves him awash in anxiety and ultimately suicidal as he has no vocabulary for such disruptions. He struggles to understand love, struggles to understand the simple biology of conception, struggles just to play along with Mary's elaborate tease and foreplay (curious over his endowments, she pesters him as he collects eels in a bucket to show her his biggest eel). Thus denied access to words, to speech, and to stories, Dick forms his deepest bond not with the randy Mary or with his long-suffering father or his book-smart half-brother, but rather with his reliable motorcycle, with whom he earnestly converses, an empty fetish for a thing that parodies the larger dramas of love (and lust) that Crick relates.

Counterpointed to a character utterly denied access to language is, of course, Swift himself. Moving Swift to the narrative center dramatically alters the novel's impact: the most stunning drama now is not so much between any of the characters (and Crick's absorbing tales surely provide much heat and friction) but rather the unsuspected interior drama of a man we never directly encounter in the text who is furiously creating, a professional writer in the late twentieth century, an unassuming, soft-spoken, massively erudite, successful career academic in his mid-thirties, an only child raised in comfortable and conventionally stable middle-class circumstances, a life bound largely within London's city limits except for excursions into the protective ivory towers of nearby universities, himself unmarried and without children, who nevertheless convincingly conjures the predicament of a late-middle-age war veteran, a tormented brother, a bereaved husband/father fingering the tassels at the end of any number of ropes, both professional and personal. Swift has long dismissed as irrelevant the presumed intimacies between writer and reader, of limiting writing to an act of veiled autobiography that restricts the creative act to dredging about the shallow reservoir of the writer's own private life. Swift prefers to conjure the interior lives of characters manifestly not drawn from personal experience, to animate their stories and chart iterations of behavior in characters who, despite being word chords, ink pressed on paper, assume evident immediacy, even poignancy and tragedy. Writing, Swift believes, must test the leaping power of the imagination. It is an audacious celebration of the medium, an elaborate reconception of the inherited form of the realistic novel that relieves the artist entirely of the responsibility (even the expectation) of establishing any authentic self within the narrative space.

Here is a writer who deliberately, even passionately discounts that most traditional of writerly bromides: Write about what you know. Rather, Swift introduces a bold reverence for the imagination and its ability to conjure a convincing simulation. "The imagination is a wonderful thing: it can cross the gap between you and some experiences you have never had personally, or to some person who is entirely out of nowhere and not someone you've known. That's the excitement and, of course, it's the real creative element of writing. Assuming you have to write about what you know—which is often the standard advice given—is rather sad. . . . sooner or later you've got to make it up" (quoted in Rosenberg). What is remarkable about Swift's fiction is the evident tension between the low-key life Swift has lived and this, his most accomplished fiction, wherein he renders eccentric lives whose anything-but-routine predicaments he has never even remotely touched, all played out in a haunting atmospheric East Britain rural landscape that he has (by his own admission) glimpsed only once or twice from a train bound for Oxford, a narrative that is (again by Swift's own admission) not a product of the sort of assiduous research such grand realistic narratives traditionally involve (he disdains such library work) but rather the result of the opportunity it provided for its author to test the reach of his imagination. Swift is not content here to restage dramas of doomed love, too hip to replay the crushing evidence of a capricious nature and the chilling reality of inevitable death: those basic contours, after all, have been fundamental to the British novel since Dickens and Hardy and their explorations of love's anticipation, expectation, detonation, and inevitable disappointment. *Waterland* becomes a text that concedes the traditional elements of character/plot/action to generate an (im)perfect lexical space that insists on its told-ness, a complex structured space that is to be admired for exactly what it is: a structure that reveals even as it conceals.

The drama of generation is not Tom Crick's generating tales for his class but a far more exacting behind-the-scenes act of generation: Graham Swift at his typewriter. That is the sole successful act of generation in a narrative that otherwise moves toward the cool stillness of sterility; all other acts of generation within the narrative itself are doomed gestures, cursed enterprises, misbegotten conceptions. Thomas Atkinson's hubric dream of a grand multigenerational financial dynasty collapses when his grandson falls in decidedly nonplatonic love with his own daughter, the offspring of that illicit union a genetic mishap, Dick. Tom, the first educated Crick, manages a cool estrangement from his own farmer-father and ultimately relocates to distant Greenwich; after Mary's abortion, that same Tom is given the traumatic responsibility of dumping the bloody fetus of what will be his only offspring into the Ouse. That pregnancy itself, as retold by Crick to his class, is little more than an adolescent exploration of "Holes and Things," a decidedly unromantic stab at grown-up loving. And that abortion leaves Mary barren until, compelled by the pressure of the closing-in of late middle age, she remedies her childlessness by the criminal act of kidnapping, the child swiftly returned to its distraught mother.

Every story related by Crick involves an inevitable sundering: the urge to procreate leaves its fevered participants ultimately abandoned within the irreversible cool of isolation. Passion, savage in its urgency, is devastating in its effects. Every gesture toward the generosity of connection, sympathy, or love is rendered ironic and fails to sustain even its premise of bonding. (In one of Crick's more elaborate asides, he mentions the geological drifting of the tectonic plates since the Ice Age as even the continents themselves inch farther from each other.) The only gesture of outreach Crick himself attempts in the narrative, with the belligerent Price, is conducted clumsily when, on his last day of teaching, he invites the student to accompany him to a nearby tavern, where, in a drunken mawkish moment, he identifies the student to the bartender as his own son.

All such gestures fail—except the confederacy of tale-teller and audience. Ironically the *stories* of such sunderings bring together in accidental confederation the writer and reader, threaded by the tensile-tough webbing of language, a love of language as a medium for connection. That love, Swift ultimately affirms. Within the narrative, forming a sort of resonant patterning, are three bodies in the water—the bloody fetus from Tom and Mary's adolescent affair, the bruised and battered corpse of Freddie Parr, and the massive bulk of the drowned Dick—that each testify to damage done by the imperfect, fractured heart born wanting the consolation of another imperfect, fractured heart. Such is the gentle terrorism implicit in the pull of beauty—Crick tells that when his beautiful mother took her place at a reviewing stand for a military parade during World War I, the soldiers were so distracted by her beauty as they filed past the stand that their careful lines collapsed into chaos as they slowed for just a glimpse. Recall the touching scene between Henry and Dick, as the father struggles to explain to his son where babies come from and stammers through a definition of how babies come from love, hopelessly lost to the dim-witted Dick and dramatically ironic given the circumstances ultimately revealed about Dick's own conception.

More to the point, storytelling alone defies not only the narrative's movement toward sterility and isolation but as well the persistent narrative push toward endings, the hunger for apocalypse, the infatuation with closure—without the framing device that compels the reader to stay outside the narrative's reach, the story here would be decidedly death-soaked. Nothing succeeds, nothing survives. A once grand family is devastated and left to extinction. Price's Holocaust Club is preoccupied with imminent nuclear devastation, suggested by Price's coating his face in a death-white color. Crick's normally jaded students are suddenly fascinated with his graphic recounting of the messy guillotine street executions during the French Revolution. A massive fire destroys the magnificent Atkinson brewery. A viral holocaust of influenza quickly, casually kills Crick's beautiful mother (and thousands of others). To this is added the vast brutal theater of two world wars, the suicides of Crick's grandfather and his half-brother, the murder of Freddie Parr, and the bloody fetus in the crude wooden bucket that Crick must dump in the river. One after another, narrative lines move toward the ignominy of death—except the impulse to tell those stories. That survives—its sheer energy often compelling the chapters to flow each into the next as the closing sentence of one chapter is completed by the chapter heading of the next, like some undammable flow.

To follow Swift's sense of narrative empowerment, the reader can use the metaphor of the eternal process of land reclamation necessary to tame the Fens. The process of controlling the river suggests the writer's ability to direct the otherwise open course of experience into the manageable tidiness of plot. The cycle of narrative, for Swift, parallels that ongoing process: we live stretches of empty time, bored by the evident press of routine, until the sheer fatigue of such calm is shattered by an intrusive stroke, what Swift terms the "surprise attacks of the Here and Now" (p. 61), inexplicable misfortune, random accident, the speechlessly quick cut of death, the shattering intrusion of love. We reel, suddenly upended, and calm is not restored until that jolting event is rendered within the steady-ing frame of a story. Settled by that calmative qua narrative, we return to our settled lives, stretches of empty time, bored by the evident press of routine, until. . . . a never-ending cycle salvaged from pointlessness and the cooling hiss of silence by the rich suasion of curiosity, the animating engine of the engaged imagination, and ultimately by the manageable intricacy of the narrative shape itself. As Crick tells his students, "Only animals live entirely in the Here and Now. Only nature knows neither memory nor history. But man—let me offer you a defini-tion—is the story-telling animal. Wherever he goes he wants to leave behind not a chaotic wake, not an empty space, but the comforting marker-buoys and trail-signs of stories. . . . As long as there's a story, it's alright" (pp. 62–63). We are all then historians of a kind, touched by the need to construct some sense, even incomplete and provisional, out of the onrush of events in our lives, with indeterminacy the only certainty. We live the amphibious life, a water-land existence as it were, at home both within the limitless stretch of a fluid reality and the story- shelters designed by the imagination. To live entirely in either is to sacrifice: pure reality grinds the heart down; pure imagination is untenable escapism. The interaction, the aware-ness that each needs the other, is Swift's larger offer. Nothing is worse, Crick counsels his students, "than when curiosity stops. Nothing is more repressive than the repression of curiosity. Curiosity begets love. It weds us to the world. It's part of our perverse, madcap love for this impossible planet we inhabit. People die when curiosity goes" (p. 206).

IMPORTANCE AND INFLUENCE

Although its relatively recent publication restricts assessing its influence, *Waterland* can nevertheless be located within an important decade-long interest in a radical sort of historical fiction that coincided with the Conservative revolution of Prime Minister Margaret Thatcher

(1979–1990) during which Britain was forced to confront its own national identity as the politi-cal, social, and economic assumptions of its postwar complex gave way to a radically new conception of how the country was to work. Caught between generations, Britain was in the grip of a deep recession, troubled by union discontent, and finding antiquated and unwork-able the postwar liberal ideals of government.

The country thus turned to the aggressive economic philosophy of Margaret Thatcher, whose blunt, confrontational, and often jarring personality made her a fitting leader to move the country in a decidedly different direction: a conservative revolution that echoed a similar political and social movement in the United States under Ronald Reagan. Following her elec-tion in May 1979, Thatcher uncompromisingly pursued principles of free market economics: reducing government control of utilities and industries, limiting the power of labor unions, enacting sweeping domestic legislation that virtually dismantled the postwar welfare state, and heading efforts to reduce taxes and cut government spending in an effort to return Britain to what she tirelessly argued were its forgotten virtues of self-reliance, personal responsibility, and hard work.

Not surprisingly, it was a time of massive cultural self-examination, a time of British investigation into its own historic identity, of radical questioning about the past and its relationship to the upheavals in the present, a crossroads moment when cultural identity itself appeared to participate in a dialogue between past and present. When Argentina invaded the British-controlled Falkland Islands in 1982, Thatcher seized on the invasion as a matter of national pride and responded with a show of military muscle that brought England a long-lost sense of nationalism (at times bordering on the jingoistic). That military campaign, coupled with the contemporaneous decision to hand over Hong Kong to the Chinese Communist govern-ment by century's end and the decade-long pres-sure over England's joining the European Union (both of which threatened the very national identity the Falklands crusade had defined), created a much- heightened interest in the identity of England, particularly in the viability of the British Empire itself, fanned by the decade's long tabloid intrusion into the formerly sacrosanct royal family. It was a time for historical inquiry, a time for a culture to reflect on its own identity by investigating the very viability, even relevancy, of the past.

Appropriately, there emerged in the 1980s and 1990s a genre of fiction, written largely by writers born in the years immediately around World War II, that centered on the role of history, that investigated the process of history writing and the need to turn to the past in order to understand the present. Swift emerged as something of a dominant voice largely because each of his six novels has focused specifically on historic inquiry and the play of past and present on multiple generations. During the Thatcher revolution, these writers—among them, Peter Ackroyd, Julian Barnes, A. S. Byatt, Peter Carey, Penelope Fitzgerald, Kazuo Ishiguro, Penelope Lively, John McGahern, Timothy Mo, Michael Ondaatje, Salman Rushdie, and Rose Tremain—were very much a generation suspended between identities, too young to recall the glory of their parents' war victory and too old to tap into the easy resilience of energy premised by the Thatcher nationalism.

Not surprisingly, their novels are similarly poised between past and present. Characteristically the novels counter- position a contemporary narrative of a central character struggling with the problem of identity or with a shattering memory/secret against an absorbing (and vividly re-created) historical narrative that, as it is gradually uncovered or retold by the central character, comes to move that character toward some satisfying (if painful) confrontation with the self. Thus private stories and public history, past and present, intertwine. These are fictions in which central characters are often intimately involved with the historic process itself: if they are not characters actually positioned in a historic period, they are present-day academic investigators, history teachers, investigative journalists, genealogists, professional historians, amateur historic sleuths, or bureaucratic archivists, thus foregrounding not merely history but also its methods, its agenda, and its responsibilities.

Unlike the straightforward (and highly successful) historic fictions of pre-World War II, such as the sprawling generational sagas of John Galsworthy or the social comedies of P. G. Wodehouse, which drew so directly from the grand Victorian realism models of Dickens, Hardy, Arnold Bennett, and George Eliot and provided accessible story lines within the verisimilitude of meticulously accurate recognizable landscapes and often set their fictional characters amid well-known historic moments for optimum effect, these contemporary works are too aware of the delicate process of historic inquiry to allow their narratives to be satisfied with simply relating the often riveting and involved plots that they offer. Influenced by the mid-century modernist studies in shifting perspective and multiple centers of perception, and schooled in the experiments in fragmented narration of Virginia Woolf, Ford Madox Ford, and William Faulkner, these contemporary writers deploy the expected elements of traditional historic realism (plot, character, suspense) but insist on braiding among them a counterplot, a sort of alternate narrative, that privileges the process itself and ultimately, by constantly shifting narrative center from present to past, shatters linearity in the narrative retelling. Thus they are more novels of ideas. By leaving the endings open, or in some cases by offering multiple endings, these works offer as thematic focus the search for meaning via the turn to the past.

These works differ too from the historical novels of a generation earlier, the postmodernist experiments of the late 1960s and 1970s most engagingly suggested by John Fowles's landmark *The French Lieutenant's Woman* (1969), works that openly parodied even the possibility of a workable history and, with the savvy guerrilla love of shattering conservative notions that defined the postmodern experiments of the mid-century, boldly dismissed history as a purely intellectual construction and compelled narratives to relentlessly expose that reality by tactics of ludic self-reflexivity (as when, for instance, Fowles introduces himself as a character in his otherwise Victorian narrative). The historical fictions of the Thatcher era, by contrast, were not so willing to dismiss outright the historic process or to happily implode such investigations. These works, Swift's among them, reflect a more sobering, less playful approach to historical fiction that offer a "yes, but" caution to their postmodern antecedents. Yes, history is a construct, but it is as well a powerful revelation of the intricate process of understanding itself and a genuine boon to those too aware of the easy slide of chaos that defines the day-to-day quotidian. History, memory, fairy tales, myth, folklore, journalism, and ultimately narrative itself: such constructs allow the past to feed into the evolving definition of the present. That awareness, far from limiting or undercutting the process, instead creates a new respect for its muscle, if contemporary audiences can accept the inevitable conclusions drawn from such tactical fictions: that truth is elusive and inevitably ironic, meaning indeterminate and shadowy, resolution unattainable and indeed unwanted, curiosity a viable sustenance, order a manageable but fragile construct, and cause and effect a bravura assertion of the imagination wrestling with chaos itself. Given the tumultuous decade, such writers, preeminently Swift, were clearly more inclined to empower rather than deride the brave edifices of history, myth, and narrative as the heroic exertions of the imagination.

Selected Bibliography

EDITIONS

Waterland. London: Heinemann, 1983. New York: Vintage International, 1992.

SECONDARY WORKS

Alexander, Marguerite. *Flights from Realism: Themes and Strategies in Postmodernist British and American Fiction.* London: Edward Arnold, 1990. Although Alexander does not directly treat Swift, a helpful introduction to the era.

Bernard, Catharine. "An Interview with Graham Swift." *Contemporary Literature* 38, no. 2 (1997): 217–231.

Brewer, John, and Stella Tillyard. "History and Telling Stories: Graham Swift's *Waterland.*" *History Today* (January 1985): 49–51.

Cooper, Pamela. "Imperial Topographies: The Spaces of History in *Waterland.*" *Modern Fiction Studies* 42, no. 2 (1996): 371–396.

Higdon, David Leon. "Double Closures in Postmodern British Fiction: The Example of Graham Swift." *Critical Survey* 3, no. 1 (1991): 88–95.

———. " 'Unconfessed Confession': The Narrators of Graham Swift and Julian Barnes." In *The British and Irish Novel Since 1960.* Edited by James Acheson. London: Macmillan, 1991.

Ireland, Kenneth R. " 'Carry On, Dickens!': Dickens in the 1980s: Peter Ackroyd, Graham Swift, Salman Rushdie." *Studies in English Literature* 69, no. 1 (1992): 45–61.

Irish, Robert K. "'Let Me Tell You': About Desire and Narrativity in Graham Swift's *Waterland.*" *Modern Fiction Studies* 44, no. 4 (1998): 917–934.

Janik, Del Ivan. "History and the 'Here and Now': The Novels of Graham Swift." *Twentieth Century Literature* 35, no. 1 (1989): 74–88.

————. "No End of History: Evidence from the Contemporary English Novel." *Twentieth Century Literature* 41, no. 2 (1995): 160–189.

Landow, George P. "History, His Story, and Stories in Graham Swift's *Waterland.*" *Studies in the Literary Imagination* 23, no. 2 (1990): 197–211. Professor Landow maintains a website devoted to Swift: http://.landow.stg.brown.edu.

Lee, Allison. *Realism and Power: Postmodern British Fiction.* London: Routledge, 1990. Pp. 40–46.

Lewis, Barry. "Graham Swift." In *Contemporary Novelists.* Edited by Susan Windisch Brown. New York: St. James Press, 1996. Pp. 964–965.

Lord, Geoffrey. "Mystery and History, Discovery and Recovery in Thomas Pynchon's *The Crying of Lot 49* and Graham Swift's *Waterland.*" *Neophilologus: An International Journal of Modern and Medieval Language and Literature* 81, no. 1 (1997): 145–163.

Marsh, Kelly. "The Neo-Sensation Novel: A Contemporary Genre in the Victorian Tradition." *Philological Quarterly* 74, no. 1 (1995): 99–123.

McKinney, Robert H. "The Greening of Postmodernism: Graham Swift's *Waterland.*" *New Literary History: A Journal of Theory and Interpretation* 28, no. 4 (1997): 821–832.

Rosenberg, Scott. "Glowing in the Ashes: An Interview with Graham Swift." The *Salon* interview. Posted 1996. http://www.salon.com.

Schad, John. "The End of the End of History: Graham Swift's *Waterland.*" *Modern Fiction Studies* 38, no. 4 (1992): 911–925.

Index

Arabic numbers in **boldface type** refer to subjects of articles.